Women and Politics in a Global World

SECOND EDITION

Sarah L. Henderson
Oregon State University

Alana S. Jeydel
American River College

New York   Oxford
OXFORD UNIVERSITY PRESS
2010

Oxford University Press, Inc., publishes works that further Oxford University's
objective of excellence in research, scholarship, and education.

Oxford   New York
Auckland   Cape Town   Dar es Salaam   Hong Kong   Karachi
Kuala Lumpur   Madrid   Melbourne   Mexico City   Nairobi
New Delhi   Shanghai   Taipei   Toronto

With offices in
Argentina   Austria   Brazil   Chile   Czech Republic   France   Greece
Guatemala   Hungary   Italy   Japan   Poland   Portugal   Singapore
South Korea   Switzerland   Thailand   Turkey   Ukraine   Vietnam

Published by Oxford University Press, Inc.
198 Madison Avenue, New York, New York 10016
http://www.oup.com

Oxford is a registered trademark of Oxford University Press

Library of Congress Cataloging-in-Publication Data

Henderson, Sarah, 1971–
   Women and politics in a global world
Sarah L. Henderson, Alana S. Jeydel.—2nd ed.
      p. cm.
Includes bibliographical references and index.
ISBN 978-0-19-538807-7 (pbk.: alk. paper)   1. Women in politics—
Cross-cultural studies.   2. Women—Government policy.
I. Jeydel, Alana S., 1968–   II. Title.
HQ1236.H45   2010
320.082—dc22   2009024993

Printing number: 9 8 7 6 5 4 3 2 1

Printed in the United States of America
on acid-free paper

*This book is dedicated to all who work
tirelessly to achieve equality of opportunity for all.*

CONTENTS

PREFACE

Mao Tse-tung used the slogan "women hold up half the sky" to promote the equality of women as part of his larger goal to restructure Chinese society radically under his vision of communism. Since then, the phrase has been adopted by a myriad of organizations around the world to highlight the fact that even though women make up half of the population, their interests—political, economic, social, and personal—are often vastly underrepresented and undervalued. While they may hold up half the sky, women are not consistently rewarded or acknowledged for their work. Across countries, women make up a disproportionate share of the illiterate, the poor, the displaced, the elderly, the underpaid, the underemployed, and the underrepresented. Even though women have gained visibility and influence in a wide array of political and economic arenas, they are still far from equal to the position and status of men in society. However, beginning in the post–World War II era an explosion of women's activism occurred globally, with the goals of equality, liberation, and better living conditions, not just for women, but for their families as well. This activism increased in the late 1960s, 1970s, and 1980s as a second wave of women's activism continued to highlight women's often separate and unequal status around the world. *Women and Politics in a Global World* is written to serve as a central text for courses that address women and politics. We provide an overview of the ways in which women participate in politics, discuss some of the key policy issues that impact women, and define some of the critical transnational issues that confront women in the international community. This book is global in its coverage, and it compares women's impact on politics and politics' impact on women from a cross-national, comparative perspective.

We decided to write this book because as political scientists, we both teach classes that address women's issues and politics from a comparative perspective. We found that while a vast literature on women and politics exists, past research tended to focus on the experiences of women in a single country. Alternatively, past comparative literature on women and politics tended to look at the experiences of women in a single region, such as western Europe, Latin America, or Asia. The few books that did offer a comparison of women's activism across continents either were outdated or were edited volumes of case studies, which also did not quite match our needs. We never found that single text that pulled together all of the themes we wanted to emphasize and described the experiences of women not just from a particular country or region but from countries across the globe.

This comparative approach comes with inherent dangers. Is sisterhood really global? Can we really generalize about women's interests, given that women come from such vastly different economic, social, and cultural backgrounds? A white, wealthy, college-educated American woman seemingly has little in common with an illiterate Nigerian woman who was born into, and will in all likelihood die in, poverty; yet we discuss the condition of both in this book. Even within countries, vast disparities are found between how women define and advocate their interests; American women's gender identities, for example, often coexist with equally important ethnic, racial, religious, and class differences. Further, how can we compare the impact of women on policy and politics when there is such wide variation around the globe with respect to types of political regimes? France and Zimbabwe both claim to be democracies, yet any observer would agree that there are significant differences in how politics function in these two countries.

Despite these concerns, we argue that a global comparison is not only possible, but necessary. Certainly, a white, wealthy, college-educated woman in the United States faces different challenges than an illiterate woman in Nigeria does, and while these women probably have many concerns that they do not share, there is a set of core issues around which women have organized. In their study of women's political engagement in forty-three different countries, Barbara Nelson and Najma Chowdury found that women around the world mobilized around four sets of common issues: ensuring their personal safety, security, and autonomy; providing reproductive rights and maternal and child health programs; equalizing access to public resources, such as education, employment, health care, and credit; and remaking the political and legal rules of the game to ensure women's access to political institutions and positions of authority.[1] In other words, women face common barriers, even though the specifics of those barriers may differ substantially from country to country. Also, cross-nationally, in broad ways, women have responded to these challenges similarly by organizing and advocating for greater roles for women in determining the direction of their lives. Of course there are numerous differences among women across nations and even within nations. But we find that women have many common experiences (being raped during war being but one example) and common ways of addressing issues they care about (mobilizing in a social movement, for example). We feel it is possible, and advantageous, to identify and discuss broad themes and experiences that women share across cultures and political contexts.

At the same time, we recognize that while sisterhood may be global, that does not mean that all women face identical situations or consistently respond in identical ways. Class, ethnic, religious, and cultural differences, for example, all intersect to enrich the variety of women's responses to issues that are important to them. A variety of scholars have tried to capture the complexity of women's diverse interests while simultaneously identifying larger commonalities. For example, Maxine Molyneux distinguishes between strategic and practical gender interests as a way to understand the varied ways in which women organize. While strategic gender interests are more explicitly feminist in orientation in that they seek ultimately to change the relations between the sexes to overcome women's subordination, practical gender interests "are usually a response to an immediate perceived need and they do not entail a strategic goal such as women's emancipation or gender equality."[2] Scholars who studied women's activism in Latin America and the Caribbean used this distinction to classify groups as "feminine" in orientation versus "feminist"; that is, "feminine" groups do not question the gender roles that men and women play in everyday life, but actually use these gendered roles as a justification for their activism. In contrast, feminist groups explicitly target issues that would change the relationship between the sexes.[3] Thus, for example, women in both the United States and Brazil may mobilize over the issue of improved access to contraception, but they may be drawn into that activism for different reasons and may use different mobilization techniques and strategies that resonate with local cultures, customs, and needs. Some of these techniques may more overtly challenge existing patterns of gender relations, while others may reinforce them. These distinctions between practical and strategic gender interests and feminine versus feminist organizations are just a few illustrations of how women around the world can care about similar issues while expressing these concerns in very different ways. Commonalities among women can coexist with marked social differences, and thinking about women's activism in this way further explores how gender interacts with other social cleavages and dispels the idea that women's interests are unified and undifferentiated, without dismissing women's broad commonalities altogether.

Further, larger structural factors, such as a country's levels of economic development and social modernization, also affect the nature and impact of women's activism and the design of woman-friendly policy. In the previous few decades, a wealth of research based on survey data drawn from citizens from countries all over the world indicated that there are significant differences in the cultural views and attitudes of people living in agrarian, industrial, and postindustrial societies. This is because economic modernization creates systematic (and predictable) social change in terms of people's values. In particular, Ronald Inglehart argues that there is a rising and clearly distinct emphasis in postindustrial societies on self-expression, subjective well-being, and quality of life concerns rather than materialist concerns of basic security and survival.[4]

In terms of cultural attitudes about gender relations, drawing from survey data from over seventy countries, Ronald Inglehart and Pippa Norris find that citizens of richer postindustrial societies are consistently more likely to support gender equality than are those in agrarian or industrial societies. As they point out, when people are no longer "restricted by widespread fears and insecurities based on life threatening challenges, then women and men gradually develop greater willingness to adopt interchangeable roles within the family and workforce."[5] Also, postindustrial societies are characterized by significantly large generational divides (which are not very large in other societies), in which younger respondents are even more likely to support gender equality than their parents or grandparents are. However, in their work only twenty countries are considered postindustrial, fifty-eight are industrial, and ninety-seven are classified as agrarian; thus, while this culture shift is significant, it is most noticeable in a minority of countries.[6] Our larger point, however, is that, certainly, these differences in broad levels of modernization and cultural attitudes, norms, and customs will manifest themselves in terms of how women participate in politics as well as in the design and implementation of policy issues that affect women. Thus, when we compare the condition and status of women in Nigeria with women in the United States, we are aware of the socioeconomic backdrops that inform people's values, interests, and identities.

In this book, we try to maintain the delicate balance between stressing the broad commonalities that women share while acknowledging the very real and substantial differences that separate them by carefully choosing which countries we discuss in each chapter. Thus, we try to avoid the "everything but the kitchen sink" approach to examples—bombarding the reader with a host of statistics and random examples from multiple countries that may bear little relation to one another. Each chapter expressly indicates which countries we are comparing and explains why those particular cases were selected. We carefully thought about which countries might illustrate broader theoretical points and when a global comparison would illuminate women's commonalities and when it would superficially impose a "woman's view" rather than "women's views." As a result, while the chapters in Part I tend to draw from the experiences of women around the world, the chapters in Part II focus on policy issues that impact women in the developed world and the chapters in Part III focus primarily on transnational issues that affect women in the developing world. Our aim in pursuing this strategy was to combine a global scope of inquiry with an appreciation for the limitations of such an approach.

Other obstacles to this type of study arise in addition to the thorny issue of defining women's interests. As political scientists we bring certain assumptions and methodologies to this research. As political scientists we have been trained to study the state as a key actor in the lives of its citizens. We also discuss the state quite frequently, since the book addresses women's impact on government institutions and policies and these institutions' impact on women. By "state" we are referring to the various institutions within a country's governing apparatus, such as the legislature, the bureaucracy, and other related policy-making and implementing bodies, as well as the people who are employed by these institutions. Thus, we tend to ask questions that involve finding out more about the relationship between the state and its citizens (in this case, women) versus the role and impact of women in families or clans or villages. We also tend toward more macro-level analysis than other disciplines do. For example, an anthropologist might be more likely to study the role and impact of women in a specific town or village rather than in one country, in several countries, or even around the world.

We also had to think carefully about whether we wanted to present an analytical or a normative work. That is, should we simply present the condition and status of women, or should we take a position on what the condition and status should be? We decided to take the following normative position: When women's access to political and economic power is increased, women and society as a whole benefit. We echo the principals of the Beijing Declaration and Platform for Action, announced at the UN Fourth World Conference on Women (1995), which maintains that "women's empowerment and their full participation on the basis of equality in all spheres of society, including their participation in the decision-making process and access to power, are fundamental for the achievement of equality, development, and peace," as is helping women shape "their lives in accordance with their own aspirations."[7] Thus, this book does advocate for women's equality, without confusing equality with "sameness." By women's equality, we mean that one sex is not superior to the other, nor should one sex have categorical control of the rights and opportunities of the other. Further, we assume that women's condition is socially constructed and historically shaped rather than preordained by God or nature.[8] Thus, while we may discuss the role of women and/or organizations that view women as separate and unequal, we do not endorse this view.

At the same time, we try to avoid presenting women's impact and concerns from an overly narrow feminist perspective only. Feminism as an ideology is quite diverse; it includes liberal feminism, radical feminism, Marxist-socialist feminism, global feminism, black feminism, ecofeminism, and gender feminism. These strands of thought differ in their assessments of the nature and source of women's oppression as well as the strategies needed to overcome it. For example, liberal feminism, the oldest and probably most influential strand of feminist thought, focuses on the importance of increasing women's autonomy through working within the existing political system and structures to allow women equal access to opportunities and resources. In contrast, radical feminists argue that liberal feminists have been co-opted by the male hierarchy since their goal is to reform the system rather than replace it. A third perspective, global feminism, critiques liberal feminism because it evolved out of a specific Western tradition of Enlightenment values that is overly focused on the individual, which does not mesh well with other cultures' focus on community, rather than individualist, values. And conservative critics charge that feminism as a whole is out of touch with mainstream society, which values marriage, motherhood, and family.[9]

While the book does advocate the promotion of women's equality, it does not take a particular position on which strategy should be used to achieve that goal, although it does present a range of differing positions on improving women's status. Many of these strategies differ on how to resolve the tension between sex and gender, which are often used interchangeably in the popular press and media. The word "sex" refers to physical and biological differences between men and women. Males and females differ most obviously in their contribution to human reproduction; for example, females are unique in their abilities to give birth and to breastfeed. In contrast, "gender" refers to "socially determined attributes, including male and female roles."[10] For example, women's roles in raising children after birth are socially defined gender roles, not physically defined biological functions. Women's inequality in society cannot be attributed to sex differences alone; rather, "it is how society interprets differences and values one quality over another that has the greatest impact on women's lives."[11]

Women activists have pursued various strategies in their quest for women's equality, and they reflect differing attitudes about addressing what one scholar has termed the "paradox of gender equality"—that is, resolving demands of gender equality with biological differences between men and women.[12] Some advocates for women's equality have argued that the best way to ensure equality is to treat men and women the same by passing gender-neutral legislation. Thus, differences must be eliminated in laws and policies in order to foster equality. Others argue that treating men and women the same, given their biological and gendered differences, amounts to unfairness. According to proponents of this view, the solution lies in designing laws and policy that account for these differences by treating men and women differently, but fairly. Throughout this book we discuss this tension and show how it has been manifested in women's battles for greater political, economic, and human rights.

The book is divided into three parts. Part I, "Women Impacting Politics," contains three chapters, all of which provide a different perspective on how women in developing and developed societies participate and achieve representation in the political arena. The first part of the book gives the reader a clear analysis of the impact of women on politics in a variety of political settings around the world. Chapter 1 looks at women's participation in political institutions. It covers women's impact in institutions such as legislatures, parliaments, executives, and bureaucracies. The increase in the number of women in public office has shaped irrevocably the way these institutions work and the policies that they produce. Chapter 2 covers women's involvement in and impact on interest groups and social movements. These organizations play a crucial role in expressing the demands of citizens to their state. Women's involvement in such groups has made a crucial difference in the actions that many states have taken regarding women's issues and concerns. Chapter 3 deals with women's roles in revolutionary movements. Lacking stable channels of participation toward the state, women have been crucial forces in revolutions, although they have not always been rewarded consistently for their efforts with policies that substantially improve their lives.

Part II, "Gendering Public Policy," moves from the topic of women's influence on politics to the ways in which public policy shapes women's lives in advanced industrialized nations. The three chapters explore the tension that exists between the quest for policy that creates gender equality (such as equal pay or antidiscrimination legislation) and the battle for policy that acknowledges the differences that exist between the sexes. Chapter 4 examines employment policy in the advanced industrialized world and its impact on women's lives. How have states attempted to ensure women's equality, and how have they designed policies to reflect that commitment? Chapter 5 explores the politics of difference. In other words, states also write gender-specific legislation, acknowledging the innate differences between men and women. Specifically, this chapter delves into how states have legislated balancing the needs of production (work) with reproduction (family care). Chapter 6 examines how states address issues of privacy by looking at ways that different countries have resolved the issue of abortion.

Part III, "Participation and Protest in the Global Community," explores a variety of women's issues that, although of global concern, tend to be concentrated in the countries of the developing world. This part is different than the first two; instead of long chapters we have chosen to write shorter chapters on a variety of issues that address critical and compelling global issues affecting women in countries on nearly every continent. Chapter 7 surveys how the international community has addressed gender issues and concerns. Chapter 8 examines the role of women in the global economy. We then turn to women and health care in Chapter 9. Chapter 10 examines women and education. Chapter 11 addresses the issue of sexual violence during war. Finally, Chapter 12 discusses women's lack of physical autonomy in issues such as female genital mutilation.

For the second edition we decided to make several key changes. First we updated the data in all the chapters to reflect any recent relevant changes. Second, we expanded the content in each of the final six chapters, not only deepening the discussion of existing issues but also integrating new topics such as international trafficking of women, the increasing incidence of women soldiers in civil conflicts, the reintegration of child soldiers after war, global migration of women, and the impact of structural adjustment policies on women's access to education. Third, we added text boxes to the chapters to enable students to get a feel for the individuals and groups relevant to the issues addressed. And finally, we added a "For More Information" section at the end of each chapter that provides links to websites where students can learn more information about these issues as well as the people and organizations working for critical change. This section also includes cites for memoirs and documentaries that may provide an alternative narrative for students. These final two changes were prompted by the desire to provide more active learning, to help the material come more alive for students.

Throughout the book we discuss a number of dilemmas that women have faced as they have battled for greater representation in political and economic institutions. As we shall see, countries differ dramatically in terms of the degree to which women have access to the state and are able to impact state policy. While there is not one correct way to resolve the demands for women's equality, hopefully we have provided enough information for you to think about various women's issues with your professor and your classmates so that you can continue to ponder your position on these issues long after the course has ended.

Sarah L. Henderson
Alana S. Jeydel

ACKNOWLEDGMENTS

We would like to acknowledge all those who supported us in the research and writing of this book. First and foremost, we would like to thank each other for providing the support, patience, and love necessary to write and revise this book while also raising small children. At different times, one of us would provide the critical push necessary, without which this book would never have seen the light of day. Alana would like to thank the Center for the Humanities at Oregon State University, which deserves special thanks for providing her with the resources needed to work on this project. Sarah would also like to thank her husband, Doug, for supporting her throughout the long process of researching and writing both editions. We would also like to thank Julie M. Bunck, University of Louisville; Marilyn Dantico, Arizona State University; Patricia F. Freeland, The University of Tennessee, Knoxville; Manjusha Gupte, North Dakota State University; Lynn H. Leverty, University of Florida; Dana Patton, University of Kentucky; Leslie Schwindt-Bayer, University of Missouri; Carisa R. Showden, University of North Carolina, Greensboro; Gina Woodall, Arizona State University; and Sharon D. Wright Austin, University of Florida, for their thoughtful comments. Finally, we would like to thank Jennifer Carpenter and Thomas Pold at Oxford University Press for believing in and supporting this project.

Sarah L. Henderson
Alana S. Jeydel

PART I

Women Impacting Politics

In this part we look at various ways in which women seek to impact the state. Drawing from countries in the developed as well as the developing world, we discuss women's involvement in institutionalized and noninstitutionalized forms of political activism. In other words, we look at women's participation in activities ranging from voting and running for office to participating in interest groups, social movements, and revolutionary movements. To what degree does women's involvement in politics and movements matter, and what barriers still stand in the way of their further involvement?

While women seek to influence the state in a variety of ways, certain common themes unite these chapters. One theme that runs through the chapters is that, while women have fought for and attained access to positions of power in elected governments, social movements, and revolutionary struggles, such access is neither widespread, uniform, nor far-reaching. Women are still marginalized in most governments and movements. They are often relegated to positions that deal with "women's issues" instead of issues like foreign policy and finances. Even in revolutionary movements that profess radical aims in terms of the redistribution of power, women's rights are often put off or ignored altogether, and women are often expected to fulfill the traditional female role of nurturer and caretaker in the movement. Further, multiple barriers still exist that bar or deter women from attaining leadership positions, and many women still attain positions of power via their roles as wives, mothers, or sisters of important male leaders or political dynasties.

Another theme that unites the chapters is the gendered nature of women's activism. That is, women's varied socially constructed roles and relationships are a constant subtext in their motivations to act. Women are often pulled into activism when their socially defined roles are threatened, and they have drawn on their status as mothers and caretakers to fight for issues, such as those involving food, shelter, health, and children, which are perceived to be of immediate concern to them. In addition, women are able to exploit societal expectations about

1

their affinity for "women's issues" to push for specific political outcomes, such as policy or regime change.

However, the ways in which women around the world define and express their gender interests vary widely. As we discussed in the preface, while women from disparate cultures often share broad, common concerns that unite them, cultural, socioeconomic, ethnic, religious, and racial differences often shape how women identify with and mobilize around these broad issues. In the chapters in this part, we try to emphasize these broad commonalities while also explaining how socioeconomic and cultural differences can manifest themselves at the local and national levels. Further, we stress that women are not necessarily united simply by the biological commonality of their sex or the status of their gender and that women can define and express their interests in diametrically opposed ways.

As we shall also see, not all women are motivated to activism out of gender concerns, and in fact, some subordinate these concerns in the face of other, larger causes, such as national self-determination, independence, and greater levels of social justice for all. Some women are conflicted by the question of "double militancy," or allegiance to two simultaneous issues (such as feminism and democracy), while others consciously choose to prioritize alternative issues. Regardless, all too often, primarily male political elites are often ready and willing to take advantage of women's contributions, while denying them substantial access to avenues of power upon achieving political victory.

Yet, as we shall see, the presence of women in political institutions and movements does matter. The increased visibility of women in a variety of political activities has led to increased attention to women's issues, the creation of women's bureaus and commissions, and the design and implementation of policy that impacts the status of women. This is not to say that women's views are always integrated or that women are consistently successful in achieving their political goals; however, having women in positions of power and influence has made a substantial impact.

This part provides a comparative analysis of women's involvement in various forms of political activism and expression. Specifically, we look at three areas of women's involvement in politics: at the institutional level, through struggles to get elected and/or appointed to government institutions, as well as women's voting behavior; at the noninstitutional level, through involvement in social movements and interest groups; and at the level of participation in movements whose aim is the overthrow of the government and the institution of a new, totally restructured government. Thus Chapter 1 covers women and institutional politics, Chapter 2 covers women in social movements, and Chapter 3 covers women in revolutionary movements.

The chapters highlight the impact that women have had on politics while also demonstrating the barriers and obstacles that remain in their way even in the twenty-first century. In the Chapter 1, "Women and Institutional Politics," we provide a comparative overview of women's representation in political institutions and their voting behavior. While the number of women elected officials has increased greatly in the past twenty years, there are still a number of countries where female representation is scant to nonexistent. Further, there appears to be a political "glass ceiling"; women are not moving up the rungs of the political ladder and are often relegated to "women's issues" departments, committees, and bureaus. Also, many barriers still exist to women's participation in politics—both cultural barriers and structural barriers. Finally, women worldwide are less likely to get involved in politics than men are—this means they are less likely to vote, run for office, and get involved in politics in general. Nonetheless, we see that women's involvement in politics does matter. Elected women officials are more likely than their male counterparts to introduce, lobby, and vote for legislation of immediate concern to women and their families. Further, in some countries, women's voting behavior has at times been decisive in election results, such that many now often talk about a gender gap. In short, women clearly have impacted institutional politics, but in most countries there is still vast room for improvement in women's representation and in addressing issues of direct consequence to women's lives.

In Chapter 2, "Women and Noninstitutional Politics," we examine women's involvement in and impact on social movements and interest groups worldwide. We see that women's movements and organizations are important players in politics around the world. From women taking over oil plants in Nigeria to Christian women fighting to limit or curtail access to abortion in the United States, women have been involved in and have impacted a wide spectrum of movements. Socially and culturally, women's groups have changed the way society perceives women, have motivated women to get more involved in grassroots politics, and have often changed the way women view themselves. Institutionally, women's groups have impacted governments by encouraging them to pass legislation directed toward women's issues and to create women's bureaus and ministries, and they have made politicians aware of the usefulness of a woman's bloc of votes. But women also have become involved in religious fundamentalist and nationalist movements that often seek to roll back or prevent any advancements that women have made. Their participation in such movements perplexes many scholars—why would women wish to maintain or return to a time when they had fewer rights and were subservient to men? We conclude the chapter with a discussion of this intriguing question. In sum, women have impacted the state in a multitude of ways via their involvement in social movements; however, this involvement is not without its contradictions, as recent years have seen a spate of religious fundamentalist and nationalist movements attracting women to their ranks.

Chapter 3, "Women and Revolutionary Movements," examines women's involvement in and impact on revolutionary struggles. In this chapter we see that despite the radical goals of most revolutionary movements, the key activists in the struggles often hold very orthodox views regarding the role of women in society and in the movement. And while some revolutionary leaders speak the rhetoric of women's rights, in practice they are more concerned with class struggle and often place women's rights on the back burner to be dealt with at some nebulous later date. Thus, it is rare that women occupy important leadership positions in revolutionary movements or the government, should the movement be successful. We do see, however, that women have played an active and important role in numerous revolutionary struggles—as messengers, fighters, and more. In sum, while revolutionary movements are not consistently revolutionary in their views of women, women have certainly impacted the course and outcome of many revolutions through the ages.

Women have had an important impact on the politics of many states in both advanced industrial and developing nations. Women are increasingly running for and winning access to political office. They are participating more frequently in the political process by utilizing their right to vote (where they have it) and by organizing around issues of interest to them. They are mobilizing in increasing numbers in revolutionary movements. In sum, their presence in institutions and movements does matter. Nonetheless, the number of women involved in politics as compared to men is still comparatively low in most countries and abysmally low in others. Further, there appears to be a glass ceiling in both political institutions and revolutionary movements, whereby women can only advance so far on the leadership ladder. This is caused, in part, by lingering societal norms about the "appropriateness" of women's involvement in politics, as well as by persistent gendered divisions of labor that keep women from exercising their full range of talents. Until societies view women as politically capable and are willing to redistribute the division of labor between men and women, women's impact on politics will continue to be hampered and countries will not experience the rich rewards that come from politically empowering their entire adult population.

1

◆❍

Women and Institutional Politics

In November 2002, Yvonne Khamati, a candidate for the Kenyan legislature, was beaten up, allegedly by supporters of one of her rivals.[1] Khamati noted, "The threat had been made on me since early October. The aspirant had been threatening to undress me in public if I did not step down for him, but I have resisted....I fear the threat itself more than the actual act."[2] This violent act was not an anomaly in the 2002 Kenyan elections. It was reported that in early December 2002, women who were waiting to hear a candidate for the Langata constituency of Nairobi were assaulted by a gang of youths who supported the opposition. Further, a parliamentary candidate and her children were attacked on the campaign trail, and another female candidate's convoy was stoned as she campaigned among her constituency.[3] And while violent attacks against candidates in Kenya are not limited to women, they are certainly a tactic used to try to prevent women in particular from seeking political office. In the 2002 elections in Kenya, 130 women expressed an interest in running for office, but ultimately only 44 did.[4] Kenya's legislature has one of the worst records in Africa regarding female representation. In the last Assembly only 9 out of 220 members were women, and at no point in Kenya's history has the number of women ever exceeded 10. A patriarchal culture, a lack of funding, and Kenya's electoral system are just a few of the variables that stand in the way of women's decision to run for and ultimately win office.

The Kenyan case is one example of a pervasive problem—women's under-representation in institutional politics. As of 2008, worldwide, women comprised just over 18 percent of members of legislatures.[5] There are also only twenty-one female heads of state and government.[6] Of that twenty-one, many serve in the more ceremonial position of head of state (often as queen or governor general) and have few real political powers. However, despite these discouraging general statistics, women's representation in political institutions varies substantially from region to region and is improving. Women constitute over 40 percent of members of parliament in the Nordic countries and at least 30 percent of members of lower houses of legislatures in twenty-two countries located primarily in Europe and Africa.[7] Further, although on average women comprise 17.9 percent of legislators in sub-Saharan African countries, countries such as Rwanda, Mozambique, and South Africa also have high percentages of women legislators. In fact, Rwanda has the highest percentage of any nation; 56.3 percent of the members of the lower house are women.[8] As a point of comparison, in the United States Congress (as of 2008) women comprised almost 17 percent of representatives and 16 percent of senators, placing it sixty-ninth out of 185 countries in terms of its representation of women.[9] These numbers improved slightly after the November 2008 elections; 17 women now serve in the Senate and 75 women serve in the House, up from 71, in the 110th Congress. Women are also increasingly visible as heads of legislatures, members of cabinets and bureaucracies, and executives. These increases are a largely recent phenomenon. For example, of the thirty-two women who have served as heads of state in the twentieth century, twenty-four were in power in the 1990s.[10]

But, as the Kenyan case suggests, there is still vast room for improvement. In a wide array of countries women's presence in government is scant. In the newly independent states of the former Soviet Union and in the former members of the Eastern bloc the number of women in political positions has dropped.[11] And women's representation in politics is extremely low in Middle Eastern countries. In Arab states, women comprise just over 9 percent of elected representatives and are barred by law from standing for parliament or voting in Saudi Arabia.[12] On a positive note, women recently won the right to vote and stand for elections in Quatar in 1999 and Kuwait in 2005; women in Oman could stand for elections beginning in 1997; in 2002 all Omani citizens received the right to vote; and finally, in 2006 the United Arab Emirates began the slow path toward democracy with the creation of an elective body in which 15 percent of the candidates and eligible voters were women.[13] But overall, while women's legislative representation is higher, at its current growth levels, women legislators will not achieve parity with men until the turn of the twenty-second century.[14] What explains women's underrepresentation, and what factors can continue to improve their status?

This chapter examines women and institutional politics. Institutional or formal politics is the realm of politics that takes place in formal governmental institutions, such as parliaments/legislatures and the executive branch, and encompasses political behavior, regulated by the state, which is geared toward electing people to those institutions. We explore women's voting behavior, their paths to political office, the reasons for their underrepresentation in office, and their political behavior once in office. In closing, we discuss a variety of strategies that have been used to improve women's representation in institutional politics.

Why study women and institutional politics? Quite simply, because the decisions made by political institutions directly impact women's lives. Political institutions were created and largely run by men for centuries, and, as a result, many women's concerns have either been ignored, forgotten, or inadequately addressed. And since men and women often experience life differently (arguably as a result of socialization and societal constraints on appropriate behavior), it stands to reason that they might have different concerns, views, and modes of behavior that might result in different voting patterns, laws, regulations, and policies. And in fact, this is the case. As we show, a significant gender gap exists in voting patterns, and this gap has been decisive in determining the outcome of elections. Further, women's presence in political office, particularly in legislatures, does matter, as does their voting patterns. When compared to men, women elected officials are often more progressive, more consensus-oriented, and more likely to introduce legislation that directly addresses women's concerns (health care, education, welfare). They also work hard to see such legislation become law. While there are individual exceptions to all of these generalizations, nonetheless, across countries and contexts, women engage in distinctly different patterns of political behavior.

WOMEN AND VOTING

The Expansion of Suffrage

Beginning in the mid-1800s women worldwide began to organize to demand the right to vote in their countries, and in some countries women are still working to gain this basic political right. In 1861, Sweden introduced limited suffrage for women in local elections. Over thirty years later, in 1893, New Zealand became the first country to grant all women the right to vote at the national level. Australia extended suffrage to women in 1902 and Finland in 1906, with a number of European countries as well as the various republics of the former Soviet Union following suit in the 1910s. By 1930, forty-two countries had granted women the right to vote, and in the ensuing three decades, from 1931 to 1960, an additional eighty-six countries widened suffrage regulations to include women. Finally, an additional thirty-eight countries extended the right to vote after 1960.[15] The end of World War I, World War II, and the ensuing decolonization (and initial democratization) in many countries around the world were some of the factors that created a wave of women's suffrage. Table 1.1 offers a glimpse of when national voting rights were granted to women around the globe. As noted, New Zealand was the first country to expand the suffrage to all women in 1893; over a century later, Qatar, Oman, Kuwait, and, to a limited degree, the United Arab Emirates, became the most recent countries to expand the suffrage to women.

Winning the right to vote was not easy, often requiring decades of struggle. For instance, in the United States women began agitating for the right to vote in 1848 but only received that right nationally seventy-two years later, in 1920. Nor did women win the right to vote for particularly noble reasons. For example, U.S. women were granted the right to vote, in part, to counteract the influx (and

Table 1.1 Year Suffrage Granted in National Elections
in Selected Countries

COUNTRY	YEAR
New Zealand	1893
Australia	1902
Finland	1906
Germany	1918
Austria	1919
United States	1920
Cuba	1934
France	1944
Japan	1946
Argentina	1951
Bolivia	1952
Nigeria (Southern)	1957
Nigeria (Northern)	1976
Iran	1963
Yemen	1967
Switzerland	1972
Jordan	1974
Zimbabwe	1982
Qatar	1999

SOURCE: United Nations Development Programme, "Women's
Political Participation," Human Development Report 2004
(New York: UNDP, 2004), 234–237.

political influence) of immigrants into the country. Further, some legislators assumed that women would vote as their husbands directed. In other countries, suffrage was gradually extended to all women. For example, while white women won the right to vote in Australia in 1902, Aboriginal women did not gain that right until 1967.[16]

In some countries, women's right to vote is still fragile. In Kuwait, the emir issued a decree in May 1999 granting women full political rights (the right to vote and to run for and hold political office). However, the National Assembly threw out this decree and then subsequently defeated a bill that would have granted women these rights. The issue, however, did not disappear, and on May 16, 2005, parliament granted women the right to vote and run for parliament. The law first went into effect in the 2007 parliamentary elections. Other Gulf nations, such as Bahrain, Qatar, and Oman, all had their first elections in recent years and allowed women to cast ballots.[17] Saudi Arabia is the only remaining Middle Eastern country where elections are permitted without women's suffrage.

Women's Political Participation

What has been the impact of women's suffrage, and how have women participated in other forms of political activities? Early research on women in the United States indicated that women voted and engaged in political activities (such as helping political parties, attending political rallies, and other such civic activities) at rates lower than men did.[18] Since women gained the right to vote in the United States they have historically lagged behind men in their rates of turnout at election time. For example, in 1964, 72 percent of voting-age males cast a ballot, versus 67 percent of voting-age females.[19] A few explanations were put forth to explain these lower rates of participation. First, some argued that women are politically passive and thus do not participate in political activities. Second, some argued that women's family responsibilities hinder their involvement in politics. Finally, some maintained that women are less likely to be found in those segments of society that are most politically engaged—the highly educated, for example. While this research was limited to the United States (and in terms of voting is no longer valid), we will show that these explanations travel well to other countries.

However, since 1980, women's turnout in U.S. elections has been greater than that of men.[20] In 2000, women led men in turnout 56 percent to 53 percent.[21] Similarly, in 2004, turnout was higher for women (65 percent) than for men (62 percent).[22] And while this difference is not great, it is interesting. It sends a message to elected officials that women are worth targeting because they will vote. In addition, the gender gap in party identification with regard to voting in the U.S. is significant; since 1980, women have been more likely than men to vote for Democratic Party candidates. In the 2000 presidential election, for example, approximately 54 percent of women voters backed Al Gore, while only 43 percent of men did.[23] In 2004, 55 percent of men voted for George W. Bush while 48 percent of women voted for him.[24] 2008 witnessed a continuation of this trend, with 56% of women voters favoring Obama and 43% favoring McCain. The media quickly labeled this emerging gender gap in voting as the "soccer mom" vote. In their depiction, these women are not only behind the wheels of suburban minivans but are also increasingly in control of the fate of presidential elections. As a result, both Republicans and Democrats have become much more attentive to women voters, and the gender gap is an incentive for them to include more women's issues on their party platforms as well as to nominate more women for office.

Interestingly, however, women's rates of participation in campaign activities (working for a candidate, contributing money, attending a political meeting or a campaign rally, trying to persuade someone how to vote, or wearing a political button or displaying a campaign sticker) consistently has remained below that of men since 1952.[25] However, when we expand participation to include involvement in community groups, women's involvement improves. Women are somewhat more likely than men to be members of and actively involved in such groups.[26] And as you will see in the chapter on noninstitutional politics, women are very involved in social movements and interest groups. Research seeking to explain women's lower levels of political participation in the United States has found that while women have as much, if not more, of some of the resources necessary for becoming involved in politics, namely education, they lack other crucial resources, such as personal income and occupations that facilitate political participation and a sense of personal efficacy.[27] Nonetheless, and no matter the explanation, with the exception of voting, women's political participation in the United States remains below that of men.

What about in other countries? What are women's rates of political participation around the globe? Some studies indicate that in advanced industrial nations, traditional gender differences in voting participation have either diminished or reversed.[28] In most countries outside of the advanced industrial world, women's rate of voting is generally below that of men. However, it is important to note that we do not have longitudinal data for many countries. We have limited longitudinal data for a few democracies, all of which are at varying levels of development: Chile (elections since 1989), Puerto Rico (1992 and 1996), and Nepal (1991–1999). And longitudinal data since World War II exists only for eight other democracies (not including the United States), only one of which would be considered a developing nation—India. Of these countries for which we have data, the evidence is inconclusive. In Chile women have voted in greater numbers than men in each election for which we have data (by about 5 percent), and in Puerto Rico women have also voted in greater numbers than men (by about 2–3 percent), but in India and Nepal men have voted in greater numbers than women (by about 10 percent and 1 percent, respectively).[29] In Israel, Arab women display a higher rate of voting than do Arab men, although there is no noticeable difference between Israeli women and men.[30] However, this is not a representative sample of developing

Kuwaiti women, long denied suffrage, vote in parliamentary elections in Kuwait City on May 17, 2008. SOURCE: YASSER AL-ZAYYAT/AFP/Getty Images

nations, and, while limited, evidence does seem to suggest that women vote in lower numbers in most developing nations.

Low voter turnout among women in developing nations is not surprising given the significant discrepancies in adult literacy rates between men and women. Further, men's longer history of political involvement provides them with the basic know-how concerning how to vote. One deterrent to voting is fear—a lack of knowledge about what to do once one enters the polling site. Nigeria is no exception to this rule. One group, the Women's Rights Advancement and Protection Alternative (WRAPA), is working to change this by educating women on how to vote correctly (e.g., how to use the machines).[31] Arab women are also working to overcome this barrier to women's participation. In some tribal communities, Arab women have provided women-only transportation and polling stations in an attempt to increase the number of women voting.[32]

However, even if women may be less likely in many countries to vote, nonetheless the gender gap in party identification is noticeable in many countries, as it is in the United States. Until 1980, the conventional wisdom was that women were more conservative than men. In fact, The Civic Culture, a comparative study of political cultures that was first published in 1963, found that "wherever the consequences of women's suffrage have been studied, it would appear that women differ from men in their political behavior only in being somewhat more frequently apathetic, parochial [and] conservative....Our data, on the whole, confirm the findings reported in the literature."[33] Yet, by the 1980s, scholars were finding signs of gender dealignment in Britain, Germany, the Netherlands, and New Zealand. Drawing from survey data collected from over seventy countries over the course of several decades, Ronald Inglehart and Pippa Norris found that in most nations surveyed, women hold more left-leaning values than men do, favoring active government intervention and public ownership. This left-leaning gender gap is most pronounced among young voters; older voters tend to adhere to pre-1980 expectations about women's more conservative political behavior.[34] Thus, the United States is not singular and is one example of a growing and enduring gender cleavage in voting.

In addition, around the world, women's participation in other forms of traditional political activity—party membership, contact activity, and community organizing—has historically been below that of men. A 1978 seventeen-nation comparative study of political activity found that, even after controlling for levels of education, institutional involvement such as trade union membership, and psychological involvement in politics, women in advanced industrial nations were less active than men were.[35] However, recent research presents a less conclusive picture. One study demonstrated that women's rates of political activity in advanced industrial nations increased in the 1980s and 1990s, and in some cases their participation surpassed that of men.[36] The Inglehart and Norris study found that while there is a gap in traditional forms of political activism, particularly in advanced industrial societies, that gap is narrowing and very modest. However, particularly in agrarian societies, the gap is more substantial, and men are much more likely to join parties, discuss politics, and work in community organizations than women are.[37]

In sum, while there still seems to be a modest gap in traditional forms of political participation, particularly in developing countries, nonetheless women's participation is increasing. This increase appears to have a few causes. One clear pattern is that the increase in participation is largely found among younger women (those under twenty-five), who are turning out in greater numbers to vote than their male counterparts are.[38] The other causes appear to be changes in social norms and in structural lifestyles, which have removed many barriers that had deterred women's participation.[39] However, it is important to remember that voting is no guarantee of political, social, or economic equality. And further, voting may mean little in authoritarian regimes where voting has no impact on the outcome or in patriarchal states where men may inform their female family members how they should vote. As a woman in Oman commented to a Reuters reporter, "Some [women] . . . follow their male relatives' lead when choosing which candidates to vote for."[40] Finally, voting is but one form of political involvement. As we will show, women increasingly are involving themselves in other forms of nontraditional political participation.

PATHS AND BARRIERS TO POLITICAL OFFICE

In the beginning of this chapter, we gave some statistics to illustrate women's persistent underrepresentation in positions of political leadership. Specifically, as of September 30, 2008, only 18.3 percent of the world's parliamentarians were women (although this was the first time that women exceeded 18 percent and was a 2 percent increase from the first edition of this book). Moreover, women comprised only 4.2 percent of the world's heads of state.[41] In sum, the higher women ascend the ladder of political power, the rarer their representation. Why has the rate of women in political office historically been so low? Cross-national research on this question has produced three general explanations for the persistent lack of women in political office. Women worldwide running for office, no matter which path they have taken, run into some common obstacles or barriers.

The first explanation emphasizes the role of structural barriers, such as levels of political and socioeconomic development, as well as women's representation in professional and managerial occupations. For example, scholars have argued that the degree to which a country is democratic is positively related to women's presence in elected office. That is, newly democratized countries are likely to promote widespread political and civil liberties, increased political party building, and other measures that would increase the involvement of women. However, the evidence to support that claim is inconclusive.[42]

Another study demonstrated that levels of socioeconomic development are significantly associated with the number of female parliamentarians worldwide.[43] In other words, in developing countries, many women are disadvantaged because they are more likely to be illiterate, have inadequate health care, and live in poverty. Further, women in the developing world are less likely to have an independent source of income, making it difficult to accumulate the funds to run for office. In Uganda, for instance, women lack the monetary resources required to dole out beer, small gifts, and contributions to fund-raising events, thus making their run for office more arduous in a society accustomed to such offerings during the campaign season.[44] All of these are barriers to running for office.

Further, studies have demonstrated that in established democracies, the presence of women in professional, administrative, and managerial occupations is critical, as these types of careers often provide the experiences, financial resources, social networks, and flexibility needed to compete for elected office.[45] However, since women have traditionally not been well represented in careers that prepare them for politics, they often have difficulty running campaigns that highlight their preparation for political office. Women also often lack the necessary resources (primarily money) required to run a successful campaign. Individuals and political parties often donate to the candidate with the greatest chance of winning, and women are still not seen in many countries as viable candidates. Further, since men traditionally have been in the paid labor force and women relegated to the home, women often do not have the same personal financial resources that men have to contribute to their own campaigns. And while money is critical, women also lack access to the "old boy's network" that has enabled men to access to political power.

This explanation, however, does not fully explain the variance in women's rates of election to office. Countries that have similar standards of living exhibit major disparities in the proportion of women elected to parliament. For example, in 2003, nearly 20 percent of Canadian parliamentarians were women, while in the United States, that figure was just under 13 percent. The countries in Europe and Africa also demonstrate great disparities in women elected to office, even when they share similar socioeconomic characteristics. Comparatively, in 2005, Rwanda had a very high percentage of women legislators, even though it is one of the world's poorest countries.

In addition, in many postindustrial societies, while women are increasingly well represented in careers, such as law, that serve as a jumping ground for political office, they are not reaping a clear increase in their political representation. For example, while almost a third of all lawyers (29 percent) in the United States are now women, the United States has not witnessed a similar surge in women's representation in the U.S. House or Senate. Nor has increased funding for female candidates in countries such as the United States led to a dramatic increase of women representatives. Thus, while improving women's socioeconomic status and career opportunities is an important condition for improving their access to political office, it is not in and of itself sufficient.[46]

A second explanation for women's underrepresentation focuses on the role of institutional design and the "rules of the game" as expressed by electoral laws and the use of what are known as positive action policies. Specifically, scholars point to the importance of proportional representation (PR) electoral systems and the adoption of gender quotas, either via internal party rules or mandated through national legislation. A PR system is one in which parliamentary seats are awarded in proportion to the vote received by each party. In addition, voters in a proportional system often choose among party lists, which are lists of candidates who would assume seats if the party is elected. In contrast, countries such as the United States use a single-member plurality electoral system, also known as a majoritarian system. That is, the candidate that obtains more votes than any other is elected. The larger difference between the two systems is that a proportional system tends to produce a multiparty legislature, in which power is shared among a coalition of varied parties, while a majoritarian system produces a two-party system, in which power usually alternates between two large catchall parties.

Proportional systems have beneficial ramifications for female candidates; research shows that women are almost twice as likely to be elected under the rules governing a proportional system.[47] The Inter-Parliamentary Union reported that in 2007 the twenty-one chambers that used proportional representation elected an average of 18.3 percent of women to seats versus 13.8 percent of the seats being won by women in chambers that do not use proportional representation (twenty-one such chambers).[48] This is because parties in majoritarian systems are less likely to nominate women, since they are afraid of losing the seat to a male competitor. In contrast, parties in proportional systems are more likely to add women to their party lists to make their ticket more diverse and broaden their appeal. Women candidates in proportional systems are perceived to be less risky because a woman is part of a larger group of candidates running for office, rather than a sole candidate competing for office.[49]

Other institutional variables, such as the adoption of various quota regulations, have also been critical in promoting women to elected office. Many parties, particularly those of the left, have moved to adopt voluntary internal quotas mandating that women must constitute a minimum proportion of parliamentary candidates or elected representatives within each party. This is usually done by requiring that a certain percentage of female candidates appear on party lists. For example, in 1980, the Green Party in Germany became the first party in Europe to institute a 50 percent quota for women on party lists. Eventually, two other major German parties moved to implement quota systems in their own party rules. Political parties in Scandinavian countries followed the Green Party model several years later; in 1983, the Norwegian Labour Party implemented a 40 percent quota for all elections, and other Norwegian parties soon followed with similar strategies. However, while this is significant, the effects can be limited by several factors. One, given that voluntary quotas are adopted by individual parties within a country, the potential benefits to women can be limited if the practice does not spread to other parties. Second, the effects can be diminished if parties decide to place women at the bottom of party lists, which lessens their chances of making the cut for political representation. In response to this problem, some parties, such as the Greens, also simultaneously adopted what is known as a "zipper" or "zebra" principle; that is, names on the party's nomination list must alternate evenly between men and women.[50] Finally, it is easier to adopt this type of quota system in proportional systems than in majoritarian ones, which govern the United States and Great Britain. However, this does not mean it cannot be done. In 1993, in response to an electoral defeat in which they failed to attract sufficient levels of women voters, the British Labour Party agreed that in half of certain categories of targeted seats, local party members would be required to select their candidate from an all-female short list. Although this provision was eventually dropped under legal challenge, the proportion of women at Westminster doubled from 1992 to 1997.[51] Around the world, 131 political parties, representing sixty-two countries, have instituted voluntary internal quotas.[52]

Other countries have moved to mandate party list quotas through passing legislation that applies to all parties.[53] For example, in the summer of 2000, the French legislature passed parity legislation, a constitutional amendment requiring parties to include 50 percent representation of women in their party lists for local, regional, parliamentary, and European elections.[54] Belgium, Italy, and various Latin American countries have instituted legal gender quotas. Further, Finland and Norway have implemented legislation that sets out gender quotas for appointments to public bodies and consultative committees.[55] Alternatively, other countries have implemented legislation that reserves a certain percentage of legislative seats for women (and in some instances, ethnic minority candidates). This system of reserving seats has been used in Morocco, Bangladesh, Pakistan, Botswana, Taiwan, Lesotho, and Tanzania. However, some argue that this is not as effective a mechanism as party quotas, for it can simply be used to sideline or appease women, particularly in countries where the women are appointed, rather than elected. While this system is most often used in countries with more limited democratic rights, a notable exception is India, where a third of seats in local municipal elections are reserved for women.[56] Despite these concerns, voluntary, internal gender quotas as well as legally mandated party quotas have been two of the most successful means for getting more women into office and are used in a total of ninety-two countries around the world.[57] Tables 1.2–1.6 provide an overview of the varied use of quota systems around the world.

Political scientist Eileen McDonagh, in her research on female leaders, has found that women are more likely to be elected head of state or government in political systems that combine both traditional and modern features. She maintains:

> Every nation where women have been elected to be head of state or government is one that combines modern guarantees of individual rights and electoral processes with the retention of at least one major traditional feature, such as a monarchy, a state religion, or a constitutional connection between the state and the family as an institution or another ascribed group.[58]

It will be interesting to see if this holds true in the twenty-first century.

Table 1.2 Quota Systems for Women's Representation

QUOTA TYPES	TOTAL NUMBER OF COUNTRIES	AVERAGE % OF WOMEN	TOTAL NUMBER OF COUNTRIES PREVIOUSLY HAVING QUOTA PROVISIONS	AVERAGE % OF WOMEN UNDER PREVIOUS SYSTEM
Constitutional quota for national legislatures	14	20.7	2	16.2
Election law quota regulation, national legislature	33	17.2	2	5.7
Constitutional or legislative quota, subnational level	17	N/A	N/A	N/A
Political party quota for electoral candidates	62	N/A	N/A	N/A

SOURCE: International IDEA and Stockholm University, "Global Database of Quotas for Women," http://www.quotaproject.org/system.cfm (July 15, 2005).

Table 1.3 Constitutional Quotas for National Legislatures

COUNTRY	% WOMEN
Afghanistan	27.3
Argentina	35
Bangladesh	2
Burundi	30.5
France	18.5
Guyana	30.8
Iraq	25.5
Kenya	9.8
Nepal	5.9
Rwanda	56.3
Serbia	20.4
Somalia	7.8
Taiwan	22.2
Tanzania, United Republic of	30.4
Uganda	23.9

SOURCE: International IDEA and Stockholm University, "Global Database of Quotas for Women," http://www.quotaproject.org/system.cfm (July 15, 2006).

Table 1.4 Election Law Quota Regulation, National Legislature

COUNTRY	% WOMEN	COUNTRY	% WOMEN
Afghanistan	27.3	Liberia	12.5
Albania	7.2	Macedonia	28.3
Argentina	35.0	Mauritania	17.9
Armenia	9.2	Mexico	22.6
Belgium	36.7	Nepal	5.9
Bolivia	16.9	Niger	12.4
Bosnia and Herzegovina	14.3	Pakistan	21.3
Brazil	8.8	Palestinian Territory, Occupied	12.9
Burundi	30.5	Panama	16.7
China	20.3	Paraguay	10.0
Costa Rica	38.6	Peru	29.2
Djibouti	10.8	Philippines	20.4
Dominican Republic	19.7	Portugal	21.3
Ecuador	25.0	Rwanda	56.3
Eritrea	22.0	Serbia	20.4
France	18.5	Slovenia	12.2
Honduras	23.4	Spain	36.3
Indonesia	11.3	Sudan	14.7
Iraq	25.5	Tanzania, United Republic of	30.4
Jordan	6.4	Uganda	23.9
Korea, Dem. People's Republic of	20.1	Uzbekistan	17.5
Korea, Republic of	13.0		

SOURCE: International IDEA and Stockholm University, "Global Database of Quotas for Women," http://www.quotaproject.org/system.cfm (July, 15 2006).

A third explanation for women's poor electoral performance focuses on the role of cultural barriers. This explanation contends that "ideas about women's role and position in society can enhance or constrain women's ability to seek political power."[59] Thus cultural norms can inhibit women's participation, as the Kenyan case certainly suggests. This explanation has recently found strong support in research done by Paxton and Kunovich, which draws on survey data from forty-six countries.[60] Further, Inglehart and Norris found that there is a strong relationship between attitudes toward women's political leadership and the actual proportion of women legislators. In other words, countries with egalitarian cultures, such as Sweden, Finland, and Norway, have more women in power. This egalitarian culture is a reflection of broader patterns of socioeconomic development and cultural modernization that are impacting many countries, not just northern European ones.[61]

Cultural norms have made it difficult for women to run in a number of ways. One barrier women encounter when running (or deciding to run) for office is that political behavior is seen as masculine because aggression and autonomy are considered requisites. These are not traits commonly associated with women,

Table 1.5 Constitutional or Legislative Quota, Subnational Level

COUNTRY	COUNTRY
Argentina	Nepal
Bangladesh	Pakistan
Bolivia	Palestinian Territory, Occupied
Bosnia and Herzegovinia	Paraguay
Brazil	Peru
Costa Rica	Philippines
Dominican Republic	Portugal
Ecuador	Rwanda
France	Serbia
Greece	Sierra Leone
Honduras	Slovenia
India	South Africa
Korea, Republic of	Spain
Lesotho	Taiwan
Macedonia	Tanzania, United Republic of
Mauritania	Uganda
Namibia	

SOURCE: International IDEA and Stockholm University, "Global Database of Quotas for Women," http://www.quotaproject.org/system.cfm (July 15, 2006).

Table 1.6 Political Party Quota for Electoral Candidates

COUNTRY	NUMBER OF WOMEN ELECTED	% WOMEN
Algeria	28 of 389	7.2
Argentina	90 of 257	35.0
Armenia	12 of 131	9.2
Australia	37 of 150	24.7
Austria	59 of 183	32.2
Belgium	55 of 150	36.7
Bosnia and Herzegovina	6 of 42	14.3
Botswana	7 of 63	11.1
Brazil	45 of 513	8.8
Burkina Faso	13 of 111	11.7
Cameroon	23 of 163	14.1
Canada	64 of 308	20.8
Chile	18 of 120	15.0
Costa Rica	22 of 57	38.6
Croatia	32 of 153	20.9
Cyprus	8 of 56	14.3
Czech Republic	31 of 200	15.5

Table 1.6 (*continued*)

COUNTRY	NUMBER OF WOMEN ELECTED	% WOMEN
Côte d'Ivoire	19 of 223	8.5
Dominican Republic	35 of 178	19.7
Ecuador	25 of 100	25.0
El Salvador	14 of 84	16.7
Equatorial Guinea	18 of 100	18.0
Ethiopia	116 of 546	21.2
France	107 of 577	18.5
Germany	195 of 614	31.8
Greece	48 of 300	16.0
Hungary	41 of 386	10.6
Iceland	20 of 63	31.7
India	44 of 543	8.1
Ireland	22 of 166	13.3
Israel	17 of 120	14.2
Italy	109 of 630	17.3
Kenya	22 of 224	9.8
Korea, Republic of	39 of 299	13.0
Kyrgyzstan	23 of 90	25.6
Lithuania	29 of 141	20.6
Luxembourg	14 of 60	23.3
Macedonia	34 of 120	28.3
Malawi	27 of 188	14.4
Mali	15 of 147	10.2
Malta	6 of 65	9.2
Mexico	113 of 500	22.6
Moldova, Republic of	21 of 101	20.8
Morocco	34 of 325	10.5
Mozambique	87 of 250	34.8
Namibia	21 of 78	26.9
Netherlands	55 of 150	36.7
Nicaragua	14 of 92	15.2
Niger	14 of 113	12.4
Norway	64 of 169	37.9
Paraguay	8 of 80	10.0
Philippines	49 of 240	20.4
Poland	94 of 460	20.4
Portugal	49 of 230	21.3
Romania	38 of 332	11.5
Senegal	33 of 150	22.0
Serbia	51 of 250	20.4
Slovakia	24 of 150	16.0
Slovenia	11 of 90	12.2

(*continued*)

Table 1.6 (*continued*)

COUNTRY	NUMBER OF WOMEN ELECTED	% WOMEN
South Africa	131 of 400	32.8
Spain	127 of 350	36.3
Sweden	165 of 349	47.3
Switzerland	59 of 200	29.5
Taiwan (UN: Province of China)	50 of 225	22.2
Thailand	53 of 500	10.6
Tunisia	43 of 189	22.8
United Kingdom	128 of 646	19.8
Uruguay	12 of 99	12.1
Zimbabwe	16 of 150	10.7
Total countries:		69
Total political parties:		169

SOURCE: International IDEA and Stockholm University, "Global Database of Quotas for Women," http://www.quotaproject.org/system.cfm (July 15, 2006).

and thus women are not seen as capable of doing the job if elected (thus people may not vote for them). And, when women do exhibit these traits, they are seen by the electorate as abnormal or deviant, which are not adjectives often ascribed to successful candidates for elective office.

In addition, voters often have trouble overcoming traditional societal norms about appropriate divisions of labor between men and women. Women are associated with parental roles, and men are associated with paid labor. Thus politics is not seen as an appropriate realm for women since it will interfere with their parental responsibilities. In Uganda, female parliamentary candidates confronted cultural prohibitions on their political activity that their male colleagues did not face: "[W]omen candidates . . . faced greater public ridicule than men, were labeled 'unfeminine' and some even risked their marriages and public discrediting by their husbands." [62] In Oman, a female university lecturer told a Reuter's reporter that "My husband stopped me from standing for elections." [63] These societal norms are even still prevalent in advanced industrial nations; female candidates with children are routinely asked how their election may impact their ability to care for their children, but male candidates with children are almost never asked such questions.

This barrier not only prevents people from voting for women but also prevents many women from running. Women often do not see elective office as an option, either because they also ascribe to this societal norm or because they choose not to come forward as candidates for office. Those that choose to run often face a negative environment. A study conducted by the Inter-Parliamentary Union found that female politicians in many countries identified hostile attitudes toward women's political participation as one of the most important barriers to running for office.

Further, holding political office is not a family-friendly job for either women or men. It is extremely difficult to parent and hold elective office. National capitals are often quite far from most people's homes, the hours are unorthodox, and there are often no on-site daycare options. Given that women are traditionally expected to be the primary caregiver in the family, prevailing cultural norms serve as a significant barrier for women wishing to hold political office.

There is some evidence that cultural values toward women in office is changing. For one, Inglehart and Norris found that there is a significant generational gap in attitudes about women's abilities. Younger, postwar generations are much less likely to believe that men make better leaders than women do. Further, there is a significant emerging gender gap; while men and women of older generations are equally likely to be suspicious of women as leaders, the gap widened substantially across generations, until by the youngest generation the gap has become considerable. Women are much less likely than men to agree with the statement "men make better political leaders than women," and as a result, they may be more likely to raise the issue of women's underrepresentation in office.[64] While changes in cultural attitudes in and of itself are not enough to improve women's access to political power, changing public opinion can also pressure parties and legislatures to institute institutional reforms, such as quotas, which we discussed earlier.

Theory aside, practically, what are the various paths that lead women to political office? There are four general paths that women have tended to take to reach political office. The first is the political family path. Women on this path come from families that have a long history of involvement in electoral politics. For example, a former prime minister of India, Indira Gandhi, was the daughter of Jawaharlal Nehru, the first prime minister of an independent India. In turn, she mentored her two sons in their political careers, and both later served as prime minister. In Asia, every past or present female executive had a male relative who at one point or another held the top executive position in that country.[65] Second, women have assumed office, often temporarily, as a surrogate for a father, husband, or brother who recently died. These women often have little or no political experience, although occasionally they find they enjoy politics and, upon the expiration of the term, run and are elected on their own merits. Mary Bono, for example, served out the term of her husband, U.S. Representative Sonny Bono, who died in a skiing accident. At the end of the term, Representative Bono decided that she enjoyed politics and sought and won election with her own political agenda. Another example is Jean Carnahan, who took her husband's place in the U.S. Senate after he was killed in a plane crash. Later, when a special election was held to fill his seat, she ran but was defeated. Corazon Aquino of the Philippines, Isabel Peron in Argentina, and Mireya Moscoso in Panama all assumed office upon the deaths of their husbands. Violeta Chamorro was elected as president of Nicaragua after the death of her husband, a noted political journalist. And in India, Sonya Gandhi rose to head the Indian National Congress after the death of her husband, Rajiv (son of Indira). However, even though her party won national elections in 2004, she declined the office of prime minister in the face of public opposition (she is Italian by birth, although she became an Indian citizen). Nonetheless, she still heads the Congress Party.

The third path is the party or political insider path, in which women come to office by starting at the bottom of the party/political ladder and working their way to the top over a number of years. In parliamentary systems this may mean decades of dedication to the party, serving whatever roles are needed. Margaret Thatcher, the former prime minister of Great Britain, ascended the political ladder of power after years of dedicated service to the Conservative Party. New Zealand's current prime minister, Helen Clark, also followed the party insider path to power. She notes that she became interested in politics early in life and became "fully committed" while at university in Auckland.[66] She joined the Labour Party in 1971 and slowly moved up through the ranks. In nonparliamentary systems this may mean beginning in local or state-level politics until one has accrued enough political experience to make one look like a savvy, qualified politician. Finally, women assume office by pursuing a political outsider path. In this scenario, they may emphasize their lack of political experience or connections, and instead run on the platform that they will bring something new to politics and will serve as an alternative to the status quo. This is the least successful path for women seeking political office.

Thus women worldwide face numerous and often similar obstacles if they seek political office. At the end of this chapter, we will discuss various ways in which women can overcome these obstacles. However, now we address the issue of women elected officials' impact on politics and whether they are as effective as their male counterparts.

THE IMPACT OF FEMALE LEGISLATORS, BUREAUCRATS, AND EXECUTIVES

How do female politicians behave in elected office? What types of legislation do they introduce and work on? Are they as effective at legislating and leading as their male counterparts are? Do women executives behave differently than their male counterparts do? And do women bureaucrats tend to emphasize women's issues? Further, if the answer to any of these questions is no, why is this so? First we examine women legislators in the advanced industrial world and then the developing world, and then we turn our attention to female executives and bureaucrats.

Women in Legislatures, Parliaments, and Cabinets

Advanced Industrial Nations
Women have a clear impact in legislatures in the advanced industrial world. There has been a substantial amount of research on women in the U.S. Congress and state legislatures, all of which demonstrate that women's presence has a demonstrable impact. Scholars have shown that female legislators tend to hold

more liberal views than their male colleagues do.[67] Women are also more likely to make feminist speeches on the floor of the U.S. House of Representatives than their male colleagues are[68] and are more likely to take the lead in advocating for women's issues bills on the Hill.[69] Further, women are also more likely to sponsor or cosponsor feminist legislation in Congress than their male colleagues are.[70] Similarly, Swers, in her analysis of voting behavior in the 103rd (1993–1995) and 104th (1995–1997) Congresses, finds that women are more likely than men to vote for women's issues bills, even when controlling for ideological, partisan, and district factors.[71] And further, she finds that gender is more likely to influence a female representative's vote when the bill deals directly with issues that affect women, such as reproductive policy and women's health concerns, rather than on issues that do not affect women as directly, such as education.[72] Thus, at the national level in the United States, the presence of women in Congress does make a difference; women are more likely than their male colleagues to introduce legislation of concern to women, to vote for women's issues bills, and to fight hard for their passage.

At the subnational level in the United States, a study in 1991 by the Center for the American Woman and Politics (CAWP) finds that women state legislators have distinct issue priorities from men and are more active on women's rights legislation than male legislators are.[73] For instance, women are more likely to sponsor or cosponsor feminist legislation than their male colleagues are.[74] And Thomas and Welch find that among state legislators, female-sponsored bills on women's issues are more likely to pass than are male-sponsored bills on men's issues.[75] Further, women actively advocating for women's issues appears to enable their passage.[76] And, legislative committees in state legislatures that blocked anti-abortion legislation had a greater proportion of women on them than in the chamber at large.[77] Thus, as at the national and subnational levels in the United States, women clearly make a difference to the legislative agenda and output of those legislatures.

There is also evidence that women in Congress and the state legislatures have different, more collaborative, consensus-oriented leadership styles than their male colleagues do.[78] Research has suggested that these differences arise out of the different ways that girls and boys are socialized[79] or that different life experiences compel women to lead differently than men do.[80] As Burrell suggests, "Gender role socialization may predispose women to certain styles of leadership."[81] Further, others find that women state legislators are also impacting the behavior of their male colleagues. Male legislators appear to be "shifting toward the adoption of 'female' types" of leadership.[82] And, male legislators who have had female mentors "indicate stronger motivations to involve people in legislative deliberations and report less dominating, more nurturing traits than men without female mentors."[83] Finally, the CAWP survey of 1991 finds that women state legislators are more likely than their male colleagues to bring the citizen into the process by advocating for greater levels of public scrutiny in the legislative process and greater levels of access to underrepresented segments of society.[84]

In gendered institutions like legislatures these differences could decrease the effectiveness of women since their mode of interaction may be seen as aberrant by many male colleagues and thus antithetical to the process of lawmaking.[85] But recent research has shown that female members of the U.S. House of Representatives are as effective as their male colleagues. It does appear, however, that to be effective, women need seniority, membership on influential committees, membership in the majority party, and leadership positions within the party and committee systems.[86] The presence of women in legislatures is important, but it is no panacea. We will see that this holds true worldwide.

Thus, in the United States it appears that women in Congress and state legislatures clearly make a difference and are as effective as their male counterparts. But what is the impact of women in legislatures in other countries? Research on female politicians in other parts of the advanced industrial world and the developing world is not as extensive as that on women in the United States, but some clear trends have been found. In the advanced industrial world many of these trends are consistent with the findings in the United States. But in the developing world we will show that while the presence of women has made a difference, women still face a variety of barriers and are often marginalized by male colleagues, who often relegate them to committee assignments and duties that revolve around issues that have traditionally been of concern to women.

In the remainder of the advanced industrial world the presence of female legislators appears to have a similar impact as in the United States. Research in Scandinavia has shown that women legislators have been successful in "bringing into the public realm the debate over what political equality of the sexes should be."[87] Bratton and Ray have found that the presence of women in Norwegian local councils positively impacted policy outcomes related to child care.[88] Interviews with Norwegian politicians indicate that women legislators introduce women's issues into debate as well as more policies favorable to women.[89] Further, these interviews suggest that women's presence has wrought a change in the way politics is conducted as well as the language used; in meetings and debates male politicians have become more polite, less direct conflict occurs, and men now excuse themselves to go pick up their children from daycare.[90] However, these same female politicians indicate that they have conflicting loyalties and demands that make it difficult for them to work as a group to influence politics. Further, many are careful not to be perceived as too feminist, as they fear this may result in negative reactions from colleagues and possibly party sanctions in the form of poor committee assignments.[91] Further, the political system, which was created by males, still continues largely to serve male interests, and while women have been able to affect some changes in the way politics is conducted in Norway, they have not substantially altered the political system.[92] As Bystydzienski notes, "Masculine values continue to be at the foundation of political structures. Masculine images of the politician prevail, and organizational arrangements that appear to be gender-neutral advantage men."[93] Thus institutional barriers still exist that prevent women legislators from having as great an impact as they might under different structural conditions.

Research on women in the British parliament had, in the past, found that women did not attempt to represent women.[94] However, this changed in 1997, when 101 Labour women members of parliament (MPs) returned to parliament, 65 of whom were newly elected. More recent research done on these women does seem to indicate that they have

> articulated women's concerns in debates, in select committees and in the Parliamentary Labour Party's women's group and that in the constituency their presence has engendered greater access between women constituents, women's organizations and women representatives and the articulation of a feminized agenda.[95]

Other recent research on the British parliament has found that women MPs in general, not just Labour, do "bring a different set of values to issues affecting women's equality, in the workplace, home, and public sphere."[96] Research conducted on the New Zealand parliament yielded similar findings as those in Britain and the United States. Women MPs in New Zealand are more active in debates on child care and parental leave than their male counterparts are. Further, they make fewer personal attacks than their male colleagues do during debates and do not interrupt as often as their male colleagues do.[97] In these examples, attaining a critical mass of women MPs was a key factor in fostering a distinctly female style of leadership.[98] All of this research indicates that women's presence in legislatures does matter and that if the numbers of women in office continue to increase, there is the potential for women to affect legislative change on women's issues and to influence the conduct of parliamentary debate.

The Developing World

In the developing world, while women have clearly impacted politics, they nonetheless still face many barriers. First we will look at their impact. Research on legislatures in Latin America indicates that despite the conservatism of many of these countries, there has been an increase in the number of laws passed that support women's equality as well as changes to political structures that can be tools for women's empowerment, such as women's franchise, quota laws, and the creation of women's ministries. These changes were correlated with increases in the number of female legislators.[99] For example, in Nicaragua, women in the Frente Sandinista de Liberación Nacional (FSLN) party succeeded in persuading the party leadership to implement quotas; currently, a minimum of 30 percent of all party positions must be reserved for women, and this same quota must be applied in the selection of candidates for elections.[100] And these same women fought to make sure that some female candidates were actually placed at the top of the lists, thus ensuring their election.[101]

Women in Latin America have also succeeded in attaining the important party leadership position of speaker of the parliament in a number of countries.

The first was in Argentina in 1973; since then women have held this position in eight more countries (six since 1990): Bolivia, Costa Rica, El Salvador, Mexico, Nicaragua, Panama, Peru, and Venezuela. In Costa Rica, since 1994 women have been given high governmental positions such as vice president of the Republic, vice president of Congress, and various cabinet nominations at ministerial and vice ministerial levels.

Further, research on women legislators in Latin America has found that they are as effective in getting all types of legislation passed as their male counterparts, in some cases more so. Research on women in Costa Rica found that female deputies have an 81 percent success rate in getting laws they have submitted to the Legislative Assembly approved, versus a 48 percent success rate for their male counterparts.[102] This is largely because "women spend many more hours in meetings with constituents and in congressional committee meetings than men.... [Men] devote much time to other economic activities such as their professional vocation or personal business."[103]

In the Middle East, women are also trying to impact the political game, although often their biggest impact is simply in getting elected. The number of female elected officials throughout the Middle East is slim (as noted previously), but nonetheless women are attempting to gain access to formal politics. In Iran in 1996, 190 women competed with 3,010 men for 270 seats in the Majlis (the Iranian parliament).[104] And while this number may seem small, it is a remarkable feat in a country that experienced a conservative religious revolution a little over twenty years ago. Thirteen women were elected in 1996, and once elected, these women were active on gender issues. Women were also actively involved as candidates and as voters in the local council elections in Iran in 1999, and won office in twenty-five provinces. Further, voters elected at least one female member in twenty-three cities and at least two females in forty-eight cities, which means that "a large number of women will be participating in decision making at both city and local council levels in economic, political, social, and cultural issues."[105] In the 2004 parliamentary elections, Iranian women maintained their presence at the national level, winning twelve seats, comprising 4.1 percent of the legislature, but 2008, saw a decline in the number of women elected to eight.[106]

While the policy impact of these female elected officials is still unclear, the importance of female voters is more visibly significant. When *Zanan*, an influential women's magazine, interviewed the two presidential candidates, Khatami and Nouri, in 1996, it asked each candidate about his views on various women's issues. Khatami's answers expressed sympathy while Nouri refused to answer.[107] Khatami was ultimately elected, and the majority of women and youth, especially young women, voted for Khatami.[108] Thus the presence of women in elective office and as active voters has signaled to the political establishment in Iran that it must begin to at least be aware of women's concerns, and this is certainly an initial step toward recognition of women's political influence.

However, women still have made few inroads in access to Iran's highest elected office. The Iranian constitution is somewhat ambiguous in its wording regarding the necessary qualifications for presidential candidates. The Arabic word *rajul*, used to define the prerequisite condition for assuming the post of president, can be interpreted to mean both a man and a renowned personality, which technically can also be a woman. A few women activists have used this ambiguity to launch unsuccessful bids to have their candidacy approved by the Guardian Council, the most influential governing body in Iran. In the 1997 presidential elections, 8 women (out of 238 candidates) declared their candidacy, although all were eventually disqualified, with no accompanying reason.[109] In the 2005 Iranian presidential elections, over 1,000 hopefuls including 93 women registered, but the Guardian Council ruled that only 6—all men—qualified.[110] This trend continued in 2009, where all women candidates were barred from running. Given that the Guardian Council is currently controlled by conservatives, women may make little progress in their quest for candidacy to Iran's highest elective office.

Elsewhere in the Middle East women are also leaving their mark on politics. In Israel, women are making strides as candidates and, once elected, as members of parliament. While the number of women elected to the Knesset (the Israeli parliament) is not vast (hovering around 14 percent), one study of Israeli female politicians found that they were more active than their male colleagues and sometimes even more successful in their legislative efforts.[111] However, female members of parliament in Israel do not focus their attention on women's issues; instead, their interest tends "toward the national flag more than toward the feminist banner."[112] As Wadie Abunassar, a political analyst at the University of Tel Aviv stated, "They [women] have not made a difference in governance.... [T]hey mainly focus on the Israeli-Palestinian issue and have neglected the bread and butter, everyday issues ordinary women face."[113] Nonetheless, the presence of active, successful female politicians is important, for it signals to society that women are capable legislators. This, in turn, may lead more women to decide to run for office and eventually build a critical mass of female legislators. Another impact that engaged female voters and politicians have had on the Knesset is the creation of a subcommittee on women's affairs, an entity that may not have been seen as necessary if women were not playing an active role in Israeli politics.

We now turn to countries in Asia. Although India has produced some very prominent female politicians, such as Indira and Sonia Gandhi, nonetheless, most women politicians do not focus on women's issues. Research on women in the Indian parliament has shown that they do not have women's issues high on their list of priorities.[114] Given their low numbers—as of 2009, women comprise only 10.9 percent of parliamentarians in the lower house—this is not surprising.[115] As previously noted, research has pointed to the fact that women often must reach a critical mass before they are not only able to affect change for women but are also interested in affecting change for women. However, trends at the local level in India may generate some change. In 1993, the Indian parliament mandated a 33 percent women's quota in rural and urban local councils, or Panchayat, creating space for over 1 million female politicians. However, efforts to introduce a 33 percent quota in the national legislature stalled in 1996 and 1998. Male politicians opposed the law, arguing that women should stay at home where they "belonged." In addition, they claimed that the bill would only benefit middle-class city women.[116] However, the issue of women's representation in India is bound to reoccur, partly as the effects of increased women's representation at the local level trickles up to impact national politics.

In the Kashmir region of India, one woman in particular is impacting politics. Mehbooba Mufti is the vice president of the region's ruling People's Democratic Party (PDP). In the region's first election in October 2002, the PDP won sixteen of the state assembly's eighty-seven seats, making it the third strongest party and a coalition partner in the government. Some political analysts believe that Mufti may be the coalition's choice as chief minister "because of her common touch and widespread popularity." [117] In an area torn by strife, where many women have lost a male relative to the insurgency that has been ongoing between Pakistan and India over control of Kashmir, Mufti is seen by the people of the region as someone who may be able to begin a dialogue with the separatist militants and bring some peace to the region.[118] While her ultimate impact is still unknown, traditional gendered beliefs in women as more peaceful, consensual communicators may have helped contribute to her rise to power and her subsequent election.

Research on women politicians in other parts of Asia is scant. However, we do know that women occupy a significant proportion of seats in a number of legislatures. Nepal leads with 33.2 percent of its legislature made up of women. It is followed by the Democratic Republic of East Timor (29.2 percent), Afghanistan (27.7 percent in lower house, 21.6 percent in upper house), Vietnam (25.8 percent), Kyrgyzstan (25.6 percent), Iraq (25.5 percent), Laos (22.9 percent), Singapore (24.5 percent), Pakistan (22.5 percent in its lower house, 17 percent in its upper house), China (21.3 percent), the Philippines (20.5 percent in the lower house, 17.4 percent in the upper house), and the Democratic People's Republic of Korea (North Korea) (20.1 percent).[119] The remaining countries in Asia all have female legislative representation at 17.5 percent (Tajikistan and Uzbekistan) or below.[120] Given the wide variety in levels of political freedoms in these countries, it is important to put these figures into context. For example, while one of five legislators in China and in North Korea are women, given the authoritarian nature of the political systems, one must question whether this figure constitutes significant representation of women's political power or any real "progress" for women's equality. In sum, while political representation can signal the advancement of women's interests, it is no guarantee of success.

Finally, let us look at the African continent. Here there is less research quantifying women's impact on political institutions. We do know that women occupy a significant number of seats in the lower houses of legislatures in twenty-five African nations, ranging from 15.2 percent for Zimbabwe to 56.3 percent for Rwanda. However, in twenty-eight other African nations, the number of women in the lower houses of legislatures is fairly low, ranging from 3 percent in Comoros to 14 percent in Guinea-Bissau, with a majority in the 9–14 percent range.[121] This, combined with other factors, including the tendency of academics studying women in Africa to focus on topics other than female politicians, has resulted in limited data concerning the impact of women in African legislatures.

However, many point to the experiences of South Africa as a model for promoting more women to formal politics. Women were always extremely active in the African National Congress (ANC), the main opposition force to apartheid rule in South Africa, and currently the dominant political party in the postapartheid era. They were a critical force in drafting the new South African Constitution, which includes many clauses guaranteeing the rights of women, and have introduced legislation to benefit women.[122] In turn, the ANC has often promoted the position and status of women in words as well as in deed. The commitment of the government to the cause of women's emancipation can be heard in President Nelson Mandela's remarks in May 1994: "Freedom cannot be achieved unless the women have been emancipated from all forms of oppression." [123] And it can be seen in its actions, too. In South Africa's first democratic elections in 1994, the ANC adopted a 30 percent quota for women on their party lists. As a result, women's representation increased from below 3 percent to 27 percent. In the 1999 elections, the ANC adopted internal party rules in which women were placed in every third position on the national party list, so that women would not be pushed to the bottom of lists, and thus in effect, denied political office. These proactive policies have generated results; of the 119 women elected to parliament in 1999, 96 (80 percent) were from the ANC.[124] And as of 2008, women make up 33 percent of elected representatives to the National Assembly, the lower house of parliament. The ANC has pushed through legislation to increase women's representation at the local level as well; the Municipal Structures Act of 1998 specifies that political parties should ensure that women comprise at least half of their party lists in local level elections, although there is no penalty if this rule is not followed.[125]

This increased representation at all levels also helped women rise to increased positions of power within the government. Ms. Gwen Mahlangu-Nkabinde was elected as speaker of the National Assembly in 2008 (this position has been held by a woman since South Africa became a democracy in 1994), a position she held till the 2009 elections. Ms. NC Madlala-Routledge was appointed deputy speaker in 2008, a position she still holds even after the 2009 elections; also, as of 2008, almost 50 percent of cabinet ministers were women. Further, the government has also established various bodies within the administration to monitor the position and status of women in South Africa. In 1996, the government established a Joint Committee on the Improvement of the Quality of Life and Status of Women in the parliament, as well as the Office on the Status of Women in the executive branch the following year.[126] As a result of this critical mass of numbers, women have taken steps to advance the cause of women, as has the government itself.[127]

Despite these gains, throughout the developing world women in politics still face barriers in politics, even once elected. Women legislators in India noted that within the political parties women are rarely found in leadership positions.[128]

And even fewer women are found in government cabinets, although this is changing. Worldwide in 1997, women made up 20 percent or more of cabinet members in only fifteen countries.[129] By 2001, women made up 20 percent or more of cabinet members in thirty-six countries.[130] Some of this increased representation is because of quota laws. For example, in 2000, a quota law passed in Colombia mandated that at least 30 percent of appointed positions in the executive branch be filled by women. When President Alvaro Uribe took office in 2002, six women were appointed to his thirteen-member cabinet and received powerful portfolios such as the Ministry of Defense.[131] However, the Colombian example is the exception, not the rule; as with committee assignments, women ministers around the world are primarily concentrated in social areas (14 percent), not in legal (9.4 percent), economic (4.1 percent), political (3.4 percent), or executive (3.9 percent) areas.[132]

Further, female legislators are still often assigned to committees and roles that "fit" their gender—committees that deal with reproduction, social welfare, and motherhood, for example.[133] While many women have a genuine interest in the issues these committees deal with, these are not the "power" committees that influence the direction of the country or serve as stepping-stones to positions of greater authority in government. In addition, while the creation of women's ministries and subcommittees is important in the struggle for women to bring attention to issues that directly impact their everyday lives, women's ministries do not always receive the status and resources necessary for them to impact politics.[134] Thus, in the developing world, while women have been active in institutional politics at all levels of government they are often concentrated in the least influential positions and have had a tough time moving up the ranks to more influential government positions.[135] To create a pool of qualified women candidates, more women will need to hold cabinet positions (and party and committee positions) of greater political importance if they are going to attempt the next step to executive office.

Further, social and cultural barriers in the developing world still inhibit women's actions in running for office and once elected. In many countries, the lack of a critical mass of women legislators makes it difficult for them to form alliances with other women on key issues. For example, in Uganda, because social and cultural barriers keep women from running for office, the chances of women elected officials having any kind of collective impact are slim.[136] Women who do choose to run and are elected note that there are many ongoing difficulties once elected. When women first entered the South African parliament there were no female restrooms. And while this structural issue has been addressed, women legislators still have a difficult time balancing family life with a work environment that includes late hours and lots of travel.[137] Women politicians worldwide often comment on the difficulty of balancing a demanding career with the demands of their families. Since women are still mainly responsible for care of the family, they are faced with demands that male legislators often do not have to consider.

A final barrier that women politicians face is that of balancing their concerns over gender issues and identities with the predominantly male world of politics. For example, they are often conflicted over conforming to male patterns of leadership behavior. Female legislators in Latin America noted the contradiction present in the traits required to be an effective MP: "the characteristics of good parliamentary practice remain male; long, unsociable work hours, aggressive in debate and a tendency to dominate."[138] To be successful, women must adopt these characteristics, which are perceived as male, while also remaining "feminine" in the eyes of their culture. Further, as Tripp found in Uganda, existing parliamentary practice makes it difficult for women to realize their interests since parliamentary rules of procedure, as they were written and currently stand, entrench particular male interests.[139] Women do manage to get these rules to work for them and do manage to "win" at times, "but rarely can they make the rules or make the rules work on their own terms."[140] Thus, while women have made great strides in legislatures, and their presence clearly impacts the proceedings and output of these legislative bodies, there are still barriers to be overcome.

Women as Executives

As of June 2008, there were 14 female presidents and prime ministers out of 189 rulers (see Table 1.7). Women rule in other capacities (as queen, for example); however, we do not discuss them as they exercise little political power. The world's first female prime minister was Siramavo Bandaranaike of Ceylon (now Sri Lanka), who was elected in 1960; a small but increasing number of female leaders have followed in her footsteps in the ensuing decades.

Table 1.7 Current Female Leaders

NAME	POSITION, COUNTRY, AND DURATION
Mary McAleese	President of Ireland since 1997
Helen Elizabeth Clark	Prime minister of New Zealand since 1999
Tarja Kaarina Halonen	President of Finland since 2000
Maria Gloria Macapagal Arroyo	President of the Philippines since 2001
Luisa Dias Diogo	Prime minister of Mozambique since 2004
Maria do Carmo Silveira	Prime minister of São Tomé and Príncipe since June 8, 2005
Angela Merkel	Federal Chancelor of Germany since November 22, 2005
Ellen Johnson-Sirleaf	President of Liberia since Jan. 16, 2006
Michelle Bachelet Jeria	President of Chile since March 11, 2006
Portia Simpson Miller	Prime minister of Jamaica since March 30, 2006
Cristina Fernandez de Kirchner	President of Argentina since December 10, 2007
Yuliya Tymoshenko	Prime Minister of Ukraine since December 18, 2007
Zinaida Greceanii	Prime Minister of Moldova since March 31, 2008
Michelle Pierre-Louis	Prime Minister of Haiti since September 5, 2008

Michelle Bachelet

Michelle Bachelet was born on September 29, 1959; on January 25, 2006, she became the first female president of Chile and the first female president in Latin America not elected on the basis of her husband's name. Bachelet rose through the ranks, following the party-insider path. She was Chile's Minister of Health in 2000 and later became the first woman ever in Latin America to hold the position of Minister of Defense. Michelle's father was arrested and tortured because of his opposition to the regime of Augusto Pinochet, the brutal leader of Chile from 1973 to 1990. He died in prison soon after in 1974. Michelle and her mother were also arrested in 1975 for their opposition to the regime and held at a torture center. She and her mother left Chile and lived in exile in Germany and Australia. While in exile, Michelle finished her medical education and became a pediatrician. She has also studied military strategy in both Chile and the United States. Bachelet's election was heralded by many as an exciting step forward for women, especially in the developing world. Bachelet's election on her own merit, and not on that of a male in her family, offers some hope that some of the barriers to women holding higher political offices are beginning to crumble.

What has been the impact of female rulers on the politics and policies of their countries? This question does not have a clear answer. First, not all prime ministers and presidents are created equal. In parliamentary systems, for example, the position of president, the head of state, is largely ceremonial, while the prime minister, as head of government, wields most of the consequential executive powers. This is the situation in Ireland's parliamentary system, where the president's role is more symbolic, while in the United States, for example, the president is vested with substantial measure of authority. Thus, while it is important that women have attained these presidential positions, their impact on governmental policy making is minimal, particularly if they have assumed the presidency in a parliamentary system. Further, because of their small numbers, very little research has been done on female executives. And given the nature of the job—one is theoretically required to act in the interests of the entire country, not in those of a subset of the population—a leader needs to have a broad-based agenda. Particularly, women leaders may not want to appear to be overly concerned with women's issues lest they be branded as too soft or unable to handle important military and foreign policy decisions. Therefore, it is difficult to discern a difference in leadership styles or issue concerns. For example, Margaret Thatcher, former prime minister of Great Britain, showed absolutely no interest in women's issues and in fact distanced herself from them. In contrast, when Gro Harlem Bruntland became prime minister of Norway for her first term in 1986, she announced her intent to represent women's concerns as a route to promoting social justice.[141]

Thus, we simply do not have enough data to know whether female leaders have impacted politics in ways that differentiate them from male leaders. But, we can argue that it is important to have female executives because their presence shows their citizens and the world that women can get elected and can lead the country on a broad range of issues, not just women's issues. This may open the doors to women's leadership roles in a host of other areas. However, to get more women elected as executives there needs to be more women elected to parliaments and appointed to cabinet posts. Women need political experience to be serious contenders for executive office worldwide. So how can more women get elected to legislatures and other positions of political power? We now turn to this question.

ADVANCING WOMEN'S EQUALITY

Advocates have been working to advance women's political equality for well over a century. What are some ways that women can increase their political representation? Simply increasing the number of women in parliament is not a magic bullet. The increased presence of women in institutional politics does not necessarily translate into concern for women's issues. Even when women politicians are interested in women's issues, they may have vastly differing opinions about what those issues should be or how they should be resolved. However, increasing women's presence is a start to ameliorating some of the inequalities that govern women's lives. A variety of strategies have been proposed; some entail implementing specific policy solutions, while other proposals involve fostering large-scale social change.

As we discussed earlier, quotas, whether encoded in constitutions, mandated by law, or adopted voluntarily by political parties when composing party lists, have been a promising way to get more women elected. Currently, fourteen countries have constitutional quotas for national parliaments, thirty-three countries have legislated quotas for national legislatures, and seventeen countries have adopted quotas for women's representation in subnational legislative bodies. In sixty-two countries, parties have established internal guidelines governing women's representation in party lists.[142] As we have discussed in greater detail in earlier sections, this has been one proven method of increasing women's presence in legislatures around the world.

Quotas, however, are no panacea. They do not necessarily translate to political power. For example, they can be used to marginalize women by symbolically supporting their progress without substantively improving their position in political power. Thus, for example, while some hailed the Argentine government when it became one of the first in Latin America to institute a quota law for women, others argued that it was a simple way for the government to show its support of women as political actors without actually addressing a women's agenda.[143] Quota laws do not necessarily combat the male culture of many parties. Even if parties have quotas on the books, they can still marginalize women by placing them at the bottom of lists, thus meeting the requirement of quota laws but not honoring the spirit of them, which is to increase women's representation. As we discussed earlier, the adoption of "zipper" laws, which prevent parties from relegating women to the bottom of party lists, has helped combat this problem.

Nor are all women convinced that quotas further women's quest for greater acceptance as equal political players. For example, the passage of parity legislation in France, which mandated women's equal representation on party lists, was met with resistance from many prominent women, who argued that "the reform would undermine the concept of universalism in political representation and therefore open the door to demands from other specific groups based on race, religion, or sexual preference." [144] Other French women argued quotas are "insulting and unnecessary." [145] Overall, however, the quota law does have overwhelming public support in France. [146]

One other method for increasing the number of women legislators is to adopt a preference vote system combined with a party-list, proportional representation electoral system. In such a system, voters are presented with a list of candidates from their political party and may choose up to a certain number of the candidates from the list (no matter where the candidate is on the list—top, middle, or bottom). Further, proportional representation rules entail that the party's share of seats in parliament is approximately equivalent to the percentage of the electorate that votes for it. This combination system, used in countries such as Belgium, Denmark, Finland, Luxembourg, and Switzerland, has been shown to assist in the election of women to parliament, whereas winner-take-all systems, like that in the United States, hinder the election of women. [147] Also, proportional representation systems, even without the preference vote system, are more advantageous to women than the winner-take-all, majoritarian system of the United States. Thus, changing the political "rules of the game," either via adopting quota laws or via adopting an alternative electoral system, has been a proven method of improving women's political representation.

However, institutional changes can go only so far. While quotas have been a very significant tool for women's advancement, advocates argue that their impact is limited in the absence of broader cultural change, in which society becomes more accepting of women as political leaders. If the public is more broadly sympathetic to getting more women into public office, they may be more likely to vote for women. In addition, politicians and parties may feel more pressure to introduce reforms and be willing to enforce them. [148] For example, while the Nordic countries are often cited for their impressive levels of women's representation, this is in part because of quota laws but also is a manifestation of these societies' strong egalitarian cultures.

Changing societal norms and values is a slow process, which often emerges via generational change, rather than over the course of a few months or years. Often, these changes are caused by broader shifts wrought by the processes of economic and social modernization. However, fostering a change in social values can be further reinforced through education. Educating children from a young age that women are not only capable of serving in government but also do an effective job at it is one important step.

Educating the public would also require the media to change the way they report on female candidates and elected officials and the types of questions they ask them. For instance, the media often focus on the clothing and physical attributes of female candidates and officials, often times, although not always, to the detriment of discussing their policy positions. This tendency is not singular to mainstream media. Even media that are supposedly dedicated to women's issues and concerns note such facts. For instance, in an article posted on the Women's eNews site regarding Argentine presidential candidate Elisa Carrio, the author, in a section entitled "From Glamour Queen to No-Frill Politician," noted that "The chain-smoking, cake-eating, plain-dressing lady is now known affectionately by some as Lilita and by others as 'La Gorda' (the fat woman)." [149] It is hard to imagine many articles about male candidates making such observations. The media also tend to ask women questions about how they will balance home and elective office, a question they do not ask of male candidates. These are just a few ways that the populace could be educated regarding the suitability of women as candidates/elected officials.

CONCLUSION

Women's involvement in politics at all levels does matter, from voting to running for office. In many countries women legislators behave differently than their male colleagues and actively work for the passage of bills that will assist women. Even where women legislators are not focused on women's issues, their presence is important. Their presence signals to society that women belong in the political, public realm, thus expanding the range of careers and lifestyles open to women. Further, given that female legislators can be as effective as their male colleagues, their presence helps dispel any myths regarding women's political abilities. The impact of women executives is a bit more difficult to gauge, but as with women legislators, their presence also has positive impacts on how society views women and their appropriate roles. However, even though increasing numbers of women are getting elected to office worldwide, their committee assignments are often to the "caring" committees, not the power committees, and they are rarely included in cabinets and other power positions within political parties. Without such power positions, women will have trouble impacting the direction of their country on issues like foreign policy, and, ultimately, politics will still be a man's world. And unfortunately, in most countries, but particularly in developing nations, the women who run for any office (or are able to run) are often from the upper class. Thus, it is not clear if their presence will alter the way society views lower-class women or if it will clear the obstacles, such as lack of monetary resources or child care, to their involvement in politics. This dilemma highlights the need for institutional and procedural political reform in many countries, as well as broad-based cultural change in the way society views women. While each of these reforms is important and necessary, none in and of itself is a sufficient means for increasing the number of women involved in politics. Improving women's representation in and impact on institutional politics involves engendering change at multiple levels over the course of multiple decades.

FOR MORE INFORMATION

The Aspen Institute Council of Women World Leaders, http://www.womenworldleaders.org

Current Women Leaders, http://www.guide2womenleaders.com/Current-Women-Leaders.htm

Database on Gender and the Empowerment of Women in the Arab Region, http://www.guide2womenleaders.com/Current-Women-Leaders.htm

Global Database of Quotas for Women, http://www.guide2womenleaders.com/Current-Women-Leaders.htm

The Inter-Parliamentary Union Women and Parliaments Database, http://www.ipu.org/wmn-e/world.htm

The Delegate—This film follows one of the first female delegates to the Republican National Convention in 1972, twenty-one-year-old Cathy Swajian. It provides an insider look at the presidential selection process and the role of women in presidential politics.

Fourteen Women—This documentary, narrated by Annette Bening, looks at the fourteen women who served in the 109th Congress in the United States.

Our Times—This documentary looks at the role of women in Iranian politics; in particular it follows a group of women who ran in the 2002 elections and one woman's unsuccessful bid for the presidency.

Recall Florida—This nonfiction movie follows former Attorney General Janet Reno in her 2002 bid for the Democratic Party nomination for Florida's governor.

Why Is Kofi Anan Not a Woman: Gender and Leadership at the United Nations—This documentary looks at the lack of female leadership both at the head of the United Nations, where a woman has never held the position of secretary general, and at its lower levels.

2

❦

Women and Noninstitutional Politics

In July 2002 a group of about two hundred Nigerian women took over a multi-national plant of Chevron-Texaco in Escravos, Nigeria, and held twelve hundred employees hostage for approximately nine days. Armed with only food and cooking pots, these women seized a boat used to transport workers to the island terminal and, upon arrival, stormed the plant.[1] The women demanded that Chevron-Texaco create more jobs for their unemployed sons and invest in their communities. After five days of occupation the women agreed to allow about four hundred workers to leave but threatened to strip naked in front of the men should any of the remaining captive workers try to escape. Discussing this strategy, a representative of the women stated, "Our weapon is our naked-ness."[2] This is because in many Nigerian tribes any display of nudity by wives, mothers, or grandmothers is considered a damning protest and shames all those who are exposed to it. After the women occupied the plant for nine days, which halted oil production, Chevron executives agreed to their demands to hire more than two dozen villagers and to build schools, water systems, a town hall, and other amenities. Further, the action by these women prompted similar occupa-tions across Nigeria, and other women seized four other oil plants during the Escravos siege.

This story illuminates important concepts and themes in the study of wom-en's roles in noninstitutional politics. Why did these women join together to challenge authority? Why did they choose the tactics they did? And why did the executives grant their demands? Or, to pose these questions differently: When/ why do social movements and interest groups form? Why do people join such groups? What strategies and tactics do social movements and interest groups employ, and why? Under what conditions do social movements and interest groups attain their demands? And, finally, how have social movements and interest groups impacted government, society, and people's lives?

Since World War II, the world has witnessed an increase in women's mobilization, not only in the industrialized nations but also in countries in the developing world. Increased social activism in the 1960s in numerous countries gave birth to a variety of groups and movements pushing for more equitable distribution of power and access. Out of this context, women's activism increased in size and magnitude, as women converged into more clearly articulated feminist movements in the industrialized Western countries that pushed for increased political and economic rights as well as long-term structural changes in gendered divisions of labor. At the same time, women in the southern hemisphere also became increasingly active in a wide array of women's issues, some of which overlapped with their fellow activists in the industrialized West and some of which took on local and regional flavor. This activism has been stimulated further by a growing international women's movement, which in turn has been facilitated by global events such as the UN Decade for Women (1975–1985), as well as a variety of international conferences devoted to women's issues in Kenya (1985), Cairo (1994), and Beijing (1995). Finally, women have become increasingly active in political movements that are neither feminist in orientation nor concerned with issues that have traditionally been considered important to women. In fact, sometimes they join movements whose goal is to act collectively against the interests of other women.

Drawing from examples around the world, this chapter looks at the role of women in noninstitutional politics. Noninstitutional politics, or informal politics, encompasses any political activity that does not take place directly within formal political institutions. Thus, actions such as voting and running for and serving in political office are not considered in this chapter because they are activities that take place directly within formal political institutions. We will examine why women's movements and interest groups form, why women join such groups, the strategies and tactics they use, and their impact on themselves, the public, and the state. In discussing women's movements in comparative perspective, we will cast a broad net and will discuss women's activism in women's movements rather than a unified woman's movement.[3] In addition, we will address the issue of "women in movement," or women's activism in other social movements, where men predominate in leadership roles and decision making.

Women's activism in social movements is often gendered. That is, their reasons for joining and their strategies and tactics often are based in, and also challenge, traditional societal expectations about women's appropriate roles in society. Women have drawn on their status as mothers and caretakers to justify their actions, and they have sometimes exploited these roles, in ways that men cannot, to attain their demands. However, the ways in which women around the world use their gender vary widely, and what may be a successful tactic in the industrialized West may not resonate with women in the countries of the southern hemisphere. The impact of women's activism has been substantial; women have lobbied successfully for legislative changes, have advocated for the creation of administrative offices to address women's issues, and have used their experiences to jump into positions of political leadership in institutionalized politics. However, it is also important to remember that women are not necessarily united simply by the biological commonality of their sex or the status of their gender and that women can define and express their interests in diametrically opposed ways.

DEFINING SOCIAL MOVEMENTS, INTEREST GROUPS, AND WOMEN'S MOVEMENTS

What is a social movement? A social movement is a group of people with a common interest who work together either to change a policy of government and/or to change how society perceives something (e.g., gay activists trying to alter how society views gays and those afflicted with AIDS). It is often made up of various organizations all working on the same topic, such as the environment, but often on different issues within that topic. For example, within the environmental movement, some groups may focus on clean air, others on clean water, and others on the issue of land conservation. Nor do all social movements utilize similar tactics; some may opt to lobby the government, while others may choose more militant strategies such as spiking trees to halt logging. In addition, some of these groups may be organized formally with an executive director, chapters throughout the country, paid lobbyists, and thousands of dues-paying members. In contrast, others may be much more informal in structure, with no clear leadership or organized chapters. Membership size is indeterminate because individuals do not pay dues or may not even need to formally join in order to be a member. In other words, the organizations that participate in social movements are incredibly diverse, often sharing few commonalities beyond their common issue.

Sometimes the groups that make up a social movement are called social movement organizations (SMOs) and other times they are referred to as interest groups, which are organizations that attempt to influence government but are not part of the government they are trying to influence.[4] As you can see, an interest group is quite similar to a social movement organization. However, while many SMOs can be called interest groups, not all interest groups are part of a social movement and thus cannot be called SMOs. For example, the American Association of Retired Persons (AARP) is an interest group but not a social movement organization because it is not part of a social movement, in the sense that we cannot say there is a retiree movement in the same way that we refer to the environmental movement or the women's movement. In contrast, the National Organization for Women (NOW) can be considered both a social movement organization and an interest group because it is part of the women's movement and attempts to influence the government with its organizational activities.

Defining a "women's movement" can be difficult, contested terrain, particularly if one is trying to generalize across a wide array of examples of women's mobilization. How can we produce a definition of women's movements that can apply to radical feminist activists in Great Britain and the Nigerian women discussed at the beginning of this chapter? Women's organizations represent a diversity of interests, ideologies, and goals, mediated by competing class, ethnic, religious, cultural, and racial identities. For example, some women's movements and organizations, like the Lesbian Avengers, who use civil disobedience to highlight what they see as a patriarchal, unjust society, are quite radical in their ideology and tactics. Others, like many women's organizations in Latin America, do not claim to be feminist or interested in changing their roles in the social order. Rather, they wish to see services for their families improved and are more conservative in their ideology and tactics. Can we discuss these movements and organizations in the same breath? The answer is both no and yes.

We cannot argue that there is a worldwide "women's movement." Cultural, religious, ethnic, and class differences result in varied interests, concerns, and needs for all people worldwide, and to expect half the world's population to feel identically about these things is unrealistic and naïve. Even within countries, these barriers create a diversity of often clashing interests. For instance, in the United States some conservative, Christian women are fighting to protect what they perceive to be the rights of a developing fetus. This movement is at odds with the traditional Western feminist movement, which has framed the issue as maintaining women's right to choose whether or not to carry a pregnancy to full term. These two groups of women within a single country do not see themselves as part of a common women's movement. These differences in interests and concerns can widen even further as we make observations about women's mobilization over a large range of countries that differ drastically in terms of levels of economic and social development, as well as cultural and religious traditions.

One way of acknowledging this problem is to distinguish more clearly between the various strands of women's activism in noninstitutionalized politics. Women's activism is not always feminist in orientation. While feminist organizations explicitly challenge the patriarchy by critiquing the gender-based domination of men over women, women's organizations often mobilize over issues considered important to women but may not go so far as to challenge broader societal or structural impediments to women's equality. Further, it is important to recognize that sometimes women organize collectively against other women; for example, as we discussed, women have mobilized on both sides of the abortion issue. To encompass these varied motivations, Karen Beckwith has defined women's movements as ones that are characterized

> by the primacy of women's gendered experiences, women's issues, and women's leadership and decision making. The relationship of women to these movements is direct and immediate; movement definition, issue articulation, and issue resolution are specific to women, developed and organized by them with reference to their gender identity.[5]

This definition allows us to encompass a wide variety of women's activism and acknowledges that how women define their issues will vary across continents and contexts. At the same time, it distinguishes between women's movements and the broader phenomena of "women in movement," in which women's activism is channeled into alternative causes, such as nationalist or religious movements. Certainly, often women's activism in these other movements is gendered, in that their biological or social status as women affects their participation. However, they are not necessarily mobilized because of their identities as women. Thus, when we discuss women's movements in this chapter, we are referring to women who are active in a variety of feminist and women's issues, which we distinguish from the more general phenomenon of women in movement, which will be addressed at the end of the chapter.[6]

Given these differences, we write about women's movements that often share broadly defined interests and utilize similar tactics rather than a global women's movement united identically around specific concerns. What commonalities can we emphasize, without obscuring the differences that separate women? Many of the issues around which women mobilize are common across cultures: to be seen as a human being, not as property; a desire for fair employment opportunities; the right to reproductive choice; widened access to health care and education; the right to vote and participate in politics; and more.[7] Second, as you will see in this chapter, across cultures women's movements form and women join them for similar reasons, no matter the goal. Third, women's movements, like all social movements, make use of a variety of tactics to achieve their desired ends. However, one tactic that is used widely by all women across cultures, and which is not available to men, is the tactic of emphasizing their gender and the rights and responsibilities that come with it. That is, women often draw their legitimacy and authority from their roles as wives, mothers, caretakers, and sometimes even sexual objects to justify their activism. As we shall see, across the world and across class, culture, religion, and ethnicity, women who are fighting for everything from educational opportunities for their children to clean water and air, equal pay, and ample food to feed their families all emphasize a common thread. That is, they are women and as such have certain responsibilities that they feel only women can fulfill. Further, as we saw with the example of women in Nigeria, they may use their bodies to emphasize their point.

Finally, women's movements across the globe have impacted their societies and the world's perception of women. Despite many societies' efforts to portray women as the weaker sex, incapable of voicing their demands and in need of protection by their male relatives (and the state), women have disproved this through action. This change in the world's view of women is a result of women's past and present mobilization, and while the extent of the change may vary across cultures, it is undeniably an important commonality among women's movements.

WHY DO WOMEN'S MOVEMENTS AND ORGANIZATIONS FORM?

Women's movements and organizations often, although not always, form for reasons that are similar to those that are found in the formation of other movements and organizations. The reasons for social movement and interest group formation often fall into three general models. The first model is a psychological model, which has a few variants, but in general argues that drastic disruptions in society such as war, economic depressions, and industrialization often lead to feelings of confusion and alienation among individuals. Individuals react to this psychological distress by forming groups in attempts to return society to "normal."[8] In contrast, proponents of the resource mobilization model maintain that movements emerge when resources in society, such as people, money, office space, and a communications network of individuals with a shared history or concern, are plentiful; people are willing to join and lead the movement; and some elite allies, such as government officials, church leaders, and corporations are interested in building alliances with the movement.[9] The third model, the political process/ political opportunity model, acknowledges the critical role of resources, leaders, and occasionally elite assistance in explaining movement emergence. However, it also maintains that these factors are not sufficient. The other crucial variable for formation is favorable political conditions.[10]

Using the psychological model we can try to understand why the women's movement in the United States developed from emerging women's consciousness in the post–World War II era to feminist mobilization in the 1970s. During the war, women became accustomed to working outside of the home and in workplaces that provided daycare and training programs. The number of women holding college degrees also increased during the war. But when the war ended, many of these women were fired to make room for the returning soldiers. Women, who had worked during World War II, saw men with similar training and education receive the jobs and benefits they once had received, at their expense. Other scholars point to the role of the civil rights era several decades later in increasing women's sense of alienation and anger at their position in society. That is, women activists who had mobilized to fight for racial equality were awakened to their own unequal status in society. According to the psychological model, this led to feelings of anger and frustration among women who then ultimately mobilized for change. However, this model lacks explanatory power because it leads one to assume that women just spontaneously organized, without leadership or assistance, in a political environment that was not particularly open to the issue of women's rights.

We can also apply the resource mobilization approach, which emphasizes the role of monetary and human resources as well as elite allies to explain women's mobilization in the decades following World War II. The economy in the United States after the war and into the 1960s was rapidly expanding; thus, individuals had excess resources in terms of money and time. In addition, a number of women working in government and corporate America had encountered numerous instances of discrimination and had the training and education to serve in leadership positions in a movement. Further, in 1961, President Kennedy created the President's Commission on the Status of Women, whose mission was to examine the legal status of women in the United States (although with the hopes of pinpointing potential minor changes in women's rights policy formulation, thus negating the need for the Equal Rights Amendment). The commission was composed of numerous women from the government sector, and it spawned the creation of similar state-level commissions in all fifty states. These national and state commissions created a communications network of women who were able to discuss their shared history and experiences of discrimination. Finally, the publication in 1963 of Betty Friedan's *Feminine Mystique,* a book that highlighted the condition of middle-class women, sparked a sense of outrage among women, many of whom had previously been unable to identify their sense of grievance.[11] Calling it "the problem with no name," Friedan detailed the unhappiness of middle-class women who were educated and raised to become housewives and mothers, rather than individuals with a capacity to work and earn incomes outside of the home.[12] When taken all together, ample resources, a communications network, potential leaders, some elite facilitation (even if unwitting), and a sense of outrage fostered the emergence of a women's movement in the 1960s. This explanation is far more satisfactory than the psychological model, but it still appears to leave out an important variable—the political situation at the time.

Political process theory, which points to the role of the larger political context, can also be used to explain the emergence of the U.S. women's movement. First, the U.S. political system, in which power is divided among a variety of branches as well as between federal, state, and local authorities, is generally open to citizen pressure. Citizens can lobby Congress and can write letters to, call, and e-mail their representatives; they can also pressure the president and the executive branch; and groups can file legal proceedings in federal courts in an attempt to challenge federal law. Further, individuals and groups can stage sit-ins, protests, and marches without fear of arrest, assuming they follow basic laws, such as obtaining a permit and so forth. Thus, the women's movement had a variety of access points through which to advocate their interests. Second, the political situation in the mid- to late 1960s and early 1970s was favorable to the emergence of social movements in general, and the women's movement in particular. The successes of the civil rights movement had, to a certain degree, paved the way for other progressive movements, such as the student movement, the environmental movement, and, of course, the women's movement. Further, the Kennedy, Johnson, and Nixon administrations were somewhat amenable to the issue of increasing citizens' rights, especially since they were involved in fighting a war in Vietnam, whose ostensible purpose was to liberate a people from a political system that denied them their rights. Finally, the Watergate scandal, in which President Nixon was found to have used campaign funds to pay individuals to break into Democratic Party National Headquarters at the Watergate Hotel, led to the defeat of many incumbent representatives in the House. Voters were disgusted with government and its members in general, even those who were not associated with the Nixon administration. The new representatives, most of whom were elected by slim margins, were eager to increase their winning margins in the next election and thus were wooing potential voters. Women fit the bill for many of these Democratic members. Thus, American political institutions and the political context of the mid- to late 1960s and early 1970s were conducive to the formation of a women's movement. The additional factors of women's rising sense of frustration, as well as their increased resources, arguably led to the emergence of a women's movement in the United States.

Let us now return to our example discussed in the beginning of the chapter. How can we explain the mobilization of the women in Nigeria? To begin with, it appears that these women were frustrated with Chevron. As one activist told a reporter, "Chevron has long been neglecting the Ugborodo community in all areas of life. They have not shown concern at all to involve our people in employment and provision of social amenities."[13] Thus, a key element of the psychological model was present. Resources were also present. A majority of the women who occupied the Escravos plant were from the same tribe, the Itsekiri, which served as a communications network among a people with similar histories, experiences, and concerns. Further, there were other, more intangible resources available to these women. Reports indicate that their men were very supportive of their actions[14] and that while the local Nigerian authorities were not encouraging their actions, they supported their demands.[15] And finally, the political situation was conducive to their siege. While local government authorities did not condone their actions, they were not going to interfere in the occupation. Thus, the system was open to their protest. Further, Chevron was willing to work with them. As Dick Filgate, an executive of parent company Chevron Texaco stated, "We now have a different philosophy, and that is do more with communities."[16] As a result, the political and corporate climate was amenable to their protest, thus facilitating the maintenance of the movement. Overall, we can see that all three models contribute to an understanding of the emergence of this social movement. We now turn to another question: Why do women join women's movements and organizations?

WHY DO WOMEN JOIN WOMEN'S MOVEMENTS AND ORGANIZATIONS?

Women join women's organizations and movements for a variety of reasons, many of which are similar to the reasons that individuals join any social movement organization. Often, a trauma or disaster has impacted their lives directly. Sometimes they are integrated into activism through their varied networks of friends and family, who encourage them to join. Alternatively, they get something out of membership, whether it is a sense of camaraderie, contribution to a higher cause or good, or a material benefit. Many of these motivations act upon a person in tandem; no one reason is often enough to explain why a woman joins a women's movement. Women's gender identity is also relevant to explaining why women join women's movements; in the following examples, we will see that women's gender, their varied socially constructed roles, and their relationships are a constant subtext in their motivations to act. Women are often pulled into activism to meet practical gender needs when their socially defined roles are threatened, as well as in response to strategic gender concerns that arise out of their frustration from their subordinate social status as women.

Much research has shown that a common thread that explains why women join movements, even in the face of political repression, is that some trauma or disaster has occurred in their life and has in a sense "woken them up" to the need to take action. In El Salvador, the Farabundo Marti National Liberation Front (the FMLN), a guerrilla organization dedicated to overthrowing the government and creating a more just and equitable society, engaged in violent conflict with an authoritarian and repressive government. The government was responsible for arresting, detaining, torturing, and killing thousands of El Salvadoran men. In this climate, women formed the organization Co-Madres to pressure the government of El Salvador to explain and discover the whereabouts of their missing relatives. Many of the women in this organization had a "disappeared," assassinated, or jailed relative.[17] It was this traumatic event that encouraged many, who had no history of political activity, to act despite the very real possibility that they might be arrested and/or jailed, heckled, and physically abused by the government for their actions.

An example from the United States also serves to illustrate this point. The founder of Mothers Against Drunk Driving (MADD) began this organization after her daughter was killed by a drunk driver with a history of arrests for drunk driving. The trauma of her daughter's death, coupled with her frustration that someone with such a deplorable driving record still had his driver's license, prompted her to take action. Many other members of MADD have a family member or friend who was killed or seriously injured by a drunk driver. Thus a traumatic, disastrous event in one's life might encourage one to take action by joining a group.

Another motivation to join women's movements appears to be encouragement from others. Recruitment by friends, relatives, or other organizations such as one's church/temple/synagogue is a commonly cited explanation for joining a movement or organization. Women also join women's movements and organizations for the solidarity benefits (feelings of camaraderie) that come from such organizations. In the 1960s, in the women's movement in the United States, women joined consciousness-raising groups in which women gathered informally and discussed issues in their lives and sought solutions to their problems through their shared experiences. An example from Uganda illustrates that such motivations are not limited to the advanced industrial world. One scholar studying the women's movement in Uganda asked women why they had joined women's organizations. Their reasons included "that they wanted to socialize, gain new ideas, and meet like minded people."[18] Thus solidarity benefits are often important factors in women's decisions regarding whether or not to join an organization.

Another common motivation appears to be the desire to do good (purposive benefits). Many of the women in the Co-Madres in El Salvador argued that they owed it to the next generation to work for change so that the horrors they had experienced would not be repeated in the future.[19] Material benefits are also often cited as a reason for joining women's movements and organizations. Women worldwide have joined movements to protest prices and rents, the loss of daycare centers, and the cost of water and electricity.[20] In Uganda, for example, research has found that women are joining women's movements so that they may improve their standard of living.[21] Thus another motivation for women in joining a women's movement is the pursuit of material gain (or protecting what material benefits they have).

Finally, a common subtext for all of these examples is the role that women's gendered identities play in informing their activism. For example, many women organize to meet what are known as "practical gender interests."[22] Practical gender interests are those interests that are traditionally considered women's realm of concern, such as issues concerning the family, children, and almost anything related to caring for them (e.g., access to food, water, shelter, health, education). Women are motivated to join organizations that fight for improvements in these areas because they feel they have a legitimate right to do so. And while stereotypes of women often impede their advancement and claims, sometimes their role as mothers gives them the authority and legitimacy to demand that the state take care of concerns that are considered "women's issues."[23] Women in the developing world, who may mobilize more frequently around practical gender interests, often embrace these categories as identities that legitimate their political activity. In a sense, women who accept the gendered division of labor have a certain legitimacy in demanding rights that pertain to their role. Further, motherhood provides a common identity for many women that can cut across race, ethnicity, and nationality.[24] Thus, many women join women's organizations to improve areas of life considered within their realm of concern and expertise as women.

For example, women joined the Co-Madres, in part, to respond to some trauma, but also because their experience of the trauma had a gendered dimension. As mothers, they were responsible for the welfare and care of their children, and they were mobilized to action in ways that men (and fathers) were not. Similarly, women in the developing world who mobilize to protest prices and rents are doing so out of a desire to improve their material conditions, but also because as women, they are traditionally responsible for care of the household and their family's immediate living conditions, which have come under threat. Thus, while women join movements for similar reasons as do men, often their gender identities further define which issues mobilize them, and often, it is when their practical gender needs and roles have been threatened. However, women who mobilize to meet practical gender needs often do not explicitly challenge larger gendered divisions of labor and women's subordinate position in society.

In contrast, "strategic gender interests" are "those fundamental issues related to women's... subordination and gender inequities. Strategic gender interests are long-term, usually not material, and are often related to structural changes in society regarding women's status and equity. They include legislation for equal rights, reproductive choice, and increased participation in decision-making."[25]

In other words, they arise out of a recognition of women's subordinate position in society, and women who are mobilized out of a concern for strategic gender interests often explicitly challenge gendered divisions of labor, power, and control, as well as traditionally defined norms and roles. For example, activism on issues such as women's legal rights, equal wages, and women's control over their bodies often uses a rhetoric that challenges societal norms about women's appropriate roles in society, rather than reinforcing them. Women's mobilization to advance strategic gender interests is more common among Western feminists, who are often trying to escape classification as mothers and wives. While women in the developing world do mobilize around strategic gender interests, more often their interests are defined by immediate needs that draw on traditional expectations of the appropriate division of labor between men's and women's interests.

We have thus far examined why women's movements emerge and the various reasons why women might join such movements. Now we turn to the strategies and tactics that women's movements utilize. Do these differ from the strategies and tactics available to other social movements? Do women have strategies and tactics available to them because they are women?

STRATEGIES AND TACTICS

Tactics are the tools a social movement uses to achieve its ends, and often movements use a variety of tactics in their quest to attain their goals. Some tactics are conventional and include such things as writing letters to public officials and meeting with public officials to express one's views. Other tactics are militant and include acts of civil disobedience (openly disobeying a law in protest) such as the Nigerian women's occupation of the oil plant in Escravos. There are also violent tactics, such as assassinations, kidnappings, and armed struggle, but these tactics are most often used by revolutionary organizations and will be discussed in the following chapter. Finally, there are tactics that are considered conventional in advanced industrial/democratic societies, such as marches, strikes, and sit-ins, but which in developing and/or authoritarian societies might be considered militant.

Women's movements and organizations have used a bevy of tactics to fight for change, which often depend on factors such as levels of repression/authoritarianism within the state, the resources of the group, the culture of the country in which the women live, and the organizational structure of the group. As noted earlier, across cultures, many women use their gender as a tactic, although varied cultural, political, and social contexts often define the appropriateness or effectiveness of varied strategies. Public attitudes about women differ across cultures, and women in the advanced industrial world may be able to use their gender in ways that women in the developing world cannot. For example, as will be discussed in greater detail later, women in the advanced industrial world can live in lesbian communes to protest nuclear weapons or they can bare their mastectomy scar on the cover of a national magazine to bring attention to breast cancer. Such use of their gender differences as a tactic is not always available to women in developing nations because of culturally accepted norms of appropriate female behavior. More will be said on this later. Let us now examine tactics available to women in authoritarian/repressive states.

Repressive states often arrest and jail dissidents; as a result, movements rarely use such tactics as lobbying or even marches, and instead move underground or use alternative means of political expression. Female activists often use tactics that are only available to them as women; that is, they are able to use gendered expectations about their behavior in order to participate in unorthodox forms of political protest. Women, in many societies, are not seen as a threat. They are often viewed as complacent, apolitical, and solely concerned with their children and home. These assumptions allow them a certain cover, and even provide them with hidden venues in which they can organize. Women active in movements in authoritarian states may gather at a seemingly benign sewing circle or tea party. As Craske notes in her research on women activists in Latin America, "women were able to be invisible simply by being women."[26] Adams shows that women protesting Pinochet's regime in Chile were able to hide subversive artwork under their skirts—something men clearly could not do![27] And women in Uganda, during the internal war to oust dictator Idi Amin, hid weapons of Tanzanian soldiers who were in the country to assist in overthrowing Amin and provided shelter and food for these men. Amin's troops never suspected women of these acts, simply because they were women.[28]

Further, since women worldwide are still primarily responsible for the care of their children and home, they have authority and legitimacy when they fight for improvements in these areas. Or, they may work in caregiving tasks to assist others less fortunate. For instance, they may work in a food cooperative or communal kitchen that provides food to the poor. Men do not have all of these tactical choices—their gender also limits the tactics and strategies they may use (as it does women). When the state does not allow people (men) to gather or form groups, women are still allowed to meet to do traditionally female pastimes because women are assumed not to be political.

Further, women in authoritarian states can conduct silent protest, as the Madres de la Plaza de Mayo (Mothers of the Plaza de Mayo) in Argentina did when they gathered everyday in the Plaza de Mayo to bear witness silently to the disappearance of their loved ones, whom had been disappeared by the state because they were seen as revolutionaries and/or potential threats. The state dared not take action against these women because it risked losing the little legitimacy that it had left. How could they justify jailing women who were doing nothing more than silently gathering to mourn for their lost family members? They were being "womanly and true" and violating no culturally held norms of appropriate female behavior. Their femaleness granted their behavior a legitimacy and protection that males did not have. As Craske argues, "It [motherhood] has a significant cultural and political currency and as such lends legitimacy to demands made within this rubric."[29]

However, utilizing motherhood and one's female identity as a tactic also has its limitations. As Craske notes, motherhood is a limited identity for politics because "the tight links between motherhood and social reproduction...are evident and for many motherhood remains an apolitical identity. Furthermore, the non-negotiable stance of many motherist demands is anti-politics. The limitations of using motherhood as the basis for female political action is apparent." [30] Thus women cannot solely rely on motherhood as a tactic or issue; doing so may provide the state with an excuse for dismissing women's concerns as nonpolitical and, thus, not important.

Yet, on the other hand, often this is women's safest choice in terms of activism. Safa and Flora argue that women have been forced into focusing on motherhood and their femaleness in authoritarian regimes because traditional avenues of protest have not addressed women's issues meaningfully and thus women are left with few other tactics when fighting for change in such settings. [31] Women in authoritarian regimes often must utilize certain tactics because they conform to culturally held norms about acceptable gender roles. Women can do things like feed and clothe the poor in an authoritarian system because these are viewed as appropriate pastimes for women. In this sense, it is important to note that even behavior that conforms to "appropriate" female roles is political because it is a tactic that often contributes to the downfall of authoritarian regimes. By providing such services women are demonstrating the inadequacies of the state and in doing so making a political statement about the need for change.

Women in authoritarian regimes and the developing world do not always emphasize their femaleness and use conventional tactics; in addition, despite their gender, many have suffered at the hands of the state for their participation and tactics. In El Salvador, the Co-Madres have combined accepted modes of female behavior with more confrontational tactics that angered the state. They have utilized conventional, accepted tactics such as distributing fliers at Sunday Mass, but they have also utilized militant tactics such as occupying government offices and staging sit-ins. [32] As a result, women have suffered, as have men, for their actions. Major Roberto D'Aubisson, the authoritarian leader of El Salvador during most of the 1980s, threatened the Co-Madres with decapitation if they kept up their work. Their office was also bombed in 1980, 1981, 1986, 1987, and 1989. Further, in 1982 three mothers were captured by death squads and detained and tortured. Others have been raped and some assassinated. [33]

Women in industrialized, democratic regimes often have a wider array of tactics available to them because there are more diverse views of acceptable roles for women, but also because the state is more open to a variety of tactics. Costain and Costain note that the women's movement in the United States has used almost every routine and nonroutine method in its attempts to gain political influence. [34] The tactics and strategies chosen, they find, changed depending on the views of the movement. In the 1960s the women's movement viewed political parties as part of the male power structure and so would not work with them and used protest instead. By the 1970s the movement saw a need to embrace all types of tactics;

however, as a result of some political gains, by the 1980s, the movement settled on lobbying and electoral politics in order to consolidate their hard-fought victories.[35] Similarly, in their comparative study of women's movements in western Europe and North America, Banaszak, Beckwith, and Rucht found that women's movements have shifted from radical tactics and suspicion of the state in the 1970s to a more moderate, state-involved, and accommodationist stance by the 1990s. In part, this shift in tactics is a tribute to women's movements' successes; in the wake of the creation of varied policy agencies to address women's issues, many activists have become inside players rather than outside agitators. In addition, however, state structures have also shifted since the 1970s, and the increased significance of international organizations, delegation of power to governments at the local level, and reliance on nonstate actors has changed how women's organizations respond to and seek influence with the state.[36]

Women in advanced industrialized democratic states often utilize their gender as a tactic. But protest by women in these states, even when emphasizing similar female traits as their fellow activists in the developing world, often takes different forms than such protest in authoritarian regimes. In advanced industrialized democracies, women may have a greater variety of tactics available to them to emphasize their gender than women in the developing world do.

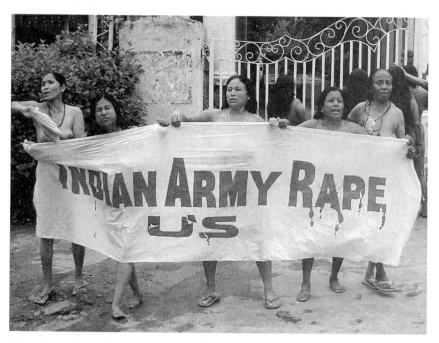

Women in India strip naked before Indian Army troops in front of a security office in the capital city of Imphal to protest and demand action over the alleged murder by paramilitary troops of a woman accused of being an insurgent. These women are using their bodies to shame the military. SOURCE: AFP/AFP/Getty Images

For example, worldwide, women are often characterized as the more peaceful sex, who, if in power, would work to prevent and end wars. Throughout the world, there are many examples of women organizing to protest wars, military build-ups, military actions, and armed conflict in general. In the United States in 1983, a group of women built an encampment near the Seneca Army Depot in Seneca, New York, to protest the deployment of nuclear missiles, as well as the patriarchal system that created these instruments of destruction. Daily, they proceeded to the depot to demonstrate peacefully against the deployment of nuclear weapons. Currently, there are still women living near the depot in a communal, nonhierarchical community. Their very presence is a form of peaceful protest against nuclear weapons. Both genders have protested actively against nuclear weapons; however, this group is different in that it is using gender as a tactic. That the group is solely made up of women is a political statement—that women are innately more concerned about preventing destruction and more adept at taking care of the problem. Further, the organizational form of their group is a tactical choice, a political statement. Hierarchy is often associated with patriarchy and male-dominated organizations, so by opting for a communal, all-female, nonhierarchical organization they are rejecting traditional male-defined organizational structures. Finally, while peaceful protest as a tactic does not often inflame public opinion, living as a communal group of women can. These women have unsettled their socially conservative rural New York neighbors with their choice of living arrangements.[37]

These women have chosen on the one hand to embrace a traditionally female characteristic—being peace-loving. At the same time, however, they have chosen a radical way of expressing it—by living only with women. So while these women share something in common with their Latin American sisters—embracing some traditional female characteristics and tactics—they are also radically different from them. It would culturally be very difficult for women in the developing world to use an all-female commune as a tactic to protest the politics of their country. Thus, we can see that women in industrialized democratic regimes have a wider array of tactics available to them, even when emphasizing a cultural norm that would be viewed as acceptable in the developing world.

The experiences of breast cancer activists also illustrate the use of gendered tactics in advanced industrialized democracies. Breast cancer activists have also emphasized their differences from men in fighting for increased funding for breast cancer research. Since breast cancer primarily affects women, this is not so odd. However, while many of the tactics of the movement have been fairly traditional—walks for the cure, bicycle tours to increase public awareness of toxic sites that may contribute to breast cancer, lobbying, and electoral politics—some have not. In May 1993, a breast cancer survivor and activist appeared on the cover of the *New York Times Magazine* with half of her white dress cut away to reveal a mastectomy scar.[38] This act was controversial in many ways; breasts are a defining feature of women, and to show a cancer survivor with a scar where a breast formerly existed publicly displayed some of the physical repercussions of breast cancer. The picture emphasized the physical differences between men and women, showing that breast cancer is something that primarily afflicts women. But breast cancer also has a psychological impact on women since breasts are seen by society as such an essential characteristic of what it is to be a woman. Once again, this is a tactic that is not as available to women in authoritarian and/ or developing nations where censorship of the press or notions of female modesty prevent such radical tactics.

Finally, in Love Canal, New York, a group of women discovered that the cause of the increasing rates of cancer among their children was the existence of a toxic waste site underneath their town. These women decided to confront the corporation responsible for the toxic waste and get them to clean up this site. This group of women emphasized their femaleness even as they became adept, somewhat radical, political actors. Kaplan, in her research on this movement, notes that they presented themselves to the corporation and to the world as helpless mothers trying to protect their children and that this approach was a key element in their stock of tactics.[39] The corporations responsible for the toxic waste had a tough time presenting their side in the face of this strategy. But, it must be noted that these women did not simply sit around and proclaim their helplessness; these women also utilized radical tactics. They burned effigies of authorities, they took mock coffins to the state capital, and they even took hostages (albeit for a short period, and not premeditated). But all along they emphasized that they were women who were doing the socially acceptable thing—protecting their children and families as good mothers ought to. So while women in authoritarian or developing nations may not always have such tactics available to them (though in some instances they do), they do share a tactic in common with women activists in the advanced industrial world—many of the women organizing in these economically, socially, and politically different societies are emphasizing their femaleness and claiming it as a source of legitimation for behavior that might not otherwise be tolerated or acknowledged by the state.

Explicitly feminist movements that seek to ameliorate women's subordinate status in society are often torn over whether explicitly to utilize strategies that draw on (and sometimes exploit) conventional norms and expectations about women's appropriate spheres of activism. For example, the feminist movement in the United States chose strategies emphasizing women's similarities to men and lobbied for the passage of laws that highlighted their equality with men. They drew primarily on classical liberalism, values embodied in the Declaration of Independence, which emphasized the importance of self-determination and individual rights. Historically, many discriminatory laws against women were grounded in the belief that women were inherently different (and often inferior) to men and that women and men should occupy separate spheres of influence, with women designated as caretakers of the home and hearth and men as breadwinners. In response to these traditional beliefs, many liberal feminists argued that equality between men and women is only possible when laws require men and women to be treated equally. Their focus was on achieving equality under the law and on pushing for equal rights as citizens to education, jobs, or political office as well as equal protection from violence or unfair treatment.[40] Thus, they were hesitant to pursue strategies that magnified women's differences or exploited their traditional roles because they wanted to emphasize the lack of differences between men and women as part of their overall strategy for improving the position and status of women. As we shall discuss in further detail in Chapter 4, this strand of the feminist movement the United States and Europe has sued companies and governments for violations of laws that grant them equal opportunity and access in employment, education, credit, housing, and more. For example, in the United States the women's movement has often used Equal Employment Opportunity laws as a tactic for gaining equality in employment.[41] Feminist organizations have also used tactics common to variety of social movements and interest groups, such as lobbying, launching letter-writing campaigns, forming political action committees to funnel money to candidates, volunteering for campaigns, mobilizing voters, and organizing marches.

In sum, women's movements and organizations have utilized a variety of tactics in their quest for their goals. Women both in the developing world and in advanced industrial nations find that using their gender as a tactic is useful because it often legitimates their actions and their cause. However, local political and social contexts often define which tactics will resonate with society. While not all women's movements use their gender as a strategy, until the burdens of raising children and caring for the home are shared more equitably in all parts of the world, gendered tactics will likely continue to be used by women's groups in a variety of contexts.

THE IMPACT OF WOMEN'S MOVEMENTS

We have looked at why women's movements and organizations form, why women join them, and what strategies and tactics they use, but what, if any, are the impacts of women's movements? Inarguably, women's movements worldwide have been successful in changing laws that impact the condition and status of women. As we shall discuss in greater detail in the chapters of Part II, some of this legislation directly affects women's status by mandating equal pay, education, and job opportunities; increased political participation and representation; liberalized divorce, contraception, and abortion rights; increased maternity leave benefits; and the criminalization of violence against women. Further, women's activism has changed legislation that often impacts women indirectly. Women's movements have successfully lobbied for increased gun control, higher levels of education funding, and better access to a wide array of social services.

Second, the efforts of women's movements have led to the creation of ministries and bureaus that address women's issues. Also known as "women's policy machineries," these agencies mushroomed in the industrialized countries in the 1970s and 1980s (although in the United States, the President's Commission on the Status of Women was created in 1961).[42] For instance, Ireland created the

Commission on the Status of Women in 1972, and Norway, the Netherlands, Australia, and France followed suit in the ensuing three years. This change is, in part, a result of feminist movements' pursuit of alliances with political parties, primarily of the left, to push for policy reform.[43] Further, particularly in industrialized nations, pressure from feminist-oriented women's movements led to the increased presence of "femocrats," a term used to refer to "both feminists employed as administrators and bureaucrats in positions of power and to women politicians advocating gender equality policies."[44] These newly emerged femocrats worked in the newly formed women's policy machineries, ranging from equal opportunity commissions and councils to departments and ministries for women, to integrate gender concerns into national policy agendas. This also granted feminist activists further access to institutional politics.[45]

This change is no longer restricted to industrialized nations; worldwide, this shift in discourse has resulted in the creation of women's ministries and bureaus and the introduction and passage of more laws positively impacting women. For example, the United Nations has its own policy machinery devoted to women's agendas; the Commission on the Status of Women and its administrative arm, the Division for the Advancement of Women, have lobbied national governments tirelessly to establish similar structures to assess the progress of women's status. In fact, the United Nations estimates that nearly three-quarters of all states have established some form of national machinery for the advancement of women, particularly in the wake of the fourth World Conference of Women, held in 1995 in Beijing.[46] The United Nations' efforts to advance women could not have happened in the absence of women's mobilization; as Enloe notes, "Part of the success of the emergent second wave of feminism has been to put women's lives and feminist questions onto the formal agendas of the foreign policy establishments of dozens of state regimes and international agencies."[47] We will discuss this phenomenon in greater depth in Chapter 12, which discusses international responses to fostering women's equality.

Also, as we discussed in greater detail in Chapter 1, women's movements and organizations have forced public officials to pay more attention to women's issues, women's organizations, and women voters. As Costain notes, in the late 1960s and early 1970s, politicians in the United States became aware of the potential electoral impact of women and made serious efforts to attract women's support.[48] This phenomenon is not limited to the United States; political parties around the world have made an increased effort to organize women's sections within their party structures and have also integrated women into party lists at election time. Despite this, increased women's activism in women's movements has not led to a significant trend toward forming women's political parties, although there are a few exceptions. For example, in Russia, women have mobilized twice to form political parties that are primarily run and staffed by women and address issues that are considered important to women.[49] Nonetheless, for the most part, women's movements have tended to work with preexisting parties rather than form a new political party devoted explicitly to women's issues.

However, these strategies of cooperation with the state have not always augured well for women's movements. Sometimes states respond to women's movements with "symbolic reform," policies that are supposed to address certain problems but fail to solve these problems, partly because governments refuse to imbue them with anything beyond rhetorical force.[50] For example, many constitutions contain wording that recognizes men's and women's formal equality, without establishing clear mechanisms to measure, monitor, or enforce this pledge. Further, in some countries, the impact of mobilization has been kept to a minimum because the state has co-opted women's organizations. Following the Cuban Revolution, the government mobilized women into state-sponsored women's organizations under the umbrella of the Federation of Cuban Women. Similarly, many authoritarian states in Africa do not wish to have their power challenged, so women's groups, since they represent a challenge to their power, are often funded by and sponsored by the state in order to keep the organizations as apolitical as possible.[51] As a result of this state sponsorship, these organizations lose their ability and leverage to place demands on it. Alternatively, sometimes a movement accepts the aid of the state and finds its goals placed on the back burner or diluted by the state. For instance, in Kuwait in the 1970s, the Arab Women's Development Society (AWDS) was able to pressure the all-male National Assembly to discuss an equal rights bill.[52] However, the state disbanded the AWDS in 1980 and was hesitant to license any women's organizations that did not have a religious purpose. Thus the impact of women's organizations can be seriously curtailed in states where groups must receive permission from the state to form.

This phenomena is not limited to countries in the developing world; advanced industrialized democracies can co-opt women's movements in more subtle ways, and some scholars argue that women's movements in western Europe and the United States moved from "an early radicalism, autonomy, and challenge to the state in the 1970s, to a more moderate, state-involved, and accommodationist stance by the 1990s," using rhetoric that would have been "unthinkable" in the 1970s. Drawing on the example of women's mobilization over daycare issues in the United States, the authors traced the transformation of a movement that once pushed for collectively run child-care centers free of state intervention into one that did not seriously oppose radical (and potentially punitive) welfare reform in the 1990s.[53] In sum, working more closely with the state, either through increased integration with political parties or women's policy machineries, has brought benefits in the form of increased legislation as well as passage of symbolic and material reforms. However, as women's movements move to a more legitimized "insider status," they have also, in many instances, moderated their demands and, in some instances, been used as a tool for the state.

Third, women's movements have also left a trail of motivated, skilled, and politically active women in their wake who have impacted politics and society in multiple ways. One way these women have impacted politics and society is that globally, participation in movements and organizations has "encouraged the development of citizenship and political subjectivity" among women involved.[54] These women may go on to lead other movements, run for political office, or just remain aware of and involved in politics. Women's participation in movements also often alters how they see themselves. In some instances, while women may have joined an organization because they felt it was their duty as mothers to protect their children and the family, through their participation they discovered a new identity—one of a political being.[55] Further, women's mobilization has encouraged other marginalized groups in society to fight for change.[56] For example, in the United States, the peace movement adopted feminist ideological frames and organizational structures built on feminist processes, and also adapted some of the women's movements' tactical innovations. In addition, women became increasingly prominent in leadership positions.[57]

Finally, women's movements have had a broad transformational effect, altering the way society views women. In many countries, women's mobilization has made a previously unseen, invisible population highly visible. When women fight for their rights and/or the rights of their family, they emerge from the woodwork and become political actors. While this is no guarantee of success, nonetheless the impact is notable. It is easy for a government to ignore a population that is complacent and quiet; it must respond in some way to a movement that is increasingly organized and vocal. Further, public opinion polls demonstrate that societies are more supportive of gender equality than in previous decades. While this change is more significant in postindustrial societies than in industrial and agrarian societies, and is also dependent on larger processes of socioeconomic modernization, nonetheless the rise of women's movements played a role in this broader process of attitudinal transformation.[58] And the proliferation of women's and gender studies programs indicate the spreading influence of the women's movement and the issues it has raised and continues to raise. There are over seven hundred such academic programs, located primarily in the United States, Canada, and Europe, but also in developing countries in Latin America (Brazil, Chile, Colombia, Costa Rica), Africa (South Africa, Uganda), eastern Europe and the countries of the former Soviet Union (Ukraine, Russia, Belarus, Croatia), Asia (China, India, Thailand, Korea), and the Middle East (Egypt, Lebanon).[59] In sum, women's movements have brought women into the public sphere, a sphere previously inhabited primarily by men, and have altered their own and society's perception of them.

THE RISE OF EXTREMIST NATIONALIST AND RELIGIOUS FUNDAMENTALIST MOVEMENTS

Not all women who join social movements are motivated by women's issues. Further, they may join movements that, as a by-product of their larger goals, often seek to impose a vision of women's roles that seem antithetical to the rhetoric of equality for women. Extremist nationalist and religious fundamentalist movements, while not primarily composed of women, attract a small but critical female constituency. Both types of movements have often emerged in societies undergoing wide-ranging social and economic changes, which have altered men's and women's traditional division of labor in society. Both movements often advocate returning to a past in which these traditional roles are restored and, in some instances, further entrenched. How can we explain why women would become involved in movements whose primary aim is often to return them to traditional divisions of labor where they know their "appropriate" role? To answer that question, we first discuss how extremist nationalist movements and religious fundamentalist movements view women, outline women's involvement in these types of movements, and then explore some explanations for their involvement.

A nationalist movement is a group of people who often feel that they have some important commonalities that unite them and make them distinct from the rest of society. This may include, but is not limited to, a common history, language, religion, and/or ethnicity. Further, they believe that as a result they should form their own sovereign nation or force the state to incorporate them more equally into society/government. Nationalist movements are often not concerned with women's issues, as independence from their "oppressor" or a more significant political role for their group is the main goal. While nationalist movements have often been channeled into peaceful demands for independence, autonomy, and democracy, they can also morph into extreme right-wing, xenophobic movements. For example, the rise of the National Front (FN) in France (which is actually a political party, although it refers to itself as a movement), the savage war in the former Yugoslavia, and the horrific genocide in Rwanda were motivated by extreme forms of nationalist fervor, which drew on and inflamed ethnic and racial divisions within society.

In these instances, women are often portrayed as the symbolic and physical reproducer of the nation. Women are expected to embrace their role as mother and find total fulfillment in that role. For example, the FN, an extreme far-right French party founded by Jean-Marie Le Pen in 1972, focuses on women as part of its larger obsession with the growing population of non-European immigrants in France, the rapidly declining birth rate in France, and the perceived moral decay of society in the face of rampant individualism. As Le Pen explained in *Le Pen Without Mask,*

> One has artificially turned women away from their natural function by offering them an illusory integration into the working world presented by pernicious ideologists as a token of dignity and liberation.... Deflected from their intrinsic social role, millions of women have found themselves pushed into a less and less open sector, contributing to the development of unemployment and—but is it really by chance?—serving against their will to create a new proletariat, easily to exploit—and manipulate—by political organizations whose aim is to destroy national harmony by constantly arousing totally artificial confrontations.[60]

In this view, women's true mission is to return to a traditional and subordinate role in the household, where they will find a higher sense of purpose than that provided by economic modernization.

To remedy the problems created by society's moral decay, the FN promotes a social order that glorifies the traditional nuclear family and "is based on the difference of the sexes—the men direct and command, in public as well as in private life. The women must obey and submit themselves to their biological destiny, that is, to have babies and raise them."[61] To better organize women to the cause, the FN founded a women's organization, the National Circle of European Women, whose stated objective is to "defend the French family, women and fundamental values of our society."[62] In addition, the FN has proposed a number of pronatalist policies, such as providing stay-at-home mothers with a monthly paid wage to take care of their children (and also to liberate jobs for unemployed men). Alternatively, they have proposed introducing "family-based voting," in which more electoral weight is given to families with children (parents should have as many extra votes as they have children below voting age).[63] Given their priorities, they are also vehemently opposed to the legalization of abortion. In sum, women are seen not as individuals but as the critical reproductive element within the family unit. They are heralded as both the symbol of the regeneration of society (if they live up to these traditional, familial roles) as well as the potential enemy of this same process (if they defy the previously described "ideal").

Worldwide, religious fundamentalist movements are often formed in reaction to what they see as an increasing level of moral decay in society, often brought on by encroaching modernization and Westernization.[64] By forming such groups the members hope to encourage government to roll back or stop any further changes that would exacerbate this decay, which, in their eyes, is partially caused by a rhetoric of women's rights that encourages women to abandon their traditional roles. And particularly in the developing world, women's movements are perceived as Western imports that are not truly reflective of the culture of their society and, in some sense, are the catalyst for this moral decay. While Muslim fundamentalist movements in countries such as Iran, Afghanistan, and Nigeria have garnered a significant amount of media attention, Hindu fundamentalist movements are a significant force in India, and Christian fundamentalist movements from a variety of denominations continue to play a strong role in U.S. politics and society.

While there are numerous differences between countries in the developing world and those in the advanced industrial world, religious movements in both are seeking a similar solution—a return to "traditional female virtues and morality."[65] Similar to the rhetoric of extremist nationalist movements, this often entails the return or maintenance of what fundamentalists view as a more moral and traditional society and family structure, where the woman's main role is as mother, wife, and caretaker of the home and where male authority is paramount. In developing countries, some fundamentalist movements have moved to impose dress codes, ban divorce, allow for honor killings of women who have dishonored the family, prevent women from leaving the home without a male family member as escort, and more. In industrialized democracies, religious movements usually have proposed less extreme measures for women, focusing on the incorporation of religious values into a society that is overly secularized.

The Islamist movement in Turkey provides an interesting example of a conservative, right-wing movement that organizes within the parameters of a secular, democratic state. Turkey has been torn between secularism and Islam since the foundation of the republic in 1923, partially because this split for much of Turkey's history has been portrayed as a struggle between modernism and Westernization and traditionalism and the Ottoman past. Women have often been caught in the middle of this struggle because both sides want to claim them as symbols of either Westernized progress or the embodiment of Islamic values. Turkey's first president, Mustafa Kemal Ataturk, launched Turkey on a path toward Westernized modernization, and as part of that goal he targeted the veil as a symbol of woman's oppression and unveiling as a sign of her emancipation. The government, often through state-sponsored women's organizations, sponsored unveiling campaigns in an effort to publicize Turkey's embrace of Western, modern, secular customs.[66] Considered by the government to be symbols of backwardness, veils were banned from public spaces, such as government offices, although women could wear them in private. In addition, women benefited from other reforms, such as suffrage, liberalized divorce laws, and other Westernized policies. The overall goal was not so much to eradicate Islam from society but to confine it to the private sphere in an effort to push Turkey closer to European standards of living.

However, Islamists, male and female, wanted to reclaim women's bodies for their own version of an ideal society, and since the 1970s there has been a revival of Islamist movements in Turkey through political organizations such as the National Order, National Salvation, Welfare, and Virtue parties. These parties at different times united religiously conservative Sunni Muslims, small businessmen, and others who had waited to benefit from Turkey's modernization policies but failed to do so.[67] Also, they channeled citizens' dissatisfaction with secularization, which was equated with a rejection of Turkish heritage. While the various strands of the Islamist movement attracted predominantly men in the 1970s, as we shall see, women became increasingly drawn to protest activities in the 1980s and participated frequently in veiling protests.

So what roles do women play in extremist nationalist and religious fundamentalist movements? Let us first turn to our example of the French FN, where women have been recruited primarily in supporting roles. When the FN first emerged as a movement in the 1970s, women candidates were few and far between. However, the FN has tried to recruit a few token women to prominent political positions, particularly at the local level, to appeal to women voters and to soften their image. Women candidates are highlighted as "family women," and they are often used specifically to propagate the antifeminist rhetoric of the FN. For example, Marie-France Stirbois, a prominent FN member, has pledged to "liberate women from feminism" and to replace feminism with femininity. She also discourages the concept of equality between men and women, arguing that it "humiliates women."[68] Thus, women in the FN are useful because they are able, as women speaking to other women, to promote a more compelling critique of feminism than the male leadership, who may not engender the same kind of legitimacy advancing similar rhetoric.

Primarily, however, women are more visible in the movement as wives to male leaders in order to emphasize the FN's focus on the traditional nuclear family. At times, these wives have been recruited to political office to serve as surrogates for the values of their spouses. And often female family members are recruited to various supporting roles in the organization to perform the "helping tasks" needed to make things run smoothly. They also carry out the movement's charitable activities, such as organizing collections for the nation's poor, organizing summer camps for children, and other "feminine" activities. However, despite its rhetoric of women's central force in society, nonetheless the FN still places women's interests behind more "important" issues, like immigration or security; out of the 426 pages of the movement's program, the chapter on the family (women don't merit a separate entry) is restricted to 14 pages.[69]

Women's involvement in religious fundamentalist movements, both in the developing world and the advanced industrial world, has increased greatly in the past few decades. In Turkey, women mobilized in response to a 1982 decision to ban the veil at university campuses. Veiled women became increasingly militant and staged sit-ins, demonstrations, and fasts. They also, through their voting power, helped sweep the conservative Welfare Party to electoral victory in 1994. Many Islamist women adopted a vision of the "ideal" Turkish woman by emphasizing the piety and obedience of the Prophet's daughter, Fatimah, rather than focusing on women's submission to patriarchy. For example, for Cihan Aktas, a prominent Islamist woman writer, the ideal Muslim woman represents "the intelligent, brave, chaste, productive and virtuous woman" who submits to Islam, while simultaneously rejecting traditional interpretations that minimize women's participation.[70] In a sense, they are advancing an "equal, but different" version of womanhood.

So why would women join these movements? While the supporters of the FN are disproportionately male, a small (but increasing) percentage of women have thrown their support behind them. In fact, in 2002, 14 percent of women cast their votes for Le Pen in his bid for the presidency.[71] Women tend to respond to the FN for the same reasons that men do; that is, they fear how immigration, crime, and unemployment will affect their lives, although some women also respond to the rhetoric of the defense of the traditional family.[72]

In the instance of religious fundamentalist movements, some join in reaction to the growth of feminist ideologies, which conservative religious women see as threatening their culture and/or position in society, or as imposed by the West or by women not in touch with the mainstream. However, other women see their adherence to Islamist values and dress codes as a choice that should not be taken as an automatic rejection of women's equality. In Muslim countries that have a dress code, and even in those that do not, many Muslim women argue that they prefer to wear conservative dress, especially in the workplace (in countries such as Egypt where they are allowed to work) because it forces men to look at them only as colleagues, to focus on what they have to offer intellectually, as opposed to physically. Writing of her own choice to wear the headscarf, Merve Kavakci, a former representative of the right-wing Virtue Party in Turkey's parliament, argued that "Mainstream Islamic tradition considers the headscarf an obligation for Muslim women because it conceals their physical allure. By covering themselves, Muslim women can be recognized not only for their religious beliefs but for their contributions to society as well; they can be judged for their intellect and not just their appearance." Further, she maintained, the headscarf is an important part of women's identity and should be a choice; simplistic interpretations of the *hijab* as a symbol of oppression reveal a "deep and growing misunderstanding between Muslim women and the rest of the world."[73]

Further, some common themes emerge between the two types of movements. As we mentioned previously, both are responses to larger processes wrought by economic and social modernization and globalization, which often have altered radically men's and women's roles in society. For both types of movements, while it is tempting to assume that women have been forced into wanting a return to traditional family structures by strong-willed, patriarchal men in their lives, that explanation is too simplistic and insulting to women. The fact is that there are women who prefer traditional roles. They feel that motherhood and taking care of the family confers a certain status upon them as well as a level of safety and security. Further, these movements do not just push a negative agenda for women; rather, they seek to legitimize and uphold the role of mother and caregiver. This can have a powerful appeal to women homemakers and mothers who feel their work is undervalued in societies in which more women are working outside the home and gaining increased levels of public visibility and power.[74] In sum, many women join these movements because they believe that their status and lives are better under more traditional codes of conduct and conceptions of rights. Further, many women are not responding primarily to the messages regarding women's roles in the household, but to the larger goals advanced by the movements. In France, women, like men, are attracted to the FN because of their affinity for the authoritarian, nationalist, and racist rhetoric of the party. In Turkey, women, are, in part, trying to establish an alternative between the secularism of the West and the more severe fundamentalism of the Middle East.

CONCLUSION

In this chapter, we have read about women who have occupied oil refineries, held silent vigils in honor of their disappeared sons, set up communes to promote peace, spread breast cancer awareness, lobbied for tougher drunk driving laws, and pushed for a variety of antidiscrimination legislation mandating equality between the sexes. As we have seen, it is more useful to look at women's activism in women's movements, broadly defined, than to impose a narrow definition on what constitutes a "legitimate" woman's issue. While women do not mobilize over identical issues or express their interests in uniform ways, nonetheless, women do tend to organize over similar concerns, many of which are not expressly feminist in orientation, but are often seen as important to women. Women have used their multiple roles of wives, mothers, and caretakers as a strategy to grant legitimacy to their demands.

Women's groups have clearly had an impact on both society and politics. They have lobbied successfully for the passage of numerous items of legislation that have directly and indirectly impacted women's status. They have pushed for the creation of women's policy machineries and have built alliances with sympathetic "femocrats," politicians, and political parties. They have created an active base of women who go on to influence and sometimes lead other movements, who remain active and aware of politics, and who may run for political office. Finally, they have changed the way society perceives women and they have often changed the way women view themselves.

Yet, it is important to recognize that women are not united simply through their common sex or gender status. Not all women agree what constitutes "progress" and "equality" for women, and as a result, women have been active in movements that seem to work against women's collective interests. Their participation in these movements poses interesting questions for scholars—why would women wish to maintain or return to a time when they had fewer rights and were subservient to men? Many such women feel that feminism is either imposed by the West or out of touch with the mainstream or believe that societies that esteem and protect the role of mother and wife are preferable to those in which the sexes are considered equal. In the former, they feel that they have a status and level of safety that they would not or do not have in the latter.

Women's movements and organizations will continue to be a powerful force worldwide. In particular, since 1985, in the wake of the third UN conference on women in Nairobi, Kenya, women's activism has become increasingly transnational, crossing borders and cultures. Globalization has both united women, by highlighting the commonalities that the process of global economic restructuring has wrought,[75] and increased the divide between the winners and losers of this process. On the one hand, some scholars have theorized that with the increasing trend toward supranationalism, women will be facing conditions that are increasingly similar. In turn, this will encourage the homogenization of women's movements.[76] The challenge for the future is to continue to forge stronger links between women across cultures, without obliterating their differences. And as power increasingly devolves to supranational institutions, global women's movements will have to respond with new strategies, tactics, and goals to keep pace with an ever-changing international structure.

Guerrilla Girls Take on the Art World

In 1985 a group of women decided that patriarchy in the art world had gone on long enough. When the Museum of Modern Art held an exhibition in 1984 titled "International Survey of Painting and Sculpture" and of the 169 artists chosen all were white and less than 10 percent were women, some female artists decided that enough was enough. Thus in April 1985 the Guerrilla Girls emerged. The movement was made up of women artists who assumed the names of dead women artists and wore gorilla masks to hide their identities. The masks and assumed names were used so that the world would focus on the women's message, not on their personalities or looks. Using unconventional tactics, between 1985 and 2000 over 100 women artists anonymously produced posters, books, billboards, and public actions to bring attention to their cause. They used humor to show that feminists could be funny, too; they protested in front of the Guggenheim; and they took part in various panels where they came dressed in high heels and their tell-tale gorilla masks and passed out pamphlets that sarcastically poked fun at the male art establishment. In one such pamphlet they facetiously commented that "I'm a Guerrilla Girl and I think the art world is perfect.... [W]omen artists make fully one whole third of what male artists make, so what's there to be mad about?"[i] By the 1990s the art world had become more accepting of female artists, partly in response to the tactics of the Guerrilla Girls. This success forced the movement to reexamine its purpose. For some, the mask, which had initially been empowering, was now a burden and had "become a projection of racist fantasies and a perpetuation of the sexual allure of the veiled woman."[ii] Nonetheless, the Guerrilla Girls continued on and still exist today, although their work and focus have changed with the times. Today they have an official website, www.guerrillagirls.com, and three of the members have formed Guerrilla Girls on Tour, which dramatizes women's history and the patriarchy that persists in all realms, including politics and the family, as well as the art world.

---

[i] "How and Why Did the Guerrilla Girls Alter the Art World Establishment in New York City, 1985–1995?," Introduction, http://womhist.alexanderstreet.com/ggirls/intro.htm, March 6, 2009, p. 4.
[ii] Ibid.

FOR MORE INFORMATION

Pambazuka News: Weekly Forum for Social Justice in Africa: Social Movements, http://www.pambazuka.org/en/category/socialmovements

Social Movements and Culture: A Resource Site, http://www.wsu.edu/~amerstu/smc/smcframe.html

Women and Social Movements in the United States 1600–2000, http://womhist.alexanderstreet.com

Beyond Bejing—This is a documentary film about the 1995 Bejing Conference and the numerous women's nongovernmental organizations that attended; produced by Women Make Movies.

Butterfly—This film looks at twenty-four-year-old Julia "Butterfly" Hill, who sat in a tree for two years to protest the clear cutting of trees in the Redwoods of California.

Not for Ourselves Alone: The Story of Stanton and Anthony—This film looks at the life and history of the two women who started the women's suffrage movement in the United States.

The Righteous Babes—This documentary film looks at the impact of the third wave of feminism on such female rock artists as Ani Di Franco and Queen Latifah; produced by Women Make Movies.

Union Maids—This film looks at the role of women in the United States in the labor and left movements of the 1930s and 1940s.

Welfare Warriors—This film looks at a grassroots movement of women on welfare who protested the 1996 Clinton Welfare reform bill.

The Women of Hezbollah—This film looks at the lives of two women who are members of Hezbollah.

3

~◦

Women and Revolutionary
Movements

Saturday, July 5, 2003, began as an ordinary day for the citizens of Moscow, Russia. Many of the city's teenagers and twenty-somethings had headed off to a rock festival to enjoy the sunshine, celebrate the summer, and listen to some Russian rock. At 2:45 that afternoon, the first of two explosions occurred, sending bodies and garbage into the air. Fifteen minutes later, a second deadlier blast ripped through the crowds. Two suicide bombers blew themselves up to protest the ongoing war between the Russian army and Chechnya, a separatist region in southern Russia.[1] However, it was not just the terrorist act that mesmerized and horrified the public; the two suicide bombers were women. This was not the first time that women terrorists had entered the conflict between Chechnya and Russia; rather, it was the latest of a series of terrorist attacks launched by Chechen women in protest of the ongoing war. These women quickly became known in the media as "black widows"; the media claimed that these women were drawn to terrorism after their Chechen husbands, and often other relatives as well, had been killed by Russian forces.[2]

Chechen women are but one example of women's activities in noninstitutionalized, often violent forms of political protest and conflict. In 1991, the Tamil Tigers, a group fighting for independence in Sri Lanka, used a woman suicide bomber to assassinate former Indian Prime Minister Rajiv Gandhi.[3] More recently, Palestinian women, previously discouraged from becoming suicide bombers, have become increasingly willing to give up their lives as the potential for a negotiated settlement between the Israeli and Palestinian governments vaporizes in the wake of continued hostilities between the two sides.[4] While the phenomenon of women terrorists has received increasing amounts of coverage in the news, these incidents are neither new nor isolated. Yet, the recent examples of terrorism in Russia and elsewhere illustrate how women participate in revolutionary movements that seek to achieve their ends through noninstitutionalized political means, often through the use of violence.

This chapter explains how women interact with the causes, processes, and outcomes of revolutions and revolutionary movements in Europe, eastern Europe, Asia, Latin America, and the Middle East. We assess how participation in this form of noninstitutionalized politics has changed women's lives, both in positive and negative ways. How do women interact with the origins, processes, and outcomes of revolution? Do they respond similarly to men in why and how they participate in revolutionary movements? Are they affected in the same ways by the new regime? The answer to all of these questions is, not surprisingly, a resounding "no."

Throughout history, women have been recruited to revolutionary movements to fight for profoundly new societies. Women have responded to the revolutionary call, fighting for women's rights, but more frequently for what they perceive to be larger struggles involving issues of class or national self-determination. While women may not have been motivated by concerns of gender equality, the ways in which they participate are rarely gender neutral. While women have masterminded complicated assassination plots, served as soldiers and tacticians, and died for their cause on the battlefield, in prison, or strapped to a bomb, more frequently, women have fulfilled critical, but often unacknowledged, supporting roles. Further, many have succeeded in their revolutionary tasks by exploiting traditional societal expectations about women's supposedly apolitical status. Gender matters, particularly given that as we march further into the twenty-first century, women have increasingly filled the ranks of guerrilla movements in Latin America, Asia, and the Middle East.

However, despite women's multifaceted and emphatic participation in altering the distribution of power, it is unclear to what degree they have benefited from such movements. Revolutionary leaders are adept at promising rewards for women in return for their support; they are much less successful in (and committed to) working to ensure that these benefits actually materialize under the new order. Disappointingly, the effects of revolution have rarely been as radically progressive for women as originally promised. While revolution has changed significantly the way that women live their lives, it is often in unanticipated ways or in ways that rarely live up to the promises issued. There is something of a "glass ceiling" for women in that they are allowed to reap the benefits of radical change, but only to a certain degree. Often, men are able to maintain crucial positions of economic, social, and political power, leaving women to serve as symbols of progress, but often, in reality, to act as maidservants to the new order. Part of this is because women themselves are often willing to sacrifice "women's" issues to a perceived "more important" cause, such as national self-determination. Thus, revolutions have been something of a double-edged sword for women.

DEFINING REVOLUTIONS

Revolutions involve more than just a change in political leadership. Most scholars agree that a revolution entails a large-scale alteration, not only in terms of who governs but also in terms of dominant cultural mores and values. This change is often implemented rapidly, over the course of months, years, or perhaps decades, but not centuries.[5] For example, the French Revolution was radical in its impact, not only because it brought new people into the hallways of political power in the space of a few years but also because it seriously weakened the power of the aristocracy and ushered in a new class of ruling elite that espoused the values of classical liberalism, popularly expressed as "liberty, fraternity, and equality."

When explaining why revolutions happen, some scholars have focused on the role of psychological factors, such as people's perceptions of deprivation. For example, in the pathbreaking book *Why Men Rebel*, Ted Gurr argued that people revolt when their expectations for a better life are not met. Often, this happens when their position in society is improving, but not as quickly as another group's in society.[6] In contrast, structuralist explanations have tended to focus on the actions of the state in explaining breakdown. Samuel Huntington, in *Political Order in Changing Societies*, hypothesized that revolutions occurred primarily in modernizing societies, when social and economic institutions developed faster than political institutions. It was the state's inability to absorb citizens' competing demands that led to political disintegration. Other theories, such as the one advanced by Theda Skocpol in *States and Social Revolutionaries*, have posited that states fell apart in response to international pressures, combined with fragmentation among the political elite. The conjuncture of these two factors created a political opening that allowed peasants to mobilize in opposition.[7] Demographic theories, such as those advanced by Jack Goldstone, have focused on the problems that arose when sustained population growth outpaced economic growth, thus undermining stability.[8] While these theories differ in their approaches, nonetheless they all tend to underplay the role of individual leaders and instead focus on broader, societal-level changes that provide openings for a variety of players to act on their frustration.

Yet, until the 1980s, researching revolutions felt like entering a museum; when studying examples of widespread and far-reaching political breakdown, one would study a select grouping of historical events. Revolutions were perceived to be something of a rarity; scholars tended to focus on the "great" revolutions, studying every nook and cranny or political upheaval in England (1640), France (1789), Russia (1917), and China (1949). The field was widened to sometimes include events such as the Mexican (1910) and Cuban (1959) revolutions.[9]

However, world events caught up with standard definitions and demonstrated that scholars needed to broaden both what they considered to be a revolution and the nature of the underlying conflict. As the text box in this chapter discusses, in the late 1960s and early 1970s, the political stability of Western democracies was rocked by a variety of radical left-wing terrorist movements that often recruited from a growing pool of disillusioned middle-class youth. And more recently, throughout the final two decades of the twentieth century, authoritarian regimes collapsed in countries in almost every continent of the globe. In the 1980s and 1990s, military regimes disintegrated in Latin America, "people power" succeeded in toppling corrupt governments in the Philippines and Haiti, communism collapsed in eastern Europe and the former Soviet Union, the apartheid regime stepped aside in South Africa, and prodemocracy movements challenged dictatorships in China, Indonesia, and Burma.

Revolutionary Movements in Advanced Industrialized Democracies

Many of the movements and activists mentioned in this chapter hail from countries either in the developing world or from what used to be known as the second world, those countries that fell within the Soviet sphere of influence. We often don't think of revolutionary movements agitating in relatively stable, wealthy democracies. After all, a hallmark of a stable democracy is its ability to absorb competing interests through the more institutionalized political processes of elections, lobbying, interest group politics, and social movement activities that practice mostly legal forms of protest. Further, what helps make stable democracies endure is a political culture in which almost all citizens choose to cooperate within the rules of democratic politics or, at the very least, choose not to defect. Many students born in the post–Vietnam War/post–Cold War era are surprised to learn that countries such as the United States, Germany, Italy, and Japan were rocked by the activities of small underground terrorist organizations such as the Weather Underground (United States), Red Army Faction (Germany), Red Brigades (Italy), and Japanese Red Army in the late 1960s and throughout the 1970s and 1980s. Other groups, such as the Black Panther Party in the United States, flitted between radical left-wing, but legal, protest activity and advocating armed uprising against legal authority. In all movements, women held important leadership positions, although for most, gender was not an important rallying cry. Rather, the enemy was usually the capitalist system, Western imperialism, and the people who enforced these systems at home and abroad.

The damage inflicted by these relatively small groups was significant: The Weather Underground, which was founded in 1969 by disillusioned members of Students for a Democratic Society (SDS), organized riots, detonated bombs in a number of public spaces, and facilitated a jailbreak of famed LSD advocate Timothy Leary in their six short years. Tired of the supposed futility of nonviolent protest to the Vietnam War and inspired by the militancy of the Black Panther Party, the Weather Underground believed in the potential of urban guerrilla actions to fundamentally reset the priorities of the U.S. military, and in 1970, they issued a "Declaration of a State of War" against the U.S. government. As Naomi Jaffe, a former member, explained,

> We felt that doing nothing in a period of repressive violence is itself a form of violence. That's really the part that I think is the hardest for people to understand. If you sit in your house, live your white life and go to your white job, and allow the country that you live in to murder people and to commit genocide, and you sit there and you don't do anything about it, that's violence.[i]

However, after the United States reached a peace accord in Vietnam in 1973, the group gradually disintegrated, as some leaders were arrested, others turned themselves in, and some refocused their militancy on other issues. Their legacy was briefly unearthed during the 2008 U.S. presidential elections when vice presidential candidate Sarah Palin accused Barack Obama of "palling around" with terrorists because of Obama's alleged relationship with a former member of the Underground.

While the Weather Underground primarily targeted buildings, rather than people, with their bombs, other radical groups in other countries were not as discriminating. For example, the German Red Army Faction (RAF, also known as the Baader Meinhof Gang), which operated from the late 1960s to 1998, was responsible for thirty-four deaths and numerous injuries from bombings, kidnappings, and other forms of armed protest over almost thirty years of activity. Their armed resistance reached a peak in autumn 1977 when, in response to the convictions of members of their group, part of the RAF tried to free their imprisoned comrades and kidnap a prominent German businessman, killing three policemen and the driver in the process. Eventually, the businessman was also executed, in the wake of an audacious hijacking attempt. Like the Weather Underground, members of the RAF cited their disillusionment with capitalist society. In addition, members felt alienated from what they perceived to be a conservative, pro-order political culture that echoed totalitarian currents from the Nazi era. This two-decades-long spasm of violence transfixed the world and shattered Germans' vision of their society as a democratic and orderly one. The RAF continued its sporadic campaign of terror into the 1990s, assassinating the head of the Treuhandanstalt, the trust in charge of privatizing East Germany's state-owned assets (and bringing capitalism to the former socialist state). Finally, in 1998, a letter faxed to the Reuters news agency, signed "RAF," announced the dissolution of the group.

Communist-inspired terrorist groups also shattered the stability of Japan and Italy throughout the 1970s and 1980s. The Japanese Red Army, whose stated goal was to overthrow the Japanese government and start a world revolution, conducted numerous hijackings, kidnappings, and hostage takings and launched a series of seventeen bombs in buildings belonging to large corporations. In Italy, the Red Brigades, in their efforts to create a revolutionary state through armed struggle and to remove Italy from NATO, kidnapped and murdered a former prime minister, in addition to conducting several high-profile political kidnappings.

Young women became increasingly active in these terrorist cells and, in almost all of these movements, assumed leadership positions. Bernadine Dohrn of the Weather Underground, Gudrun Ensslin and Ulrike Meinhof of the RAF, and Fusako Shigenobu of the Japanese Red Army were all key public faces and behind-the-scenes organizers of their respective organizations. Their female status was often a source of great fascination to the public, in part because they completely upended gender expectations about "appropriate behavior" for middle-class, college-educated women. Bernadine Dohrn, for example, had been a cheerleader in high school, something perceived as American as apple pie, before becoming radicalized in college and law school. Ensslin was a pastor's daughter pursuing her Ph.D., and Meinhof was the daughter of an art historian and a teacher, and herself was studying at university when she became much more polarized in her political beliefs. Media coverage of the women often mentioned their attractive physical appearance, as if this was somehow unexpected or noteworthy about their terrorism (male terrorists were rarely described in any fashion). Further, Ensslin and Meinhof had both married and had children before pursuing a life underground as terrorists and had decided to leave their children behind, which was seen as "unwomanly" and "unnatural," even though this was a common decision made by male activists who chose political violence over their children. Further, these women's recruitment to political violence was often portrayed as being an outgrowth of a "love connection" with a male member, rather than a carefully considered political choice.

Although there was a gendered component to how the public perceived these women, the activists themselves rarely pursued a gendered political agenda. Certainly, given that they were active in radical, Marxist-inspired movements, they were well versed in the Marxist critique of women's subjugation. And women active in the Weather Underground connected the battle against sexism with their violent activities, arguing that 'the struggle against sexism demands the destruction of the American state, and…the immediate personal nature of sexism requires struggle against men who enforce that oppression as well as its institutions."[ii] Yet, for the most part, women active in these movements subjugated their gender concerns to their larger struggle against what they perceived to be an oppressive state.

Has the evolution of time, and world events (such as the collapse of communism in the former Soviet Union and Eastern Europe) changed these women's views? Many of the women of the Weather Underground went underground themselves, although almost all eventually resurfaced, either when they voluntarily turned themselves in or were arrested. Bernadine Dohrn, a former leader once on the FBI's Ten Most Wanted List, eventually turned herself in and served a commuted sentence; she currently teaches law at Northwestern University and heads a nonprofit organization that advocates for the reform of the juvenile court system. Gudrun Ensslin and Ulrike Meinhof both committed suicide in the 1970s under suspicious circumstances in prison while awaiting trial for their participation in terrorist attacks. And Fusako Shigenobu, founder and leader or the Japanese Red Army, was finally arrested in 2000, after spending over twenty-five years in hiding. She vowed to continue her revolutionary goals from prison, although this time through the establishment of a political party rather than from the barrel of a gun. Although media attention has shifted to covering female suicide bombers in the Middle East, it is important to recognize that women, from all classes and all backgrounds and from many different countries, have been recruited to political violence and will probably continue to respond to armed revolutionary calls, even if peace in the Middle East is ever achieved.

---

[i] As quoted in the documentary film *The Weather Underground,* produced by Carrie Lozano, directed by Bill Siegel and Sam Green, New Video Group, 2003, DVD.
[ii] "Women of the Weather Underground," *Ms. Magazine,* February 1974, p. 105.

While many countries were moving toward implementing Western-style political and economic systems, other areas of the world were gripped by movements that questioned or rejected these same values. In Latin America, guerrilla movements that challenged the benefits of globalization and integration continued to spring up in Mexico, Colombia, and Brazil as the promise of better lives failed to materialize for many of its citizens. Fundamentalist movements grew in pace and popularity in the Middle East and Africa, as the rhetoric of political inclusion failed to encompass varied demands for political, cultural, and religious self-determination. Many of these movements incorporated a powerful anti-Western theme to accompany their ideological message. For example, in 1979, Islamic-inspired forces overthrew the corrupt Western-allied government of the Pahlavi family and replaced it with an Islamic theocracy. In 1987, Palestinians launched an "intifada" (uprising) against Israeli occupation that continues to this day, with no foreseeable end to an increasingly polarized conflict. Several years later, in 1992, Algeria was gripped by a deadly revolt when a general election won by an Islamist party was annulled.[10] In addition, ethnicity became an increasingly compelling rallying cry for the world's dispossessed, as conflicts over class diminished in the wake of the Cold War. Civil war and ethnic genocide in Bosnia, Kosovo, the Sudan, Rwanda, and the Congo were the horrifying accompaniment to the more positive democratization developments elsewhere in the world.

In addition, new actors became critical players in revolutionary movements. Specifically, since the 1970s, women have been recruited in rapidly multiplying numbers to guerrilla and revolutionary movements in countries such as Nicaragua, El Salvador, Mexico, and Iran. As the beginning of this chapter notes, women are increasingly recruited as suicide bombers. Despite this increasing participation of women, nonetheless, one observation remains constant; while revolutions have been waged in the name of many different ideologies, such as liberalism, communism, and various forms of nationalism, they have never been waged exclusively in the name of feminism.

In response to changing events, one could currently say that "a revolution is an effort to transform the political institutions and the justifications for political authority in a society, accompanied by formal or informal mass mobilization and noninstitutionalized actions that undermine existing authorities."[11] This definition can cover disparate events that all share a core set of characteristics: They are efforts to change the political regime by drawing on a competing vision of justice and a just society, they involve a substantial amount of both formal and informal means of citizen mobilization, and they encompass efforts to change politics through noninstitutionalized means, such as the use of mass demonstrations, protests, strikes, riots, and more violent forms of political expression. This definition allows us to unite a diverse array of events—ranging from the "classic" revolutions such as the French Revolution and the democratic transitions in countries all over the world to the chaotic periods of state breakdown in Africa and guerrilla movements that spring up in Latin America and the Middle East. At the same time, it allows us to exclude protests and movements, which seek to work within the system or through the ballot box. As we shall see, however, this means that it becomes harder to distinguish clearly the social movement activity in authoritarian or semi-authoritarian countries described in the previous chapter, for example, from the revolutionary activity outlined in this chapter. Repertoires of protest have expanded and range from nonviolent protest and peaceful demonstrations to the burning of effigies, the building of barricades, and the plotting of terrorist activities. A wider range of actors has been critical in revolutions. And in this latest stage of democratization, revolutions have morphed from violent upheavals into primarily peaceful transfers of power. Thus, for the purposes of our discussion in this chapter, revolutionary activity proceeds along a continuum of activities rather than belonging in a discrete category.

WHY DO WOMEN JOIN REVOLUTIONARY MOVEMENTS?

Why do women become involved in revolutionary movements, and do they respond for reasons similar to those of men? Women rarely join in order to fight for greater levels of gender equality, and instead tend to subjugate their concerns to perceived "larger" struggles. When women do mobilize out of a concern to improve women's lives, it is often to meet practical gender interests, immediate needs around issues that are traditionally perceived as being important to women and mothers. Part of this trend is because very few revolutionary movements target gender inequality as a salient issue. Even those that do, such as communist movements, subjugate these concerns to perceived "more important" struggles. Women themselves have often acquiesced to this choice and are often rarely in agreement about whether there is an essential woman's identity and about how central women's concerns should be in the face of a wide array of competing political, economic, and social demands. While it is important to look at how women participate in and benefit from revolutions, it is also important to recognize that women themselves experience a diversity of reactions to revolutionary ideology.

While this chapter discusses the myriad ways that women participate in and are affected by revolutionary movements, it is important to recognize that women have been and still are a minority in these movements. While women have become increasingly active in guerrilla struggles, particularly in Latin American countries, nonetheless, in only a few examples do women's representation in revolutionary movements constitute even a third of participants.[12] Why is there a gender imbalance in this area of political participation? As in other areas of women's participation in political and economic institutions, there are serious barriers and impediments to women's inclusion.

As we have seen, across contexts, women occupy a subordinate position in almost all realms of the public sphere because of their duties in the private realm. In other words, many women are simply too busy with their domestic responsibilities of raising children and tending to the household to organize. This sometimes extends to the direct family of revolutionary leaders. A wife often shares her husband's political beliefs but remains out of the political limelight, caring for the family. For example, Joshua Nkomo, head of Zimbabwe African People's

Union, which fought for the overthrow of white rule in the former Rhodesia, commented:

> My marriage was the best thing I ever did in my whole life. In the thirty-four years of our marriage we have spent less than half the time together, but we have had a perfect understanding all the time. My wife has always borne the main responsibility for such property as we have owned: more, she has kept our family together, because all of us have always been confident that she would be there whatever happened.[13]

Further, in his memoir covering his participation in South Africa's struggle for justice, Nelson Mandela talks eloquently of the sacrifices his wife made so that he could pursue his political activities. While Winnie Mandela also emerged as a prominent opposition leader, nonetheless, she was also responsible for caring for the children, the house, and other family obligations.[14] Many women participated in revolutions by staying out of them or by occupying supporting positions, allowing their spouses or partners to engage fully in the struggle by taking full responsibility for activities in the household.

In addition, many women have less access to education and, as a result, receive less exposure to revolutionary ideas and plans. Women's lesser integration into the workforce also diminishes their opportunities to become exposed to revolutionary ideas of change. However, joining the workforce in and of itself often is not a sufficient catalyst for change. Class issues further complicate women's participation. Middle- and upper-class women often encounter fewer barriers to participation than do working-class women, who often have little education, meager incomes, few marketable skills, and sometimes sole responsibility for the domestic sphere. Even though their levels of deprivation and exploitation may be higher, they have less opportunity to voice their frustration. In this sense, women's experiences in revolutionary movements mirror men's in that revolutionaries often come from the middle and upper classes. Greater levels of economic independence, more education, and potential access to daycare have all helped wealthier women organize for other women (and men) who are less advantaged.[15] In sum, despite women's desire to participate in movements of political change, often women are unable to participate in the same ways that men do.

For the women that do answer a revolutionary call for action, what prompts them to get involved? Is it for the benefits that could potentially accrue to them as women, or are they motivated by other concerns that override gender identity? The following sections discuss three types of revolutionary movements—Marxist, liberal and democratization movements, and nationalist and religious movements—and explains what they offer women and why women have responded to them. Because Marxist movements have most explicitly targeted women and women's equality as a revolutionary goal, we shall start our discussion there.

Marxist Revolutionary Movements

Overcoming the contradictions of capitalism and freeing the worker are the primary goals for socialist revolutionaries. In peasant-based, agrarian societies, such as those in Latin America, Marxist revolutionaries sought to rectify the unequal distribution of land, which helped maintain the power of a small, privileged landholding elite over a relatively landless and powerless peasantry. However, Marxist-inspired ideologies also directly addressed and critiqued women's status within the larger framework of capitalism. Many Marxist theorists argued that women are doubly burdened—as workers they are exploited by the capitalists, and as wives and mothers they are further exploited, for they are still responsible for the cooking, sewing, child-rearing, and cleaning. Marxists argued that marriage is, in fact, often a form of prostitution, as women marry out of economic necessity rather than choice and "earn their keep" by performing essential domestic and sexual tasks. This double burden of production and reproduction further prevents them from entering the public realm in positions of power on an equal footing with men. This Marxist critique of class and gender relations was used widely among revolutionaries in the Soviet Union, China, Cuba, and Vietnam and, more recently, in guerrilla movements in Nicaragua, El Salvador, Peru, and the Chiapas region of Mexico. As we shall see, many of these more recent movements also incorporated strong nationalist ideologies; fighting economic injustice often was combined with a rhetoric of national self-determination, and imperial powers, such as the United States, were condemned for their overbearing role in directing domestic politics.

Marxists theorists proposed a variety of solutions to the "woman question." For example, the Bolsheviks in Russia painted a Marxist utopia in which household cares would be transformed to the public sphere. Paid workers would assume the duties that wives had once fulfilled, and communal dining rooms, laundries, and child-care centers would ensure that women could be freed to enter the public sphere, unburdened by duties at home. Marriage, even, would become superfluous, and men and women would come together and separate as they wished, no longer shackled together because of economic dependency.[16] In China, Mao Tse-tung supported women's right to vote and run for office, to hold land on equal terms with men, to reject forced marriages, and to initiate divorce proceedings.[17] In Chiapas, Mexico, on the first day of the 1994 rebellion, the Zapatistas distributed pamphlets listing their demands, many of which related to issues of gender equality. Known as the Revolutionary Women's Law, the list included an affirmation of a woman's right to an education and primary health care. In addition, it affirmed a woman's right to choose how many children to have and when to have them, to choose her spouse without forceful intervention, and to live free from violence both in and out of her home.[18] Across contexts, many Marxist-inspired movements offered a postrevolutionary society that included increased political opportunities for women, increased access to professional opportunities (which would thus make women less economically dependent on men), and a variety of social reforms (increased access to higher education, better health care, increased maternity benefits, and daycare) to make this possible.

In practice, Marxist-inspired revolutionaries turned to women, actively recruiting them by acknowledging their importance to the struggle. Lenin claimed that "there can be no socialist revolution, unless a vast section of the toiling women takes an important part in it...and the success of a revolution depends on the extent to which women take part in it."[19] Mao echoed these sentiments when he said that "women have an urgent need for revolution.... [T]hey are a force that will decide the success or failure of the revolution."[20] Further, he argued, man could not be free unless woman was liberated. Fidel Castro declared the quest to end women's subordination within the household as a "revolution within the revolution."[21] Abimael Guzman, the leader of the Peruvian guerrilla movement Shining Path, was fond of quoting Lenin directly regarding his policy toward women. And Daniel Ortega, the leader of the Sandinista Front (FSLN), which eventually overthrew the corrupt Samoza regime in Nicaragua, proclaimed that "the FSLN commits itself to guaranteeing women's rights and to struggle energetically against the residual sexism inherited from our past."[22] Revolutionary leaders, most of them male, who borrowed their inspiration from Marx, certainly knew the rhetoric of gender equality. Later on, we will discuss whether women responded to this call to gendered revolution and how willing male revolutionaries were to implement gender equality in practice.

Despite the explicit critique of women's position in society, Marxism has never been the panacea for women that leaders have claimed. Ultimately, the enemy to defeat, according to Marxist theory, is the capitalist system and the bourgeois class. Thus, despite the rhetoric of gender equality, women have often been recruited in the name of overall class struggle, rather than the battle of the sexes. Women's liberation was part of a more important cause, the rights of the worker, and women were to identify as workers first, rather than as women with separate agendas, identities, and reactions to revolutionary policy. Despite the gendered critique of the capitalist system, the struggle for workers' rights was preeminent, and once that was won, Marxists argued, gendered oppression, similar to the state, would simply wither away. Thus, while Marxism is one of the few revolutionary ideologies to critique women's position in society explicitly, nonetheless the demands of class struggle usually trumped gender concerns.

There are a few signs that this may be changing as Marxist-inspired revolutionary movements unfold in the wake of national and international women's movements. For example, Lisa, an activist in the Zapatista Front for National Liberation (FZLN), connected gender concerns with the larger struggle for increased autonomy. Putting the Zapatista movement in context with other Latin America guerrilla movements, she explained:

> I think it [the FZLN-led struggle] has learned from the earlier processes and it has gone beyond them. Obviously as a woman I am very interested in taking on women's struggles. [In FZLN meetings] we have begun to talk about the fact that one cannot be a Zapatista and an oppressor. And it is incongruent to be a revolutionary and to block women's liberation.[23]

It is hard to tell whether this quote represents one individual's thought process or is indicative of a larger change in the way that Marxist-inspired revolutionaries interpret class and gender relations. Another interviewee had a different perception of the FZLN's commitment to gender issues. In her view:

> What I think is that the FZLN is not a feminist movement but rather a movement that is military, hierarchical, and authoritarian. Not all of them have gender consciousness but some of them do. The FZLN is not against working with women, but I think that it has been a little careless about work with women. The topic of women is always treated as less important than other topics. But it does try to break with the patriarchal system.[24]

While the second participant presents a less rosy view of the FZLN's integration of gender interests, she does acknowledge that the FZLN is making an effort to balance gender with other issues. Nonetheless, Marxist revolutionary ideology, of all the revolutionary ideologies discussed here, most explicitly critiques the status of women and seeks to rectify imbalances with proactive policies.

Liberal/Democratization Movements

Classical liberalism is a political and economic philosophy that emerged in seventeenth- and eighteenth-century Europe. Liberalism focuses on establishing an array of individual rights and liberties to counteract the actions of an often too powerful state. Revolutionary movements that profess the ideology of classical liberalism focus on the need for greater political inclusion as a way to wean power away from traditional elites and stress themes such as democratic government, individual liberty, and laissez-faire economic growth. While Marxists saw the division of wealth as the obstacle to equality, liberals identified political lack of freedom and an authoritarian political system as the main impediment to progress. John Locke, Jean-Jacques Rousseau, Adam Smith, Benjamin Franklin, and Thomas Jefferson all came to be identified with a wide variety of ideas associated with classical liberalism, and liberalism was the inspiration for revolutionary movements in America, France, and more recent democratization movements, such as those that toppled communist regimes across eastern Europe and the former Soviet Union, as well as authoritarian regimes in South Africa and the Philippines. Democratization movements led to the collapse of repressive regimes on nearly every continent in the world in the 1980s, 1990s, and the first decade in the twenty-first century.

However, revolutionary movements that espouse liberal ideologies rarely focus specifically on women's rights (or the lack of) as a critical problem to be rectified. Rather, revolutionary leaders have tended to pitch their rhetoric to women as citizens, rather than as women with specific gendered interests. For example, some revolutionary movements that fought for greater political inclusion, such as the French Revolution, sought broader changes within the political system in an attempt to wean power away from traditional elites, such as the monarchy and the nobility. Thus, they appealed to women as citizens to support the larger goals of "liberty, equality, and fraternity." They did not address the reasons that might make it problematic for women to participate equally with men in the political realm. Two hundred years later, when democratization movements were sweeping communist regimes from power across eastern Europe, the leaders of these movements were appealing to all citizens to unite to topple authoritarianism, rather than targeting women in particular and communism's failure to address women's inequality. However, many feminists active in women's movements, particularly in the West, have used liberal ideology to fight for greater women's rights, by arguing that women, like men, should be valued as individual, autonomous agents deserving of equal rights, rather than targeted as justified cases for discrimination. Thus, liberalism has been something of a double-edged sword for women; on the one hand, it has been used to justify women's equality in the sense that it supports equality for all citizens, but on the other hand, liberal-inspired movements fighting for greater political inclusion have tended to blur the distinction between genders in the search for a widened space for political participation for all citizens, thus obscuring the reasons why women may be unable to participate equally.

In practice, leaders of liberal movements could be ambivalent, even hostile, about the gains of women's participation. In the French Revolution, the male leadership always treated women gingerly, despite women's enthusiastic participation. Overall, women were tolerated only as long as their help and activity were necessary. When they were not perceived as necessary they were excluded from participation in the newly formed clubs and political organizations.[25] Robespierre, one of the leaders of the Revolution, thought women's involvement in political debate "unnatural" and "sterile." [26] The Republican Convention outlawed women's clubs at the height of Revolution, perceiving them as dangerous and counterproductive.

Unfortunately, the passage of time (and the greater awareness of women's rights) did not necessarily ameliorate the tension between supporting gender equity and the larger political struggle of increased citizenship rights for all. Women participated actively in mass demonstrations and protests against communist regimes in eastern Europe and the former Soviet Union. Many joined in the hopes of installing a new, liberal, democratic regime. In fact, women made up half the membership of Solidarity, the trade union turned opposition movement in Poland.[27] Yet, as we shall see, women's concerns were virtually ignored in the aftermath of the overthrow of the communist system.

In fact, many women would not have been interested in, and would have even been alienated by, promises for gender equality in the democratization movements that felled communist regimes across eastern Europe and the former Soviet Union. In part, the authoritarian communist systems they were trying to topple had enforced a strong rhetoric of gender equality, and many women were uninterested in lining up behind a rhetoric that now seemed dated and insincere. Under communism, women were told they were equal to men and that the communist state would provide them with advantages that would afford them higher standards of living than experienced by their counterparts trapped in the capitalist West. Reality was very much at odds with the official myth, however, as the rhetoric of women's equality under communism translated into long work days on the job followed by equally weighty responsibilities in the home. Furthermore, the heightened, yet essentially symbolic, political status of women in communist regimes simply loaded them down further as they faced a triple burden of work, home, and public life. Consequently, many women, particularly those old enough to remember the communist era, did not respond, and would not have responded, to a Western liberal feminist rhetoric of equality, for it seemed to echo the empty promises of the Soviet past. Shana Penn, who interviewed many women who had been active in the Polish movement against communism, found that many felt that the communists had not really succeeded in solving the various conflicting demands on women's lives; rather, they had profoundly silenced discussion about it. In fact, most of her interviewees "forthrightly declared that they were not feminists and had no intention of adopting another ideology when they had just discarded one." [28]

In addition, many women who grew up in the drab uniformity of the communist period reacted positively to the promise of a new consumerist culture of postcommunist society. Many women initially embraced makeup, high heels, and tight clothing as a welcome change from the drab uniformity of the Soviet era. Thus, Western feminist concerns about social pressures on women to conform to narrow standards of beauty fell on deaf ears. Moreover, one mobilizing factor for the women's movement in the West—a woman's right to choose to have an abortion—did not exist in countries of the former Soviet Union and eastern Europe. Women during much of the Soviet era could choose to terminate their pregnancies with an abortion, and most were forced to do so in the absence of other forms of reliable contraception. Furthermore, women across the eastern bloc enjoyed relatively generous maternity leave benefits. Thus, many of the issues that mobilized women in the West either did not exist or were subverted by Soviet ideology, thus making it difficult for a new wave of female activists to appropriate the rhetoric of feminist principles of liberation and equality. [29]

Finally, women participants saw the goal of overthrowing the previous regime as more important than ensuring their rights as women. Commenting on her own role in the opposition to communist rule in Poland, Joanna Szczesna noted the discrimination against women in society. However, she noted, "I considered feminism a needless luxury in those days. I'd rather get involved in activities protesting the use of physical violence by the police than in a struggle for the equal distribution of a policeman's blows." She went on to add, "It happened that once in my life, I put out a lot of fires, but please believe me, it was not because of gender discrimination that I didn't become a fireperson. I didn't become one because I didn't want to be one." [30] In the democratization movements that swept communist governments from power across eastern Europe and the former Soviet Union, neither male revolutionary leaders nor female participants were interested in appealing to women along gender concerns. As we shall see, some women soon regretted their rejection of women's issues as important ones once they saw their economic, social, and political status slide under the newly minted democratic regimes.

Religious Fundamentalist Movements

A third type of revolutionary movements has been formed in the name of establishing a theocracy, a form of government in which religion and government are intertwined. In a theocracy, some, if not all, civic leaders are identical with leaders of the dominant religion, government policies are identical to or are strongly influenced by religious principles, and often the leader claims to rule on behalf of God or some alternative religious authority. The main qualification is that there is little or no distinction between religious and government authority. While many Western countries contain small Christian movements that push for a greater role for the church in determining state policy and while the Vatican City is an example of a Christian theocracy, recently, many revolutionary theocratic movements have been centered on various tenets of Islam. In addition, these movements have melded a powerful vision of an alternative society guided by religious precepts with another potent ideology, nationalism, often defined with an anti-Western bent. Revolutionary movements have been successful in establishing theocracies in Iran under the Ayatollah Khomeini and in Afghanistan under the Taliban. There are also strong Islamic revolutionary movements in Algeria and Bahrain, and the Kingdom of Saudi Arabia is a theocracy.

There is widespread discussion about the position and status of women in Muslim societies. It is important to remember that countries that are predominantly Muslim vary extensively in their political systems and their design of public policy toward women, ranging from democratic and secular Turkey to the semi-authoritarian clerical rule of Iran, which has enforced Islamic law. This chapter is not meant to address the very complicated and complex issue of Islam and women's rights. As with all religions, there is a host of contradictory evidence about how Islam defines a woman's role, position, and status in society. However, in this section, we will discuss women's participation in movements that seek the imposition of an Islamic state, for many argue that countries such as Iran, which have moved to implement Shari'a, or Islamic legal code, proscribe a role for women that is not only different from men but also inferior.[31] Shari'a, as it has been interpreted and implemented in various countries, has tended to minimize women's rights in areas such as marriage, divorce, child custody, inheritance, access to higher education, employment, and political office.[32]

The Iranian Revolution (1979) provides an interesting example of women's mobilization in support of a regime that promised to radically alter (and, as some would argue, reverse) women's recently gained political, economic, and social opportunities. In 1979, the world's attention was riveted on Iran. A broad alliance of liberal, leftist, and religious groups ousted Shah Mohammed Reza Pahlavi, who had been in power since 1941. While the shah had implemented a variety of Western economic and social reforms to modernize Iran, his rule primarily benefited a small, wealthy elite. Further, he was widely perceived to be a stooge for the Western powers, primarily the United States. In the face of widespread protests in which millions of citizens filled the streets, the shah fled the country in January. However, in the wake of his abdication, the alliance of opposition forces further fragmented, leading to the eventual rise of the Ayatollah Khomeini, an Islamic fundamentalist who had spent the previous fourteen years in exile in Iraq and France because of his opposition to the Pahlavi regime. On April 1, less than three months after the toppling of the shah, a referendum led to the proclamation of the Islamic Republic of Iran, with the Ayatollah Khomeini as supreme leader.[33] As we shall discuss in greater depth later in this chapter, Khomeini moved to implement a variety of changes that would bring women's status in line with Islamic law, which is unfavorable to women with regard to marriage, divorce, and inheritance. Yet, many women supported Khomeini and mobilized extensively to support his rule. Why would women support a leader that expressly argued for their diminished rights?

As in other movements, many women did not respond to a revolutionary call for action out of a desire to change their own gendered status; many were temporarily united in their opposition to the rule of the shah. While still in exile in France, the Ayatollah presented a vision of an Islamic state in which the political and social rights of women would be guaranteed and women would gain true freedom, dignity, and respect. In addition to endorsing women's political rights, Khomeini declared that "democracy is incorporated in the Quran and people are free to express their opinions and to conduct their acts. Under the Islamic government, which is a democratic government, freedom of expression, opinion, and pen will be guaranteed for everyone."[34] In part, Khomeini's vision of Iran was attractive to women because his rhetoric presented a rosier picture for citizens than what eventually ensued after the installation of an Islamic government. In addition, however, after attaining power, Khomeini announced several jihads—one against illiteracy, another to rebuild the country, and a third against foreign invasion and the possibility of a coup. Millions of women joined up, not for religious reasons, but because they believed in the goal of rebuilding the country in the wake of a tumultuous revolution.[35]

Further, women responded to the gendered elements of an Islamic state, such as wearing the veil, as a vehicle to express their frustration at the failures of corrupt, Westernized elites that were perceived to have sold their country's national interests to an all-powerful, decadent West. Reclaiming their country from their rulers also entailed embracing an alternative to Westernization. In this sense, gender motivations were important to the revolution in that women took to wearing the veil as a symbol of opposition to the decadence of the Pahlavi regime as well as of Western values, and the middle- and upper-class, Westernized woman came to embody the corruption of the old system.[36] As Valentine Moghadam notes, "the idea that women had 'lost honour' during the Pahlavi era was a widespread one."[37] Other women initially embraced Islamic dress code, such as the veil, because they were tired of constant and public sexual harassment as a result of their Western clothing. Adopting Islamic cultural customs was a way of reclaiming national pride and heritage. As Afsaneh Najmabadi editorialized in *Zan-e Rouz,* a popular women's magazine:

> [W]omen serve as the unconscious accomplices of the power-that-be in the destruction of indigenous culture.... In Islamic countries...Islamic belief and culture provide people of these societies with faith and ideals....Woman in these societies is armed with a shield that protects her against the conspiracies aimed at her humanity, honor and chastity. This shield verily is her veil.[38]

In other words, women themselves were conflicted about the symbolic meaning of the veil, and many adopted it to reclaim a national identity that they felt had been subverted under Pahlavi rule. Later in this chapter, we will discuss how the revolutionary regime impacted women once the leadership implemented Islamic law and made issues that had once been a matter of choice compulsory.

In sum, how have women responded to these various ideological pitches? One common theme is that few women joined revolutionary movements in order to fight specifically for greater levels of gender equality (or inequality). Even in Marxist-inspired revolutions, which most directly addressed women's issues, few if any women saw their actions as connected to feminism.[39] For example, after interviewing over two hundred women who were active in the guerrilla movements in Nicaragua, El Salvador, and Chiapas, only one woman had joined out of a desire for increased gender justice.[40] Women joined guerrilla movements in Latin America for other reasons not related to women's rights. Similar to the men, they wanted to end the dictatorship, end the exploitation of the poor or the indigenous, or create a more just country for their children.[41] Further, the example of Leila Khaled, a Palestinian who was part of a team that hijacked a TWA flight in 1969 and who, the following year, led an attempted hijacking, further illustrates many revolutionary women's priorities. She explained her motivations in the following way:

> We wanted to put the Palestinian question in front of international opinion. All the time we were being dealt with as refugees who only needed human aid. That was unjust. Nobody had heard our screams and suffering. All we got from the world was more tents and old clothes. After 1967, we were obliged to explain to the world that the Palestinians had a cause.[42]

Throughout history, many women, including Leila Khaled, have been motivated by causes such as nationalism, self-determination, and greater political autonomy for all, rather than gender equality.

However, many women in various movements have been recruited out of what Maxine Molyneux terms practical (as opposed to strategic) gender interests. That is, they have organized to meet immediate needs that arise out of issues that are traditionally perceived as being important to women and mothers. For example, as the ones primarily responsible for gathering food, making meals, and overseeing the household, women often became involved because their abilities to perform their gendered duties at home were threatened. The most notable expression of women's participation in the French Revolution was expressed by a women's march to Versailles to petition King Louis XVI for change; they were upset about the availability of food, which dramatically affected their ability to feed their families. Many women joined Latin American movements to alleviate the sense of fear they felt for the well-being of their families.[43]

Yet, there has been an undeniable increase in the number of women active in underground movements. Revolutionary movements in the eighteenth, nineteenth, and first half of the twentieth centuries tended to produce a few high-profile female revolutionaries; however, women were not systematically incorporated into the rank-and-file opposition. For example, female revolutionaries such as Alexandra Kollantai in the Soviet Union, Vilma Espin of Cuba, and Nguyen Thi Binh in Vietnam were the exception, not the rule. However, increasingly, women have made up the ranks of soldiers in various guerrilla movements across Latin America. For example, while some estimate that 5 percent of the Cuban revolutionary movement was female, women's participation in Latin American guerrilla movements from the 1970s onward ranged from 20 to 30 percent.[44] In Peru, an estimated 35 percent of leaders of Shining Path were women, primarily at the underground cell level.[45] We should treat these numbers with some caution since they have been contested; actual visitors to guerrilla camps reported having seen few female combatants.[46] However, whatever the numbers, it is true that significantly more women are involved in revolutionary movements than in previous decades.

What explains this dramatic increase? Various scholars have posited a number of factors that have converged to facilitate women's increased participation. Ilya Luciak argued that part of this increase is because of the rise of the international feminist movement.[47] Karen Kampwirth, in her research on Nicaraguan, Salvadoran, and Mexican women, attributed women's increased presence to four related trends. First, the economic changes after World War II in Latin America increased land tenure inequality. This forced many women to move to the cities, where they were exposed to new organizing opportunities that had not been available in the countryside. In addition, the emergence of liberation theology in Latin America, which stressed social justice and human rights issues, meant that the church was much more active in organizing activists, and women in particular. This opened up new opportunities that helped women gain organizational experience, which in turn facilitated their transition to more revolutionary political movements. Third, Kampwirth noted that many guerrilla movements in Latin America switched organizational strategies from the "Cuban model," which emphasized mobilizing a small cadre of tightly trained revolutionaries, to one that involved mass mobilization and the need to recruit as many people as possible. Finally, she argued that women became recruited for a variety of personal factors—early childhood experiences of resistance, participation in preexisting networks, higher levels of education, and youth—which contributed to high levels of participation.[48] All of these factors point to the fact that women's involvement in revolutionary movements has increased dramatically in scope.

However, we still do not know if this increase in women's mobilization will result in an increased focus on practical or strategic gender interests.

REVOLUTIONARY STRATEGIES AND TACTICS

Once women are recruited to revolutionary movements, do they contribute to the cause differently than their male counterparts do? On the one hand, some women have assumed traditional "male" roles and have made bombs, masterminded plots, and led troops into battle with equal zealousness. However, the high-profile female revolutionary is the exception, not the rule, and women rarely hold positions of power within the movement, instead serving as crucial assistants. Further, women have assumed traditionally female, nurturing roles as helpers in revolutions by raising money, giving shelter, teaching, and nursing. Revolutionary leaders, in turn, have been ambivalent about women's participation in the movement. On the one hand, they have exploited society's traditional visions of women's femininity by assigning women difficult and dangerous decoy assignments. However, many leaders are hesitant to put their revolutionary rhetoric of equality into practice; they rarely appoint women to true leadership positions and save the most visible and high-ranking jobs for their male colleagues.

History is not lacking examples of exceptional women who rose to prominence in a "man's world" of revolutionary combat. For example, in the French Revolution, Theroigne de Mericourt fought for the right to form a women's battalion to fight.[49] In Russia, Vera Figner was born into the privileges of the aristocracy in 1852, but by the age of thirty-two had become one of Russia's most vocal revolutionaries. She was a member of the Executive Committee of the People's Will Party, an underground organization that masterminded the successful plot to assassinate Tsar Alexander II. She was eventually sentenced to life imprisonment for her involvement.[50] Speaking of her own experiences in the Cuban Revolution, Haydee Santamaria professed that "I believe it takes a great effort to be violent, to go to war. But one has to be violent and to go to war when there is good reason.... It is painful to kill, but if it is necessary, you must do it."[51] In the long struggle for Vietnamese independence and the subsequent battle against American involvement in Vietnam, Nguyen Thi Dinh fought with the Viet Minh forces against the French while still in her teenage years. After her release from imprisonment, she went on to help lead various armed insurrections against the French- and American-supported governments.[52] Another Vietnamese woman, Nguyen Thi Binh, eventually became a member of the Central Committee for the National Front for the Liberation of Vietnam and played a major role in the signing of the Paris Peace Accords on Vietnam, which ended the war in 1973 (although only Henry Kissinger and Le Duc Tho received the Nobel Peace Prize and were named *Time* magazine's Men of the Year for their roles in the process).[53]

More often, however, women did not assume prominent leadership positions but instead worked in critical (but often undervalued) secondary roles and engaged in tasks such as weapons transport, intelligence gathering, or recruitment. Often they performed these activities precisely because tacticians counted on their opponent's gendered expectations about "appropriate" areas of activity for women (which did not include joining revolutionary movements). As a result, women were crucial as decoys and as on-the-ground agents because they often attracted less suspicion. For example, in the Cuban Revolution, in Castro's first attempt to overthrow the Batista regime, two women went by train to Santiago carrying weapons in a suitcase and a flower box. One of his mistresses typed and mimeographed copies of a manifesto written by Castro. Women also stored weapons, smuggled messages, and played vital roles as arms runners in the name of the Cuban Revolution.[54] Vilma Espin, Cuban revolutionary and sister-in-law to Fidel Castro, would smuggle political pamphlets into Santiago. As she explained, "It seemed easier for us because we could carry papers in our skirts."[55] In more recent guerrilla struggles in Latin America, women continued this trend, participating in supporting roles, such as keeping safe houses, acting as messengers and decoys, and transporting weaponry and communications equipment in the guise of going to the market.[56]

In the anticommunist struggle in Poland, when many prominent men were arrested in the wake of the imposition of martial law in 1981, women single-handedly started the underground paper and, after 1989, created the first free press, *Gazeta Wyborcza*.[57] Polish women were also used to smuggle dissident pamphlets in their heavy shopping bags, which was not questioned because authorities were used to seeing women haul around heavy shopping bags and assumed that women were too occupied with feeding their families to express political opinions.[58]

In the Iranian Revolution, women were critical to the Ayatollah Khomeini's rise to power. Millions of women ignored night curfew and took to the streets when the Ayatollah called on them to attend public demonstrations. Further, their presence at the front lines of the demonstration kept them relatively peaceful, as soldiers were hesitant to fire on fellow Muslim women to protect a corrupt, Westernized regime.[59]

In the increasing wave of violence subsuming the Middle East, terrorists are recruiting women because border guards are still not accustomed to viewing women as potential terrorists. Palestinian women, who are often draped in bulkier, less form-fitting garb, can carry the necessary explosives under their clothes without arousing suspicion.

Women often become the symbols of revolutionary movements, and leaders manipulate the image of the self-sacrificing woman to rally and mobilize support. In Vietnam, women were used prominently in propaganda posters, not only to rally citizens behind the concept of the nurturing mother but also to exemplify the bravery of the Vietnamese, the totality of national mobilization, and the extent of sacrifice demanded by the struggle. Women were also used by the Vietnamese to mock the weakness of the enemy; one popular and ubiquitous cartoon portrayed a small Vietnamese woman holding a rifle on a much taller and bulkier U.S. pilot as she marched him off to a POW camp.[60] In this scenario,

Although women still are a minority in guerrilla armies, their presence has increased steadily in the twentieth and twenty-first centuries. In this photograph, a small group of North Vietnamese women receive rifle training before joining Viet Cong forces during the Vietnam War. (September 11, 1967) SOURCE: Central Press/Hulton Archive/Getty Images

even the powerful United States could be brought to its knees by the determination of an organized resistance movement, even one populated by women giving selflessly to the cause.

Yet, even as women have used gender stereotypes to their advantage in one area of revolutionary activity, they have fulfilled them in others. In addition to their roles as fighters, women still found time to fulfill their traditional roles as caretakers, even in guerrilla camps, serving in less visible roles as cooks, health providers, and sex providers/workers.[61] These roles often were endorsed enthusiastically by leaders who were equally comfortable talking about gender equality in theory. Castro, in a letter to Celia Sanchez, commented that "Your absence has left a real vacuum. Even when a woman goes around the mountains with a rifle in hand, she always makes our men tidier, more decent, gentlemanly—and even braver.... But what would your poor father say?"[62] Che Guevara, another famed guerrilla warrior, found women valuable because they would do the tasks and chores that men spurned in favor of more traditionally male roles of active combat.[63] Although he considered women to be indispensable to the revolutionary struggle, nonetheless, as he wrote in *Guerrilla Warfare,* women were valuable for their specific "female" traits:

> The woman can also perform her habitual tasks of peacetime; it is very pleasing to a soldier subjected to the extremely hard conditions of this life to be able to look forward to a seasoned meal which tastes like something. One of the

great misfortunes of the [Cuban] war was eating cold, sticky, tasteless mess. Furthermore, it is easier to keep her in these tasks; one of the problems in gue-rilla bands is that they [men] are constantly trying to get out of these tasks.[64]

While Guevara may have spoken the rhetoric of gender equality, he was also capable of making breathtakingly stereotypical assumptions about the "appro-priate" gendered division of labor.

He was not alone; male leaders often spoke the rhetoric of equality, even gender equality, while simultaneously maintaining traditional views of appro-priately gendered divisions of labor within the movement. Despite an increas-ing acceptance of women as colleagues in the struggle, women active in Latin American guerrilla movements in the latter half of the twentieth century still met resistance from their male colleagues. For example, men were hostile to women leaders and resisted taking orders from them.[65] In the Nicaraguan strug-gle, when Monaca Baltodana, a high-ranking commander in charge of the final push to take Managua, went to negotiate, a guard refused to speak with her because she was a woman.[66] Nicaraguan activists faced resistance within their own party cadres; the Association of Nicaraguan Women (AMNLAE), the wom-en's arm of the Sandinista National Liberation Front (FSLN) pushed the leader-ship to include women in the draft. However, FSLN leadership resisted this push, arguing that women were needed at home to care for their children.[67] Speaking of her own experiences working with the revolutionary movement in Nicaragua, Margaret Randall observed that "only one, perhaps two, have the slightest inter-est in or respect for the feminist agenda. I do not know if any of them under-stands a feminist agenda as something beyond the proverbial 'equal rights for women.'"[68] Revolutionary actions rarely matched the discourse of gender equal-ity in movements.

The few women who were also included in the leadership circles often did little to overturn these attitudes because they felt that sexism was not an issue in the struggle. When Fidel Castro created the Federation of Cuban Women and appointed Vilma Espin, part of the inner circle of leadership, to head it, she objected vehemently. As she commented, "Why do we have to have a wom-en's organization? I have never been discriminated against. I had my career as a chemical engineer. I never suffered."[69] Drawing from the experience of women revolutionaries in Cuba, Nicaragua, and El Salvador, Karen Kampwirth argued that high-powered women did not see sexism as much "because the advantage of their prestige overrode the disadvantage of their sex."[70]

Nonetheless, Kampwirth notes that while sexism still did exist within rev-olutionary struggles, for women these struggles still offered unprecedented opportunities. Many women experienced more equal treatment than they had before. Further, male leaders for the most part were not ideological feminists but pragmatic strategists. They needed more participants, and to exclude women just because they were women would have been inefficient.[71] Thus, while condi-tions for women may not have matched the rhetoric of equality, these revolutions nonetheless presented women with opportunities and, as we shall see, transformed the women as a result of their experiences.

THE REVOLUTION'S IMPACT ON WOMEN

Revolutions, which often result in a totally transformed state, seemingly offer a window of opportunity in which women can take advantage of the opening of political space to fight for increased benefits and representation.[72] After all, old structures and ideologies are swept aside, political authority is weakened, and women have an opportunity to take advantage of these uncertainties. Women potentially have easier access to political roles, and women's activities can expand as the boundaries between "men's work" and "women's work" blur. As Barbara Jancar concludes, "because the new order has not yet been established the real possibility of change still exists."[73] Or, as Nikki Craske maintains, "moments of revolution and periods of transition provide opportunities and open up the political system when changes can be made that are positive to women." However, she goes on to add that "once the system begins to consolidate the opportunities for change decrease and in some situations women's positions erode."[74]

How did women benefit from the various revolutions we have covered? Did the transition open up opportunities for women, and did these opportunities eventually erode as the new political system consolidated its authority? The impact of various revolutions has been mixed for women. On the one hand, the new leadership has often designed policy that has had a substantial impact on women. For example, they set up ministries to address women's issues or improve women's access to education and employment opportunities. However, revolutionary regimes, even communist ones that directly address women's interests, rarely result in a clear-cut victory for women. Women rarely advance to formal positions of policy-making power in the new leadership of postrevolutionary regimes. If they do, they are often put in charge of overseeing "women's issues" in the new regime. Women's organizations, particularly those set up by the state, can easily be co-opted, and women's interests are often subordinated to other goals. In the face of scarce resources, women's needs are rarely met with ambitious state programs. Thus, while women's condition does often improve, many times it is as a by-product of larger, more encompassing goals. Despite the gains that women have experienced, the impact of revolutionary policy on women is rarely as emancipatory in practice as was promised, and women's activism in the revolutionary struggle does not neatly translate into participation in the new, postrevolutionary regime.

Political Impact

Revolutions have ushered in greater levels of political participation through an opening of the political process. Women are often guaranteed greater participation—either through increased suffrage, through the creation of state-facilitated organizations to represent women's interests, or through women's increased elevation to elected office. Yet, while women increasingly have become recruited to the cause of foot soldier in revolutionary struggles, they have rarely received political promotions for their loyalty, and they remain excluded from top leadership positions. Their participation in the revolutionary struggle often represents the zenith of their influence in formal mechanisms of power. Once a new regime comes to power, women historically have been marginalized or pushed off into gender-specific positions, heading departments of women's affairs or formulating policy for women, children, and the family, which are positions that are accorded relatively little political power or significance. They are rarely allowed into other areas of policy making. Alternatively, when they gain political access, it often is a result of their status as spouses, lovers, daughters, or sisters of leaders rather than through their merits as political operatives.

For example, Alexandra Kollantai, a Bolshevik feminist, theorist, and politician, was initially on the Central Committee of the Bolshevik Party and on the Central Executive Committee of the Petrograd Soviet. But under the Soviet regime, she was put in charge of the "women's section" of the party, a position that eventually was taken from her.[75] Similarly, despite the fact that many in Castro's closest circle were women, once he assumed power, most of the women who had participated in the guerrilla struggle disappeared from public view.[76] Castro then created the Federation of Cuban Women and appointed his sister in law, Vilma Espin, to head the organization. Although she had been part of Castro's inner circle, her appointment was perceived (particularly by her) as a political demotion, since women's issues were not considered to be as important as key policy areas such as foreign policy, defense, or other pressing national issues.[77] In Latin American countries, women's organizations, which had been formed to harness women's support for the revolution, fought against efforts by the state to co-opt them in the wake of the revolution, as newly formed postrevolutionary parties saw them as a conduit to potential voters.[78] Further, postrevolutionary regimes were suspicious of autonomous women's organizations and tried to contain women's activism by organizing them into state-sponsored groups, thus limiting their independence.[79]

In liberal-inspired revolutions, particularly those that occurred in the countries of the former communist bloc, women benefited, as did men, from the opportunity to participate in meaningful democratic elections. However, after these revolutions women lost their previously high levels of political representation. While under communism, women were often allotted quotas in legislatures; the installation of new, quota-free legislative systems led to their representational decimation in elections. While their previous levels of political representation under communism were essentially symbolic, given that legislatures served as rubber stamps for state policy, nonetheless the new reality of women's lack of political voice in the legislative arena was sobering to many female activists. This was particularly evident in Poland, for example, when the fledgling, male-dominated parliament proposed a ban on abortion. When the women's section of Solidarity, the opposition movement turned leading party, objected to the bill, they were shut down.[80] Sidelined by the power of the Catholic Church, women were unable to register much impact with their opposition to a further change in legislation, which replaced the word fetus with "conceived child."[81] While the previous communist regimes often failed to acknowledge their failures in advancing gender equality, the male-dominated regimes that replaced them simply ignored or overrode women's concerns.[82]

In Russia, some Soviet era women's organizations eventually responded to this by forming their own political party, Women of Russia. Although the party enjoyed some initial electoral success in 1995, it soon faded from political prominence. More recently, the Russian social movement Committee of Soldiers' Mothers organized more formally into a political party to advocate more forcefully for the end of the war in Chechnya. However, they have not yet competed in national-level elections, so it is difficult to predict their impact.[83] Not all democratization movements registered such a negative political impact on women; as we discussed in Chapter 1, the South African transition resulted in significant levels of female representation in the legislature. However, for postcommunist transitions, women must also confront the baggage of communism's rhetoric of women's equality and its subsequent delegitimation in the new democratic era.

In the wake of the Iranian revolution, women maintained their political rights, although they lost many of their civil rights. However, women's representation in the years following the revolution was minuscule; women parliamentarians comprised about 1.5 percent of the seats in the Majli in 1979, 1983, and 1987.[84] However, women's issues and the presence of women in public spaces became more prominent following the end of the Iran-Iraq War (1980–1988), which had mobilized much of both countries' material and human resources. Women's political representation in ensuing elections rose to 3.3 percent in 1992 and 4 percent in the 1996 elections (for a total of ten seats). Despite their minimal representation, the increased presence of women was felt in policy; two female representatives presented a motion in January 1993 to create the Special Commission of Women's Affairs. Although this proposal failed, women continued to push for change. In the fifth Majli, another deputy argued that "I believe that half of the deputies should be made up of thoughtful and specialist women who are aware of women's sufferings. In countries where women's rights are respected, a growing number of women are elected to the parliaments."[85] While the 2008 legislative elections resulted in a decrease in their numbers (from 13 to 8), nonetheless they have become increasingly vocal in bringing a woman's voice to policy. While women's voices still tend to be marginalized, in that they are circumscribed to advocating primarily on women's issues, nonetheless this is better than having no voice at all.

Further, Iranian women have maintained a political presence in civil society. Women's press continued to serve as a discussion forum for secular women and addressed critical contemporary political and social issues. For example, in the "Necessity for the Reform of Laws Concerning Divorce, Polygyny, and Child Custody," published in the magazine *Payam-e Hajar,* the author presented an analysis of Quranic verse to demonstrate that women's equality and Islamic values are not inherently contradictory. Many other articles have tried to demonstrate how Islam favors the equality of men and women.[86] It is important not to overstate the condition of women's political rights in postrevolutionary Iran; however, women have been able to maintain alternative spaces of expression in a regime that is hostile to a Western definition of women's equality.

Economic Impact

Economically, women often are enlisted in larger projects of economic modernization instigated by the revolutionary regime. This was particularly the case in the Soviet Union, China, and Cuba. Women's entry into the workforce was facilitated through legislation, such as maternity leave or child care, which ensured greater access to employment possibilities. Women initially benefited from the potential economic gains and resulting independence that financial wealth brought. In addition, women benefited in more indirect ways. The need for a better educated, more skilled labor force led to dedicated drives to educate women in order to meet the demands of industrialization.

However, familial relations within the household often remained embedded in more traditional settings. The result is that women ended up doubly burdened, working full-time outside of the house as well as within, by caring for the cooking, housework, and child-rearing. Often, the habit of using women's unpaid labor to fuel greater change became the convenient fallback strategy.[87] In analyzing the impact of guerrilla struggles in Latin America, scholars such as Craske concluded that while postrevolutionary regimes were able to make improvements in women's lives, they failed to address gender inequalities in the private sphere. Women still had to do all or most of the work in the home, which limited the ability of revolutionary regimes to foster gender equality.[88]

In the wake of the collapse of communism in eastern Europe and the former Soviet Union, women bore the brunt of the costs of economic transition. The economic impact of revolution was particularly harrowing because reforming former communist economies into capitalist ones involved a series of structural reforms that proved much more problematic than attempting to make underdeveloped economies more competitive. While the former communist regimes prided themselves on full employment and relatively equal divisions of wealth, the new democratic regimes had to implement reforms that led to massive joblessness, underemployment, and burgeoning poverty rates for large segments of the population. Initially, women were on the front lines of the unemployed; they were the first fired and last to be rehired and were further ghettoized into low-paid jobs with few opportunities for advancement.[89] While more recent analyses indicate that women's economic position, particularly in eastern European countries that are seeking entry into the European Union, has improved from the initial chaotic years of reform, nonetheless women face substantial hurdles in the labor market. The reduction in cradle-to-grave social benefits, such as maternity leave, child-care subsidies, family benefits, and pensions, that impact women have significantly complicated their efforts to combine work and family responsibilities.[90]

In the initial wake of the Iranian Revolution, women were dismissed from administrative positions and encouraged to assume their suitable positions of influence in the home, where they were to focus on their familial roles as mothers and caretakers. In addition, given the high levels of unemployment among men, the government did not want to encourage women's participation in the labor force. As a result, the government introduced a variety of policies to reduce the number of women in the labor market, such as offering early retirement and the option of transferring their salaries to their husbands if they choose to leave their jobs. The effects of these policies, however, are unclear.[91] One difficulty for the government has been in resolving their dual aims of reducing women's participation in the paid workforce with their simultaneous aim of maintaining their gendered ideology, which requires separate facilities for men and women in many spheres of life. If, for example, women are not to be seen or touched by men who are not kin (as Ayatollah Sanei, a powerful member of the leadership, proclaimed), then this requires the hiring of female teachers, doctors, and so forth.[92] As a result, the government has effectively removed women in more visible, high-level jobs, particularly in the public sector, while maintaining their participation in domains exclusive to women. Thus, while women's employment is low (about 30.5 percent of women are integrated into the paid labor force), nonetheless the government has had to compromise on its initial plans to return more women to the exclusive domain of the home.[93]

Social Impact

Finally, postrevolutionary regimes usually implement a wide array of policies that impact women's social status. They often pass wide-ranging legislation that redistributes power among families. Women are often granted new rights, such as suffrage, the right to divorce, child support, or abortion. However, these initial gains for women are often rolled back or reversed as governments attempt to consolidate power and appease old political enemies. Some revolutionary movements, such as the ones that came to power in Iran, are built around explicit ideologies that return women to traditional roles in the household and negate women's presence in the public sphere.

Often, radical and far-reaching social policies are scaled back in the face of larger political, economic, and social needs. For example, women's opportunities in the Soviet Union were scaled back as Stalin reprioritized Soviet goals. In the initial heady months following the Bolshevik rise to power, the new Soviet administration pushed through a variety of social reforms. It removed legal restrictions to divorce; secularized marriage; established paternal responsibilities for all children, whether born under wedlock or not; legalized abortion; recognized unregistered marriages; and enforced men's alimony obligations. In short, the Soviets envisioned a radical redistribution of power in an area usually shrouded in privacy—the household. Just over a decade later, many of these policies were being cut back or reversed altogether. Women's political organizations, the Zhenotdel, were abolished in 1930. By 1936, abortion was outlawed. By the end of

World War II divorce was nearly impossible, and unregistered marriages were no longer legally recognized. Womanhood and motherhood were glorified.[94]

Similarly, leaders of the Chinese Revolution, another Marxist revolution that directly appealed to women, implemented radical reforms at first, only to back off as they faced looming obligations during World War II. Initially, women's feet were finally unbound and such basic rights, such as the right to mobility, were ensured. The communists also enacted legislation backing free choice marriages and access to divorce. But the party also had to continuously compromise on the "woman question," and women within the Communist Party and at large acquiesced to these compromises.[95] In Vietnam, in the wake of the independence, the new government outlawed polygamy, although they did not work particularly hard at enforcing the law, making it an important step for women on paper but a toothless idea in practice.[96]

In the more recent guerrilla struggles in Latin America, women responded more vociferously to the new governments' weak commitments to gender issues. In Latin America, Kampwirth argues, an unintended legacy of the revolutionary struggle was that it radicalized women and helped create a feminist consciousness and the seeds of a feminist movement. This trend developed after the overthrow of various authoritarian regimes, when women guerrillas were expected to return to "normal" gender relations after the conclusion of the war. Many women were transformed personally by their participation in the movement and gained new skills and confidence in their abilities. In particular, Kampwirth argues that what she terms "mid-prestige" women formed the bulk of this unanticipated feminist movement. That is, these women were members of the rank and file who had experienced some authority in carrying out their duties but were not important enough to overcome the culture of machismo. Nor were they so powerless in the movement that they didn't develop important skills. In other words, their work was important enough that they got the opportunity to make decisions and develop some authority, but they were not important enough to carve out spheres of political influence after the revolution ended, and as a result, they became more aware of issues of sexism.[97] For example, Letty Mendez, member of the Farabundo Marti Front for National Liberation (FMLN) of El Salvador and later head of the women's secretariat of the FMLN, commented:

> We did not have a gender consciousness, before and during the war, but unconsciously we hoped that with change in society and from the class struggle, there was going to be a situation of equality for women. Unconsciously that was the feeling.... They [the men on the left] always said that this [the women's] struggle was secondary; always they said the problem was capitalism and I think we believed that because we didn't know the depth of our situation.[98]

This activist subsequently developed a gendered consciousness after her participation.

Further, an independent women's movement may be a necessary outgrowth of revolutionary movements. Because of the new government's tendency to scale back on promises in various Latin American regimes, Craske argues that independent women's organizations are necessary as an alternative to the regime's plans for women. As she points out, "even the most 'women-friendly' regimes seem to harbour an antipathy towards feminism, particularly among the male leadership; consequently an independent, grassroots movement is needed to promote this particular perspective." [99] In sum, one unintended consequence of the revolution has been increased autonomous women's organization around women's and feminist issues.

Liberal and democratization movements also have curtailed more progressive policies regarding women's status. In the wake of the French Revolution, women's rights were curtailed as Napoleon sought to return France to a more traditional, less tumultuous path. Women were enshrined in their roles as traditional wives and mothers, and with the Napoleonic Code of 1804, women found themselves legally and socially to be more powerless than before the Revolution. [100] In the wake of the collapse of communism in eastern Europe, as we mentioned previously, the Polish government quickly moved to place further restrictions on abortion, despite women's protestations, although this also sparked the beginnings of a postcommunist feminist movement. [101] In Russia, in the wake of severe economic dislocation, many women chose not to have children, causing the birth rate among the Russian population to decline rapidly. Male politicians quickly responded with a nationalist rhetoric, urging women to fulfill their "natural" responsibilities, and some proposed banning access to contraception or restricting access to abortion as a potential solution. Further, across many postcommunist countries, women lost their cradle-to-grade social benefits as governments attempted to scale back and meet "more important" targets, such as economic growth or increased employment. Yet, women were initially ambivalent about the changes in their social status. Many, exhausted from years of communist propaganda that stressed women's invincibility on all fronts, initially embraced a pronatalist rhetoric that sought to return women to the sanctity of hearth and home, which would potentially scale back their enormous work load. However, as the reality of the implications of lessened social benefits became more obvious, women began to organize, either in social movements or in political parties, as in Russia.

Women's social status in society was radically altered in postrevolutionary Iran, when women were governed under the jurisdiction of Shari'a law. Officials imposed an Islamic dress code and made covering of the hair and body compulsory, first for active women and then for the entire female population. Women's access to higher education was limited. The implications of Shari'a law were manifested most radically in family law. The husband was declared the head of the household, and the wife was obliged to submit to her husband. Her failure to comply can result in sanctions, or even divorce. Overall, men were given overwhelming privileges in matters of marriage, divorce, child custody, and so on. Further, the minimum age of marriage for girls was lowered to nine years of age. [102]

Women in Motion: Shirin Ebadi

"With a correct interpretation of Islam, we can have equal rights for women."[i] Shirin Ebadi, an Iranian lawyer and human rights activist, has a fascinating life story that bridges Iran before and after the revolution. Raised in a middle-class family, Ebadi was the first female judge in her country, until the Iranian revolution derailed her career plans. An initial supporter of the revolution, Ebadi became one of its early victims as the regime soon implemented a system that was punitive to women. Yet, rather than emigrate to the West, as many of her friends and colleagues did, Ebadi chose to stay in Iran and has since devoted her career to working within the repressive laws of the regime to bring about change. In 2003, she became Iran's first Nobel Peace Prize winner in recognition of her campaigns for increased rights for Iranian women and children and greater levels of democracy. Respected internationally, Ebadi has faced increasing levels of harassment at home, as her work places her increasingly at odds with a regime controlled by conservative clerics.

Shirin Ebadi was raised during the Westernized reign of the shah and benefited from many of his modernizing reforms, which opened up education and career opportunities for women. After receiving her law degree from Tehran University, she became the first woman judge to preside over Tehran's legislative court in 1975. However, larger political events—namely, the Iranian Revolution of 1979—soon stopped her promising legal career in its tracks. A practicing Muslim, Ebadi was initially attracted to the aims of the revolutionaries. Like many other Iranian women, Ebadi was alienated from the shah's corrupt regime, which was increasingly propped up by military aid and assistance from the United States, and initially welcomed the nationalist Islamic rhetoric of the revolutionaries. However, after the overthrow of the shah, she soon became one of the revolution's victims; the regime of the Ayatollah Khomeini soon decided that Islam forbade women to serve as judges, and she and other female judges were dismissed and given clerical duties. In fact, they made Ebadi serve as a clerk in the court she had once presided over. Frustrated by the lack of professional opportunities, Ebadi took early retirement, focused on raising her two daughters, and became an independent scholar, writing out of her home.

In the wake of the election of a reformist president, Ebadi applied for a lawyer's license and set up a private practice in 1992. Since starting her practice, Ebadi has also taken on various child abuse cases and has worked to improve the rights of girls and women in a system in which they legally have lesser rights than do boy children and men. For example, Ebadi represented the family of an eleven-year old girl who was raped and killed. Although three men were eventually found guilty of the crime, Iran's laws proclaim that a woman's life is worth half that of a man's. As a result, the bizarre outcome of the guilty verdict was the following: The girl's family was required to come up with thousands of dollars for the "blood money," or the price of a human life, for the execution of their daughter's killers. The family of the victim soon sank further into poverty as a result of this verdict; they eventually sold their house and most of their possessions before moving into a tent outside the local courthouse during the trial. Further efforts to sell their kidneys to raise money ended in failure. After seven years of legal efforts, Ebadi succeeded, in addition to raising an enormous amount of public awareness and unprecedented media coverage on the issue, in forcing the state to pay one-third of the sum required, an extremely unusual concession given the conservativeness of the regime.[ii] Further, Ebadi has defended a number of pro-Western liberal and dissident figures that have fallen afoul of the regime. Most recently, she has taken on the defense of seven Bahai leaders accused of spying for Israel.

Perhaps what is most interesting about her work is her approach, which seeks to work within the rules of the Islamic system rather than import solely Westernized models of law, justice, and gender equality. She has always worked from the premise that Islam and democratic principles are not mutually exclusive belief sets. As she wrote in her autobiography, *Iran Awakening,*

> In the last 23 years, from the day I was stripped of my judgeship to the years of doing battle in the revolutionary courts of Tehran, I had repeated one refrain: an interpretation of Islam that is in harmony with equality and democracy is an authentic expression of faith. It is not religion that binds women, but the selective dictates of those who wish them cloistered. That belief, along with the conviction that change in Iran must come peacefully and from within, has underpinned my work.[iii]

Further, in interviews, Ebadi has referred to herself as a "traditional Iranian woman" whose duty is to take care of the housework and the children, work that she enjoys after her often psychologically rough and bruising work as an attorney. In sum, equality between men and women can be accomplished in many ways and in ways that may draw on, rather than repudiate, traditional and/or Islamic values.

Her work, while praised by international human rights agencies, has won her few friends in the ruling regime in Iran, and as her international reputation has increased, she has faced increasing levels of political repression at home. In 2008, the Iranian news agency criticized Ebadi for defending homosexuals, appearing in public abroad without an Islamic headscarf, questioning Islamic punishments, and defending CIA agents. In addition, the Iranian police have shut down the office of one of her human rights groups, citing irregular paperwork. In 2009, proregime "demonstrators" attacked her home and office, accusing her of being insufficiently critical of Israel's actions in Gaza and their effects on children. Despite the increased levels of harassment, Ebadi has vowed to continue her work in her fight to demonstrate that Islam, women's rights, and democracy can be mutually compatible concepts. In a recent interview, she noted that "I don't feel secure, but this will not cause me to leave the country or to stop my activities. The Iranian government knows very well that as long as I am alive, I will do my duty."[iv] Certainly, millions of Iranian women and scores of human rights activists are counting on her to continue her pioneering work.

---

[i] Radio Free Europe/Radio Liberty, "Interview: Iranian Peace Prize Laureate Shirin Ebadi on Women's Rights," March 15, 2006, http://www.rferl.org/content/article/1066743.html.

[ii] Dan De Luce, "Iran Girl's Murder Spurs Debate over Blood Money," Women's e-News, December 1, 2003, http://www.womensenews.org/article.cfm/dyn/aid/1619/context/archive.

[iii] Ebadi, Shirin, *Iran Awakening: A Memoir of Revolution and Hope,* by Shirin Ebadi with Azadeh Moaveni, Random House, 2006, p.204.

[iv] Mike Shuster, "Iran Cracks Down on Human Rights Activists." NPR July 24, 2009. http://www.npr.org/templates/story/story.php?storyId=100780499

At the same time, the postrevolutionary leadership in Iran became more pragmatic in its treatment of women. The government also readopted family planning and birth control in 1989, after discouraging it in the previous decade. A high birth rate, combined with a depressed economy, threatened the leadership's ability to build a just Islamic society that could provide for its citizens. As a result, some religious leaders reasoned that the Prophet allowed Muslims to practice contraception during times of economic hardship. The result was a successful, government-sponsored family planning program. Further, the government, partially in response to its family-planning policies, has increased efforts to improve the low female literacy rate. Although this has been accompanied by sex segregation, veiling, and enforced religious education, nonetheless women's literacy has increased more rapidly than has men's.[103] Further, women continued to seek access to higher education, and in 1998–1999, for the first time since women entered the University of Tehran in 1939, 52 percent of the admitted students were women, although they remain barred from certain areas of study.[104] Further, under heavy public pressure, the government has introduced some moderate reforms to divorce law. Most controversially, in December 1992, legislation passed that granted women wages for housework in the event of divorce.

While it is important not to overstate the liberalism of the Iranian leadership, nonetheless, it has been much more pragmatic in its policies toward women than initially feared. This has also opened a small space for Iranian women activists, who may support the regime but reject its vision of women's status in Islamic society. They have been able to use a woman-centered interpretation of Islamic text to push for incremental reforms within a system that, in its early years, was much more fundamentalist in its approach to women's issues.

In sum, the political, economic, and social impact of successful revolutionary movements has been mixed for women. However, Marxist-inspired movements have historically directly addressed the lesser condition and status of women by trying, perhaps imperfectly, to address this lesser status with proactive policy. This has not been the case with liberal/democratization movements, which have tended to see women as citizens that are in theory equal to men. As a result, they have not been as effective in dealing with the frequent reality of women's secondary status. And finally, religious fundamentalist revolutionaries have consistently put into place a system that often severely curtails women's rights in both the public and the private realm, although this policy shift has sometimes been initially actively supported by women themselves. However, as the work of Shirin Ebadi illustrates (see text box), reform that works in favor of women can be implemented, often incrementally, even in more repressive societies.

CONCLUSION

Throughout history, revolutionary leaders pushing for the radical redistribution of power—political, economic, and social—have targeted women as enemies, victims, allies, and saviors. As wives, lovers, and relatives of imperfect political leaders, they have been reviled for their tainted pasts and supposed excesses under corrupt and bloated prerevolutionary political regimes. They have been recruited to revolutionary movements to fight for profoundly new societies, with greater women's rights dangled in front as an ideological carrot. They have been enshrined as the symbol of a brighter and better future under a new and more enlightened leadership.

In conclusion, were women included or excluded from the unmaking of the old regime and the remaking of the new one? Are women manipulated or transformed by their participation in revolutionary movements? Perhaps the answer lies in the nature of women's exclusion and inclusion in revolutionary origins, processes, and outcomes, rather than the presence or absence of their influence. As events past and current demonstrate, women have participated actively in radical processes of political change. Women, however, often join causes, not because they are fighting for greater rights and access for their sex, but because they identify with a larger cause. Thus, often women willingly surrender specific gender concerns to larger, more encompassing political struggles. Once a new regime takes control, women often are pushed out of or denied real leadership positions. While a movement headed by a woman makes great material for the newsroom, the actual incidences of female leadership are relatively few. Loyal foot soldiers, women rarely make the transition into political office, and thus have a muffled impact on the design of the new state. The few women that do make the cut are often designated to token "female" positions of power and are appointed to various committees in charge of women's and children's affairs.

It is important not to overlook the numerous organizations, social programs, and economic opportunities that have been designed for women, and sometimes by women. But at the same time, it is important to acknowledge that rhetoric toward women's greater participation has always outpaced the reality of programs offered. Part of this is because women themselves have often not been united on what it means to be a woman in revolutionary times. A large part, however, also is because for women to gain or advance in society, another social group, often men, has to lose something in return—a position of power, a job, a certain status in society or the family. Throughout history, people have been willing to offer women reforms until another group loses. Acknowledging that women's gains may end up costing another segment something (but is still worth it) is a revolutionary idea whose time is yet to come.

FOR MORE INFORMATION

Gioconda Belli. *The Country Under My Skin: A Memoir of Love and War* (New York: Anchor, 2003). A first-person account of one woman's journey from upper-class wife and mother to armed revolutionary in Nicaragua's Sandinista movement.

Jung Chang. *Wild Swans: Three Daughters of China* (New York: Anchor, 1992). An autobiographical family history of three generations of women who survived China's tumultuous century of political upheaval and revolution, from the collapse of the Imperial order to the fallout from Mao's cultural revolution.

Angela Y. Davis. *Angela Davis: An Autobiography* (New York: International Publishers, 1989). Covers the life and early career of left-wing activist and scholar Angela Davis, including her association with the Black Panther Party and the Communist Party of America.

Bernadine Dohrn, Bill Ayers, and Jeff Jones, eds. *Sing a Battle Song: The Revolutionary Poetry, Statements, and Communiques of the Weather Underground, 1970–1974* (New York: Seven Stories Press, 2006). A collection of three complete and unedited publications by the Weathermen during their most active period underground.

Slavenka Drakulic. *How We Survived Communism and Even Laughed* (New York: Harper Perennial, 1993). A series of essays that portrays that daily struggles women faced in communist eastern Europe.

Shirin Ebadi with Azadeh Moaveni. *Iran Awakening: One Woman's Journey to Reclaim Her Life and Country* (New York: Random House Trade Paperbacks, 2007). A first-hand account of the 2003 Nobel Peace Prize laureate's life and work in Iran both before and after the revolution.

Barbara Alpern Engel and Clifford N. Rosenthal, eds. *Five Sisters: Women Against the Tsar* (New York: Routledge, 1987). The memoirs of five young anarchist women who participated in Russia's underground revolutionary movements in the 1870s.

Rigoberta Menchu, Elisabeth Burgos-Debray, and Ann Wright. *I, Rigoberta Menchu: An Indian Woman in Guatemala* (New York: Verso, 1984). The life story of a Quiche Indian woman and her family's struggle to survive the repressive military dictatorship in Guatemala.

Marjane Satrapi. *The Complete Persepolis* (New York: Pantheon, 2007). A personal account of life in Iran before and after the revolution, portrayed through the format of a graphic novel.

PART II

✦◯

Gendering Public Policy

In the previous part, the three chapters focused primarily on ways in which women try to influence the state. As we have seen, they have gained access to political institutions by running for office, by participating in social movements and interest groups, and through joining revolutionary movements in the hopes of bringing about radical change. Despite the myriad of ways in which women are active in both institutionalized and noninstitutionalized forms of political activism, common themes link all forms of women's activities. Certainly, women's participation in institutionalized and noninstitutionalized politics has had an impact. Yet, while women have played an important role in gaining access to formal positions of political power, that access is neither widespread, uniform, nor far-reaching. Nonetheless, as we saw with their activities in social movements, women are often able to use their gender to their advantage by successfully exploiting traditional expectations of women's and, particularly, mothers' "appropriate" spheres of activity. However, even in revolutionary movements, which profess radical aims in terms of redistributing power, women's rights are often sacrificed to larger, "more important" revolutionary goals, and revolution's impact on women is never as significant as promised by charismatic leaders. In sum, while the increased presence of women in all levels of activity has resulted in more women-friendly policies, it has come as a result of a long and protracted struggle for influence, and the push for women's equality is a slow, trickle-up process that is still met with great resistance.

We now turn to look at the other side of the equation, moving from an examination of women's influences on the state to looking at the impact of state structures and policies on women. One of the key themes that cut across the chapters of this part is that of "the activist state." Often, we don't think of states as actors, with specific interests, agendas, and concerns. Rather, we view the state as an arena in which interests battle for influence and control. Yet, it is the various institutions and organizations within the state that are in charge of making and enacting policies, and these policies are often shaped to further specific state goals, interests, and targets. For example, when the U.S. government issues policies on affirmative action, they are not only regulating terms of employment but are also pushing a certain vision of an equitable, diverse society. When the French government bans headscarves from public schools, they are, on the one hand, designing school policy. But this policy also is a statement about the French government's views on the separation of religion and state and the methods by which Muslim minorities should integrate into French society. Thus, by looking more closely at policy, we can learn a lot about state visions of "ideal societies" and the policies they pursue to bring the real closer to the ideal.

In the following three chapters, we examine how states have designed policies that impact the position and status of women in society. We assess the degree to which states have sought "to advance women's status and condition as a group...and/or to strike down gender-based hierarchies."[1] Primarily in the 1970s, many states started "feminizing the state" by founding offices, advisory councils, and administrative bureaucracies to deal specifically with gender concerns. Further, bureaucrats sympathetic to women's issues, also known as "femocrats," began to fill various positions within the emerging policy machinery. In addition, as a result of pressure coming from women voters, activists, and bureaucrats, states began to embed gender issues in national policy agendas by adopting legislation that addressed women's inequality in such areas as political representation, equal employment, family law, education, health care, and reproductive choice. This has led a number of scholars to define this trend as "state feminism" as a way of describing this institutionalization of policies that promote women's status and strike down gender hierarchies.[2] The chapters in this part explore this trend toward state feminism by looking at three policy areas within advanced industrialized nations: equal employment, reconciliation (balancing the demands of work and family), and reproductive choice. Thus, Chapter 4 deals with issues of equality in the public realm, Chapter 5 addresses bridging the public and the private divide, and Chapter 6 addresses the challenge of passing policy to govern issues of privacy that are contested areas of government intervention.

As we shall see, across all our policy issues, states have responded to the problem of gender inequalities with varying levels of commitment. They have issued symbolic statements, encoded new rights into the constitution, passed legislation, issued plans and reports, and installed government machineries. But some countries are more dedicated to rectifying gender imbalances than others and demonstrate varying levels of commitment to enforcing existing legislation. In addition, some states are more proactive than others in implementing policy that not only protects women from discriminatory practices but also actively attempts to redress past imbalances with affirmative policies. Throughout the three chapters, we will see that states are somewhat contradictory in their policies. Often, they advance the rhetoric of gender equality but then do not put policy in place that can realistically assist women in achieving that equality. Alternatively, they advance the rhetoric of gender equality while simultaneously enacting policies that actively discourage women from achieving equality. Issuing the rhetoric of gender equality has become almost required of advanced industrialized nations; achieving that equality has been a much more uneven process.

Another important theme that runs throughout all the chapters of this part is the intentions of the state. Policies tell us something about how various governments view women's appropriate position in society, and state policies often send subtle (and sometimes not so subtle) messages through the enactment of specific policies, which legitimize or challenge existing social and economic inequalities. Rhetorical support of women's equality that is not accompanied by strict enforcement mechanisms can indicate that a state does not see women's equality as a policy priority. Policies that encourage women to leave the workforce to become mothers can tell us something about how states view women's participation in the workforce. Sometimes states send contradictory, mixed messages about the ideal position of women in society by designing policies to strengthen traditional family values while simultaneously enacting other programs that try to ensure women's economic equality.

The following chapters demonstrate the difficulties states have in matching their rhetoric of gender equality with significant results. In Chapter 4, "Women and Employment," we provide a comparative overview of equal employment policies in Japan, the United States, and the European Union. Our three case studies demonstrate varying levels of commitment to ensuring women's equality in the workforce. Further, equal employment policy can only go so far in correcting women's subordinate position in the labor market. In all countries, women occupy a separate and unequal status. Women's pay for positions of equal value still lags behind that for men. Women are persistently marginalized in workforces; there is both a "glass ceiling" that keeps women from attaining a large share of top management positions as well as a "sticky floor" that relegates many women to low-paying jobs and positions of borderline poverty. In short, passing legislation to ensure equality has been easier than ensuring that that equality will automatically follow from activist policy. Much of this is because equal employment policy does not address the inequalities in the division of labor outside of the work force.

Chapter 5, "Women, Work, and Family," acknowledges that equal employment policies that address equality issues in the public realm often ignore the fundamental causes that affect men's and women's unequal position in work, politics, and public society. This is particularly true in the areas of balancing production (work) with reproduction (family care). Because women are biologically responsible for activities related to pregnancy and childbirth and still take care of many of the "nurturing" responsibilities of child-rearing, they often are unable to compete equally for competitive jobs or perform to their fullest potential. In response, states have enacted legislation that provides various benefits, such as parental leave and child-care provisions to help citizens manage the competing demands of public and private life. In this chapter, we compare the varying policy approaches of the United States, Germany, France, and Sweden with regard to parental leave and child care. As we shall see, the design of these policies can either enforce existing gendered divisions of labor or help redefine them, for example, by encouraging men to become more active in parenting.

Chapter 6, "Abortion Politics," addresses the state's increasing involvement in enacting policies that limit or expand women's reproductive choices. Drawing from our case studies of Ireland, the United States, and the Netherlands, we explore the varying outcomes of the abortion debate. While Ireland has implemented one of the most conservative laws in terms of restricting access to abortion services in Europe, the United States has designed relatively liberal laws that have been challenged repeatedly in all political arenas. As a result, abortion practices have been restricted significantly in the ensuing decades following legalization. In contrast, the Netherlands has implemented a liberal policy that has not been challenged significantly since it was approved in the 1980s.

You may notice that all of the case studies are from advanced industrialized nations and may wonder why we are not covering the countries of the developing world in this chapter. After all, women in these countries also face employment discrimination, juggle work with child-care responsibilities, and struggle to control their fertility. There are several answers to this question, which we also addressed in the preface. First, there is a wide disjunction between state policy and state action in developing countries. One of the enduring characteristics of developing countries is the weak state. That is, governments exist, but they are often too weak and fragmented to design and then effectively implement policy. They lack what is known as "capacity." In effect, laws that exist on paper often are not enforced in reality. Thus, we felt that comparing government action in these policy areas would tend to overemphasize similarities while obscuring very critical differences in terms of policy implementation and impact. In addition, as we have argued elsewhere, while these issues are of concern to women everywhere, the ways in which women vocalize and act on that concern often differ as a result of economic, cultural, ethnic, racial, and religious differences. For example, while women around the world have mobilized over issues of reproductive choice, many women in the southern hemisphere still face enormous health risks in even bearing children, while women in the northern hemisphere may be more concerned about access to abortion services. Again, trying to generalize across these policy issues would obscure interesting differences in women's responses and make facile generalizations about their commonalities. However, the final part of the book will discuss many of the issues that affect women in the developing world. Thus, the reader will still get an opportunity to learn about how women in the southern hemisphere are affected by a variety of issues.

4

❧

Women and Employment

When Gretchen Swan, a part-time employee, was asked by her employer to take on a few more hours of work, she accepted but she asked for something in return—benefits, including a pension. Swan is currently lobbying her company to provide benefits to all part-time employees, the majority of whom are women.[1] In Great Britain, Citigroup recently paid 1.4 million pounds (about $2.8 million) to a former employee, Julie Brower, "whose track record had been described by her manager as 'had cancer, been a pain, now pregnant,'" and Deutsche Bank paid 500,000 pounds to Kate Swinburne, "who was described, among other things, as 'hotty totty.'"[2] In Scotland, male government workers recently lodged discrimination complaints because of a dress code that insists that men wear ties at all times, whereas women have no dress code and can show up to work in T-shirts.[3] And in the United States, Wal-Mart is facing a class-action suit from up to 1.6 million present and former employees who claim they were routinely underpaid and overlooked for promotion because they were women.[4] All of these stories indicate that women and men are still not treated equally in the workforce and that, despite numerous gains, (primarily) women face different, unequal, and, at times, hostile working conditions. Cultural attitudes about women's abilities, gendered divisions of labor within the workforce, and lack of government enforcement of existing legislation are just a few of the variables that stand in the way of women's equal treatment in paid employment.

The economic emergence of women has been one of the most significant developments in the post–World War II era. Between 1970 and 2000, women's participation in the workforce in Organisation for Economic Co-operation and Development (OECD) countries increased from nearly 45 percent to just over 60 percent, and those numbers have not changed in recent years.[5] Yet, in country after country, women earn substantially less than men.[6] Part of the problem is that women are often segregated into low-paying "female" professions such as secretarial work, sales, teaching, and other service-oriented and caregiver industries. Further, women are less likely to ascend to positions of power and authority and are passed over for promotions more frequently than equally qualified male counterparts are. In addition, women are often clustered in part-time or temporary jobs that offer less financial reward and fewer opportunities for advancement. Nor are working conditions ideal for women. For many decades, employers could discriminate against women because of their reproductive capabilities, and sexual harassment was often a by-product of a predominantly male working environment. By the end of women's lives, these disadvantages take their toll on working women, and, upon retirement, women make up the vast majority of the elderly poor.

How have governments tried to address these inequities in the workforce? The increase in the number of women in the workforce, the emergence of feminist movements in the 1970s, the creation of women's policy machineries, and the increasing numbers of women politicians led many governments to pass equal employment policies to address the barriers that prevented women from participating in employment in the same way that men did. These laws have focused on establishing a more level playing field by mandating equal treatment and equal opportunities for women at work and by criminalizing forms of discrimination such as sexual harassment. The rationale for many of these policies has stressed a liberal, gender-neutral rhetoric. That is, the assumption is that the pathway to better employment conditions lies in stressing women's legal equality with men.

As we shall see, although important, equal employment policies are limited in their impact, for while they can address direct barriers that operate in the job market, they do not address the indirect obstacles, such as gender inequities involved in family life or socialization to gendered divisions of labor, that affect women's abilities to perform equally to men on the job.[7] As one scholar commented, "The design of equal employment policies still needs to recognize that inequities in wage labor are actually a product of forces outside of the labor market."[8] As a result, state activism regarding equal employment legislation has not "solved" the problem of sex discrimination in the workplace. However, equal employment legislation does legitimate the problem of discrimination, demonstrates to society at large that the problem will not be tolerated by the government, and penalizes firms and individuals who engage in blatant acts of prejudicial behavior. It is a necessary tool in the battle for women's equality; however, equal employment legislation in and of itself will not result in economic equality for women.

In this chapter we look an array of equal employment policies that address the following issues: pay; hiring, promotion, and firing; sexual harassment; and retirement income. We use Japan, the United States, and the European Union (EU) as case studies of how states have designed and implemented policy to further women's status in the workforce. Japan has made the least progress in advancing gender equality in the workforce, having implemented equal employment legislation that is merely symbolic in its support for women's equality because it lacks critical enforcement mechanisms. In contrast, the United States has been more successful in implementing a variety of policies to encourage equal employment practices. While government support for this was initially symbolic, a well-mobilized women's movement actively lobbied the state to enforce its own regulations. The European Union provides an interesting example of policy design and implementation at the supranational level, which has, in turn, impacted individual policies adopted by member countries. While the EU has been hospitable to women's demands and lobbying, nonetheless it has been more adept at urging nations to pass equal employment legislation than pressuring them to enforce it. Across our cases, we find that many states are better at advancing the rhetoric of gender equality in the workforce than they are at designing and enforcing policy to ensure a more equitable employment outcome for women.

THE DEBATE OVER EQUAL EMPLOYMENT POLICIES

One of the most significant demographic trends of the post–World War II era has been the massive influx of women into the paid workforce. As we mentioned previously, in OECD countries in 2005, 61.5 percent of women were employed. Certainly, that broad average masks a number of differences between the thirty member states of the OECD; for example, in Turkey, 27.2 percent of women were working, in comparison to a high of 80.5 percent for women in Iceland. However, most countries are somewhere between these two end points; one OECD country has a female labor participation rate of 44.2 percent (Mexico), six are in the 50–59 percent range, thirteen are in the 60–69 percent range, eight are in the 70–79 percent range, and two (Iceland and Luxembourg) have female labor participation rates at over 80 percent. This 2005 figure is a substantial increase even from the previous decade; for example, from 1995 to 2005, female labor participation rates increased over 30.9 percent in Luxembourg and 13.1 percent in Ireland. Only a four states had a decrease (the Czech Republic, Iceland, Poland, and Turkey).[9]

Despite this increase in women's participation, women have often had a separate and unequal experience in the paid labor force. Despite their increasing participation, there are significant employment gaps between men and women. Women are less likely to be employed than men are and are more likely to make less money and advance less quickly when in the workforce; as a result, women are at a higher risk of poverty throughout their lives.[10] For many years, particularly before the passage of antidiscriminatory legislation, these problems could be partially attributed to blatant acts of discrimination. Companies openly refused to hire women, paid them less for identical jobs, and fired them when they got pregnant, often under the rationale that women were less competent, capable, or able to perform their work responsibilities.

Equal employment was one of the early mobilizing issues for feminist movements, and it became one of the earliest targeted areas for state activism in advancing gender equality in the 1960s, 1970s, and 1980s. Equal pay laws were

often the first to be legislated, followed by equal treatment laws that criminalized direct discrimination against women in hiring, promotion, and firing.[11] Yet,
legislation outlawing direct discrimination did not immediately solve women's
experiences in the workforce. While women continued to experience direct discrimination (which was illegal), the larger problem was in designing policy to
combat less obvious forms of indirect discrimination.

For example, the vast inequalities between men's and women's salaries are
often attributed to women's occupational segregation in careers that are less
highly valued and mimic women's "caring" and "nurturing" functions in the
household. Various nations' economies are literally divided between "wom-
en's jobs" and "men's jobs," in which women are overrepresented in low-paying
professions, such as teaching, secretarial work, sales, and domestic services
while men predominate in more remunerative careers, such as management,
administration, policy, and industry. Such is the case in the member countries
of the European Union; 52 percent of all employed women are concentrated
in the services sector, while men are disproportionately employed in agriculture and industry, which are "male" areas of employment that tend to be more
financially rewarding.[12] In the 1990s in the United States, women comprised
98 percent of the nation's preschool teachers, 96 percent of its child-care workers, and 79 percent of its health-care workers. In contrast, 98 percent of the
nation's firefighters, 74 percent of its physicians, and 97 percent of its construction workers were male.[13] Women also tend to be overrepresented in low-
skilled, low-wage jobs, such as low-tech assembly line workers, and in jobs such
as clerks, service workers, and shop assistants. At the EU level, 34.4 percent of
women work in low-paying occupations compared to 19.9 percent of men.[14] In
addition, women are much more likely to work part-time than are men, in part
because they still assume primary responsibility for child care, elderly care, and
housework. For example, in Japan 40.9 percent of the part-time workforce is
female; in the Netherlands that number is 59.7 percent.[15] In the European Union
in 2006, 31.7 percent of working women worked part-time, while only 7.1 percent of men did so.[16] As a result, women become segregated in jobs that are more
disposable and, hence, are less well paid. This matters because, as the opening
story about Gretchen Swan indicates, part-time workers often do not receive
the benefits that their full-time counterparts receive. All of these factors mean
that women enter their retirement years in a much more financially precarious
situation than men do.

Further, a glass ceiling keeps women from ascending the corporate ladder
to important management positions. For example, women account for less than
15 percent of board directors, less than 16 percent of executive officers, and only
2.7 percent of chief executives of Fortune 500 companies.[17] As we shall discuss
in greater detail in the next chapter, women who have children tend to take
more time off from work, often at times when they are in the midst of climbing
the career ladder, and thus tend to miss out on critical opportunities that could
launch them into higher management positions. A study of American graduate

managers found that women returning after a break of three years or more lost an average of 37 percent of their earnings.[18] In addition, indirect social barriers continue to impede women's progress. Women for many decades have been shut out of the "old boy's network" and all of the accompanying activities, such as informal lunches, golf games, and trips that mix business and pleasure. As we shall see, it is harder to devise strategies to counter these forms of "indirect" discrimination because they are not a product of blatant, illegal hiring practices but rather emerge from a variety of societal norms that steer women into occupations, career paths, and work networks that do not advance them as quickly as men.

What are the arguments in support of equal employment policies? Some advocates for women's equal treatment in the workforce frame the issue as one of fairness; as human beings men and women share a common humanity and should treat each other, and be treated by business, government, and social institutions, equally. Second, potential differences in ability are because of socialization patterns, rather than as a result of biological sex, and thus are not valid reasons for discrimination. Women's increased presence in higher education and advanced study demonstrate that, when given the opportunity, women can excel as frequently as men can. Third, discrimination is bad for a nation's economy, for it does not tap the full potential of a nation's citizenry. For example, evidence indicates that hiring women makes good business sense; *The Economist* reports that research results from America, Britain, and Scandinavia demonstrate a strong correlation between shareholder returns and the proportion of women in high-level executive positions. There are a variety of explanations for this; some posit that women tend to be better at team building and communications, which indirectly can increase profits. Others maintain that a homogeneous white male executive culture stifles the diversity needed to generate new, innovative ideas.[19] On a more general level, the World Bank notes, "It [gender equality] strengthens countries' abilities to grow, to reduce poverty, and to govern effectively. Promoting gender equality is thus an important part of a development strategy that seeks to enable all people—women and men alike—to escape poverty and improve their standard of living."[20]

However, while many agree on the need for equal employment policies, there is less agreement on potential policy solutions to rectify women's unequal status. States have faced numerous dilemmas in designing equal employment policies. For example, how should equal employment be promoted? Should states simply outlaw discriminatory practices, or should they more proactively ensure that women have equal opportunity to compete in the paid labor force, such as through the use of affirmative action policies? And to what degree should states attempt to correct for gender imbalances in the division of labor in the household, in which women carry the burden of child-rearing and family care? While the next chapter addresses the latter question, in this chapter we address the former ones. Similarly, advocates for women's equality in the workforce also differ on which policies should be implemented under the rubric of equal employment. Does "equal employment" mean that men and women should have similar employment profiles in lifetime work patterns—that is, comparable occupational distributions, job status, salaries, and promotions? Extending this logic, many advocates for women's equality pursue strategies that tend to emphasize men's and women's innate commonalities, rather than their differences, and target abolishing laws that distinguish between men and women based on sex.

Not all proponents of women's advancement believe that focusing on treating women in the workforce equally is an appropriate strategy. For example, difference feminists such as Carol Gilligan argue that men and women are developmentally different.[21] Women's ways of knowing and thinking, and their caring abilities, should be preserved and honored, and difference feminists argue that gender-neutral legislation may dilute differences that should be honored and preserved. Difference feminists argue that policies should not try to treat women and men equally in certain areas, but instead should compensate women for the ways their biology makes them different from men, particularly with regard to their reproductive roles. Further, women's socially constructed roles as nurturers and caretakers further hinder their abilities to participate equally in the workforce, which also should be taken into account. In this view, gender-neutral laws are detrimental since they merely perpetuate and exacerbate inequalities in the household. Difference feminists advocate for differential treatment in the workforce through the passage of protective legislation, specific maternity leave benefits, or affirmative action policies to redress past imbalances. Let us now turn to how states have attempted to rectify inequalities in men's and women's experiences in the workforce.

POLICY AREAS

Equality in the workplace encompasses a number of topics, among them equal pay; equal treatment in hiring, promotion, and firing; the right to a harassment-free working environment; and equality in retirement benefits. We will now examine each of these four issues in greater depth in our three case studies—Japan, the United States, and the European Union.

Japan has made the least progress in advancing gender equality in the workforce, implementing equal employment legislation that is merely symbolic in its support for women's equality in that it lacks critical enforcement mechanisms. This can be attributed to a variety of factors. For one, Japanese society is, compared to other advanced industrial nations, more accepting of traditional gendered divisions of labor. Women are expected to leave the labor force after marriage, and particularly after having children. In addition, Japan's small women's movement mobilized much later on employment issues and has struggled to gain access to important decision makers in the Japanese state. As a result, the movement has used Japan's participation in international treaties as a pressure point to facilitate domestic reform. In turn, the government has been unwilling to offer more than symbolic policies, which are stronger on rhetorical support for women's equality and much weaker on enforcement mechanisms that could advance that equality. In sum, as Joyce Gelb has argued, legislation to improve women's equality "has produced only limited gains in employment opportunity for a small number of Japanese women and, arguably, has created even worse conditions for many."[22] Larger contextual factors, such as Japan's ongoing economic woes and declining birth rate, have created a backlash against further implementation of equal employment policy.

In contrast, the United States has implemented a variety of policies to encourage equal employment practices. While government support for this was initially symbolic, a well-mobilized women's movement actively lobbied the state to enforce its own regulations. Further, the U.S. system of litigation, in which claimants can sue for substantial monetary damages, has encouraged a number of government agencies and businesses to address the issue of equal employment with proactive policies. While the government has tended to design policy that is gender neutral, it has also introduced various affirmative action policies to promote women, which is still a controversial issue in the United States. Yet, as we shall see, the impact of equal employment policy has been limited in that women still face substantial barriers in breaking the glass ceiling in a number of professions.

Finally, the case of the European Union illustrates efforts to resolve gender inequalities at the supranational level. The European Union is an intergovernmental and supranational union of twenty-five member states (and four candidate countries). Although the EU is not intended to replace the nation-state, its member states have set up common institutions to which they delegate some of their sovereignty so that decisions on specific matters of joint interest can be made democratically at the European level. While enforcement issues are problematic (as they are with all international organizations), the member nations have transferred more sovereignty to the EU than to any other regional organization. Thus, the EU provides an interesting point of comparison with our other two case studies; although it does not act as a traditional nation-state, it has significant and growing influence on the politics of the various countries of Europe.

The European Union repeatedly has advanced a progressive rhetoric regarding equal employment. It has placed pressure on member countries to institutionalize equal opportunity policies, particularly in Mediterranean countries, which lagged behind other member countries in designing policy. However, member states have responded to various directives to improve their legislation with mixed levels of enthusiasm. And while the European Parliament and the European Commission have been hospitable to women's demands and lobbying, nonetheless the European Union has been more adept at urging nations to pass equal employment legislation than at pressuring them to enforce it.[23] We now turn to how our three cases have designed and implemented a range of policies related to equal employment.

Equal Pay

Over the years all advanced industrial nations have enacted legislation designed to eradicate the differentials in pay between men and women, which are substantial. The short-term and long-term impact of this pay gap on women, families, and countries is significant. For example, women's low income increases the incidence of poverty, which often has a female face. In the United States, women's advocates argue that if women received the same pay as men "who work the same number of hours, have the same education, union status, are the same age, and live in the same region of the country, then these women's annual family income would rise by $4,000 and poverty rates would be cut in half."[24] Other issues, such as women's overrepresentation in part-time labor and time taken off from work to raise a family, compound this problem. As Britain's Equal Opportunity Commission noted, "taking time off work to bring up children, the average gender-pay gap and the large number of women working in part-time or low-paid jobs all contributed to their poverty."[25] Further, women live longer than men and are increasingly swelling the ranks of the elderly. Since many women who worked did not earn as much as men throughout their lives, their savings and pension benefits tended to be much lower. Thus, the pay gap between men's and women's salaries is a significant policy issue for states. We now turn to how states have tried to legislate equal pay and the effectiveness of their policies.

Japan

Japan's approach to addressing equal pay has lagged behind that of other industrialized countries. While the Japanese Diet adopted weak equal employment legislation in the 1980s, it did not specifically address the issue of equal pay for equal, or comparable, work. As we shall see, compared to other countries, women's mobilization in Japan has been lower, and much of the pressure to reform Japan's equal employment laws came from external, international pressure. Finally, the government has not been committed to passing and enforcing legislation relating to a wide array of workforce issues that might advance women's equality.

Technically, the Labor Standards Act of 1946 required equal wages for women and men. However, because the equal pay clause only applied to the same type of labor, employers often paid women less by segregating them into separate jobs than men.[26] The passage of the 1985 Equal Employment Opportunity Law (EEOL) prohibited gender discrimination in training, pension allocation, and employee dismissal, but did not specifically address the issue of equal pay. Thus, Japanese policy mandating equal pay for equal work is somewhat murky; although the EEOL does not mention equal pay for equal work, it is the most visible policy that addresses the broader issues of gender equality in employment.

The passage of the equal employment legislation occurred much later in Japan than in other countries and evolved from a combination of international and domestic pressures. While there are organized women's groups in Japan, they did not mobilize as early as those in the United States and Europe. Further, the

Japanese government has been slower to respond to their demands and has established relevant women's political machinery much later. In contrast to the U.S. feminist movement, which had developed a well-honed strategy to promote equal opportunity legislation by the 1970s, in contrast, in Japan, the small feminist movement was relatively quiescent until its participation in the 1975 UN Decade for Women. Their participation in this event exposed them to international women's networks and new rhetorical frames and strategies, which in turn acted as a mobilizing force. In addition, the Decade for Women resulted in the establishment of women's political machinery in the Japanese bureaucracy, creating an access point through which women's advocates could lobby for change. Finally, in 1985, Japan ratified the UN Convention on the Elimination of All Forms of Discrimination Against Women (CEDAW), which requires the eradication of all legal, political, social, and cultural structures that prevent women from enjoying full equality with men. According to the provisions of the treaty, the Japanese government is legally obligated to aim for actual, not just formal, equality between men and women. This gave advocates of antidiscriminatory legislation a further weapon; given that government officials had committed themselves to enacting certain policies, activists could now pressure them to honor their commitments. Thus, in Japan, pressure for change came from international influences, which women's organizations exploited for further leverage.

Because of Japan's international obligations, the government was required to take positive action to achieve gender equality, and a coalition of progressive social scientists, sympathetic bureaucrats, and feminist organizations successfully lobbied for the passage of the EEOL in 1985, which prohibits discrimination in hiring and firing, promotion, and pension benefits. Further amendments passed in 1997 provided additional refinements to the law. In 2000, the government adopted the "Basic Plan for Gender Equality," and a Gender Equality Bureau was created within the Cabinet Office. As a result, while Japan has moved to remedy issues of discrimination, the EEOL does not address directly the specific issue of pay equity and the Gender Equality Bureau does not appear to have helped decrease the pay gap between men and women. In sum, the government's commitment to pay equity has been primarily symbolic in that it has expressed support for women's equality but has failed to give the legislation substantial "teeth" by supporting it with enforcement mechanisms.

The United States

In contrast, in the United States, women's organizations mobilized in the 1960s on the issue of equal pay. The government responded with a series of policy reforms, which initially served a symbolic function because government agencies were unwilling to enforce the legislation. However, increased pressure from women's movements helped encourage government agencies to enforce existing legislation, creating opportunities for women's progress.

Equal pay for women became a contentious issue in the United States in the early 1960s. Although there were a few government initiatives to address the issue of discrimination, equal pay legislation was not passed at the federal level until 1963, when President Kennedy signed the Equal Pay Act into law, which provides for equal pay for equal work. Although advocates of the bill, such as the Women's Bureau, had wanted the wording to be equal pay for work of comparable worth, they acquiesced to the present wording in order to get the bill passed. The act "provides that when an employer has men and women doing the same or substantially the same job (that is requiring the same or substantially the same skill, effort, and responsibility) at the same location and under similar working conditions, the employees must receive equal pay." [27] However, employers could still base pay differentials on factors such as seniority, merit, and measures related to the quantity and quality of the work. This continued to hurt women who often were segregated in low-prestige jobs, which continued to reinforce pay inequities between men and women.

Improvement upon the Equal Pay Act came the following year, with the passage of the Civil Rights Act of 1964. The initial intent of this act was to end discrimination based on race or religion. However, Representative Howard Smith (D-VA), an opponent of the law, proposed an amendment that he was sure would lead to the act's failure; he added sex to the list of groups protected by the legislation. Much to his chagrin, the amendment passed and so did the act. Thus women attained additional rights in an odd fashion. However, even some women's groups, including the President's Commission on the Status of Women, the Women's Bureau, and the American Association of University Women, also opposed the inclusion of sex in the wording of the act, fearing that protective legislation barring women from certain occupations would then be declared unconstitutional.

Title VII of the Civil Rights Act, among other things, prohibits discrimination on the basis of race, color, sex, religion, or national origin in determining wages. The act is in many ways stronger than the Equal Pay Act because of its enforcement measures. It created the Equal Employment Opportunity Commission (EEOC) to handle complaints, and those found violating its provisions could be subjected to judicially issued cease and desist orders.

However, the impact of the law in its initial decade was limited. First, coverage of legislation was not universal; it did not (and still does not) provide equal opportunity and nondiscrimination protections in pay and benefits for part-time workers. [28] Further, for many years, the EEOC did not respond to complaints. It ignored claims until the National Organization for Women (NOW) formed in 1970s (in part, in reaction to this lack of enforcement) and actively pursued the enforcement of the Equal Pay Act and Title VII.

Women's groups have drawn on strategies used by the civil rights movement and have used the courts actively since the 1960s to advance their interests. One landmark Supreme Court decision, *Frontiero v. Richardson*, established the precedent that preferential treatment given to military men in pay and benefits was unconstitutional. In 1970, Sharon Cohen, then Lt. Sharon Frontiero, opened up her paycheck at Maxwell Airforce Base in Alabama to find that she had not received the expected increase in housing allowance or medical benefits for her new husband. At the time, federal law treated men and women in the military differently. It stipulated that male servicemen could receive an increase in pay for housing costs and health benefits for their wives; however, the same was not the case for women unless they could prove that their husband relied on them for more than half their support. In 1973, the Court ruled that such discrepancies were unconstitutional. While this case specifically pertained to the U.S. military, the decision has been used as precedent in cases arguing for equal pay and benefits for women in the private sector as well. In 2008, in a blow to women's ability to sue for pay discrimination, the Supreme Court ruled in *Ledbetter v. Goodyear* that employees have 180 days from the first act of pay discrimination to sue, not 180 days from the first discovery of pay discrimination. Lilly Ledbetter had been working for Goodyear for almost twenty years before she discovered that she had been discriminated against. As one journalist noted regarding this decision, "The Supreme Court's rulings strayed from years of precedent. And it now guarantees corporations the freedom to discriminate with impunity, while restricting access to the civil court system for many ordinary Americans who often have no other legal recourse." [29] However, in a historic move in 2009, the U.S. Congress passed the Lilly Ledbetter Fair Pay Act. This act amends the Civil Rights Act to allow employees 180 days to sue from the discovery of pay discrimination. President Obama signed the bill into law immediately. This bill is certainly a step in the right direction, but in itself it will not end pay discrimination. Pay discrimination lawsuits are costly and emotionally draining, so many employees who suspect pay discrimination will never seek recourse. What might be helpful is pay transparency. In public universities, government jobs, and much of the nonprofit world, salaries are public information. Transporting this transparency to the private sector would help alleviate some pay discrimination.

In sum, while U.S. government action on equal employment issues was initially symbolic, in that it professed support for equal pay, pressure from women's groups eventually led the state to enforce their laws more actively. Women's groups have pursued a predominantly gender-neutral strategy that assumes women and men experience the workforce in similar ways. Later on, we will discuss whether these efforts helped promote equal pay for equal work.

Lilly Ledbetter

In 1979 Lilly Ledbetter began working at the Alabama Goodyear Tire and Rubber Company. Immediately before her retirement in 1998 a colleague slipped an anonymous note into her mailbox. The note informed her that, while she had been earning $3,727 a month, male colleagues doing the same job were earning anywhere from $4,286 to $5,236 per month. Ledbetter filed a complaint with the Equal Employment Opportunity Commission (she had filed earlier complaints with them regarding sexual harassment in the workplace and her supervisor had been reassigned) soon after she found out about the pay discrepancies. Ledbetter also sued Goodyear for pay discrimination. Goodyear countered that she was not a good worker, despite her Top Performance Award in 1996. Ledbetter was awarded $3.3 million by a jury, but that amount was later reduced to approximately $300,000. Ledbetter appealed her case to the Supreme Court, who heard it in 2007. The Supreme Court, in a 5–4 decision, ruled against Ledbetter. They argued that anyone filing for pay discrimination had to file their complaint within 180 days of their *first* paycheck. The Supreme Court decision created quite a public outcry from women's groups and other citizens because the decision effectively meant that any employee, male or female, would have to know of discrimination within six months of a new job. Such knowledge is rare. Most employees of private companies are told not to discuss their pay with colleagues, so discovering pay discrimination is difficult to impossible and often only emerges from anonymous tips like the one Ledbetter received. Soon after the Supreme Court decision the U.S. House of Representatives passed the Lilly Ledbetter Fair Pay Act. This act changes the Civil Rights Act so that employees can sue employers for pay discrimination within 180 days of receiving *any* discriminatory paycheck. The bill was filibustered in the Senate, however, and eventually died. In 2009, the bill was reintroduced and passed the House on January 9 and the Senate on January 22. Soon thereafter President Obama signed the bill into law; it was the first piece of legislation he signed as president.

The European Union

The European Union integrated equal employment concerns into its early treaties and has continued to support increased gender equality at all levels with its current policy of gender mainstreaming, which involves the integration of equal opportunity rules into other areas of policy making. In addition, various branches of the EU, such as the European Commission, the European Parliament, and the European Court of Justice, have been responsive to women's mobilization at the national and supranational levels. Yet, many individual member countries were slow to respond with legislation, although they increasingly have recognized, primarily through rhetorical support, the importance of equal rights for women.

Article 119 in the Treaty of Rome (1957), the founding treaty of the European Community (which became the European Union in 1993), provides that women and men should receive equal pay for equal work. In the treaty's words, "Equal pay without discrimination based on sex means: (a) that pay for the same work at piece rates shall be calculated on the basis of the same unit of measurement; (b) that pay for work at time rates shall be the same for the same job." [30] This clause was inserted largely because of French pressure. France had already passed equal pay legislation and wanted to ensure that other member states were required to adhere to a similar standard. However, the initial commitment of member states to equal pay was lukewarm; according to the European Parliament, they showed "little enthusiasm for implementing this provision." [31] Thus, Article 119 was essentially symbolic; it existed on paper but was not implemented in practice.

However, beginning in 1975 a number of directives were adopted in an attempt to force the issue. A directive is a legally binding joint decision made by the Council of the EU or the Parliament that sets common objectives for member countries. Failure to comply with appropriate legislation or regulations can result in sanctions placed by the European Court of Justice. In 1975, The European Council passed Equal Pay Directive 75/117, which broadened the definition of *pay* and *equal work*. Specifically, the Council clarified that equal work did not have to mean same work, but rather "work to which equal value is attributed." By including equal value in the wording, the council was prohibiting indirect discrimination, such as prejudicial job classification schemes. Further, the directive ordered member states to pass necessary legislation to implement the principle of equal pay for equal work or value and directed states to report on their application of the directive. However, the directive did not define what was meant by "work of equal value," thus limiting the impact of the potential policy.[32] The European Parliament has also issued resolutions backing various commission communications on eradicating pay inequalities.[33]

Further, the EU has taken action on other factors that indirectly address equal pay. Further directives issued in the 1970s broadened the principle of equal treatment for men and women.[34] In the 1980s and 1990s, frustrated with the slow pace of reform, the European Commission, the EU's bureaucratic arm, issued four Action Programmes to foster equal opportunity for women in the workforce, which, although not binding, placed pressure on member countries to act more proactively in advancing equal employment policies.[35] And as we shall discuss in greater detail in the following section, in 1999, the Treaty of Amsterdam inserted into the EU treaty the principles of equality and nondiscrimination based on sex or sexual orientation. Finally, the EU Social Charter now guarantees equal rights to part-time workers, and the European Court of Justice has ruled that "unfair treatment of part-time workers can constitute indirect sex-discrimination against women."[36] While these policies do not directly discuss equal pay, they do address issues of discrimination, which often lead to inequality in salaries. Continued pressure from varied offices of women's policy machinery within the EU, such as the Committee on Women's Rights and Gender Equality of the European Parliament and the Equality for Women and Men unit of the European Commission, also kept women's issues on the EU agenda. However, while women's groups were able to access the EU policy machinery by participating in hearings, writing policy briefs, and so forth, it has been harder to translate advocacy into policy gains at the national level. Thus we see that the issue of equal pay in the EU and its member states has received a great deal of legislative attention over the past twenty-five years, even if the member states are not always so keen on following the EU's lead.

Impact

How has all of this legislation impacted women? Given the vast increase in women's activism, government policy, and corporate efforts to remedy women's often second-class status in the workforce, one might think that the pay gap between men and women is a relic of the past. However, the data indicate otherwise. In no advanced industrial nation do women earn the same as men, even for work in similar or identical occupations.

Equal pay legislation has not been able single-handedly to close the pay gap between men's and women's salaries. This is particularly true in Japan, where working women still earn only 66 percent of the average man's pay.[37] In the United States, according to research done by the General Accounting Office, in 1979 women full-time wage and salary workers earned only 63 percent of their male counterparts; by 2000 this gap had decreased to 76 percent.[38] And in 2008 in the United States, women still earned 22.4 percent less than their male counterparts, according to a report from the International Trade Union Confederation.[39] Finally, as Table 4.1 indicates, a 2003 survey of the existing fifteen member states of the European Union found that, on average, women's average earnings were 16 percent below those of men, although this number had decreased to 14.5 percent by 2008.[40] This figure, however, masks large differences between employment patterns in the private and public sectors; while women earned 89 percent of men's salaries in the public sector, the pay differential was 78 percent in the private sector.[41]

Table 4.1 Gender Pay Ratios in the European Union, 2003

COUNTRY	PAY RATIO (BASED ON HOURLY EARNINGS)
European Union members (2003)	.84
Austria	.80
Belgium	.88
Denmark	.85
Finland	.83
France	.87
Germany	.79
Greece	.85
Ireland	.81
Italy	.95
Luxembourg	N/A
Portugal	.92
Spain	.85
Sweden	.82
The Netherlands	.79
United Kingdom	.79

SOURCE: Commission of the European Communities, "Gender Pay Gaps in European Labour Markets—Measurement, Analysis, and Policy Implications." Brussels, April 9, 2003, SEC(2003)937.

Some might argue that the pay gap does not mean that women do not have pay equity. They note that the figures used to measure pay inequalities are averages across all work categories and do not take into account important intervening variables, such as years of employment and experience. Yet, even when age, educational background, and years worked are taken into account, there is still a disparity between men and women. For example, in Japan, in the 45–49 age group women earned 82 percent of their male colleagues in 1997.[42] A recent report by the U.S. Census Bureau found that the pay gap persists, even when years of employment and experience are taken into account. The Census Bureau reported that in six major employment categories women still earn less than men do. Further, women working in management, professional, and related fields suffer the biggest gap; the median income in 2000 for men in these categories was $50,034, while women with same jobs and levels of experience received a median income of $35,654.[43] Also, between 1995 and 2000, the earnings gap between full-time female and male managers widened.[44] The 2003 study of EU member nations echoed these findings; even in identical occupations, women made less than their male counterparts, even controlling for years of employment and experience.[45] And a 2007 survey in Great Britain of 42,000 managers found that the gap between male and female managers had widened to 12.2 percent from 11.8 percent in 2005 and from 20 percent to 23 percent among directors.[46] Thus, the pay gap between men and women, while diminishing, is still significant, despite legislation efforts to correct for it. While it is impossible to determine to what degree antidiscrimination legislation has helped close this gap, nonetheless, it has helped change some of the more obvious prejudicial employment policies against women.

Part of the problem lies in the fact that the persistence of the gender pay gap also can be attributed to indirect discrimination. An EU study linked the pay gap to the pervasive problem of gender segregation in the workforce, women's concentration in low-paying sectors and occupations, and the added responsibilities that women shoulder in child-bearing and child-rearing.[47] And an article by the Japan Times argues that "seniority systems at most companies, especially large scale ones, ensure that men are promoted more often than and receive extra allowances for dependents and housing. These fringe benefits, including higher bonuses, are often significantly less for women."[48] Further, women working part-time suffer even greater pay discrimination. Women make up a majority of part-time workers in Japan, the United States, and Europe and often are not paid as well as their full-time female or male colleagues are. Can broader policies that address equality in hiring, promotion, and firing address some of these deeper problems that lead to women's unequal status in the labor market?

Equality in Hiring, Promotion, and Firing

For decades, women have been the last hired and the first fired. Deemed "the weaker sex," women were "protected" from certain occupations because of supposed limitations on their physical capabilities or because the job could potentially interfere with their reproductive health. In fact, it was only recently that Belgium repealed nineteenth-century restrictions on women working at night.[49] Such protective legislation kept women from being hired for many jobs and from advancing if hired. Further, many women remained unhired or were fired after announcing their pregnancies; they were perceived as a threat to profits, and employers assumed that they would "naturally" choose to leave the workforce to devote themselves to motherhood. And while most protective legislation such as this no longer exists, certain barriers still keep women from being hired and promoted. Even when women embark on a career path, they rarely advance far. A glass ceiling still keeps women from achieving the highest positions, with the accompanying prestige, power, and pay. States have responded with legislation that bars employers from discriminating against women. Further, some have more proactively implemented affirmative action policies to promote women's advancement. We now turn to our three case studies. How has each designed policies to combat discrimination, and what has been the impact of these policies?

Japan

As we discussed in the previous section, the UN Convention to End Discrimination Against Women created the international pressure that prompted the Japanese Diet to pass the Equal Employment Opportunity Law in 1985. For the first time, Japanese law prohibited discrimination in termination of employment and encouraged equal treatment in recruitment, hiring, job assignment, and promotion. However, the law, as originally written, was essentially toothless; there were no sanctions for employers who refused to comply.[50] The law "only required that employers 'endeavor' to treat men and women the same in terms of hiring and promotion." [51] Nor were courts given the power to mediate by issuing orders to cease and desist or award punitive damages. And the law did not establish an administrative agency, such as the U.S. EEOC, to enforce compliance. Rather, the Ministry of Labor's Women's Bureau was charged with establishing "administrative guidelines" and "ministerial ordinances" to clarify the legislation. Finally, the legislation established a cumbersome, three-step system of mediation (as opposed to litigation) to attempt resolve disputes. The final third step involved the Equal Opportunity Mediation Commission (EOMC), which would handle the dispute only if one party requested mediation and both parties agreed to it. Yet, at most, mediation bodies could only provide advice, guidance, and recommendations, rather than legal resolution. The law was further amended in 1997 to, among other things, simplify the mediation process and provide for the publication of the names of companies violating the EEOL provisions and the nature of the violation. Nonetheless, twenty-three years later, the law still lacks significant enforcement mechanisms.[52] In addition to the EEOL, the Japanese Diet passed amendments to the Labor Standards Law, which abolished various protective measures for women related to overtime, late night, and hazardous work.[53] Thus, while the government has become more proactive in making symbolic efforts to advance women's equality, the lack of enforcement mechanisms severely weakens the impact of the law.

The United States

In the United States, until legislation deemed otherwise, employers were permitted to refuse to hire women in a variety of positions, many of them the higher-paying, managerial ones. It was not uncommon for newspaper advertisements to specify men only. Women were often paid less than men even for identical work.[54] The United States began addressing the issue of equality in hiring, firing, and promotion with Title VII of the Civil Rights Act of 1964 as amended in 1972. Title VII states that discrimination on the basis or race, color, religion, sex, or national origin is unlawful in hiring or firing; determining wages (as discussed previously); providing fringe benefits; classifying, referring, assigning, or promoting employees; and more. Most lawsuits concerning discrimination are brought under the auspices of this act. In 1978, the act was further amended; the Pregnancy Discrimination Act declared that classifications based on pregnancy and pregnancy-related disabilities fell within the meaning of "sex" under Title VII.

However, the language of Title VII was open for interpretation. While the law banned discrimination of the basis of an individual's race, color, religion, sex, or national origin, it also specified an important exception, known as the Bona Fide Occupational Qualification (BFOQ), which allowed employers to take factors such as sex into account where it was deemed "a bona fide occupational qualification reasonably necessary to the normal operation of that particular business enterprise."[55] This clause often pulled the courts into the debate, for the wording is open to interpretation. For example, in 1977, the Supreme Court ruled in *Dothard v. Rawlinson* that an Alabama state penitentiary could refuse to hire women as prison guards because, they maintained, women might not be able to maintain order as effectively as men because women were at risk of assault from inmates "deprived of a normal heterosexual environment."[56] On the other hand, the courts have also found that other employers' policies did not meet BFOQ guidelines and were thus discriminatory. For example, the courts have repeatedly found that employers cannot bar women from holding positions that required lifting more than a certain weight. In addition, men have successfully used the BFOQ clause to take on airlines that pursued a policy of hiring only female flight attendants. The BFOQ clause has been important because courts have often ruled against companies' discriminatory policies under the rationale that limits are often based on stereotypes of women's (and men's) abilities, rather than on factual evidence.

Further, a series of executive orders addressing equality in hiring, firing, and promotion became quite controversial because they sought to not only bar discrimination but to also remedy past inequalities by taking proactive measures to increase women and minority representation. Executive Order 11246 prohibited discrimination regarding race in hiring, firing, and promotion by contractors and subcontractors with federal or federally funded contracts (this encompasses a massive number of businesses and places of higher learning). This executive order was amended in 1967 by Executive Order 11375 to include sex. These executive orders are often referred to as affirmative action because of the wording of Executive Order 11375, part of which states that "The contractor will take affirmative action to ensure that employees are employed and are treated during employment, without regard to their race, color, religion, sex or national origin." [57] Many people have come to see affirmative action as preferential treatment for women at the expense of men and have been able to frame the policy of affirmative action as one of reverse discrimination. In their interpretation, businesses and places of higher learning use quotas to ensure the promotion of minorities and women, despite their supposed inferior qualifications. The Supreme Court has ruled repeatedly (most recently in the summer of 2003 in a lawsuit against the University of Michigan) that quotas are unconstitutional but that race and sex can be taken into account in hiring and admittance decisions.

A final piece of legislation that might have assisted women in the United States with their claims of equality was the Equal Rights Amendment (ERA). The text of the ERA is as follows: "Equality of rights under the law shall not be denied or abridged by the United States or by any state on account of sex. The Congress shall have the power to enforce, by appropriate legislation, the provisions of this article. This amendment shall take effect two years after the date of ratification." [58] Depending on the design of resulting policy, and the government's willingness to enforce these policies, the ERA potentially also could have been used as an equalizing force in employment. In fact, the ERA passed Congress in 1972 and was sent to the states in search of ratification by three-fourths of the states. However, by 1982 the ERA failed to attain ratification by the requisite number of states and thus did not become an amendment to the U.S. Constitution. Thus, in the United States, litigation has been a successful method of punishing some discriminatory hiring practices; however, more proactive policies, such as affirmative action and constitutional amendments, have been much more controversial.

The European Union

The European Union, as previously discussed, has attempted to integrate equal employment policy into its laws and treaties from its inception. However, the member states have not been too eager to follow the lead of the EU. Throughout the 1970s, the European Community continued to issue directives related to equal opportunity employment issues. As we mentioned in the previous section, a 1976 directive broadened the principle of equal employment for men and women to cover the issues of equal access to employment, which included promotion, as well as job training, and barred discrimination on grounds of sex, particularly with regard to marital and family status.[59] Further, the directive allowed for positive action measures (which in the United States are known as affirmative action policies) to address gender inequalities in the labor force. However, the directive did not contain clear implementation directions for member states, which weakened the directive's force. In addition, the section addressing affirmative action measures were recommendations, and thus were not binding on member nations.

The 1997 Amsterdam Treaty (which took effect on May 1, 1999) extended the EU's abilities to take action to foster gender equality beyond the issue of equal pay for equal work. The treaty's broader purpose was to update and clarify the conditions of the Maastricht Treaty (which created the European Union), prepare for EU enlargement, and clarify the powers of the European Parliament and the Council of Ministers on a range of issues, including social policy.[60] In terms of fostering gender equality, Article 13 empowered the Council of Ministers, the executive branch of the EU, to take "appropriate action" to combat discrimination based on sex, racial or ethnic origin, religion or belief, disability, age, or sexual orientation. The Council of Ministers and, to some extent, the European Parliament are vested with the power to design and adopt legislation that goes beyond ensuring equal pay, but also encompasses equal treatment and equal opportunities.[61]

In addition, the European Court of Justice (ECJ), the judicial branch of the EU, has grown more proactive in enforcing the directives and advancing women's equality through its decisions in important cases. Initially, the ECJ was relatively conservative in its approach, issuing two judgments that in essence ruled that affirmative action hiring policies, such as quotas, were contrary to European equal opportunities legislation.[62] However, in the wake of the Amsterdam Treaty, and its expanded definition of gender equality, the court has pursued a more proactive strategy and has recognized that member states can take action to improve women's ability to compete in the labor market so that women with the same qualifications as men can receive preference for promotion in areas in which they are underrepresented.

Thus, equality in hiring, firing, and promotion is protected in various EU treaties, directives, and decisions of the European Court of Justice. Yet, because of the relative youth of the European Union, continuously evolving policies, and changes in leadership style of the European Commission, it is important not to overemphasize the presence of directives, legislation, and court rulings. Certainly, directives oblige all member states to adopt or amend existing legislation to ensure compliance with EU rules. And the rhetorical leadership of the EU on various equal employment policies sets an important example to member nations and can provide further pressure on member countries to implement national-level legislation to meet EU standards. This can also encourage women's organizations at the national level to lobby their governments for prompt legislative initiative, as well as the formation of transnational networks of women's activists. For example, the founding of the European Women's Lobby in 1990 was in response to support from the European Commission and the Committee on Women's Rights of the European Parliament.[63] However, implementation of policy at the national level will be the key challenge.

Impact

What has been the impact of all of this legislation on women? In Japan, despite the EEOL, women still lag behind men in promotions and hiring. While in 1985 women held just 6.6 percent of all management jobs in Japanese companies, that number had risen to only 10.1 percent by 2005 even though women make up nearly half of Japan's work force.[64] This is in part because of holes in the legislation. For example, the law fails to guard against indirect discrimination. Many companies initially responded to the EEOL by establishing a dual career track system for men and women, with men hired in managerial track positions and women relegated to clerical positions. While managerial positions involve complex judgment, involuntary transfers, and unlimited access to promotion, the clerical track, although often full-time, involves less time, commitment, and thus opportunities for advancement.[65] Given that many Japanese companies operate on an informal policy of "lifelong employment," which offers high job security, demands high worker commitment, and involves extensive worker training, this dual model often places women in a long-term disadvantageous position from which they are unable to extricate themselves.[66] Further, the lack of strong enforcement measures limits the impact of the EEOL. The Equal Opportunity Mediation Commission can only recommend and encourage parties to resolve their differences, but businesses are under no legal obligation to follow the advice of the commission. In addition, the worst the Ministry of Labor can do is publish names of violators, which it has never done.[67] Instead, it has taken a cautious route and has attempted to appeal to employers' goodwill in complying with the law rather than fighting for greater enforcement mechanisms.[68]

This has not stopped a few women from attempting to fight for more equitable working conditions. Indirectly, the passage of the EEOL, which heightened women's awareness of discrimination issues, led a few to pursue litigation through other means, such as Article 14 of the Constitution, which provides for equality between the sexes, or Article 4 of the Labor Standards Act, which prohibits gender-based discrimination at work.[69] In 1995, four women who worked at Sumitomo Metal Industries Ltd. filed a lawsuit claiming that the company uses a sexually discriminatory employment system that in practice kept women's wages much lower than men's in similar jobs with similar qualifications.[70] Nine and a half years later, the Osaka District Court ruled in their favor and ordered the company to pay compensation. Sumitomo is appealing the ruling.[71] The increased use of lawsuits, even if not under the auspices of the EEOL, point to the greater consciousness surrounding issues of employment.

However, women are still blocked by a very thick glass ceiling. The International Labor Organization, a United Nations agency, found that in 2005 women occupied only 10.1 percent of managerial positions, compared to 42.5 percent in the United States.[72] And the Japanese government's White Paper on Equal Gender Participation found that 67.7 percent of Japanese women believe that men are given preferential treatment at work.[73] Women's under-representation, in part, can be attributed to pervasive cultural attitudes about women and work; women seeking jobs in Japan are described by employers as "too ambitious" and/or "uncooperative" and "too proud to listen to their colleagues' advice."[74] This is coupled with the persistent social belief that "women should be the primary caregivers for children and sick or elderly family members."[75] Given these impediments, women will need more than symbolic policy to change their unequal position in the labor market in Japan.

In the United States, while Title VII and affirmative action policies both have aided women in their quest for equality in hiring, firing, and promotion, their impact is limited. Women slowly are increasing their numbers among the top employees of companies and among chief executive officers. Since 1992, the number of female CEOs of large nonprofit organizations has increased significantly.[76] And women have clearly increased their numbers among the middle to upper ranks of companies. However, as of December 2008, only fourteen Fortune 500 companies had female chief executive officers or presidents.[77] And a survey conducted by the General Accounting Office found that "women who are full time managers are paid less and advance less often than male managers."[78]

The state of hiring and promotion practices in the EU is also quite poor. In the member states of the European Union, according to the European Parliament, women are still to be found in the basic career grades and "women eligible for promotion are less likely than men to actually get promoted."[79] In fact, women hold only one-third of managerial jobs and account for only 10 percent of board members and 3 percent of CEOs of large companies.[80] Further, according to the European Trade Union Confederation, women remain sequestered in a narrow range of occupations (one in six women works in health and social services) and primarily at the bottom of the ladder.[81] As the EU noted of its own performance, "despite all the efforts of the past decades, complete equality of opportunity has not yet been achieved....In other words, there is still work to be done in the EU to implement equal opportunities in practice."[82]

Further, as the European Union expands to encompass candidate countries in eastern Europe, its abilities to enforce its rulings will be tested to the limit, as these countries will have to bring their equal opportunity legislation (which is often nonexistent) into line with European standards. Discrimination in hiring is still blatant in eastern Europe, even though some of these nations have recently been admitted to the European Union. Employment advertisements, for instance, still ask for such things as "attractive female receptionist" or "girl under 25," and sometimes women must promise to not get pregnant for five years.[83] For those nations that have recently been admitted to the EU, these practices will need to end because of EU legislation that prohibits such practices.

However, EU policy has affected some countries' domestic policies on equal employment dramatically, which probably could not have changed in the absence of EU pressure. For example, the EU did have an impact on Irish women's equal access to employment. As Julia O'Connor found,

> The Community has brought about changes in employment practices which might otherwise have taken decades to achieve. Irish women have the Community to thank for the removal of the marriage bar in employment, the introduction of maternity leave, greater opportunities to train at a skilled trade, protection against dismissal upon pregnancy, the disappearance of advertisements specifying the sex of an applicant for a job and greater equality in the social welfare code.[84]

In this example, the presence of EU directives pushed an individual member country to change its policies to align with European standards.

Sexual Harassment

A third crucial issue for women in the workplace is that of sexual harassment. Sexual harassment is not a new problem; however, it was not seen as an issue for many years because of women's limited participation in the workforce. Further, for many years, it was treated as an unpleasant working condition to be tolerated. However, beginning in the 1960s and 1970s, women's movements raised the consciousness of many women and many began to question patriarchy and its attendant trappings. By the 1980s women began to believe that sexual harassment was not something they had to accept and slowly began to work toward changing laws as well as attitudes. Men are certainly subject to sexual harassment as well; however, since it predominantly affects women, women will be our focus here.

Before delving into the topic of sexual harassment it would be helpful to have a working definition of it. What is sexual harassment? One definition, used by the U.S. Equal Employment Opportunity Commission, states that sexual harassment includes

> unwelcome sexual advances, requests for sexual favors, and other verbal or physical conduct of a sexual nature when submission to or rejection of this conduct explicitly or implicitly affects an individual's employment, unreasonably interferes with an individual's work performance, or creates an intimidating, hostile, or offensive work environment.[85]

One problem with sexual harassment has been deciding what actions constitute it. This definition helps but still leaves some people confused. Do dirty jokes told around the water cooler at the workplace constitute sexual harassment? What about statements made regarding one's appearance? The story at the beginning of the chapter about the employee who was called a "hotty totty" by her employer appears today to be a fairly straightforward example of harassment, but other examples are not so clear-cut. However, we adopt the preceding definition because it offers a fairly comprehensive definition that can guide the discussion of this issue.

Another complication is that harassment can be hard to prove, since it often happens in the privacy of someone's office, rather than in public, in front of

Anita Hill testifies before the Senate Judiciary Committee on charges that she was sexually harassed by her former boss, Clarence Thomas, while working for him at the Equal Employment Opportunity Commission. Thomas, at the time a nominee for the Supreme Court, was ultimately confirmed to the Court in a contentious 52–48 vote by the U.S. Senate. SOURCE: Brad Markel/Getty Images

witnesses. This can make it difficult for women to come forward, as illustrated by the Anita Hill and Clarence Thomas hearings. In 1991 Clarence Thomas was nominated to the U.S. Supreme Court. During the confirmation process allegations arose by his former aide, attorney Anita Hill, that Thomas had sexually harassed her when they worked together at the Department of Education and later at the Equal Employment Opportunity Commission during the early 1980s. Hill underwent grueling cross-examination by the Senate Judiciary Committee, which was made up of all men. They queried her as to why it took so long for her to say something about this harassment and whether she had invented the incidents. Ultimately, the Judiciary Committee confirmed Thomas. The topic of sexual harassment stayed in the public's mind when Paula Jones charged that President Clinton had sexually harassed her when he was governor of Arkansas.

And, as the story at the beginning of the chapter illustrates, the problem is certainly not confined to the United States. What laws have been passed to assist women in their quest to end this form of discrimination, and what has been their impact?

Japan

The concept of sexual harassment is still relatively new to Japanese workers. The Japanese language does not even have a word for sexual harassment—the word used, *seku-hara,* has been derived from the English term. And the EEOL, as it was originally written, said nothing specifically about sexual harassment. However, the 1997 amendments to the EEOL make employers responsible for the prevention of sexual harassment. Yet, as we discussed previously, the amendments (and the original law) lack significant punitive measures to enforce compliance. The Ministry of Labor can publicize the names of companies that violate the conditions of the EEOL.[86] In addition, women can use the cumbersome mediation process specified in the EEOL. Thus, as in other areas, the policies are primarily symbolic and lack "teeth" that could enforce new standards of equal employment. Instead, they rely on the Ministry's abilities to cajole good behavior out of companies.

The United States

In the United States, sexual harassment is considered to be a form of gender discrimination that is covered under Title VII of the Civil Rights Act of 1964 as well as under Title IX of the Education Act of 1972. According to the EEOC, sexual harassment includes instances of quid pro quo (e.g., requiring the provision of sexual favors as a term or condition of one's employment) as well as the creation of a hostile working environment. As in many countries, it is often difficult to prove harassment; in the United States, the plaintiff must show that

> (1) she was subjected to unwelcome sexual conduct; (2) these were based on her sex; (3) they were sufficiently pervasive or severe to create an abusive or hostile work environment; and (4) the employer knew or should have known of the harassment and failed to take prompt and appropriate remedial action.[87]

The courts have used a "reasonableness" standard to determine what defines an unwelcome sexual advance and a hostile work environment. That is, under similar circumstances, would a "reasonable person" have identified the behavior as unwelcome? As one can imagine, this does allow for a wide degree of latitude in terms of what constitutes "reasonable." However, the federal courts in the United States have made it clear that companies are financially liable for the actions of their employees. As a result, many employers conduct extensive training and educational outreach with their employees in hopes of halting the problem. Much of this is because of the efforts of the women's movement; NOW and other women's groups litigated and lobbied extensively in the 1970s (and beyond) and as a result were successful in expanding the interpretation of Title VII. Thus, the U.S.

system of litigation, the state's willingness to enforce the law, and active women's mobilization have forced many companies and institutions to take the issue of sexual harassment seriously.

The European Union

European countries have been much slower in addressing sexual harassment. However, studies conducted in the 1980s in individual member countries indicated that the problem was severe, and another report published in 1988 revealed that no member state had an express legal prohibition against sexual harassment. In fact, in only two countries—the United Kingdom and Ireland—did courts accept the argument that sexual harassment constituted discrimination. However, the European Commission was divided on whether they needed to issue a directive, which would be legally binding on member states, to address the issue. Some members argued that the 1976 directive on equal treatment, which banned sex discrimination, could be used to sanction harassment. Finally, in 1991, the commission adopted a recommendation (which is not legally binding) on the protection of the dignity of women and men at work and added it to a code of practice on measures to combat harassment. In essence, the commission urged member states to take the matter of sexual harassment seriously, without providing the clarity or enforcement mechanisms that could have made it an effective Europe-wide policy tool. As a result, while member states responded with various legislative acts addressing harassment, the acts are often weak, unclear, or put an undue burden on the woman to prove her case.[88] Thus, while initial efforts heightened awareness of sexual harassment as a problem and led to initial legislation to address the issue, nonetheless most national-level policies lack strong sanctions against offenders.

The EU raised the issue again, when it amended the 1976 directive on equal treatment in 2002. Currently, "binding legislation defines sexual harassment and outlaws it as a form of discrimination based on sex. It bans any form of unwanted sexual behavior that creates an intimidating or degrading environment and also urges employers to take preventive action against all forms of discrimination and to compile regular equality reports for staff."[89] Under the conditions of the amended directive, when an employee files a sexual harassment claim with an employer, that employer is required to prove that it has done all they could to prevent sexual harassment. Further, employers are financially liable when sexual harassment allegations have been shown to be true. Finally, the directive gives courts a freer hand when awarding financial compensation to victims of sexual harassment. Member states have until 2005 to comply, and some have already passed relevant legislation. For instance, France has made sexual harassment a criminal offense, the only nation in the world to do so. However, not all women's equality advocates have supported this move. Some argue that the criminalization of sexual harassment in France will make it harder for women to bring charges. They argue that a civil law approach, where one uses a lawsuit to threaten a firm, is more successful in getting firms to take the issue seriously. Finally, women in France whose sexual harassment charges against men fail can be hit with a defamation lawsuit by the men and then forced to pay damages.

Impact

What has been the impact of these laws on women's lives? In Japan it appears that sexual harassment is still widespread. A 1997 survey by the Ministry of Labor reported that "62 percent of women claimed to have experienced at least one act of sexual harassment."[90] On a positive note, another survey indicates that some of the more extreme forms of sexual harassment may be on the wane in government workplaces. Female government workers reported a decline in their bosses pressuring them to have a sexual relationship—from 17 percent in 1997 to 2.2 percent by 2000.[91] And there has been a 35 percent increase in the number of women reporting sexual harassment in the workplace since the EEOL revisions went into effect in 1999.[92] Further, as in other areas of equal employment policy, women's disenchantment with the EEOL's mediation process has led women to use other antidiscrimination legislation to press sexual harassment suits. From 1989 to 1997, women brought forward fifty-eight lawsuits related to sexual harassment charges. Thus, the weakness of the EEOL in many ways spurred women on to exploit alternative venues of leverage. While the number of women coming forward pales in comparison to, say, the United States, nonetheless it marks a very small but significant cultural shift in the acceptability of harassment on the job.

In the United States the number of sexual harassment claims to the EEOC more than doubled between 1990 and 1996, from about six thousand to fifteen thousand.[93] While this may be because of the existence of laws allowing women to sue their employers, it also may be, in part, because of the media attention paid to the topic in the 1990s. The Clarence Thomas confirmation hearings were televised, and the allegations by Paula Jones against President Clinton received a great deal of media attention. Some speculate that after these nationally televised events regarding sexual harassment, the cases brought to the EEOC increased dramatically.

The EEOC has also been willing to enforce legislation criminalizing harassment and has charged a number of large corporations with sexual harassment. One of the largest suits it brought was against the Mitsubishi Corporation alleging sexual harassment against more than 350 women. The suit was settled in June 1998 and Mitsubishi was ordered to pay the plaintiffs over $34 million, end sexual harassment in the workplace, and make sure that no retaliation against these women occurred. A team of monitors was established to ensure that Mitsubishi complied. The EEOC has also successfully led a case against the largest lettuce grower in the United States on behalf of female migrant workers who alleged that they had been sexually harassed. The company, while not admitting to any wrongdoing, agreed to pay $1.85 million, fire one manager, reprimand another, and train and monitor all other supervisors and employees. This is an important victory because migrant women have few resources to battle sexual harassment. They often do not know the law, fear losing their jobs, and lack the language fluency to facilitate acting on harassment. The deck is stacked against them even more so than it is for middle-class women.

The number of sexual harassment cases heard in U.S. federal courts has also increased. The Supreme Court has handed down numerous rulings on the topic beginning in the mid-1980s. The first rulings dealt with what behaviors constituted unlawful sexual harassment. More recently, the Court has begun handing down decisions regarding legal responsibility for sexual harassment. In one of the first cases addressing sexual harassment, *Meritor Savings Bank v. Vinson* (1986), the Supreme Court recognized as unlawful both types of sexual harassment defined in the EEOC guidelines. This decision and others, as well as the fact that the Supreme Court is hearing sexual harassment cases, are significant indicators that the courts take the issue of harassment seriously. The Supreme Court can pick and choose which cases it hears, and if it is choosing to hear sexual harassment cases and upholding EEOC guidelines, then this indicates that it views such cases as involving important legal questions, thus granting legitimacy to women's claims.

While sexual harassment persists in the United States, some improvements have occurred. Women are stepping forward to charge their employers with sexual harassment, the EEOC is successfully waging battles against these employers, the Supreme Court has upheld the EEOC guidelines and handed down decisions that assist women alleging sexual harassment, and companies are creating their own guidelines and holding training sessions to educate their employees on the topic. However, sexual harassment does persist. The laws and the legal decisions have assisted women and scared corporations who do not wish to suffer large monetary losses because of the behavior of some of their employees. It will very likely take time and more education to further decrease the incidence of sexual harassment.

The European Union only recently has devoted concerted attention to policy pertaining to sexual harassment, and, as a result, policies still differ significantly at the national level. And sexual harassment is rampant in Europe. One survey indicates that up to 50 percent of European women have experienced some type of sexual harassment (ranging from sexual verbal remarks to assault or rape).[94] However, national estimates vary widely, from 11 percent in Denmark to 54 percent in the United Kingdom to 81 percent in Austria.[95] This discrepancy is largely because of a lack of an agreed-upon idea of what constitutes sexual harassment. In some of the southern European countries women feel sexual harassment is an unfortunate but enduring part of the work environment that must be tolerated. Further, many men do not see their behavior as inappropriate. This is different than in northern Europe, where sexual harassment is recognized more widely and is not condoned by women (or men). So, sexual harassment persists throughout Europe, although in varying degrees from country to country. The attitude of the country, as well as the legal recourse available, have impacted whether or not women have filed suit against harassers and how successful these suits have been. The stories at the beginning of this chapter indicate that women in Europe are bringing suit against their employers for sexual harassment and winning. The EU directive discussed earlier adopts a common definition, which should assist women in identifying what it is and in bringing suit against employers. A common EU policy, accompanied by a public relations campaign designed to educate the populace about the policy, should further assist women by making lawsuits easier to wage and hopefully decreasing the prevalence of sexual harassment in the workplace.

Retirement Income

We now move on to examine our final area of policy in which women have strived to attain equality—retirement income. Retirement income usually refers to income that one receives from the state after one retires, such as Social Security in the United States, pensions that one's employer provides to its workers, and any money that one may have saved over the course of one's life. Retirement income is of crucial concern to all people, but especially to women, in part because women tend to live longer than men and thus need income for a longer period of time than men do. However, for a variety of reasons that we shall discuss in this section, women earn much less than men in retirement income. For example, on average, women's government pensions in Europe are significantly less than men's—the gap between what women and men receive ranges from a low of 16 percent in the United Kingdom to 45 percent in Austria.[96] And in the United States, at the end of 2003, women's average monthly retirement benefit was $798, compared to $1,039 for men.[97] The result is the feminization of poverty among the elderly. While this is a critical issue for women, there have been fewer efforts to design policy to address this issue. Thus, this final section diverges from the previous ones in the sense that we discuss why retirement is a gender issue rather than discuss the design and impact of policy reforms in our three case studies.

Why is retirement income a women's issue? For one, women who do work often work fewer years than men because they assume the tasks of child care and care of elderly relatives, and the amount of retirement income that one receives from the government is dependent on the number of years that one has participated in the workforce. Thus, women have usually paid less into the government system and get less back upon retirement. As the European Institute for Women's Health finds, "In Italy...only 20 percent of women have a 30-year contribution record compared to 60 percent of men."[98] In Australia, for the year 2000, men averaged thirty-eight years in the workforce while women averaged only twenty.[99] In countries such as Japan, women's participation in the workforce is perceived as a reason to potentially deny women their benefits, for they have shunned the more valued occupations of wife and mother. For example, a former prime minister of Japan noted in public that women who did not bear children were not worthy of public (government) pensions. He said: "The government takes care of women who have given birth to a lot of children as a way to thank them for their hard work.... It is wrong for women who haven't had a single child to ask for taxpayer money when they get old, after having enjoyed their *freedom and fun* (emphasis added)." [100]

The effects of private pension plans on women are similar to government pension plans. One's retirement income from a private pension plan with one's employer is often dependent on the number of years that one has been with a specific employer. Because women move in and out of the workforce more frequently than men do (often because of family commitments), they often don't stay long enough in a job to become eligible. Among all racial groups only 28.5 percent of women even have a private pension, compared to 45.4 percent of men. Second, women are still relegated to lower-paying jobs than men, and even when they have jobs similar to those of men their income is often less. This means that they often pay less into public and private pension plans and get less back. Finally, many service sector, retail, and part-time jobs—jobs primarily occupied by women—offer no pension plan. In the Netherlands, "of women working part-time and in low paid jobs, more than one-third (37 percent) are not in occupational pension schemes." [101]

The laws governing spousal pension rights in the circumstance of marriage, divorce, and death also often work against women, particularly those who spent their working years caring for their families rather than in the paid labor force. They have accrued little if any retirement income over the course of their lives and thus are often almost entirely dependent on their husband's income. Yet, for example, in the United States, if a couple has been married for less than ten years and they divorce, the ex-wife receives none of her husband's Social Security benefits upon his retirement. Alternatively, if the husband dies, the wife is under sixty, and there are no children under the age of eighteen, the wife receives none of her husband's benefits until she turns sixty. Further, with regard to private pension plans in the United States, for many years men could waive their wife's survivor benefit without her consent. On the positive side, this bolstered a couple's monthly income when the husband retired. However, when the husband died the payments ceased. This was not a problem if the wife died before the husband, but since women often outlive men, this left a great number of women with no retirement income in old age. Thus, women are often placed in a precarious financial situation upon divorce or the death of their husband. Inequality in the distribution of bereavement benefits isn't solely a problem confronting women. In the United Kingdom, until recently men whose wives died were not entitled to a widower benefit; only women could receive benefits when their husbands died. However, the United Kingdom has changed their pension system so that now, should a man outlive his wife, he can receive widower's benefits.

Since women often live longer than men, retirement benefits, particularly those provided by the government, are of crucial importance to their lives. For example, research on elderly women in the United States found that they rely heavily on Social Security for their retirement benefits—only 13 percent of elderly women receive a private pension compared to 33 percent of older men.[102] And, in the United States, "Nearly two-thirds of all women 65 and older receive half or more of their income from Social Security, and for nearly one-third of older women, Social Security is 90 percent or more of their income." [103] Yet, because women receive substantially less in benefits than men do, the result is the feminization of poverty among the elderly. For example, 1994 U.S. Census Bureau figures show that nearly three-quarters of the elderly who live below the poverty line are women and "two-thirds of women over age 65 have no pension other than social security." [104] In the United Kingdom, one in four pensioner women lives in poverty.[105] According to a report by the Economic and Social Research Council in the United Kingdom, these inequalities are the result, in part, of gendered divisions of labor at home; "mothers who take career breaks to bring up their children are seven times as likely to face hardship and poverty when they reach their 60s than single women." [106] The United States and the United Kingdom are just two examples in a larger trend affecting all European countries, where, in general, older women are more likely than men to rely on social assistance for their needs.[107]

In contrast to our other equal employment policy issues, there have been fewer concentrated efforts to address this imbalance, in part because the inequality in retirement benefits is often the result of indirect forms of discrimination. However, there are a few examples of policy reform that may have a limited impact on women's economic status in their retirement years. In Europe, the European Court of Justice has taken a positive step to improve the lot of part-time workers. They have ruled that part-time workers must be included in private pension schemes on a pro-rata basis. But this still leaves many women without pension plans and so, as the story at the beginning of the chapter regarding Gretchen Swan indicates, women often do not receive pension benefits and must fight for them. The U.S. Retirement Equity Act of 1984 was designed to help widows win more spousal benefits from private pension plans. It "made it mandatory for workers with private pension plans to get the written consent of their spouses in order to waive their survivor benefit." [108] The act also helped divorced women because it requires private pension plans to honor state court orders that divide pension plans in settlements. However, these isolated acts tend to respond to specific issues rather than broadly address issues of gender inequality. As a result, the issue of retirement income is of ongoing concern for women, with few legislative changes in sight.

ADVANCING WOMEN'S EQUALITY

In this chapter we have surveyed the current status of women in their search for equality and examined some of the legal remedies that have been enacted in hopes of attaining equality between the sexes. Despite improvement in women's working conditions, there is still much room for improvement in all of the areas we have discussed. What are some further suggested reforms? We will briefly examine this question in light of each of the broad areas we have covered in this chapter.

As we discussed earlier, many women are paid less than men because they are segregated into predominantly "female" professions. As a result, they work in different positions than men, and it is thus hard to prove overt discrimination in pay scales when women are paid less for their work. As a result, some women's groups have stressed the importance of "comparable worth," a proposal to pay different job titles the same based on their value. For instance, in a law firm a legal secretary is of vital importance to the firm and in the contracting industry a carpenter is also vital. However, carpenters make significantly more money than legal secretaries even though both jobs may be of comparable importance to their respective employers. As a result, one change that women have fought for is making comparable worth the benchmark for pay. Companies would have to rate the importance of certain jobs; all jobs rated a "5," for example, no matter the description, would receive comparable pay. In this scenario, while factors such as years of experience and performance reviews would affect salary, the gendered divisions with regard to pay inequality would be lessened. However, while women's groups in most advanced industrial nations have lobbied for comparable worth policies, they have been unable to make much legislative progress on the issue.

In our three case studies, women's groups have worked on a variety of specific policy proposals to further the cause of fair pay. In Japan, women's groups have lobbied for the abolition of the "two-track" personnel administration system found in most corporations, in which women form the overwhelming majority of general track (as opposed to management track) jobs, which tend to be lower paying and do not lead to promotions to management positions. Abolition of this system would assist women in gaining equality in the workplace. In the United States, members of the 110th Congress were considering two bills, the Paycheck Fairness Act and the Fair Pay Act. Both of these acts would amend the Fair Labor Standards Act of 1938. The former would amend it to provide for more effective methods of redress for victims of wage discrimination, and the latter would prohibit discrimination in the payment of wages on account of race, sex, national origin, and for other purposes. As of November 2008, the Paycheck Fairness Act had passed the House and was awaiting a vote in the Senate, but President Bush had promised to veto the bill. The Fair Pay Act was introduced in the Senate, but as of November 2008, it had not made it out of Committee. Further, women's groups advocate the continued use of affirmative action policies in hiring and promotion decisions to assist women in achieving equality in the workplace. In the past, affirmative action unquestionably has assisted women in gaining greater access to a variety of jobs and entrance into institutions of higher learning. Finally, the European Union and its member states continue to work toward improving gender equality in pay and hiring and promotion. One improvement for women would be making the European Charter on Human

Rights legally binding, which would provide the EU with more tools for ending discrimination.

There are fewer solutions to the ongoing problem of sexual harassment. While many companies are taking necessary steps by educating their workers about what constitutes sexual harassment and methods of communication, broader cultural norms are slower to change. While the U.S. system of litigation has encouraged companies to move more rapidly on implementing harassment policies, there has been less progress on this matter in Europe, where there is less agreement on what constitutes harassment and fewer legislative efforts to combat it.

In terms of retirement benefits, advocates have pushed for a variety of reforms. For example, greater protections for part-time workers in the United States would improve the pay and benefits of part-time workers, the majority of whom are women. Other countries have moved to implement changes that would reward women for their years off from work for raising children. For example, Germany has reformed its pension system to grant women a three-year pension credit if they are the primary caretakers of their children (and thus not employed in the paid labor force). While this amount is more symbolic than significant, it nonetheless acknowledges the contribution of women who are not consistently working outside the home. Further, private pension accounts (worldwide) could be made more female-friendly by shortening the time one has to work until becoming vested. And all retirement schemes would greatly benefit women if women were paid the same as their male colleagues. The pay differential is one of the biggest contributors to women's poverty in their later years.

CONCLUSION

Despite the strides made with equal employment policies, this chapter also illustrates the limits of equal employment policies in many countries. These policies do not address the fundamental inequalities between men and women outside the workforce; women's caretaking and nurturing responsibilities have a dramatic effect on their abilities to compete in the realm of work, as we shall see in the next chapter. Further, laws can only go so far in ameliorating women's separate and unequal status in the absence of significant cultural change about the acceptability of discriminatory practices. Education is one key to this cultural change, as well as an educational system in which the topic of equality is at the heart of its curriculum and in which women's achievements and contributions are a regular part of the curriculum, not just during Women's History Month in March. Until more cultural change occurs, women will still be fighting an uphill battle for equality. Laws and their enforcement are important, and additional legal changes could assist women in their quest for equality. But societal change must come as well. And while this may be slow in coming, the rewards to individuals and society will be worth the time and effort.

FOR MORE INFORMATION

The European Commission: Employment, Social Affairs, and Equal Opportunity: Gender Equality, http://ec.europa.eu/employment_social/gender_equality/index_en.html

The International Labour Organization, http://www.ilo.org/public/english/region/eurpro/geneva/what/events/malta/equal.htm

The United States Equal Employment Opportunity Commission, http://www.eeoc.gov

The World Economic Forum—The Global Gender Gap, http://www.weforum.org/en/initiatives/gcp/Gender%20Gap/GenderGap

Clarence Thomas and Anita Hill: Public Hearing, Private Pain—This film, made in 1992, looks at the intersection of gender, race, and sexual harassment.

Elechek—This film made in Krgyzstan in 2006 looks at the life of a woman whose husband has decided to take a younger second wife. The film addresses the difficulties and abuses that women face often as a result of a lack of economic opportunities.

Women and Public Policy: The Actors and the Issues—This film discusses the role that women have played in the public policy that impacts their lives.

Women's Happiness or Men's Dignity—This film, made in Armenia in 2006, looks at the lives of two women, one divorcee and one widow, and their very different views on the appropriate role of men and women in the economy and the family.

5

✦

Women, Work, and Family

Rocco Falivena, the mayor of Laviano, a small Italian town outside of Naples, was trying to solve a serious demographic problem. When he took office in 2002 in this sleepy village of sixteen hundred residents, two numbers worried him: four, the number of babies born in the town the year before, and five, the number of children enrolled in first grade (the school also served two additional communities). In other words, women were not having babies. In a desperate move to encourage more women to have babies, he offered them a fairly substantial financial incentive to reproduce. He announced he would pay 10,000 euros (over the space of the child's first five years) for every woman who would bear and raise a child in his village. The demographic crisis is not contained to the village of Laviano; in the 1990s, demographers noted plummeting birthrates across many of the countries of Europe. In 2002, birthrates in southern and Eastern Europe dropped below 1.3—a rate that indicates that a country's population rate will be cut in half within forty-five years, creating a massive demographic crisis. And similar to the mayor of Laviano, governments have scrambled with a package of incentives to encourage women to have more children, ranging from cash payments to women and increasing maternity leave benefits to boosting subsidies and financial support for families to help cover the costs of raising children. Yet, it is not necessarily true that women want to have, on average, 1.3 children; a 2006 Eurobarometer survey by the European Commission found that when asked how many children they wanted to have, the average result for women respondents was 2.36—well above replacement level and actual birthrates anywhere in Europe.

The traditional explanation for falling birthrates has been that as women enter the workforce, they delay having children and have fewer of them. Certainly, women's increased employment opportunities have acted as an informal, yet highly effective, contraceptive. However, studies also show that in Europe, high fertility rates are associated with high female labor force participation and that countries that had lower female labor force participation also had lower fertility.

In other words, working and mothering is not the obstacle to increasing the birthrate. Rather, studies have found that governments with a greater commitment to state-supported programs such as daycare and other institutional supports enable women to choose to have that second, or third, child. Further, they found that another significant determinant was culture; women who do more than 75 percent of the housework and child care are less likely to want to have another child than women whose partners participate more equally in caregiving and housework tasks.[1] Thus, national cultural values and institutional levels of support from the state make all the difference in whether women will choose to have more children, as well as how (and whether) they combine that choice with working outside of the home.

The previous chapter discussed how states often become involved in public policy to ensure that men and women are treated equally in the workforce. However, women's biological differences, combined with their responsibilities in the private sphere, often affect their abilities to interact on an equal basis in the public sphere. This has been particularly evident in the struggles to reconcile work and family duties, what is also known as balancing the demands of production and reproduction. While this is a problem for both men and women, historically it has impacted primarily women. Women are biologically unique in that they alone can become pregnant and give birth. Once the child is born, women often assume primary responsibilities for caring and feeding the infant, particularly in the initial months when many children are breastfed. As the infant develops into a child, constraints of tradition overtake those of biology, and women often assume primary care responsibilities in many countries, not only in raising their children but also in maintaining the household by doing much of the shopping, cleaning, and cooking for the entire family. Thus, child-bearing and child-rearing have serious ramifications for women's equality in the workforce; women with children often work less, advance much more slowly, and accumulate fewer earnings and hence less retirement benefits. As a result, granting formal equality in the work sphere often does not translate into actual equality, since women's responsibilities in the private realm affect their abilities to compete at work. Thus, many feminists maintain that policies that increase work opportunities for women, without targeting gender bias in responsibilities at home, will yield, at best, a flawed form of gender equality.[2]

States have responded to this dilemma with activist public policies that grant maternity, paternity and parental leaves, and federally funded child-care options, which help women (and men) reconcile work and family life. However, not all states respond in the same ways, and they have designed various policies depending on beliefs about the "appropriate" role of the welfare state in society and which societal issues should be considered public or private responsibility.[3] For example, some states, such as the United States, the United Kingdom, and Australia, are oriented around an ideology that stresses the primacy of the market and the privacy of the family, which often leads to policies in which government intervention is minimal in the economy and family life. Many European states are more interventionist and try to moderate the harmful consequences of the market through transferring money and benefits, such as pensions, insurance, and welfare payments, to citizens. Finally, nations such as those in Scandinavia have a much more proactive model of state intervention in order to achieve greater levels of social equality, providing cash benefits as well as a wide array of social services to its population to bring about a more equal society. Each one of these approaches to the welfare state has implications for women.[4]

These differing concepts of the welfare state intersect with state attitudes toward the "ideal" family and "appropriate" gender and family relations, and states enact policies that can reinforce, alter, or transform existing gender relations. For example, some states enact policies that encourage strict divisions of labor, with the husband as earner and the wife as carer, while a few states have enacted policies that have helped redistribute responsibilities and roles within the home, so that both men and women can be workers as well as carers.[5] Often, states send mixed messages regarding their attitudes about managing the balance between women's productive and reproductive roles. They are inconsistent on what aspect of women they value more, and there is a tension between ensuring women's full participation in their domestic and work responsibilities.

In this chapter, we ask how different states have legislated the politics of sex and gender difference with regard to motherhood. We will address these issues by comparing and contrasting what are known as reconciliation policies of various advanced industrialized countries in two areas: parental leave and child care. We discuss four different approaches to balancing the demands of work and parenting: the profamily noninterventionist approach of the United States, the traditional breadwinner model exemplified by Germany, the profamily/pronatalist model of France, and the egalitarian model of Sweden. While all of our case studies (except the United States) have improved their commitment to public spending to help bridge the divide between private and public divisions of labor, designing policy that encourages the redistribution of that divide is a more elusive task.

THE DEBATE OVER RECONCILIATION POLICIES

Welfare state activism regarding family policy precedes the rise of the women's movement, and states historically have been motivated by a variety reasons, many of which are not related to advancing gender equality, to assist families. For example, for many decades, family policies were part of larger, pronatalist campaigns to encourage women to have babies, as well as to maintain the family unit. However, in the post–World War II era, a variety of demographic changes caused states to shift their rhetorical approach. As we discussed in the previous chapter, women's participation in the labor force increased dramatically in the decades following World War II. In particular, women, who had previously left the workforce upon marrying or having children, are now returning to work after getting married and having children. In the United States, 68 percent of married/cohabitating and 66 percent of lone mothers are employed; in France, 68 percent of married/cohabitating mothers and 82 percent of single mothers work; and in Denmark, 85 percent of married/cohabitating mothers and 69 percent of single mothers work, either as full-time or part-time workers.[6] Part of this is because of the satisfaction women receive from employment, and part is because of the increasing difficulties that families face in surviving on one income. This shift in women's employment has brought about increasing demands on the state to help women balance the demands of production and reproduction.[7]

At the same time that women were entering the workforce, feminist movements emerged in many OECD countries and lobbied for policies to address gender inequities in the workforce. In addition, more women were filling the ranks of government bureaucracies and advocating for more female-friendly policies. Finally, in response to these trends, governments were also establishing special commissions, departments, and other bureaus to deal specifically with the condition and status of women in society.

Why should states create policy to help women balance these two parts of their lives? As we learned in the previous chapter, there are numerous laws in place in all of the OECD countries to protect women's equal treatment at the workplace. Shouldn't this be enough to protect women? Further, should we really be talking about parental rights, as opposed to maternal rights, as fathers become more involved in parenting? As we mentioned earlier in this chapter, women are biologically different than men, and thus child-bearing and the early development stage affects them differently. The nine-month process of pregnancy often affects women's health. In addition, the period of childbirth often requires substantial periods of rest and recovery for the mother. The early months of a child's life places further demands on a mother's time and energy; babies need to be fed frequently, and many women breastfeed, meaning that mothers must be in relatively close physical proximity to their newborn infants (although in some Western industrialized countries, the breast pump has helped alleviate this problem for some women). Women simply must perform a larger portion of the responsibilities associated with these activities not because of choice, but because of sex, which is not chosen.

But the demands of motherhood do not end after the initial few months. Traditional gender roles often mean that women carry a "double burden"; not only are they responsible for a variety of duties at work, but they are also responsible for many of the child-rearing and child-care responsibilities at home. If a child becomes sick, it is often the mother who takes off from work to shuttle the child to the doctor, to home, and to bed. Without adequate or affordable day-care or nearby family that can serve in that capacity, many women have trouble working full-time. Many compromise and choose to work part-time in order to balance their varied responsibilities. In fact, many more women than men are employed in part-time labor.[8] In 2000, they made up nearly 68 percent of the part-time labor force in the United States, almost 70 percent in Denmark, nearly

80 percent in the United Kingdom, and just over 80 percent in France. This is not an isolated phenomenon; on average, women in OECD countries make up 71.6 percent of the part-time workforce.[9] As a result, even though women are protected from formal discrimination, many do not advance in their careers as quickly as men or fathers do because the demands of their home lives have taken a toll on their abilities to advance professionally. Women all too often have a different and unequal condition in the home, and inequalities in the home often translate into inequalities at the workforce, despite formal mechanisms that legislate against discrimination.[10]

As discussed in the previous chapter, employers have historically treated women, particularly women of child-bearing age, differently than male colleagues. Employers have an interest in ensuring smooth and uninterrupted periods of work from their workforce in order to facilitate the continued stability of their businesses. Thus, businesses, without the presence of antidiscrimination legislation, have tended to treat women employees gingerly, as they are perceived as a potential business "risk" in that they may need substantial time off to give birth to and care for children. In countries where employers, rather than the state, are responsible for paying benefits, having to provide maternity benefits is also perceived to be a greater financial burden that can be avoided by employing men. Alternatively, businesses underpay women to make up the cost of employing someone that may need more time off or additional benefits. It is only recently that many businesses have realized that in avoiding women employees, they also miss out on tapping some of the most talented people in the application pool. Thus, ensuring that women's differences, whether a result of biology or gendered expectations, do not result in inequality in the public sphere is a challenge.

As we discussed in the previous chapter, some advocates for women's equality argue that states should help women (and men) balance productive and reproductive responsibilities. In addition, they point out that this will be difficult to achieve without changing gender inequalities in the household division of labor. Yet, many disagree about the appropriate solution to resolving the tension between productive and reproductive responsibilities. Should advocates for women's rights support "special treatment" for women or equal treatment for women in the workplace? Historically, as women joined the workforce, states began to pass protective labor legislation based on women's reproductive capacities. Convinced that women needed special treatment, policy makers excluded women from a variety of jobs that might be considered hazardous to their health, allowed them to be paid less than men, or placed them in menial positions. In practice, protective legislation often enforced inequalities between men and women. Women were ghettoized into jobs that were considered women's work, which translated into less desirable jobs with little to no opportunity for advancement. Underneath the veneer of progressive rhetoric, much protective legislation codified a belief that women's appropriate place was at home, raising children, or in temporary jobs that could withstand a revolving workforce.[11]

As a result, advocates for increased attention to the issues of child-rearing faced a dilemma. One the one hand, women's abilities to bear children do make them different, but should legislation then be passed to treat them separately, with explicit maternity benefits? Given that states had historically used women's biological "destiny" as a reason to deny them equal treatment in access to education, employment, and social benefits, activists disagreed on whether to highlight women's biological singularities. On the other hand, women experience a burden that is substantially different from that of mothers, and thus not to acknowledge that in policy design simply creates an extremely uneven playing field in the workplace.

Other women's rights advocates argue that the work involved in raising children is undervalued (most mothers who work in the home are not paid for raising their children). Further, they question the prevailing model of women's participation in the workforce, which often merely pushes them to adopt to a "male" model that values competition and defines "success" in overly narrow, materialistic terms. Working to ensure women's participation in this system merely forces them to adapt to already established "male" rules of the game, rather than transforming them into more humane conditions for all. Some argue that parents (primarily women) who choose to raise their children should receive a yearly allowance or income, thus elevating and highlighting the work of those who choose to define their careers as raising their children. Yet others point out that this solution glorifies the traditional view of motherhood without necessarily challenging the traditional division of labor between men as breadwinners and women as caregivers. In sum, the debates range, not about whether men and women are different, but about what ways this should be acknowledged and remedied in public policy and about which "ideal" family model the state should promote. The tension between balancing work and family, particularly in the public sphere of politics, became a significant campaign issue in the 2008 U.S. presidential elections, as the accompanying text box indicates.

POLICY AREAS

In the following sections, we look at two family policy issues: maternal/parental leave and child-care and preschool provisions for children from birth through age six. Because of the wide variation in countries, we will look at the politics behind these three policy arenas in four types of countries. Each country illustrates a different approach to resolving the tension between production and reproduction and proffers different answers on whose responsibility it is to resolve these questions. States are rarely passive regarding family policy, and resulting programs can both assume and reinforce a family breadwinner role for men and a maternal, wifely, caring role for women or can design policy to help diminish the potency of some of these gendered divisions of labor by redefining traditional roles within the household. The potential effects of these policies can not only enable women to make choices about their lives but can also help ensure equality,

Sarah Palin

Alaska Governor Sarah Palin's bid for the vice presidency of the United States in the 2008 race marked a series of firsts: Palin is the first female governor of Alaska and the first female vice presidential nominee of the Republican Party. Her bid also was extremely controversial; as a working mother of five children, Palin reignited a fiery debate about the issue of women, family, and the workplace in unexpected and unusual ways. While the concept of the female politician as working mother is not new, Palin's bid to become a working mom second in line for the Oval Office was fairly unusual. For one, many female politicians have entered politics when their children are either older or out of the house completely. Palin, mother of five, had, at the time of her nomination, an infant son diagnosed with

Governor Sarah Palin's efforts to balance work and family life touched off numerous debates among women's rights advocates. Here, Palin holds her youngest son, born during her time in office as governor of Alaska. SOURCE: PAUL J. RICHARDS/ AFP/Getty Images

Down's syndrome. In addition, during the campaign, it was revealed that her seventeen-year-old daughter was expecting a child with her boyfriend. Many questioned whether a woman, no matter how talented at multitasking, could successfully serve in such a high-powered office with a small infant with special needs and also tend to the needs of her other four children, one of whom was expecting a baby of her own at a fairly young age. But what was particularly interesting about the public debate was how traditional left-wing and right-wing views flip-flopped. Palin, a Republican candidate who represented the social conservative, religious wing of the party, had a life narrative that seemed to contradict the stated platform of her own party. Traditionally, the Republican Party, as well as Republican voters, has been more leery of the qualifications of working mothers running for office. Surveys conducted by the Pew Research Center[i] found that Republicans were far less likely to support a female candidate who is the mother of young children than were Democrats and were more likely to believe that it was "bad for society" when mothers of young children work outside the home. Yet, Republicans swarmed to her defense, while many Democrats questioned her ability to be both mother of five and serve in such a high-powered position. Supporters of Palin decried the sexism behind the critique; would opponents really have had a problem with her profile if she had been a father, rather than a mother, of five? And women, many of whom were mothers themselves, had strongly held views that polarized them on Palin's candidacy. While Palin was a controversial candidate for women as well as men for many reasons; her personal life history added even more fuel to an already combustible mix of political positions, statements, and actions.

Palin's candidacy also raised, but did not answer, uncomfortable questions about gender equality. Men and women are biologically different, and despite the greater involvement of fathers in traditional "women's activities," studies show that the reality is that parenting and household maintenance is still primarily women's work. Women still shoulder the heavier burden of child-care, housework, and other important caretaking responsibilities. As one columnist asked during the election season, given this reality, "[D]o such obligations make women less suited than men for certain professions or roles?…[W]hen do someone's family commitments rule her out as a strong candidate for a highly responsible position?"[ii] In other words, can women politicians transcend gender when we are still enmeshed in a reality so unequally structured by it?

Politicians who are also women and mothers must maintain a precarious balance. On the one hand, they often have to assert their motherliness—thus Palin described herself on the campaign trail as "just a hockey mom," a traditional, family first kind of woman. Nancy Pelosi, the first woman Speaker of the House and the highest-ranking woman to achieve elected office in the United States, has referred to her journey from "kitchen to Congress," playing up an "I'm just a mom at heart" image. Yet, most female politicians, to succeed in what has traditionally been a "man's world" of politics, have had to pursue unusual trajectories to realize their aspirations. Palin was back at work as governor of Alaska three days after giving birth to her fifth child, as was New York Senator Kirsten Gillibrand. Is it really progress for women, and all working parents, that now women, like men, can also take relatively short breaks from the labor market? Or is this a sign of the relative inflexibility of many careers when it comes to the demands of parenting and work? Alternatively, if this represents these women's authentic choices, is this progress, or does it demonstrate that women still have to adapt to "men's game rules" to compete? Nor is this a uniquely American phenomenon; when French justice minister Rachida Dati returned to work just five days after giving birth by cesarean section (and thus declining to take the sixteen weeks of maternity leave offered to French women), French women (and presumably men) were split over whether this was a feminist breakthrough or a betrayal.

Sarah Palin may have been one of the most recent examples of the ongoing tension between balancing work and family, but she won't be the last. What do you think? Is there a time when a person's family situation makes him or her ineligible for a job that involves significant levels of responsibility, even if he or she freely chooses that option?

_____

i As cited in Lisa Belkin, "Palin Talk," *The New York Times*, October 5, 2008. www.nytimes.com/2008/10/05/magazine/05wwln-lede-t.html?_r=1
ii Christina Bielaszka-DuVernay. "Sarah Palin, Working Mother." *Business Week*, September 9, 2008. http://www.businessweek.com/managing/content/sep2008/ca2008099_703240.htm

not only in the public sphere but in the private realm as well. As a result, we will also delve into whether countries in these regimes enforce traditional visions of appropriate division of labor, tinker with them, or try to alter them.

Maternity, Parental, Paternity, and Family Leaves

Paid maternity leaves were part of a larger movement in the creation of the welfare state in Europe in the latter half of the nineteenth century; in the 1880s, Chancellor Otto von Bismarck in Germany instituted maternity leave benefits as part of a larger package of social insurance programs to prevent worker radicalism from infecting the country. In 1883, the world's first national social insurance law provided for health insurance, paid sick leave, and paid maternity leave. France, facing its own struggles with recalcitrant workers, followed soon after.[12] International organizations picked up the rallying cry for greater rights for women workers in the early twentieth century; in 1919 the International Labor Organization (ILO) adopted a resolution stating that women working in industry or commerce should be entitled to twelve weeks of maternity leave. The ILO also advocated for a cash benefit for mothers.[13] However, widespread adoption of leave policies relating to women did not flourish until the 1960s and 1970s, following the unprecedented rise of labor force participation rates among women in many of the advanced industrial countries, coupled with the rise of women's movements and women's policy machinery that advocated for change.

What do countries currently grant to mothers and fathers of newborns? Around the world, some 128 countries provide paid and job-protected childbirth-related leave. Leave is calculated to be the minimum time considered necessary for the rest and recuperation of the parent. Thus, states define this period of time in different ways, with some states legislating a few weeks' worth of leave, while other states provide several months, even up to a year, of leave. On average, leave is for about four months and includes time off both before and after the birth. For the twenty-nine OECD countries, the average childbirth-related leave, including paid and unpaid, is almost one and a half years. In a few instances, leave is mandatory.[14]

Most parents cannot afford to take time off from work unless they are paid some level of compensation; thus, continuity of income during leave is a critical issue. In most cases, this leave is paid, and in half of the countries that provide maternity leave, leave replaces the full wage.[15] Other states issue a flat monthly benefit, regardless of the women's previous earnings. More frequently, however, states calculate benefits according to past earnings. In many countries, benefits are paid for by the state, through national social security agencies. In over forty countries around the world, the employer pays benefits. Finally, in about fifteen countries, the responsibility for covering the costs of maternity leave is shared between social security and the employer.[16] However, relying on employers to cover the costs of maternity leave is problematic. As mentioned previously, this added cost often discourages firms from recruiting women and may be a factor in explaining why women's wages are lower than men's: Firms are trying to find a way to recoup the "loss" of potentially paying out maternity benefits.

Countries have also become increasingly flexible in defining who is eligible for leave. In the 1980s and 1990s, as feminist movements pushed for, among other things, the redistribution of responsibilities within the home, some states began enacting policies that encouraged male as well as female participation in the task of child-rearing by granting parental leaves, paternity leaves, and family leaves. This trend is most well developed in the Scandinavian countries, as well as in a few other industrialized nations.[17]

Maternity leave, which is the most common policy, provides job-protected leaves from employment for employed women at the time they are due to give birth as well as an amount of time following the birth. Other countries grant parental leaves, which are gender-neutral, job-protected leaves from employment that follow the same guidelines as maternity leaves or offer additional time off to care for an infant, toddler, or sick child. However, in this scenario, either men or women may share the leave or choose which one of them will use it. Recently, in some countries, part of the parental leave is reserved for fathers on a "use it or lose it" basis to encourage fathers to play a more active parenting role. While maternity leave is usually paid, the conditions accompanying parental leave are more varied and tend to be less generous. Many countries provide unpaid parental leave, which places severe constraints on families in need of a continued income. For example, in the United States, where parental leave is unpaid, 63.9 percent of workers with family responsibilities and in need of time off chose not to take advantage of the benefit because they could not afford to do so.[18] In contrast, other countries provide specific paternity leaves, which are job-protected leaves for fathers. The conditions behind the leave are similar to maternity and parental leave, but specifically target men to encourage them to be more engaged in family life. However, they are usually much briefer than maternity leaves, supplement maternity leaves, are more likely to be unpaid, and are usually important for families in which a second child is born. In this scenario, for example, the father may take time off to care for the eldest child as well as provide help to the mother and the newborn. Finally, family leaves are granted to care for an ill child or to meet parental obligations, such as parent-teacher meetings once the child is no longer covered by various maternity/parental leave policies. This benefit is also often covered under parental leave policies.

Table 5.1 provides a summary of how some OECD countries have resolved the issue of maternity, parental, paternity, and family leave. It is important to remember that even in countries with generous provisions, all women are not covered. Home workers are frequently excluded, as are women employed in small enterprises. In sum, how countries define leave is critical. Vital issues to consider are whether leave is paid or unpaid, levels of payments as well as duration of benefits, and the beneficiaries of the leave.

Table 5.1 Parental Leave Policies in OECD Countries, 1998–2002

COUNTRY	DURATION OF CHILDBIRTH-RELATED LEAVE	% OF WAGE REPLACED
Australia	1 year parental	Unpaid
Austria	16 weeks maternity; 8 weeks before/ 8 weeks after birth (mandated)	100% Flat rate
	Parental leave replaced by child-care allowance for 30 months if child care is shared by both parents	Higher rate for single- and low-income parents
Belgium	15 weeks maternity	75–80%
	3 months parental for each parent	Low flat-rate benefit
	3 days paternity	
Canada	17 weeks maternity	55%
	35 weeks parental for each parent	55%
	3 days paternity	
Czech Republic	28 weeks maternity	69%
	37 weeks for multiple births or single mother	Unpaid
	Parental leave until child turns 3	
Denmark	18 weeks maternity including 4 weeks prebirth	90%
	10 weeks parental	60%
	2 weeks paternity	100%
	Child-care leave up to 52 weeks for either parent up to child's 8th birthday	60%
Finland	18 weeks maternity	65%
	26 weeks parental	
	Child-rearing leave of absence until child is age 3, or can opt for home-care or child-care allowances (under age 7)	Flat rate

Table 5.1 (*continued*)

COUNTRY	DURATION OF CHILDBIRTH-RELATED LEAVE	% OF WAGE REPLACED
France	Guaranteed right to part-time work	
	Paternity: 18 days	
	16 weeks for first 2 children including compulsory 6 weeks before birth	100% for maternity and paternity leaves; flat rate, income-tested
	26 weeks for 3rd child	
	Postbirth leave applies to adoptions as well	
	3 days paternity	80%
	Parental leave with two or more children up to child's 3rd birthday	
Germany	14 weeks maternity including 6 weeks before birth	100%
	13 years parental/child-rearing leave full- or part-time up until child's 8th birthday	Flat rate/income-tested for 2 years; unpaid for 3rd year
Greece	17 weeks maternity	50%
	3.5 months parental leave for each parent	Unpaid
Hungary	24 weeks maternity	70%
	Child-rearing leave up to a child's 3rd birthday	Flat rate/income-tested
Iceland	3 months each for mother and father; one parent also can take an additional 3 months, for a total of 9 months parental leave; the 9-month leave may spread over the first 18 months after birth	80%
Ireland	18 weeks maternity including up to 4 weeks before birth	70%
	14 weeks parental leave	Unpaid
	Maternity and parental leave cover adoption	
	3 days paid family or emergency leave	
Italy	5 months maternity including 1 month prebirth	80%
	Additional 10 months parental leave, 20 months for multiple births	30%
	Fathers applying for 3-month leave be granted an extra month	
	Unused parental leave can be taken until the child's 9th birthday	
	Family (sick) leave: 5 days/year for children 3–8 years old	Paid
Japan	14 weeks (6 prebirth and 8 postbirth)	60%
	Additional year up to child's first birthday	Unpaid

(*continued*)

Table 5.1 (*continued*)

COUNTRY	DURATION OF CHILDBIRTH-RELATED LEAVE	% OF WAGE REPLACED
Korea, South	8 weeks maternity	Unpaid
Luxembourg	16 weeks maternity	100%
	Parental leave is 6 months full-time or 12 months part-time or prorated up to child's 5th birthday	Flat rate
	2 days/year family leave	
Mexico	12 weeks maternity (6 weeks prebirth)	100%
Netherlands	16 weeks maternity	100%
	16 months parental leave per parent	Unpaid
	2 days paternity	Paid
	Family leave: 10 days/year	
	12 days emergency leave	
New Zealand	12 weeks paid parental leave (July 2002); may opt for parental tax credit in lieu of paid parental leave	Lower of 100% wages or flat rate
	Extended parental leave	Unpaid
Norway	52 weeks parental leave (or 42 weeks at 100%), including maternity	80%
	Child-rearing leave up to age 2	Flat rate
	4 weeks paternity leave, "use it or lose it"	
Poland	16 weeks maternity leave; 18 for subsequent births; 26 weeks for multiple births	100%
	Additional 24-month leave, 36 months for single parent	Flat rate
	Additional 12 months for single parent	
Portugal	6 weeks mandated maternity leave postbirth	100%
	Additional 6–24 months parental leave; includes adoption	Unpaid
	5 days paternity leave	
	Up to 30 days/year family leave for children under age 10 and 15 days for over age 10	
	Special leave up to 4 years for sick child	
	Right to part-time work	
Spain	16 weeks maternity; may transfer up to 10 weeks to father; 2 additional weeks maternity per child in multiple births	100%
	Additional parental leave until child is 3	Unpaid
	2 days paternity leave	100%
Sweden	Full parental leave until child is 18 months; includes adoption	80%
	13 months	Flat
	13 months	Unpaid

Table 5.1 (*continued*)

COUNTRY	DURATION OF CHILDBIRTH-RELATED LEAVE	% OF WAGE REPLACED
	Maternity leave may begin 60 days prior to expected delivery and 6 weeks after birth	
	Parental leave can be used full- or part-time until child's 8th birthday	
	Additional 6 months for each child if multiple births	
Switzerland	16 weeks maternity	Varies by canton
	Right to part-time work until child is 8	
Turkey	12 weeks maternity	66 $\frac{2}{3}$%
United Kingdom	18 weeks ordinary maternity leave (up to 11 weeks prior to birth); includes adoption	6 weeks at 90%, 12 weeks at flat rate; varies by employment
	Additional maternity leave of 11 weeks for women who've completed 1 year service with employer	
	13 weeks parental leave up to child's 5th birthday	Unpaid
	18 weeks parental leave for disabled child up to child's 18th birthday	Flat rate
United States	12 weeks family leave, includes maternity	Unpaid

SOURCE: The Clearinghouse on International Developments in Child, Youth and Family Policies at Columbia University, http:///www.childpolicyintl.org/maternity.html (January 6, 2004).

Family Allowances

In addition, many states provide a wide array of child and family cash and tax benefits to defray the costs of child-rearing. Worldwide, eighty-eight countries provide some form of child or family allowances.[19] Allowances vary, depending on family size, family income, and employment status. For example, in a study of twenty-one industrialized countries, thirteen provided child and family allowances to all families, regardless of income, while eight based eligibility and benefit levels on income. Only one country (the United States) provided no form of family allowances to defray the costs of child-rearing.[20] Benefits are generally extended to children from birth to the age of majority or completion of formal education. The maximum age limit is twenty-six, although disabled children may qualify regardless of age. Some countries provide a uniform rate per child, regardless of the number of children per family, while other countries increase the rate after each additional child. For example, in France, benefits are not issued until the birth of the second child.[21] The benefits are usually relatively small (often less than 10 percent of average wages), but they are nonetheless a vital part of family income. Allowances are often further supplemented by birth grants (a lump sum granted at the birth of the child), prenatal and breastfeeding allowances, school grants, child-rearing or child-care allowances, adoption benefits, supplements for single parents, and so on. A few states make the collection of supplemental parental benefits contingent on other factors. For example, the French government will revoke the benefit of a flat-rate prenatal allowance from women who fail to undergo the prescribed prenatal medical examination.[22] Finally, some countries provide tax benefits to parents for having children. All of these benefits and services can help ease the financial burdens of child-rearing.

Governments have been motivated by a variety of factors. Initially, many of these policies were designed not to help women balance work and family life but as part of larger pronatalist campaigns to encourage women to have children. However, these policies did not encourage women to substantially increase the size of their families, and in fact, birthrates have continued to fall across Europe despite the increasing generosity of benefits. In addition, child and family allowances are part of an effort to redistribute income from childless households to families with children, given the increased financial burden associated with child-rearing. Alternatively, states are motivated to supplement the incomes of poor or lower-income families as a means of reducing or preventing poverty. Other countries want to encourage parents (primarily women) to engage more fully in the task of child-rearing, and thus offer incentives for a parent potentially to stay at home with the child rather than return to the workforce. In contrast, other countries are trying to facilitate greater participation in the labor force, and offer generous benefits so that parents can balance work with family life. Finally, these policies are not necessarily motivated by gender concerns; states support child and family allowances to increase social cohesion, particularly among families. It is only in the past few decades that debates over family benefits have become tinged with gendered concerns about women's responsibilities at work and in the home.

If we look more closely, how do our four case studies interpret the responsibilities of the welfare state, and how do these policies in turn reinforce or transform gender relations? The following section contrasts the policies of the United States, Germany, France, and Sweden.

Profamily/Noninterventionist Model: The United States

The United States is singular in its treatment of parents; of the OECD countries, it has the least generous maternity or family leave policy and, until 1993, when the Family Medical Leave Act (FMLA) was passed, did not have a federal policy defining and granting parental leave. The policy that did pass is extremely limited. The act applies only to employers with fifty or more employees. In addition, although employees are allowed to take twelve weeks off a year to care for a newborn, newly adopted, or foster child; a child, spouse, or parent with a serious health condition; or a serious health condition of the employee, the leave is unpaid. As a result, many people cannot afford to take the time off. Further, employees may be required to first use up accrued sick leave or vacation time to cover part or the complete duration of the leave. Finally, employers may deny leave to an employee within the highest paid 10 percent of its workforce, if letting the worker take leave would create a problem for the firm. With all of these adjustments and further specifications, 45 percent of workers are not covered by the act.[23] Nor does the law cover care for grandparents, grandchildren, in-laws, or domestic partners. Even with these limited provisions, the bill was vetoed twice by President George H. Bush. Upon its passage (for the third time) by Congress, it became President Clinton's first signed piece of legislation in 1993.[24]

In fact, in 1985, when Congresswoman Patricia Schroeder (D-CO) introduced the nation's first family leave bill (and the first version of what was to become the FMLA), 135 countries had established maternity leave benefit programs, and of those, all but 10 provided for some form of paid leave.[25] Of the OECD nations, the United States and Australia are the only nations that do not offer federally mandated paid leave for parents (although Australia offers up to a year of unpaid parental leave, in comparison to the U.S. policy of twelve weeks). This policy inaction is not for lack of trying; since 1942, various government agencies have attempted to implement a family leave policy. The U.S. Department of Labor originally proposed a fourteen-week leave, in which women could take the six weeks preceding and eight weeks following the birth of a child. However, the United States did not follow in the footsteps of its European counterparts in the 1960s and 1970s, which substantially redesigned their national policies toward working mothers. Rather, policy evolved at the state level. However, even in the 1980s, states were slow to enact legislation; by 1987, only nine states had a maternity leave law in place, and by 1989, another fourteen states had added provisions for maternity (three) or parental (eleven) leave. All of these policies granted unpaid leave only.[26] In fact, in 2004, California made history when it became first state in the nation to provide its workforce with comprehensive paid family leave.

Although the federal government did not pass legislation until 1993, many businesses had already begun to offer leave options. According to one study of 279 U.S. businesses, in the late 1950s, only 5 percent of companies offered leave; however, by 1985, over half offered it. Nonetheless, this increase was not because companies voluntarily decided to help women and men balance family responsibilities with work. Rather, most implemented leave policies in response to a 1972 EEOC ruling that stated that companies that offered leave for temporary disability had to also allow leave for maternity. Although this requirement was later overturned by the Supreme Court (but was then subsequently voted into law by Congress in 1978), nonetheless many companies in the early to mid-1970s implemented leave policies out of fear of lawsuits or as a result of the negative publicity generated by lawsuits.[27] In fact, besides taking sick leave, claiming temporary disability benefits is currently one of the few ways that women can receive financial remuneration during their leave; unless an individual company offers paid leave, or one lives in California, there is no other option for recouping some of the income lost from time off from work.

Nor was the FMLA touted as a feminist bill; in fact, neither political party was willing to frame it as a "prowoman" issue. Instead, the Democratic Party claimed it as a "prolabor" measure, while the Republicans who helped pass it used the legislation to bolster their image as a "profamily" party.[28] (In fact, Henry Hyde, a Republican, switched his vote to supporting the bill because he thought that it would discourage women from having an abortion.[29]) In the end, both labor and families ended up with the least generous benefits of any country in the OECD. Further, women's groups argued over the conditions and framing of FMLA; some advocated for wording that would grant women leave, while others wanted to make the language gender neutral and applicable to either men or women. The battle over whether leave should be defined as "special treatment" for women versus "equal treatment" for everyone was eventually won by the "equal treatment" advocates, who argued that benefits should go to all workers, and not just parents. While this may have seemed like a reasonable strategy in the wake of charged arguments about affirmative action, it ended up creating less advantageous benefits for women than policies created by states, such as California, that offered a specific maternity leave policy.[30]

Why has the United States tended to lag behind other countries in this area, especially in an era when "family values" are omnipresent in political debate? For one, the United States has long exemplified a political culture that is suspicious of an interventionist state, or what is more often framed in the press as "big government." In addition, it embraces an individualist culture and touts a free market rhetoric, which also emphasizes the negative aspects of an interventionist state. Thus, when President George H. W. Bush vetoed the FMLA for the second time in 1992, he commented that "I want to strongly reiterate that I have always supported employer policies to give time off for a child's birth or adoption or for family illness and believe it is important that employers offer these benefits. I object, however, to the Federal Government mandating leave policies for America's employers and workforce."[31] Similarly, Bob Dole, in the first presidential debate against President Bill Clinton in 1996, declared his opposition to the FMLA; he also argued that Congress should not have used the "long arm of the federal government" to pass FMLA to make employers offer leave.[32] Both Bush and Dole offered a variety of other incentives that would encourage businesses to grant leave, while stopping short of mandating it; both echoed suspicion of an overreaching federal government and worried about the effects of federal governments "tampering" with business practices. A second potential answer lies in the nature of the decentralized American system, in which much policy is left in the hands of individual states. Finally, unions, which have been a driving force in advocating for greater levels of worker benefits, are relatively weak in the United States, compared to other European countries. As a result, another pressure point that had been utilized by other countries was not really an option for U.S. workers.[33] The result is that the United States has a very limited family policy, and pervasive cultural values that emphasize individualism and limited government interference in family matters further enforce America's singular approach to reconciliation policies.

Traditional Breadwinner Model: Germany

Germany implements a different approach to maternity and family leave. The German model of benefits is one that encourages a two-parent, one-earner family and reinforces a traditional division of labor between men and women in the household. Reunification, in which East and West Germany merged into a united Germany, further complicated Germany's benefits model, as two distinct cultures (and benefits models) had to be merged into one.

Germany was the trailblazer for the concept of the modern "welfare state"; Otto von Bismarck was the mastermind behind Germany's fledgling social insurance system, which laid out the framework for a variety of benefits for the unemployed, the sick, and, for our purposes, the pregnant. In the post–World War II era, two systems of benefits evolved. East Germany (GDR) adopted a Soviet-style system of benefits that encouraged women's full-time employment in the workforce with generous leave benefits. Thus, in the 1980s, the GDR had a nearly 90 percent female labor force participation rate, and women were also entitled to twenty-six weeks of leave with a 90–100 percent wage replacement rate. In 1986, three years before the collapse of the GDR, East German women were granted an additional seven months of paid leave. They were also given one day of additional leave per month for housework, a reduced work week for having two or more children, and additional weeks of leave to care for sick children. The model, though generous, did not challenge the division of labor in the household by designing policy to encourage fathers to participate in child care or housework. In West Germany (FRG), a much lower percentage of women worked; in 1990, before unification, the female labor participation rate was about 58 percent.[34] Further, unemployment among women was high, and the government did relatively little to address this issue with proactive policy.

When Germany unified in 1990, West German policy replaced that of the East. The West German policies were designed to preserve the traditional nuclear family, with a single breadwinner and an "at-home" mother caring for the children. Maternity leaves are paid, job-protected leaves for fourteen weeks (including six weeks before childbirth). Further, in the 1980s, Germany implemented a parental leave policy (*Elternzeit*) in response to women's growing demands for better services to accommodate their work schedule, and since 1992, parental leave covers the child's first three years, although this leave is accompanied by a much smaller financial benefit. Both mothers and fathers who work in firms that have more than fifteen employees are entitled to this parental leave, and, as of 2001, both parents can take leave at the same time.

In addition, the German government offers a child-rearing allowance (*Erziehungsgeld*). This allowance, about $300 a month, subsidizes the care needs of the first two years of a child's life. However, it requires that one parent (overwhelmingly the mother) be designated the full-time caregiver or work part-time.[35] This is just one part of a larger, more complex system of child benefits known as *Kindergeld.* As we shall discuss later in the chapter, these benefits are generous, but they also encourage primarily women to take three years off of work, and then to return to work part-time afterward. As a result, women tend not to advance as far in their careers, and the end result is that the German model reinforces a family model of a male breadwinner and female caregiver.[36]

Profamily/Pronatalist Model: France

France has implemented a very different system from those implemented in America or Germany. The French policy is designed simultaneously to attract women to the workforce during times of labor shortages while also encouraging higher birthrates. The pronatalist goal originated in the Napoleonic era, when large armies were needed for various military campaigns, but was also encouraged by a large and vocal Catholic population.[37] However, the pronatalist policies have done little to increase France's fertility rate. In fact, fertility rates continue to drop from 2.3 in 1970–1975 to 1.9 in 2000–2005 (which is lower than the U.S. rate of 2.1).[38] Nonetheless, France has one of the most generous family policies in the world, which supports parents and children from infancy to adulthood.

France implemented a maternity leave policy in 1928 and rapidly expanded its family policies in the post–World War II era. Currently, job-protected maternity leave extends for sixteen weeks (six of which are taken before birth) at 80 percent of earnings for the first and second children. That leave is extended for third and fourth children. Parental leave, which follows maternity leave, was introduced in 1985 and further modified in 1994. Workers have the right to take unpaid leave (and with the second and subsequent children, leave is paid) for up to three years and then return to the same or a similar job at the same pay. Unlike in the United States, employers cannot refuse the leave (although workers must give at least one month notice before taking the leave). Further, men may take paternity leave, which as of January 2002 granted fathers fourteen days of paid, job-protected leave. Finally, all working parents can take up to five paid days a year to care for a sick child under the age of sixteen. In addition, a parent may claim four months of job-protected, paid leave to care for a seriously ill child.

France continues to implement policies to encourage women to have more children. In the early 1980s, the government implemented a "third child package," which extended benefits in three ways. First, the duration of maternity leave was increased from sixteen to twenty-six weeks for the third child and any subsequent births. Second, women's cash benefits were increased substantially for the birth of a third child and subsequent children. Third, mothers of three children were given an old-age pension credit (previously available to mothers who had raised four children).[39] France also offers a child-rearing benefit, which is a flat rate amount awarded to parents, regardless of income, if they have at least two children. The benefits continue until the child turns twenty. The amount is adjusted yearly but amounts to about one-half of the French minimum wage.

There are additional benefits, such as increased allowances for families with three or more children, a young child allowance, a single parent allowance, an allowance to subsidize costs of in-home care for children under three, and a housing allowance. These benefits, although usually not enough to equal an income, nonetheless comprise a crucial part of family budgets: 14 percent for those with two children, 29 percent for families with three children, and 45 percent for those with four or more children. There are also child-care tax credits to offset some of the costs of child care for working parents.[40] Despite the enduring pronatalist legacies of these policies, as we shall see later on in the chapter, these policies, combined with early childhood education programs, promote a system in which parents can choose to work or stay at home. Nonetheless, it is usually women who make the choice to opt out of the workforce.

Egalitarian Model: Sweden

Finally, in contrast to the other three models, Sweden has designed a series of policy initiatives to encourage an egalitarian model of child-rearing. First, the Swedish model is based on the presumption that children will be better off both economically and developmentally if they bond early with both parents in a family that is financially stable. Second, Sweden encourages a "dual breadwinner" model, in which pay equity between men and women is a major goal. Third, Sweden designed a parental leave policy to encourage men to take more time off from work.

Sweden's approach to maternity and parental leave policy evolved out of the Great Depression, when birthrates were considered to be dangerously low. Two academics, Alva and Gunnar Myrdal, in their book *Crisis in the Population Question,* urged increased government intervention to improve the well-being of families, and hence their desire to bear children. The Swedish government responded with legislation that encouraged society as a whole, rather than just women, to display a commitment to family life.

Currently, Sweden has a complex policy that includes stipulations for maternity leave, parental leave, and several provisions specifically addressed to fathers. All women are guaranteed fourteen weeks of leave (including up to seven before childbirth), including some wage replacement. Fathers are granted two weeks of paternity leave after childbirth. Parental leave was initiated in 1974 and has changed numerous times since then. Currently, each parent can take an additional eighteen months of full-time leave that includes a benefit allowance. This also includes wage replacement of 80 percent for the first year, with a flat rate for the following months. Although there is a cap of about $33,000 a year on benefits, nonetheless, this represents a substantial investment from the state in supporting parenting. Further, the Swedish model of benefits is quite flexible; parents may work half-time or quarter-time and receive partial financial benefits. However, what separates the Swedish model from others is its approach to encouraging fathers to take leave. Under law, 30 of the 450 days of parental leave must be taken by the father. They are not transferable to the mother and are lost if not used by the father. This policy was designed to encourage fathers to take advantage of parental leave; past experience had demonstrated that parental leave, unless specifically directed at fathers, was overwhelmingly taken by women. Further, working parents (and grandparents) may take up to 60 pays a year of paid leave to care for a sick child (and grandchild). Finally, Sweden grants parents a cash allowance to any family with one or more children under the age of sixteen. In 2001, this amount equaled about $100.[41]

As we shall discuss, in combination with their early childhood education and care system, the Swedish model promotes a more egalitarian division of labor between men and women rather than reinforcing traditional gendered divisions of labor. This fits in with a Swedish culture that stresses the importance of maintaining a balance between work and family life.

Impact

All of these policies tell us something about how states view the challenge of balancing public and private responsibilities for parenting and the "appropriate" division of labor within the household. Of all of our case studies, the United States has provided the most minimal intervention in terms of facilitating parents' abilities to manage work and family, despite the recurring invocation of family values in political discourse. The lack of accompanying financial benefits makes it difficult for poor and lower-income families to take advantage of the FMLA. In contrast, our other case studies provide much more generous support to enable families of all income levels to take time off from work, thus minimizing the incidence of child poverty.

Yet, often, policies can be deceiving. For example, what are we to make of generous maternity benefits? Certainly, they can help ease women's responsibilities at work and acknowledge that giving birth to a child, and then raising that child, is a difficult, time-consuming process that is also extremely valuable to society. However, policies can also be interpreted as a statement about where women "should" be spending the majority of their time once they have children. For example, Germany has a generous leave policy because historically, women have not been expected to return to work or to return to a full-time position, and the assumption has been that the man will continue to be the primary breadwinner.

A maternity leave policy that allows women significant amounts of time off from work may help her balance the varied competing demands placed upon her, but it may not advance her long-term economic interests. For example, on the one hand, one study of women workers in Britain, Japan, and the United States demonstrated that granting leave has encouraged women to return to work after the birth of their child.[42] Presumably, this is because they know that their job will still be available to them. Thus, despite business fears that mandating leave would result in increased complications because of a constantly changing workforce, in fact, most employers did not use up their full leave time and returned to work when they were ready. However, women with children who do work are still less likely to advance as quickly as men, even men who also have children. Thus, while various leave policies have helped protect women in the workforce, the policies have not altered their position of power within the workforce significantly. Women who have children make significantly less than men, while men actually receive a pay boost after they have children. This can be because of a variety of reasons; traditional gender roles often place pressure on men to be even more productive after the birth of a child to "provide" for their families, while it is more socially acceptable for women to ease out of a grueling work schedule. Alternatively, when women have children, employers see them as an employment risk, while they interpret the same development as a sign of stability and commitment from a male employee. Regardless, while maternity leave policies have helped women stay active in the workforce, either as part-time or full-time employees, they have not necessarily helped women earn more at the workplace vis-à-vis men or advance in other ways in their careers.

In fact, research shows that the more generous the leave policy, the less likely that the woman will return to full-time work.[43] Thus, the United States, which has the least generous leave policy, also has the highest percentage of women employed full-time in the workforce. Certainly, we are not arguing that progress for women is solely exemplified by their abilities to work full-time outside of the home; many women choose different work paths to meet their personal wants and needs, and many freely choose to scale back work responsibilities in the face of family needs. However, there are ramifications for women who choose to work part-time or to leave the paid workforce completely. This often lessens their financial independence, increasing their reliance on a male "breadwinner" model of family relations, as well as their dependence on the state. While women may be choosing to work less, the side effect of this decision is less economic power within the household, which can have serious implications if the family unit dissolves or is reconfigured. Further, it has serious ramifications for the level of women's pension benefits when they retire. Thus, it is important to evaluate varying parental leave plans carefully and to think about the long-term ramifications of each system for reinforcing or reconfiguring family dynamics.

Some of this impact could be lessened by radically restructuring the division of labor within families. You may have also noticed the overwhelming focus on women in this chapter, even though many countries are now implementing paternity, parental, and family leave policies. Why all the discussion of mothers' rights if states are making leave an option for so many men? Although some states have been very proactive in terms of encouraging the redistribution of labor within the area of child-rearing by extending parental leave to fathers, men have been slow to take full advantage of the opportunities available to them. For example, look at the information presented in Table 5.2. Even when men have the opportunity to take parental leave, they rarely take it. The reasons for this are multifaceted; when given the option of who should take leave, couples may fall back on traditional societal norms in which it is more accepted for women to take time off. Also, given that, on average, men make a much higher salary than women,

Table 5.2 National Take-up Rates of Parental Leave

COUNTRY	PERCENT TAKE-UP RATE BY WOMEN	PERCENT TAKE-UP BY MEN	PATERNITY LEAVE PERCENT TAKE-UP
Austria	90%	1%	
Denmark	93%	3%	58.2%
Finland	99%	64%	64%
Germany	95%	1%	
Netherlands	40%	9%	
Norway	94%	33%	80%
Portugal	100%	N/A	
Spain	100%	N/A	
Sweden	90%	78%	
United States	36%	34%	

SOURCE: Columbia University, The Clearinghouse on International Developments in Child, Youth and Family Policies, http://www.childpolicyintl.org/ (April 22, 2006).

it may be more difficult for families to absorb the costs of paternal leave unless the benefits are quite generous. Research has demonstrated that policy design also matters; men are much more likely to take advantage of leave benefits when they are framed as paternity leave benefits rather than the more neutral "parental leave."[44] This points to the limitations of designing "gender-neutral" policies in a context of extreme gender imbalances. Sometimes more proactive policies are necessary to change long-standing habitual actions. Regardless, unless fathers use their benefits or find alternative ways to be more involved in parenting, the unequal distribution of labor that pervades the household will continue to impact women's abilities to participate successfully in the workforce.

Early Childhood Education and Care

Women's work, however, does not end after the birth of a child. Parental obligations continue to complicate workers,' particularly women workers' lives, as they search to balance family obligations with professional responsibilities. Because women are still often responsible for child-rearing activities, the presence of daycare (usually available for children from birth to age three) and preschool education (usually available for children age three to six), its availability, and the degree to which it is funded by the state have significant implications for women and their reintegration into the workforce. Child care has become increasingly important in the wake of significant demographic and attitudinal shifts: Women's entrance into the workforce, the need to keep women in the labor market at a time when skilled labor is at a premium, an increase in single-parent households, as well as the importance attached to good educational services for young children have all led to a marked increase in demand for state services.[45] Thus, another critical question is the role of the state in providing public child-care facilities.

Historically, daycare for children grew out of the charitable movement to help poor and working-class mothers. In the wake of World War II, governments began to take over the costs and responsibilities for providing daycare in the wake of the large influx of women workers into economic activity.[46] States rapidly increased their commitment to providing daycare in the 1970s, partly in response to the critical mass of women in the labor force as well as their demands for more services. Currently, all OECD countries provide universal, publicly funded education for children starting at the age of five to seven, and most provide some form of publicly funded and publicly delivered daycare in order to lessen the financial burdens on parents. As one can see in Table 5.3, however, the countries differ substantially with regard to the scope of the daycare policy, the source of funding for daycare, as well as in the eligibility, access, and coverage for daycare. In addition, across all countries, despite the strides countries have made in providing daycare, demand in many countries outstrips supply. While there is adequate daycare in many countries for children ages three to six (of the nineteen countries for which we have data, over 80 percent of children from the ages of three to six are in part-time or full-time daycare), providing good care for infants and toddlers is still a challenge for almost all OECD countries. The result is that many women choose to opt out of the labor market or work part-time until their children are old enough to stay in care full-time. Again, this is problematic in the sense that it tends to lessen women's abilities to advance their careers, which in turn has consequences for their short-term and long-term financial autonomy.

We shall discuss three approaches to the task of balancing production and reproduction. The United States provides minimal coverage, assuming relatively little responsibility for the task of daycare. In this scenario, the government leaves it to the private sector and to individual parents to provide daycare, and the financial burden of daycare falls primarily on the parents' shoulders. Other countries, such as Germany, are more proactive in providing publicly funded daycare. However, often this coverage does not start until age three or is provided in such a way to encourage male full-time employment and female part-time employment. A third group of countries, such as France and Sweden, have attempted to provide comprehensive daycare so that either parent may enter the workforce with the greatest freedom possible.

Profamily/Noninterventionist Model: The United States

The United States stands alone in its record of support for working mothers. While the government subsidizes the cost of daycare in most OECD countries, in the United States parents are responsible for covering the majority of the costs. Further, while in many OECD countries the coverage of the programs is universal and all children are eligible regardless of parents' income or employment status, the United States provides federally funded daycare for neglected, abused, and/or low-income children only, as well as a part-day educational nursery school for middle- and upper-class children ages five and up. Britain and Canada

Table 5.3 Child-Care Provisions in Selected OECD Countries

COUNTRY	LOCUS OF POLICY MAKING—NATIONAL OR LOCAL	AGE GROUP SERVED	ELIGIBILITY CRITERIA—UNIVERSAL, POOR, WITH SPECIAL NEEDS, WORKING PARENTS	FUNDING SOURCES (GOVT., EMPLOYER, PARENT FEES, COMB.)
Austria	State/local	3–6	Working parents	State and local govt., parent fees
		0–3	Working parents	
Belgium	State	2½–6	Universal	Govt.—free to parents
		Under 3	Working parents, special needs, poor	Multiple, including govt., employer, parent fees (income-related)
Canada	State	5–6	Universal	Govt.—free
		Under 5	Special needs, poor, working parents	Mixed; largely parent fees
Denmark	National and local (primarily)	5–7	Universal	Govt.
		6 mos.–6 years	Working parents	Govt. (local), parent fees (income-related—max. 20–30% of costs)
Finland	National and local	6	Universal	National and local govt., parent fees (income-related—approx.10% of costs)
		1–7	Universal—priority for working parents	
France	National (primarily) and local	2–6	Universal	Govt.—free to parents
		3 mos.–3 years	Working parents, special needs	Mixed; local govt., family allowance funds parent fees (income-related— max. 25% of costs)

Country	Level of government	Age group	Target population	Funding
Germany	State	3–6	Universal	State and local govts. plus parent fees (income-wrelated—max. 16–20% of costs)
		Under 3	Special needs, poor, working parents	
Italy	National	3–6	Universal	Nat'l govt., free
	Local	Under 3	Working parents	Local govt., parent fees (income-related—average 12% of costs, max. 20%)
New Zealand	National	Under 6	Universal	Nat'l govt., parent fees
Spain	State/local	0–6	Universal	Govt., free
		Under 3	Universal (3–6)	Govt., parent fees (income-related—max 20% of costs)
Sweden	National and local (primarily)	0–6	Universal, working parents, special needs	National and local govt., parent fees (income-related—about 13% of costs)
United Kingdom	National/local	3–4	Special needs, poor	Govt., free
		0–4		Free or income-related fees
United States	National/local	5	Universal	State and local govt.
		0–4	Special needs, poor, welfare, working parents	Federal/state/local govt. Parent fees cover approx. 76% of costs

SOURCE: Adapted from Sheila B. Kamerman, "Early Childhood Education and Care (ECEC): An Overview of Developments in the OECD Countries." Unpublished paper, date not provided.

also subscribe to a model that conflates federally funded daycare with welfare programs.[47] The only system of benefits that the United States does offer for parents with children in daycare is a variety of indirect tax credits. The IRS offers a credit against owed taxes equal to the percentage of a family's income spent of child care, although the amount is capped at $4,800.[48] In sum, the expectation is that the state should intervene only in the event of market or family breakdown. Otherwise, families and individuals are expected to support and care for themselves. For those who cannot provide for themselves, the state has provided a minimum safety net.

In the United States, federal funding for child care has been used to respond to perceived emergency situations and pressing social problems. The first federal investment in child care was made during the 1930s, during the years of the Great Depression, as a way to provide jobs for the unemployed and to provide child care assistance to poor families. However, as the economy improved, the program was canceled.[49] The U.S. entrance into World War II, which generated an enormous demand for female labor, once again brought the issue of publicly funded daycare to the fore of the political arena, and for a brief period during World War II, child-care services were subsidized with public tax dollars. From 1942 to 1946, the federal government financed a preschool program for children of working mothers in "war impact areas." This wartime federally funded child-care service expanded to more than three thousand centers in forty-seven states. While congressmen initially were reluctant to fund the program, they were eventually persuaded by the practical problems presented by women's influx into the labor market as men left to fight the war in the Europe. Despite widespread protest from mothers, federal policy makers moved to terminate the program at the war's end.[50]

The rise of the feminist movement in the late 1960s rekindled the issue, and in the 1970s, local feminist groups were active in building community daycare centers, run cooperatively by parents. In addition, the National Organization for Women fought for the passage of the Comprehensive Child Development Act of 1971, which would have provided federal funding for daycares, open to all parents, on a sliding fee basis. Although Congress passed the bill with bipartisan support, President Nixon vetoed the measure.[51] Similar to the rhetoric used two decades later by President Bush to veto the FMLA, Nixon expressed symbolic support for working parents but stopped short of offering federal financial support. Arguing that the government's intervention should be kept to a minimum, he vetoed the legislation on the grounds that "for the Federal Government to plunge headlong financially into supporting child development would commit the vast moral authority of the National Government to the side of communal approaches to child rearing over against [sic] the family centered approach."[52] Since then, there has been no similar attempt to mandate federal support for comprehensive child-care policies.

In the United States, the limited discussion over the provision of federally funded daycare for all was replaced by a policy strategy in which public child-care funds became entangled with debates over welfare reform. Publicly subsidized daycare became framed as part of a broader policy package to cure welfare "dependency." This approach to federal daycare funding was reintroduced in 1962 through the Aid to Families with Dependent Children (AFDC) program, but was only available for a limited number of families with working mothers whose children were identified as "at risk" and in danger of neglect.[53] The creation of early childhood education programs in the mid-1960s, such as Head Start, furthered the focus on assisting very low-income families. In 1996, Congress passed a radical welfare reform bill, and the Temporary Assistance for Needy Families (TANF) program replaced AFDC. TANF stressed, among other things, ending poor families' reliance on federal assistance by making eligibility for cash aid dependent on participation in the workforce. Thus, at least for poor women, the government designed a policy explicitly to encourage them to work more in an effort to reverse their perceived "unproductivity" under the previous system. Although in 2002, about 19 percent of TANF dollars were allocated for child-care support,[54] demand vastly outstrips supply of actual services. The increased work requirements, combined with inadequate child-care assistance, often encourage the proliferation of poor mothers who work.[55] Further, single mothers (except in the state of Wisconsin) currently lose some of their benefits if they cannot identify the father of their children.[56]

In short, the United States follows a model in which managing work and child care is relegated to the private domain and parents are left to purchase child-care services on the private market. Publicly funded daycare has become intertwined with various welfare reform programs. While this approach has less of an impact on middle- and upper-class women who can afford to pay for care, this approach to family policy has been particularly difficult for low-income families and has compounded the incidence of child poverty.

Profamily/Breadwinner Model: Germany

Other child-care systems encourage a division of labor with the man as breadwinner and the woman as caretaker, at least for the first years of a child's life. This type of system couples generous maternity leave provisions and cash benefits with limited publicly subsidized child-care support, particularly for daycare for children from birth to age three. For example, in Austria, only 3 percent of children in this age range are in part-time or full-time daycare, but that number changes to 80 percent for children ages three to six. Other countries combine generous maternity leave with even less support for daycare options. Norway has extremely generous maternity leave policies, but it offers relatively low levels of support for public child care for children under the age of three and only modest investments in preschool. This is particularly hard on Norwegian working mothers since children there do not start school until the age of seven. This system indirectly discourages women's full-time return to work until the child is of school age.

The German system is a good exemplar of this approach. In line with Germany's pro–single breadwinner family policy, publicly subsidized day-care options, particularly for parents with children from birth to age three, are extremely limited, although there are growing state levels of support for child-care programs from children from the ages of three to six. Rather, the German state is more willing to give financial assistance to those taking on the task of child or elder care in the family, as opposed to investing in expanded social ser-vices (such as access to daycare).

In the German "breadwinner" model, the work involved in child-rearing is considered an alternative to paid employment, and, as we discussed earlier, par-ents on leave from work (primarily women) may receive a stipend (*Erziehungsgeld*) for the first few years of a child's life. The allowance that a parent may receive for the care of a child is more symbolic than real; it does not fully cover the costs of raising a child nor does it equal a salary. However, it is intended as a symbolic rec-ognition for the work of child care and child-rearing.[57] In the government's own words, "bringing up a child is a great responsibility," and "Children are a won-derful gift, but they do cost money."[58] Further, to lessen the long-term impact that loss of wages can have on pension plans, the German government grants a pension credit to mothers who spend up to three years at home rearing a child. The value of the credit is equal to up to three years of work at average wages.[59]

Why did this type of male breadwinner model emerge in Germany in the postwar era? For one, German political culture, particularly in its attitudes about the family, has always been conservative. The rise of center-right Christian Democratic parties in the postwar years further cemented the emphasis on the preservation of traditional family structures, defined as a working father, a stay-at-home mother, and children. Further, the government took an antiwoman stance when women did join the workforce in increasing numbers. In public campaigns, the family ministry portrayed working mothers as greedy "double earners" who were pursuing their selfish personal aspirations at the expense of fulfilling their family obligations. The government also pursued a policy of rely-ing on foreign "guest workers" to fill the demand for labor rather than encourag-ing women into the workforce.[60]

Nor did the West German feminist movement focus on child-care provision as a means to advance women's equality. Rather, women's and feminist organiza-tions focused on women's increased access to part-time employment so that they could continue to meet their care responsibilities in the home but also achieve some level of economic independence in the workforce. The issue was framed as one in which the government should provide sufficient levels of material support so that mothers would not be forced to work out of economic necessity. The result of this framing was that for the most part, feminist organizations did not chal-lenge women's traditional roles in the family and home.[61] The few radical femi-nist organizations that did mobilize on issues of daycare as a means to advance women's autonomy found little public support, since they were deeply suspicious of a paternalistic, authoritarian state and thus advocated for collective child care.

This suspicion of the state kept them from working with potential allies within key government policy agencies. In addition, German feminists chose to focus on abortion and the right to choose *not* to become a mother and *not* to have children. Thus, the women's movement overall was fractured between the "new maternalists," who did not directly challenge women's traditional roles, and in fact, pushed for society to place more value on them, and the more radical feminists, who questioned the entire family structure and whether women could truly emancipate themselves and simultaneously continue to bear children.[62]

The return of a center-left governing coalition, increased pressure from women, as well as demographic pressures resulting from reunification in 1990 prompted the state to revisit the issue of publicly subsidized child care, where demand vastly outstripped supply. The merging of two welfare systems—the East German one, with a much more extensive and comprehensive system of daycare for children from birth to age six, with the West's much less extensive one—highlighted the realities of an increasingly active female workforce, which was out of step with Germany's "breadwinner" model of welfare policy. In 1996, the government moved to extend daycare options to accommodate funding for half-day kindergartens for children between the ages of three and six, although this still did not fully ease the burden of dual-career couples who worked full-time. Further reform was implemented in 2004, when the ruling leftist coalition partners, the Social Democratic and Green parties, pushed through new legislation to increase full-time daycare offerings for children under three years of age. (In western Germany, the situation is particularly dire, with only 2.7 percent of children younger than three having spaces in daycare; the hope is to provide an addition 230,000 more spaces by 2010.[63])

While it will take time for the effects of these changes to be felt, nonetheless, for much of Germany's post–World War II history, one scholar has argued that "the institutional framework not only reconstructs traditional gender roles, but it also enhances new forms of social inequality among women."[64] In sum, while this model of benefits (generous maternity leave combined with little support for daycare) tends to keep women in the workforce over the long term, it also encourages them to take a "baby break" for several years or to work part-time for numerous years until returning to work full-time.[65] This, in turn, tends to support a family structure in which one parent serves as the breadwinner while the other provides care and supplementary income.

Egalitarian Model: France and Sweden

A few countries, primarily the Scandinavian countries of Denmark, Finland, and Sweden, as well as France and Belgium, have taken great strides in ensuring that with state support, families can balance work with parenting. All of these countries have implemented a wide array of policies to provide strong coverage for children from birth through age six. Denmark, Finland, and Sweden even adopted legislation in the 1980s that established daycare as a right for all children under the age of six.[66] In addition, particularly in the Nordic countries, the state has assumed the financial burden of providing these services, rather than relying on fees from parents. How much money is this? It is difficult to generalize across countries. However, Scandinavian countries such as Denmark and Sweden each spend about $13,000 per child per year.[67] We now turn to the individual cases of France and Sweden.

The French system of early childhood care consists of crèches for children from three months old through age two and a single model of preschool education for children ages two to six. Crèches usually operate ten to twelve hours a day. On average, the family pays about one-quarter of this cost; low-income families send their children for free. France's preschool program (*Ecole Maternelle*) is a publicly funded preschool program that is free for an eight-hour school day. The programs are available to all children regardless of parents' income or employment status. Although demand for spaces still outstrips supply for spots for two-year-olds, all three-, four-, and five-year-olds are enrolled.[68] In addition, France offers a variety of family allowances to defray the costs of child-rearing.

Sweden has even more generous benefits and is one of the few countries that spends about the same amount on child-care services as on family benefits. Swedish child-care policy is designed with twin aims: "one is to support and encourage children's development and learning, and help them get a good start in life, while the other is to enable parents to combine parenthood with employment or studies."[69] Since the 1970s, the Swedish government has focused increasingly on providing quality child care, with full access to all and financed by public funds in order to improve "the well-being of the young and a desire for greater equality between the sexes."[70]

Initially, Sweden's child-care program was designed to meet the needs of poor, working, and single mothers. However, as more women entered the workforce in increasing numbers in the 1960s and feminist groups agitated for increased government support for daycare options, the government moved to update its approach to the provision of daycare. In 1968, the government appointed a special commission, the National Commission on Childcare, to compile proposals for an overhaul of the current system. Out of this came the foundations of the Swedish model, which emphasized an integrated system of care for infants and education for small children, with the goal of enabling parents' work needs. As the government explained, "Without such a highly developed childcare system, the changes in family patterns and gender roles that have occurred since the 1970s would not have been possible." Thus, they consciously linked their policy design with a stated goal of advancing women's equality in the labor market and encouraging a more equitable distribution of labor at home.[71] However, in the 1970s, the government's performance often lagged behind its rhetorical commitment, and demand vastly outstripped supply. For example, in 1972, there were 95,000 child-care spaces available and demand for 400,000. Women's groups played a critical role in staging sit-ins and other forms of protest to highlight the gap between the government's symbolic versus real levels of support.[72] Since the 1970s, the state has increasingly emphasized universal coverage so that all parents, working or nonworking, can access child-care services and all children, regardless of income, can access education. Reforms from 2001 to 2003 increased both the scope and the scale of coverage. Preschool programs are universal and serve all children under age seven, with priority for children with working mothers, with single mothers, from immigrant or low income families, or with a disability. In addition, there is a cap on the amount that parents must contribute to the costs of daycare. The aim, according to the government, is to "make public childcare a part of the general welfare system, available to all. The basic principle is that all children in Sweden shall have access to childcare and that fees shall be so low that no child is excluded." [73] Further, all families with children qualify for a monthly allowance until the child reaches the age of sixteen (or twenty if a student, twenty-three if attending a school for the mentally retarded).[74]

Why did Sweden design such generous policies, in comparison with some of our other case studies? Like the other countries, political culture, institutional design, political opportunities, and levels of women's mobilization all provide keys to answering this question. For one, the Swedish government made several critical policy decisions. In response to labor shortages in the 1960s, the Swedish government consciously tapped the reserve of married women, who had previously chosen to withdraw from the labor market upon marrying and bearing children. Further, labor unions, which played a much more powerful role in policy formulation, agitated for better daycare, partially in response to increased female membership, as well as because they felt that employed women were the "lesser evil" when compared to relying on guest workers (the German strategy). At the same time, Swedish society was more accepting of a dual-income family model that advanced gender equality vis-à-vis the division of labor. This trickled up to political parties, and by the mid-1960s, parties on both the left and the right acknowledged the need for public child care in principle. Finally, the different strands of the women's movement in Sweden were more united around the idea that combining family and full employment were not contradictory aims. In addition, they did not adopt the antistatist rhetoric of the radical German feminists, and thus actively courted allies with key government policy positions, with the end goal of the establishment of state-supported child-care services. In turn, the government was relatively open to the demands of the women's movement. The increasing number of women in decision-making positions in political parties and labor unions facilitated this access.[75]

Impact

Similar to our discussion regarding maternity leave policies, child-care policies also tell us something about how states view the challenge of balancing public and private responsibilities for parenting and the "appropriate" division of labor within the household. In the United States, little attempt is made to encourage women's departure from the workforce, although there is also little attempt to subsidize child care for working parents to facilitate women's increased participation. Rather, the government simply stays out of that arena and looks to the

market, rather than the state, for solutions unless it needs to step in and provide a minimal social safety net for the neediest families. In contrast, Germany
until recently actively encouraged a "mommy" break through its combination of
maternity and child-care policies. While France's parental policies are pronatalist in intent, the generous child-care provisions allow women to choose whether
to rejoin the workforce after the birth of their child. Finally, Sweden has moved
furthest in their efforts to design policy that encourages full employment for men
or women as they balance work responsibilities with child-rearing.

Drawing from the data presented in Table 5.4, there is widespread variation
in the number of children who have access to daycare in each of the countries
studied here. Further, there is widespread variation within countries in children's access to daycare from birth through age three and age three to six. Thus,
for example, while Germany ranks last in our country case studies in terms

Table 5.4 Percentage of Children in Daycare

COUNTRY	PERCENTAGE OF CHILDREN IN PART-AND FULL-TIME DAYCARE		COMPULSORY
	BIRTH TO AGE THREE	AGES THREE TO SIX	SCHOOL AGE (YEARS)
Australia	—	80	—
Austria	3	80	6
Belgium	30	97	6
Denmark	58*	83	7
Finland	48*	73	7
France	29	99	6
Germany	5	85	6
Ireland	2	55	6
Italy	6	95	6
Japan	21	52	6
Luxembourg	N/A	N/A	6
Netherlands	8	71	5
New Zealand	25	85	6
Norway	N/A	N/A	7
Portugal	12	48	6
Spain	5	84	6
Sweden	48*	79	7
United Kingdom	2	60†	5
United States	26	71	5–7 (varies by state)

* FROM AGE ONE, WHEN BASIC PAID LEAVE ENDS, BUT ALL THREE HAVE SUPPLEMENTARY PAID AND JOB PROTECTED PARENTAL OR
CHILD-REARING LEAVE.

† THREE- AND FOUR-YEAR OLDS, AS COMPULSORY SCHOOL BEGINS AT AGE FIVE.

SOURCE: Sheila B. Kamerman, "Early Childhood Education and Care (ECEC): An Overview of Developments
in the OECD Countries." Unpublished paper, date not provided.

of children in care from birth through age three, that number increases significantly for children ages three to six. In France, while less than a third of children from birth through age three are in daycare, 99 percent are integrated into the preschool education system for ages three to six. Sweden has the highest percentage of children in daycare from birth through age three, but not as high a percentage as Germany or France from ages three to six. And despite the absence of uniform publicly subsidized care for children in the United States, parents are finding ways to piece together daycare for their children, although they trail France, Sweden, and Germany's numbers (but only for ages three to six.) However, given the lack of substantial federal funding, daycare in the United States is something of a class issue and is more readily available to those who can afford it.

What has been the impact on women's employment? Women's advocates have long argued that the availability of child care is strongly linked to women's access to paid employment. Further, promoting maternal employment is important for increasing women's financial autonomy and is also critical in preventing child poverty, particularly in families that are headed by a single parent.[76] Has increased child care kept women in the workforce? In the United States, 68 percent of married/cohabitating mothers work and 66 percent of single mothers work. In Germany, the profamily model, 41 percent of married/cohabitating mothers work and 40 percent of single mothers work. The figure for France is 68 percent and 82 percent, respectively, and Sweden is 80 percent and 70 percent. While correlation does not equal causality (we cannot determine if daycare policy is the primary force driving women into or keeping them out of the workforce), we do know that women who live in systems with generous benefits, such as Sweden's and France's, are able to balance work and parenting more readily than those in Germany's single breadwinner model, where women tend to take time off during their child-rearing years.[77] In profamily/noninterventionist states such as the United States, families are finding ways of coping, although the incidence of child poverty in the United States is much higher than in the other countries, where there is a more generous system of social benefits. Further, although employment rates for women are high in the United States, this figure is much lower for women with young children, particularly those with infants under the age of three.[78]

What political conditions are conducive or, alternatively, pose obstacles to policies reducing gender inequalities? What determines whether states will promote "equity for breadwinners or parity for caregivers"?[79] The prevailing societal vision of the "ideal family" is critical. In the United States, suspicion of "big government," individualist values, and suspicion of alternative care providers combine to create a model in which the federal government is hesitant to intervene. Germany's conservative family culture, combined with an acceptance of the welfare state, helped foster policies that reward caregiving activities and support a "male breadwinner" family structure. Sweden's relatively tolerant political culture, combined with an acceptance of a strong welfare state and active state intervention in social policy, helped create more egalitarian policy that also sought to foster more equal divisions of labor within the family.

Second, the nature of the women's movement in each of our cases was also critical. In each of these countries, the prevailing belief system of the feminist lobby has affected which measures groups will push in order to bring about gender equality. For example, some movements have stressed the differences between the sexes and women's special capacities and have fought for policies that acknowledge that. In contrast, other women's movements have tried to frame women's issues as a matter of gender equality and equal rights. These two approaches engender different visions of gender relations. Thus, for example, women's movements in Germany, the United Kingdom, and Norway have tended to take the gender difference argument, pushing for recognition of women's caregiving activities and for benefits that financially reward caregivers. In contrast, equal rights advocates have been influential in the United States, Netherlands, and Sweden, although women's demands have been spun differently in the countries. While the United States has tended to focus on the equality of women at work while pushing for their abilities to also be breadwinners, women's movements in the Netherlands and Sweden have focused on trying to redistribute tasks of breadwinning and caring so that men do more caring and women have more access to breadwinning than before and both parents perform both careers equally.[80]

The presence or absence of a strong labor movement has also affected the scope and nature of policies that affect balancing productive and reproductive responsibilities. In countries with strong unions and/or collective bargaining, the differences between male and female wages are much smaller for full-time workers. Nonetheless, unions do vary to the degree to which they promote women's interests. Often, this is based on the extent of women's labor market participation, as well as their participation in unions. Women's share of total union membership has increased; in Finland, Sweden, and Denmark, women account for roughly half of union membership.[81]

Finally, parties and the political makeup of governments matter in terms of pushing for policies that encourage balancing production and reproduction. Traditionally, left-wing parties have been much more receptive to implementing policies that encourage female equality, while right-wing parties have been more skeptical, even hostile. Left-wing parties in various countries have introduced child-care services, equal taxation, women's policy machinery within the administration, policies that reduce gender pay differentials, and lower poverty rates among women and children. However, left-wing parties are not the only avenues for women's participation. Women's entry into all parties can make a difference. For example, a Republican woman in the United States headed a movement to change taxation for married women, against the wishes of the male leadership.[82]

ADVANCING WOMEN'S EQUALITY

What are some further potential solutions to the dilemma of balancing work and family? What issues are still on the horizon? Women's equality advocates do not all agree on appropriate strategies for advancing women's equality. One of the biggest divisions has been whether to focus on further integrating women into the workforce while simultaneously pushing for a more equitable division of labor in the household or to push states to value the task of child-rearing, which often falls on the shoulders of women. Still others advocate combating what they see as an overly materialistic focus on accessing traditionally male institutions of work. But all of these scenarios are fraught with difficulties. Does integrating women into the workforce merely push them to further adopt a flawed, patriarchal approach to work? If a woman willingly chooses to stay at home and engage in caregiving as a career, is the fact that she chose this path more empowering than the critique that this type of family arrangement reinforces traditional divisions of labor in the household? What is the alternative to a rejection of work-centered modern societies and male-dominated work norms? We try to take no position on this. However, we do take the position that women who work are an increasing reality and that currently, the design of a wide array of policies has serious implications for women who also choose to parent. Despite the improvement in policies, women who work are still penalized (in terms of income and career advancement opportunities) more so than men for having children.

What are ways to ease this tension? Particularly in noninterventionist states such as the United States, advocates have focused primarily on extending the provisions of FMLA and pushing for partially paid leave for parents and secondarily on better levels of federal support for early childhood education. After signing the FMLA, President Clinton hoped to expand leave entitlements for parents by expanding the application of the legislation to companies that employ twenty-five workers or more (as opposed to the current fifty) and by providing some sort of wage replacement, perhaps through focusing on increased coverage of Temporary Disability Insurance. From 1993 to 1999, almost twenty initiatives were put forth by members of Congress to expand FMLA.[83] However, the dominance of the Republican Party, which is suspicious of increasing government intervention, along with a renewed focus on foreign policy concerns, has put the domestic issue of parental leave on the back burner. As a result, the debate over the expansion of benefits has moved to the state level; it may, however, create some impetus for revisiting the issue at the federal level under the Obama administration.

For European countries that have more significant levels of federal support for both leave and child-care provisions, emphasis has focused on improving the conditions of the benefits, either through increased financial support, longer and more flexible conditions of leave, and/or improved access and coverage of child care. Advocates have focused on lobbying businesses for increasingly flexible work conditions to meet parental demands. In particular, countries such as Germany have struggled to update and modernize their profamily/breadwinner structure, which tends to discourage women from fully participating in the workforce. This issue has become part of the national discourse, in part, because many young German women are choosing not to have children. A 2002 study found that 27.8 percent of German women born in 1960 were childless, a figure far higher than in any other European country. In addition, 16.6 percent of German women ages eighteen to thirty-four, when asked their ideal number of children, responded "none." [84] Further, the German government, in response to Germany's ongoing economic slump, has realized that it needs to harness the productivity of all of its citizens, not just its male ones. As a result, in January 2007, the government announced several policy changes to encourage women to return to the workforce sooner, to increase fathers' involvement in child care, and to increase state involvement in early childhood care and early childhood education.[85] Germany is slowly moving toward a more equitable model that does not rely on a male breadwinner and a stay-at-home mother.

In the future, states will have to respond more coherently to the issue of single-parent households. In the post–World War II era, governments had to adjust policy to absorb the relatively new trend of the dual-income family. Since then, countries have had to adjust to further changing demographic trends. Household size has decreased in recent decades, and in all industrialized countries (except the United States), women have been having children later. Fewer individuals have chosen to marry, and a higher percentage of marriages end in divorce. Births outside of marriage have grown, and single-parent households are increasingly common. The rise of same-sex unions across OECD countries has further stretched traditional definitions of the family unit. All of the trends have led to a rapidly changing definition of the family, and states will have to continue to adjust to these changes with new policy.

CONCLUSION

How have varied policies relating to parental leave and early and childhood care affected parents' abilities to manage work and family and reduce gender inequalities? Noninterventionist approaches to this dilemma, exemplified by the United States, have enacted minimal gender-neutral policies to ease the tension between work and family but have done little to implement more proactive policies. In contrast, the German model consists of policies that, while generous, tend to encourage traditional views about the appropriate division of labor within households. The state tends to adhere to a "male breadwinner" model of social benefits, and mothers are given strong maternity benefits, not because they are to return to the workforce, but because upon becoming pregnant, they are to leave work and engage themselves in caring activities of home and hearth, or *kinder, kuchen,* and *kirche.* France and Sweden both have designed policies that help men and women combine careers with family responsibilities by providing generous leave benefits with comprehensive child care. Sweden has gone furthest in designing proactive policy to encourage fathers to contribute to a more equitable distribution of labor in the household.

However, it is important not to overemphasize the effects of trends to ease the tension between parenting and working. Most countries' policies have been reworked and are gender neutral in language, giving both parents equal rights to take leave or draw benefits. However, gender-neutral policies, even if written with the idea of encouraging fathers to share more equally in the burden of care, still have gender-specific results. Even though states increasingly are legislating on parental, as opposed to maternity, leave, fathers are still hesitant to take advantage of the benefits offered them, and women continue to shoulder the burden of care responsibilities. The European Union is also aware of the problem and has acknowledged that "there is broad agreement on the need to encourage fathers to make use of the opportunities for child care that are available to them. Whilst short-term leave at the time of a child's birth is becoming more popular, longer-term care options seem to be ignored by the vast majority of fathers." While citing a need for a "radical shift in attitudes," the EU was less aggressive in addressing the means to facilitate this and merely acknowledged that member states had launched "information campaigns" to address the issue.[86] However, this is only the beginning. As one scholar noted: "Mothers have changed the gender balance in breadwinning. Changing the gender balance in caring remains a challenge for parents, work organizations and policy reform."[87]

In closing, the degree to which states provide parental benefits is of enormous significance to women. In the absence of generous benefits, women often end up in low-paid, part-time, and irregular jobs.[88] Yet, talk is cheap; providing the resources, such as publicly funded leave as well as universal daycare, is easier to promise than to provide. While states have improved their commitment to public spending to help bridge the divide between private and public divisions of labor, designing policy that encourages the redistribution of that divide is a more elusive task. However, passing policy to do such a thing has been a contentious process. Even in states that have designed policies that provide incentives for men to take a more proactive role in assuming traditional women's duties, men have been slow to respond. Policy in some ways is only the first step; changing people's habitual behavior is the ongoing challenge.

FOR MORE INFORMATION

The Clearinghouse on International Developments in Child, Youth, and Family Policies at Columbia University, http://www.childpolicyintl.org

International Mothers Network, http://www.internationalmothersnetwork.org/home.html

MomsRising, http://www.momsrising.orgMothers Ought to Have Equal Rights, http://www.mothersoughttohaveequalrights.org

National Association of Mothers' Centers, http://www.motherscenter.org

6

◦

Abortion Politics

On February 23, 2005, a pharmacist in Chicago refused to fill two customers' prescriptions for emergency contraception, also known as the "morning after pill." Although the morning after pill is medically classified as a contraceptive, it is usually taken after sexual activity to prevent a fertilized egg from implanting in the uterus. It is a contraceptive because most doctors maintain that pregnancy begins with implantation, not fertilization, and that therefore, morning after pills prevent pregnancy rather than end it. However, another Illinois pharmacist, Luke Vander Bleek, who also refused to sell the morning after pill, argued that "the risk is that it is going to take a human life, and I don't think an individual should be allowed by law to draw me in to that activity." In response, Governor Rod Blagojevich issued a ruling ordering pharmacists to make the contraceptive available by ensuring that another pharmacist is on hand to fill the prescription if a colleague is unwilling to do so. In response, Vander Bleek filed suit to challenge the state government's order. In addition, opponents of the state ruling argue that it conflicts with the Illinois Health Care Right of Conscience Act, which allows medical professionals to opt out of medical practices with which they are uncomfortable.[1] In December 2008, the Illinois Supreme Court overturned an appellate decision dismissing the pharmacists' case (and thus ordering the appellate court to issue a decision), ensuring that the conflict will continue to enflame the nationwide discourse on who should define women's reproductive choices.[2]

We now move to one of the most contentious issues in the realm of women, policy, and politics—legislating reproductive rights and, specifically, abortion. Beginning in the 1960s, women's movements in many of the advanced industrialized countries successfully lobbied for liberalized contraception and abortion policies. However, these debates are not resolved; in particular, the abortion debate has opened deep divisions within societies and has occupied legislative, executive, and judicial branches of government as well as interest groups and bureaucratic agencies at the national, regional, and local levels. The issue has become entangled with policies touching on education, welfare, sexuality, science and medical research, licensing of professionals, health care, the military, foreign aid, labor, and taxation. It involves making decisions about the regulation and legalization of funding for and access to medical services, limits on protest, family planning, reporting requirements, advertising, fetal research, parental consent and notification, and spousal consent and notification.[3] The abortion issue has involved all branches of government at multiple layers and has cut across numerous policy issues.

In addition, the abortion issue illustrates the complexity of balancing demands for women's autonomy with a variety of diverse and often warring interests. On the one hand, many feminists argue that abortion is primarily a woman's issue about personal autonomy and choice over one's body. Alternatively, the medical industry has often framed the debate as primarily a potentially dangerous, life-threatening health issue that is best left to medical experts to regulate. Religious figures have couched abortion as a moral conflict and proclaim the universality of all living beings', born as well as unborn, right to life. Alternatively, abortion is also framed as a government issue; governments have a responsibility to regulate the welfare of their citizens, although there is no agreement over how to balance the rights of the mother with the rights of the fetus. Further, because reproduction includes other people, should the rights and interest of others, such as the father, the extended family, and society, be taken into account?

The abortion issue has been more successful at raising very complex questions than resolving them. Very few countries have navigated a policy that has pleased all interests. Part of this is because the varied sides of the debate share almost no common language. For example, while anti-abortion activists begin by stipulating that the embryo is an unborn child, prolegalization activists view this initial premise as highly problematic. While abortion foes may see the presence of a fetal heartbeat as evidence of life, abortion legalization supporters may respond that the fetus does not breathe independently until birth. At heart, the debate centers around how society should define personhood, which theoretically grants one an array of inalienable and acquired rights. And this decision is based on interpretations of the meaning of personhood rather than lining up clear "facts."[4]

The abortion debate has enormous implications for women and their ability to choose to subordinate their reproductive roles to other roles. The abortion debate is not gender neutral, and legislating abortion involves a fundamental recognition of women's biological distinctiveness. For example, because women alone can give birth to children, should they then be given full choice as to controlling what happens in that body? It also raises difficult questions about how states should ensure women's autonomy in making choices about their bodies. To what degree should the state intrude into "the private" to regulate how women make these choices? In sum, at issue is the question of who gets to make the final decision about regulating women's bodies—should it be the state, the doctor, the woman, or some other configuration?

In this chapter, we find that while nearly all OECD countries have liberalized their policies regulating reproductive rights, the scope of the legislation varies dramatically from country to country, as do governments' commitments to designing and enforcing policy on these areas. We highlight the varied experiences of Ireland, the United States, and the Netherlands. The Irish government has not implemented policies that increase women's control over their own bodies. The United States has exhibited mixed results. In the Netherlands, the debate largely has been settled, both in terms of battles within the government system as well as with public opinion. We find that the strength of the women's movement, prevailing cultural norms, and government policies all play a role in determining the outcome of this policy struggle. In closing, however, it also important to acknowledge that women are not uniformly in favor of the legalization of abortion, and we will discuss the multiplicity of women's view regarding their "right" to have full access to terminating a pregnancy.

THE DEBATE OVER ABORTION

Abortion was not always perceived as a contentious or thorny moral issue. Abortion techniques are described in some of the earliest medical texts of China and Egypt; ancient Greeks argued that abortion was an appropriate method for regulating population size. During the Roman Empire, it was used with few if any restrictions; abortion was considered not as a crime but as an "immoral act." The fetus was considered to be part of the "mother's viscera" and thus was within her sphere of influence. Nor were abortion prohibitions part of the indigenous cultural, religious, and legal traditions of most of the non-Western world; rather, they were imported as part of colonial, imperial, or Western influences in the previous two centuries, when legal restrictions increased in the colonial countries themselves.[5] Thus, historically, abortion was practiced in virtually every society, despite the great variation in cultural and moral views about it.

However, with the advent of Christianity came a new focus on souls and on humans in general as God's creatures. Nonetheless, it took centuries for the church to settle the debate about when fetuses became "human," endowed with souls, and thus connected to God. In the twelfth and thirteenth centuries, Pope Innocent considered that the fetus had life, or a soul, only when "quickening" (movement of the fetus) was felt, which occurs around twenty-four weeks. In the sixteenth century, Popes Sisto V and Gregory XIV argued that the fetus has a life or soul from the beginning of conception. The Catholic Church became more firmly entrenched in this second view when, in 1869, Pope Pius IX further emphasized the idea of the immediate animation of the fetus by accepting the dogma of the Immaculate Conception. Since then, the Catholic Church has espoused the protection of human life since conception, and Catholicism is unique in that it presents unified and nearly absolute opposition to induced abortion in nearly all circumstances.[6] Other religious traditions are more varied in their stances on abortion. Nothing in Confucian and Shinto ethics or in the Hindu religion forbids abortion. Different Islamic legal schools give varying interpretations on the moral issue of abortion, especially in the early stages of pregnancy. Buddhism is generally interpreted to be opposed to abortion.[7] In sum, the equation of abortion with murder is a relatively new phenomenon.

For centuries, the state stayed out of regulating reproduction. For example, before the nineteenth century in Great Britain, there were no statutes relating to abortion, and it was not considered a crime to abort a fetus before "quickening."[8] States began to legislate abortion in the nineteenth and early twentieth centuries by criminalizing or recriminalizing the issue. At the time, abortion was not framed primarily as a religious issue, but by the emerging medical profession as a protective one. Women needed to be protected from nefarious doctors, who were performing dangerous operations on women and deterring them from performing their natural mothering functions. States responded with legislation that began to lay out a framework regulating the conditions under which women were allowed to terminate their pregnancies. The most common allowances for abortion were in cases where carrying the child to term threatened the health and/or life of the mother. In many countries, both the doctors performing the abortion as well as the women undergoing the medical process were punishable, although different countries pursued this with varying degrees of zeal. In an era when contraception was not widely available, abortion also served as a method of birth control, and criminalizing the process often drove the process underground, or to backstreet alleys.

Although some countries liberalized abortion policy in the early to mid-twentieth century—most notably many communist countries as part of other reforms designed to unlink law from religious influences, improve the status of women, and get women into the workforce—for the most part, abortion did not reappear as a political issue until the 1960s. England was one of the first countries to liberalize its abortion policies; in 1967, it passed the Abortion Act, which decriminalized abortion and broadened women's choices by widening the conditions under which women could have abortions. In the ensuing three decades, abortion policy was challenged, and mostly widened, in every Western industrialized country. Ironically, the medical profession, which in the nineteenth century had been one of the forces to push for criminalization of abortion, a century later played a central role in overturning these same laws.[9]

Abortion debates raged around several issues. First, under what conditions could women have an abortion? Many countries already did provide for abortions in order to save the life of the mother. Additional permissible conditions were to preserve the woman's physical health, in the case of rape or incest, or in the case of fetal impairment. While many countries already granted exceptions in these three areas, movements in the 1960s began to stress new reasons why an abortion might be necessary. While some countries had allowed abortion to preserve the physical health of the mother, supporters of legalized abortion emphasized the need to broaden definitions of what constitutes "health." Advocates introduced the idea that mental health was also a necessary consideration and that many women, while physically able to have a child, would be placed under enormous emotional stress if forced to carry the child to term. In addition, advocates also argued that women should be able to terminate pregnancies for economic or social reasons. That is, lack of financial means to support a child should be a legitimate reason to terminate a pregnancy. In addition, the social stigma attached to young mothers and single mothers meant that women of all ages, but particularly young women, should be granted more choice in whether to carry the fetus to term. Finally, the concept of "abortion on demand" became increasingly common. That is, advocates argued that it is the woman's choice to have an abortion and that there do not have to be "extenuating circumstances."

In addition to debating the reasons why women could terminate the pregnancy, advocates and opponents argued about when women could legally terminate a pregnancy. Even in countries that provided abortion without asking for extenuating circumstances, there was disagreement about how far into the pregnancy the woman exercised control over choice and when the state needed to intervene to protect the rights of the fetus. Many feminists argued that since only women can experience pregnancy, they should then have complete control over deciding the fate of their bodies. However, many countries adopted a version of the trimester system, in which women had a wider latitude of choices in the first twelve to fourteen weeks. After the first trimester, many states restricted access to abortion. Particularly in the third trimester, when the fetus is theoretically "viable" (potentially able to survive outside the womb, although often with extensive medical intervention), abortion was restricted to very specific circumstances, such as to save the life of the mother. Thus, models were set up that gave women more choice and control in the first part of the pregnancy, but then followed this with a more assertive role for the state in the second and third trimesters.

Governments have regulated abortion in other ways. Some decreed that women needed first to undergo counseling in order to understand the full range of issues involved and the various alternatives to abortion. In other countries, women had to go before a committee to make their case for terminating pregnancies, even if the decision ultimately was theirs to make. Still others legislated that women could have an abortion, but only after observing a specified waiting period during which they could reconsider their choice. Alternatively, women had to verbally and in written form request an abortion. Other countries were concerned with the right of the partner who had helped conceive the child and enacted policy in which women had to get permission from their spouse, who presumably had been the partner in conception. For teenagers, states grappled with whether teens should be vested with the power to make this decision on their own or whether, as minors, they should have to inform their parents of the decision. Additionally, the issue of state funding arose. Should state funds be used to finance such a divisive medical procedure? A refusal to finance abortion could turn it into a class issue, in which wealthy women could afford abortions, while poor women would be forced to forgo them for financial reasons.

But would state funding be interpreted as state endorsement of abortion? Finally, access became a big issue. While states may have legalized abortions, ensuring that women had access to them was a separate issue. For example, while many U.S. states have legalized abortions, fewer doctors can be found to perform them, effectively denying women access to the procedure. In sum, abortion is not a "yes/no" issue; rather, it involves a wide array of issues beyond simply deciding the legality of the procedure.

Given this background, what is the current status of abortion worldwide? According to the World Health Organization, abortion is one of the most widely used medical procedures by women; about one in five pregnancies worldwide end in abortion. Abortion is least prevalent in Western European countries, where nearly all abortions are safe and legal, and more frequently used in developing countries, where more than half of all abortions are unsafe and illegal. Nonetheless, the number of induced abortions has declined worldwide between 1995 and 2003.[10]

Despite the universality of the practice of abortion, there are wide variations across countries with regard to the legality of the practice, access to the procedure, societies' acceptance of abortion, and the prevailing moral and ethical views concerning its practice. While about 39 percent of the world's population live in the fifty-six countries that grant access to legal abortion without restriction as to reason, this is geographically concentrated in the countries of Europe, the former Soviet Union, and North America. However, most of these countries impose a limit on the period during which women can readily access the procedure. The rest of the world's population faces differing degrees of restrictions. A second category of countries allows abortion if the woman has justifiable grounds, which are related to her physical well-being and overall emotional health and are often broadly interpreted. Fourteen countries (21 percent of the world's population) allow abortion on socioeconomic grounds. These laws are often interpreted liberally, allowing for such considerations as a woman's economic resources, her age, her marital status, and the number of children she has. In a similar vein, an additional twenty-three countries (4 percent of the world's population) allow abortion in situations that would preserve a women's mental health, allowing for such factors as psychological stress suffered by a woman who is raped or severe strain caused by social or economic circumstances. A third group of countries allows abortion in quite limited circumstances. Thirty-five countries (10 percent of the world's population) allow abortion to preserve the physical health of the mother. The most restrictive laws are those that ban abortion altogether or permit the procedure only to save a woman's life. Sixty-eight nations, representing 26 percent of the world's population and located primarily in the developing world, have enacted these laws. Of these sixty-eight countries, thirty-three do not permit abortion under any circumstance.[11] Table 6.1 provides an overview of the world's abortion laws as of 2008.

Table 6.1 The World's Abortion Laws, 2008*

TO SAVE THE WOMAN'S LIFE OR PROHIBITED ALTOGETHER*

Afghanistan	Gabon	Malta	Senegal
Andorra	**Guatemala**	Marshall Islands	**Solomon Islands**
Angola	Guinea-Bissau	Mauritania	Somalia
Antigua & Barbuda	Haiti	Mauritius	**Sri Lanka**
Bangladesh	Honduras	**Mexico**	**Sudan**
Bhutan	**Indonesia**	Micronesia	Suriname
Brazil	**Iran**	Monaco	**Syria**
Brunei Darussalam	Iraq	**Myanmar**	**Tanzania**
Central African Republic	**Ireland**	Nicaragua	Tonga
Chile	**Kenya**	**Nigeria**	**Tuvalu**
Congo	**Kiribati**	Oman	**Uganda**
Cote d'Ivoire	Laos	Palau	**United Arab Emirates**
Democratic Republic	**Lebanon**	**Panama**	**Venezuela**
of the Congo	Lesotho	**Papua New Guinea**	**West Bank & Gaza Strip**
Dominica	**Libya**	**Paraguay**	**Yemen**
Dominican Republic	Madagascar	Philippines	
Egypt	**Malawi**	San Marino	
El Salvador	**Mali**	San Tome & Principe	

TO PRESERVE PHYSICAL HEALTH (AND TO SAVE THE MOTHER'S LIFE)

Argentina	Costa Rica	Kuwait	Qatar
Bahamas	Djibouti	Liechtenstein	Republic of Korea
Benin	Ecuador	Maldives	Rwanda
Bolivia	Equatorial Guinea	Morocco	Saudi Arabia
Burkina Faso	Eritrea	Mozambique	Togo
Burundi	Ethiopia	Niger	Uruguay
Cameroon	Grenada	Pakistan	Vanuatu
Chad	Guinea	Peru	Zimbabwe
Comoros	Jordan	Poland	

TO PRESERVE MENTAL HEALTH (AND TO SAVE THE MOTHER'S LIFE AND PHYSICAL HEALTH)

Algeria	Israel	New Zealand	Sierra Leone
Botswana	Jamaica	Northern Ireland	Spain
Colombia	Liberia	Portugal	Swaziland
Gambia	Malaysia	Saint Kitts & Nevis	Thailand
Ghana	Namibia	Samoa	Trinidad & Tobago
Hong Kong	Nauru	Seychelles	

Table 6.1 (*continued*)

FOR SOCIOECONOMIC REASONS (AND TO SAVE THE MOTHER'S LIFE, PHYSICAL HEALTH, AND MENTAL HEALTH)

Australia	Fiji	India	Taiwan
Barbados	Finland	Japan	Zambia
Belize	Great Britain	Luxembourg	
Cyprus	Iceland	Saint Vincent & Grenadines	

WITHOUT RESTRICTION AS TO REASON

Albania	Czech Republic	Kyrgyzstan	Slovak Republic
Armenia	Dem. People's	Latvia	Slovenia
Austria	Republic of Korea	Lithuania	South Africa
Azerbaijan	Denmark	Moldova	Sweden
Bahrain	Estonia	Mongolia	Switzerland
Belarus	France	Montenegro	Tajikistan
Belgium	Former Yugoslav Republic	Nepal	Tunisia
Bosnia-Herzegovina	of Macedonia	Netherlands	Turkey
Bulgaria	Georgia	Norway	Turkmenistan
Cambodia	Germany	Portugal	Ukraine
Canada	Greece	Puerto Rico	United States
Cape Verde	Guyana	Romania	Uzbekistan
China	Hungary	Russian Federation	Vietnam
Croatia	Italy	Serbia	
Cuba	Kazakhstan	Singapore	

* COUNTRIES IN BOLD ALLOW AN EXCEPTION TO SAVE THE MOTHER'S LIFE.

SOURCE: Center for Reproductive Rights, "The World's Abortion Laws." May 2008, http://reproductiverights.org/en/document/world-abortion-laws-2008-fact-sheet (March 18, 2009).

Despite the numerous laws that have criminalized abortion, this has not stopped women from having them. Because of the varying nature of laws regulating access and availability of abortion, the World Health Organization estimates that around two-fifths of all abortions are clandestine and are carried out in countries that, because of the circumstances surrounding the pregnancy, render the abortion illegal or in which the provider is not legally qualified. This has important ramifications for women; clandestine abortions are often unsafe abortions, and women often pay with their lives. Thus, abortion accounts for about one-third of maternal mortality worldwide. This mortality has an economic and geographic face; 99 percent of this mortality occurs in countries of the developing world, which is also where 90 percent of the world's unsafe abortions are performed.[12] However, making abortion legal, particularly in the developing world, does not always make it open. India has a relatively liberal abortion law. Yet, an estimated 90 percent of abortions in India are illegal and clandestine and are not performed by qualified medical staff because the priority is not on safety or cost, but on secrecy.[13] In Western countries where abortion is legal, it is not so much social mores but lack of access that restrict women from choosing safe methods of abortion.

Around the world, women choose abortion for a variety of reasons. Particularly in the absence of widely available or affordable contraception, many women use abortion as a form of birth control. This is particularly true for women in some developing countries, who often do not have the means to effectively control the timing and sequencing of their pregnancies. Further, women may be motivated to protect the family economy from having to make outlays on education or life course rituals or ceremonies in close succession. In places such as Russia or eastern Europe, where housing is extremely limited and married couples live in small apartments with their parents, abortion is a choice motivated by a housing shortage. In developed countries, where contraception is more widely available, women may choose abortion because of concerns over increased financial and social responsibilities that come with additional children.[14]

The demographics of abortion worldwide also give a sense of the varying reasons why women choose not to go forward with a pregnancy. In countries of the West and sub-Saharan Africa, three out of every four abortions are to single women or to women under the age of twenty. The majority of women have borne no children. In contrast, in eastern Europe, Latin America, and much of Asia, three out of every four abortions are to married women and to persons over twenty years of age. In some cultures, premature motherhood (before marriage) is the taboo to be avoided, while in other countries, the concern over the increased responsibilities, financial as well as social, that come with added children predominates.

In the following section, we turn to three case studies of abortion policies in OECD countries. Specifically, we look at the debates over abortion in Ireland, the United States, and the Netherlands. Each case demonstrates a different outcome and illustrates larger lessons about why and how some states have resolved the abortion issue. Ireland is unique in that not only has it not liberalized abortion, but it has also taken further steps to strengthen legal prohibitions against abortion.[15] In contrast, while the United States has a relatively liberal abortion law, the success of the law has been mixed, in that it has been faced with constant legal challenges and implementation problems. Finally, we will look at the case of the Netherlands, where abortion policy was resolved relatively quickly and has not been challenged. What explains the varying array of policy outcomes in each country?

IRELAND

Unlike other countries that enacted significant abortion reforms, abortion in Ireland has been a criminal act since 1861. This act remained intact until an anti-abortion movement successfully mounted a campaign for a constitutional prohibition on abortion in the early 1980s. Since then, the abortion debate has revolved around several issues: Does an Irish woman have a constitutional right to seek an abortion in another country? Can women seek information about abortion in Ireland in order to successfully procure a safe one abroad? Can a woman seek an abortion if there is a real and substantial risk to her life, including a risk of suicide? While other European countries significantly reformed their abortion laws in response to public opinion, women's groups, and other prolegalization lobbies, there was no similar cultural shift in Ireland. Thus, Ireland is unique in that not only has it not legalized abortion except to save the life of the mother, but it has also taken steps to strengthen legal prohibitions against abortion. This is backed by a majority of citizens and has not been strongly opposed by the women's movement, which has not significantly raised the issue of gender into the debate. Rather, the abortion debate has been tentatively gendered over time, with a focus on the mother's right to life and a more empathetic understanding of crisis pregnancies.[16]

As a former subject of the United Kingdom, Ireland based its legislation on abortion in the 1861 Offences Against the Person Act. According to the act, performing and procuring an abortion "unlawfully" is a crime, although the act does not specify which abortions are to be considered unlawful.[17] This legislation remained in effect after the country gained its independence. When Great Britain became the first country to decriminalize abortion to any great extent in 1967, Ireland maintained its steadfast position on the criminalization of abortion.[18] With an overwhelming majority of practicing Catholics, many citizens followed the church's injunctions regarding contraception and abortion. Even the provision of contraceptives in Ireland was a topic of great controversy. It was not until 1973 that the Supreme Court, basing its decision on a right to marital privacy, ruled that adults be allowed to import and possess contraceptives. Nonetheless, the sale of contraceptives was still illegal until 1979, when Parliament allowed pharmacists to sell contraceptives with a prescription. In 1985, it expanded its categories of people who could sell contraceptives and allowed persons over eighteen years of age to buy condoms and spermicides without prescription. These reforms in the contraceptive law were not based on feminist arguments, but were a response, in part, to a rise in the incidence of sexually transmitted diseases.[19] Given that contraception is still heavily regulated, efforts to widen access to abortion were much more protracted, with fewer successes.

In addition, unlike other countries, which often have settled difficult moral issues through the courts or the legislature, the Irish government has put the issue before the people in a series of public referenda. Abortion was not the only issue put forth before the voter; this heavily Catholic nation also voted on whether to legalize divorce. In 1986, voters rejected legalization of divorce by a landslide. Nearly a decade later, voters legalized divorce, but only by a margin of 0.7 percent. In sum, Ireland has implemented a variety of family policy reforms much later than other European countries have, and these decisions have been much more divisive.

Ireland grappled with the issue of abortion regulation in early 1980s, when conservative Catholics, in response to the Supreme Court's decision to legalize contraception, tried to find a way to ban abortion in such a way that it could not be overturned by either the Supreme Court or the European Court of Justice. Given that the Supreme Court had, similar to the United States, based its decision to legalize contraception in a right to privacy, conservative Catholics formed the Society for the Protection of the Unborn Child and worked to avert what they feared would be a repetition of the American path to legalization of abortion through the justification of a right to privacy. They campaigned for a constitutional amendment that would prevent the legalization of abortion. In 1983, the issue was put before the public in a referendum and was worded as follows: "The state acknowledges the right to life of the unborn and, with due regard to equal right to the life of the mother, guarantees in its laws to respect, and as far as practicable, by its laws to defend and vindicate that right." [20] In sum, the amendment placed the lives of the mother and the unborn child on an equal level, rather than specifying under which conditions the state could place the life of the mother above that of the fetus. The wording of the Irish amendment obligated the state to adopt measures to protect the life of the fetus and, in effect, banned legislators from passing any law to loosen the abortion ban.[21] Women's groups tried to oppose the bill, although with a rhetoric that emphasized the inadequacies of the bill rather than by framing it as a woman's right to choose. Thus, their arguments tended to focus on the fact that the amendment made no provisions for exceptions, was a waste of public funds, and would prevent possible future legislation on the issue. Although this helped build opposition to the amendment, it still passed easily, with 66 percent of voters in favor and 33 percent against, although the voter turnout was relatively low, at 50 percent.[22] Thus, abortions were completely prohibited in Ireland, with no exceptions.

Nonetheless, Irish women still found ways to access abortions. England had liberalized its abortion laws in 1967; as a result, many Irish women traveled yearly to England to have a legal and safe procedure. By the 1990s, four thousand Irish women were traveling to England for abortions each year.[23] Further, in 1990 the European Community (EC) defined abortion as a commercial service; thus, as citizens of a member country of the EC, women had a right to access services, including abortion, available in other member states.[24] In addition, various public agencies such as clinics, student groups at universities, and bookstores in Ireland continued to distribute information that touched either tangentially on abortion or gave specific information about accessing abortion abroad. Once again, opponents of abortion mobilized, arguing that these services were in violation of the 1983 amendment, and, at the request of the government, the Supreme Court of Ireland banned the provision of these services by family planning groups and student groups, arguing that the government had a duty to defend and vindicate the rights of the unborn. Thus, by the beginning of the 1990s, all information on abortion, even in magazines and books, was illegal. Copies of *Our Bodies, Ourselves,* a woman's health manual, were removed from public libraries, and

British editions of fashion magazines, such as *Vogue* or *Elle,* were censored to fulfill Irish abortion regulations.[25] Eventually, the Council of Europe, which monitors human rights in member states in light of the provisions of the Convention
for the Protection of Human Rights and Fundamental Freedoms, ruled that the
denial of information violated the right to impart and receive information contained in the convention. Thus, they ruled, Ireland was obligated to change its
law to correct this violation.[26] However, like many international organizations,
the council cannot coerce countries to abide by its rulings, and while it sent a
strong message to the Irish government, the government did not immediately act
on the ruling.

Other events in Ireland continued to generate controversy over the issue of
abortion and over the right of women to travel to procure an abortion. The plight
of a suicidal fourteen-year-old girl who had been raped by an older man caught
the attention of the public. The parents wished to take their daughter to England
for an abortion because the daughter claimed she would kill herself if forced to
carry the pregnancy to term. However, the attorney general sought to block the
family from leaving the country, arguing that the state had a responsibility to
defend the right of the unborn in light of the terms of the 1983 constitutional
amendment. The "X case," as it was known in the media, made its way to the
Supreme Court in 1992. The Court allowed the family to go to England, arguing
that even under the 1983 amendment, an abortion could be legally performed if
there was a "real and substantial risk" to a pregnant woman's life, including a risk
of suicide (although the girl eventually miscarried).[27] This reading of the amendment opened up a new debate: What did the court mean by "real and substantial
risk," and how liberally or conservatively should this be interpreted? The government was not in a hurry to write legislation further defining the parameters
of what constituted a "real and substantial risk" (including suicide), and, as of
summer 2009 (seventeen years later) no legislation has been passed to flesh out
this court decision.[28]

Abortion foes continued to mobilize to close what they perceived to be
loopholes in various laws restricting abortion access. This time, they chose to
focus on restricting women's abilities to travel abroad to procure an abortion.
Women feared that there would be pregnancy tests given to all women leaving
the country. The government put the issue to the public once again in a series
of referenda. Voters approved amendments guaranteeing rights to travel and to
information, which were signed by the president in December 1992. The voters
rejected the third amendment, which would have specifically allowed abortions
to be performed to save the physical, rather than mental health, of the mother,
although the wording also excluded suicide as a justification for having an abortion.[29] Thus, the Supreme Court's interpretation of the amendment remained
intact, and, further, women were allowed to access information about abortion
in Ireland and to travel abroad to procure an abortion.

However, the government was unwilling to design policy quickly to reflect the
referendum decisions, which guaranteed women's right to access of information

and travel, and thus did not announce proposed legislation to implement the results of the referendum until 1995. Further, the legislation placed restrictions on information distributed about abortion; information may not advocate or promote abortion, be displayed by notice in a public place, or appear in publications that are distributed without having been solicited by recipients. Organizations and individuals providing information, advice, or counseling on pregnancy may not advocate or promote abortion. They must provide information on all possible options, and they may not make any arrangements for the woman seeking an abortion, among other restrictions. The Supreme Court later upheld these regulations, disappointing both those who thought the laws were too liberal and those who felt the laws were overly restrictive.

In 1997, a similar case to the 1992 case reopened the issue of abortion. A thirteen-year-old girl was pregnant as a result of an alleged rape and said that she would kill herself if she could not have an abortion. However, because she was under the medical care of the Eastern Health Board, a state agency, they could not assist in the procurement of an abortion. In addition, the girl's father did not wish for her to have an abortion. The Court upheld the girl's right to have an abortion; the case also brought the issue of "crisis pregnancies" to public debate once again and highlighted the government's inaction on passing legislation outlining the parameters of the 1992 X case. In response, the government commissioned a working group to produce a Green Paper on the issue in the hopes of eventually drafting further legislation clarifying the legality of abortion. In September 1999, the government finally published the results, outlining seven possible legislative options. The options included an absolute constitutional ban on abortion, an amendment to the constitution to restrict application of the X case, maintenance of the status quo, legislation to allow abortion in circumstances such as those specified in the X case, and permitting abortion on further grounds, such as risk to the mother's mental health, pregnancies resulting from rape or incest, and on request. However, while the paper generated public and political debate around the issue of abortion, it did not push the government to formulate or propose legislation detailing under what conditions a woman may seek to terminate her pregnancy.

On March 6, 2002, voters once again went to the polls for a referendum on abortion. Voters were asked to decide on the Protection of Human Life in Pregnancy Bill, which, if passed, would have reversed the 1992 X case ruling, thus making all abortions once again illegal, regardless of circumstances. The bill was narrowly defeated by a margin of less than 1 percent (and about ten thousand votes), although voter turnout was quite low at 43 percent.[30] In other words, the original conditions of the 1992 Supreme Court ruling still stand; abortions are technically still legal if a woman's life is at risk from continued pregnancy, including cases of threatened suicide. In light of the divisiveness of the issue, Prime Minister Bertie Ahern continued to postpone writing legislation further defining the 1992 court decision and instead announced the establishment of the Crisis Pregnancy Agency to help women deal with the ramifications of unplanned pregnancies.[31] In March 2005, a spokesperson for the Department of Health reaffirmed the government's decision not to pursue legislation, stating that "the government has no plans to introduce legislation regarding abortion and there is no plan to legislate for the X case."[32] Thus, there has been no significant movement breaking the stalemate. Technically, abortion under very limited circumstances is legal in Ireland; however, few doctors will provide an abortion without stronger legal parameters defining what constitutes a "real and substantial risk" to a woman's life. However, increasing numbers of women are traveling to Great Britain to have the procedure; in 2002, the United Kingdom's Office for National Statistics found that 6,214 women who could not get an abortion in Ireland went to England for the procedure.[33]

There have been international efforts to highlight the issue of the status of reproductive rights in Ireland. In June 2001, a Dutch organization called Women on Waves docked their hundred-foot converted trawler in Dublin. Their mission, in part, was to dispense contraceptives and family planning advice. They were also licensed to use the drug RU-486, which is a pill that induces abortion in the first two months of pregnancy (also known as the "abortion pill"). In addition, the ship was also equipped to administer surgical and medical abortions. While Women on Waves did not intend to carry out surgical abortions, the group did plan on administering RU-486 to pregnant Irish women under Dutch law. Because they anchored their ship twelve miles offshore, they were located in international waters and thus were not subject to Irish law.[34] Further, in 2005, the Irish Human Rights Commission, a government commission that monitors Ireland's adherence to the UN-sponsored Convention on the Elimination of Discrimination Against Women (CEDAW), criticized the government for not doing enough to combat discrimination against women. It also specifically urged the government to pass legislation specifying the precise circumstances under which an abortion could take place in Ireland.[35] And in July 2009, the European Court of Human Rights, which adjudicates on human rights issues among the 47 states of the Council of Europe, agreed to hear a challenge by three Irish women (known only as A, B, and C) who argue that the ban jeopardizes their health, their wellbeing, and violates their human rights. Any court decision at this level will be binding on the Irish government. However, regardless of the outcome, the cases have generated additional publicity for and attention to the unresolved issue of abortion in Ireland.[36]

Yet, there is little indication that Irish society is ready to tackle decisively the issue of abortion, and citizens are still enormously conflicted, more so than in other European countries, about when a woman can terminate her pregnancy. For example, in 1990, a European Values study found that 65 percent of Irish respondents approved of abortion when the mother's health was at risk. In contrast, 95 percent of Europeans approved of abortion under these circumstances. Support for abortion crumbled in the face of other potential scenarios; only 32 percent approved of an abortion when it was likely that the child would be handicapped, and only 8 percent supported a woman's right to have an abortion when the mother was not married or when a married couple did not want to have more children. Thus, the public's approval of liberalized abortion law was highly dependent on a specific set of circumstances and did not encompass the feminist rhetoric of personal autonomy and a "woman's right to choose." [37] Other data indicate that an even lower percentage of Irish citizens support abortion rights; according to the 2000 World Values survey data, 51 percent of those surveyed thought that abortion was never justifiable, while only about 3 percent of the population felt that it was always justifiable. [38] These figures also indicate that public tolerance for abortion is substantially lower in Ireland than in other European countries. The government has reflected this ambivalence by attempting to resolve the issue through public referenda and by delaying the implementation of legislation that would further clarify the issue.

In addition, the coalition of organizations opposing abortion has been extremely well organized and influential. For example, the Irish Medical Council has been a central player in maintaining a unified stance against substantially liberalizing the practice. The council was established by law in 1978 to register and discipline doctors and provide guidance on professional standards and ethical conduct. They are the main state-sanctioned regulatory agency for the medical profession. Until recently, the council took an express position against any kind of abortion, and their ethical guidelines contained the statement, "The deliberate and intentional destruction of the unborn child is professional misconduct." [39] While the 2004 edition of the *Guide to Ethical Conduct and Behavior* has been updated to reflect the changing nature of abortion policy in Ireland, nonetheless the current language states that "We consider that there is a fundamental difference between abortion carried out with the intention of taking the life of the baby, for example for social reasons, and the unavoidable death of the baby resulting from essential treatment to protect the life of the mother." [40] Thus, while the Medical Council has softened its opposition to abortion, it has been a major force in advocating for a more restrictive policy, unlike medical associations in other countries that have sided with substantially liberalizing abortion laws. The church has also been a central player in a country that is overwhelmingly Catholic. However, according to World Values survey data, in the previous decade, the public's level of trust in the Catholic Church, one of the leading forces arguing against liberalization of abortion laws, declined and only 30 percent of those surveyed thought that churches gave answers to moral problems, compared to 42 percent in 1990. [41] It is unclear whether this will have any effect on the church's leadership on the abortion issue in the coming years.

In contrast, the women's movement has struggled in mounting a well-organized opposition along themes that resonate with the public. While there are numerous women's organizations that advocate for liberalizing the abortion laws, they have been unable to generate massive support for widened access to abortion by framing the issue around feminist arguments regarding women's autonomy over their own bodies. Rather, they have tried to soften laws by appealing to a public sense of compassion for women in crisis. Further, because the state is heavily influenced by antiliberalization forces, the women's movement in Ireland has been more active internationally, advocating for the EU to put increased pressure on the Irish government or working with the organization Women on Waves to bring attention to the situation of women seeking abortions in Ireland.[42]

THE UNITED STATES

While the United States, compared to other countries, has enacted relatively liberal abortion laws, these laws have come under some of the most sustained and vigorous attack of any nation that has legalized abortion. The debate has occupied nearly every branch of the government and civil society, ranging from the legislative, executive, judicial, and bureaucratic bodies at the federal state and local levels. While women's organizations have made a substantial impact on abortion policy, that impact has constantly been under attack, and the issue continues to divide American politics, holding up judicial nominations and determining nominations for political office at all levels of politics. In addition, although a relatively liberal abortion law has been in effect in the United States since 1973, a variety of forces—political, economic, geographic, and medical—ensure that while women have a legal right to abortion, in practice, many women, particularly low-income women, are unable to access abortion services.

Historically, abortions were permitted in America before "quickening." However, in the nineteenth century, many states, at the urging of the American Medical Association, began passing laws prohibiting all or most abortions.[43] Part of this stemmed from the emerging profession's attempts to establish greater authority over the area as well as to professionalize a field still populated with quacks, traditional healers, and semi-trained practitioners. By 1900, all but six states had designed legislation that gave doctors discretion in deciding when abortion was necessary (usually to save the life of the mother), and thus legal.[44] This model remained in place up to the early 1960s, and in all but nine states, abortion was permitted only if the woman's life was in danger. Reform was implemented in many states in the five years before the landmark 1973 *Roe v. Wade* decision; eighteen states reformed or repealed their anti-abortion legislation. In the remaining thirty-two states and the District of Columbia, laws that criminalized abortion unless performed to save the life or health of the mother remained on the books. The pregnant woman's mental health also became more accepted as a justification or abortion.[45]

However, the 1973 Supreme Court decision, which legalized abortion throughout the United States, tipped off a nationwide debate, which continues still without resolution. The *Roe v. Wade* decision was the culmination of a variety of trends in social movement mobilization, previous court decisions, and statewide trends. The National Organization for Women, formed in 1966, was one of the early proponents of legalized abortion. Drawing from the experiences of the civil rights movement, which had achieved numerous movement goals through constitutional litigation through the court system, the women's movement adopted a similar strategy. An early success was the 1965 Supreme Court case *Griswold v. Connecticut*, which legalized contraception for married couples under the argument that the Constitution protected a couple's "right to privacy." Finally, reform of abortion laws at the state level created a momentum, which crested with the 1973 *Roe v. Wade* decision.

Margaret Sanger (1884–1966)

"A woman's body belongs to herself alone. It does not belong to the United States of America or any other government on the face of the earth. Enforced motherhood is the most complete denial of a woman's right to life and liberty. Women cannot be on an equal footing with men until they have full and complete control over their reproductive function."[i]

Abortion policies have become such a controversial issue that many forget that the various sides in the debate often have a similar goal—to reduce, if not end, the need for women to terminate their pregnancies. Women's activists often point out that one way to reduce the number of unwanted pregnancies is to increase the availability of contraceptives, as well as education for women, men, and families about family planning options. As we shall see in Chapter 9, women's right to control the timing and number of their children has been affirmed at numerous international conferences. Yet, we forget that for many years, women lacked (and still lack) this basic freedom; the state often restricted women's access to birth control, as well as any information about family planning. In the United States, up until 1965, a Connecticut law prohibited the use of contraception, even by married couples, until the Supreme Court struck it down in *Griswold v. Connecticut*. This right to contraception wasn't extended to unmarried couples until 1972.[ii]

Although hundreds of men and women worked to increase women's access to information about and means to use birth control, Margaret Sanger was the public face and driving force behind the movement to legalize contraception in America. Sanger's public drive was very much influenced by events in her own life; she was deeply influenced by watching the experiences of her devoutly Catholic mother, who endured eighteen pregnancies, eleven births, and seven miscarriages before succumbing to tuberculosis from the ravages of so many births. Sanger, who wanted a different life for herself and for other women, went to nursing school in the hopes of expanding her own and, by extension, other women's medical knowledge about pregnancy. She was further radicalized by the experiences of working in the slums of New York City's Lower East Side, where she was inundated with requests from mothers desperate for information about and means to prevent (or at least plan) future pregnancies. Further, she saw firsthand the terrible results when women took medical matters into their own hands and resorted to illegal or self-induced abortions, often dying from their efforts. This was at a time in America when buying even a single condom made one a criminal in thirty states.[iii] Sanger also became convinced that poverty was a driving force in constraining women's choices.

In response to her experiences, Sanger launched a variety of newsletters publicizing information about contraception. At the time, this violated New York state law, and she was arrested and served time in jail in 1913 and 1916 for her efforts to educate women. After a state judge allowed doctors to provide birth control information to married women, Sanger worked tirelessly to found a network of clinics to serve women. Her efforts eventually led to the establishment of Planned Parenthood Federation of America, as well as Planned Parenthood International. She then turned her energies to spearheading the effort to create America's first nearly 100 percent reliable oral contraceptive, the birth control pill. She worked tirelessly, lecturing not only in the United States but also abroad in Europe and in Japan, in her efforts to enable women to make their own reproductive choices.

Most of us don't realize how much this tiny pill has transformed society after it was approved by the Food and Drug Administration in 1960; over the following decades, it redistributed power in so many places—the bedroom, the classroom, and the workplace, to name a few. Women, on a mass level, had the ability to choose when and whether to have children, to marry, and to work. Perhaps the pill has helped create the current situation in which women outnumber men in colleges and graduate degrees. In 1931, H. G. Wells wrote the following about Margaret Sanger's crusade to legalize birth control: "The movement she started will grow to be, a hundred years from now, the most influential of all time. When the history of our civilization is written, it will be a biological history, and Margaret Sanger will be its heroine."[iv]

---

[i] As quoted in Nancy Woloch, *Women and the American Experience* (New York: Alfred A. Knopf, 1984), 369.
[ii] Gloria Steinem, "Margaret Sanger," The Time 100: The Most Important People of the Century, www.time.com/time/time100/leaders/profile/sanger.html, March 21, 2009.
[iii] "Margaret Sanger: Birth Control of a Nation," *BusinessWeek* (September 13, 2004), www.businessweek.com/magazine/content/04_37/b3899026_mz072.htm, March 21, 2009.
[iv] As quoted in Steinem, "Margaret Sanger."

In *Roe v. Wade*, the Court established the framework for deciding the legality of abortion. There were several larger issues at stake: For example, when does a fetus become a "person," and thus a citizen of the United States deserving of rights and protection of those rights? The Court held that a fetus is not a person, and therefore is not entitled to protection under the United States Constitution until it reaches the point of viability, or the point at which the fetus is sufficiently developed that it could live and develop in normal conditions outside of the uterus. The Court defined viability as occurring between twenty-four and twenty-eight weeks of gestation. It then set up a trimester system, which outlined the changing balance between a woman's right to choose to terminate her pregnancy and the state's interest in regulating the procedure. The justices ruled that a woman's decision to have an abortion in the first trimester was a decision to be made by a woman in consultation with her doctor. However, the Court ruled that individual states could regulate abortion in the second trimester in ways that would preserve and protect the woman's health. In the third trimester of pregnancy, which was after fetal viability, the Court ruled that states could regulate or even outlaw abortion unless the procedure was necessary to preserve the life or health of the mother. In the 1973 case *Doe v. Bolton,* the Court defined "health" to include "all factors—physical, emotional, psychological, familial, and the woman's age— relevant to the well-being of the patient."[46] In sum, the Court required states to justify interfering with a woman's decision by showing that it had a "compelling interest" in doing so and that restrictions on abortion before fetal viability were limited to narrowly and precisely defined concerns about maternal health.

Writing for the majority, Justice Blackmun based the Court's decision on the "right to privacy." The Court did not invent this right in 1973; it was drawing on a legacy of court decisions dating back to 1891 that had articulated the boundaries of government intervention in private affairs. A right to privacy had been used to defend people's rights to refuse medical treatment, not to undergo forced sterilization, and to access birth control. However, *Roe v. Wade,* by arguing that a woman's decision to continue her pregnancy was protected under the constitutional provisions of individual autonomy and privacy, extended this right to privacy to encompass a woman's right to choose whether or not to terminate a pregnancy.

This decision had an immediate effect. On the one hand, thousands of women who before might have undergone a dangerous, illegal, and potentially life-threatening medical procedure now had access to legal, safe, and relatively simple methods to terminate a pregnancy. Within a few years following the decision, the mortality rate for women undergoing legal abortions was ten times lower than the rate for women who had illegal abortions. It was also five times lower than that for women undergoing childbirth.[47]

However, rather than settling a nationwide debate, *Roe v. Wade* actually launched and mobilized a divisive struggle between pro-abortion and anti-abortion forces. The anti-abortion forces, who had been a small, relatively disorganized contingency, became much more organized and active after the ruling and began a campaign aimed at reversing *Roe v. Wade* and creating as many legal barriers to abortion as possible. The pro-abortion rights organizations similarly mobilized to protect a woman's right to choose to terminate a pregnancy on her own terms.

This battle has been waged in small and large ways in the various arenas of American politics. In terms of the judicial arena, the Supreme Court has ruled repeatedly on the abortion issue. The most significant case in terms of affecting the reach of *Roe v. Wade* was the Webster ruling of July 3, 1989 (*Webster v. Reproductive Health Services*). By a one-vote margin, the Court upheld a Missouri law that barred the use of public funds, employers, or buildings for abortions. As we will discuss later in greater depth, the effect of this was to restrict the availability of abortions, as well as who could access them. In addition, the law required abortion providers to conduct tests to determine whether a fetus was viable at twenty weeks. In upholding the Missouri law, the Court's decision weakened the trimester framework outlined in *Roe v. Wade.*

This also signaled the Court's willingness to allow individual states greater latitude in designing abortion policy. In fact, following the *Webster* ruling, many states interpreted this as a green light to pass more restrictive legislation. For example, Pennsylvania soon enacted a law requiring a woman to notify her husband, receive state-prepared information on alternatives to abortion from her physician, and wait an additional twenty-four hours before obtaining an abortion. Kansas, Mississippi, North Dakota, and Ohio also required the provision of alternative information as well as waiting periods. Louisiana, Utah, and the territory of Guam enacted more punitive abortion bans, narrowing the conditions under which women could seek an abortion. Less than two decades after writing his original opinion in *Roe v. Wade,* Justice Blackmun wrote in his dissent on the *Webster* ruling: "For today, the women of this Nation still retain the liberty to control their destinies. But the signs are evident and very ominous, and a chill wind blows."[48] For the first time, only four justices voted to uphold *Roe* in its entirety.

The Supreme Court further adjusted the conditions set down by *Roe v. Wade* in its June 1992 ruling, *Planned Parenthood of Southeastern Pennsylvania v. Casey.* The Court upheld a woman's constitutional right to an abortion before viability and ruled that a state may prohibit abortion thereafter only if it provides exceptions for the life and health of the mother. However, the Court also rejected the trimester framework established by *Roe v. Wade* and argued that states have legitimate interests in protecting the health of the woman and the life of the unborn fetus from the outset of pregnancy. In addition, the Court adopted more lenient standards under which to evaluate the constitutionality of state restrictions on abortion. Under this new ruling, the state may regulate abortion throughout pregnancy as long as it does not "unduly burden" a woman's right to choose. An undue burden was defined as a substantial obstacle in the path of a woman seeking to terminate an abortion before fetal viability. For example, in this case, the Court ruled that a Pennsylvania law that had imposed a twenty-four hour waiting period before attaining an abortion, required a woman to receive alternative information, and mandated that teenagers receive the consent of at least one parent did not constitute an "undue burden." It did, however, find spousal consent to be an undue burden on a woman's right to abortion and struck down that portion of the law.[49]

Once again, taking the lead from the courts, individual states moved to implement more restrictive abortion laws. As of 2009, thirty-four states require parental consent or notification for minors seeking an abortion; twenty-four states have enforced mandatory delays and state-directed counseling providing alternative options to termination, and four states (Idaho, Kentucky, Montana, and North Dakota) prohibit private insurance coverage for abortion unless the woman's life is endangered if she were to carry the pregnancy to term.[50]

The U.S. Congress has also gotten involved in the abortion issue. In 1976, Congress passed the first Hyde Amendment, which banned the use of federal Medicaid dollars, essentially health insurance for the poor, and other federal funds for almost all abortions, except when the pregnancy was terminated as a result of rape or incest or endangered the life of the mother. As of March 2009, only seventeen states covered abortion under Medicaid for reasons beyond rape, incest, and life endangerment.[51] In later years, other restrictions on use of federal funds for abortion were placed on other federal spending measures, which covered federal workers, military personnel, women on reservations, and inmates. The effect of the Hyde Amendment was to make abortion unfeasible for many poor women, whose health benefits were covered under Medicaid. While abortion costs $300–$500 during the first trimester, the fees escalate precipitously after the first twelve weeks. Thus, even though abortion is legal, for many poor women, it is financially out of reach and not an option. The Supreme Court upheld this ban in *Harris v. McRae* (1980), reasoning that government could distinguish between abortion and "other medical procedures" because "no other procedure involves the purposeful termination of a potential life."[52]

Abortion foes in Congress also lobbied to have their views implemented in U.S. foreign policy. Senator Jesse Helms of North Carolina, in response to the *Roe v. Wade* decision, introduced the "Human Life Amendment" to the Constitution, which would have overturned *Roe v. Wade*. It failed to pass. However, he did successfully insert restrictions on foreign assistance, which prevented the use of federal funds for "abortion as a method of family planning." President Clinton lifted this ban, also known as the Global Gag Rule; in 2000, President George W. Bush reimposed the ban and tied development dollars once again to domestic demands. President Obama, upon assuming office in 2009, lifted the ban, once again freeing up federal funding for international nonprofit organizations that provide a full range of information on women's reproductive choices.

Presidents have gotten involved in the abortion debate in other ways. When President Clinton took office in January 1993, he rescinded several of the policies of previous administrations designed to discourage women from obtaining an abortion. The president lifted restrictions on abortion counseling at federally financed family planning clinics and also allowed federal research using fetal tissue from aborted fetuses. He also reversed a 1979 decision and allowed physicians at U.S. military hospitals to resume abortion provision services for armed service personnel and their dependents who paid the cost. Finally, the president asked the Department of Health and Human Services to review the import ban of RU-486, the French-manufactured "abortion pill," and to rescind it if there was cause to do so.[53]

However, Congress mobilized in response to these steps and soon moved to impose more restrictions on abortions. Congress reinstated the prohibition against physicians at U.S. military hospitals performing abortions for armed services personnel and their dependents who paid for the procedure. They also passed legislation prohibiting federal employees' health insurance from including abortion coverage except in cases of rape, incest, or danger to the life of the mother.[54]

Congress also passed legislation banning certain abortion procedures, specifically, the performance of the dilation and extraction procedure for the performance of late-term abortions. Although this procedure accounts for approximately 0.03–0.05 percent of all abortions, abortion opponents were successful in mobilizing support against the procedure. Using extraordinarily graphic images, many of which had been enhanced and altered, and naming the procedure a "partial birth abortion," anti-abortion advocates portrayed the practice as a bloody and brutal act of violence on both the mother and the unborn child. Opponents of the ban contended that the procedure, used in a handful of cases, was both necessary to protect the health of the mother and was safer than the other alternative methods. This legislation was approved by wide margins twice and was vetoed twice. Congress was unable to override the veto and waited until a president who was more sympathetic to the legislation took office. In November 2003, President George W. Bush signed into the law the Partial Birth Abortion Ban Act, stating that "at last, the American people and our government have confronted the violence and come to the defense of the innocent child." He went on to state that the "right to life cannot be granted or denied by government, because it does not come from government, it comes from the Creator of life." [55] The following year, three district courts declared the ban unconstitutional because it did not include an exception for the women's health and also because the language defining the procedure was so broad that it could be used to outlaw a range of second-trimester procedures.[56] Appeals to these decisions were filed, and in 2007 the Supreme Court ruled in *Gonzalez v. Carhartt* that the legislative ban does not represent an undue burden on women, and as a result is constitutional. Thus, the Partial Birth Abortion Ban Act stands.

On the other hand, Congress has also acted to protect the right of access to abortion services. In response to the growing militancy and extremism of anti-abortion advocates picketing abortion clinics, Congress passed the Freedom of Access to Clinics Act in 1994. The act establishes federal criminal penalties and civil remedies "for certain violent, threatening, obstructive, and destructive conduct that is intended to injure, intimidate, or interfere with persons seeking to obtain or provide reproductive health services." [57] Despite the legislation, abortion providers are continuously harassed by anti-abortion forces. In a 2000 survey of abortion providers, 80 percent reported that they had been picketed, 28 percent had been picketed and their patients had had physical contact with the protesters, 18 percent had experienced vandalism, 14 percent said the homes of staff members had been picketed, and 15 percent had received bomb threats.[58] Despite the legislation protecting them, women seeking abortions as well as abortion providers face severe verbal and physical harassment. And in some extreme circumstances, they face death. In June 2009, Doctor George Tiller, one of the few remaining doctors in the United States who performed third trimester pregnancies, was gunned down in the lobby of his church Sunday morning as he handed out the bulletin. [59]

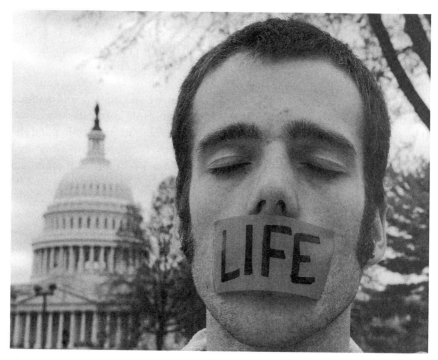

The abortion debate in America has been waged in all branches of government at both the national and state levels. Here, an anti-abortion protester prays outside of the Supreme Court building, where the Court, in a 5–4 ruling, upheld a federal partial birth abortion ban. (April 18, 2007) SOURCE: Jonathan Ernst/Getty Images

As a result, even though the United States has, on paper, a relatively liberal abortion law, it is harder for women to access these services. For one, women are discouraged from having abortions in a variety of ways; many states have imposed legislation requiring women to undergo mandatory counseling, endure a waiting period, or acquire parental permission. Further, the various restrictions on the use of federal funds for abortion services essentially place abortion beyond the financial parameters of poor women, who ironically take on the long-term financial burden of raising a child with inadequate resources because they lack the short-term resources to make preventing that pregnancy possible. Finally, despite the legality of abortion, abortions are increasingly difficult to procure because many doctors are no longer willing or able to provide them. Increasingly, abortions are provided at abortion clinics (defined as facilities where half or more of patient visits are for abortion services) rather than at hospitals or doctor's offices. For example, while about fifteen hundred hospitals performed abortions in 1980, that number fell to about six hundred by 2001.[60] Many doctors were intimidated by the constant harassment and violent methods of certain factions of the anti-abortion movement, who were willing to picket doctors at work as well as at their homes. In addition, abortion providers are aging, and newer colleagues are not entering the field; fewer than half (46 percent) of residency training programs in obstetrics and gynecology routinely provide training in first-trimester abortion.[61]

As a result, many women, despite their legal right to an abortion, cannot exercise that right. In 2000, 87 percent of U.S. counties had no abortion provider. In nonmetropolitan areas, 97 percent of counties had no provider. Thus, it is no surprise that about one in four women who have an abortion travel fifty miles or more for the procedure or that the percentage of women in counties without a facility that provides even one abortion a year climbed to 34 percent in 2000. This percentage of unserviced areas is steadily climbing.[62]

THE NETHERLANDS

The Netherlands represents an interesting case study of abortion politics and policies. One the one hand, the government liberalized its abortion policy later than many other western European countries did. Abortion was not legalized until 1981, and the legislation did not come into effect until 1984, although in practice, abortion services were liberalized a decade before these changes were legalized. In addition, while women have the right to terminate their pregnancy until viability (about twenty-four weeks), they must receive counseling from their doctor and must undergo a five-day waiting period. Thus, the Netherlands provides a slightly modified version of abortion "on demand" by involving the medical establishment more thoroughly in a woman's decision than in countries such as the United States. However, since the passage of the Pregnancy Termination Act, abortion has not been challenged seriously by any social group within the Netherlands. In addition, the Netherlands has one of the lowest abortion rates in the world, despite the widespread availability and public financing of the procedure.[63] What accounts for this particular outcome in the Netherlands?

Abortion was criminalized in the Netherlands in 1886. However, the law required proof that the fetus was alive at the time of the abortion as a requirement for conviction; because such proof was difficult to obtain, it was nearly impossible to convict anyone for performing the procedure. This legislation was amended in 1911 to try to further regulate abortions, and in practice, abortions were outlawed except when performed to save the life of the mother.[64] However, few people were convicted under the laws; in 1973, when the abortion debate returned to the public arena, only three people had been convicted.[65]

As in many other countries, challenges to and efforts to revise the criminalization of abortion surfaced in the late 1960s and throughout the 1970s. For one, Dutch society in the 1960s was in the midst of massive attitudinal changes. Traditionally, family planning had been discouraged, for it interfered with the objectives of marriage and supposedly encouraged promiscuity. However, the birth control pill was introduced in 1964, and contraceptives in general became more readily available. In addition, England liberalized its abortion laws in 1968, and Dutch women began to travel there to terminate their pregnancies. Further, there was emerging pressure from women's groups, academics, and the medical industry to update legislation to accommodate current practice. In particular, the medical industry argued that existing legislation did not adequately allow for abortion under conditions of medical necessity and that doctors should be able to decide when an abortion was necessary. Starting in 1967, with the tacit approval of the relevant legal authorities (even though no new legislation had been passed), several university hospitals created "abortion teams" to reach consensus on the conditions under which an abortion would be medically necessary. By 1973, teams were essentially allowing all abortions if the woman requested it, and throughout the 1970s, doctors openly defied the law by opening private clinics providing abortion on demand. In essence, the Dutch government had to address the abortion issue because practice was in direct conflict with written legislation.[66]

The government first delved into the issue in 1967, when members of parliament first considered reforming abortion; three years later, in 1970, the Cabinet appointed a special commission to study the issue. However, the main obstacle to passing reform lay in the Dutch multiparty, parliamentary system. In parliamentary systems, no one party is usually able to win a majority of seats. As a result, coalition governments are often the only way to build a parliamentary majority. The leadership of the various coalition parties negotiates a pact for each new cabinet, which sets the political agenda for the next four years. Party discipline is strict, and adherence to the pact is expected and is relaxed only in the event of individual conscience. This negotiation process can take weeks, even months to hammer out so that all parties reach agreement.

In addition, this process is complicated by the fact that until 1994, coalition governments always involved the three main religious parties, which had united into a coalition called the Christian Democratic Appeal (CDA). The CDA often served as the critical coalition partner with either of the two major ruling parties, the Liberals and the Social Democrats, and was able to veto abortion reform, even if their larger coalition partner was in favor of such a development. As a result, from 1971 until 1984, the abortion issue was raised but not resolved in the negotiations of coalition pacts. On several occasions, the issue threatened to endanger the life of incumbent cabinets.[67]

Throughout the 1970s, the Dutch government unsuccessfully tried to resolve the issue of abortion. An initial liberalization of the abortion law, which would have permitted the procedure only where pregnancy posed a threat to the women's physical or mental health, was presented to parliament in June 1972 and was met with strong opposition from both the left, who felt it did not go far enough, and the right, who felt it had gone too far. However, before the parliament could vote on it, the cabinet fell because of an unrelated fiscal policy issue, and the bill died a silent death. The bill was also the last time that the Dutch government tried to contain abortion; afterward, the debate moved on to an issue of who decides when women can get an abortion, as opposed to under what conditions women may get an abortion. In the next coalition government, the relevant parties could not come to an agreement, and legislation foundered once again.[68] However, coalition partners were able to agree not to prosecute clinics that were performing abortions except in cases of medical malpractice.

After a flurry of coalition negotiations, in 1980 the government finally succeeded in introducing abortion legislation to the parliament. In May 1981, the Dutch parliament passed the Pregnancy Termination Act, which repealed the restrictive 1911 regulations. However, it took another three years for the legislation to be translated into administrative regulations. Further, the legislation passed with the smallest majority of votes possible, mainly because those who voted against the law felt it was not liberal enough.

The legislation essentially affirmed abortion practices that had been implemented over the previous decade.[69] Currently, abortion is permitted virtually upon request between conception and viability, which the legislature set at twenty-four weeks, although in practice this was translated into twenty-two weeks. According to the law, abortion is allowed if the woman is in an "emergency situation," which is to be determined by a woman together with her physician. In practice, this has been loosely interpreted, and abortion is permitted virtually on request. However, the woman must also accept counseling from the physician to ensure that the decision to terminate the pregnancy is taken carefully and that the woman feels that this is her only viable choice. After the initial visit, women must wait for five days before undergoing the procedure. After the abortion, a woman must be given access to adequate aftercare, including information on how to prevent unwanted pregnancies in the future. Physicians in a clinic or hospital may only perform abortions with the appropriate permit from the Ministry of Health, Welfare and Sport. Finally, if a doctor has a conscientious objection to providing abortions, he or she must immediately inform the woman of this fact, and the doctor may also choose not to perform the procedure. Since November 1984, the government-sponsored national health insurance system has covered the costs of abortion for Dutch women. Despite initial fears, this did not result in an immediate rise in the number of abortions.[70]

In the wake of the law's implementation, there has been relatively little opposition. There has been concern expressed over the fact that technically, women cannot seek an abortion (unless her life is endangered) once the fetus is considered viable (which, at the very latest, is twenty-four weeks). In practice, abortions are only allowed after viability if there are very serious defects, which in effect means that the fetus will die in the womb or shortly after birth (thus, it is not viable).[71] However, in many situations, doctors are unable to detect severe (but not life-threatening) diseases or impairments such as Down Syndrome or spina bifida until about week twenty-four, thus eliminating abortion as a legal option.[72] Women who find out after viability that they their fetus has severe (but not life threatening) developmental issues then have to travel abroad to seek a late-term abortion if they choose to terminate the pregnancy.

Yet, for the most part, abortion has been a noncontentious social issue. Why is this? There are several significant themes that emerge from the Dutch case study. For one, legislation legitimized a decade of abortion practice that was much more liberal than existing law dictated. In some ways, legislation enforced an already evolving social acceptance of the practice, rather than exacerbating existing social cleavages. The main impediment to legislation was not public opinion but, rather, the complexities of the Dutch parliamentary system, which gave disproportionate amounts of power to smaller coalition partners, who could often derail legislative initiative. Further, a key player, the medical industry, which had derailed reform in countries such as Ireland, was a major proponent of reform in the Netherlands.

In addition, the Netherlands has always combined a liberal abortion policy with strong support for contraception programs. The Netherlands has one of the lowest abortion rates in the world; up until the end of 1996, it had the lowest rate in the world. In 1997, the abortion rate in the Netherlands was 6.5 per 1,000 women, compared to 22.9 in the United States.[73] In addition, 95 percent of abortions are performed within the first thirteen weeks of pregnancy.[74] Abortion has never been intended as a method of family planning; given the strong family planning programs that exist, Dutch women are able to exercise more choice and control over their fertility and, thus, perhaps, do not have to face the decision of whether to abort as often as women in other countries do.

There has been a recent rise in the number of abortions, threatening the Dutch reputation of liberal abortion laws but low rates of provision. In 2003, the rate had risen to 8.7 abortions for every 1,000 women of child-bearing age.[75] The rise in abortion rates is most significant among young girls and immigrant women. Of the teenagers seeking to terminate a pregnancy, 60 percent had an ethnic background from traditional immigration countries such as Suriname, the Dutch Antilles, Turkey, Morocco, and countries of Africa, eastern Europe, and Asia. Many of these women came to the Netherlands as asylum seekers or refugees, were raised in different cultural contexts, and also have less knowledge, as newly arrived citizens, of Dutch family planning services. A sizeable number of women seeking abortion in the Netherlands are also traveling from other countries.[76]

GENERAL THEMES

What larger lessons can we learn from the cases of the Ireland, the United States, and the Netherlands? What explains the varying outcomes of abortion policies in these three countries? While Ireland has moved to further restrict access to abortion, the United States wrote one of the most liberal laws, although the law has been under sustained attack for the past three and a half decades. Finally, the Netherlands has implemented a law that places some restrictions on woman's full autonomy but has also encountered relatively little resistance. What lessons can we draw from these differing outcomes?

One explanation may lie in prevailing attitudes about the justifiability of abortion. The World Values survey tracks attitudinal changes among populations in more than eighty countries on a wide array of social, economic, and political issues. One of the questions asked in the 2002 survey delves into people's tolerance for abortion. The question reads: "Please tell me for each of the following statements whether you think it [abortion] can always be justified, never justified, or something in between, using this card" (scale is 1 = never justifiable to 10 = always justifiable).[77]

As demonstrated in Table 6.2, the responses to this question from citizens in Ireland, the Netherlands, and the United States reveal marked differences in the public's acceptance of abortion. In Ireland, just over half of the population feel that abortion is never justified; the United States is in the middle, with less than a third of the population feeling that it is never justifiable; and the Dutch are most tolerant in their attitudes toward abortion, with 15.3 percent of respondents answering that abortion is never justified. Despite these figures, abortion for most citizens of these three countries is not a black or white issue; support for or opposition to the practice is contingent on a variety of extenuating circumstances, as the data indicate. Except for Ireland, the bulk of the citizenry differ, not so much in whether they support or oppose abortion, but under which conditions. Nonetheless, it is true that the citizenry in Ireland is most consistently opposed to liberalizing abortion laws; in the United States, public opinion seems to indicate more tolerance for the practice; and in the Netherlands, citizens are most tolerant, with just over 29 percent of the population placing themselves on the upper third of the ten-point scale of acceptance. Thus, some of the variation in policy outcomes potentially can be explained by variations in public opinion.

In addition, in our varied cases, the venues used for decision making were critical to the outcome of the debates. In Ireland, many of the decisions were made through the use of public referenda, and the government repeatedly distanced itself from the debate by delaying legislating the matter further. Thus, the debate was waged primarily in the court of public opinion, with some assistance from the Irish Supreme Court. Because the government has refused to design or enact policy, this has forced the issue into the broader arena of European politics. In the United States, the relatively open system, with power divided between the varied branches and among federal and state authority, allowed a variety of interest groups to lobby for policy in all possible arenas, thus prolonging the battle. Finally, in the Netherlands, the major policy decisions were left to the prime minister and the legislature, although the Dutch parliamentary system of coalition governments impeded the formulation of abortion policy for quite some time.

In addition, levels of social mobilization differed in our case studies. In particular, women's groups differed in their abilities to "gender" the debate and frame it as a woman's right to personal autonomy and choice with regard to her body. In Ireland, the women's movement for much of the debate was unable to present a unified position on abortion. Further, they had relatively few allies within the

Table 6.2 Acceptance of Abortion in Ireland, Netherlands, and the United States

			COUNTRY/REGION		
Justifiable: Abortion		IRELAND	NETHERLANDS	UNITED STATES OF AMERICA	TOTAL
Never justifiable	Count	498	152	354	1004
	% Within country/region	50.7%	15.3%	29.7%	31.7%
2	Count	79	57	84	220
	% Within country/region	8.0%	5.7%	7.0%	6.9%
3	Count	78	75	74	227
	% Within country/region	7.9%	7.5%	6.2%	7.2%
4	Count	43	59	66	168
	% Within country/region	4.4%	5.9%	5.5%	5.3%
5	Count	160	171	184	515
	% Within country/region	16.3%	17.2%	15.4%	16.3%
6	Count	26	97	145	268
	% Within country/region	2.6%	9.8%	12.2%	8.5%
7	Count	27	91	69	187
	% Within country/region	2.7%	9.2%	5.8%	5.9%
8	Count	24	114	85	223
	% Within country/region	2.4%	11.5%	7.1%	7.0%
9	Count	16	51	34	101
	% Within country/region	1.6%	5.1%	2.9%	3.2%
Always justifiable	Count	31	127	97	255
	% Within country/region	3.2%	12.8%	8.1%	8.0%
Total	Count	982	994	1192	3168
	% Within country/region	100.0%	100.0%	100.0%	100.0%

SOURCE: World Values Survey, "1999–2002 World Values Survey Questionnaire." http://www.worldvaluessurvey.org/statistics/index.html. (April 22, 2006).

government. As a result, they have been hesitant to frame the issue of abortion as a feminist issue, but have instead focused on invoking sympathy and tolerance for women in crisis pregnancies and improving women's access to abortion abroad. They were never able to fully counter the power of the Catholic Church and the medical profession, two potent lobbies in opposition to liberalized abortion policy. In the United States, women's organizations framed abortion as a women's rights issue. However, they were soon countered by an increasingly powerful and well-organized countermovement. Further, abortion became an increasingly partisan issue, with anti-abortion advocates dominating the Republican Party and prolegalization advocates influential in the Democratic Party. As a result, the debate increasingly has been framed as one that weighs competing rights of women with the status of the fetus. Although the Democratic Party reclaimed the Presidency, as well as majority in Congress in 2008, it is unclear whether the administration will revisit the issue, given its priorities on economic policy and health care. Given the current role of the Republican Party in national politics, it is doubtful that women's organizations in favor of abortion will be able to recapture the framing of the debate. Finally, in the Netherlands, women's groups succeeded in defining abortion as a women's issue and in winning most of their demands on access to services. The increasing presence of women in parliamentary parties, key cabinet positions, and a women's policy agency ready to advocate for abortion helped settle the debate by the 1980s. Further, the medical industry strongly favored reform, and opponents to liberalization did not organize or mobilize effectively.

ADVANCING WOMEN'S EQUALITY

The broader issue of reproductive rights is central to women's equality. Only women are biologically capable of giving birth, and they are often responsible for many of the tasks associated with child-rearing and family care. As we have seen, this has enormous ramifications for women's advancement in the realms of work and politics. However, it is important to recognize that not all women agree that improving access to abortion is the only way to increase women's abilities to make autonomous decisions about their bodies or that abortion is synonymous with advancing women's equality. What are the varied ways in which women's groups have sought to increase women's decision-making autonomy over their reproductive rights?

Feminists who advocate for a women's right to choose an abortion have emphasized increasing state support for abortion services, so that it is not a medical practice available to predominantly middle-class women. This is particularly the case in the United States, where access also continues to be a critical issue. In addition, numerous organizations, which may differ on widening access to abortion, agree on the need for increased funding for family planning. Many point to the Netherlands as an example of a country that, through its focus on sex education and responsible contraception programs, has enabled women to choose when to have children, so that they are less likely to be confronted with the difficult choice of whether or not to terminate a pregnancy. However, this has not been embraced universally across the political spectrum (particularly in the United States), as some Christian organizations have objected that it encourages promiscuity and teenage sex rather than abstinence before marriage. Alternatively, opponents of abortion have lobbied for increased funding for crisis centers and counseling for women to help them manage their conflicted reactions to a pregnancy so that they can come to terms with the ramifications of their pregnancy for their lives.

Finally, there are women's groups who do not view reproductive rights as a compelling women's issue. For example, in the United States, conservative organizations such as Concerned Women for America (CWA) self-consciously identify themselves as women's organizations that address women's issues from a conservative woman's point of view. The CWA is opposed to abortion and most forms of birth control, lobbies for legislation to limit or fully criminalize abortion, and opposes the use of federal funds for most domestic and international family planning programs. Their position is that abortion and family planning programs ultimately hurt women. First, they argue that abortions are psychologically damaging to women and can lead to "postabortion syndrome," in which women may suffer from something similar to posttraumatic stress disorder. They base their opposition to family planning in the argument that it increases negative health side effects for women. While the CWA does not speak for all women who oppose abortion, it is an example of a woman's group that opposes contraception, abortion, and other family planning services from a "woman's perspective."[78]

CONCLUSION

In the past forty years, abortion has moved from an issue that was considered to be a private dilemma to one of public controversy. In deciding who ultimately gets to make the final decision on women's control of family planning, women's groups, governments, religious organizations, and the medical industry have all become key players in advocating what they feel to be the appropriate balance between a woman's right to control her own body and fetal rights to survival.

Abortion is merely one issue in an increasingly contested domain of reproductive rights. Dramatic leaps in technological and medical innovation have further complicated a variety of issues. Better fetal testing blurs the line between parental concerns over raising a child with a significant disability with more blatant eugenic motivations. Improved prenatal care has improved premature babies' chances at survival outside of the womb, even if those chances are heavily dependent on technology rather than internal levels of fetal development. States eventually will have to assess what this will mean for legislation that bases access to abortion on "viability." Strides in stem cell research and alternative conception methods have complicated a host of issues related to women's reproductive abilities and also challenge traditional notions of what constitutes the family. While abortion currently may be one of the more visible issues concerning reproductive rights on which states are expected to legislate, it will not be the last.

FOR MORE INFORMATION

Abortion Rights, United Kingdom, http://www.abortionrights.org.uk

Catholics for Choice, http://www.catholicsforchoice.org

International Planned Parenthood Federation, http://www.ippf.org/en/What-we-do/Abortion

The National Abortion Rights Action League, http://www.prochoiceamerica.org

The National Organization for Women, http://www.now.org/issues/abortion

The National Right to Life Council, http://www.nrlc.org

Operation Rescue, http://www.operationrescue.org

Planned Parenthood, information on Ireland, http://www.plannedparenthood.org/issues-action/international/articles/irelands-rights-6470.htm

Women on Waves, a Dutch NGO working to prevent unwanted pregnancy and unsafe abortions throughout the world, http://www.womenonwaves.org

Information on a number of films dealing with the topic of abortion can be found at http://www.abortionfilms.org/?lang=en.

4 Months, 3 Weeks and 2 Days—A Romanian film by director Christian Mungiu that won the top prize at the 2007 Cannes Film Festival, the film tells the story of a student who goes to great lengths to help her friend have a secret abortion.

Vera Drake—A British film by director Mike Leigh that tells the story of a woman who provides illegal abortions in 1950s England.

PART III

*‿○

Participation and Protest in the Global Community

In the previous part, the three chapters focused on ways in which advanced industrialized states have designed policies that impact the position and status of women in society. We focused on three areas of government action. First, we discussed varying equal employment policies. We then turned to how states try to balance the demands of production and reproduction by enacting legislation governing maternity leave and childcare. Finally, we looked at how states police the private realm by legislating issues such as reproduction that had once been considered private concerns. We found that while many states advance the rhetoric of gender equality, ensuring that that equality exists is a different matter. Providing equal employment opportunities, generous maternity leave benefits, comprehensive daycare, and control over reproductive choice often butts up against cultural values about appropriate divisions of labor between men and women in the family and poses difficult questions about whose interests, and whose welfare, should truly be at stake.

In this final part, we now turn to exploring a variety of women's issues that, although of global concern, tend to be concentrated in the countries of the developing world. For many of the world's citizens—men as well as women—overcoming the varied manifestations of poverty defines their daily lives. Poverty is a constant for much of the world's population—more than 1.2 billion people survive on less than $1 a day.[1] However, levels of economic deprivation are not the sole indicators of poverty; poverty also encompasses other dimensions, such as lack of empowerment, opportunity, capacity, and physical security. Thus, economic scarcity is a problem, not only in and of itself, but also because it often robs people of the abilities to make decisions about the ways in which they want to live their lives.[2] Further, as we shall see in the following chapters, while it is a constant for many people, poverty, and the problems that arise from it, also has a female face. Women participate in and benefit from the process of socioeconomic development in different and unequal ways. Not only do these gender inequalities exacerbate the varied facets of poverty, but the varied facets of poverty also, in turn, exacerbate gender inequalities.

We want to underscore that many of the issues we will discuss in the ensuing chapters are universal to women all over the world; access to education, stable employment, adequate political representation, and physical and mental well-being are important goals that all women share, in all countries. Yet, a variety of problems—colonial legacies, weak governments, endemic poverty, and some traditional cultural values—ensure that many women in the developing world have a fundamentally different experience from Western women in achieving these goals. For example, while women all over the world struggle to secure their own reproductive health, many women in the developing world face challenges in gaining control and choice over this basic element of their lives that are fundamentally different from those faced by women in advanced industrialized nations. A woman in Africa faces a 1 in 16 chance of dying in childbirth, while a woman in a developed country faces a 1 in 2,800 risk. The reasons behind this figure are numerous: women's lack of power in the household, lack of government funding of public health care, and endemic poverty all play a role in ensuring that women in the developing world lack access to choices, opportunities, and services to improve their lives. Thus, it is important to underscore that while women are unequal in status in almost all societies, the depth, nature, reasons for, and solutions to that inequality differ substantially in various countries and contexts.

In addition, while these issues tend to be concentrated in the countries of the developing world, this does not mean that these issues are not of global significance. The effects of increased globalization and migration, resulting in large immigrant populations in Western countries, as well as greater interdependence among nations, also mean that few problems are entirely "local." Many of the issues discussed in this final part are not constrained by national borders; sweatshop labor, trafficking in women, or HIV/AIDS transmission do not stay contained within the boundaries of nation-states. Nor can the problem always be resolved solely by any one government. Further, many governments in the developing world lack the capacity to tackle these issues on their own and need assistance, technical as well as financial, to address many of the social dimensions related to poverty. Thus, the scope and nature of the problem as well as the nature of the remedy increasingly demand concerted, international, coordinated action. Efforts to ameliorate these problems also extend beyond traditional nation-state borders—international organizations, such as the United Nations, foreign governments, and nonprofit organizations have all become involved in trying to improve the quantity and quality of women's lives in the developing world. In turn, women's organizations, either at the grassroots level or through their participation in transnational networks, have lobbied these same agencies to incorporate gender concerns more thoroughly into their development projects.

In this final part, we look at a variety of issues that affect women globally. You may notice that the chapters in this final part are quite short. They are meant to be. In this final part, we wanted to devote our time and energy to highlighting a variety of issues rather than delving in depth into a select few. As a result, the chapters may not treat topics as deeply as the previous chapters do, but they do provide a telling snapshot of some of the most critical issues facing women around the world.

We start off by surveying the wide array of international organizations that are involved in addressing gender issues and concerns. Organizations such as the United Nations, the World Bank, the European Union, Human Rights Watch, and Amnesty International have all targeted improving the position and status of women as a goal in its own right as well as a means to foster greater levels of economic, social, and human development for all. These organizations have worked to pass international treaties, conferences, and declarations on the rights of women, in the hopes of encouraging global standards of gender justice. They have also launched numerous programs to address women's unequal status in access to critical political, economic, and social positions of power. These efforts have met with mixed levels of success. Designing international policy that effectively addresses and ameliorates, for example, women's inequality in the home, the workplace, or society is a difficult task for all societies; doing so in a context of extreme income inequality, ethnic diversity, or state collapse can stymie the most well-meaning development project. Thus, international organizations face an uphill, although by no means insurmountable, battle.

The material presented in the following chapters addresses critical and compelling global issues affecting women in countries on nearly every continent. For decades, international agencies have addressed the issue of women's economic disempowerment in much of the developing world. Despite the fact that women are increasingly active in the labor force, economically, worldwide, women are poorer than men, even though, on average, they work longer days. Women are often stratified in low-paying "female" jobs or work outside the formal economic sector, and are thus not protected by legislation. In particular, we discuss in Chapter 8 the emerging role of women in the global economy. As countries struggle to provide greater levels of economic growth for their countries, women have become the engine of this growth, serving as cheap but reliable labor in garment and low-tech industries that are located in the developing world but export their products to wealthier nations. Alternatively, thousands of other women from less developed countries, searching for a better life, work as maids, nannies, and cleaners for wealthier patrons in the developed world. What do these women contribute to the global economy, and is the global economy, in turn, improving their lives?

We then turn to the issue of women and health in Chapter 9. While women's life expectancy has improved, they experience more chronic, debilitating diseases than men do. In other words, they live longer, but less healthy, lives. While contraception has become widely available in most of the developed world, many of the world's women still do not have the means to control their own fertility. Giving birth is a dangerous procedure, and women take a substantial health risk when they become pregnant. Further, the persistent undervaluation of girls poses persistent risks to their health throughout their adolescence and young adulthood. In addition, the rise of HIV/AIDS in African nations, as well as much of Asia, impacts women in different and unequal ways. In sum, poor women are doubly disenfranchised; not only are they poor, but their gender also gives them low social status and few rights that would give them a more proactive role in making decisions about their own health.

As we describe in Chapter 10, education is often seen as the panacea of underdevelopment; give people an education, and you give them the tools to overcome persistent poverty. Yet, around the world, girls are persistently less educated than boys, and thus, they are much less likely to be literate and therefore able to enjoy the benefits that literacy can bring to an improved quality of life. Education for women is important, in part, because educated women are more able to engage in economic activities, find formal employment, earn higher incomes, and enjoy greater returns on their skills than women without access to education. This, in turn, gives women greater positions of power in the household. Once they become financial providers, they in turn are accorded more respect, independence, and weight in terms of making important family decisions. Further, educating girls and women is important because of the ways in which these women then impact other facets of human development, particularly for their children. Studies have shown that low maternal levels of education often translate into malnutrition and poor quality of care for children.

We then turn in Chapter 11 to the topic of women and war. Despite, or perhaps because of, the end of the Cold War, regional and civil warfare has increased.[3] In the past two decades, the world has witnessed horrifying conflicts in war-torn areas such as the various republics of the former Republic of Yugoslavia, East Timor, Cambodia, Guatemala, Colombia, the Democratic Republic of Congo, Liberia, Rwanda, Sierra Leone, Somalia, Israel, the occupied Palestinian territories, Afghanistan and Iraq. While all conflict involves destruction, dislocation, and incalculable levels of human loss, nonetheless, women and men experience conflicts in different ways. While men are often forced to kill and be killed in war, women by no means are isolated from the ravages of war. Women frequently experience violence, rape, forced pregnancy, sexual abuse, and slavery during times of war. Their bodies, whether deliberately infected with AIDS or host to a baby conceived in rape, have become an alternative frontier in warfare with the enemy. Women also deal with the consequences of war, and their caretaking responsibilities for their families are often stretched to the limit as they deal with their status as refugees. Gender-based violence has become an integral method of waging war; rape, forced pregnancy, and deliberate infection of HIV/AIDS are new tools of modern warfare, with women as weapons and as objects.

This leads us to Chapter 12 and our final topic for discussion—women and physical autonomy. Women are often subjected to violence and mutilation in the name of tradition, custom, and culture. Violence against women in all of its forms has reached epidemic proportions and is a pervasive human rights violation that consistently denies women and girls "equality, security, dignity, self-worth, and their right to enjoy fundamental freedoms."[4] In particular, this chapter addresses the practice of female genital mutilation, virginity testing, and "honor" rapes and the causes and consequences of such practices on women around the world.

In each chapter in this part, we describe how numerous international organizations and development agencies are working to address the various ways in which women experience poverty, as well as the manifestations of poverty, such as the lack of adequate employment, health care, education, or bitter civil strife over control of economic, political, and social resources. International agencies have made great strides in improving the conditions of many women's lives. However, the international community is better at promising change than delivering on it; international agencies have the power to lobby, pressure, and embarrass national governments, but they do not have the power to coerce. However, in countries plagued by weak governments, miniscule budgets, and fragmented societies, international organizations can step into the void to provide support, moral and financial, to women around the world seeking better lives for themselves and their families.

7

Gender, Development, and International Organizations

Sierra Leone has the dubious honor of ranking last in the world in terms of gender equality, according to the UN Human Development Report, an annual UN publication that presents data on the economic and social status of the world's citizens. One in eight women die during pregnancy or childbirth, and women can expect to live, on average, to age forty-three, one of the lowest life expectancies in the world. Girls receive, on average, just six years of education. In addition, women are struggling to recover from the horrors of Sierra Leone's ten-year civil war, in which an estimated one-third of women and girls were victims of sexual violence. As abysmal as these statistics are, Sierra Leone is not alone in offering substandard lives to its female citizens. In Haiti, the country with the worst gender equality ranking in the Americas, nearly half of the young women and girls in the capital's Cite Soleil shantytown have been raped or sexually assaulted. Yet, little has been done to address the problem to date because many Haitians don't consider nonconsensual sex to be rape unless the victim was a virgin, although rape was finally categorized as a criminal offense in 2005. Nonetheless, the laws regulating violence against women overwhelmingly favor men; if a husband finds his wife engaging in adultery in his home, the criminal code excuses him if he kills her, but if a wife kills her husband in the same circumstances, she is liable for prosecution. Moving to the Middle East, in Yemen, 48 percent of girls are married by the time they are eighteen, and some begin their lives as brides as early as the age of twelve. Perhaps this explains why one in thirty-nine women die during pregnancy or childbirth, and why one in ten children don't make it to their fifth birthdays; young women, already undervalued, underfed, and often physically underdeveloped, are often unable to ensure different life circumstances for themselves or for their children. These statistics also demonstrate women's general lack of power in their own homes; for example, Yemeni women must receive their fathers' or husbands' permission to get a passport or travel abroad.[1] These are just a few snapshots of women's lives in a variety of countries in the developing world, where powerlessness in the household and in the public sphere often translate into economic poverty, poor health, low levels of personal safety, and an overall inability to make choices about one's life.

But the United Nations, in cooperation with other development agencies, national leaders, and NGOs, is trying to change this. In 2000, a record number of world leaders and development agencies renewed their efforts to integrate gender concerns into development strategies with the Millennium Declaration, a set of ambitious goals to advance development and reduce poverty in all areas of the world by 2015. Leaders pledged to work for eight outcomes: to eradicate extreme poverty and hunger; achieve universal primary education; reduce child mortality; combat HIV/AIDS, malaria, and other diseases; ensure environmental sustainability; and develop a global partnership for development by working on issues such as debt relief for the world's poorest countries. Two additional goals specifically target women; Goal Five pledges to improve maternal health, and Goal Three promises to "promote gender equality and empower women," with a focus on achieving educational parity for girls, equalizing women's representation in parliaments, and increasing the share of women in wage employment in the nonagricultural sector.[2] In addition, drafters of the Millennium Development Goals stressed how gender inequality had, in the past, hampered levels of human development around the world and how gender equality is critical, not only as a goal in its own right, but also as an essential ingredient for achieving all of the other seven Millennium Development Goals. Because women play such a strong role in ensuring the well-being of their families and their communities, development agencies argue, they also need to be at the center at any development effort to raise the quantity and quality of life for all the world's citizens. This represents one of the most ambitious international efforts to date to eradicate hunger, poverty, poor health, and other problems related to economic deprivation and to do so by looking at these issues through the prism of gender. However, we are now past the halfway point to the target year of 2015, and while we'll see in this chapter that there has been significant progress in some targets, such as increasing primary school enrollment rates for girls, there is little to no improvement in other key goals, such as maternal mortality. For many international organizations, it is easier to set targets than to design effective policy to achieve them.

This is not the first time that the United Nations has tried to foster gender equality or to address issues of particular concern to women, although as we shall see, international approaches to advancing gender equality have shifted substantially over time, as have some of the issues that women confront. The United Nations, soon after its formation in 1945, made gender equality a central concern and has remained a crucial international player in fostering international dialogue, policy, and law that fosters that equality. It has spearheaded a number of treaties, conferences, and campaigns aimed at bringing increased attention to pervasive gender inequalities, and as the United Nations family has grown, so has the number of UN-sponsored development agencies devoted to gender and gender equality. In addition, many governments, particularly those of the advanced industrialized nations, have established gender offices within their overall development assistance programs. And a number of other international organizations and nonprofit organizations, from Amnesty International, the Ford Foundation, the Global Fund for Women, and Human Rights Watch to the Women's Environment and Development Organization (WEDO), focus on the position and status of women as an integral part of their work. Finally, since the 1970s, a plethora of southern hemisphere–based women's NGOs have mobilized to provide better input and feedback into these international efforts, to give women in the developing world a voice in shaping their own futures, and to place greater levels of domestic pressure to come up with local solutions to global problems. All of these organizations work on a wide array of issues that impact the position and status of women in society, ranging from improving women's access to employment and promoting gendered health initiatives to increasing female literacy and ensuring women's physical autonomy and safety. Further, the previous decade has brought new challenges, such as the gendered impact of globalization, international migration, and war. As international organization and law have evolved against a constantly shifting backdrop of global events, so too have approaches to address the discrepancy between men's and women's quality of life.

In the following pages, we discuss why international organizations have increasingly focused on gender equality as both a means and an end of development strategies. We cover how they have translated these concerns about gender inequality into programs that can impact the lives of millions of women around the world. We shall see that in response, women themselves have increasingly participated in setting the development agenda, rather than merely being subjects of a process discussed solely among development practitioners. And finally, we assess the impact of some of these efforts to improve both women's lives and their abilities to choose the kinds of lives they value.

THE EVOLUTION OF GENDER EQUALITY IN THEORY AND PRACTICE

While international efforts to improve women's quality of life existed in the nineteenth and early twentieth centuries, nonetheless, concerted, systematic, and wide-reaching efforts to improve the position and status of women around the world gathered momentum in the post–World War II era, when decolonization, the creation of the United Nations, and the rise of women's movements created new opportunities for mobilization around women's issues. While women had fought valiantly to develop an international language of women's rights in other international organizations such as the League of Nations or the Pan American Union, nonetheless earlier efforts were hampered by the lack of legitimacy accorded to international organizations. However, the devastation wrought by both world wars signaled the need for more coordinated, transnational efforts at facilitating peace and prosperity for all of the world's citizens. In addition, the independence movements in many of the colonized areas of the world following the end of World War II created a much larger number of fledgling nations in need of assistance in making the transition away from colonial rule toward establishing functioning political and economic systems. These trends stimulated a renewed interest in creating a world body such as the United Nations, as well as an international set of norms, to help foster a sense of global governance. As we shall see, these larger global trends helped create an infrastructure in which women's interests and concerns could be developed at the international level. We will also discuss how the rise of women's activism, particularly in the 1960s and 1970s, not only in the industrialized North, but also in the global South, also empowered women to seize the initiative and more proactively shape international development agendas.

Why should we care about gender equality or—as is the case in current times—gender inequality? As we have discussed in previous chapters, gender inequalities, although lessening, are still pervasive throughout the world. Yet, as the examples in the beginning of this chapter illustrate, the inequalities often become more severe as one travels to the poorest regions of the world. For example, in many developing countries, women still lack independent rights to own land, manage property, conduct business, or even travel without their husband's consent. Nor do they have equal access to the resources, such as education, information, and financial opportunities, that could help them exercise greater autonomy over their lives. This lack of access in turn limits women's power to influence decision making, whether it is in the home or the public realm of politics. These disparities, which already are exacerbated in middle-income and low-income countries, widen even further as one travels to the least developed countries in the world, which are located primarily in sub-Saharan Africa. For example, while the adult literacy rates in all developing countries are, on average, 70 percent for women and 77 percent for men, when one moves to the least developed countries, the rates widen to 44 percent for women and just over 55 percent for men.[3] Discrepancies such as these severely constrain a woman's right to make choices about her life, whether it's where to live, whom to marry, how many children to have or not to have children at all, or how to ensure one's financial livelihood.

While woman and girls shoulder many of the direct costs of these inequalities by often living less healthy, more constrained lives, the indirect costs of women's lesser status hurt everyone. China, Korea, and South Asian countries have excessively high female mortality rates as a result of the social norm of boy preference, leading to 60–100 million "missing girls" who could potentially be alive in the absence of a culture of boy preference. In Chapter 9, we'll see how this preference is creating a demographic crisis of unparalleled proportions in China, India, and other parts of Asia that will impact everyone, not just girls. Further, because women often perform many of the nurturing, caring tasks within households— growing, buying and preparing food; tending livestock; providing heath care to ailing family members, raising children, and ensuring familial survival—they serve as a crucial conduit in terms of fostering the human development of the members of their family. Thus, it is no surprise that mothers' lack of access to critical human resources, such as education, disadvantages their entire families. As we shall see in the following chapters, mothers with more education are more likely to use contraception and space the births of their children further apart when they have access to knowledge about how to do so. They are more likely to nurture healthier babies that are more likely to be immunized and better fed. But gender discrimination also has an economic cost; countries need to harness women's abilities to promote economic growth and, most importantly, living standards. One study showed that closing the gender gap in education increases a country's growth rate by almost 1 percent a year. And promoting women's political voice has obvious benefits as well. A World Bank study showed that where the influence of women in public life is greater, the level of corruption is lower. Other studies indicate that women in business are less likely to pay bribes to government officials. In sum, holding onto discriminatory practices against women hurts not only the women themselves but also their families, their communities, and their countries.[4] The costs of ignoring the existing situation are high, particularly in comparison to the costs of trying to ameliorate the situation through investing more resources in education, public health, and economic planning. As the World Bank argued in an influential 2001 report, "gender equality is a core development issue—a development objective in its own right. It strengthens countries' abilities to grow, to reduce poverty, and to govern effectively. Promoting gender equality is thus an important part of a development strategy that seeks to enable all people—women and men alike—to escape poverty and improve their standard of living."[5]

MEASURING GENDER EQUALITY

So how do we get a sense of how the world's women are faring in terms of achieving gender equality? How can we collect data that would allow us to compare how women live their lives in Zambia, India, and Indonesia, for example, in any meaningful way, and how can we track these trends over time to assess the changing magnitude of the problem? The narratives presented at the beginning of the chapter refer to data collected by the United Nations and used by multiple agencies that fall within and outside the UN family of organizations. As discussed in the Introduction to Part III, the United Nations Development Program (UNDP) publishes an annual *Human Development Report,* which provides a narrative of the state of the world as well as statistics culled from 177 different countries along 35 different indices, ranging from health indicators such as life expectancy and child and maternal mortality to social statistics such as access to education and literacy levels and more standard economic data such as gross domestic product (GDP), growth rates, trade flows, and poverty rates.

While the UNDP's Human Development Index (HDI), which attempts to capture and quantify levels of quality of life of citizens from 177 countries, is perhaps best known, the UN has also developed two weighted indices to capture levels of equality between men and women. The first, the gender-related development index (GDI), which we referred to in the beginning of the chapter, compares men's and women's access to knowledge (measured by comparative adult literacy rates and school enrollment rates for men and women), quality of life (measured by life expectancy at birth), and economic opportunity (measured by estimated earned income for men and women). The results can reveal illuminating differences regarding how governments design social and economic policies that impact men and women. For example, Saudi Arabia's per capita GDP is $15,711, a number similar to the relatively prosperous Baltic and Eastern European countries currently integrated into the European Union. Yet, adult literacy rates for women in Saudi Arabia (76 percent) are much lower than those of men (88 percent), and women's estimated earned income is a paltry $4,031 in comparison to men's estimated average of $25,678. In contrast, Poland has a similar per capita GDP but has ensured universal literacy for all of its citizens, and women's enrollment in educational institutions exceeds that of men. While there is still a significant estimated income gap between the sexes ($10,414 for women versus $17,493), women in Poland enjoy a more equal status than Saudi women do, despite the two countries' similar economic indicators. There is also a geographic component to the GDI rankings; out of 157 countries for which the UN has adequate data, the bottom twenty-nine are all located in Africa.[6] Unfortunately, for many of the citizens who live in countries that are ranked by the UN as having "low human development," the quality of life for all of the citizens is abysmally bad; but consistently, for women, it is even worse. Indices such as the GDI help development agencies get a sense of how a country's economic assets are being reinvested to ensure better and more equal standards of living for all citizens. As you can see from Table 7.1, according to GDI scores, in no country of the world do women achieve parity, although they come much closer in the developed regions of the world.

The UNDP also designed a second index, the Gender Empowerment Measure (GEM), which measures levels of inequality between men's and women's opportunities. It captures this by assessing gender inequalities in three areas: political participation and decision making (measured by percentage of seats in parliament held by women as well as senior officials), economic participation and decision making (measured by percentage of female professional and technical workers), and power over economic resources (measured by ratio of estimated female to male earned income). Here, the UN only has data for ninety-three countries, but by these measures, men in all countries have greater access to and voice in major political and economic institutions and reap more benefits from their participation in the economy. However, the inequalities are smallest in Western Europe, and the ten worst offenders are scattered across Asia (Sri Lanka, Nepal, and Kyrgyzstan) and the Middle East and North Africa (Qatar, Iran, Morocco, Turkey, Egypt, Saudi Arabia, and Yemen). Many of the African countries are not ranked, primarily because the data are incomplete. However, although the GEM rankings aren't as comprehensive as those of the GDI, some

Table 7.1 Gender-related Development Index (GDI)

COUNTRY	GENDER-RELATED DEVELOPMENT INDEX (GDI) RANK	LIFE EXPECTANCY AT BIRTH FEMALE	MALE	ADULT LITERACY RATE FEMALE	MALE	ESTIMATED EARNED INCOME IN U.S. $ FEMALE	MALE
Iceland	1	83.1	79.9	..	..	28,637	40,000
Japan	13	85.7	78.7	..	..	17,802	40,000
United States	16	80.4	75.2	..	...	25,005	40,000
United Arab Emirates	43	81	76.8	87.8	89	8329	33,555
Russia	58	72.1	58.6	99.2	99.7	8476	13,581
Turkey	79	73.9	69	79.6	95.3	4385	12,368
Iran	84	71.8	68.7	76.8	88	4475	11,363
Algeria	95	73	70.4	60.1	79.6	3546	10,515
South Africa	107	52	49.5	80.9	84.1	6927	15,446
India	113	65.3	62.3	47.8	73.4	1620	5194
Pakistan	125	64.8	64.3	35.4	64.1	1059	3607
Nigeria	139	47.1	46	60.1	78.2	652	1592
Ethiopia	149	53.1	50.5	22.8	50	796	1316
Sierra Leone	157	43.4	40.2	24.2	46.7	507	1114

SOURCE: United Nations Development Programme, United Nations Human Development Report 2007/2008, http://hdr.undp.org/en (March 21, 2009).

common themes emerge. One is that relying on economic data alone, or data that are not further broken down by sex, can often obscure severe gender inequalities. For example, the highly industrialized country of Japan ranks fifty-fourth according to its GEM cores because, despite its powerful economy, women there are still excluded from positions of political and economic power and make an estimated 45 percent of men's earnings. Similarly, Qatar's oil earnings often obscure the fact that women hold no seats in parliament, comprise less than a quarter of professional and technical workers, and make about 24 percent of men's income. Thus, it ranks eighty-fourth. Saudi Arabia also ranks at the bottom of the list because no woman has received political representation in its parliament, women represent a paltry 6 percent of the professional and technical workforce, and they earn approximately 16 percent of men's income. In contrast, in countries such as Vietnam, economic indicators may not be as impressive as those of Saudi Arabia, but women there may have more equality of opportunity; they hold almost 26 percent of seats in parliament, comprise just over half of the professional and technical workforce, and make about 70 percent of men's earnings. While women's status is unequal in both countries, in which country would you rather be a woman? While the UN cautions that indices such as the GDI and the GEM serve as rough proxies for measuring women's standards of living, nonetheless they represent important international efforts to collect and standardize data in order to quantify levels of inequality between men and women. Other agencies such as the World Bank also collect data that are disaggregated by sex, and thus provides a sense of how women have a separate and usually unequal political, economic, and social status.[7]

These data are invaluable, not only for research but also for tracking progress and setbacks within countries over time, to compare countries within and across regions, and to hold governments and agencies accountable for implementing programs to improve people's lives. Until the 1970s, many countries, and development agencies, did not collect data on women, particularly in the developing world. As a result, it was extremely hard at first to design effective programs to improve the position and status of women or to pressure states to improve their programs. In the past thirty years, the collection of data on the position and status of women has improved immensely, although in extremely poor and often war-torn countries in areas such as those in sub-Saharan Africa, data collection is not only difficult but also life-threatening at times. These statistics have also been invaluable in terms of tracking the UN's progress toward meeting the Millennium Development Goals. Increasingly, women's groups and activists have used the findings as pressure points on governments that are stronger on rhetoric than action. In short, data collection and measurement are invaluable, not just to academics but also to practitioners at the domestic and international levels and activists working to improve the lives of the men and women in countries in every region of the world.

So judging from statistics, what can we say about the position and status of women? As we will discuss in greater detail in the following chapters, worldwide, women are poorer than men, even though, on average, they work longer days, particularly if one factors in their responsibilities for keeping their families fed, clothed, and sheltered. Part of this is because almost two-thirds of employed women in the developing world are in vulnerable jobs as self-employed or unpaid family workers. Women also are more likely to suffer from gendered health problems and, in particular, to face desperate circumstances when giving birth. Unfortunately, maternal mortality rates in sub-Saharan Africa and parts of Asia have remained virtually unchanged over two decades. And women have to worry about other health problems; in every region of the world, women represent a growing share of people living with HIV. A large factor in explaining women's economic and social poverty as well is their lack of access to education; around the world, 10 million more girls than boys are out of primary school. This lack of access to education has life-threatening ramifications; the greatest progress in reducing child mortality has been in the richest 40 percent of households, where mothers have some education and basic health-care access. Yet, women's political voice is often silenced; in one-third of developing countries, women constitute less than 10 percent of the members of parliament, making it more difficult to design and pass legislation that could address some of these inequalities.[8] At the same time, at the end of this chapter, we'll also discuss how this situation,

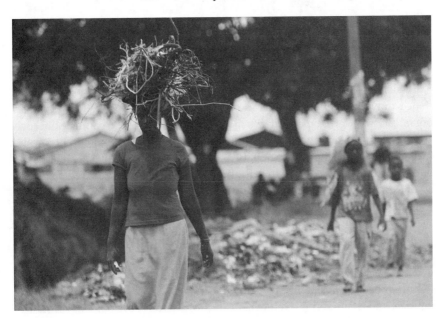

A Zimbabwean woman carries wood to boil water at home in Harare. For many of the world's women, readily accessible fuel, clean drinking water, and other devices that could improve their quantity and quality of life are out of reach. (December 13, 2008) SOURCE: ALEXANDER JOE/AFP/Getty Images

although still unequal, has improved in certain areas. There has been progress on achieving gender equality, and it has often come as a result of dedicated lobbying from women both outside and within the development community.

International Development: Designing Policy to Promote Gender Equality

We now turn to how development organizations have designed programs to improve women's lives. This task is complicated; as you can imagine from reading through some of data already presented, women (and men) are faced with innumerable obstacles to making choices about leading lives they value. And for development specialists and NGO activists, this has set off heated debate over the years. What should be the focus of aid to women and, for that matter, the developing world as a whole? Meeting basic needs, such as ensuring food, shelter, and water? Improving access to critical human resources, such as education and health? Focusing on gender specific issues, such as violence against women or rape as a tool of warfare? Should development agencies fix the symptoms of women's lesser status (economic poverty, poor health, etc.) or design more far-reaching but less focused programs that get to the reasons behind women's lack of empowerment (lack of influence in the household and/or the political sphere, for example)? How should one design a program to address women's lack of power in the private and public realms? And how should one distribute technical and financial assistance? To the governments themselves, or to local NGOs? None of the answers are obvious, and development agencies themselves have switched strategies several times in the previous five decades.

In the initial decades of development work, international organizations did not consider gender to be a salient analytical tool. As former colonies transitioned into independent nations in the 1950s, 1960s, and 1970s, international organizations' work expanded exponentially. Many of these countries needed assistance in designing economic and social institutions that would create the income needed to improve the quality of lives of its citizens. The primary task of development agencies was to help stimulate economic growth, and men were assumed to be the breadwinners and women were perceived as homemakers. Thus, the focus was on improving opportunities for wage-earning men, and until the 1970s, development policies, if they targeted women at all, tended to do so in their roles as wives and mothers, and programs focused on improved maternal and child health or on reducing fertility. Not only did this approach assume that women would naturally benefit as income trickled down through the household (which ended up not being the case), but it also often bypassed women without husbands, who didn't even benefit indirectly from development assistance. This basically ignored many of the women in the most vulnerable positions in society—the widowed, divorced, or abandoned. And for those women who were part of a family unit, it tended to reinforce a Western middle-class view that men made the money and women were housewives—a gross oversimplification of the situations of families living in fragile, politically unstable, resource-poor, under-developed newly independent nations. In sum, development practitioners at the national and international level largely ignored women, both as participants in development and as subjects of the same process. Women were often absent from the policy-making process, and gender often was ignored when designing policy or assessing impact. Nor did development agencies collect much data on the position and status of women, so it was hard even to assess the impact of larger economic development programs on women. In fact, some leading development theorists such as Walter Rostow and Edward Banfield viewed women as antithetical to development, assuming that their support for traditional values and religion would impede "progress."[9]

The assumption that overall economic growth would naturally affect women in positive ways was challenged by Ester Boserup, an anthropologist, in her book *The Role of Woman in Economic Development* (1970). Drawing from her research on rural African economies, Boserup contested the predominant assumption that the development process affected men and women in the same way and argued that development projects actually hurt women in some ways. She maintained that development theory had underestimated the role of women in agricultural production and that development projects redefined the division of labor between the two sexes in ways that deprived women of their previous productive functions, thus retarding the overall process of growth.[10] Development programs, which often encouraged the cultivation of cash crops for export rather than small-scale food production, favored men and squeezed women out of the areas where they had previously been productive. Women often could not hold title to land or get access to credit, two critical inputs that promoted men's advancement in large-scale agricultural business. Nor did extension services target women, despite the fact that they were the ones in many regions in the world who were responsible for growing food. The fact that many extension workers were male exacerbated the problem in cultures where strict norms dictated that male-female interaction outside the immediate family circle is unacceptable. Boserup and others were publishing an emerging body of critical literature that led many development agencies to reassess the assumption that women will inherently benefit from a "trickle-down" version of economic growth as well as assumptions about how women participate in and contribute to predominantly rural economies.

In addition, dedicated female development practitioners lobbied for increased funding and attention to women, arguing that the process of development is not gender neutral, in process or in impact, and that women participate differently in and benefit unequally from the process of socioeconomic development, and thus need specific programs that address their position and status in society. Inga Thorsson first proposed the idea of using development aid money for women to the Swedish Parliament in 1963, and six years later, the Swedish International Development Agency funded two positions in the UN family to ensure a voice for women at the policy level. In the United States, Mildred Marcy of the U.S. Information Agency argued that the issue of women must be included in the legislation revising the U.S. Foreign Assistance Act. Working through her connections in the Senate, Marcy succeeded in securing support for an amendment to integrate women into U.S.-funded development programs. Known as the Percy Amendment, the legislation dictated that women had to be included specifically in all development projects sponsored by the United States Agency for International Development (USAID).[11]

As development agencies began to accept that women do not automatically benefit from overall levels of economic growth, they turned to what became known as a "women in development" (WID) approach. The WID approach arose out of the second wave of feminism that was sweeping across the industrialized North, and was based in the ideological tenets of liberal egalitarianism. That is, one could not just assume that women would be positively impacted by gender-neutral economic development projects; one had to explicitly include women in the development approach by focusing on harnessing women's productive labor and promoting them into the workforce.

These projects tried to integrate women into economic development in a variety of ways. For example, development projects began to focus on income-generating projects for women, such as sewing, embroidery, or handicraft businesses. The idea was to find ways to build on women's income-generating possibilities despite the fact that most of them possessed few skills to compete in the formal labor market. Alternatively, development agencies, under the WID approach, began to fund projects that focused on providing labor-saving technologies, such as grinding mills, pumps, or cooking stoves, in an effort to reduce women's work loads.

This policy focus on explicitly acknowledging women in the development process was buttressed in the 1970s and 1980s by UN-sponsored international conferences that addressed women's issues within the development process. Once again, change in policy was often in response to women mobilizing on behalf of women, although certainly, sympathetic male colleagues were crucial to this policy shift as well. For example, a few women on the UN Commission on the Status of Women, led by Finnish feminist Helvi Sipila, succeeded in getting the General Assembly to pass a resolution calling for the "full integration of women in the total development effort." [12] This then prompted the Assembly to declare 1976–1985 the Decade for Women: Equality, Development, and Peace.[13] The start of the Decade for Women was marked by the First World Conference on Women, held in Mexico City in 1975. Two further gender-related conferences were held in 1980 in Copenhagen (the Second World Conference on Women) and in 1985 in Nairobi to review the achievements of the previous ten-year campaign, galvanize public interest, raise awareness of women's issues, and adopt international plans of action relating to gender.

These conferences were critical in stimulating a focus on women in development. For example, these conferences brought together hundreds of senior government officials in charge of making policy, which not only increased attention to gender issues but also led governments to create or bolster domestic-level agencies devoted to women's issues. For example, the 1975 Mexico City conference attendees passed a Plan of Action, which instructed governments to prepare a report on the status of women in their country, to set up a bureau or office dedicated to women's issues, and to ensure that women are included in their economic planning. As a result, the 1975 UN Year for Women and the International Women's Decade led many countries to establish women's ministries, which in turn created access points for domestic women's movements to lobby, advocate, and work for explicit policies impacting women's status. Major bilateral donors, such as the United States, developed programs that could reach poor women in the developing world. Further, the Mexico City conference led to the creation of gender offices at the international level as well; the UN Voluntary Fund for Women (currently known as UNIFEM) and the International Research and Training Institute for the Advancement of Women (INSTRAW) were created to address directly the specific issues facing women in development. The creation of these additional agencies and programs at the domestic and international levels also led to the influx of primarily women to staff, direct, and oversee these programs, helping to create critical mass of women in development. While not all women employees advocated for or worked for women's programs, nonetheless, enough women did that it made advocacy of women's issues within the institutions themselves much more acceptable.[14] And as we shall see in the next section, these conferences also formed the base from which evolved an increasingly articulated set of international norms and laws related to gender equality.

Finally, the array of global conferences helped facilitate the emergence of transnational feminist networks in the 1970s and onward. Each of the conferences was complemented by a major NGO forum, which brought together thousands of women's activists, giving them an opportunity to meet, exchange experiences, and, gradually, over the course of several decades, build important transnational alliances. The initial NGO meetings held before the 1975 Mexico City conference were not promising; while they signaled some of the first international gatherings of women activists, sisterhood did not feel global. Instead, the rise of the second wave of feminism in North America and Europe seemed to highlight the differences between women's activism in the industrialized northern hemisphere and the economically underdeveloped southern hemisphere. Many women from the South rejected Western-style feminism, which they perceived to be hostile to men and the family. Further, women were not united on which issues should be of primary concern to the world's women. While European feminists fought for issues revolving around women's legal equality and reproductive rights, Southern activists focused on underdevelopment, colonialism, and the exploitation of the global south by an industrialized north as impediments to women's (and men's) progress, rather than patriarchy. However, the increased prevalence of inter national conferences devoted to women's issues, such as the UN-sponsored conferences in Copenhagen (1980) and Nairobi (1985), helped women from around the world network and identify common areas of concern, such as violence against women, while acknowledging their differences. The rapid growth of a globalized economy also created similar conditions for many women around the world, which further underscored women's common agenda on certain issues. As a result, transnational organizations, such as Development Alternatives with Women for a New Era (DAWN), the Sisterhood Is Global Institute (SIGI), and the Women's Environmental and Development Organization (WEDO), became increasingly active in advocating women's interests at the international level.[15]

Women's grassroots mobilization, combined with the efforts of primarily women development specialists, helped bring further changes in how development agencies tried to foster better development outcomes for the world's women. By the 1980s, women had become increasingly vocal in their critique of the Women in Development approach discussed earlier, arguing for a new "Gender and Development" (GAD) framework to guide policy endeavors. Many argued that WID, although an important first step in increasing attention to women's roles, nonetheless served primarily as a band aid by treating the symptom of women's poverty, without really addressing the illness, diagnosed by some as capitalist development. Others maintained that while a WID approach was an improvement, in that it recognized that women deserved additional policy focus beyond family planning services controlling their fertility, it also treated women as an untapped source of development, with free time that could be diverted into paid labor. But activists pointed out that a WID approach simply ignored all of women's unpaid labor, which often kept them busy from morning until night, day after day. They called for a deeper gender analysis, one that viewed women's and men's roles as socially constructed, not biologically determined. Without acknowledging larger gender power relations that held women back, they argued, development projects focused on increasing women's access to the economic sphere, for example, would just increase their already substantial division of labor within the household. They also urged development agencies to recognize the diversity of women's experiences and that factors such as class, age, marital status, religion, and ethnicity or race impact women's issues. In sum, while a WID approach focused on meeting women's "practical" gender needs—that is, steps that would improve women's lives within their existing roles—some activists stressed the importance of meeting women's "strategic gender needs" by increasing women's abilities to take on new roles and ultimately empowering them.[16] Proponents of a GAD approach urged development programs to challenge gender roles by training women in "male" skills, working for women's ownership rights to land and housing, and providing child-care and transport facilities that suited women's specific needs.

As in the previous two decades, this evolution in policy in part was facilitated by women's networking at a variety of international conferences, which were all accompanied by NGO forums. The United Nations held another major Conference on Women, in Beijing, China, in 1995 to assess progress in achieving women's equality worldwide. The term "gender mainstreaming" came into widespread use among development policy makers with the adoption of the Platform for Action. Gender mainstreaming as a strategy sought to avoid the segregation of women into "gender projects" by integrating gender into all development projects, such as increased literacy, better access to health care, or improved public services. As the United Nations argued, "gender mainstreaming entails bringing the perceptions, experience, knowledge and interests of women as well as men to bear on policy-making, planning, and decision-making." [17] For example, a program sponsored by the United Nations Development Fund for Women (UNIFEM) works with governments to design gender-responsive budgets, that is, budgets that take into account women's concerns across all expenditures (health, pensions, public utilities, tariffs) rather than segregating funding for women's issues solely into one office of department (which can often marginalize women's concerns).[18] Gender mainstreaming is the latest iteration of a development philosophy that attempts to come to grips with the ways that women differ in their experiences of the social, economic, and political transformations wrought by modernization. In addition, women's issues were integrated into a number of other UN-sponsored conferences. While gender was not the organizing theme, it was often the implicit subtext. Global meetings, such as the International Conference on Population and Development, held in Cairo, Egypt, in 1994 or the World Summit on Social Development, held in 1995 in Copenhagen, inherently involved a discussion of women's rights and resulted in explicit calls for women's equality.

Further, as the United Nations has increased its support for women's rights, its agencies have broadened their mission to encompass a varied array of issues that impact women's status, such as the increased prevalence of civil strife and warfare within developing nations. In October 2000, the UN Security Council unanimously passed Resolution 1325 on Women and Peace and Security. This resolution recognized the importance of women in resolving issues of peace and security by discussing their role in negotiating peace agreements, planning refugee camps and peacekeeping operations, and reconstructing war-torn societies.[19] Development agencies are also recognizing the gendered aspects of civil strife and warfare within developing nations by focusing more explicitly on issues such as rape as a war crime. As we move forward in the twenty-first century, development agencies will continue to grapple with how gender intersects with poverty, political instability, and social inequality.

In sum, development agencies themselves have moved through a variety of frameworks through which to improve women's lives. At first, they assumed that women would benefit from large-scale development efforts and that benefits would trickle down. They then moved to implementing a Women in Development approach, which focused directly on programs designed to improve women's lives. After a decade or so, however, WID was replaced by a growing awareness, referred to as a Gender and Development approach, that development policies needed to address the preexisting gender imbalances between men and women. The extension of this line of thinking has been gender mainstreaming, a set of policy prescriptions in which gender concerns need to be integrated into all programs, rather than ghettoized into a separate portfolio. We have also seen that women's transnational activism has had an indelible impact. Increased international networking has helped foster greater public awareness of women's issues at the local level; transnational advocacy networks have teamed up with local activists to organize public information campaigns or stimulate greater levels of domestic activism. Also, international women's organizations increasingly have been active in lobbying development agencies, such as the United Nations, the World Bank, and the European Union, to devote more time, rhetoric, research, and money to advancing gender equality. They have been critical players in developing and filling spaces in women's policy machinery at the international level, which has had a strong influence on development policy.[20]

International Norms and Law

In addition to sponsoring development programs, conferences, and research related to fostering gender equality, the family of organizations under the UN umbrella has steadily constructed a body of international norms and law. International efforts to agree upon common standards to ensure gender equality started in the 1920s, when the International Labor Organization attempted to regulate the conditions under which women could be employed at night (a time, women's advocates argued, that women needed to be at home, caring for their families.) The evolution of international legislation rapidly multiplied with the creation of the United Nations in 1945, and since then, almost fifty resolutions addressing gender equality have been passed by a variety of international organizations. If you look at Table 7.2, you can see some of the landmark resolutions and treaties (also known as conventions) in gender equality that have been passed by a range of international organizations in addition to the United Nations. As the decades have passed, so too have interests changed regarding the core issues involved in promoting women's equality. Early resolutions focused on ensuring women's access to basic political, economic, and social rights. Starting in the 1970s, we can see increased attention given to issues that revolve around women as mothers. In the 1990s, violence against women emerges as an enduring international issue. In addition, acknowledging the diverse experiences of women around the world became a more key priority, with resolutions passed regarding older women in development and rural women, for example. In addition, regional international organizations, such as the African Union, have become more vocal about weighing in on issues that impact women in their particular geographical part of the world. In addition, the Commission on the Status of Women, housed within the UN, promotes, reports, and monitors the progress of the wide array of treaties that touch on women's equality.

Table 7. 2 Selected International Resolutions on Gender Equality

YEAR	RESOLUTION	ACTION
1948	Resolution on the Universal Declaration of Human Rights	United Nations General Assembly; arguably the world's most translated document
1949	Convention for the Suppression of the Traffic in Persons and the Exploitation of the Prostitution of Others	UNGA; against the trafficking of women
1951	Convention concerning Equal Remuneration for Men and Women Workers for Work of Equal Value	ILO General Conference
1952	Convention on the Political Rights of Women	UNGA; affirmed women's right to vote and hold public office without discrimination
1957	Convention on the Nationality of Married Women	UNGA; gave women the right to choose their nationality upon marriage
1960	Convention against Discrimination in Education	United Nations Educational, Scientific and Cultural Organization (UNESCO) General Conference
1962	Convention on Consent to Marriage, Minimum Age for Marriage and Registration of Marriage	UNGA
1974	Declaration on the Protection of Women and Children in Emergency and Armed Conflict	UNGA
1979	Convention on the Elimination of All Forms of Discrimination Against Women (CEDAW)	UNGA; the central women's rights convention

Table 7. 2 (*continued*)

YEAR	RESOLUTION	ACTION
1981	Convention concerning Equal Opportunities and Equal Treatment for Men and Women Workers with Family Responsibilities	ILO General Conference
1989	Convention on the Rights of the Child	UNGA; protection of children from early and forced marriage, recognition of adulthood as eighteen years, rights to education
1993	Declaration on the Elimination of Violence Against Women	UNGA; to support and complement CEDAW
1994	International Conference on Population and Development Programme of Action	UN global conference; places women's rights, health and empowerment at the center of efforts for human rights and sustainable development
1995	Beijing Declaration and Program for Actions	UN Fourth World Conference on Women; international commitments to equality, development and peace for women
1999	Resolution on Traditional or Customary Practices affecting the Health of Women and Girls	UNGA
2000	Resolution on Improvement of the Situation of Women in Rural Areas	UNGA
2000	Resolution on Violence Against Women Migrant Workers	UNGA
2000	United Nations Millennium Declaration	UNGA; sets out an international development agenda—Goal 3 is to promote gender equality and empower women
2000	Security Council Resolution 1325 on Women, Peace and Security	UN Security Council; first Council resolution that specifically addresses the impact of war on women, as well as women's contributions to conflict resolution and sustainable peace
2002	Convention on Preventing and Combating Trafficking in Women and Children for Prostitution	The South Asian Association for Regional Cooperation (SAARC)
2004	Resolution on Conflict Prevention and Resolution: The Role of Women	Council of Europe's Parliamentary Assembly
2005	Resolution on Trafficking in Women and Girls	UNGA
2005	Resolution in the Elimination of All Forms of Violence Against Women	UNGA

Condensed from Annex 2, "Selected Landmark Resolutions on Gender Equality," in UNIFEM, "Who Answers to Women? Gender and Accountability. Progress of the World's Women 2008/2009," pp. 135–136. Available at http://www.unifem.org/progress/2008/media/POWW08_Report_Full_Text.pdf.

What has been the effect of these international laws? A quick perusal of the language of many of these treaties reveals high-minded ideals and profuse commitments to equality. Turning commitment into policy, however, is a much stickier proposition. The following example is illustrative of the difficulties involved in transforming principle into action.

In 1979, the United Nations adopted the Convention on the Elimination of All Forms of Discrimination Against Women (CEDAW), an "international women's bill of rights that obligates governments to take actions to promote and protect the rights of women."[21] The convention defines what constitutes discrimination against women and sets up an agenda for national action to end such discrimination. This convention stretches beyond access to economic resources; it also contains provisions to confirm a woman's right "to decide freely and responsibly on the number and spacing of...children and to have access to the information, education and means to enable [exercise of] these rights."[22] By signing on to the convention, countries are agreeing to incorporate the principles of equality between men and women in their legal system, to establish tribunals and other public institutions to ensure the protection of women from discrimination, and to ensure elimination of all acts of discrimination against women. States that have agreed to the terms of the convention are legally bound to put its provision into practice. In addition, they are committed to submitting national reports at least every four years on measures they have taken to honor their treaty obligations.[23] In other words, CEDAW is an ambitious piece of international legislation that requires significant commitments from signatory nations to implement effectively.

First, a large hurdle to surmount in successfully drafting, passing, and implementing a convention such as CEDAW is finding treaty language that can inspire consensus among a very diverse array of countries. Countries often disagree on how compliance with convention terms should be monitored. Negotiations often continue for several years as members hammer out agreements. For example, how should countries interpret the phrase "full equality among men and women"? What does this require governments to do to ensure that this happens? For non-Western cultures in which there is a more rigid division between men and women's spheres of appropriate activity, how can treaty writers respect a diversity of cultural norms while at the same time upholding the general principle of equality? Thus, for example, the assembly voted to adopt CEDAW by a vote of 130 to 0 after a five-year drafting and negotiating process. Yet, countries were also given the option of voting separately on several controversial paragraphs. Nearly forty countries expressed reservations.[24] On the one hand, this practice helps hold together an often fragile and tenuous coalition of governments; on the other hand, it can decrease the legitimacy of the treaty by allowing countries to opt out of important principles and norms.

Also, what force do the treaties have? While 173 countries had ratified CEDAW as of May 2003, the United States, arguably the most powerful country in the world, has not ratified CEDAW, and is in the company of countries such as North Korea and Iran, two other countries that have declined to ratify the treaty.[25] While President Carter signed the convention on behalf of the United States in 1980, Congress has not ratified it. In fact, the Senate Foreign Relations Committee did not even hold a hearing on the treaty until 1990. Finally, in 1994, the committee forwarded CEDAW to the Senate for a floor vote, where it was blocked by a group of senators. In 2002, the Foreign Relations Committee once again sent CEDAW to the Senate for ratification, but the Senate was unable to vote on it before the end of the 107th Congress. The committee will have to once again vote in favor of sending the treaty forward for another vote in the Senate. Politicians have opposed the treaty for a variety of reasons, ranging from concerns about infringement on national sovereignty to beliefs that the treaty encourages abortion, interferes with the family, and will legalize prostitution, despite the fact that there is nothing in the treaty language that indicates support for any of these concerns.[26] The U.S. decision to ignore the treaty hurts the legitimacy of CEDAW, despite the large number of signatories. When powerful and influential countries opt out of international agreements it lessens the force of treaties because the authority of such treaties mostly resides in the power of widespread global agreement, particularly among the world's most powerful nations.

The legitimacy of international law is also hurt when nations commit to a treaty but then do not make efforts to implement the terms of the treaty. Countries such as Haiti, Rwanda, and Iraq have ratified CEDAW, yet research on the position and status of women in these countries indicates that they have not done much to turn promise into proactive policy.[27] For example, a quick look at UN statistics for many of the countries that have signed on to CEDAW reveals that women live substandard lives, whether it is in access to education, work, or adequate health care. This further erodes a treaty's legitimacy; passed but all but ignored, what use is international legislation? States have been more willing to promise to implement women's equality than to actually pass the legislation and commit the funds to do so.

On a positive note, international law can help to change norms slowly over time by putting pressure on governments to honor their commitments. While policy results are slow to catch up to policy ideal, nonetheless, many activists credit international law with setting the bar that nations must at least pay lip service to meeting. In other words, particularly for women activists in the developing world, the legislation of the United Nations has provided them with the tools by which to lobby, slowly and painstakingly, for change. When a nation professes to support the ideas of equality, this gives activists a foot in the door; they can critique leadership for not living up to its promises. In addition, this international legislation led many countries to establish Commissions on the Status of Women, relevant cabinet positions on women's issues, and other women's policy machineries within their own countries, thereby leading to further pressure on governments to pass domestic legislation. Thus, even though international treaties are not, in practice, always implemented, international law is an important starting point from which local activists can build momentum for further change. This has been particularly important in places where domestic women's movements are often too weak to make significant policy gains on their own or where semi-democratic governments limit domestic organizations' access to the policy-making process. Further, some scholars argue that these international norms and networks can create change even when national governments are not responsive to local activists; the international arena is sometimes the only means by which domestic actors can gain attention for their issues when government interest is lacking or weak. This is known as the "boomerang" effect; local activists team up with international networks, which, in turn, place pressure on domestic governments to respond to their own constituents.[28] In sum, while international legislation can be more difficult to craft and to enforce at the global level, at times, it can also push the evolution of norms, patterns of behavior, and domestic legislation in countries where it otherwise would not have passed. And it has helped show that, despite cultural differences among the many countries of the world, human rights are universal and that international organizations can walk the often sticky line between respecting cultural diversity while simultaneously maintaining a commitment to the equality and dignity of all living beings.

CONCLUSION

Over sixty years after the passage of the UN Declaration of Human Rights, the foundation of the Commission on the Status of Women, and the passage of numerous resolutions, conventions, and treaties, the international community is still calling for women's equality. In addition, a plethora of international agencies have collected data, funded development programs, sponsored conferences, and worked for the passage of international law and the development of international norms in their efforts to acknowledge that women's rights are human rights. Increasingly, in response to grassroots mobilization by women from the global south, they have turned from viewing women as subjects of the development process to seeing them as agents responsible for important and dynamic social change. The Millennium Declaration of 2000 represents the latest (but hopefully not the last) effort to systematically address women's secondary status in every country of the world. Throughout the document, gender equality is emphasized as an end in and of itself as well as a means to better standards of living for all the world's citizens. What can we say about international organizations' efforts to bridge the gender divides separating men and women?

As we shall see in greater detail throughout the following chapters, it is easier to promise gender equality than to attain it. However, development agencies, women's NGOs, and individuals have made a tremendous difference in changing both women's quantity and quality of life over the past five or six decades, although progress continues to unfold unevenly, often at slower rates that originally hoped. For example, the proportion of people living on less than $1 a day fell significantly from 31.6 percent in 1990 to 19.2 percent in 2004, although as the world enters a potential global recession, this figure may once again reverse itself. In part, perhaps this is because disparities in levels of employment between men and women are shrinking, granting women greater levels of control over income and decision making. However, women are still more likely than men to be poor and at risk of hunger because of their consistent lack of access to education, health care, and control of assets. Thus, even though the gender gap in primary school enrollment is shrinking in most regions, as is the gender gap in literacy, of the estimated 72 million primary school–age children that were not in school in 2005, 57 percent were girls. In terms of women's health, the picture is less rosy. Maternal mortality has remained relatively unchanged. The proportion of women living with HIV/AIDS has increased, and in sub-Saharan Africa, three out of every five adults living with HIV are women. Violence against women, which is a major constraint on women's abilities to contribute to their own or their families' well-being, is still at epidemic proportions. The following chapters delve further into the position and status of women in developing countries by focusing on the issues of women in economic development, health, education, war, and physical autonomy.

What Will $1 a Day Buy?

The United Nations has placed the international poverty line at $1 a day. Some of you may be thinking that $1 will go much further in Brazil, potentially, than in the United States. That's why the $1 figure has been adjusted to Purchasing Power Parity (PPP). That is, the United Nations makes that $1 universal. So you, too, could experiment with living on less than $1 a day to get a sense of the challenges that one in five people around the world face on a daily basis. In the fall of 2008, a couple, both high school social studies teachers, decided to conduct their own experiment and live on $1 a day for food (the average American eats about $7 worth of food per day). Overnight, their diets, and lives, changed dramatically. Most store-bought foods—even bread and canned goods—became too expensive. Fresh fruits and vegetables were not an option. Instead, they relied primarily on buying foods in bulk, such as beans, rice, cornmeal, and oatmeal, and on making their own bread and tortillas. To get some vitamin C, they made room for Tang orange drink mix in their budget. Not only were their food choices and levels of consumption narrowed, but they also found they had to spend much more of their time on food preparation. Further, although they lost weight, they also lost significant stores of energy eating a diet rich in empty calories. They pursued their experiment for one month.[i]

One in five of the world's citizens lives below this international poverty line, and a majority of these are women. Unlike the couple cited here, those who live below the international poverty line must also find ways to feed, clothe, and house their families on $1 a day. Nor can they choose to return to their "normal" lives after a month, as the couple here did—malnutrition, lack of secure employment, and poor health is a d aily reality for them. Women are more likely to be poor, and in addition, because they are the caretakers of their families, they must deal with the logistics of feeding, clothing, and caring for their families on this figure. How long do you think you could subsist on $1 a day?

---

[i] Tara Parker-Pope, "Money Is Tight, and Junk Food Beckons," *New York Times*, November 4, 2008, D6.

FOR MORE INFORMATION

Center for Women's Global Leadership, http://www.cwgl.rutgers.edu

Development Alternatives with Women for a New Era, http://www.dawnnet.org/about.html

Gender in the World Bank, http://go.worldbank.org/7KV4UHJ5W0

Millennium Development Goals, http://www.un.org/millenniumgoals

Siyanda, Online Database of Gender and Development materials from around the world, http://www.siyanda.orgUnited Nations Commission on the Status of Women, http://www.un.org/womenwatch/daw/csw/index.html

United Nations Development Fund for Women (UNIFEM), http://www.unifem.org

United Nations Development Programme, http://www.undp.org

United Nations Division for the Advancement of Women (DAW), http://www.un.org/womenwatch/daw/daw/index.html

United Nations Publications, Women2000 and Beyond, http://www.un.org/womenwatch/daw/public/W2000andBeyond.html

Women Watch, UN Internet Gateway to the Advancement and Empowerment of Women, http://www.un.org:80/womenwatch

Women's Environment and Development Organization, http://www.wedo.org

8

◆◯

Women and the Global Economy

Lufta, a mother of two, lives in a slum on the western edge of Dhaka, Bangladesh's capital city. Lufta, however, is better off than many women raising a family in the slums of the city. During a good month, she can earn up to 3,000 takas (about $50) a month, working in Bangladesh's export-oriented garment industry, which is barely enough to feed her family. She is not the only woman turning to this occupation; out of the 180 million people employed in Bangladesh's garment industry, 80 percent are women.[1] Many of you reading this book are probably wearing an item made by a woman in a developing country. Roshinara Begum lives in rural Bangladesh, in the village of Kalimajani. Surrounded by paddy fields, dotted by huts made of corrugated iron, Kalimajani is isolated from the outside world; there are no roads or phone lines to connect villagers to the outside world. Like many rural women in poverty-stricken Bangladesh, Roshinara could have spent her life hovering just above or below the poverty line, working tirelessly (but without remuneration) to keep her family at the subsistence level for another day. Instead, Roshinara makes a good living, earning $60–$70 a month selling calls on a cell phone she acquired through a microcredit loan from the Grameen Bank, a nonprofit organization that offers small loans to primarily women in an effort to change women's position and status in society, one loan at a time. Like Lufta and Roshinara, nineteen-year-old So-Young of North Korea was also searching for employment and the opportunities that paid wages could potentially bring, not only to her, but also to her struggling family. Illegally crossing the border into China, she was soon offered approximately $1.40 per day in exchange for "work." In reality, she was sold to a forty-year-old Chinese man. Although she escaped, traffickers kidnapped her once again, raping her multiple times before selling her to another man, who in turn, repeatedly raped her before her escape.[2] So-Young remains in hiding, unwilling to return home to North Korea but unable to search out legal employment opportunities in China. These women's life stories illustrate the ways in which an increasingly globalized economy can offer both potential promises as well as increased dangers to often undereducated, traditionally disempowered women in search of better lives.

This chapter provides an overview of the economic position and status of women in the developing world. Economic development is important because it is often a means to enabling all citizens—male as well as female—to live the kinds of lives they value.[3] Access to paid income not only can help ensure people's abilities to meet their basic needs but also ensures that they have greater latitude to make choices about the direction of their lives. Yet, economic development is not a gender-neutral process. Women participate in and benefit from the process of socioeconomic development in different and predominantly unequal ways, which have resulted in enormous gender gaps in access to and control of resources. This in turn has fueled women's disproportionate burden of poverty around the world.

In particular, this chapter addresses how globalization, the increasing integration of and rapid interaction between economies through production, trade, and financial transactions, has dramatically reshaped women's lives. We focus on a few critical trends. For example, we discuss how outsourcing, primarily in labor intensive fields such as garment manufacturing, has led to increased employment opportunities for women, but also to the feminization of the flexible labor. Is this an opportunity for further economic development, or is it the exploitation of cheap, predominantly female workers who have little choice in determining their own futures? We then turn to women's migration; in search of better lives, not only for themselves but also for their families, women form the bulk of transnational migrants. On the one hand, employment overseas can offer opportunities not available to women in poverty-stricken, tradition-bound societies. On the other hand, demand for cheap unregulated labor from the North feeds a massive underground trafficking industry in bonded workers in which women are often targeted for the sex trade. Can legal migration offer women better lives, or do they merely form a new global underclass? Third, we look at how globalization has impacted rural women. Women are responsible for approximately half the world's agricultural production, and as the primary cultivators and gatherers of food, water, and fuel for family consumption they are the first to notice and feel the effects of environmental stress and unsustainable economic development practices. How are women differently impacted by unsustainable development, and how is their activism gendered? Finally, we turn to the embrace of free market principles at a global level; the rise of international financial institutions, such as the World Bank and the IMF; and the increased vulnerability of southern countries to global financial trends. In times of financial crisis, women often have to bear the social and financial costs of economic reform. Why is economic restructuring gendered, and how have women responded in gendered ways to economic downturns? In closing, we turn to how development agencies, NGOs, and activists have worked to break the vicious cycle of poverty by increasing women's participation in and equality within the labor market. While globalization has launched some alarming economic trends, it has also opened up opportunities, both for women and for the transnational activists and organizations working to ameliorate the negative ramifications of globalization.

WOMEN AND WORK

Gro Harlem Brundtland, former prime minister of Norway and director general of the World Health Organization, once commented, "In many countries, women own nothing, inherit nothing, and earn nothing."[4] As we shall see, this is changing somewhat; one of the most dramatic changes to developing economies has been the rapid influx of women into paid employment. However, the relatively recent increase in women's participation in the paid labor force does not mean that women previously didn't work. Women have always worked, throughout history and all over the world. For most of history, however, the bulk of this work has been and continues to be unpaid and, as a result, undervalued. That is because women's work is often seen as an extension of their "natural" roles as mothers, nurturers, and caretakers of hearth and home. Yet, in countries of the developed world, while tasks such as cooking, cleaning, and caring take up hours of women's lives, cost them income in terms of the ever-pervasive wage gap, and often diminish their status, women's unpaid work loads only increase as we travel to the south. Grinding poverty, lack of or low literacy skills, absence of labor-saving technologies, and a culture that reinforces a strict household division of labor all combine to make women's days filled with time-consuming, back-breaking feats of manual work. In an effort to convey the critical yet undervalued role that a "housewife" plays in a predominantly rural, poor country, the Food and Agricultural Organization profiled one woman's day in Sierra Leone, one of the world's poorest countries. Rising at 4 a.m., the woman fishes in the local pond for food for her family, returning to light the fire, heat the washing water, cook breakfast, clean the dishes, and sweep the compound. At 8 a.m., she straps her baby on her back and takes her four-year-old son with her to work in the rice fields. After three hours, she returns home, collecting berries, leaves, and bark on her way to prepare for and clean up from the next meal. After washing clothes by hand, fetching more water, and cleaning and smoking the fish, she works for the rest of the afternoon in her small plot of land, which she uses to feed her family. She returns to fish in the pond before dinner, and then starts the two-hour preparation and cleanup process again before cleaning the children and getting them ready for bed. For two hours, she may converse around the fire, shelling seeds and making fishnets before extinguishing the flames and going to sleep at around 11, only to get up five hours later to repeat the same process.[5] All of this is done without the benefit of modern conveniences such as running water, prepackaged food, fuel stoves, electricity, or modern plumbing. Try this schedule for a week, and you'll quickly discover how much of this "housework" is actually back-breaking labor! Certainly, not all women in the developing world live this way. According to the United Nations Human Development Report, Sierra Leone has the unfortunate distinction of having the worst gender inequality in the world; female literacy hovers around 24 percent, and one in eight women die during pregnancy and childbirth, which may explain why women have a life expectancy of just forty-three years.[6] However, the example of this woman's day underscores that fact that much of women's work is unpaid and physically punishing. Yet it is of tremendous importance to the well-being of families, communities, and countries.

Unfortunately, this unpaid labor is often to the detriment of the women performing the work. Particularly in very low-income countries, the long hours spent collecting fuel and water often cuts into time that could be spent engaging in activities that could improve the quality of women's lives. This situation is particularly dire for young girls, who often have to lessen their time in or forgo school altogether to help with household work.[7] Further, performing women's work in the home can be a serious health hazard. More than half the world's households cook with wood, crop residues, or untreated coal. Because work in the home is often women's work, women and children are the primary targets of indoor air pollution, which can lead to a number of health problems, such as respiratory infections and blindness. It can, and often does, lead to death. In developing countries, nearly 2 million women and children die each year as a result of exposure to indoor air pollution.[8] In developing countries, performing ordinary "housework" is not only physically demanding and exhausting but can also be deadly.

Given the importance of this work, as well as the high costs it can impose on those performing it, what is its economic worth? We don't know for sure. Women's "housework" has typically been excluded from economic analysis because economists have tended to view women's work in maintaining the household as a "natural" aspect of women's roles and as not being "work" because it is so often unpaid. As a result, much of the economic data collected on countries (and presented in this book!), particularly in the developing world, misrepresent women's participation in and contribution to a country's economy. This is particularly true, given that women are much more likely to work within the informal sector, subsistence economies, and the unpaid work involved in reproduction and care of the household. In fact, the UN Development Programme has estimated that women's "invisible" output amounts to $11 billion. Expanding the definition of work to include women's full range of caretaking responsibilities adds up to the equivalent of an extra 48 percent of the world's gross domestic product.[9] That is a lot of unpaid hours. In addition, broadening our definition of what constitutes "labor" also causes us to reassess the level and nature of women's participation in workforces all over the world. For example, in the Dominican Republic census in 1981, the rural female labor force participation rate was 21 percent. However, one study included activities such as homestead cultivation and livestock care, an area of unpaid household labor traditionally assigned to women. This broadened definition raised women's participation rates to 84 percent. In India, narrow and extended definitions of labor place women's participation rates at 13 percent and 88 percent, respectively. And in Pakistan, a separate survey documented a

45.9 percent participation rate (as opposed to the official 13.9 percent rate) when labor was broadened to include such tasks as rearing livestock, collecting firewood and fetching water, making clothes, and undertaking domestic work on a paid basis.[10] In fact, if one factors in women's work loads outside of paid employment, women work longer hours than men.[11] In sum, it is critical to acknowledge both that we need to think broadly in terms of what constitutes "work" if we are to capture accurately the situation many women in the developing world face and that women work in many ways outside of the formal paid sector. However, as we shall see, gaining access to paid work can be a crucial step to advancing women's status.

Why should we worry about women's access to paid employment? From a human rights perspective, women's status should be a source of concern, particularly if women have unequal access to economic opportunities and benefits. There are also a number of practical arguments for improving the economic position and status of women, particularly in the developing world, where it is even more challenging for women to transform their labor into paid work and their paid work into better lives, not only for themselves but also for their families. For one, increasing a woman's access to paid work and income often increases her autonomy and power within the household, giving her a more equal status in decision making within the family. In addition, because women tend to be the primary caretakers of hearth and home, they also are more likely than men to reinvest their income into the well-being of their families, specifically their children. While men tend to spend more of their income in leisure activities, cigarettes, and alcohol, women are more likely to allocate their resources toward better nutrition, health care, and provisions for household members. Also, women's access to paid employment is important because it usually puts some money directly into their own hands, thus increasing their abilities to make more decisions about their own lives. Finally, improving women's access to paid employment also contributes to larger national trends; large-scale entry of women into the workforce can help stimulate economic growth, which in turn, is critical for reducing overall numbers of people living in poverty. Many developing nations need to harness the full potential of all their citizens, not just predominantly their male ones, in the search to turn economic growth into better lives for all. Thus, while there are certainly many things that money can't buy, in some respects, particularly for poor women in poor countries, the ability to earn money can provide enormous tangible and intangible benefits. It can enable women to provide food, clothing, shelter, and educational opportunities, not only for themselves but also for their families. And it can also engender increased social status, influence, and a heightened personal sense of empowerment and ultimately shift and redefine the division of labor in traditional households.

So what is the economic status of women? On a positive note, during the 1980s and 1990s, women's paid labor force participation rates increased substantially in almost every region of the world, although these growth rates have leveled off in the past decade. Hopefully, these gains will translate into lower

Table 8.1 Women's Employment Figures (number of economically active females per 100 economically active males, 2007)

World	66.9
Developed Economies and European Union	82
Central and South Eastern Europe (non-EU) and Commonwealth of Independent States	80.5
East Asia	78.9
South-East Asia and the Pacific	73.2
South Asia	41.7
Latin America and the Caribbean	70.5
Middle East	38.7
Sub-Saharan Africa	75
North Africa	34.8

International Labor Organization (ILO), Global Employment Trends for Women (Geneva, Switzerland: ILO, March 2008).

levels of female poverty and higher levels of economic and social independence for women. Further, the gap between female and male participation rates has narrowed, although in every region of the world, women are still less likely to be employed than men are. Globally, sixty-seven women per one hundred men were economically active in 2006. Take a moment to look at Table 8.1 to learn more about the regional variations between labor participation rates. For example, why do you think the gap between male and female participation rates is so much smaller in the industrialized countries of Western Europe than in the Middle East and North Africa, where just thirty-seven women per one hundred men are active in the labor force? [12] While not all women of working age may wish to work, nonetheless, the more common scenario is that women would like a job but are unable to find one.

Particularly in the developing world, women face more barriers to entering the formal paid labor force. A complex web of social norms often reinforces the idea that women's main responsibilities should revolve around reproduction and care of the family. Particularly in countries in South Asia, the Middle East, and North Africa, norms of female seclusion seriously limit women's physical mobility outside of the home, which makes paid employment extremely difficult. Further, a pervasive culture that undervalues girls ensures that women, if they enter the labor force, do so in poorer health, with less education, and with fewer skills than their male counterparts. As a result, women are often segregated into low-paying, low-skilled jobs, and, despite women's increased economic activity, women worldwide make less than men; on average, women earn about 75 percent as much as men.[13] Of course, this average masks substantial differences; for example, while women in Sweden receive about 83 cents for every dollar that men make, these differences widen as one moves to developing countries. See Table 8.2 for further examples of the pay gap between men and women in countries around the world.

Table 8.2 The Income Gap: The World's Worst Offenders

COUNTRY	ESTIMATED RATIO OF MALE TO FEMALE INCOME	COUNTRY	ESTIMATED RATIO OF MALE TO FEMALE INCOME
Saudi Arabia	0.16	Georgia	0.33
Oman	0.19	Syria	0.34
Egypt	0.23	Algeria	0.34
Qatar	0.24	Paraguay	0.34
Morocco	0.25	Cape Verde	0.35
Sudan	0.25	Turkey	0.35
United Arab Emirates	0.25	Bahrain	0.35
Pakistan	0.29	Kuwait	0.35
Swaziland	0.29	Malaysia	0.36
Tunisia	0.29	Samoa	0.38
Sao Tome and Principe	0.3	Iran	0.39
Yemen	0.3	Mexico	0.39
Botswana	0.31	Korea	0.4
India	0.31	Chile	0.4
Lebanon	0.31	Belize	0.4
Jordan	0.31	Suriname	0.4
Nicaragua	0.32	El Salvador	0.4
Guatemala	0.32		

SOURCE: United Nations Human Development Programme, *UN Human Development Report 2007/2008*, pp. 330–333.

However, despite the previous discussion, it is difficult to quantify the value of women's activities within countries' economies because much of women's paid labor either is expended in the informal sectors of the economy or is hired illegally without notifying the proper authorities or paying the relevant taxes. In fact, in developing countries, a much higher percentage of women who are active wage earners are informally employed. Sixty percent or more of women workers in the developing world are in informal employment (outside agriculture).[14] This is a growing area of women's employment, and the proportion of women who are self-employed in nonagricultural work is increasing faster than men's share. Most women who turn to the informal sector for their livelihood are self-employed, for example, as street vendors rather than engaged in wage work, such as domestic work or day labor.[15] Their income for the day rests on their abilities to sell their skills, products, or other services for whatever fee they can negotiate. Some of these women are visible. They often line the streets of cities, towns, and villages in developing countries, selling their wares. Other times, they are busy at home, engaged in activities such as sewing, embroidery, or cigarette or incense rolling, and are paid usually per unit produced. Those that work for wages are visible in the developing as well as developed world as casual work-ers in hotels and restaurants, as piece rate workers in sweatshops, as temporary office helpers or off-site data processors, and as maids, child-care providers, and sex workers.

Women are overrepresented in the informal sector in part because it is more flexible, which may help them balance paid employment with their caretaking responsibilities in the home. In addition, however, women have a much more difficult time gaining access to formal employment in developing countries because these jobs are coveted by and primarily filled by men, and so informal labor markets are often their only outlets for ensuring their economic survival. Another problem with the rising numbers of informal sector jobs is that the pre-dominantly female workers that fill these positions are often denied all of the benefits—secure contracts, unemployment, disability, and maternity—that can accrue from a position in the formal economy. While this has opened doors for women, the absence of social safety nets makes it a short-term rather than a long-term solution for women's lack of economic independence. Yet, the dynamics of the globalized, export-led economy, as we shall see, are creating more jobs than ever that provide fewer labor rights and little social protection.

In sum, over the past few decades there has been some progress in that more women than ever are participating in the paid workforce, although the female labor participation rate has stopped growing in the past decade. However, women are more likely to work either in the informal sector or in low-paying jobs, such as agriculture and services. In the following sections, we turn to look more closely at some of the ways in which women increasingly participate, will-ingly and unwillingly, in the global economy.

GLOBALIZATION

Globalization broadly refers to the growing integration of economies and socie-ties around the world. Although early forms of globalization have existed since the Roman Empire, the current debates that swirl around globalization refer to the massive changes in economic, social, and political interaction from the 1980s onward. As Thomas Friedman explained in his bestselling book, *The Lexus and the Olive Tree*, globalization is "the inexorable integration of markets, nation-states, and technologies to a degree never witnessed before—in a way that is enabling individuals, corporations and nation-states to reach around the world farther, faster, deeper, and cheaper than ever before.... [It is] the spread of free-market capitalism to virtually every country in the world." [16] As you can imagine, globalization has wrought profound change in the international system, domes-tic government policies, and our day-to-day lives. The founding of international organizations such as the North American Free Trade Agreement (NAFTA) and the World Trade Organization (WTO), as well as the expansion of the European Community into a much broader and more powerful European Union, has fur-ther eroded trade barriers and tariffs and facilitated the easier movement of goods and services across borders. International financial institutions that lend money and provide technical assistance to primarily developing countries, such as the International Monetary Fund (IMF) and the World Bank (WB), have become much more influential in designing domestic economic policies that, as we shall discuss later in this chapter, have directly impacted the lives of millions of citizens living in these countries, who must live through the consequences of these policies. Further, domestic economies have become increasingly vulnerable to stresses and strains in the global economy; economic crashes in Mexico (1994), Thailand (1998), and the United States (2008) had far-reaching consequences, not only for neighboring countries but also for the entire global financial system. Alternative ideologies to free market capitalism have collapsed; China has all but abandoned its communist economic principles, and the disintegration of communist economic and political systems in eastern Europe and the former Soviet Union prompted scholars such as Francis Fukuyama to posit that liberal democracies run on market economies were the only viable political and economic options. Consumers could hardly miss the impact of globalization, as manufacturing and even customer service went global, in search of lower labor and production costs.

The backlash against the economic, political, and social implications of globalization have been just as momentous. New movements, which focus on fair trade, not free trade, increased awareness of the excesses of sweatshop labor and increased activism at international conferences have all arisen in response to globalization. On a much more ominous note, the rise of fundamentalist and extremist movements in reaction to the perception of a secularized, Western hegemony over diverse political and cultural environments was instrumental in fueling movements such as Al Qaeda. In terms of government economic policy, proglobalization views translated into significant shifts in downsizing the role that governments played in managing the economy; in the 1980s and 1990s, governments everywhere reduced trade barriers, focused more heavily on attracting foreign investment, and encouraging export-led growth. As a result, globalization has also become one of the most charged issues of the past two decades, and debating aspects of this phenomena, such as the merits of free trade, foreign direct investment, and multinational corporations, has become commonplace on TV, on the Internet, in corporate boardrooms, and at labor union meetings and has often become a divisive political issue, particularly during election years. Proponents promise that globalization has and will continue to improve people's lives around the world by providing numerous economic opportunities, jobs, and income that will inevitably reduce poverty rates. Opponents charge that globalization simply further impoverishes the world's poor, enriches the already rich, devastates the environment, and alienates already marginalized citizens around the world. We now turn to how this increasingly integrated economy has impacted women by looking at women's participation in the global assembly line, the issue of migration, and women's role in sustainable development.

Women in the Global Assembly Line

In many developing countries, particularly ones that have focused on manufacturing and export-led growth, young women are often the unsung heroes behind the rapidly expanding economy. For example, China has emerged as a global economic power, fueled by its enormous workforce and low labor costs. Much of its rise can be attributed to the 130 million migrant workers who have moved from rural poverty to the cities to help build the new industrial skylines, fill the factories, and churn out cheap goods in rapidly multiplying quantities. Many of these migrants who staff the assembly lines are young women who move from the hinterland to new industrial cities like the Pearl River Delta of southern China. As Leslie Chang narrates in her book about these workers, they are the invisible but crucial drivers of China's economic boom, working tirelessly, often making great sacrifices to escape the poverty of their rural origins. The book centers on Dongguan, a massive factory town where the economy has grown at 15 percent every year for two decades. Seventy percent of the population of the town is female. Life in the factories can be harsh; shifts last for twelve hours, fines are assessed for talking on the job, and bathroom breaks are allowed only every four hours. The young women make about $100 a month and usually must commit to a minimum of six months or forfeit their first two months' salary, which is withheld upfront. They live in spare dormitories, and their lives revolve around

Young women are the unseen engines of China's thriving export-oriented economy. In this photograph, Chinese workers make Beijing 2008 Olympic mascots at a factory east of Beijing. (December 1, 2005) SOURCE: Guang Niu/Getty Images

work. Yet, many women continue to work, either because it is better than the alternative of returning to a rural life of poverty or because they believe that through hard work, their current jobs will serve as temporary stopping places before they hopefully move into a management position or even a highly coveted white-collar job.[17]

China, while perhaps the most dramatic example of a country harnessing its future to manufacturing and export-led growth, is not alone in pinning its hopes to joining the global assembly line. In the effort to attract foreign capital, the low cost of labor, especially cheaper female labor, combined with little to no regulation, is often one of the lures governments have to attract outside funds. This is especially true in the growing world of Export Processing Zones (EPZs), special manufacturing enclaves that are exempt from environmental and labor regulations. The number of EPZs has increased dramatically in the past thirty years. While only 25 countries had EPZs in 1975, in 2006, 130 countries had established thirty-five hundred zones that employ 66 million workers. While almost two-thirds of these workers come from China alone, nonetheless EPZs are a phenomenon that affect workers in nearly every developing country.[18] The rise of these free trade zones is part of a massive increase in world trade flows, particularly in manufactured goods. Exports in labor-intensive manufacturing have been rapidly expanding, with electronic components and the garment industry as the fastest-growing industries. These manufacturing jobs grew first in east Asian miracle economies and Mexico but soon spread to other parts of Asia and Latin America. In particular, the garment industry has taken off in Bangladesh, as well as in Indonesia, Malaysia, Mauritius, the Philippines, Sri Lanka, and Thailand.[19] This growth marks a shift away from male-dominated heavy industrial production of the post–World War II era and toward the repetitive assembly line work in export-oriented "light" industry subsectors of garments, textiles, shoes, and electronics. Further, in the current era of open economies and market deregulation, governments have focused on creating a market environment designed to attract investors, which can often come into the conflict with the goal of managing the market for social ends—that is, providing an adequate standard of living and a safe working environment for adults.

There is a gendered component to this economic growth; women tend to be ghettoized in these industries. While in the industrialized West much attention is paid to the "glass ceiling" that prevents women from being promoted to the highest echelons of power, we sometimes forget that there is also a "sticky floor" that keeps millions of women in developed and developing countries trapped in low-skilled, low-paying jobs in light manufacturing and service industries. For example, the garment industry in many countries in Latin America, the Caribbean, and Asia or the electronics industry in Asia are industries that rely on cheap, unskilled labor provided predominantly by women to fuel profits. Women comprise 65 percent of the garment industry in Honduras, 70 percent in Morocco, 85 percent in Bangladesh, and 90 percent in Cambodia.[20] The field of data entry and processing is populated overwhelmingly with women; for example, in the

Caribbean, they make up the entire labor force.[21] As we discussed in Chapter 4, women in the advanced industrialized countries are also often relegated to sex-segregated occupations that pay less and offer less job security. But this trend has been fostered further by the increased globalization of trade, in which goods and services are outsourced to far-flung regions of the world where labor costs are lower. These jobs are increasingly offered to women with no accompanying contract or benefits. Is this an opportunity for further economic development, or is it the exploitation of cheap, predominantly female workers who have little choice in determining their own future? Not surprisingly, the answer can be found in both interpretations.

On the one hand, women often work under worse conditions than men do; they almost always work for lower pay than it would cost to employ a man. Yet, from an employer's perspective, they often provide better service than men; one study of the *maquiladora* industry in Mexico found that employers chose women employees over men because they were more dexterous and skilled at assembling small components at a rapid pace. In addition, employers prized women for their perceived submissiveness. Because fewer young women had had experience living on their own outside of the home, they rarely questioned the policies set down by management, often acquiescing rather than fighting decisions that would affect them adversely. Alternatively, older women who were the single providers for their small children recognized the nature of their poor working conditions but continued to work so that they could feed and clothe their families. Fighting for better working conditions threatened the livelihoods of their families, for whom they were responsible. For many, the costs of protesting were simply too high.[22] Further, it is difficult for women workers to implement reform from within; they are still overrepresented at the bottom rungs of specific careers and underrepresented in positions of power in the areas of management or administration. As a result, they often do not occupy positions in which they could impact labor policy. For many laborers, women as well as men, all they have to offer is their cheap, predominantly unskilled labor, which often is not much of a bargaining chip for better conditions. There are often other people, desperate for paid employment, willing to take their places. Further, as previously mentioned, much of this employment is informal, has no benefits, is accompanied by pitiful working conditions, and comes as an additional work burden to women who are already overburdened with household and family responsibilities. And studies have shown that while these jobs do put money in women's hands, nonetheless the salaries are rarely enough to lift women out of poverty; it simply moves them up the economic ladder to the "working poor."

Yet, as the Chinese example illustrated, however bleak, many women perceive these conditions as an opening to increased opportunities. While the conditions under which they work often violate international labor standards, nonetheless these employment options still offer an improvement on their precarious lives. Ana, a worker in a Honduran *maquila*, commented that "Even though the salaries are low, the *maquilas* give us employment—they help us to make ends meet."[23]

And this increasing economic power has implications for how women are treated in the family. According to one woman worker in a Bangladeshi factory, "in my mother's time...women had to tolerate more suffering because they did not have the means to become independent. They are better off now, they know about the world, they have been given education, they can work and stand on their own feet. They have more freedom."[24] A study of more than thirty Bangladeshi garment factories found that two out of three women had some control of their earnings. This translates into increased decision-making power in the household and, sometimes, a shift in gendered divisions of labor.[25] And for many women, the alternative of working in the global economy, however fraught with uncertainty, poor conditions, and unequal outcomes, it is nonetheless better than the offerings of the domestic economy, where high unemployment, poor government regulation, corruption, and weak government capacity further undermine women's opportunities to participate in the labor market. Conditions in these factories tend to be better than what the domestic economy can offer. Factors such as these have prompted *New York Times* op-ed columnist Nicholas Kristof to argue, "[T]he central challenge in the poorest countries is not that sweatshops exploit too many people, but that they don't exploit enough." Using the example of Cambodia, where five-year-old children scour toxic garbage dumps for recyclable material to sell for 5 cents a pound, Kristof argues that manufacturing jobs offer a potential alternative route out of poverty, particularly for women.[26]

Perhaps the reality is that these jobs both exploit women and simultaneously open up new opportunities for greater levels of economic independence and autonomy in decision making in the household. Particularly for students living in a country in the developed world, it can be hard to see the benefits of working in a factory for little pay under little to no regulation. But most students aren't faced with the alternative of scouring a garbage dump, illiterate, barefoot, poorly nourished for salvageable refuse. Sweatshops often are a symptom of poverty, not a cause, and, despite their shortcomings, they are still out of reach as a development option to the world's poorest countries, which are often hampered by unreliable governments, transportation, and energy systems. As we shall see in the next section, economic opportunities for women in the developing world are still scarce, and increasingly thousands of women journey to other countries in search of better opportunities. We now turn to the issue of women and international migration.

WOMEN AND MIGRATION

Saokham, a young woman who grew up in poverty in a mountain village in Myanmar, emigrated to neighboring Thailand to work at assembling costume jewelry for export to North America. She earns 140 Thai Bhat a day—about U.S. $3.50—a respectable wage, particularly given the economic conditions of her village. Nor did she face many prospects if she were to have stayed in rural Myanmar; although she completed eight years of free schooling, she had to leave school because her parents could no longer afford to pay her school fees. With few economic opportunities in sight in her home environment, at the age of fourteen she set out for neighboring Thailand to join her older sister who had left two years previously. She now lives with her husband in a community of fellow compatriots. Reflecting on her new life, she said, "Living in Thailand, we have money for food and to spend. Life is convenient. Back home we didn't have any work except farm work." [27] Increasingly, women from the developing world are migrating to richer, more developed countries in search of increased opportunities. They may move to marry, to rejoin migrant husbands and family, or to find work as domestic workers, cleaners, or caregivers. Some work in low-skilled jobs found in the peripheral world of sweatshops; others work as migrant farm laborers, while those with skills come to fill the growing need for qualified teachers and health-care workers. In today's globalized economy, transnational migration is increasing, both among men and women. Almost 100 million, or about half, of the world's migrants are women.

This migration has had a significant impact, not only on the women themselves but also on the families they leave behind. For one, the economic impact of this global migration is significant; in 2004, the World Bank estimated that migrant workers sent $126 billion home to their families in developing countries. This is particularly impressive given that many of these workers are working in unskilled or low-skilled jobs, with annual incomes that can range between $1,500 and $4000. These remittances add up to almost double the amount of Official Development Assistance (ODA) and approximately 75 percent of total foreign direct investment. [28] In late 2007, the United Nations estimated this figure to be even higher ($300 billion) and argued that remittances represent "one of the world's largest poverty reduction efforts" that contributes to "grass-roots economic development." [29] According to one Ethiopian woman who migrated (undocumented) to Yemen, "There are very limited job opportunities in this country [Ethiopia]....I remember how I suffered before securing a job in Yemen....[T]hings would have been worse for me and my family had I not gone abroad to work." [30] Although we don't know how much of this money is being sent by women migrants, available data indicate that women send a higher proportion of their earnings back to their families and that women tend to invest the remittances meeting daily needs, health care, and education for their families. In contrast, men tend to spend remittance income on consumer items such as cars and TVs or on investments such as property and livestock. [31] Although the data are spotty, nonetheless it is clear that the money that female migrants send back home (and that female caretakers receive) can make a substantial impact on the daily lives of families and sometimes entire communities.

The women themselves can benefit from the transnational move; it can expose them to new ideas and norms about their rights and enable them to participate more fully in society. Also, if and when they return to their home country, they take those new norms back with them, and these norms can directly improve the lives of their families. For example, a World Bank report found that female migrant workers from Guatemala, Mexico, and Morocco, as a result of the health education they received while working abroad, improved their children's health and experienced lower mortality rates. Migration can also redefine traditional gender norms of behavior between men and women. In particular, women who migrate alone (rather than as part of a family) are more likely to report a positive experience and may even be reluctant to return home and potentially relinquish some autonomy. Women earning income abroad report receiving greater levels of respect and household help from their husbands.[32] And many do live better lives in their new countries. One Venezuelan domestic worker living in the United States, who fled with her two children from an abusive husband, commented, "Here there were a lot of opportunities for my children, so they could have a different kind of life. For all the opportunities, all the good things that my children have, I love this country, I love it. I am very thankful."[33]

However, many women have also paid a high price for this decision to often leave family, spouses, and children in search of better economic opportunities. Particularly for women who are migrating illegally, they often face sexual harassment and abuse or may be forced to provide sexual favors in return for transport. Further, upon reaching their host country, they may face increased discrimination as migrants and as women, particularly if they are of a different race, class, or religion than the dominant culture of the host country. Particularly if they are there illegally, many have no recourse to social, legal, or health services and may be afraid to contact the police if facing violent or predatory conditions. And as we shall discuss in greater detail, many women, in leaving their families and children behind, usually pass on the task of care to other female relatives, thus reproducing, rather than changing, gendered household divisions of labor.

We now move to some of main reasons women are pushed and pulled into transnational migration. For each example, take a moment to think about the impact of these women's choices on their own lives and their communities. Whose lives are being improved most? Are these situations "win-wins" for everyone, or does the transaction primarily benefit the host community in the wealthier country? How free are these women to choose their own futures, given the often bleak economic and social conditions that they face back in their home countries? Certainly, there are no right answers to these questions, but they are issues to ponder as you explore women as domestic workers, skilled professionals, mail order brides, and sex providers.

Demand for domestic work in the wealthier countries is one of the largest factors driving female migration. In many ways, this global migration is a result of the strides that feminist movements have made in the more developed economies of North America, western Europe, and East Asia. As more women move into the workforce, they have had to contract out and pay for the labor that they once had performed for free, such as caring for their children and elderly and infirm relatives. For example, in the United States in 1950, only 15 percent of women with children under the age of six worked; that number has since soared to 65 percent. While many feminists advocated for a more equitable distribution of labor between spouses in the household, in reality, fathers and husbands have not fully compensated for this shift by assuming more responsibilities in the home. The result, as one scholar claims, is a gaping "care deficit," and many middle-class families pay poorer women to shoulder the burden of balancing work and family life.[34] Thus, in some ways, women's abilities to advance in the industrialized northern hemisphere are dependent on their abilities to transfer gendered divisions of labor to poorer women in the southern hemisphere who are looking for better employment opportunities than those that their own countries can provide them.

This phenomena tends to create what is termed a "global care chain"—a situation in which migrant women, having left their own homes to care for others abroad, pass on their domestic caregiving responsibilities to other female relatives or, sometimes, hire lower-income domestic workers. These women often end up running two households—their employers' as well as their own from abroad. Women who make the difficult decision to leave their families in order to sustain them also pay a significant psychological and emotional price for their decision. Often, they provide love and affection to their employer's children to earn enough money to improve the quality of the lives of their own children, whom they may not get to see for many years.

Some female migrants possess enough skills and education to parlay their strengths into relatively stable careers in the West. Increasing numbers of female professionals—particularly teachers and nurses—are choosing to emigrate to wealthier, more economically and politically stable countries. For example, since the early 2000s, about one-quarter of employed migrant women in Finland, Sweden, and the United Kingdom have been working in either the health or the education sectors. Since 2001, the United States and United Kingdom have been recruiting Caribbean teachers directly out of high school and college. And the ever-increasing demand for nurses in the wealthier countries has fueled a significant migration of qualified women from Africa, Asia, and the West Indies. In fact, more than one in four nurses and aides working in major cities in the United States is foreign born.[35]

While this influx of foreign workers may help relieve pent-up demand for more health care in the industrialized West, it has also created a huge brain drain from the poorer regions of the world, many of which are facing severe health crises with even fewer human resources. The World Health Organization recommends a minimum ratio of 100 nurses for every 100,000 people. Many developing countries, particularly those in sub-Saharan Africa, do not even come close to meeting that goal. For example, the ratio is less than 10 nurses per 100,000 people in countries such as Uganda, while there are more than 2,000 nurses per 100,000 people in wealthier countries such as Finland or Norway. The yearly migration of 20,000 trained nurses and doctors from Africa further exacerbates what was already a dire situation. The lack of trained health professionals is particularly problematic given the skyrocketing incidences of malaria, HIV/AIDS, and maternal mortality. While nurses are in extremely short supply in the developing world, their reasons for emigrating are not; collapsed health systems, underfunding and chronic shortages of basic supplies, and poor pay are all common scenarios for nurses who stay behind. But who will take care of the population of the countries they have left? In 2003, an estimated 85 percent of employed Filipino nurses were working abroad, a factor that has made an indelible impact on the quality of care available to Filipino citizens.[36]

A third major motivation for female migration is marriage. Further, advances in technology, such as the rise of the Internet, have aided the rise of the mail order bride and arranged and forced marriages. As we shall see in Chapter 9, the undervaluation of girls in some cultures, such as India and China, has led to millions of "missing girls," those who are aborted while still in the womb in favor of producing only boy children. But this has also led to an unprecedented shortage of marriageable women and has fueled the growth of international marriages, as families comb regions such as South East Asia for brides.

Yet, given the futures that they face in their home countries, women are often willing participants in this business. Whether it is based in a desire to find a supportive partner, economic security, or a means to gain legal entry into another country, thousands of women are choosing to market themselves to the increasingly international marriage market. In the United States alone, according to the Department of Justice, 80,000 Russian women have entered the United States in the past ten years looking for companionship and, hopefully, a brighter economic future than what may have faced them if they stayed behind in Russia. At the same time, some women face such extremely circumscribed options that it is somewhat hard to view their decisions as freely made "choices." A 2005 study of Vietnamese migrant women who had once lived in China found that most entered into unions because of poverty or to provide for elderly parents back home. Would they have made the same choice if coming from a position of economic security, not only for themselves, but for their families as well?[37] And unfortunately in some cases, the growing industry of mail order brides can serve as a front to the illegal sex industry, and thousands of women, who may expect (and accept) to exchange sex for marriage, end up providing sex against their will as unwilling participants in the sex trade.

Unfortunately, millions of people—men, women, boys, and girls—are caught up in the transnational trafficking chain. U.S. law defines trafficking as "the recruitment, harboring, transportation, provision, or obtaining of a person for labor or services, through the use of force, fraud, or coercion for the purpose of subjection to involuntary servitude, peonage, debt bondage, or slavery."[38] A fundamental element of this definition is that there is a substantial power differential; while the trafficker is aware of the exploitation, the victim has at best only partial information and at worst none at all. In sum, fundamentally, trafficking is not considered to be a consensual employment agreement, given the imperfect information available to the victim.[39] This phenomenon is relatively widespread; the International Labor Organization, the UN agency that addresses labor standards, employment, and social protection issues, estimates that 12.3 million people are in forced, bonded labor. Further, every year, approximately 800,000 people are trafficked across borders, in addition to the millions trafficked within their own countries. Trafficking has a gendered component; 80 percent of transnational victims are women, and up to 50 percent are minors. Many of these women are trafficked into some form of the burgeoning and extremely profitable sex industry, although they are also trafficked into migrant labor, bonded labor, and domestic servitude (as opposed to consensual domestic service). This underground, highly illegal business is also highly profitable. Human trafficking is the third most profitable illicit business in the world, edged out only by arms and drug trafficking.[40] Conservative estimates place the money generated by sex trafficking alone at $7 billion per year, although Interpol puts the estimate at $19 billion; the ILO argues that each victim generates, on average, $23,000 a year in profits.[41] About half of the victims end up in industrialized countries and almost one-third in Asia.[42] The largest numbers of trafficked persons come out of Asia; an estimated 225,000 are taken out of South East Asia, while another 150,000 come from South Asia. More than 100,000 persons are trafficked from the former Soviet Union, and 75,000 come from eastern Europe.[43]

In reading through the testimony of rescued workers, a familiar narrative emerges. Most victims come from an entrenched environment of poverty and lack of opportunity, combined with a dearth of education or other tools to give them skills to compete in an already extremely underdeveloped job market in their countries of origin. Women's lack of economic and social rights and access to opportunities often serve as a root cause of their trafficking, and many are lured by promises of fabricated jobs as hostesses, waitresses, nannies, or entertainers. The experiences of Sylvia, a nineteen-year-old living in Ungheni, Bulgaria, illustrates an all too common narrative facing many young women searching for employment. Unemployed, broke, with no job prospects but a baby daughter to support single-handedly, Sylvia was thrilled when a neighbor told her he could help her find a good job as a sales girl in Moscow. Sylvia first traveled to Chisinau, the capital of Moldova, to meet two men who would arrange for her travel to Russia. Instead, she was beaten, raped, and eventually smuggled with eleven others to Moscow, and straight into prostitution. Now living in a safe house, she reflected, "I thought all the stories about trafficked girls were fake, a scare tactic. But now I know better.... [I]t is real and can happen to anyone."[44] And even if victims do manage to escape, for many, the nightmare has not ended. Particularly for victims of sex trafficking, they are too ashamed to return home, often prompting their reentry into the sex industry. This is particularly true for young boys, who face even greater levels of stereotypes that entrench the idea that they cannot be exploited in prostitution.

It is important to acknowledge that not all women in the sex trafficking industry are victims; they also work the other side of the industry as recruiters, brothel operators, and "clients." For example, women often recruit other women in Europe and Central and South Asia. Frequently, they themselves were victims of the system, but through a system of physical and psychological pressure, as well as the offering of limited incentives, become part of the system, recruiting fresh victims through stories of having had ideal experiences in legitimate jobs in the West or elsewhere. In addition, women serve as pimps and madams, and often broker the transactions. Some hypothesize that this has become a deliberate hiring strategy for the industry; criminal organizations may hire female traffickers because they believe that governments will exhibit greater leniency toward female criminals. Further, in some countries, particularly in Eurasia, female traffickers are released from serving prison time when they are pregnant or mothers of young children, and thus are actively recruited by organizers higher up in the trafficking industry as a way to minimize risk to their profits.[45]

As with mail order brides, the trafficking of women, as well as the burgeoning underground industry of sex tourism, has been spurred by advances in technology. The Internet has been a critical force in easing the illicit purchasing of sex, facilitating foreign travel with the express purpose of purchasing sex, often with what is legally considered underage girls. And the Internet is teeming with websites that provide potential sex tourists with accounts written by other tourists and supply information on destinations, prices, and procurement. In 1995 alone, there were over twenty-five U.S. businesses that offered and arranged sex tours; one business promised sex with two young Thai girls "for the price of a tank of gas." And although almost all countries have laws on the books outlawing prostitution and underage sex, lax government regulation, poor enforcement, and/ or lack of resources to tackle the problem all conspire to make domestic laws in some developing countries relatively useless. Places such as Thailand, Indonesia, Malaysia, and the Philippines have become hubs of the sex tourism industry, and unfortunately the profits are so substantial that they represent anywhere from 2 to 14 percent of the gross domestic product of these countries.[46] This encourages governments to turn a blind eye to the crimes committed, out of a need for the larger profits generated by visiting tourists, given the paucity of other economic development strategies.

The other factor that drives the sex industry is a relentless flood of demand. Sex tourists are typically male and come from all income brackets, usually from nations in western Europe and North America. Many may even perversely justify their actions as "humanitarian." Thus, one retired U.S. schoolteacher, traveling with the express purpose of purchasing sex, commented, "On this trip, I've had sex with a 14 year-old girl in Mexico and a 15 year-old in Columbia. I'm helping them financially. If they don't have sex with me, they may not have enough food. If someone has a problem with me doing this, let UNICEF feed them."[47] Others convince themselves that children in foreign countries are less sexually inhibited and that culturally, the destination countries do not have the same taboos against what is considered underage sex in their home countries. Many simply rely on the anonymity that foreign travel provides, releasing them from the usual moral constraints that may check their behavior in their homes.

In closing, millions of women migrate annually in search of better lives, often motivated to leave their home countries because of severe levels of gender inequality, whether in education, economic, or social opportunities. The impact of the growing feminization of migration is complex; on the one hand, migration can open up new vistas for women who otherwise might have faced a life of penury and social disempowerment if they had stayed behind. On the other hand, their secondary status can often continue on in their new host countries, and, at times, their situations can worsen if they are trafficked into labor against their will. Globalization has been and will continue to be a critical force in shaping women's lives; the increased interconnectedness of national economies, advances in technology, and spread of cultural values have all pushed and pulled women to cross borders for better opportunities.

RURAL WOMEN, THE ENVIRONMENT, AND SUSTAINABLE DEVELOPMENT

Increasingly, international organizations, policy makers, and activists have rallied behind the concept of sustainable development, which the United Nations defines as "development that meets the needs of the present without compromising the ability of future generations to meet their own needs."[48] Yet, economic development, seen by these same agencies as the engine behind greater levels of human development, often has negative environmental consequences and can imperil both long-term human and ecological health and survival. Further, the environmental impact often disproportionately affects some regions of the world; poorer countries in the South pay the environmental and human costs of the richer northern countries' incessant desire for cheaper goods in the context of a high consumption lifestyle. For example, the housing boom of the previous decade in the United States fueled demand for lumber, much of which is harvested in developing countries. Deforestation often leads to soil erosion, which lowers agricultural yields, which in turn can prompt a series of suboptimal practices, such as the increased reliance on fertilizers, which can increase soil salinity, which can lead to desertification, polluted waterways, and shortages of drinkable water and edible fish. This has an enormous impact, not only on the ecosystem but also on people's livelihoods, health, and life trajectories. Deforestation also contributes to global warming, as there are now fewer trees to absorb excess carbon dioxide. As you can see, consumer choice in the United States can have far-reaching implications for people living in the global south. Certainly, citizens in less developed countries also play a role in perpetuating unsustainable development practices; however, the damage done in terms of exhausting local renewable resources such as water and land is often prompted by the quest to meet basic needs, not to sustain a consumer lifestyle. Many people in the developing world have constrained choices and thus contribute to resource depletion and pollution in their larger struggle for survival.[49]

Women are particularly impacted by the environmental impact of larger development processes because millions of women in the developing world live in rural areas and ensure their families' survival through paid and unpaid agricultural work in activities such as food production, animal husbandry, and fuel collection. Yet, globalization has penetrated to even the most rural of areas and has redefined, in both positive and negative ways, women's roles in the rural economy. Further, we shall see that women are particularly vulnerable to the impact of pollution, soil erosion, and environmental degradation and that their response to these problems has also been deeply gendered, often rooted in their roles as caretakers of "mother earth."

Until 2005, agriculture was the main sector of employment for women worldwide. Although the service sector now provides most jobs for women (42.2 percent), 40.4 percent of working women around the world are employed in agriculture. This number increases substantially as one moves from developed to developing countries (61 percent), and then to the least developed (79 percent) countries in the world.[50] In fact, women have a higher share of agricultural employment than men in East Asia, South Asia, sub-Saharan Africa, and the Middle East and North Africa.

Women are critical to the sustainability of rural economies and communities, although their roles are rapidly shifting in response to the larger forces of globalization. As caretakers of hearth and home, they are often responsible for growing the food, and some estimate that women agricultural workers produce half of the world's food. In particular, women are the main producers of stable crops such as rice, maize, and wheat, which form the basis of diets in most developing countries. And in the least developed countries of sub-Saharan Africa, the United Nations estimates that about 60–70 percent of all food production is done by women.[51] In many developing countries, they also responsible for caring for animal livestock; in sub-Saharan Africa, 50 percent of all animal husbandry is done by women. Women are also the main food producers in terms of preparation; as the caretakers of the household, women are primarily responsible for ensuring that their families get enough to eat. Further, in order to prepare the food, women spend hours a day collecting water, gathering fuel sources, and cooking and cleaning up, in addition to their care work in tending to children, the elderly, and the sick. As a result, they are critical to ensuring food security and fighting to keep their families out of poverty.

Yet, despite the fact that women are an essential part of rural economies, and produce a significant amount of the world's food, many women are excluded from opportunities to capitalize on their roles. Despite the fact that women work the land, local custom and/or law can deny women equitable access to and control over land. Women often do not hold formal and clear land titles, and women own less than 2 percent of land in the developing world. This lack of ownership puts many of the women who work the land in an extremely vulnerable position because they can be evicted, or simply because they lack the ability to make long-term plans to maximize their economic options. And without a strong tradition of land ownership, and the ability to claim it as an asset, it is difficult for women to gain access to other essential resources, such as credit. As a result, many women, if they need to borrow, must resort to informal methods, which often are accompanied by higher interest rates. Further, women's unequal and constricted access to education can limit their abilities to learn new technologies to increase production. Nor have development projects consistently addressed these problems; a study of women in agriculture in Africa found that while women produce about 70 percent of Africa's food, only 20 percent of these women are the direct recipients of extension advice.[52] As we discussed earlier in the chapter, much of women's work goes unnoticed because it is considered "housework," and therefore is unpaid. This oversight is even more problematic for rural women in that rural residents in particular struggle for daily survival; 75 percent of the poor in developing countries live in rural areas, and rural women are particularly vulnerable.[53] In particular, indigenous women, widows, and female-headed households are even further marginalized in rural economies.

Globalization has significantly impacted domestic agrarian economies, and women's roles in them. Consumer demands from industrialized nations, spurred on by increased efficiency in communication and transportation, has led to the increasing reliance on large-scale plantation farming as well as a focus on nontraditional exports and high-value foods, compared with the traditional exports of coffee, tea, sugar, and cocoa. The rise of chains such as Whole Foods, where shoppers can buy blueberries, exotic fruits, boutique coffees, and fresh flowers at any time of the year, has dramatically shifted how things are grown and who cultivates them. For example, in Africa, there has been a shift in focus to produce goods such as cut flowers in Zimbabwe, tobacco in Mozambique, and vanilla in Uganda. Fruit and flower production has also become much more important for Latin American economies. In Asia, shrimp farming has become increasingly important, and former rice farms are being taken over by shrimp farms that export to Europe and the United States.

Women in Movement: Wangari Maathai

"The planting of trees is the planting of ideas. By starting with the simple act of planting a tree, we give home to ourselves and to future generations."[i]

Nobel laureate, activist, politician—Wangari Maathai, mother of three, has accumulated a long list of firsts in her remarkable quest to revive the connection between thriving ecosystems and health, justice, and peace. Raised in rural Kenya in the waning days of the British Empire, Maathai, with the support of her mother and older brother, was one of the few girls who attended school beyond the primary level. Marked early on as an exceptionally bright student, Maathai was selected as part of a U.S. program (known as the Kennedy Airlift) to send young Africans to American colleges for further education in the hopes that they would return to assume leadership positions in the soon-to-be independent African states. Combining her academic interest in science with her deep love for the lush rural environment of her girlhood in Kenya, Maathai returned with a master's degree in biology, to which she soon added a Ph.D. in veterinary medicine from the University of Nairobi. She was the first woman in East and Central Africa to receive her doctorate. She became professor of veterinary anatomy at the university and went on to chair her department. In 1977, Maathai founded Kenya's Greenbelt Movement to mobilize thousands of women to plant trees in an effort to revive the country's forest lands, which had been transformed from the lush, green, fertile land of plenty from her childhood to a deforested nightmare in her adulthood. Since founding this organization, the Green Belt Movement has planted more than 40 million trees across Africa. In addition, what began as a targeted program to address the challenges of deforestation, soil erosion, and lack of water developed into a means of female empowerment, supporting and nurturing women's roles as champions for sustainable development, equitable economic growth, and responsible political governance. Maathai underwent a political transformation as well, eventually connecting Kenya's environmental degradation with the irresponsible policies of a corrupt government, and her Greenbelt Movement also became part of the broader campaign for democracy in Kenya. When a new government came to power in 2002, she was elected to parliament and appointed assistant minister in the Ministry for Environmental and Natural Resources. Although she lost her bid for reelection in 2007, she continues to be an impassioned advocate for environmental conservation, democratic governance, and human rights for women and men.

As a woman, Maathai often had to fight against gender discrimination, sometimes within her own family. In the 1980s, her husband, a politician whom she had married in 1969, divorced her, maintaining that she was too strong-minded for a woman and that he was unable to control her. The judge agreed with the husband, and eventually jailed Maathai for speaking out. Her willingness to speak out also prompted political enmity; President Moi denounced her as a "wayward" woman and jailed her several times for her prodemocracy activities.

---

[i] Wangari Maathai, *Unbowed* (New York: Knopf, 2006). As quoted in The Green Belt Movement, http://www.greenbeltmovement.org/a.php?id=183.

On the one hand, globalization has helped diversify rural livelihoods and increase labor mobility. Women increasingly make up the bulk of migrant labor in fresh produce global supply chain, comprising 65 percent of the labor force in Colombia, 75 percent in Kenya, and 87 percent in Zimbabwe.[54] These jobs in the global food production chain offer paid employment and the opportunity to work for waged labor, as opposed to what is often the norm—unpaid labor in service to the family. Research on female employment in the flower plantations in Ecuador, where two-thirds of all workers are women, for example, showed that the presence of the industry did increase incomes and, indirectly, led to important changes in gender roles within the household. Some of the trends noted were changes in spending patterns, the division of work, and decision making regarding education and health. Men tended to increase their contributions to housework after women began work. In addition, the marriage rate among women working on the plantation dropped, as marriage became less an economic necessity and potentially more of a choice.

However, the study found that the entry of women, specifically mothers, into the paid labor force had a negative impact on their daughters, who often took on increased work loads at home, particularly with regard to child care of younger siblings. This often harmed their educational prospects. Second, because women are hired and are willing to work as temporary workers, many did not qualify for social benefits, such as health care, or fair labor practices, such as regulated work shifts. In turn, employers point out that the demands of the increasingly global-ized economy means that they must continue to find ways to slash production costs. As one South African apple farmer, who exports to the United Kingdom's biggest supermarket, Tesco, explained, "The only ham left in the sandwich is our labour costs. If they squeeze us, it's the only place where we can squeeze." Thus, hiring women on temporary contracts, with few to no benefits, is the only way they feel they can compete.[55] While the globalized economy enables wom-en's employment, it is often on the punishing terms of free trade rather than fair trade. However, women themselves prefer the work to the alternative—work as a domestic or seasonal worker—which potentially requires moving away from their families in search of better opportunities.[56]

In addition, liberalization policies, which are an essential element of the free trade argument of globalization advocates, eliminate trade and market barriers as well as reduce government-funded price supports for basic agricul-tural commodities. The adoption of these policies has encouraged the priori-tization of large-scale farming in support of cash and export crops over food crops for household and local consumption. This means that commercialized agriculture is squeezing out subsistence agriculture and that preference is given to export-oriented crops rather than domestic markets. This shift also requires greater investments in expensive inputs such as fertilizers, seeds, and farming equipment.

This has had a profound effect on domestic livelihoods, and also on women specifically. The shift away from producing food for individual consumption has created a food shortage for those living in the developing world. For example, the shift toward shrimp production for export in much of Asia has led to decreased availability of fish for low-income consumers, diminished availability of land for local food production, and increased levels of soil salinity, which has led to decreased food crop yields.[57] This problem of falling levels of local food produc-tion is not isolated to a few Asian countries; in 1960, developing countries had an overall agricultural trade surplus of almost $7 billion per year; by 2001, the sur-plus had reversed into a deficit of more than $11 billion. This has created a serious food security issue, particularly for women, who are primarily responsible for cultivating, buying, and cooking food for their families.

Further, the increasing scarcity and degradation of land, water, and other property resources have affected women's caring work. Women have to spend more time coaxing smaller plots of overtaxed, overfarmed land to produce food. They also have to spend more time and energy searching for fuel, water, and other essentials that keep their families alive, given that deforestation and water contamination are increasingly common. Women, who had maybe once spent one hour gathering local firewood or fetching water from the local pump, may now need to walk several miles to find the same resources. The search for these necessary inputs often diminishes the time they can spend on farming and caring for livestock, which simply increases the vicious cycle of food insecurity. Further, women's health, and the health of their families, may deteriorate, as women must carry heavier loads for longer distances; cook, drink, and wash with polluted water; and burn increasingly toxic fuel sources.

WOMEN AND ECONOMIC CRISIS

Women's role as caretakers is also called upon (and stretched to the limit) in times of economic crisis. Further, women respond differently to and are affected differently by economic downturns. This was particularly so in the 1980s and 1990s, when many countries began to implement what are known as structural adjustment programs (SAPs). Initially pushed by international lending agencies such as the International Monetary Fund, structural adjustment programs were the expression of a neoliberal, promarket approach that emphasizes making internal economic and political reforms to help the domestic economy be more competitive in the global marketplace. In particular, lending institutions such as the IMF advanced loans to countries only when they could meet certain conditions that theoretically would reduce trade barriers and stimulate economic growth. Some of these conditions were reduced social expenditures, increased focus on export-led growth and resource extraction, currency devaluation against the dollar, removal of import and export restrictions, opening of domestic markets to foreign investment, balancing budgets, privatization of critical state-owned industries, and removing price controls and state subsidies. In sum, SAPs called for decreased government intervention in the economy, decreased government spending in favor of balanced budgets, and an embrace of global free market forces.

The results of these reforms for many countries were devastating and caused many to go more deeply into debt without reaping the rewards of economic growth. Many countries' increased focus on export-led growth reaped few rewards, given that prices for commodities and raw materials on the global marketplace were falling, rather than rising. Devaluation often severely weakened domestic currencies, and domestic prices spiraled in turn, leading to rampant inflation. Privatization often resulted in a net loss of jobs, as new owners in the private sector laid off workers to try to reduce costs. And cuts on government expenditures slashed services to citizens often most in need. Finally, corrupt governments squandered or embezzled the loans, ensuring that future generations would be held hostage to crippling debt loads.

Women were particularly vulnerable to these reforms, which increased their work load, not only in their paid work responsibilities but also in their unpaid responsibilities in the home. Women tried to increase their paid work to compensate for rising male unemployment and increased cost of living. In addition, women's unpaid labor increased to compensate for cutbacks in public services. For example, women assumed the responsibility of caring for sick relatives, who previously might have received care from a doctor or hospital. In addition, women had to find ways to substitute for the food and clothing the household could no longer afford.[58] In sum, the financial backlash when fragile economies in newly opened societies fail creates new stresses and strains for women, who must often bear the brunt of financial dislocation.

As the global recession continues in 2009, it looks as if women will once again bear the brunt of the social costs of financial collapse. Rising food prices, spiraling unemployment, and slashed social services are just a few of the manifestations of a larger economic meltdown. Yet, because women have been primarily affected by trends such as the dramatic rise in food prices, they have also been at the forefront of protests. In April 2008, more than one thousand women protested the lack of accountability and action from their government regarding the food crisis by banging empty pots and pans. Similarly, women in Haiti protested by making biscuits outs of mud, salt, and vegetable shortening. These protests were not isolated phenomena; in the first months of 2008, there were protests in over thirty-four countries over the spiraling costs of food.[59] As the implications of the U.S.-led recession deepen, so too will the gendered impact, as well as the response to the crisis.

ADVANCING WOMEN'S EQUALITY

Women's economic status in the developing world is slowly improving, in that a higher percentage of women have access to the paid labor force, and thus to the advantages that monetary income can bring to their personal well-being and their families. Yet, women are also more likely to be trapped in low-paying, unstable, and insecure jobs, leaving them mired in poverty. It is harder for them to translate their labor into paid work, and their paid work into secure, living wage incomes. Development agencies are aware of the gendered nature of these economic inequalities; however, it is often easier to recognize the problem than design an effective solution. A good place to start is identifying the reasons why women's inequalities exist; if we can address some of these underlying factors, then perhaps it will be possible to then change employment patterns. However, there is no single reason why women often come out as second-class citizens with regard to economic development. Depressingly, the World Bank estimates that only about one-fifth of the wage gap can be explained by gender differences in education, work experience, or job characteristics; rather, they argue, the pervasive power of prejudice and discrimination against women accounts for much of women's second-class economic status.[60] Other issues, such as the unequal division of labor in the household, further impact women's abilities to gain equality in the workforce. This suggests that the target of development policy needs to be focused on society at large, rather than solely on women.

However, education still is a factor in explaining women's unequal access to economic resources, and according to the World Bank's World Development Report 2000/2001, closing the gender gap in education would significantly increase and, in some instances, double economic growth in sub-Saharan Africa, South Asia, the Middle East, and North Africa.[61] As a result, as we will discuss in greater detail in Chapter 10, development agencies have focused on increasing women's access to education, which is still quite low.

Another factor that inhibits gender equality is access to the appropriate resources, such as land and credit. In particular, land titling is particularly problematic. Women are often barred from owning the title to land, even when they are its primary users. This means that they are then unable to use the land as collateral for credit, a strategy available to many male farmers trying to expand their business. In addition, women's access to land is often based on their marital status; as a result, unmarried and divorced women are rarely named on title deeds. The World Bank has begun to address this issue by sponsoring a pilot project in north central Vietnam that gives both women and men rights to use land. In two rural communities in Nghe An province, land tenure certificates (LTCs) for households are being reissued with the names of both the wife and the husband, allowing both to take advantage of the opportunities that such property rights can bring to the well-being of the rural economy.[62]

In addition, women are barred from other forms of borrowing, and thus are unable to start up small businesses that would help stimulate economic growth, not only for them, but also for their country's economy. One popular solution to this issue has been the funding of microcredit programs, which give very small loans primarily to women who are too poor, and thus lack collateral or traditional risk indicators, to qualify for traditional bank loans. Microcredit programs have shown some impressive results; many programs not only demonstrated that the poor were credit-worthy in that they could repay their loans but also showed that the loans can catalyze wider impacts, such as female empowerment, increased use of contraceptives by women, and better health outcomes for children of borrowers. In addition, the ideological premise of microcredit—that the poor have underutilized skills that, if fostered with small amounts of funding, can be used to lift them out of poverty—appealed to a wide range of development specialists and political actors on the left and the right. As a result, microcredit has become extremely popular with development agencies as a poverty reduction strategy, and organizations such as the World Bank, the United Nations, and the United States Agency for International Development have devoted millions of dollars to funding microcredit projects as a way to reduce not only women's economic vulnerability but also their higher levels of social exclusion. Despite some impressive results, microcredit is no panacea. Critics warn that microcredit alone is not sufficient to overcome the many social, political, and economic obstacles that the poorest confront on a daily basis. In addition, others warn that the focus on women, although important, may not be as empowering as supporters claim; men sometimes force their wives to take out loans only so that they can take control of the money themselves. Further, in some cases, a rise in household income was accompanied by the abandonment of more nutritious foods in favor of more prestigious, but less nourishing, prepackaged Western foods, which hold higher status in many communities.[63] Nonetheless, microcredit still remains an inspirational example of the implementation of an idea that was once deemed unrealistic, unworkable, and untranslatable as a widely used development strategy. The accompanying text box on Muhammad Yunus and the Grameen Bank describes one of the most well-known examples of microcredit.

Men in Movement: Muhammad Yunus and the Grameen Bank

Muhammad Yunus, founder of the Grameen Bank and co-winner of the 2006 Nobel Peace Prize, became an unlikely banker in 1976. Born to a middle-class family in Bangladesh and educated in the United States, Yunus returned to Bangladesh in 1972, where he soon became head of the Economics Department at Chittagong University. Increasingly aware of the gap between the lofty economic theories he taught in the classroom and the impoverished status of millions of citizens of his own country, Yunus became involved in local community efforts to stimulate economic development. But his plans soon changed when he interviewed an impoverished woman in a rural village in Bangladesh and learned that she lacked the 22 cents she needed to buy bamboo to weave stools. As a result, she was caught in a cycle of continuous poverty; she had to borrow the cash from a moneylender to buy her own raw materials. She would then sell her bamboo stool back to the money lender, for a profit of about 2 cents, ensuring that could never escape the vicious cycle of poverty. Yet, women such as her, desperate for credit at a fair price, could never get it from traditional banks, who saw poor people, with their lack of assets, as loan risks. Professor Yunus responded by loaning $27 from his own pocket to a group of forty-two villagers, who successfully repaid their loans. Realizing that serving as a personal banker to the local village was not a long-term solution, Professor Yunus set out to design a banking system that could loan small amounts of money to the poor. In 1977, he founded the Grameen Bank to make loans to poor, primarily female Bangladeshi women. By the end of 2008, the Grameen Bank had grown from a pilot project to meet the needs of local villagers to a bank with 2,535 branches, working in 83,343 villages, providing services to 7.61 million borrowers, 97 percent of whom are women. Since its inception, the Bank has loaned out over $7 billion, with a repayment rate of over 98 percent. Yunus proved that one could make very small loans (as of 2008, the average loan size was just under $350) to the very poor, the same group that traditional banks had deemed not credit-worthy.

What is it that makes Grameen Bank distinctive? One of the main things that distinguishes the bank is its creative use of incentives to encourage repayment, given the absence of traditional sources of leverage, such as collateral. Yunus devised a system whereby borrowers were divided into support groups of five members. Each group is loaned money, but the whole group is denied further credit if one person defaults. Social pressure from one's peers replaces the monetary pressure of forfeiting on assets in this system. And small repayments are made on a weekly, rather than monthly or quarterly, basis to encourage clients to keep up a steady, incremental habit of repayment. Another distinctive feature is the bank's focus on women; they comprise 97 percent of the Bank's clientele. Yunus made a conscious decision to focus on women; not only are they in greater need of assistance, he reasoned, because of their secondary status in society, but they also are more likely to repay their loans. And finally, the bank is more than a financial program; it also asks that members abide by what are known as the "Sixteen Decisions," a set of principles designed to advance overall levels of well-being among women and their families. For example, women must promise to strive to keep their families small, to grow nutritious food, to educate their children, and to decline to participate in the dowry system. While the bank does not enforce these decisions, nonetheless it sees its loans as a small part of a larger process of changing the way that women and men live their lives in Bangladesh.

Yunus also helped expand the bank's activities, creating a number of other socially conscious enterprises underneath the Grameen name. For example, Grameen Bank established a program, discussed in the opening of this chapter, to bring telephones to distant villages, loaning money to almost 139,000 poor women in rural areas to pay for the phones. They also established Grameenphone, the leading telecommunications service provider in the country. Grameen has also expanded the reach of their clientele, starting a program for beggars.

The tireless work of Yunus and the Grameen Bank was recognized by the Nobel Prize Committee, who awarded them the Nobel Peace Prize in recognition for "their efforts to create economic and social development from below. Lasting peace cannot be achieved unless large population groups find ways in which to break out of poverty." And the larger idea of microcredit, or very small loans to the poor, has become a popular poverty fighting strategy, funded by development agencies and other nonprofit organizations in over 130 countries around the world. And it all started with the effort to figure out a solution for one disempowered female basket weaver in the village of Jobra, Bangladesh, in 1972.

The Self-Employed Women's Association (SEWA) of India is another example of an organization that works to improve the lives of poor, self-employed women workers, who, as mentioned previously in the chapter, work without the stability of salaried wages, benefits, insurance, or, in most cases, representation. Founded as an independent trade union in 1972, SEWA emerged when a small group of migrant women working as cart-pullers in India's vast textile industry approached the women's wing of the Textile Labour Association, India's largest and oldest union of textile workers, to ask for help in finding housing. At the time, they were living in the streets without shelter. Ela Bhatt, the head of the Women's Wing with the TLA, went with the women to the areas where they were living to assess the situation, and there she met with another group of women who were working as head loaders, carrying loads of clothes between the wholesale and retail markets. Collectively, they discussed their jobs, their low and erratic wages, and their larger problems with translating their capacity for work into stable, wage-paying employment. The ensuing proposal to form an association of their own was a novel idea at the time, for the self-employed had no real history of organizing, because unlike other unions, they had no recognized employer. SEWA argued that a union was necessary to promote the unity of workers, rather than fight against an employer. In April 1972, the union was born. In addition to its efforts to improve the working conditions of its members, SEWA has expanded to provide services to its members such as savings and credit, health care, child care, insurance, legal aid, capacity building, and communication services. Like the Grameen Bank and its Sixteen Decisions, which emphasize the need to reinvest higher incomes into better life decisions for the loanees and their families, SEWA emphasizes the importance of its members' abilities to answer positively to eleven questions that assess women's abilities to lead secure lives, not only for themselves, but also for their families. Thus, the questions ask whether the women's income has increased, whether they have obtained food and nutrition, are safeguarding their health, are obtaining child care, are improving their housing, or are increasing their literacy, for example. Like the Grameen Bank, SEWA sees increased employment opportunities for women as a means to a healthier, more autonomous life, rather than an end expressed solely in higher income.

As we discussed earlier in this chapter, many women, desperate for increased earning opportunities, are either pushed or pulled, often against their will, into the sex industry. While poverty and lack of opportunity help create a supply of sex workers, ever-increasing levels of demand (often from the industrialized world), combined with lax local laws and corrupt officials, seriously compound the problem.

And finally, women have been at the forefront of organizing to protest the negative human impact of environmental degradation. For example, the Chipko (which literally means "embrace") movement was started by Indian villagers, primarily women, in the 1970s and 1980s to protest the impact of deforestation on their livelihoods.

CONCLUSION

Even though women are entering the labor force in increasing numbers, they are paid less than men and are segregated into low-skill, low-paying jobs. The reasons for women's differing status in the economy are varied; persistent cultural values, discriminatory practices, and undereducation are just a few reasons women are underutilized in some areas of economic production and overutilized in others. As the global economy becomes increasingly interdependent, women have become the lynchpin of the economy. As wage laborers, they fuel the global economy by working primarily in low-skilled, low-wage jobs outsourced from the West. Alternatively, they travel to Western industrialized nations, willing to work for low pay, in search of better lives. In their traditional roles as wives and mothers, they hold the family together in times of economic crises. While women have improved their economic status, they have yet to reach any form of gender parity with men.

FOR MORE INFORMATION

Born into Brothels, http://www.kids-with-cameras.org/bornintobrothels
Chipko Movement, http://uttarakhand.prayaga.org/chipko.html
Coalition Against Trafficking in Women, http://www.catwinternational.org
Global Alliance Against Traffic in Women, http://www.gaatw.org
Grameen Bank, http://www.grameen-info.org
The Greenbelt Movement, http://www.wangarimaathai.com
International Labor Organization Bureau for Gender Equality, http://www.ilo.org/gender/
    lang—en/index.htm
International Poverty Center, Report on Gender Equality, http://www.undp-povertycentre.
    org/pub/IPCPovertyInFocus13.pdf
Self-Employed Women's Association, http://www.sewa.org/aboutus/index.asp
Sixteen Decisions, http://www.berkeleymedia.com/catalog/berkeleymedia/films/global_
    and_development_studies/sixteen_decisions
United Nations Development Programme (UNDP), Gender and Poverty Reduction,
    http://www.undp.org/poverty/genpov.htm
Women's Environment and Development Organizations, http://www.wedo.org

9

꩜

Women and Health

Abeba Zerehun lives in Ethiopia. She got married at the age of fifteen to a man that her parents chose for her, whom she met for the first time on her wedding day. She left school in the seventh grade to start her new life as a married woman, and she became pregnant within a year. When it came time to deliver, she labored unsuccessfully for many hours at home in her village with her mother and husband by her side, until she was eventually taken to a hospital, where they removed her baby, which had already died. But Abeba's pain was not over; she soon discovered that during her long and difficult labor, she had developed a fistula, or hole between her birth passage and one or more of her internal organs. Left incontinent and unable to bear more children, her husband, who married another woman, abandoned Abeba; after that, Abeba faced a future life of physical disability, shame, and destitution. However, she traveled from her village in southern Ethiopia to the Addis Ababa Fistula Hospital in the capital, which provides free fistula repair surgery to about twelve hundred women every year. When she returns home, she hopes to resume her education so she can someday become a doctor to help girls, such as her, who have developed fistulas.

Abeba's story is, unfortunately, not unique. Fistulas, which rarely happen any longer in the industrialized West, afflict approximately 100,000 women in Nigeria alone and approximately 2 million untreated women in the developing world. They occur when women are in difficult labor; babies become lodged in narrow birth canals, and the resulting pressure cuts off blood to vital tissues and rips holes in women's bowels or urethras, or both. The result is that the babies die during labor and the women become incontinent for life and are unable to bear more children. The women often become societal outcasts because they are perceived by their communities to be unfit to fulfill their traditional roles as wives and mothers. In addition, they are shunned because they are often severely disabled from injuries sustained during labor and are unclean as a result of their incontinence. Many live the rest of their lives sequestered in their huts, with rags stuffed between their legs to catch their urine and feces. But fistulas are also entirely treatable, which is why they disappeared as a medical issue in the wealthy, industrialized West nearly a hundred years ago. Access to trained medical staff that can perform cesarean sections, or even the $300 operation to repair fistulas, would dramatically improve women's lives.

But the high incidence of fistulas points to the larger problems that women such as Abeba face. For example, a woman born in Ethiopia is expected to live to age forty-one. She has a 35 percent chance of being literate and a 50 percent chance of living below the poverty line. She will marry at seventeen and give birth to six children, not counting the ones that will die during her pregnancy or not survive the first five years of life. Moreover, giving birth in Ethiopia is somewhat similar to playing Russian roulette; one in eighteen women die while giving birth. In part, this is because of the chronic undervaluation of girls in society; underfed from birth, a woman's growth will be stunted, and she will have difficulty, particularly if she starts bearing children at a young age, pushing them successfully down and out of her birth canal. In sum, poverty; early marriage; a lack of rights, independence, and education; and a generally low standing within society all collude to rob women of the ability to make decisions about how to live long and healthy lives.

Women around the world face serious impediments to living long and healthy lives. In this chapter, we will focus on several issues that threaten women's health: inadequate access to family planning, maternal care, and other reproductive health services; societal preferences for boy children; and the spread of HIV/AIDS and its impact on women. In closing, we look at international efforts to improve women's quality of life.

THE STATUS OF WOMEN'S HEALTH

Living a long and healthy life is now seen as an integral component of human development; the United Nations uses longevity as one of its three measurements (along with literacy/enrollment figures and gross domestic product) to rank countries in its Human Development Index (HDI), a ranking of citizens' levels of well-being and quality of life in countries around the world. The HDI, combined with many other measurements and statistics relating to women's health, indicates that men and women live different lives. In some ways, women are biologically built to survive. Women outlive men in almost every country in the world and, on average, live about three years longer than men. Males are more vulnerable both before and after birth. Worldwide, more girls are born and more boys die in the early years of life. Women are hardier and more resilient to external crises. However, while women on average live longer lives, they are less healthy. This, in part, is because culturally, females are often undervalued in society. As a result, they are often poorly fed, nourished, and nurtured, whether as mothers or as daughters.

Why should we be concerned about women's health? From a human rights perspective, women's unequal status should be a source of concern. In addition, however, improving women's health is important, not only because women, like all citizens of the world, deserve to live long and healthy lives, but also because healthy women have a significant impact on the world around them. Because

Although women live longer lives than men, they are often less healthy, usually because they have been malnourished since childhood. Nor do they have access to adequate medical treatment and facilities in many developing countries. Here, a little girl is treated in the hospital of the Ehtiopian city of Kabridahar for malnutrition and tuberculosis. (April 15, 2005) SOURCE: JOEL ROBINE/AFP/Getty Images

women often form the heart of the family by cooking the food, caring for sick relatives, and maintaining the household, healthy women are critical for raising healthy children. In particular, when women die in childbirth, from AIDS, or from other health complications, the children left behind are more likely to suffer health problems, fall into poverty, or even die. The story of Fatima, a mother of nine from Afghanistan, illustrates how a mother's death usually has dire consequences for her family and her community. When Fatima became pregnant with her tenth child, family resources were stretched to the breaking point; the family was already barely surviving on the husband's salary as a security guard. Yet, the stability and heath of the family unit plummeted precipitously when Fatima died giving birth to twin boys, a not uncommon fate for women giving birth in Afghanistan, where a shattered health care system multiplies women's risks to astronomical levels. Fatima's hospital expenses put her husband deeper in debt, so he took their thirteen-year-old son out of school to work. The twins, who survived, were sickly, often ill with diarrhea or acute respiratory infections, the most common killers of infants worldwide. As a result, their eleven-year-old daughter was taken out of school to care for them. Nonetheless, the smaller twin died at seven months of a respiratory infection. The father, still mired in debt and poverty, married off his oldest daughter when she turned thirteen. Pregnant by the age of fifteen, her body struggled to deliver her baby successfully; her baby was born brain damaged, and she was left with a fistula (described at the beginning of the chapter). Her husband abandoned her, and she had to return to her father's home.[1] Unfortunately, this story, while harrowing, is all too common in the developing world. Why do so many women like Fatima have so few options in terms of determining their own reproductive health?

Women and Reproductive Health

Bearing, birthing, and nurturing a newborn baby should be a joyous event in any woman's life. Yet, for millions of women around the world, the time from conception to the month following the birth of a child can be the most dangerous period of her life. For women who live in the countries of sub-Saharan Africa, this is a long period of life-threatening danger, as a woman might spend two-thirds of her time between the ages of seventeen and thirty-five pregnant or lactating. Thus, maternal mortality is an ever-present possibility for women, who, if they had been born in a wealthier country, would be potentially enjoying the healthiest years of their lives. Maternal mortality, defined as the death of a pregnant woman during her pregnancy or within four days of pregnancy termination, remains a leading cause of death for women in the countries of the developing world. Every minute, a woman dies in pregnancy or childbirth; this means that on average, 1,400 women die daily and more than 536,000 women die yearly.[2] Ninety-nine percent of these deaths occur in the developing world. Of the estimated 529,000 maternal deaths in 2000, 95 percent occurred in Africa and Asia, while 4 percent occurred in Latin America and the Caribbean.[3] The situation is worst in sub-Saharan Africa, where a woman has a 1 in 16 chance of dying in pregnancy or childbirth. In comparison, the risk of dying from similar complications in a developed country is 1 in 3,800.[4] Young girls are particularly vulnerable to the dangers associated with pregnancy; their bodies, already stunted from years of malnutrition, are not sufficiently developed to consistently push a baby through small birth canals. As a result, adolescent mothers are twice as likely to die in childbirth as women in their twenties, and women under fifteen are five times more likely to die in childbirth.[5] Even these brutal statistics mask the more far-reaching health risks associated with pregnancy for millions of the world's women; for each woman who dies as a result of complications, about twenty women survive but suffer from serious disability or physical damage, as the opening narrative of this chapter illustrated.[6] Depressingly, maternal mortality figures have remained relatively unchanged over the previous two decades, despite the fact that the United Nations has made reducing maternal mortality a key element of the Millennium Development Goals discussed in Chapter 7. Table 9.1 shows how women in different countries fare in measures of maternal mortality.

A variety of factors impact the quality of women' reproductive health. Family planning is a critical first step in ensuring safe motherhood. Ideally, families, and women in particular, should be able to plan how many children they want and when they want them. There are compelling reasons for why family planning, when centered on women and their needs, benefits not only the

Table 9.1 Rank by Lifetime Risk of Death from Pregnancy-Related Causes*

RANK/COUNTRY	LIFETIME RISK	RANK/COUNTRY	LIFETIME RISK
1. Ireland	1 in 47,600	52. Russian Federation	1 in 2,700
2. Bosnia and Herzegovina	1 in 29,000	61. China	1 in 1,300
3. Italy	1 in 26,600	69. Mexico	1 in 670
4. Greece	1 in 25,900	84. Iran	1 in 300
5. Austria	1 in 21,500	92. Egypt	1 in 230
6. Germany	1 in 19,200	103. Nicaragua	1 in 150
7. Czech Republic	1 in 18,100	119. Iraq	1 in 72
8. Denmark	1 in 17,800	127. Bangladesh	1 in 51
9. Sweden	1 in 17,400	143. Nepal	1 in 31
10. Spain	1 in 16,400	152. Congo	1 in 22
17. Japan	1 in 11,600	160. Rwanda	1 in 16
18. Canada	1 in 11,000	169. Afghanistan	1 in 8
41. United States of America	1 in 4,800		

* In 2007, using a new method of calculation, a joint UN agency working group released new estimates on maternal mortality worldwide. This methodology takes into account both the probability of getting pregnant and the probability of dying as a result of pregnancy, cumulated across a woman's reproductive years. This is called the lifetime risk of maternal mortality.

SOURCE: Women Deliver, Maternal Mortality Scorecard; http://www.womendeliver.org/resources/Maternal_Mortality_Scorecard.htm (March 21, 2009).

women, but also the families and communities within which they are embedded. For one, maternal health improves when women can control the timing, spacing, and total number of their children. High-risk pregnancies are often those that come too early, too frequently, or too late in life, and maternal mortality drops significantly when births are spaced out to at least fifteen months. Also, increased family planning reduces women's recourse to abortion, particularly in the developing world, where abortions are largely illegal and/or unsafe. As a result, almost all abortion-related deaths occur in developing countries. Further, better timing and spacing of births reduces the risks posed to the estimated 15 million women who face illness or disability from pregnancy-related complications every year. But focusing on better timing and spacing of births also has dramatic effects on child health and survival. In some countries, infants born less than two years apart have almost twice the risk of dying than those born under greater birth intervals. In fact, if women in developing countries could space their births three years apart, mortality rates for infants and for children under five would fall by 24 percent and 35 percent, respectively. Better spacing could also improve perennial problems such as stunting and underweight children, since parents have longer to focus on the nutritional needs of each individual child. Because families with more children have a risk of falling into poverty, having fewer children allows parents to invest in adequate nutrition, housing, and education for the whole family. And finally, empowering women to make choices about their own fertility is an important step in raising their status in society. Women who have the ability to decide the timing and number of children they want are also in a stronger position to negotiate other decisions in their households as well as ones that involve how they want to lead their lives.[7] This right, not just for women but also for all couples, has been affirmed numerous times at the international level. In 1968, the UN International Human Rights Conference declared family planning to be a human right, and this declaration has been revisited and reemphasized at numerous international conferences, such as the UN-sponsored 1994 International Conference on Population and Development in Cairo, Egypt. As we will discuss later, one of the biggest shifts in international family planning efforts has been to place women and their choices at the center of family planning, rather than as objects that need to have their fertility "controlled."

Worldwide, women, when they are able to choose, are choosing to have fewer children; women in the developing world are currently having half as many children as they did in the 1960s.[8] Yet millions of women and families still lack access to all of the goods and services associated with family planning and reproductive health; an estimated 228 million women who want to delay or cease childbearing (about one in six women of reproductive age) are in need of effective contraception.[9] As a result, women are still unable to plan their pregnancies; an estimated 38 percent of all pregnancies are unintended, and the World Health Organization estimates that as a result, around six out of ten such unplanned pregnancies end in an induced abortion, which, as we mentioned previously, often ends up in death for women of the developing world.[10]

Women's limited access to family planning services is in part the result of undersupply and underfunding of family planning services in the developing world. There is also still a dearth of family planning information in many countries; many women in the developing world who do not want more children but are not using contraception report that it is because they believe they are not at risk of getting pregnant. They believe they are too young, too old, are nursing, or are practicing what they believe to be an effective form of birth control (such as early withdrawal). In addition, women may not be presented with a full range of contraceptive options, so that they may match a method with their needs. And despite the label "family planning," this is still primarily women's work; fewer than 5 percent of couples in the majority of developing countries use male methods of birth control, such as the condom, withdrawal, or vasectomy.[11]

In addition, women's limited access to family planning services is symptomatic of a much larger problem—women's lack of power and choice within the household. Although a woman's role as a reproducer has been a source of status, it has also largely been a reason for her disempowerment, and in truth, despite much of the rhetoric about the essential importance of mothers to society, millions of women around the world lack the freedom to control whether, when, how many, and under what circumstances they will bear children. In some parts of the world, women's bodies are still perceived, and in some circumstances legally recognized, as being the property or under the jurisdiction of their husbands.

Women may need to get their husband's permission to use contraceptives, pursue sterilization, or receive an abortion. Even if women are legally free to pursue their own reproductive choices, cultural norms, which place decision-making power in the hands of the male head of the household, may prohibit this. As one woman in Pakistan stated, "In our home, the household head decides about the attainment of healthcare. If he is not home, we have to wait." And in some countries, such a Taliban-controlled Afghanistan, women many have extremely limited freedom of movement, which directly impacts their ability to seek medical help. Thus, often it is the husband who ultimately decides whether the woman will gain access to family planning services, or when and how the couple will have sexual relations. This is particularly problematic for many girls who are married off at a young age and are unable to exercise choice over these issues. Further, male partners often resist the adoption of contraceptive methods because of the fear that access to birth control will lead to the woman's promiscuity and potentially will encourage her to have sex for pleasure with other men as opposed to for procreation with her husband. Other cultures equate multiple offspring with male virility, or with impotence if multiple pregnancies in as many years is not the result. The pervasive belief that women should remain virgins until marriage also inhibits the spread of information about various family planning methods, since girls are often sheltered from this information under the fear, again, that it will lead to promiscuity. In sum, lack of power over making decisions about reproductive choice is also embedded in larger patterns in which women have little control over making decisions about their lives, whether it involves the timing and spacing of their own children, going to the doctor, purchasing medication, buying better food for their families, or making other decisions about the household's economic resources. And gendered inequalities in other areas of their lives impact their abilities to make choices about their health. For example, women are less likely to be literate than men; educated women generally have more access to information about family planning.

Once women become pregnant, many lack access to prenatal care; in 1996, in low-income countries such as Yemen, Ethiopia, and Sierra Leone, only 62 percent of women received prenatal care.[12] Further, a significant proportion of women deliver without trained medical attendants. Only 58 percent of women in developing countries deliver with the assistance of a trained midwife or doctor, and even less (40 percent) do so in a hospital or other medical facility.[13] In fact, five complications, which are largely medically preventable, account for 70 percent of maternal deaths: hemorrhage (25 percent), infection (15 percent), unsafe abortions (13 percent), eclampsia (a condition resulting from high blood pressure—12 percent), and obstructed labor (8 percent). In addition, over 20 percent of women die as a result of diseases that are aggravated by pregnancy, such as malaria, anemia, tuberculosis, and HIV/AIDS.[14]

In part, women lack access because there is a limited supply of trained medical staff and facilities in countries of the developing world. For example, there is a global shortage of 4 million health care workers, which is most severe in rural parts of developing countries.[15] But a variety of other issues impact women's abilities to access medical services and care before, during, and after the delivery of a baby, even if that care is available. For example, maternal survival rates are often dependent on the distance and time a woman must travel to get to skilled emergency care. Yet, many women do not or are unable to seek care because they may have to get permission from family members, may not recognize the emergency, or may fear hospital practices. For example, in Bolivia, indigenous traditions proscribe that women give birth at home with only family members to help. When Albina Chambe, fifteen, went into labor, her fiancé wanted to take her to a hospital. But Albina's mother had delivered thirteen children at home, without medically trained birth attendants, and felt that Albina should follow tradition. After unsuccessful labor at home, Albina's fiancé helped her hike to the nearest dirt road, where they spent more than a day's pay on a taxi to the hospital. While she eventually delivered a healthy baby and suffered no long-term consequences herself, a variety of factors associated with Albina's status as a woman impacted her abilities to seek out the care that was available. Lack of knowledge, lack of decision-making power, and lack of economic resources all complicated her ability to successfully deliver a healthy baby and emerge a healthy mother.

In sum, women's abilities to choose whether, when, and how many children to have, as well as the circumstances under which to bear them, are still extremely constrained. Their access to family planning services, as well as to prenatal and postnatal care, are still extremely limited. Part of the problem is undersupply. But this constrained access is also a symptom of a larger problem—women's social, political, and economically disadvantaged position in society. As we shall discuss later in the chapter, improving women's reproductive rights will require a multipronged approach that addresses the short-term and long-term reasons for women's disempowerment.

The Problem of Boy Preference

Mothers are not the only women at risk in the developing world; their future daughters are also at risk. Often girls are systematically undervalued and, at times, unwanted; traditional cultural values often put a premium on boy children. Boy children are traditionally expected to take over the family livelihood and care for their parents when they reach old age, and, given the wide and pervasive employment participation and income gaps between men and women, it is true that men are usually financially in a better situation to care for their parents, particularly in poorer countries where state-funded social security systems are nonexistent or poorly funded. In contrast, girls are seen as a financial burden on families in countries such as Bangladesh or India, where a dowry system, although illegal, still flourishes. While male children, when they are grown and married, bring a woman into the household to help with running the family, girls traditionally join their husband's family, bringing a dowry that can be a cash settlement or a pre-agreed list of valuables to contribute to the household. Thus, traditionally, boy children potentially will grow up to add to the household economy, and girls are perceived to be a financial drain. A few proverbs illustrate this traditional preference for boys: A Hindu proverb claims, "They who are full of sin beget only daughters"; a Chinese proverb states, "A stupid son is better than a crafty daughter"; and a Sanskrit proverb declares, "A virtuous son is the sun of his family." [16] Alternatively, as an Indian proverb states, raising a daughter is like watering the neighbor's garden—an activity that produces no gain for the family. These sayings still express deep-seated beliefs about ideal family structures and the roles that women play in them.

These cultural norms of strong preferences for sons can endanger the lives of millions of unborn girls every year. Around the world, there are an estimated 100 million "missing" women; fully half of them are estimated to come from India. [17] Because girls are often unwanted, parents resort to infanticide or sex-selective abortions in the hopes of having a boy. This problem is also severe in China, where a strictly enforced one-child policy, enacted in 1980, has led many parents to resort to extreme measures to ensure that their one child is a boy. Thus, in some societies, men outnumber women. A "natural" ratio is about 105 girls born for every 100 boys, and this is the figure that predominates in areas such as Europe and North America, where sex-selective abortion is relatively uncommon. However, in the Middle East, the northern areas of Africa, the Indian subcontinent, and China, there are more than 105 males to 100 females. [18] In fact, in China, the figures rose to 120 males for every 100 females born in 2005, and as high as 130 in some provinces. In India, the ratio has risen to 120 to 100 in some northern and western states. These figures are particularly disheartening, given that, as discussed at the beginning of this chapter, girls are biologically built with stronger survival abilities. Thus, these figures point to girls' unequal and lesser status in family hierarchies. Nor are the problems of boy preference necessarily lessening; Vietnam and Nepal are following in India and China's footsteps, with similar demographic patterns emerging. Let's now take a closer look at sex-selective abortion and the problem of boy preference in India, where strongly embedded cultural practices of dowry devalue girl children, and China, where coercive government policy, along with traditional values of boy preference, create tragic results.

"Spend 3,000 [rupees] now and save 300,000 later": Before sex-selective abortion was outlawed in India in 1994, this type of advertisement was displayed at clinics to entice parents to find out the sex of their baby in utero. While the overt advertisements have all but disappeared, the problem of sex-selective abortion in India has not, despite the fact that it is also now illegal in India to tell parents the sex of their fetus. Yet, in 2006, two journalists working for an Indian TV channel found one hundred doctors, in both private and government hospitals, who were willing to perform illegal abortions of girl fetuses. Although the TV images, shot from hidden cameras, were somewhat grainy, the information captured on them was indisputable; doctors willingly agreed to help parents terminate their pregnancies, even advising them about where to deposit the remains. Although the doctors were caught on tape, the police have been slow to act on the report, and a year later, only seven doctors had been suspended. Nor was the report an isolated incident; the following year, police officers recovered almost four hundred tiny bones believed to be from newly born female babies or fetuses. And parents resort to other options as well; when girls are born, they are much more likely to be dropped off at an orphanage by parents unwilling to incur the perceived costs of raising girl. For example, of the forty children at Mother Theresa's Missionary Sisters of Charity, thirty-seven are girls.[19] Confirming the data discussed earlier, girl children are not wanted in many Indian families.

Women who bear girl children are also at risk, and the inability to produce sons may increase the incidence of what has been termed "dowry death," murder or induced suicide as a result of continual harassment by husbands and in-laws disappointed with the short-term and long-term gains of the marriage settlement. For example, when Varsha Hitkari failed to produce sons after bearing two daughters, the husband's family demanded additional dowry, and eventually beat her into an unconscious state before trying to hang her by a noose from a shower head. Women face other forms of physical abuse for bearing daughters; one husband poured hot coals on his wife's abdomen after she bore a daughter, and another tortured his wife with cigarette burns. Still other mothers are discouraged from feeding or educating their daughters, under the mistaken belief that such investments are wastes of time and money. Although it's the man, not the woman, who contributes the Y chromosome that determines the baby's sex, women are often the ones blamed for being unable to produce the invaluable son.[20] Those who hoped that India's economic boom over the previous fifteen years would usher in more egalitarian attitudes and practices have been sadly disappointed. While GDP growth rates have skyrocketed, so have the costs of traditional, but illegal, customs, such as dowry, which is estimated to be at about five times the average annual salary in India.[21] And the increased availability of technology, such as early sonograms, as well as parents' abilities to pay for them, has simply accelerated the rate of sex-selective abortion. Depressingly, the data indicate that wealthier and better-educated Indians—the ones predicted to shun "traditional" cultural values—still want sons. In fact, a study found that sex-selective abortion was highest among women with university degrees.

While China does not practice the custom of dowry, cultural traditions value boys over girls. Sons are particularly valued in China because they are seen as the ones who will care for the parents when they become old. As one farmer explained, "The worst situation to be in is to have no son and no money. That's when you have nothing at all."[22] Thus, while boy preference is more common among better-off urban families, in China it is much more of a rural phenomenon. And the government's one-child policy has meant that, when faced with the possibility of having only one child, parents want to ensure that it is a boy. As a result, the problem of boy preference is even more severe in China than in India. As in India, using scanning technology such as sonograms to determine the sex of the child is illegal. So are sex-selective abortions. But like in India, doctors, if caught, face only a fine and suspension, which has not stopped many doctors in search of making extra income in China's booming economy. Often, the interaction can be accomplished without even any verbal communication; to avoid getting caught for revealing the sex of the fetus, a doctor may resort to sign language, nodding his or her head to indicate a boy, and shaking the head to signal a girl. One report found that retired doctors would perform abortions for as little as $20.[23] And like in India, even when girls are birthed, they face a separate and unequal care situation. A study conducted in Shanxi province, where death rates for girl children are higher, found that after birth, the survival environment was much more unfriendly to girls. Boys tended to be birthed in hospitals, where mother and child could receive care, while girls were birthed at home. Boys were fed better and more nutritious food than girls, and they were sent to the hospital more quickly when they became ill, while girls were cared for at home and expected to rely on their own resistance to illness.[24]

The tragic consequences of boy preference in both India and China are beginning to emerge. Many demographers warn of an impending social crisis of too many men and not enough women to marry them. Not only will this shake the stability of the entire marriage system, they argue, but it will also create tides of social unrest, as men, particularly the poorest with the least options, will be unable to marry. In fact, in their book *Bare Branches: The Security Implications of Asia's Surplus Male Population,* authors Valerie Hudson and Andrea Den Boer argue that throughout history, men who were unable to marry and create families (called "bare branches" in China because they are branches of a family tree that will never bear fruit) have played a role in instigating societal instability, violent crime, and gang formation. The cumulative effect of this is increased levels of insecurity, violence, and internal threat. This threat is particularly severe for China and India, where "bare branches" are projected to comprise 12 to 15 percent of the young adult male population.[25] Further, demographers argue that the lack of women will simply drive up the demand for (and supply of) young girls for sexual trafficking, as well as the kidnapping and selling of women to provide brides for those who can pay the fee. In sum, boy preference is a problem that has significant repercussions, not only for girls and women but also for overall levels of democracy, stability, and peace, and the low status of women in developing countries will impact the health not only of those societies but potentially the world as well.

As girls move from infancy to young adulthood, their health continues to suffer because of the cultural norms of undervaluing females. While girl infants have a biological advantage over boy infants in the first year of life, that advantage disappears as cultural norms of discrimination result in less healthy lives for girls. Even malnutrition among children is gendered. Women and girls are more affected by hunger than men and boys because females often eat last, as well as least, in households.[26] As girls grow older and begin to bear children, the cycle of ill health begins anew; poorly fed mothers give birth to underweight children; low-birth-weight children are three to four times more likely to die from diarrheal diseases, acute respiratory infections, and, if not immunized, measles. By the time they reach the age of five, low-birth-weight babies may have had more cyclic episodes of infection and malnutrition and may be severely stunted. This will be carried into adult life, potentially to be repeated on yet another generation of young girls.[27]

Women and HIV

Increasingly, the spread of HIV/AIDS has come to be perceived as the next looming health crisis that will require concentrated, coordinated, international attention. The global statistics are overwhelming; as of 2007, an estimated 33 million people were living with HIV, and over 95 percent of them were in developing countries. While these numbers are terrifyingly high, nonetheless the global percentage of people living with HIV has stabilized since 2000, although the number of people living with HIV has increased, partly because the increased availability of successful antiretroviral therapy. Sub-Saharan Africa is most heavily affected by HIV; the region accounts for 67 percent of all people living with HIV. Statistically, it would seem as if the virus was gender blind; women account for about 50 percent of people living with HIV.[28] However, as we shall see, the transmission and impact of HIV are deeply gendered.

HIV specialists and women's rights advocates are concerned about the gendered impact of HIV for several reasons. First, while infection rates seem to have stabilized, nonetheless transmission rates for women have risen, and in sub-Saharan Africa, women currently account for about 60 percent of people living with HIV.[29] Further, transmission is rising rapidly in people ages fifteen to twenty-four, particularly among girls; in some countries, females ages fifteen to twenty-four have infection rates that are six times higher than those of males of the same ages. There are several reasons why women are particularly vulnerable to HIV. For example, even transmission is not gender neutral; for a variety of physiological reasons, the transmission of the virus through sexual contact is more efficient from men to women than vice versa. HIV transmission from male to female is seven times more likely than transmission from female to male.[30] But the rapid rise in women's transmission rates is not only an expression of biology; women's unequal social status also fuels the transmission of HIV. That is, women's unequal social, economic, and legal status increases their vulnerability to AIDS. As Jonathan Mann, the former head of the UN global HIV and AIDS program, argued, "When women's human rights and dignity are not respected, society creates and favours their vulnerability to AIDS." In other words, the central AIDS issue is not biological—it is rooted in the deep-seated discrimination that women face on a daily basis.[31] For example, women's lack of power in their relationships increases their risk of contracting AIDS. Cultural values often designate men as the initiators of sexual activity. Promiscuity is often condoned in men but condemned in women. In practice, this means that women lack the power in relationships to either refuse sex or negotiate protected sex. The high incidence of child marriages and forced marriages also contribute to women's lack of influence in negotiating their sexual relationships. Further, the traditional focus on preserving women's innocence with regard to sexual relations often means that they lack adequate knowledge about preventing the transmission of HIV and other sexually transmitted diseases. And in some cultures, the pervasive but patently untrue belief that sex with a virgin will cure AIDS has put many young women at risk for infection. As rape increasingly becomes used as a tool of war, women in conflict zones and refugee camps are also particularly vulnerable to the virus.[32]

Once women contract HIV, they often are further victimized by their families, who may turn them out of the house, deprive them of their property, and cut them off from loved ones. For example, the story of Rajni, a young Indian mother, illustrates the plight of many women in the developing world. She was married at fourteen and became a widow at twenty when her husband, who ran a small business, died of AIDS. She too, tested positive for HIV. Her son, now twelve, is also HIV positive; her nine-year-old daughter, who is healthy, was given to her sister to raise so that she does not have to bear the social stigma of the disease. She and her extended family live in poverty, having been forced to sell their home to pay for her husband's medical bills.[33] Widows of AIDS victims, even if they are not infected, often face a dire future; unable as women to inherit or own property or land in many countries, they often become destitute, many at a young age, given the high incidence of child marriages in many areas of the developing world.

But AIDS has a female face in other ways as well, in terms of how it impacts primarily women by adding to their already high levels of household responsibility. When AIDS arrives in a household, it is primarily the women who take on the added responsibilities of caring for the infected family members, particularly in developing countries where access to medical services are extremely limited. Yet, women are already overburdened in terms of their responsibilities in raising, feeding, and clothing their often extended household. Particularly in regions where women not only prepare the food but also grow it and care for the livestock, the arrival of AIDS, and the caring duties that come with it, adds on to women's already overloaded days and takes them away from other critical household production tasks. And when they are pulled out of their work in household production, the whole household suffers, falling further into poverty, ill health, and potential starvation. As students primarily located in wealthy developed nations, we easily forget how lack of basic amenities can quickly overwhelm already overextended women. For example, one rural woman from southern Africa estimated that it took twenty-four buckets of water a day to care for an AIDS patient in her household. She estimated twenty-four because the severe diarrhea that afflicted her relative required that she bathe the patient and wash the bedding and clothes five to six times a day. In the absence of washing machines, cooking stoves, running water, and potentially electricity, the work involved in this caring activity is intense—and remember that women must walk ever increasingly long distances to fetch water (every day in South Africa, the country's women walk the equivalent of going to the moon and back sixteen times over to fetch water). In addition, this work keeps her from all the other life-sustaining tasks she must normally perform. And even if the patient is lucky enough to receive medical care in a hospital, women still spend countless hours bring food and providing care, given the understaffed, overtaxed status of many of the medical facilities that service severely ill patients.[34]

And when the women themselves become ill with HIV, the problem of the overtaxed caretaker worsens exponentially. As women succumb to the effects of the virus, many are unable to perform their normal household activities, which, in turn, impacts the well-being of the entire family. One news story covered one woman's struggle to raise her family while coping with HIV. Often sick and exhausted, she must still somehow find a way to get out of bed to feed the children, fetch water, and keep house. In her weakened circumstances, she cannot feed her own family and depends on the help she gets from well-wishers.[35] Further, the loss of mothers can have drastic effects on the families they leave behind; of the million children who are left motherless per year, they are three to ten times more likely to die within two years than are children with two living parents.[36] For those children who survive, life is still difficult, particularly when AIDS robs them of one or both parents; 11 million children have been orphaned as a result of AIDS.[37] Finally, as HIV shifts toward being a young person's affliction—nearly 12 million fifteen- to twenty-four-year-olds are living with AIDS or HIV—young women already infected are increasingly more likely to give birth to children who are HIV positive, thus compounding the infection rate. As of 2007, about 2 million children under the age of fifteen were living with HIV.[38] Not only do these trends create new depths of human tragedy, but they also put new stresses and strains on governments with inadequate budgets to absorb the effects of these demographic changes. As we will discuss in our next section, it is only recently that the international community has mobilized around the issue of women's unequal caring burdens and the dramatic impact that this can have on families' livelihoods.

ADVANCING WOMEN'S EQUALITY

How have international development agencies, states, NGOs, and individual activists addressed women's health, and what has been the impact of their work? Numerous international organizations address issues of family planning and reproductive health. The United Nations Population Fund (UNFPA) is the world's largest international source of funding for population and reproductive health programs. Since it began operations in 1969, the fund has provided nearly $6 billion in assistance to developing countries.[39] It works with governments and nongovernmental organizations in 150 countries, at their request, to, in their words, ensure that "every pregnancy is wanted, every birth is safe, that every young person is free of HIV, and that every girl and woman is treated with dignity and respect."[40] The International Planned Parenthood Federation, the world's largest voluntary organization working on issues of family planning and sexual and reproductive health, links autonomous family planning agencies in over 180 countries.[41] The World Health Organization also promotes family planning by working to help improve the safety and effectiveness of contraceptive methods, widen the range of family planning methods available to women and men, and improve the quality of family planning service delivery.[42]

In addition, the UN and its umbrella organizations have continued to highlight the unequal status of women and their health by organizing conferences; building consensus among spiritual, political, and cultural leaders; and using their persuasive powers to cajole governments into honoring the international promises they made. For example, in 1994, the United Nations sponsored the International Conference on Population and Development, held in Cairo, which brought together eleven thousand participants from over 180 countries to discuss and formulate a Program of Action in the area of population and development for the next twenty years.[43] NGOs from all over the world, often representing women's voices and providing another avenue for women's participation, arrived to provide input and feedback to government delegations. All attendees, representing what seemed like diametrically opposed religious, social, and cultural orientations, grappled with controversial issues such as abortion, female circumcision, and violence against women, as well as the larger contextual issues that define women's fertility choices, such as their access to education and economic opportunities. This was certainly a strong precursor to building consensus around making gender and gender equality a centerpiece of the Millennium Development Goals. In particular, Goal 5 explicitly pledges to improve maternal health by working to reduce the maternal mortality ratio, increasing the proportion of births attended by skilled health personnel, and improving antenatal care coverage, among other things.

The overall impact of this renewed focus on reproductive rights has been mixed. Discouragingly, despite the strong rhetorical support for reducing maternal mortality, the two regions of the world with the worst maternal health status—South Asia and sub-Saharan Africa—show only small signs of improvement.[44] And in some places, such as war-torn Afghanistan, the rates are truly abysmal—one out of every eight women will die of pregnancy-related causes. However, the international community has also focused with renewed energy on several issues related to maternal health that have made a real difference in women's lives. The UNFPA has launched their Campaign to End Fistula in thirty countries in sub-Saharan Africa, South Asia, and some Arab states. Part of their funding supports the work of dedicated doctors and health professionals in Ethiopia. The accompanying text box describes the significant difference that the founders of the Addis Ababa Fistula Hospital have made in the lives of thousands of young women and their families. Numerous individual examples such as these demonstrate that, with determination and effort, institutions and individuals can make a difference in many people's lives, which isn't necessarily reflected in the aggregate data.

Women in Action: Doctor Catherine Hamlin

The narrative about fistula repair surgery that opened this chapter illustrates how a few dedicated individuals can effect substantial change. Responding to an advertisement in the British medical journal *Lancet*, Catherine and Reginald Hamlin traveled from Australia to Ethiopia to establish a school of midwifery in Addis Ababa in 1959. Originally planning on staying for three years, their plans changed when they saw the plight of so many young girls suffering from inadequate prenatal and postnatal care, as well as the sacrifices many had made to search for treatment. Many young women had walked for days through rough terrain, were carried by relatives, or had sold the one piece of family livestock crucial to the family economy to buy the bus fare in hopes of receiving treatment. Reflecting on her experiences, Catherine Hamlin said, "I had never seen injuries like that before. Our hearts broke at the sight of these women and what they were experiencing, and we knew we could not ignore it."[i] Fifteen years later, deeply dedicated to their efforts to provide better medical care for women in Ethiopia, they decided to found the Addis Ababa Fistula Hospital. Speaking of her motivation to help, Catherine Hamlin noted that "Childbirth should be a joyful occasion, but for these fistula girls it has developed into a nightmare and a horror—to suffer the agony of days of labour, with nobody but the village women to help and nothing to relieve the pain, to deliver their longed for child as a stillbirth, and then to experience the awful consequences of this ordeal....The whole picture is an unimaginable plight, and one which no woman should be called on to endure, but one that is being repeated all over the Developing World, where women have no access to any medical help." Discussing her motivation to work in the face of what must be extremely difficult circumstances, Hamlin notes that "every day our hearts go out to them as they arrive at our hospital with nothing in this world except their faith and hope in us, and their urine soaked clothes—young beautiful girls with a life shattered and in ruins....Each one pulls at our heart strings and calls forth the utmost compassion."[ii]

[i] Kate Benson, "Australia's Mother Theresa," *The Sydney Morning Herald*, March 29, 2008, http://www.smh.com.au/news/world/australias-mother-teresa/2008/03/28/1206207412966.html
[ii] Dr. Catherine Hamlin, "United Nations Population Award Acceptance Speech," July 6, 2004, http://www.fistulafoundation.org/press/tools/transcripts.html.

The compassion of Dr. Hamlin and her staff has significantly changed the lives of thousands, and promises to continue to do so. Since opening, the hospital has treated over thirty-two thousand women. All medical students specializing in obstetrics and gynecology in Ethiopia are required to train for two months at the hospital; in addition, staff train doctors from all over the developing world. They have also built Desta Mender (which means Village of Joy), a village of ten cottages and two common buildings to house long-term care patients. The hospital is now building five mini fistula hospitals throughout Ethiopia in the hope of reaching more rural patients, most of whom do not have the financial or personal resources to make the arduous journey, often alone, to the capital city for treatment. And to help staff them, Dr. Hamlin has opened the Hamlin Midwifery College, which accepted its first twelve students in 2008. The students will undergo a three-year diploma program in midwifery before returning to their villages to provide medical care. Eventually, Dr. Hamlin hopes to train a midwife for every village in Ethiopia.

Dr. Hamlin ultimately traces the problem of fistulas to the pervasive undervaluation of girls in Ethiopia and many other areas of the developing world. Part of the problem, she feels, is the tradition of early marriage, in which girls are betrothed at eight or nine years old. At this point, the girl moves to the mother-in-law's house until she reaches puberty and is ready for marriage. In the meantime, she often works in the mother-in-law's household, performing extremely demanding labor, but often with few nutritional resources to fuel that labor because she is a girl, and thus the last one in the family to be fed. The result is that her growth is stunted, and her pelvis is too small to successfully deliver a baby. Dr. Hamlin would like to improve girls' access to education so that girls have alternative options to early marriage. The impact of the Hamlins' work is significant. Not only have they healed the physical scars of thousands of poor women from predominantly rural areas of Ethiopia, but they have also helped emotionally heal these young girls, who would have faced a life of potential social ostracism and severe physical disability. As one health worker commented, Dr. Hamlin "pulls these untouchables back into society." [45]

On a positive note, women's access to contraception has increased, and women are now choosing to have fewer children, spaced more widely apart. As mentioned earlier, families are half the size they were in 1960.[46] There has also been a significant shift in the attitudes and beliefs of development policy makers, state officials, and demographers—that population growth rates cannot be dictated to women but that women and men have the right to choose the appropriate size of their own families and that when they do choose, everyone is better off. Many countries are turning away from the policies of forced population control to focus on larger strategies such as increasing girls' access to education, and eventually employment opportunities, as a more effective means of controlling population growth.

However, despite increasing international rhetorical support for a woman's right to control various aspects of her body and her health, international reproductive rights efforts often become mired in domestic political struggles between social conservatives and liberals, and funding for international family planning programs has been held hostage by governments with conservative agendas. "Family planning" covers a variety of practices and issues, such as contraception, abortion, and women's rights, that make many governments uncomfortable. The Catholic Church has been extremely active in trying to narrowly define "family planning," with a focus on abstinence as a form of birth control. In addition, religious organizations have successfully lobbied the U.S.

government to attach conditions to international family planning funds. Since 1973, the Foreign Assistance Act has prohibited the use of U.S. funds for any abortion services overseas. President Reagan imposed further restrictions in 1984 when he issued an executive memorandum, which became informally known as the Global Gag Rule. Under these stipulations, family planning agencies may not receive U.S. assistance if they provide abortion services, which includes counseling and referrals on abortions. Nor can they lobby to make or keep abortion legal in their country. In effect, if they want U.S. assistance, they may not refer to, advocate for, or mention abortion as an option, regardless of the circumstances (such as to save the life or health of the mother or in instances of incest or rape). This rule was revoked by President Clinton in 1993 but reinstituted by President George W. Bush on January 22, 2001.[47] Family planning advocates worried that this would increase the number of unplanned pregnancies and would drive women to resort to backstreet abortions in the absence of reliable medical information. When President Obama assumed office in January 2009, he promptly reversed the ban, once again freeing up funding for a variety of family planning NGOs around the world.

In addition to the gag rule, the U.S. president is authorized under the 1985 Kemp-Kasten Amendment to prohibit U.S. foreign aid for any organization that he or she determines "supports or participates in the management of a program of coercive abortion or involuntary sterilization." President Bush also wielded this power, and in July 2002, despite congressional approval, the Bush administration cut off funding for UNFPA's work, arguing (inaccurately) that the UNFPA supports China's coercive abortion policies (the UNFPA does work in China). The administration has continued to withhold funding, totaling $235 million as of 2008, from the UNFPA. It will be up to the Obama administration to decide whether the United States will resume its annual contribution.[48] However, this ambivalence about funding reproductive rights is not a singularly American phenomenon; donors' share of funding for family planning has steadily fallen since 1995, in part to fund other critical initiatives such as the fight against the high incidence of STDs/HIV/AIDS.

Despite these financial concerns, or perhaps because of them, citizen activism has become a critical source of support. For example, Jane Roberts, a retired schoolteacher, and Lois Abraham, an attorney, cofounded the NGO 34 Million Friends of UNFPA in reaction to President Bush's withdrawal of $34 million in funding for the UNFPA in 2002. Both wrote to friends and the local paper, asking fellow citizens to send $1 and a message of support for the UNFPA's work. Soon, they started a website, www.34millionfriends.org. As of the end of November 2008, individuals, many donating just $1, had sent in almost $4 million. While this represents just a fraction of what the U.S. government owes the UNFPA in withheld funding, in the words of Abraham and Roberts, it nonetheless demonstrates "the growing power of citizen efforts in an information age that daily draws people and countries closer and closer together.... [W]e hope that our grassroots efforts will serve as an example for citizen action around the world on behalf of women's health, the environment and other common causes that serve the global good."[49]

In terms of changing the culture of boy preference, the Indian and Chinese governments have adopted a variety of policies, with mixed success. In India, although the government has tried to become more proactively involved in discouraging the practice, they also seem to condone the undervaluation of girls. Renuka Chowdhury, India's minister of state for women and child development, urged parents to give up their children to state-run orphanages instead of aborting them in the womb. In a public statement, she urged parents who "don't want a girl, [to] leave her to us." The government, she promised, "will bring up your children. Don't kill them."[50] Although this proposal was later abandoned, the Indian government has attempted to apply additional sanctions and incentives to encourage parents to shift their beliefs to value girl children. The government is proposing to stiffen the sentences against the doctors who perform sex-selective abortion. In the fourteen years since the practice was outlawed, only two doctors had been convicted of the crime, a sign that various offices of the government did not take the exiting law very seriously.[51] At the regional level, some state governments have offered free immunizations, no school fees, and free books for girls and an age allowance to take care of parents to lessen the financial burden on parents of having a girl.[52] The Indian government has also liberalized inheritance laws, equalizing sons' and daughters' claims to land and other immovable property. However, designing policy to discourage powerful customs, such as dowry, continues to be a severe challenge to fostering gender equality in India.

The Chinese government has also begun to realize that its policy of population control, which essentially coerces parents into having one child (rather than persuading them to want fewer children), will have dramatic consequences. In 2003, the government launched a "Care for Girls" campaign to change the pervasive culture of boy preference. In addition to public education, the campaign includes a set of financial incentives to offset the costs of raising a girl. Families with only daughters can qualify for small loans to help them develop income-generating projects or support schooling for girls. Girls are offered additional medical examinations to ensure that they are receiving adequate care from their families. And the program has provided additional training to girls to help them find employment, and thus give them the ability to contribute to the family economy. Other measures include pension payments for parents of girl children to offset the pressure to produce a son as an informal social insurance mechanism.[53] Both the Indian and the Chinese examples illustrate how governments can provide incentives to foster changing cultural values; yet, both examples illustrate how difficult it can be for governments to demonstrate the political will, and capacity, to truly effect a shift in deeply embedded values.

Finally, combating the spread of HIV/AIDS has become one of the most prominent campaigns waged by development agencies. The Joint United Nations Programme on HIV and AIDS, or UNAIDS, is the primary international effort to provide coordinated international action on the HIV epidemic. UNAIDS is a partnership between eight United Nations agencies: United Nations Children's Fund (UNICEF); United Nations Development Programme (UNDP); United Nations Population Fund (UNFPA); United Nations Office on Drugs and Crime (UNODC); International Labour Organization (ILO); United Nations Educational, Scientific and Cultural Organization (UNESCO); World Health Organization (WHO); and the World Bank. By taking collective action, these organizations hope to better coordinate their response to the AIDS crisis and avoid duplicating each others' work and projects unnecessarily. They focus primarily on sponsoring programs to prevent the transmission of HIV, offering care to these already living with HIV by providing antiretroviral treatments, and reducing the negative impact of HIV on individuals and communities. UNAIDS has also launched a Global Coalition on Women and AIDS. Its efforts focus on preventing new HIV infections among women and girls, promoting equal access to HIV care and treatment, protecting women's property and inheritance rights, and eliminating violence against women.[54]

The impact of these effort has been significant; the global percentage of adults living with HIV has leveled off since 2000. By the end of 2007, nearly 3 million people were receiving antiretroviral treatment in developing countries—an marked improvement from just a year previously. Nonetheless, the UN estimates that this is still only meeting an estimated 31 percent of global need. However, treatment coverage has been higher for women than men, and there has been particular progress in providing pregnant women living with HIV with antiretroviral treatment to prevent mother-to-child transmission. UNAIDS has also focused on the disproportionate burden of care that women shoulder in tending to people living with HIV, as well as the reduced circumstances that many widows face once their husbands succumb to AIDS. In particular, they have focused on providing microcredit, or small loans, to these women to increase their independent income-generating potential.[55]

Yet, similar to reproductive rights issues, the global AIDS campaign is also affected increasingly by conservative domestic agendas. In 2003, President Bush announced an "Emergency Plan for AIDS Relief" and pledged $15 billion over five years to the campaign. However, conservative groups in the United States that are interested in the issue of AIDS have also been hostile to AIDS-prevention strategies, such as comprehensive sex education and condom distribution. As a result, they have lobbied successfully for increased funding for abstinence promotion programs. When Congress passed the United States Leadership Against HIV/AIDS, Tuberculosis, and Malaria Act of 2003, conservatives in the House were able to dedicate one-third of the AIDS-prevention funding toward programs urging abstinence before marriage. They were, in part, inspired by the success of Uganda's ABC (Abstinence, Be Faithful, and Use Condoms) program. Uganda's HIV infection rate peaked at about 15 percent (30 percent among pregnant women in urban areas) in 1991, and then declined significantly through the mid-1990s and reached 5 percent (14 percent for pregnant urban women) by 2001.[56] However, aid workers on the Ugandan project attribute the success of the program primarily to the increased use of condoms and partner reduction, rather than solely to the abstinence component. Further, research on abstinence-only programs in the United States finds that they have little impact on the sexual behavior or contraceptive use among sexually active teenagers. Yet, despite little evidence supporting the effectiveness of abstinence-only programs, they are becoming a critical part of U.S. AIDS prevention programs overseas.[57] It will be interesting to see whether the Obama administration will focus on a different approach to funding AIDS prevention programs.

Finally, development agencies have become concerned increasingly with putting women's unequal health status in a broader context of larger gender inequalities. Thus, they have focused on larger themes, such as women's access to education, as a way of improving women's reproductive health. Women with less education are more likely to have children at a young age, when their risks for complications are particularly high. Further, studies have shown that low maternal levels of education often translate into malnutrition and poor quality of care for children. Demographic and health surveys from more than forty developing countries show that the mortality rate for children under five is lower in households in which women have some primary schooling. This figure drops even lower in households in which mothers have benefited from secondary schooling.[58] Another study of sixty-three countries showed that gains in women's education accounted for 43 percent of the decline in malnutrition from 1970 to 1995, although food availability and the government's commitment to health were also important.[59] Thus, as we discussed in Chapter 7, gender mainstreaming, or focusing on the status of women in society across all development programs, has become an increasingly common approach.

CONCLUSION

Women have made strides in improving the quality of their health. With international support for various family planning initiatives, women have more choice over the timing and spacing of their children. Women are choosing to have fewer children, and fertility rates are steadily declining. However, some indicators have barely changed; women are still at risk at all stages of pregnancy, childbirth, and recovery. Nor do broader cultural values that place a premium on boys appear to be disappearing soon. And as international donors gain more experience in battling the AIDS crisis, they are beginning to recognize and address the gendered dimensions of the virus. We do know that educating women is central to improving not only their own health but also the health of their immediate family. In sum, addressing these issues requires multifaceted, multilateral action.

FOR MORE INFORMATION

Center for Health and Gender Equity (CHANGE), http://www.genderhealth.org

Eldis Gender and HIV/AIDS Resources, http://www.eldis.org/go/topics/resource-guides/hiv-and-aids/gender

The Fistula Foundation, http://www.fistulafoundation.org

Gender and Health Equity Network (GHEN), http://www2.ids.ac.uk/ghen

International Women's Health Coalition, http://www.iwhc.org

34 Million Friends of UNFPA, http://www.34millionfriends.org

UNIFEM Gender and HIV/AIDS Web Portal, http://www.genderandaids.org/index.php

United Nations Environment Program, Women and the Environment, http://www.unep.org/Documents.Multilingual/Default.asp?DocumentID=468&ArticleID=4488&1=en

A Walk to Beautiful, http://www.pbs.org/wgbh/nova/beautiful/program.html

Women, Health, and the Environment: At a Glance, http://www.ourplanet.com/imgversn/152/glance.html

Women Won't Wait (End HIV and Violence Against Women), http://www.womenwontwait.org

World Health Organization, Department of Gender, Women, and Health, http://www.who.int/gender/en

10

~⚬

Women and Education

It was only the school fees that made it difficult for me to continue studying. When you don't pay your fees, the teacher in charge comes and calls out the names, and then you go home. He tells you to take home the message, that when you come back to school you must come with money.[1]

My parents feel that girls should be married; that they are not like boys who need education. Every month they plan my marriage. They don't help me. I can't talk about my ambitions with them.[2]

These quotations illustrate just two of the continuing barriers to women's education in the developing world—school fees and cultural views of appropriate roles for women. Development agencies emphasize that achieving parity in education, not only in primary school but at all levels, is critical if women are to engage fully in society. Yet, all too often girls are denied access to education and all of the benefits that accrue from formal schooling. Fifty-five percent of the estimated 75 million children who are out of school are girls.[3] Further, 64 percent of the world's 781 million illiterate adults are women.[4] Despite the fact that the gap between boys' and girls' enrollment figures is narrowing, the problem is significant enough that the United Nations pledged as part of the Millennium Development Goals to eliminate gender disparities in primary and secondary education by 2005 and in all levels of education no later than 2015.[5] In this chapter, we will focus on the status of women's education, discussing several issues that threaten women's access to education as well as international efforts to reverse women's unequal status.

THE STATUS OF WOMEN AND EDUCATION

There are many reasons why women (and by using this term we also mean girls) should be educated. First, education is a fundamental human right. In 1948, the Universal Declaration of Human Rights became the international standard for human rights law. One of its tenets was that education is a human right and thus elementary education should be free and compulsory while higher education should be made accessible to all on the basis of merit. Since this declaration, numerous other treaties have reiterated this right. Most recently, the Convention on the Elimination of All Forms of Discrimination Against Women (CEDAW, 1979) and the Convention on the Rights of the Child (CRC, 1990) set forth "the most comprehensive set of legally enforceable commitments concerning both rights to education and to gender equality."[6] As of mid-2003, CEDAW had been ratified by 173 nations and the CRC had been ratified by all nations worldwide except Somalia and the United States. Thus, education is a legally sanctioned human right that applies equally to men and women.

Second, educated girls have more choices about their futures. If they work, they will be able to earn higher wages (even though those wages will be lower than those of their male counterparts with a similar level of education and experience). Not only does this add to their household income, thus reducing poverty, but it also increases their status in the family. Education also empowers women to participate more fully in public life; for instance, women in Bangladesh with a secondary education are more likely to attend a political meeting than are those with no education.[7] Education also enables women to make autonomous choices about their personal lives; educated girls marry later and have fewer children. This is a benefit not only to them and their health, but also to governments that are straining to provide adequate services to all of their citizens. In addition, educated girls and women have a dramatic impact on their families. Educated women have healthier, better-nourished children because while they are pregnant, lactating, and beyond, they have the ability to gain the knowledge required to care adequately for themselves and their children. They are more likely to send their children to school, especially their daughters, and their children are more likely to do well there. Thus, there are multiple compelling reasons to invest in the education of girls and women. As Greg Mortensen, founder of the Central Asia Institute, a nonprofit that builds schools in central Asia, argues, "If the girls aren't educated, nothing will change.... We can drop bombs, we can build roads, or we can put in electricity. But unless the girls are educated, the world won't change."[8]

There has been some clear progress in educating girls in the developing world over the past few decades. To begin with, since 1990, 44 million more girls are attending primary schools.[9] Further, the gender gap, particularly in access to primary education, is narrowing. By 2005, about two-thirds of countries had attained gender parity in education at the primary level. Gender parity is the term used to describe how well a country is educating both girls and boys. To have attained gender parity means that boys and girls are attending schools at the same rate. It does not tell us anything about what percentage of a country's children are in school, it just tells us if boys and girls are in school at the same rate. Table 10.1 gives you a snapshot of some of the countries with the worst levels of gender parity, most of which are in Africa; in all of them, girl's enrollment is less than three-quarters that of boys.[10] In the countries of southeastern Asia, Latin America and the Caribbean, the former Soviet Union, and eastern Asia, the goal of gender parity in education is almost realized. Of sixty-five developing countries for which the United Nations has data, about half have achieved gender

Table 10.1 Poorest Performers in Terms of Girls'
Access to Primary School

COUNTRY	GENDER PARITY INDEX
Chad	0.63
Yemen	0.63
Guinea-Biseau	0.67
Benin	0.68
Niger	0.68
Ethiopia	0.69
Guinea	0.72
Mali	0.72
Pakistan	0.74

parity in education.[11] Nevertheless, there is still far to go. The gap in gender parity in education is still significant in the countries of southern Asia, sub-Saharan Africa, and western Asia. For example, a six-year-old girl in southern Asia will spend six years in school, three years less than her male counterpart.[12] These gender disparities widen even further when combined with the urban/rural split in access to education; a girl living in a rural area is three times more likely to drop out of school than is a boy living in a city.[13] And, in some countries (Algeria, the Congo, the Islamic Republic of Iran, Oman, Saudi Arabia, the Sudan, Thailand, and the United Republic of Tanzania) there has been real decline in gender parity in access to education since 1990.

Further, it is important to recognize that while increasing numbers of girls are gaining access to primary education, gender disparities tend to increase at higher levels of education. While in Latin America more girls than boys are enrolled in secondary school, this is the exception, not the rule. Girls in southern and western Asia and in sub-Saharan Africa are the least likely to advance beyond primary school. As we mentioned previously, while about two-thirds of countries have achieved gender parity in primary education, only 37 percent have done so in secondary education and less than 3 percent in higher education (Botswana, China, Mexico, and Peru).[14] As Pape Snow, former director of planning and reform in the Senegalese Ministry of Education points out, parity in primary education was attainable, but the number of girls in secondary schools drops off dramatically as many leave school to become domestic workers—the government can remove fees, but it cannot control demand for education.[15] In addition, completion of primary education in many countries does not necessarily guarantee literacy or adequate educational skills needed to progress in life.

Why has it been so difficult for girls to gain access to education? As the quote at the beginning of chapter demonstrates, one barrier to educating children, boys as well as girls, is school fees, which can include tuition, cost of books, required school uniforms, and community contributions. Many governments that lack the budgetary resources to offer free universal primary education charge students fees to attend school, and since household income is often quite low in many developing countries, fees place education out of reach for many children. Parents faced with multiple children and school fees often opt to send the male children to school instead of the female children. Daughters are expected to perform household chores as well as care for the young, the elderly, and the sick. Thus school fees are a greater barrier to girls than to boys. The World Bank notes that the elimination of school fess benefits all children, but as shown in Uganda and Tanzania, the impact is greater for girls.[16] One nonprofit advocacy group argues that when school fees were eliminated in Kenya, enrollment shot up and gender disparities in education almost disappeared because families with financial difficulties no longer had to decide which children to educate.[17] Nonetheless, school fees persist in more than eighty-nine countries despite the existence of human rights instruments that "commit states to free and compulsory education at [the] primary level." [18] Part of the reason for the persistence of school fess is that their removal is costly and difficult for countries that are struggling economically. Togo was able this past year to remove school fees because of an $80 million investment in the education system, but school administrators worried about how they would pay for supplies, cultural activities, sanitation, and assistants in the long term.[19]

While eliminating school fees will certainly help improve access to education, it will not entirely eradicate it. Many children must work, in addition to or instead of attending school, to supplement low family incomes. According to recent estimates, "18 percent of children aged 5–14 are economically active, amounting to some 211 million children, about half of whom are girls." [20] While we do not know what percentage of these children are unable to attend school, we do know that it certainly complicates their abilities to access an education. This is compounded by lack of government enforcement of compulsory education laws and labor laws.[21] On top of this, many children must perform unpaid domestic labor, and a much larger proportion of these children are girls.[22] When family incomes are limited, it is often the girls in the family who are kept back from school instead of the boys. And it is often the girls who must stay home to perform domestic labor and care for the younger children. Further, many girls, some as young as age eight, are given or sold by their families to others as domestic laborers, with no access to education. A recent report by Human Rights Watch concerning girl domestic workers in Guinea documents the numerous girl domestic laborers who work as much as eighteen hours a day for no pay, are often raped by their employers, and suffer other forms of abuse.[23] Thus the problem is much greater than just school fees.

Further, cultural, social, religious, and political beliefs about women often keep girls at home. As a result of cultural and social norms, girls are often *expected* (no matter the household income) to stay at home and help with the household chores and raising younger children. In addition, in many cultures girls are often forced to marry young; in Nepal, 40 percent of girls are married by the age of fifteen, and in Ethiopia and some countries of western Africa, some girls are married off as early as seven or eight.[24] Many families do not want to invest in their daughter's education because they perceive it to be a wasted expense. Given that girls become part of the husband's family and household upon marriage, they are often treated as a financial drain, in comparison to boys, who bring in an extra pair of hands upon marriage to aid in maintaining the household economy. Religious beliefs about the appropriate role of education in girls' lives also complicate matters. Specifically, Islam has come under attack in recent years as a barrier to girls' education. Briefly stated, some followers of Islam argue that secular education is antithetical to the Islamic faith and that girls should not receive any education other than religious education, while other followers (the majority) argue that Allah, and thus Islam, supports both boys and girls receiving a secular education. One of the notable examples of the former school of thought is the Taliban. When the Taliban ruled Afghanistan, girls were forbidden to attend school and even the curriculum for boys was tightly controlled and limited. In December 2008, one Taliban group (the Tehrik-Taliban Swat) in northwest Pakistan issued an order that girls are not to attend schools in the region, arguing that girls should only receive religious education. But other, larger, Taliban groups in the area have refused to follow the order and argue that Islam is supportive of both boys and girls receiving a secular education.[25] In June 2008, some followers of Islam destroyed two dozen girls' schools in Pakistan, and in November 2008, Islamic extremists sprayed acid on a group of schoolgirls in the Kandahar province. These are but a few examples of the various ways that some fringe elements of the Islamic faith have tried and are continuing to try to prevent girls from receiving a secular education. That said, the majority of the followers of Islam worldwide are supportive of girls having access to education and work hard to ensure girls' access to schools. One such example is Shaukat Ali, a former Kashmiri freedom fighter and member of the Taliban who is now a teacher. Ali teaches at school built by the Central Asia Institute. He argues that education is crucial as a weapon to fight extremism (and misunderstandings of the true nature of Islam): "If you can't read, then you must believe what the Imam tells you....If you cannot read the language, you can get the wrong idea....If we invest, it will come back to us. We have to deal with problems of tradition and culture. But we can stop extremism. If people are educated, we can fight against poverty, cruelty and injustice."[26]

There are also a variety of problems related to infrastructure, both material and human, that impact girls' access to education. In particular, while inadequate roads and transportation are problematic for all children, this particularly impacts girls since many families abstain from sending their daughters away from home for fear for their physical and sexual safety.[27] The Central Asia Institute lists proximity of schools to girls' homes as one of the six key ingredients to building successful girls' schools. When roads are poor, schools are far away, and there is not adequate public transportation to and from school, many families prefer to keep their daughters at home rather than risk their being raped, kidnapped, or killed while walking to school. Further, the lack of female teachers impacts girls' access to education; in some Muslim states only female teachers are permitted to educate girls, and in all countries female teachers serve as role models to young girls and thus help them see the relevance of an education and help keep them interested and enrolled. A report by UNICEF on Yemen finds that, "The causal link between recruitment of female teachers and girls' enrollment and retention is direct and very significant.... Many Yemeni families would like to see their girls continue schooling beyond the age of 11, provided there are female teachers. From the family's point of view, female teachers offer a safe environment for girls' education. At the same time, from the girls' perspectives, the work of female teachers inspires them and the teachers become role models."[28] Second, female teachers generally do not sexually harass their female students (or their male students), and so parents do not fear sending their daughters to school. The fear of sexual harassment and the attendant possibly of pregnancy is a real concern for many parents and is often enough to keep them from sending their daughters to school once they reach puberty. As the World Education Forum noted, "parents who willingly send their daughters to school remove her at puberty, for fear of an unwanted pregnancy, and marry her off early instead."[29] The presence of female teachers is another of the six key ingredients for success of schools for girls listed by the Central Asia Institute. A lack of female teachers results in many girls not receiving an education.

Nor are girls necessarily safe from their fellow students. Sexual harassment by male students is also a barrier to girls' education, and parents often do not trust the education system to protect their daughters from possible pregnancies and sexually transmitted diseases. The increased prevalence of HIV/AIDS has made girls' safety even more pressing; one report found that "In South Africa and the Caribbean, girls between 15 and 19 are infected by HIV/AIDS at rates four to seven times higher than boys, 'a disparity linked to widespread exploitation, sexual abuse and discriminatory practices.'"[30] A report done for USAID on the topic of school-based violence against women in developing countries sums up much up what we have discussed regarding the impact of sexual violence on girls in schools and the ways it serves as a barrier to girls' education. The quote is lengthy, but it hammers home the importance of safe learning environments for girls. The report finds:

> Many studies we reviewed have documented that SRGBV (school-related gender-based violence) is perpetrated on female students by their male peers and teachers in school. Outside of school, girls can fall prey to "sugar daddies," older men who can provide favors and financial assistance with school fees. Several studies point out that the consequences of SRGBV adversely affect girls' educational attainment. Girls report losing their concentration in class, feeling bad about themselves, missing school, and even dropping out. The health consequences in terms of increased exposure to sexually transmitted infections (STIs), including HIV/AIDS, and unwanted pregnancies are also devastating. Schools in many countries turn a deaf ear to the female students' complaints

and many girls do not even complain because of a fear of reprisals, especially from teachers, but also because they believe that nothing will be done. In many countries SRGBV goes unchecked in the face of indifference from school administrators, the larger community, and the ministries of education.[31]

Until girls are safe in schools, they will often be kept home.

A final barrier to girls' (and boys') education is the increased prevalence of civil conflicts and international war. Girls are voluntarily or involuntarily swept up in violent conflicts as sex slaves, fighters, cooks, and so on, and as a result do not attend school (see Chapter 11 for more on the topic of girls during war). Further, violence often causes large segments of the population to flee the war-torn region, and women and girls disproportionately make up most refugees and internally displaced persons. One report published by UNESCO estimated that nearly 100,000 girls "directly participated in conflicts in at least 30 countries during the 1990s…and the vast majority of the world's estimated 25 million internally displaced persons are women and children."[32] Many of these children grow up in refugee camps, denied an education, and thus all the lifelong benefits that can accrue from it. While in these refugee camps they are often lured into the sex slave trade or into child labor scams. A report from Kenya suggests that many girls ages twelve to eighteen who fled to camps for displaced persons after the recent postelection conflict in Kenya have been taken out of these camps by men offering to take them to lunch or the hairdresser and then find themselves in brothels for the day.[33] Civil conflicts also result in the destruction of schools and the murder of teachers. In Nepal, Maoist rebels targeted teachers and schools, killing an estimated 150 teachers as of 2004 and closing 187 schools and fifteen district offices.[34] Thus, civil conflicts and international war are a grave barrier to girls education.

While this is not an exhaustive discussion of the barriers to girls' education, it highlights many of the major barriers that still exist in many developing countries. These barriers certainly impact boys, too, but reports by international organizations repeatedly show that these barriers disproportionately impact girls. Next we turn to examine efforts to improve girls' access to education.

ADVANCING WOMEN'S EQUALITY

International organizations, nongovernmental organizations, and national and local governments have worked for decades toward removing barriers to women's education, and their efforts range from international treaties and laws to community programs. One international organization committed to advancing women's equality is the United Nations. As we mentioned previously, in 2000, as part of the Millennium Development Goals (MDG), the United Nations targeted the elimination of gender disparities in primary and secondary education by 2015. As part of this goal, in April 2000, representatives from 164 countries met in Dakar, Senegal, at the World Education Forum to discuss the various problems they all confront regarding educating the children of their respective countries and to launch their Education for All—Fast Track Initiative (FTI).[35] The FTI is an organization that raises money from donor countries and then doles this money out to low-income countries "which demonstrate serious commitment" in attempting to meet the MDG of universal primary education.[36] The FTI is made up of about thirty major countries and donor agencies such as the United States, the European Commission, France, Greece, The Netherlands, Portugal, Spain, Russia, the World Bank, and UNICEF, just to name a few. Countries may apply for aid; if aid is offered, it is contingent on the country signing a memorandum of understanding that binds the country to using the money only for specific actions and items. The FTI currently supports thirty-six countries around the world (twenty-three in sub-Saharan Africa).

The overall progress toward the MDG of universal primary and secondary education has been uneven. The FTI notes that on the positive side, between 2000 and 2006 15.2 million more children in Africa enrolled into primary schools in African FTI countries, about half of whom are girls (48 percent).[37] And according to the United Nations, gender parity in primary education "is 95% or higher in six of the ten regions, including the most populous ones."[38] But, as stated earlier in the chapter, a number of countries did not attain the goal of ending gender disparities by 2005. As the 2008 Millennium Development Goals Report states, "Of the 113 countries that failed to achieve gender parity in both primary and secondary school enrollment by the target date of 2005, only 18 are likely to achieve the goal by 2015."[39]

Why has attainment of the MDG of universal primary education been so hard to attain? Part of the problem lies with the countries themselves (discussed earlier when describing barriers to education and in greater detail later in the chapter), but part of the problem also lies with donor countries who have promised funds but have not delivered: "Four of the richest nations—the U.S., Germany, Japan, and Italy—have been among the slowest to offer their share of the necessary funds."[40] Another problem is that donor countries and the World Bank are reluctant to provide funds for such important items as paying teacher's salaries; they would rather fund tangibles such as desks and chairs. But funding teacher's salaries is crucial to nations struggling economically. One report found that a large amount of the money the World Bank spent on education "from the early 1990s onwards had been wasted on building schools that were closed within a few years due to a lack of teachers."[41] Certainly, some states have trouble attracting teachers because of civil strife, but many have trouble recruiting teachers because salaries are so poor. Thus, donor countries and institutions need to reexamine their policies regarding use of funds. To build schools only to see them shut down for lack of teachers is problematic.

Despite these problems, the Millennium Development goals and the FTI are important because they commit the participants to the goal of gender equality. And while compliance with the MDGs is not mandatory, agencies like UNESCO use it as a yardstick by which to measure countries' progress. The embarrassment that may result from being shown to be lagging behind one's compatriots

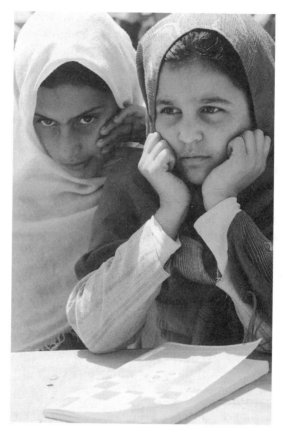

Girls in Afghanistan sit and listen at an opening ceremony for a school in Kabul. Today 5.4 million Afghani children are in school; only 35 percent of them are girls. SOURCE: MASSOUD HOSSAINI/AFP/Getty Images

may be enough to prod countries into working harder to meet their international commitments.

Another program is the Girls Education Movement (GEM) launched in 2001 by the United Nations Children's Fund (UNICEF). This project recruits young women in school to encourage other girls to attend school, improve their study habits, and gain confidence.[42] The U.S. Agency for International Development (USAID) has established a Girls' and Women's Education Initiative. It "supports advocacy for girls' education and helps decision makers at the national, regional, and community levels identify the barriers and it strengthens the capacity of individuals and groups to finance and implement girls' education projects using their own resources."[43] The efforts of these development agencies are important in the struggle to improve women's access to education because they indicate that the international community is committed to improving women's access to education.

The World Bank is another player in attempting to advance women's equality. The World Bank has emphasized the importance of expanding education as a means of reducing overall levels of poverty. To facilitate this goal they have combined grants and interest-free loans with debt relief. Debt relief is the forgiveness of often billions of dollars of debt owed to international lending institutions, like the World Bank. For instance, in 2005, G8 finance ministers agreed to cancel up to $55 billion in debts owed to the World Bank and the African Development bank by poor countries.[44] The intention of debt relief is to rid poor countries from crippling debt service payments, thereby freeing up large chunks of money for countries to redirect toward social services. Many argue that it is of great benefit to countries and has greatly enhanced access to education, especially for girls, in countries receiving it. One of its biggest supporters is the Irish rock star Bono, from the band U2. Bono has been at the forefront of international efforts to raise awareness about debt relief. In 2002, Bono and former U.S. Treasury Secretary Paul O'Neill toured countries in Africa that had been recipients of debt relief. In Uganda they visited schools that were built from savings that arguably accrued to Uganda as a result of debt relief.[45] Bono's attention to the plight of poor countries has aided their efforts to gain more public awareness around the problem of debt and poverty and the relationship between the two.

Uganda is an example of a country that has been the recipient of grants, interest-free loans, and debt relief. In 1998, the World Bank approved a $155 million package of grants and interest-free loans to support universal primary education in Uganda. In particular, the World Bank emphasized securing education for girls, orphans, and children from poor or rural families. Recent debt relief in Uganda began in the late 1990s when $650 million in debt to external creditors was written off under the Initiative for Heavily Indebted Poor Countries (HIPC). Uganda qualified for this debt relief after meeting stringent requirements for a poverty reduction plan set forth by the International Monetary Fund (IMF) and the World Bank. In 2000 Uganda again benefited from another round of relief granted by the World Bank and the IMF as a result of its efforts to reduce poverty. And in 2006, Uganda's $4.5 billion in foreign debt was reduced to $1 billion through a debt waiver granted by the World Bank.[46]

What has been the impact of these grants, interest-free loans, and debt forgiveness? Has it been used to reduce poverty, as was intended?

In 1997, Uganda was able to launch universal primary education (a requirement for receiving debt relief) and saw enrollment increase from 2.5 million to 6 million, the ratio of boys to girls narrow drastically, and annual expenditures on education increase by 9 percent (secondary education was made free in 2007).[47] Net enrollment rates for primary schooling (the total number of children in school) in Uganda increased from a total 62.3 percent in 1992 to 96 percent girls and 95 percent boys in 2005.[48] Further, the gender gap in primary and secondary schooling closed significantly: For primary school, Uganda has reached near parity, advancing from 93 percent in 1992 to 99 percent in 2005. Figures for enrollment in secondary education have also improved, with the ratio of girls to boys rising from 67 percent in 1997 to 86 percent in 2005.[49] Uganda's finance minister, Ezra Suruma, has argued that because of the debt forgiveness, Uganda has been able to free up a lot of money that would have gone to debt repayment that instead has now been directed toward increased funding for universal primary and secondary education, as well as other social services.[50] A report written by a U.K.-based organization that watches G8 promises to Africa notes that Uganda has effectively utilized its debt relief savings, as evidenced by "doubling the school enrollment rate to 94 percent, which has contributed to Uganda's remarkable decline in HIV rates."[51] Elsewhere in Africa, Zambia and Tanzania have both used savings from debt relief to build schools, and Simon Maxwell, director of Britain's leading aid think tank, the Oversees Development Institute, argues that, "Millions of children in Africa are now at school, because debt relief has given governments the resources to pay for teachers and school buildings."[52]

On the downside, while more children were going to school in Uganda, there are not enough resources to ensure that they are receiving a quality education. They face overcrowded classrooms, shortages of materials and, most importantly, shortages of teachers.[53] The World Bank notes that as of 2007 there are still approximately ninety-four students in each classroom and three students per book in Uganda.[54] Many Ugandans echo these concerns. They argue that the lack of resources has led to students who are learning nothing.[55] Minister of Education Gerard Namirembe Bitamazire, when asked about these problems, replied that Uganda's priorities in education were "access, equity and quality," in that order, and that "What was the point of quality education for a proportion of the population if it left plenty of children out?"[56] Further, the Canadian International Development Agency notes that the enrollment numbers given here can be misleading because they hide huge discrepancies between those children living in war-torn northern Uganda and those in the South, with enrollment figures being much lower in the North.

There are other problems with debt relief. The auditor general notes that money saved from debt relief—over $2 trillion—is sitting in the state's coffers, not being utilized.[57] Other critics argue that previous debt relief to Uganda resulted in money being skimmed off the top by local governments that were given funds intended to be utilized for education. One report found that "only 13 percent of central government grants for nonsalary education spending in Uganda...actually made it to the local schools that were the intended beneficiaries.[58] Thus the merits of universal primary education as well as the merits of debt relief in Uganda are more nuanced than one might expect.

There are also some general problems associated with debt relief. William Easterly of the World Bank's Development Research Group argues that debt forgiveness has a lot of pitfalls, one of which is that when a country's debt is forgiven, that country often goes out and borrows more money, thus beginning the cycle all over again. Easterly notes that "From 1989 to 1997, debt forgiveness for the 41 nations now designated as HIPCs reached $33 billion, while new borrowing for the same countries totaled $41 billion."[59] Creating new debt is not the point of providing debt relief. But when debt relief is offered to countries whose regimes may be corrupt or suffer from severe mismanagement, this may be one of the results. Easterly goes on to note that even in Uganda, where President Yoweri Museveni is a vast improvement over the dictatorial rule of Idi Amin, "Museveni's government continues to spend money on questionable military adventures in the Democratic Republic of Congo."[60] While debt relief offers promise and has clearly shown some positive results, it is not without its critics and is unlikely to be the sole answer to the problem of increasing access to education for girls.

Other efforts to improve access to women's education are conducted at the domestic level by nongovernmental organizations (NGOs) and by national and local governments. NGOs in several African countries have set up programs to educate people about sexual harassment, teach girls to resist unwanted sexual advances, and make male students sensitive to the rights of women and girls.[61] National and local initiatives to improve girls' access to education are numerous, so we will just highlight a few:

- In Chile, the Women's Institute "promotes educational activities to enable women to take an active public role and to deal with social and political issues."[62]
- Malawi has eliminated school fees and abolished compulsory school uniforms, thus making an education more affordable to many citizens.[63]
- In Mashan County in China, priority loans or development funds are awarded to villages and households that successfully take measures to send girls to school.[64]
- Guinea has raised the marriage age, and it is now illegal for male teachers to harass female pupils; Benin is now offering some basic education opportunities to girls who drop out of school.[65]
- In Mali, a community-based project works to alter traditional beliefs about women and girls by involving women in literacy and income-generating activities, after which they usually support the education of their girls. The results are promising—daily visits were made to homes of girls who were absent from school, and the girls were accompanied to school. Enrollment in eighteen villages doubled to 44 percent, and girls' enrollment rose to 33 percent from 18 percent in just three years.[66]

Overall, NGOs, local and national governments, and international organizations are actively working toward improving the state of women's education. Yet, it is clear from the discussion that while important strides have been made in removing barriers to women's education in developing nations, international pledges, treaties, and increased legislation will not be sufficient to close the gap.

Central Asia Institute

The Central Asia Institute (CAI) was founded by Greg Mortensen in 1996. Mortensen, a son of Lutheran missionaries who spent fourteen years of his youth in Tanzania, was a climber who was injured on a climb in Afghanistan. Locals found him and nursed him back to health. When it was time to leave, Greg asked them what he could do to thank them, and they asked for schools. Thus began a one-man mission to bring education to the children, especially the girls, of war-torn Afghanistan and central Asia. As of 2008, the Central Asia Institute has established seventy-eight schools, which have educated 28,000 students, including 14,000 girls. At a time when girls' schools are being destroyed in Afghanistan and Pakistan by extremists, these schools have remained untouched. Mortensen argues that the reason CAI schools are left alone is in part because, when they come close to an area where a CAI school is, extremists leave it alone because the schools built by CAI have "resounding community support."[i] CAI is a nonprofit grassroots organization that has been able to help people in an area of the world that most don't want to set foot in. Mortensen attributes CAI's success to that fact that "We have no political, religious, ideological, or western agenda.... We just try to help people with what they want and empower them to help create their own solutions."[ii] Mortensen currently lives with his family in Montana but spends a significant portion of the year traveling to central Asia. His book, *Three Cups of Tea*, has been on the New York Times bestseller list for twenty-two months. His work is clear evidence that one person truly can make a difference.

[i] Karin Ronnow, "Journey of Hope: An In-Depth Report, Educate Girls, Change the World" (Central Asia Institute, 2008), 1.
[ii] Ibid., 5.

Most of the discussion so far has focused on primary education. We noted earlier that gender parity in secondary education is still elusive; only one-third of countries have gender parity in secondary education. Why do enrollment levels drop so significantly for girls once they enter secondary school? The reasons don't differ terribly from what has been discussed earlier, the key factors being school fees and families' beliefs that daughters should remain at home to help with chores, younger children, the sick, and the elderly. Families that may be willing to send young children to primary school balk at sending older daughters, who can contribute to household chores and who will eventually be married off to another family. And, if the school is not free, then there really is no reason to send one's daughter and waste one's money. As long as these barriers exist, girls will not attend secondary school.

On a practical level, a number of specific proposals would help remove barriers to girls' education. First, increasing household income results in a huge benefit to girls. For example, in Ethiopia "increasing a household's wealth index by one unit enhances a boy's chances of attending school by 16%, against *41% for girls*" [67] (emphasis added). An increase in household income can reduce or remove the need for children to work. Further, a variety of improvements are needed in schools, such as increased teacher training on gender awareness, higher numbers of female teachers, and the elimination of school fees. Gendered classroom practices need to be altered; for example, girls in school are more often than boys sent to fetch water, sweep floors, and other such chores. [68]

A critical player in advancing all of these reforms is the government. Further, this requires coordinated commitment from a variety of agencies, given that "a massive expansion of basic education is required." [69] This can often require the redirection of the state's resources from some areas, like defense, to education, and also entails a crackdown on government corruption.

Finally, writing proactive legislation is often not sufficient; local practices, customs, and beliefs about girls' rights and abilities must also change. This can be accomplished through the use of campaigns, role models, and working directly with adolescent girls to strengthen their voice. [70] This also means that donors must be careful in making sure that they are not imposing overly Westernized visions of girls' equality and that the people and culture of each country also drive efforts for change. For example, one important lesson that USAID states that it has learned from its years of work in this area is that its programs are most effective when they are "owned" by the citizens of the country, not the donor community, and they must fit the country's economy, political system, culture, and such. [71] While the international community can stress the importance of improving girls' access to education, until local communities, NGOs, and domestic governments share this goal, gender parity in education will remain an elusive goal. However, judging from the improvements made in many areas of the world, improved access to education has been one of the more successful development campaigns with the UN's Millennium Development Goals.

CONCLUSION

Educated children, both girls and boys, will help many countries escape poverty. Educated girls have fewer children, have better nourished and healthier children, bring in more income to their families, are more likely to participate in the political process, value themselves more, and live longer and healthier lives. There are obvious and proven benefits to educating girls; yet, local communities and governments do not always prioritize improving access to girls' education in the face of multiple, competing needs. While the international community successfully has prodded governments to increase girls' access to primary education in many countries, ensuring that girls are integrated into the education system at all levels is still a future target rather than a successfully completed campaign.

FOR MORE INFORMATION

Interested in finding out what citizens in the United States are doing to let their voices be heard? Go to, http://www.endpoverty2015.org and find out about the various actions taken by regular people to try to help end poverty in the developing world.

Education for All, Fast Track Initiative, http://www.education-fast-track.org

UNICEF, http://www.unicef.org/girlseducation/india_39596.html?q=printme; "Girl Stars" take their show on the road to highlight the importance of girls' education in India

UNICEF, Gender Parity and Education, http://www.unicef.org/progressforchildren/2005n2/gender.php

The United Nations, Progress Toward the Millennium Development Goals, Education, http://www.undp.org/mdg/basics_ontrack.shtml

The World Bank, Information about Girls' education, http://web.worldbank.org/WBSITE/EXTERNAL/TOPICS/EXTEDUCATION/0,,contentMDK:20298916~menuPK:617572~pagePK:148956~piPK:216618~theSitePK:282386,00.html

The Debt Police—This documentary describes the role of debt relief in Uganda.

Educating Lucia—This documentary shows the life of three sisters in Zimbabwe and their hopes and aspirations.

Girls Can't Wait—This documentary looks at the status of girls' education in India.

The New Sudan—This documentary looks at girls and education in Sudan; http://www.nadusfilms.com/education.

11

Women and Sexual Violence During War

It was April 14th when we left our house and on the 15th we were walking near Djakovica....We met Serb paramilitaries....They approached my uncle and separated him....They came up to me....He took my hand and told me to get in his car....He told me not to refuse or there would be lots of victims....He told me not to scream and to take off my clothes. He took off his clothes and told me to suck his thing. I did not know what to do. He took my head and put it near him. He started to beat me. I lost consciousness. When I came to I saw him over me. I had great pain....Another man came with a car and he got over me.... I was crying with pain and he was laughing the whole time....He told me not to tell anyone or they would take me for good and shoot my family.[1]

They put us in a small barn with hay in it. Then the four men came into the barn and slammed the door and pointed machine guns at us....Then they took me. I was pregnant. I was holding my son. They took him away from me and gave him to my mother. They told me to get up and follow them. I was crying and screaming, "Take me back to my child!" They took me to another room. It was so bad I almost fainted. I can't say the words they said....Because I was pregnant, they asked me where my husband was....One of them said to another soldier, "Kick her and make the baby abort." They did this to me four times—they took me outside to the other place. Three men took me one by one. Then they asked me, "Are you desperate for your husband?" and said, "Here we are instead of him." [2]

While these two testimonies from Kosovar Albanian women are quite graphic, they clearly illustrate the atrocities that women and girls have suffered and continue to suffer during times of war. And while such atrocities have been committed against women during wars for centuries, it is only recently that sexual violence against women during times of war and displacement has received any attention from the international community. In this chapter we will look at the issue of sexual violence against women during times of war and displacement. This will include examining sexual violence against women in their home countries and as refugees fleeing their countries (sometimes because of war, other times because of forcible expulsion). We will discuss the intent of sexual violence, examine varying manifestations of sexual violence in four countries, discuss the impact it has on women's lives, and analyze what is being done about it.

THE INTENT OF SEXUAL VIOLENCE

Sexual violence against women and girls during times of war generally takes the form of rape. Human rights organizations have documented cases of individual and gang rape of women and girls by soldiers and rebel groups and rape with objects such as firewood, weapons, and umbrellas. Females who have suffered sexual violence are often also forced to serve as slaves or "wives" to soldiers and are often subject to a life of permanent sexual slavery. Even females who become fighters report being forced to serve as sexual slaves and soldier's "wives" in addition to fighting.[3] Such violence is often committed by government soldiers, rebel forces, and even government and international peacekeeping forces. It is also committed against women in refugee camps by locals of the country in which the refugee camp is located.

Why do soldiers and others commit this type of violence against women? First and foremost, it is not for sexual gratification. Rather, rape during war and in refugee camps is about the display of power and is a way of letting one's enemy know who is in control. However, the reasons for needing to display this power are often varied. To this end, rape is often:

- Committed in homes in front of male relatives to humiliate the men. It is used to shame them because they are unable to protect their women.
- Committed while the woman is fleeing war-torn areas and in detention centers as a form of political terror and intimidation.
- Committed against women as a way of terrorizing communities into accepting the control of the aggressor or to punish a community for assisting opposing forces.
- Committed against women by their husbands and male relatives in refugee camps. Refugee life often leads to stressful situations that erupt into violence. Further, the extended network of family and friends is not present to act as a deterrent to sexual violence.
- Committed against women who had held positions of power prior to the war. These women are often raped by men who had felt inferior to them.
- Committed against women by their husbands when they return from war angry, confused, and armed.
- Used as a method of revenge, which is often inflicted on the women of the oppressor's ethnic group. Sometimes, media coverage of victimized women fuels the anger of the ethnic group that is being oppressed.
- Used as a method of ethnic cleansing. Women are often forced to bear the children of the enemy that has raped them. Thus, the child will be the nationality of the man who impregnated the woman.

While power is the primary motivator for rape as a tool of war, the reasons for needing to display this power are varied.

Many women who have survived sexual violence have relatively few options in seeking legal retribution. Some countries lack specific legislation that criminalizes rape and sexual assault; the legislation that does exist does not clearly articulate provisions regarding rape. Women often do not know how to pursue prosecution in criminal courts; as refugees, women are unfamiliar with the local legal system and may be wary of police and judicial authorities. For years, adjudicators rejected women's claims of being raped by soldiers and police. They treated these acts as "private moments" not open to public scrutiny.[4] Further, international groups are not always receptive to or experienced in addressing rape and sexual violence. For example, in Indonesia, women were sexually abused by Indonesian security forces. When some women decided to report this abuse, a human rights NGO agreed to bring the women to the provincial capital, where the case and their identities were widely publicized. As a result, when the women were taken into custody and questioned about the incidents of abuse, not surprisingly, they recanted their stories. In this instance, women essentially became pawns of the police as a result of the lack of protection for victims of sexual violence and NGO inexperience in dealing with the issue in such a politicized context.

There is also often a cultural taboo against speaking about rape and so women keep silent after it has occurred. Many societies still function around an honor ethic in which a man's honor depends on female chastity. If a woman is raped and the rape becomes public knowledge, a man's honor is marred in multiple ways. It displays to the community that he was unable to protect the females in his family, and/or the man may see the raped woman as having "encouraged" the rape with her actions. Thus, many women who are raped but are not killed afterward or impregnated as a result die with their secret. And finally, when sexual violence has occurred during war, women often fear retaliation against their families if they tell others. This retaliation could come from soldiers (as the quote at the beginning of the chapter indicates), or it could even come from family and others in the refugee community. For example, Burundian refugees in Tanzania often rely on the *abashingatahe* system for dealing with internal matters. The *abashingatahe* is a group of respected, mostly male elders, who act as an arbiter of disputes. Fellow refugees expect women who have been raped by other refugees to take their complaints to the *abashingatahe,* even though this group is not supposed to deal with serious criminal matters like rape.[5] If women choose to take their cases to government authorities, they suffer at the hands of their own people. In sum, women who have been raped by soldiers, fellow refugees, or government or international actors have few resources for addressing the violence. The victims are wary of local police and judicial authorities, they fear retaliation by their aggressors and sometimes by their own people, and international agencies and NGOs have little experience in handling such crimes. Later we will address some recent efforts to amend these problems.

INCIDENTS OF SEXUAL VIOLENCE

Let us now turn to some specific documented incidents of sexual violence against women refugees and during times of war. There are numerous cases, but we will focus on four: the former Yugoslavia (including the Kosovo and Bosnian conflicts), the Democratic Republic of Congo, Sierra Leone, and Tanzania. The first three cases focus mainly on sexual violence during wartime. The last case is an example of the sexual violence that women face in refugee camps when fleeing war-torn countries. These cases were chosen because they are some of the most horrific examples of sexual violence in recent decades and because of the extensive amount of information available documenting the atrocities.

The Former Yugoslavia

The republics of the former Yugoslavia erupted into violent conflict in the early 1990s, as the country quickly polarized along ethnic lines. Slovenia, Croatia, Macedonia, and Bosnia and Herzegovina were recognized as independent states in 1992, while the remaining republics of Serbia and Montenegro formed the Federal Republic of Yugoslavia (FRY) under President Slobodan Milosevic. Under his leadership, the army led various campaigns to unite ethnic Serbs (and destroy the Muslim population) in neighboring republics in the name of forming a "greater Serbia." Further, in 1989–1999, FRY military and paramilitary forces launched massive expulsions of ethnic Albanians living in the Kosovo region of Serbia, which in turn prompted further NATO intervention the stationing of NATO forces in Kosovo.[6]

Bosnian Serb soldiers drove 1.5 million non-Serbs (mainly Muslims) from their homes and villages in an egregious example of ethnic cleansing. In particular, women were targeted as pawns of war and were raped in their homes, while fleeing the conflict, and in detention centers as part of a "well planned strategy of national humiliation," many experts claim.[7] Many women and girls were held in camps that were run like brothels, where Serb soldiers could come and rape women and girls as often as they liked. In the indictment filed with the War Crimes Tribunal for the former Yugoslavia in the Hague, a fifteen-year-old girl testified about her eight-month ordeal in such a camp. Raped and tortured by Bosnian Serb soldiers on a regular basis, she was finally sold by one of her captors to two Montenegro soldiers for 500 deutschmarks (about $280).[8] Further, one Serb leader, Radomir Kunarac, was reported to have "taunted one of his victims by telling her she would carry Serb babies and would not know who the father was because of the number of men who raped her."[9] A report by the European Commission (the executive arm of the European Union) estimated that "as many as 20,000 Bosnian women—including girls as young as six and women as old as 80—were raped by Bosnian Serbs during the war."[10] No woman or girl was immune or safe.

The use of rape in the Kosovo conflict several years later was similar in its form and intent. Serbian and Yugoslav forces used the rape of women as a way to terrorize the Albanian population (largely Muslim) and force them to flee the country in their campaign to "ethnically cleanse" Serbia. Women were raped in their homes in front of male relatives, on the road while fleeing, and in detention centers, often multiple times. Further, in this conflict, no woman was safe, and the oppressed also used rape against the aggressor. As the testimonies at the beginning of this chapter indicate, many Serbian, Albanian, and Roma women were raped by ethnic Albanians, sometimes members of the Kosovo Liberation Army.[11] The Yugoslav case illustrates a majority of the varied reasons for sexual violence against women during war—to induce humiliation, intimidation, and terror as part of an overall project of ethnic cleansing. We will discuss this case further when we look at the role of the international community in addressing this problem.

The Congo

The next case we will examine is the war in the eastern Democratic Republic of Congo (Congo). The massive inflow of refugees in 1994 from neighboring Rwanda and Burundi sparked ethnic strife and civil war within Congo, as the aging dictator, Mobutu Sese Seiko, slowly lost his grip on power. In May 1997, Mobutu was toppled from power by a coalition of forces led by Laurent Kabila. A mere fifteen months later, his regime was in turn challenged, when in August 1998 Rwandan- and Ugandan-backed forces invaded eastern Congo. Troops from Zimbabwe, Angola, Namibia, Chad, and Sudan entered the conflict on the side of Kabila's regime. Although a cease-fire among the relevant parties was signed in 1999, sporadic fighting continued, and the eastern Congo was in effect controlled by the Rwandan-financed Rassemblement Congolais Pour la Democratie (RCD) from 1998 to October 2002.[12] The war went on, however, with fighting continuing "among dozens of militia groups—mostly consisting of poor young men who prey upon impoverished villagers—despite the presence of the largest U.N. peacekeeping mission in the world." [13] On January 21, 2008, warring militia groups signed an agreement to end the fighting, which had claimed, by some estimates, more than 5.4 million people; the agreement was signed on January 23 by President Kabila and other militia leaders.[14] But in the fall of 2008 rebels advanced toward the eastern provincial capital; the UN estimated that more than 200,000 people were displaced from their homes in September and October 2008 alone.[15]

All groups involved in this war have used rape as a weapon. One NGO estimates that in the Northern Kivu province alone there have been 14,000 rapes since 2004.[16] In some instances rape has been used as part of a broader attack on a village, designed to terrorize local communities into accepting the aggressor's control, and in other instances it has been used to punish a village for allegedly supporting an opposing militia.[17] Dr. Denis Mukwege, director and founder of the Paniz General Referral Hospital in the eastern Congo town of Bukavu, argues that "Rape and sexual violence are now used as a war strategy. . . . It is a tactic of war. It is not rape as understood by many

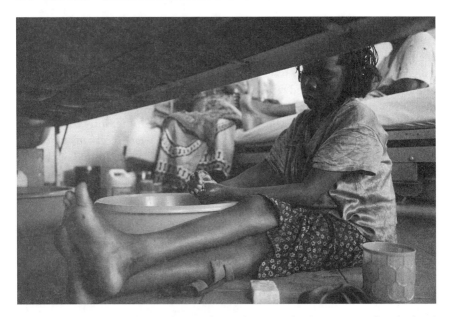

A ten-year-old girl who was raped twice during the war in the Congo sits under a bed and washes her hands in a clinic set up by an NGO for rape victims of the war. The girl was first raped by soldiers in her hometown and somehow made her way to the capital, Goma, where she wandered the streets and was raped again by soldiers. A woman found her and brought her to this clinic. SOURCE: ROBERTO SCHMIDT/AFP/Getty Images

parts of the world, as a violation of the rights of a human being. It is rape used as a weapon of mass destruction.... It is sexual terrorism that seeks to destroy the identity of the individuals and their communities."[18] Women and girls are also assaulted as, in an attempt to feed their families, they venture off to fields to cultivate produce, into forests to make charcoal, and to town to sell their wares. Further, many women have been raped as they fled, with other members of their villages, into the forests in hope of escaping the terrors of war, only to be met by another terror—the abduction of women and girls. Human Rights Watch, an interest group dedicated to documenting human rights abuses worldwide, found that these acts of sexual violence are often aggravated even further by additional acts of brutality including shooting victims in the vagina or mutilating them with knives or razor blades.[19] One young woman reports how soldiers raped her with a pestle, "One of them restrained me, while another took my pili pili pestle and pushed it several times into my vagina, as if he was pounding.... For two weeks my vagina was discharging.... They also killed my husband and my son."[20]

Further, women who have been abducted are often kept as sexual slaves by members of the various militias. One survivor recounts her story as follows:

> Fifteen men with guns and bows and arrows surrounded us. We had to walk for three days through the jungle to the village that was the Mai Mai headquarters.

I was there for three months—five men took me as their "wife" and their slave. I saw one woman killed because she refused; they cut off her breasts. My daughter died while we were there. We got home eventually. It's because of God that I'm alive. But no-one will want me now.[21]

This horrific tale documents only too well the horrors that women in this war-torn region face on a daily basis. These women have little recourse for the damage that has been done to them. A law on sexual violence was passed in 2006 by the parliament. The intent of the law was to speed up the prosecution of rape cases and to increase penalties against those found guilty. However, many NGOs argue that the law has had little effect, that it was a nice symbolic gesture, but that it has not made a difference in the lives of female rape victims. Dirk Deprez of Rejusco, a European-funded organization designed to help the justice system, argues that "It was an ambitious law in an understaffed and underequipped system.... [W]e don't see a lot happening in the field since the law came out."[22] Further, while local courts have punished rapes conducted by private citizens, soldiers and other combatants have historically not been tried. Police and judicial authorities do not take these rape cases seriously. As a result, few women come forward to charge their rapists; they fear that authorities will not act on the charges, and they fear the social stigma attached to having been raped.[23] Female rape victims also argue that they see no point in bringing their cases to court in a system that responds to the highest bidder and where there are few to no courts, police, or lawyers in the rural areas, where most rapes occur.[24] Later we will discuss what is being done to help these women and girls.

Sierra Leone

In 1991 a former army corporal, Foday Sankoh, and his Revolutionary United Front (RUF) informed the one-party government that if it did not institute multiparty politics within ninety days the RUF would take up arms to overthrow the government. The Lome peacekeeping agreement was agreed to by all sides in 1999 but was not terribly successful, as fighting continued, fueled in part by conflicts in neighboring countries like Liberia. In 2002 democratic elections were held and a government was elected, which brought a modicum of stability. Eighteen years and a few governments later, the war is essentially over, and UN peacekeeping forces are slowly withdrawing. Nonetheless, during the twelve years of conflict tens of thousands of citizens were killed and over 2 million people (about one-third of the population) fled the country and are now refugees in surrounding states. This has been one of the bloodiest, most brutal wars of the twentieth century, and the gradual withdrawal of UN forces as well as poverty and ethnic and political tension within Sierra Leone and the deteriorating conditions in surrounding countries, present ongoing challenges to the maintenance of Sierra Leone's stability.[25]

Both government forces and the RUF used notoriously horrible tactics, usually upon the civilian population. The RUF specifically targeted civilians and terrorized the population of Sierra Leone through acts of bodily mutilation (such as the amputation of hands and arms) and forced recruitment of child soldiers. Given the brutality of this war it is not surprising that sexual violence against women was one of the tools adopted by government and rebel forces.

Women and girls in Sierra Leone have reported grotesque abuses of their human rights by both government and rebel forces. Human Rights Watch collected testimonies from numerous girls and women who reported how they were rounded up by rebel forces, brought to their command centers and subsequently subject to individual and gang rape, in addition to rape with objects such as pestles, firewood, and weapons. Rapes were often accompanied by other physical abuses—including the hacking off of limbs. Physicians for Human Rights also conducted research in Sierra Leone into the use of sexual violence. One young woman they interviewed was named Bola N. Bola had been abducted four times by 2001. During her first abduction she tells of how she and other villagers ran off into the bush when the soldiers attacked the village. The soldiers followed them and captured many of them. They held some of the villagers down, cut off some hands, killed some, and raped some. She reports her own rape in the following words, "We were taken to the bush where the sexual act was forced on us.... Nine men raped me.... After they had raped me to their satisfaction, they left me in the bush. I was beaten, bruises on my body, part of my body. Some around me were amputated. I was not well." [26]

Further, these women and girls were also expected to serve as slaves to the rebel soldiers, performing housework and farm work. [27] Human Rights Watch comments that the point of this sexual violence was

> to dominate women and their communities by deliberately undermining cultural values and community relationships, destroying the ties that hold society together. Child combatants raped women who were old enough to be their grandmothers, rebels raped pregnant and breastfeeding mothers, and fathers were forced to watch their daughters being raped. [28]

Thus this sexual violence was a calculated tactic; rape was used as a means to destroy a population and overthrow a government. Later we will discuss what, if any, recourse these women and girls had after the war ended.

Tanzania

On October 21, 1993, Melchior Ndayaye, Burundi's first democratically elected Hutu president, was assassinated by army officers after having served only one hundred days in office. This launched a period of intense ethnic violence between Hutu and Tutsi factions. (The ethnic makeup of Burundi is similar to Rwanda, with approximately 85 percent of the population Hutu and 15 percent of the population Tutsi. Tutsis dominated the armed forces). The violence has claimed over 200,000 Burundian lives; in addition, some 350,000 Burundians are living in exile in Tanzania alone. A new government (Tutsi dominated), inaugurated in November 2001, signed a power-sharing agreement with the largest rebel faction

(Hutus) in December 2003. A new constitution was ratified in 2005 and a Hutu-dominated government was democratically elected that same year. The president of the government, Pierre Nkurunziza, brokered a peace agreement, with the assistance of South Africa, with the country's last rebel group in 2006, but many challenges still remain.[29] The violence in Burundi has resulted in a massive influx of refugees into neighboring Tanzania. These refugees have been subject to horrid conditions, but in particular women have been found to be the victims of sexual violence.

In 1997, Human Rights Watch received reports that many women refugees were suffering human rights abuses in the camps, primarily sexual violence, and that the response of the United Nations High Commissioner for Refugees (UNHCR) and that of the Tanzanian government was inadequate. Human Rights Watch and other human rights groups investigated these reports in 1998 and 1999. They found that Burundian women in Tanzanian refugee camps had suffered from a great deal of sexual violence at the hands of both Burundian male refugees as well as Tanzanian nationals, soldiers, policemen, husbands, and relatives.[30] The International Rescue Committee researched similar complaints about the refugee camps and determined that "Burundi refugees have suffered a high degree of sexual and gender violence. The initial results of the IRC assessment suggest that approximately 26% of the 3,803 Burundi refugee women between the ages of 12–49 in the established camp of Kanembwa have experienced sexual violence since becoming a refugee."[31]

These women, like those in the Congo, were often attacked while carrying out daily tasks, such as gathering firewood, harvesting vegetables, or looking for employment in nearby town. They often did not report the attacks because they were either unfamiliar with the local legal system and/or were wary of local police and authorities. Human Rights Watch argues that the sexual violence that these women have suffered is the consequence of the "absence of well-designed and concrete programs to protect women refugees from violence and to punish the perpetrators of such violence when it occurs."[32] We will examine the shortcomings of the UNHCR response to the problem a bit later in the chapter. No matter the shortcoming, this case illustrates the sexual dangers that female refugees face on top of the daily attempt to survive harsh circumstances far from home.

These four cases clearly illustrate the use of sexual violence against women and girls as a deliberate tool during war. Rape during war and in refugee situations is not random, nor is it a result of overly keyed-up men with weapons. It is a tactic that military leaders have chosen to use to attain their desired end—military victory and total submission of a defeated population. The main victims of modern warfare are the civilians of the countries at war, and no one is safe and no tactic is out of bounds, including mutilating a woman's vagina. How do women, assuming they survive, cope with such abuses? We now turn to discussing the impact of this sexual violence on the remainder of their lives.

THE IMPACT OF SEXUAL VIOLENCE ON WOMEN

The impact of sexual violence on women is far-reaching. Women who have been raped suffer physical, psychological, and social consequences. The physical impacts are many. Pregnancy is one obvious impact. Many rapes result in pregnancy, and rape victims are often forced, either by societal pressure or lack of access to health care, to carry the pregnancy to term. Many of these women end up as poor single mothers (if married, they are often cast off by their husbands) shunned by society because of the circumstances of their pregnancy. Or, sometimes these babies are given up for adoption, thus swelling the ranks of victims of these crimes. And even when an abortion is an option, the procedure still leaves emotional scars on its recipients.

Other physical impacts include sexually transmitted diseases such as AIDS and salpingitis. In the Congo, it is estimated that upward of 60 percent of the military forces are infected with HIV, thus exposing their rape victims to this dreadful disease.[33] Salpangitis is a sexually transmitted disease that causes pain, infertility, and a foul-smelling discharge. Further, the international group of doctors who help in war-torn countries, Médecins Sans Frontières, notes that many women are so badly damaged by the sexual assaults that they will require surgery to repair them physically.[34] These women end up suffering incontinence because of a fistula forming between the anus and the vagina. According to one health worker interviewed by Médecins Sans Frontières, "There is no life for a woman with a fistula. They smell so bad, they will not be accepted by society, maybe, just maybe, their mother will stand by them. But no one will want to approach them."[35] There are often no facilities or money for these women to be treated, so they must live with this physical pain.

In addition to the physical scars are emotional and psychological impacts. The National Center for Post Traumatic Stress Disorder states that women who have been raped during war suffer permanently from shock, intense fear, tearfulness, anger, shame, helplessness, nervousness, numbness, confusion, disorientation, unwanted memories, decreased ability to concentrate, and self-blame.[36] They note that these symptoms were found in up to 75 percent of Bosnian female refugees, even among those who did not report being raped.[37] A recent study of fighters in Liberia exposed to sexual violence echoes these findings. Kirsten Johnson, M.D., M.P.H., of the Harvard Humanitarian Initiative, Harvard University, found that "Seventy-four percent of female former combatants who experienced sexual violence had symptoms of PTSD, compared with 44 percent who did not experience sexual violence."[38] The emotional and psychological ramifications of sexual violence should not be ignored when analyzing its impact, since many of these scars do not heal easily, if at all.

Finally are the social impacts of rape during war. Rape survivors often are rejected by their families and their villages. Sometimes this rejection is because they are suspected of having been infected with AIDS or other STDs. Médecins Sans Frontières notes that in many African countries, husbands often turn out their wives and even if they let them return home "it is normal for him to find a new wife, moving the old one into a different room and ignoring her. Fear of disease, real or perceived, is often given as the reason for this rejection."[39] Other times the rejection is just because of the stigma attached to having been raped. Jeanette, a young woman who was raped by a member of the local militia in her village in the Congo, reported to interviewers that her family had rejected her, saying that "she offered herself to her attacker."[40] Because of this, many women never report their rapes or seek medical attention.

We can see that the impacts of rape during war are far-reaching. Not only do these women suffer from the well-known horrors of war—the slaughter of family members, the destruction of villages, food scarcity, and refugee status—but they have also an additional, often not discussed, horror to face, that of being raped. The consequences are many, and thousands of women and girls live with these consequences every day. We now turn to international and domestic efforts to address the problem.

ADDRESSING SEXUAL VIOLENCE AGAINST WOMEN

International law increasingly has been used as a tool to combat and criminal-ize sexual violence against women. One of the more far-reaching developments in dealing with sexual violence against women was the verdict rendered against some of the Bosnian Serb leaders for their role in the rapes of women during the war in Yugoslavia. In February 2001, the International Criminal Tribunal for the Former Yugoslavia convicted Dragoljub Kunarac, Radomir Kovac, and Zoran Vukovic for their role in the rape, torture, and enslavement of women during the conflict in Bosnia. They received sentences of twenty-eight, twenty, and twelve years, respectively. These three cases are the first time in history that an inter-national tribunal has brought charges against military leaders solely for crimes of sexual violence against women. And it is the first time that an international tribunal has found rape and enslavement a crime against humanity. Building on this record, in 2007, the International Criminal Court filed charges against men in two high-profile war crimes cases: that of two Sudanese suspected of mass rape and other war crimes and that of the leader of the Lord's Resistance Army in Uganda, who was charged with sexual enslavement and rape. Further, in 2008 the UN Security Council voted officially to recognize rape and sexual violence as war crimes and to prohibit postconflict agreements from granting amnesty to those perpetrators of sexual violence. The decision of the International Tribunal for the Former Yugoslavia, the actions of the International Criminal Court, and the UN vote are important because they establish legal precedents for charging soldiers and combatants who use sexual violence against women during war. Nonetheless, they will not end the use of sexual violence against women during war. Nor will they necessarily eradicate the climate of indifference surrounding sexual violence against women during war. Further, women will still fear coming forward and reporting rape because of the anticipated reaction of their husbands, families, or communities.

Truth and reconciliation commissions (TRCs) have been popular ways to heal the wounds of civil conflicts, like the one in Sierra Leone. Women have testified before Sierra Leone's TRC about the multitude of abuses that they suffered during the many years of conflict. Initially, investigators had a tough time getting women to speak up about sexual violence. As has been discussed elsewhere, women fear discussing sexual violence because of the stigma that will be attached to them. To aid the TRC in Sierra Leone, the UN Development Fund for Women provided support and training for TRC staff and for the women themselves.[41] As a result of this outreach and help from other NGOs, more women felt safe speaking up and a record of the abuses now exists. However, the Lome Peace Accord (which created the TRC) has an amnesty clause, which granted immunity to the perpetrators of war crimes between 1991 and 1999. Such deals leave the victims of sexual violence with no recourse. Nonetheless, some perpetrators of sexual violence have been tried and convicted. In 2007, the Special Court for Sierra Leone found three senior members of the armed forces guilty of eleven out of fourteen counts of war crimes and crimes against humanity, including sexual slavery and rape.[42] Many, however, have gone free and will never be tried.

International agencies such as the UNHCR also work on issues of sexual violence against women, although not always with great levels of success. Since 1950, the UNHCR has been charged with leading and coordinating "action to protect refugees and resolve refugee problems worldwide. Its primary purpose is to safeguard the rights and well being of refugees."[43] In particular, it has written directives protecting women from gender-based violence in refugee camps. However, while the existence of this agency is useful, it also has its shortcomings. Human Rights Watch regularly monitors the actions of the agency and has found some serious problems. For instance, in 2002 some UNHCR refugee aid workers were charged with sexual exploitation of children in Nepal. UNHCR subsequently removed these workers; nonetheless, the very fact that some of its staff were guilty of the very crimes they were supposed to prevent is disconcerting. Further, Human Rights Watch has charged UNHCR with ineffectual enforcement of the guidelines concerning gender-based violence, in particular in Tanzania.[44] Thus, the UNHCR has the potential to be a useful tool for protecting women from gender-based violence in refugee camps, but it needs to monitor its staff more forcefully and to ensure the strict enforcement of its own directives.

A number of international groups work to assist women who have been sexually violated during war and in refugee situations. Three such groups are Human Rights Watch, Amnesty International, and Médecins Sans Frontières. The first two groups visit war-torn areas and refugee camps to document human rights abuses against women (and others). They, in turn, put pressure on the national government where the abuses have occurred to end the practices and to punish those who have committed them. They also urge other nations and individuals to put pressure on the country to end the abuses. The third group sends doctors into war-torn areas to administer medical aid to those in need. They have assisted numerous women with physical healing after being harmed by sexual violence. Local groups also have emerged to assist women who have been victims of sexual violence. In the Congo one such group is Amaldefea. This is a nongovernmental organization that supports mothers and children through such acts as teaching them skills so that they can be self-supporting. All of these organizations, international and local, are crucial in assisting women who have been victims of sexual violence. Through the work of such groups, perpetrators are charged with their crimes and women are assisted in their attempts to rebuild a life for themselves.

WOMEN AS COMBATANTS

Until recently it was assumed that women's and girls' only role in armed conflict was that of victim. Recent research has begun to dispel this myth.[45] As we discussed in Chapter 3 on women and revolutionary movements, women have played and do play a variety of roles in armed conflict. Research has begun to document the number of girls and young women who have played an active role in terrorizing and destroying their communities in armed conflicts in numerous countries, including Cambodia, Colombia, Chechnya, Israel, Sierra Leone, and Uganda. Peter Singer's work on child soldiers finds that "roughly thirty percent of the world's armed forces that employ child soldiers include girl soldiers. Underage girls have been present in the armed forces in fifty-five countries. In twenty-seven of these, girls were abducted to serve and in thirty-four they saw combat."[46] And one survey found that at least 25,000 women and girls participated in the fighting forces in the conflict in Liberia.[47] Girl soldiers have taken up arms; led forces on the frontlines; mutilated and killed friends, family, and civilians; and served in more expected roles such as cooks, cleaners, and wives to rebel soldiers.

While it might sound as if this role might be empowering for women and girls and a step toward being on equal footing with men, this assumption would be mistaken. As Singer's work reveals, most of these female fighters did not join voluntarily (they were abducted), especially the children, and most experienced sexual violence during their time as soldiers. Singer argues that, "The fact that sexual abuse is often a common part of the child soldiering experience for these girls debunks any idea that their recruitment is somehow progressive."[48] And a survey conducted by Liberian Coalition of NGOs in collaboration with Amnesty International found that female soldiers in Liberia often experienced rape and use as sex slaves and cooks.[49] The survey corroborates Singer's findings that female soldiers often did not join "voluntarily," nor do they see it as a way to attain equality—rather, the "majority were forced to participate in the war, although some opted to take up arms to protect themselves against sexual violence and to avenge the death of family members."[50] Other females in Liberia joined because they were promised cash, education, or jobs (and would be willing to take up arms again to escape poverty).[51] The UN, in their research on the conflict in Sierra Leone, found that while some women joined the armed forces voluntarily, most were forced to join and almost all were forced to take drugs. Many of them remain addicted today. The UN argues that these women bear a triple burden because they were forced to fight and then when the war was over they were ostracized by society for having been a combatant and were marginalized for having been sexually violated.[52] A young woman who was recruited as a child soldier into the Lord's Resistance Army in Uganda told the international child aid agency, Plan, that the war followed her home: "People say we have ghosts attached to us because we have killed."[53] And another young woman, Bintu from Liberia, told Plan that she was abducted by soldiers when she was a child and raped repeatedly during her captivity and "service" as a child soldier.[54]

Finally, because girls are seen as victims, not as combatants, these girl soldiers are being ignored in the disarmament, demobilization, and reintegration (DDR) plans being conducted by the international community at the end of a conflict. For instance, in Sierra Leone, 6,052 boys went through DDR, while only 506 girls did.[55] The result of this is that girls who have been socialized to kill, have seen untold horrors, and are ostracized by their community after the war are not receiving any assistance in reintegrating back into life after war. Boys, because they are assumed to be the vast majority of combatants (although this isn't always the case) are receiving the vast majority of the training, schooling, and reintegration efforts (discussed in the next section), while girls are left to fend for themselves and the children they often bore during the conflict. While the presence of female combatants in armed conflicts forces us to rethink women's roles in armed conflicts; they clearly are not solely victims nor do they all think of themselves as such, but it would be a mistake to see this new role as one on a path toward liberation.

What Happens to the Boys?

While this chapter is primarily focused on the sexual violence experienced by females during war, we find it important to discuss the boys and men who have been trained to commit this violence. What happens to them when the armed conflicts are over? How can we expect sexual violence (and violence in general) to end when wars are over if generations of men and boys have been taught that violence is acceptable? While this topic alone could be a book, we will attempt to highlight a few of the key concerns and issues with child soldiers and with reintegrating boys and men back into society who have been trained to rape, mutilate, and kill.

Child soldiers are a fairly recent phenomenon. For most of history a general rule of warfare was that children would not be conscripted, especially for combat.[56] The reasons for this were based on both principal and pragmatism.

Most cultures believed that it was not appropriate for children to carry weapons and engage in warfare and, pragmatically speaking, most children could not physically carry premodern weapons.[57] There are some exceptions to this rule, but as Singer notes, "while there were isolated instances where children did serve in armies or other groups at war, a general norm held against child soldiers across the last four millennia of warfare."[58] In the late twentieth century this all began to change as nonstate militias began to recruit (often via abduction) child soldiers, the majority in most cases being boys. One of the most well-known examples of the use of child soldiers is in Sierra Leone. It is estimated that 80 percent of the forces of the Revolutionary United Front, the militia that instigated the violence, were children ages seven to fourteen.[59] The RUF was not the only group to use child soldiers in this conflict; all sides did, and it is estimated that close to ten thousand of the fighters in Sierra Leone were children.[60] Sierra Leone is but one place where child soldiers have been used extensively. Other countries that have made use of child soldiers span the globe and include, but are not limited to, Algeria, Angola, Bosnia, Cambodia, the Central African Republic (the Congo), Chechnya, Colombia, Lebanon, Liberia, Kosovo, Nepal, Rwanda, and Turkey (in the Kurdish Worker's Party). Child soldiers are used extensively by nonstate actors (rebel groups, militias, ethnic groups) with one study finding that 60 percent of nonstate armed forces (77 of 129) use child soldiers (the United Nations estimates this to be about 300,000 child soldiers).[61] But they are also used by state military and paramilitary forces that are currently at peace (the UN estimates this number to be around half a million).[62] Finally, it is important to note that these child soldiers are not solely made up of children on the verge of adulthood; their ranks include vast numbers of children age fifteen and under. Singer, in his seminal work on child soldiers, finds that "Twenty-three percent of the armed organizations in the world (84 total) use children age fifteen and under in combat roles. Eighteen percent (64) use children twelve and under."[63] Child soldiers are becoming the norm and are presenting the world with new challenges.

Child soldiers have normally been abducted or have "chosen" to join because their parents have been killed and they have no other recourse. While surveys have shown that many children are joining voluntarily, Singer argues that to phrase their joining as voluntary is misleading—children are defined as children because they are deemed to be unable to make mature decisions (like the decision to go to war and risk one's life).[64] Many child soldiers are fed alcohol and drugs and often are victims of sexual abuse (both girls and boys, although the number of girls is higher). One boy in Sierra Leone, Abu, reports that he and thirty other young boys were kidnapped in 1991, forced to join rebel forces backed by Liberia's Charles Taylor, and fed alcohol and drugs while being trained to kill. He tells his story like this:

> People were fleeing from the fighting. They raided the place. They took all the
> young men. I was about 13.... First of all, they made us carry loads, things that

were stolen when they raided. If you did not do it, they would kill you....That was the first killing I saw. That made me silent and made me obey orders."[65]

Another young man in Guatemala reports:

they killed my parents in front of me, my uncle's hands were cut off and my sister was raped in front of us by their commander called "Spare no Soul." After all this happened, they told us, the younger boys, to join them. If not, they were going to kill us.[66]

These stories highlight many of the key themes that surround the recruitment of child soldiers in armed conflict. The recruitment is often forced, and when abduction is not the method, joining is often the result of children seeing no other option aside from death.

Child soldiers are not just fetching water and cleaning weapons—child soldiers are trained to mutilate and kill. Many have been forced to kill their parents and family members, have mutilated citizens, have cut unborn fetuses out of pregnant women, and have disemboweled victims and eaten their organs. We discussed women and girl soldiers earlier and the difficulties surrounding reintegrating them back into society; now we will look at the problems associated with reintegrating into society those boys who have been trained to live a life of violence.

Most efforts to reintegrate boys and men back into society have focused on providing psychological help as well as educational training. The psychological problems faced by former boy soldiers are great. One study found that "as many as 97 percent of child soldiers may suffer from PTSD, regardless of the time they spent in violence."[67] In Bukavu, Congo, one facility is staffed with counselors who strive to help the boys "'discharge negative energy,' teach them respect for women, find out and encourage their aspirations, and eventually place them with relatives or foster parents."[68] The counselors note that the boys have been severely traumatized and that they, the counselors, end up traumatized as well.[69] The extreme trauma suffered by former combatants is a pervasive theme in all reports of efforts to reintegrate boy and adult male soldiers back into society. It is a challenge that will remain for years to come. And for male combatants who suffered sexual violence, the road to recovery is even tougher. Recent research done by the Harvard Humanitarian Initiative at Harvard University indicates that male combatants who suffered sexual violence have worse mental health outcomes than the general population and than other combatants. This finding, the authors argue, compels the international community to rework its gender-based programs to deal with males who have suffered sexual violence as combatants during war.[70] Trauma is compounded for children who either lost their parents or whose parents do not wish to be reunited with their former combatant children. Thus the psychological trauma suffered by male combatants (as well as females, discussed earlier) is far-reaching and unimaginable, and the timeline for recovery is lengthy, and possibly never-ending.[71]

Education and vocational training is also seen as key to helping former combatants, and many efforts have focused on providing this education. The challenges are extensive, as many of these children have missed years of schooling and lack a basic primary education (they are often illiterate and have no basic math skills). In Liberia, demobilized fighters were given money ($300) and scholarships that could be used for either vocational training or three years of formal education.[72] And Sierra Leone has implemented a fairly successful education program aimed at former soldiers who need to catch up. The program provides intensive six-month schooling designed to get former fighters up to par with students in their age cohort, so that they are not going to school with children years younger than them. A problem that schools are facing, however, is that parents do not wish to send their children to a school that has former combatants in it. In Liberia, one school, St. Peter's Episcopal School, struggles to overcome its bad reputation. St. Peter's principal, Edward Fayia, notes that "Other schools refused to accept (ex-combatants) students because they threatened to burn the building.... [I]f you saw what they did to this country—small, small children. Some parents were very skeptical about sending ordinary children here."[73] Another problem is that many of the programs instituted at the end of armed conflicts have directed most of their funding and efforts toward adults. It is not clear yet, and may not be for years to come, what the impact of these reintegration efforts will be. But in countries with struggling economies and few employment options after school, the outlook is not bright. One boy who fought in Sierra Leone and received some schooling through a UN program left school because he "missed the fighters life, 'we used to be free, go to the clubs, get money, get women.'"[74]

CONCLUSION

Sexual violence against women and girls has been a tool of warfare for centuries and will likely continue to be used in the future. However, rape and sexual enslavement are now considered crimes against humanity, and thus perpetrators can be tried in international courts and potentially convicted. Further, international groups like Human Rights Watch and Amnesty International are working diligently to pressure governments to prosecute incidents of sexual violence during war and in refugee camps to end such incidents and are working to educate the public at large about these crimes. These groups also are monitoring and pressuring international organizations, like UNHCR, to enforce their regulations on gender-based violence strictly. These efforts provide some relief to women seeking to rebuild their lives after living through the horrors of war and refugee status. The use of child soldiers in recent conflicts has added to the horrors of war and has presented new challenges to the international community. The success of their response remains to be seen.

A Typical Rape in Darfur

In March 2004 a sixteen-year-old young woman in West Darfur was out collecting firewood for her family when three armed men on camels surrounded her. Two men held her down and tied her hands while the other proceeded to rape her; they then each took turns raping her. When the rapes were over, the young girl returned home and told her family about what had just taken place. Her family kicked her out of the house, instructing her that she had to build her own hut away from them. This young girl was also engaged to be married, but upon finding out about the rapes her fiancée ended the engagement, saying that she was no longer clean and that she was disgraced. The rapes resulted in a pregnancy; when she was eight months pregnant the police came to her home and forcibly brought her to the police station, where they proceeded to question her about her pregnancy. She told them that she had been raped, but they did not care. They told her that since she was not married she would be delivering the baby illegally; they then beat her with whips and put her in jail. While in jail she met many other women in her situation. Her time in jail was spent cooking and cleaning for the policemen. She and the other women had to walk to a well four times a day to fetch water; the only food the women received was that which they could find during the day, and the only water they received was that which they could drink while at the well. The young girl spent ten days in jail and still was required to pay a fine of 20,000 Sudanese dinars ($65). She gave birth to her child soon after.[i]

This story was told by a young woman to interviewers with the medical group Médecins Sans Frontières (MSF; Doctors Without Borders), which has been working extensively in Darfur to help all victims of the violence there. Her story is, unfortunately, not unique. It painfully illustrates the multiple horrors that women victims of sexual violence must endure: the rape(s) itself, the rejection by family, the impossibility of marriage, lack of recourse with the state (and abuse by state actors), mental anguish, malnourishment, and rejection by society as a whole. On top of these horrors, many victims suffer physical wounds, such as fistulas. Groups like MSF are working hard to assist these victims in Sudan, but unfortunately some of their work has recently been halted. The International Criminal Court in the Hague issued a war crimes warrant in March 2009 for President Bashir of Sudan. The Sudanese government seemed unfazed by the warrant, saying that they would pay it no heed. But MSF said that they were told by the Sudanese government to shut down their operations and get out of the country shortly after the warrant was issued.

---

[i] Médecins Sans Frontières, "The Crushing Burden of Rape: Sexual Violence in Darfur," A Briefing Paper, Amsterdam, March 8, 2005.

FOR MORE INFORMATION

Amnesty International, http://www.amnestyusa.org/violence-against-women/sexual-violence/page.do?id=1108442

Human Rights Education Associates: Crimes of War; an Educators Guide: Sexual Violence, http://www.hrea.org/index.php?base_id=126

IRIN, The Shame of War: Sexual Violence Against Women and Girls in Conflict, http://www.irinnews.org/IndepthMain.aspx?IndepthId=53&ReportId=71974

Sexual Violence: An Invisible War Crime, http://www.un.org/ecosocdev/geninfo/afrec/v0118n04/184sierraleone.htm

Stop Rape Now: United Nations Action Against Sexual Violence in Conflict, http://www.stoprapenow.org

United Nations Development Fund: Facts and Figures on Violence Against Women, http://www.unifem.org/gender_issues/violence_against_women/facts_figures.php

WomenWarPeace.org, http://www.womenwarpeace.org/issues/violence; a portal on women, peace, and security

At the End of a Gun: Women and War—This film looks at the impact of the separatist war in Sri Lanka on women's lives.

All Different, All Equal—This documentary examines the global progress toward ending violence against women both during war and in general.

Lumo—One Young Woman's Struggle to Heal in a Nation Beset by War—This documentary film follows Lumo, a twenty-year-old woman in Eastern Congo who was raped by soldiers. As a result of the rape she develops a fistula, her fiancée abandons her, and she makes her way to a hospital for rape survivors on the border with Rwanda.

Women in War Zones: Sexual Violence in the Congo—This documentary looks at the sexual violence committed against women during the war in Eastern Congo.

12

⤙◦⤚

Women and Physical Autonomy

I was taken to a very dark room and undressed. I was blindfolded and stripped naked. . . . I was forced to lie flat on my back by four strong women, two holding tight to each leg. Another woman sat on my chest to prevent my upper body from moving. . . . I was genitally mutilated with a blunt penknife. After the operation no one was allowed to aid me to walk. . . . These were terrible times for me. Each time I wanted to urinate I was forced to stand upright. The urine would spread over the wound and would cause fresh pain all over again. . . . Afterwards I haemorrhaged and became anaemic. This was attributed to witchcraft. I suffered for a long time from acute vaginal infections.[1]

Increasing reports of parents beating daughters who flunk the exams have given some virginity testing supporters pause and opponents new ammunition. Publicly labeling girls virgins is also not without danger. An African folk belief that sex with a virgin can cure AIDS puts virgins here at risk of rape. Already, a few certified virgins in KwaZulu-Natal Province have been attacked by HIV-positive men hoping for the spurious cure. The girls managed to escape.[2]

On June 22, during a Mastoi tribal council meeting . . . four men, including one of the tribal council members, allegedly raped Mukhtaran Bibi, a thirty year old member of the Gujjar tribe. The rape, which occurred in the presence of a large number of villagers, was intended as "punishment" for the conduct of her brother . . . who had been seen with an unchaperoned woman from the Mastoi tribe.[3]

These three quotes all relate different tales: One is about female genital cutting, one is about virginity testing, and the third is about a woman being raped as punishment for her brother's indiscretions. So what could they all share in common? They all share the fact that women and girls often have no say regarding what is done with their bodies. Women often lack physical autonomy, a basic human right that is enshrined in many international treaties and declarations. Women's bodies are used as scapegoats for the indiscretions of male relatives, are mutilated to control their sexuality, are stoned or flogged for breaking laws that do not apply to men, and are forcibly examined to ensure their chastity. In this chapter we will examine three practices that violate women's physical autonomy: female genital cutting, virginity tests, and physical violence against women either as a form of punishment for their own or their family's actions or as domestic violence. We conclude with a discussion of international and domestic efforts to address these problems.

FEMALE GENITAL CUTTING

Female genital cutting (FGC), also known as female circumcision, is the removal of all or part of the female genitalia. There are different types of FGC. The most common form of FGC is an excision of the clitoris accompanied by a partial or total excision of the labia minora. It is estimated that about 85 percent of genital cuttings are of this type.[4] The most severe form of genital cutting, and least widely practiced (about 15 percent of all) is an infibulation, which "consists of a clitoridectomy (where all, or part of, the clitoris is removed), excision (removal of all, or part of, the labia minora), and cutting of the labia majora to create raw surfaces, which are then stitched or held together in order to form a cover over the vagina when they heal. A small hole is left to allow urine and menstrual blood to escape."[5] No matter which form of FGC is done, the procedure is extremely invasive.

The age at which the procedure is performed, which procedure is performed, and exactly how it is performed depend on what country the girl lives in, which ethnic group she belongs to, her family's socioeconomic status, and whether she lives in a rural or urban setting. The procedure can be done anytime after birth through a woman's first pregnancy but is most commonly performed in prepubescence, between the ages of four and eight. The procedure can be done in a girl's home, at a neighbor's home, or at a site with some special significance like a tree or river. Very occasionally it is done at a hospital or health clinic. FGC is usually done to a group of girls of the same age at the same time, although occasionally it is done to a girl alone. The procedure is generally performed by women, most of whom have no medical training. They are village elders, healers, and occasionally trained midwives or doctors. Girls often have little information beforehand regarding what is going to happen to them, and the procedure is often carried out with some type of cutting instrument, ranging from a razorblade or a penknife to broken glass and tin can lids. Very seldom is there any kind of anesthesia to numb the area or any type of antibiotics to prevent infection afterward.

The World Health Organization estimates that as of 2008, 100–140 million women had undergone the procedure worldwide.[6] FGC is most prevalent in Africa (it is done in at least twenty-eight African nations), and it is also prevalent in some countries in the Middle East and Asia. Its usage varies widely from a low of 5 percent in Ghana and Niger to highs of 92 percent and 97 percent in Mali and North Sudan, respectively. In Europe, the United States, and Latin America it occurs primarily in immigrant communities. Further, the United Nations Fund for Population Activities estimates that every year another 3 million girls are at risk.[7] Why is FGC practiced? What could be the reason for performing such a grisly procedure on young girls?

The most common explanation for why FGC is conducted is tradition; it is part of a community's culture and custom. As one Egyptian woman commented about her own daughters, "Of course I shall have them circumcised, exactly as their parents, grandparents, and sisters were circumcised. This is our custom."[8] Further, it is often argued that it is an initiation right into adulthood and that women who are not circumcised will not be considered adults in the village and will not be allowed to perform tasks like cooking, fetching water, or participating in certain dances because they will not be seen as "clean." Further, uncircumcised women are often not considered fit for marriage or, if married, will be ostracized by their husbands. On top of this there is concern that uncircumcised women will be too sexual and mentally unbalanced. As Lukman Hakim, chairman of the Assalaam Foundation in Indonesia, an Islamic educational and social services organization, stated, "One, it will stabilize her libido.... Two, it will make a woman look more beautiful in the eyes of her husband. And three, it will balance her psychology."[9] While there is no evidence to support the first and third points, educating people around these issues is a slow process. Later we will discuss efforts, many successful, by groups such as Tostan to educate communities about the impact of FGC on women's bodies.

Some of the other rationalizations for FGC are grounded in inaccurate understanding of the female genitalia or of how the female reproductive system works. In some cultures, parts of the female genitalia are considered male and thus must be removed. As one Egyptian woman stated, "We are circumcised and insist on circumcising our daughters so that there is no mixing between male and female.... An uncircumcised woman is put to shame by her husband, who calls her 'you with clitoris.' People say she is like a man. Her organ would prick the man."[10] Others believe that FGC enhances fertility, that an unmutilated woman cannot get pregnant, and that it makes childbirth safer.[11] As noted earlier, education to eradicate these misunderstandings is integral. But it is crucial to remember that people tend to believe information that fits into their cultural lens, so change may be slow in coming in some areas.

Fundamentally, FGC is also about control over women's sexuality. FGC allows a man to know that his bride is a virgin at the time of marriage. Many societies believe that FGC decreases a woman's desire for sex, thus decreasing the likelihood that she will be promiscuous before or after marriage. In some societies women are sewn up again after intercourse. And, in many societies it is argued that their religion dictates that it be done to keep women chaste until marriage. Yet, although FGC is often practiced in Muslim and some Christian communities, neither the Quran nor the Bible say that women should be circumcised. And numerous Muslim leaders are now speaking out against its connection to Islam and are condemning its practice. In Egypt and Kenya, many Muslim leaders have publicly stated that FGC is a cultural tradition that has no

A girl bleeds after a female circumcision ritual in Kenya. SOURCE: Stephanie Welsh/Getty Images

ties to (and actually predates) the teachings of Islam.[12] This is a crucial step to eradicating FGC. Where people feel a deep connection to their religious and cultural belief systems they are likely to listen to those they respect and look up to. The role of religious leaders in ending FGC will be quite important if we truly wish to see this practice eliminated.

The impacts of FGC on women range from physical to emotional to social. The physical impacts include the possibility of hemorrhaging after the incision, urine retention, ulceration of the genital region, injury to adjacent tissue, severe pain and shock, and damage to the urethra that can result in urinary incontinence, sexual dysfunction, urinary tract infection, infertility, and complications during childbirth.[13] The procedure also increases the risk of contracting AIDS when unsterilized instruments are used on multiple girls. Statistics on how often these complications occur are scarce because these complications are not often reported. Thus, opponents of FGC say these complications are frequent and proponents argue that they are rare. Emotional and psychological scars also result from the procedure and may include shock and an increased tendency for girls afterward to be more docile and calm. Women also report feelings of anxiety and terror, humiliation, and betrayal.[14] Some women also note that they feel shame and a physical incompleteness after the procedure. Princess Euphrasia Etta Ojong from the South West Province of Cameroon, who now campaigns to end the practice, states that "Today, I feel ashamed when I am with other women. I do not feel like a complete woman."[15] (Conversely, some women report feeling accepted by society once the procedure has been completed and they have survived.[16]) Finally, there are some social scars that result from FGC. As Princess Ojong notes, "Even the boys from my area are not interested in me because they think that the sexual urge is not there since I was circumcised."[17] Thus the scars to women are many and the benefits to society are primarily the maintenance of a tradition grounded largely in inaccurate religious interpretations or beliefs about the female reproductive system.

VIRGINITY TESTS

Virginity tests are tests where the hymen of a girl is examined to see if it is still intact. If it is intact then the girl is deemed to be a virgin. The administrators of the test make no allowances for the fact that the hymen can be torn in ways other than intercourse and some girls are not born with one at all. The practice is used in some African and Asian nations such as South Africa and India, has been used in the past in Turkey (and continues to generate political discussion), and was also proposed in Jamaica and Indonesia.

Why are virginity tests conducted? Like FGC, virginity tests are a way to limit women's physical autonomy and to control their sexuality. The rationale for using them, however, is often the claim that it is in women's best interests to abstain from intercourse because of the risk of AIDS. This is the cry that is being used in many African nations such as South Africa, which conducted these tests on both girls and boys as young as six (although most forms of virginity testing were banned by the parliament in 2005). In 2004, President Zuma of South Africa spoke out in favor of virginity tests as a way to curb the spread of AIDS/HIV and decrease teenage pregnancy. He further argued, in what has become a controversial statement, that if girls valued their family's honor, then they would abstain from sex: "Girls knew that their virginity was their family's treasure.... They would only have sex when permitted to do so by their families after marriage."[18] But, while the practice has been essentially outlawed in South Africa, Zulus actively defy the ban and continue to do testing and issue certificates to girls who pass.[19] Some Zulu girls appear to be in favor of the testing and the celebrations that take place for the girls who have passed. One girl commented that "They [the South Africans] didn't come up with it [virginity testing].... So why should they stop it? It could just be that they don't give the Zulu culture dignity."[20] But when pressed about how they would feel if they had failed the test one said, regarding the usefulness of virginity testing, that "I really don't know what to believe."[21] And another fourteen-year-old girl who failed her test was devastated and told reporters that "I feel very bad because I haven't done anything."[22] But Zulu leaders state that they will continue to practice the tradition of virginity testing because it is an important part of their culture, one that the state has no right to try to end.

In Zimbabwe, a country with one of the highest rates of AIDS/HIV infection in the world, voluntary virginity tests were recently imposed by Chief Naboth Makoni in the Makoni district in a controversial attempt to combat AIDS. His order also includes men providing documented proof that they are HIV negative if they wish to marry a "documented" virgin.[23] Chief Makoni argues, in response to critiques of his policy, that "it is unfair to allow a marriage between a person living with the virus and a virgin who has tested negative.... So far 3,500 girls have been tested, on their own insistence, and some have been awarded certificates.... That's why we're demanding proof of a man's HIV-status if he wants to marry any of these angels."[24] The district also holds a "feast for the virgins" once a month that is designed to honor those girls who have passed the test. People complain that anyone can forge a document and so there really is no proof that the men who claim to be HIV free truly are. Thus the men are on the winning end, so to speak, but the girls who fail the tests, even if they are virgins, must suffer the public humility and the stigma that result from the failure.

Virginity tests were also recently proposed in Jamaica by two legislators who felt that they (as well as sterilizing women with three or more children) would help curb the growing number of unwanted pregnancies and thus the welfare burden on the government.[25] And in Turkey, where the tests were proposed again in 2001 after their use had been banned, advocates claimed that they would protect minors from prostitution and underage sex.[26]

While preventing AIDS, prostitution, and unwanted pregnancies is generally viewed as a positive end, the method is suspect. Virginity tests impact girls in a few ways. First, in African nations now using them there is some evidence that rape is on the rise since it is believed that having sex with a virgin will cure AIDS. Thus many girls are not safe on their way to and from school or doing other daily chores. Public celebrations of the girls who have passed their tests is akin to advertising which girls would be good to rape. There are also reports of parents beating children who failed the test and girls feeling isolated and outcast by their community if they fail (and it must be noted that there is no foolproof way to prove that a girl is a virgin).[27] Second, teaching girls to remain virgins is just that, teaching them to be virgins; it does nothing to teach them how to prevent AIDS, which is arguably a crucial step in curbing the spread of the AIDS epidemic.

Given that AIDS is often spread to married women by their husbands who do not remain faithful or who come to the marriage already infected, virginity testing is going to do little to truly curb the spread of AIDS. Chief Makoni did not have a very good answer when asked about this. He could only say that failed marriages are usually the result of women who come to the marriage not a virgin, that "if a young woman is not a virgin she is considered to have less value. This often leads to her being abused by her husband, and sometimes results in divorce."[28] Virginity testing as a way to combat AIDS puts the onus on women and girls and absolves men of any responsibility for the spread of AIDS. As Netsai Mushonga of the Harare-based Women Coalition of Zimbabwe (a nongovernmental organization) pointed out, "Virginity testing leaves a man free to roam, without enforcing any similar checks and balance on his, while it strips girls of their dignity."[29]

Finally, in Turkey, the tests were going to be used as part of the admissions procedure for nursing school, and girls who failed the tests would be denied admittance. Thus girls' education was going to be held captive by the state. And, some girls attempted suicide when they thought they would be subjected to the tests.[30] When death is seen as preferable to the method used to protect girls from supposed evils, then it becomes necessary to examine the method closely. Finally, it impacts girls in that their bodies, and hence their futures, are subject to regulation by the state. While some boys have been subject to these virginity tests, no one is suggesting that castration be used as a method to curb unwanted pregnancies or that male virginity be required for admission to university. Although these tests are no longer being used in Turkey and the proposal in Jamaica appears to have foundered, they are still used in countries in Africa and India.

WOMEN'S BODIES AS WHIPPING POSTS

Women's bodies are also often used, literally, as whipping posts for their partner's anger or for their family's actions or their own. Stoning and flogging, rape, domestic abuse, and honor killings are common actions inflicted on women on a daily basis. Here will we address stonings and honor killings and attempt to understand why they are used.

Stoning, or lapidation, is a method of execution where a group of people throw stones at an individual until he or she is dead. Stoning as a method of execution is an ancient one. There are records of it across cultures and across religions. The practice was used by the ancient Greeks to execute adulterers, prostitutes, and murderers. Discussion of stoning can be found in the Jewish tradition in the Torah and the Talmud and in the Old Testament of the Bible, which both Christians and Jews follow. There is no mention of stoning in the Quran, but the practice of stoning has increasingly become associated with Islam, primarily because of its use in Iran (to be discussed later). Stoning is a controversial topic among Muslim clerics. Some argue that it should not be used because it is not prescribed in the Quran, and they add that any action that reflects poorly upon Islam should not be practiced. Others, however, cite passages of the Hadith, the acts and sayings of the Prophet Mohammed, as evidence that stoning is a legitimate punishment for certain acts. The Hadith prescribes stoning specifically for Jews found guilty of adultery, and others add that Mohammed had both men and women stoned in his time, so he must have intended it to be used.[31] Stoning is used today as a "legal" form of punishment for the crime of adultery in Afghanistan, Iran, Nigeria, Pakistan, Sudan, and the United Arab Emirates. The states of Iraq and Pakistan have never officially carried out a stoning decree, but there is evidence that local communities have done so on their own. Stoning violates a number of international treaties, including the International Convention of Civil and Political Rights (ICCPR; 1966), which states that in states that have not abolished the death penalty, the death penalty may only be used for the most serious crimes, of which adultery is not one. The ICCPR goes on to state that no state shall use cruel and unusual punishments. Iran, Iraq, Sudan, and Afghanistan are all signatories to the ICCPR. The other international treaty that addresses the issue of stoning is The Convention Against Torture and Other Cruel, Inhuman, or Degrading Treatment or Punishment (1987). Over fifty countries are signatories to this convention, including numerous Muslim nations. But as you will read, the use of stoning continues despite these international conventions and even in light of laws in some states that ban it.

In December 2001, the criminal court in Nyala, southern Darfur, Sudan, sentenced Abok Alfau Akok (a Christian) to death by stoning for having engaged in sex outside of marriage. She was pregnant at the time of the sentence. An appeals court later overturned this sentence and "reduced" the punishment to seventy-five lashes. The lashings were carried out immediately upon the decision being handed down. At the time of the lashings she had already given birth. No action was taken against the man with whom she allegedly had sexual relations. In March 2002, a Shari'a (Islamic) court in the state of Katsina in northern Nigeria sentenced Amina Lawal to death by stoning for having committed adultery. Amina Lawal was pregnant at the time of the sentence and her pregnancy was taken as evidence of her having committed adultery. Amina Lawal gave birth more than nine months after she had obtained a divorce from her husband. In August 2002, an appeals court upheld the sentence. In September 2003, another appeals court finally overturned the stoning sentence, arguing that the conviction was invalid because she was pregnant at the time the conviction was handed down. One can assume that had she not been pregnant then the conviction would not have been considered invalid by the appeals court. The alleged father repeatedly asserted that the baby was not his. Three men testified that he had not had sexual relations with Lawal, and under Shari'a law this was enough to corroborate his story and free him.

Lawal's stoning sentence is the second in Nigeria since 2000, when more than twelve of Nigeria's thirty-six states adopted strict Islamic Shari'a law. The sentence of Safiya Hussaini Tungar-Tudu was reversed by an appeals court in March 2002 after a great deal of international grassroots pressure and a warning from the president of Nigeria, Olusegun Obasanjo, who warned the states that Nigeria faced international isolation as a result of the case.[32] And while stoning sentences have thus far not been carried out, flogging (whipping) sentences for charges of having sex outside of marriage have been. In September 2000 in Nigeria, Bariya Ibrahim Magazu was charged with sex outside of marriage and received a flogging of one hundred lashes in January 2001, even though an appeal was pending.[33]

In December 2008 two men convicted of adultery were stoned to death in Iran despite a moratorium on the use of stoning handed down by the state's judiciary chief Ayattollah Mahmoud Hashemi-Sharoudi in 2002. As per Iranian law, they were buried up to their waist in a pit, and then people hurled rocks at them (rocks that, according to the law, must not be large enough to kill them immediately) until they died. If they could escape the pit, then they were free. A spokesman for Iran's judiciary said the moratorium on stoning was purely advisory and not an edict; "Judges can't act based simply on advisories by the head of the judiciary, since judges are independent," he said.[34] Human rights activists, like those with Amnesty International, argue that eight women and two men are still awaiting stoning in Iran, despite last August's commutation of stoning sentences for four people (instead of stoning two received three hundred lashes each and the other two were sentenced to ten years in jail).[35] Amnesty International notes that, while both men and women receive stoning sentences, stoning disproportionately impacts women. They note that the majority of those awaiting stoning are women and that the court system does not treat women the same as men. Women often have unfair trials, largely as a result of their higher rates of illiteracy, which lead them to be more likely to sign confessions for crimes they did not commit.[36] Further, the way stoning is implemented is different for men and women. In Iran, a woman who is stoned to death is buried up to her neck, whereas a man is only buried up to his waist, thus giving him a greater ability to escape.

Finally, in 2008, in Kismayo, Somalia, a thirteen-year-old girl who had been raped was stoned to death. A witness to the stoning told the BBC that she first pleaded for her life, crying, "Don't kill me, don't kill me."[37] She was then forcibly placed in a hole and buried up to her neck; fifty people stoned her until she died. Amnesty International reports that while she was initially reported to be twenty-three years old, she was in actuality thirteen.[38] According to the girl's family, she was raped by three men; when her family tried to report the rape, the girl was accused of adultery and detained. The port of Kismayo is not under government control but rather under the control of forces loyal to the country's main radical Islamist insurgent organization. Thus, while stoning a thirteen-year-old to death is illegal under Islamic law, these forces have no regard for the law. And while it is reported that citizens present at the stoning were mortified at the action, they did nothing to stop it, fearing for their lives. One boy who ran forward was shot by armed forces. As we can see, punishments that have been deemed cruel and inhumane by the international community continue to be imposed on women in numerous locales.

Another punishment occasionally inflicted upon women who defy their family's code of honor is an honor killing. Honor killings occur when women behave in ways that are unacceptable to their family or as a way to deal with the alleged indiscretions of their male relatives who have brought dishonor to the family. As the story at the beginning of the chapter relates, women's bodies are used as literal whipping posts for the actions of their male relatives. In honor killings, a woman may be killed (or severely maimed) by a relative or a hired hit man, as was the case with Samia Sarwar, who was gunned down in her attorney's office in April 1999 in Pakistan because she was seeking a divorce from her estranged husband.[39] More recently in 2006, a sixteen-year-old Turkish girl was shot by her family for the perceived dishonor she brought to them from a pregnancy and birth that resulted from a rape. She had tried to hide the rape but it was discovered when she was hospitalized for a severe headache. Because of threats made by the family to try to get her out of the hospital, the hospital decided to keep her and only let her go home after the birth when her father promised that no harm would come to her. She was shot dead by her brother shortly after she returned home.[40] In a rare occurrence, the entire family was convicted, three of them receiving life sentences (including the brother who shot her). Normally these killings are not dealt with in the judicial system since they are seen as family matters. Or often the family member chosen to do the killing is the youngest male, since male youth often receive much lighter sentences (sometimes as little as three months in jail) than adult family members do. Finally, in 2007, a Kurdish Muslim woman was killed by her father and uncle in Great Britain. Both were arrested and convicted, which is not generally the case in countries in the developing world. Women may also be maimed by male relatives because of actions the men deem as having brought dishonor to the family. Specifically, in South East Asia male relatives often throw acid on women who have allegedly brought dishonor to the family. The resulting injuries are gruesome.

According to reports submitted to the United Nations Commission on Human Rights, honor killings have been documented in Bangladesh, Great Britain, Brazil, Ecuador, Egypt, India, Israel, Italy, Jordan, Pakistan, Morocco, Sweden, Turkey, and Uganda.[41] In Pakistan alone it has been estimated that every day three women, including victims of rape, are killed via honor killings.[42] Among countries that do not submit reports to the UN, honor killings were condoned in Afghanistan under the Taliban and have been reported in Iraq and Iran. Honor killings have even been alleged in the United States, as the case of Yaser Abdel Said, discussed in the text box for this chapter, indicates. Honor killings typically occur in countries where the notion of women as property and as a vessel of the family still dominates, and their use travels across cultures and religions. In some places they are referred to as honor killings, but in other places their form may take that of a dowry death (when a bride is murdered because her dowry is seen as insufficient), as in India, or as a crime of passion, as in Latin America. According to UNICEF, more than five thousand brides in India are killed annually because their dowrys are not big enough, according to their fiancées.[43] These acts are condoned by family and friends, including female relatives, which is part of the reason they are so hard to eradicate. As Zaynab Nawaz, a program assistant for Amnesty International, points out, "Females in the family—mothers, mothers-in-law, sisters and cousins—frequently support the attacks. It's a community mentality."[44] The presence of this community mentality exacerbates the notion that women are property and that these acts should be dealt with via the family and not via the judicial system. When women are viewed as the property of the males in their family they have no autonomy whatsoever. Further, the very idea that a human is a piece of property makes it easier to think about exterminating her—people can do with their property as they wish. Thus, it is crucial that laws that perpetuate women's status as the property of the males in their life are removed and that women are educated about and assisted in the securing of employment because we know that when women have an independent source of income they have more autonomy in the household. Until then, women who engage in sex outside of marriage or defy their family's moral code (something that men are allowed to do) may receive the ultimate punishment for their actions—death.

Why are all of these practices (FGC, virginity tests, stoning, and honor killings) committed upon women? While each abuse is different, a common thread that unites them is control. These physical abuses are all ways to control women's actions, whether sexual or otherwise. Stoning, flogging, and honor killings are generally used to punish women for having sex outside of marriage (or being accused of it) or for attempting to end a marriage. It is hoped that the possibility

---

Honor Killings Come to the United States

On January 1, 2008, Yaser Abdel Said, a taxi driver, took his two teenage daughters for a drive. He drove them to Irving, Texas, where he is alleged to have murdered them. The girls' aunt and close friends argue that he was angry with them for wanting to wear Western dress and for dating non-Muslim boys. In Jonesboro, Georgia, in July 2008, Chaudhry Rashid allegedly strangled his daughter, Sandeela, with a bungee cord for filing for a divorce from her husband (their arranged marriage had been conducted in Pakistan). In upstate New York in summer 2008, Waheed Allah Mohammad was charged with the attempted murder of his sister, who, he argued, had angered him because she was going out dancing, was wearing Western clothing, and was planning on moving to New York City. All of these murders took place on U.S. soil and arguably fit the definition of honor killings put forth in this chapter. While these murders appear to have been fairly actively discussed in the blogosphere, their coverage in mainstream U.S. newspapers was minimal. The little coverage there was focused on whether or not labeling them as honor killings was useful or not. The arguments against labeling them as such focused on the fact that the term distracts from the larger issues of patriarchy, male control, and domestic violence and that the term is inherently racist (because these killings get covered as a "Muslim" phenomenon, which they are not, as we have discussed in this chapter). Proponents of the term argue that if we classify honor killings as a form of domestic violence then we end up lumping crimes together that are not the same. The circumstances surrounding domestic violence are often different from those surrounding an honor killing. A man who beats his wife or kills his wife because she is having an affair may look similar to a father killing his married adult daughter who is having an affair, but the two cases are not the same. In an honor killing a woman is killed because she has disgraced her family's honor; this murder is not generally done by her husband but, rather, by her own blood family. Proponents of using the term "honor killings" argue that we need to look at these crimes as different from other killings because they have different motivations. Whatever the merits and demerits of the term, the fact is that honor killings, once seen as a phenomenon that occurred outside the United States, are now a U.S. phenomenon, too.

of such punishments will be a deterrent to women acting in an independent fashion. Thus, while these abuses are all different, they share a common thread—that men can and often do control women's bodies, thus leaving women lacking the most basic of human rights.

The impacts of these actions on women are many. At the extreme end is death. But in instances where death is not the result, the impact of FGC is physical, emotional, and psychological. Physically, flogging and the like leave women's bodies battered and bruised and, at times, permanently damaged. Emotionally and psychologically, these abuses leave women permanently scarred. The trauma of experiencing such abuses cannot be forgotten. And when death is the result, the impact is obvious—a human being has been denied her life to preserve the alleged honor of a family. The acceptance of these acts by all family members and by the community means that many women will continue to suffer similar fates in the future. At the end of the chapter we will discuss efforts to improve women's physical autonomy.

ADDRESSING WOMEN'S PHYSICAL AUTONOMY

A number of international conferences have been held in recent years regarding women's human rights. Further, a few international treaties ban violence against women and require signatories to respect the civil rights of all of their citizens. A few important declarations and treaties are the Universal Declaration of Human Rights, which is seen as the bedrock of the human rights system because it protects people from being subject to cruel and inhumane or degrading treatment; the UN Convention on the Elimination of All Forms of Violence Against Women (CEDAW), which provides specific steps for signatories to take to eliminate violence against women; the International Covenant on Civil and Political Rights, another important treaty in international law; and the 1993 United Nations World Conference on Human Rights, which called for the "elimination of violence against women in public and private life...and the eradication of any conflicts which may arise between the rights of women and the harmful effects of certain traditional or customary practices." [45] While there are other declarations, covenants, and treaties, these are among the most applicable to the issues addressed in this chapter.

These important works require nations (signatories) to protect women from the type of abuses that have been discussed in this chapter, but unfortunately many nations do not adhere to the terms of the treaties. In the absence of an international police force to enforce international law obligations, it is difficult to ensure compliance. Compliance, if it comes, often comes only after human rights organizations make public their violations and conduct a grassroots campaign regarding the infringement(s). Even then, there is no guarantee that the violation will not occur again. This is largely because the nation, assuming it wishes to end the practice, has a difficult time changing old cultural practices like FGC, honor killings, and even domestic violence, which are culturally accepted in many places, particularly in small towns and villages far from the capital. Even in the major cities, many people, including those in positions of power, still ascribe to views of women that permit the continuation of such actions. For instance, Human Rights Watch interviewed a policeman in Pakistan who believed that "in practically all cases of alleged rape, women had consented to the act of intercourse and then lied to incriminate their male partners."[46] Until societal views regarding women's rights change, international treaties and similar efforts will make little headway in eradicating the actions discussed in this chapter.

Possibly more promising than international treaties, declarations, and similar efforts are bans initiated by the state and/or local communities and individuals. For instance, at least fourteen countries in Africa have banned FGC, and many communities have replaced the act with a coming of age ceremony. Further, in 2003, the Pan African Committee on Traditional Practices met in Addis Ababa, Ethiopia. Delegates from thirty African countries attended and declared February 6 the international day on zero tolerance for FGC. And, in southwestern Cameroon, a local princess works to end the practice of FGC in her ethnic group, the Ejagam. Efforts like these may bear more fruit in the long run because they are less likely to be seen as imposed by the West.

Other efforts to end the practices discussed in this chapter are often initiated by human rights groups like Human Rights Watch and Amnesty International. Both groups monitor nations for abuses of international human rights treaties, write extensive reports detailing any abuses found, and then conduct campaigns to end the abuses. The campaigns often consist of writing letters to the leaders of nations found in violation, issuing press releases regarding the violations, and conducting grassroots campaigns in which citizens from around the world are educated about the issue and urged to write a letter to the nation in violation. Such efforts have arguably assisted in overturning the stoning sentences we discussed earlier and Turkey's efforts to reinstate virginity tests, but they are not as likely to be successful in eradicating FGC, domestic violence, and honor killings. This is largely because stoning and virginity tests are actions often initiated or at least under the control of the government. Actions by international groups that publicly humiliate a government in front of the international community may be effective. However, FGC, domestic violence, and honor killings are cultural practices over which the state often has little control. Certainly the state can pass laws outlawing them, educate police and doctors on how to handle domestic violence and other reports of violence against women, and conduct campaigns to educate the public about the inhumanity of such acts, but these efforts, while necessary steps, may be very slow in effecting change. And the efforts of human rights groups to pressure governments to do something about such practices may be of limited use. Nonetheless, their efforts are worthwhile since they educate people about the abuses, bring attention to the issue, and, in some instances, effect change.

CONCLUSION

In sum, there is a solid basis in international law for protecting women from the practices discussed in this chapter. Further, local efforts in many nations have sprung up to end the various practices discussed, and international human rights groups continue to work to educate the public about abuses and to urge nations to comply with international law. All of these efforts have met with varying levels of success. Arguably, local efforts will ultimately prove the most successful since they will not be seen by locals as attempts by the West to eradicate their culture. Ultimately, success will be attained only when citizens view such practices not only as unacceptable but also as unnecessary parts of their culture.

FOR MORE INFORMATION

CARE, http://www.care.org/newsroom/specialreports/fgc/index.asp; the site contains information on the work they do to end FGC

The Female Genital Cutting Education and Networking Project, http://www.fgmnetwork. org/intro/fgmintro.html

Human Rights Watch, http://www.hrw.org

International Campaign Against Honour Killings, http://www.stophonourkillings.com

Tostan, Community-Led Development, http://www.tostan.org; organization that works to end FGC

United Nations Development Fund for Women, http://www.unifem.org/gender_issues/ violence_against_women/facts_figures.php; facts and figures on violence against women

Death by Stoning: Justice, Punishment, and Human Rights—This ABC news program discusses the stoning case of Amina Lawal in Nigeria.

Ayse Onal. *Honour Killing: Stories of Men Who Killed* (Saqi Books: London, 2008). This book provides interviews with Turkish men who killed women in the name of honor.

Karen Tintori. *Unto the Daughters: The Legacy of an Honor Killing in a Sicilian-American Family* (St. Martin's Press: New York, 2007). In this book, Tintori tells the story of the honor killing of her great-aunt.

Notes

PREFACE

1. Najma Chowdury and Barbara J. Nelson, with Kathryn A. Carver, Nancy Johnson, and Paula L. O'Loughlin, "Redefining Politics: Patterns of Women's Engagement from a Global Perspective," in *Women and Politics Worldwide*, ed. Barbara J. Nelson and Najma Chowdury (New Haven, CT: Yale University Press, 1994), 10–15.
2. Maxine Molyneux as quoted in Ibid., 18.
3. For example, see Sonia E. Alvarez, *Engendering Democracy in Brazil: Women's Movements in Transition Politics* (Princeton, NJ: Princeton University Press, 1990).
4. See Ronald Inglehart, *The Silent Revolution: Changing Values and Political Styles Among Western Publics* (Princeton, NJ: Princeton University Press, 1977); Ronald Inglehart, *Culture Shift in Advanced Industrial Society* (Princeton, NJ: Princeton University Press, 1990); Ronald Inglehart, *Modernization and Postmodernization: Cultural, Economic and Political Change in 43 Societies* (Princeton, NJ: Princeton University Press, 1997).
5. Ronald Inglehart and Pippa Norris, *Rising Tide: Gender Equality and Cultural Change Around the World* (New York: Cambridge University Press, 2003), 36.
6. Ibid., 21.
7. "Beijing Declaration and Platform for Action. Fourth World Conference on Women," September 15, 1995, http://www.unesco.org/education/information/ nfsunesco/pdf/ BEIJIN_E.PDF (August 22, 2005).
8. Nancy F. Cott, *The Grounding of Modern Feminism* (New Haven, CT: Yale University Press, 1987), 4–5.
9. Lynne E. Ford, *Women and Politics: The Pursuit of Equality* (New York: Houghton Mifflin, 2002), 20–27.
10. Mayra Buvinic, "Promoting Gender Equality," *International Social Science Journal* 162 (1999): 573.
11. Ford, *Women and Politics*, 8.
12. Ibid., xiii.

CHAPTER 1

1. Frederick Nzwili, "Women Candidates in Kenya Assaulted, Under-Funded," December 27, 2002, Women's eNews, www.womensenews.org (December 27, 2002).

2. Ibid., 1.

3. Ibid., 1.

4. Ibid., 1.

5. "Women in National Parliaments," http://www.ipu.org/wmn–e/world.htm (October 13, 2008).

6. "Women Rulers Currently in Office," http://www.terra.es/personal2/monolith/00women5.htm (October 14, 2008).

7. "Women in National Parliaments."

8. Ibid.

9. Ibid.

10. Jane Jaquette, "Women in Power: From Tokenism to Critical Mass," *Foreign Policy* 108 (Fall 1997): 23–38.

11. Ibid.

12. "Women in National Parliaments."

13. "Voters in United Arab Emirates Set to Vote in Historic Elections," http://www.dubaicity.com/news/historic-elections12–16.htm (October 14, 2008).

14. Pippa Norris, *Electoral Engineering: Voting Rules and Political Behavior* (New York: Cambridge University Press, 2004), 180.

15. United Nations Development Programme, *Human Development Report 2004* (New York: Oxford University Press, 2004), 234–237.

16. Ibid., 234–237.

17. Diana Elias, "Kuwait Appoints Its First Woman Cabinet Member," The Associated Press, June 12, 2005.

18. Susan Welch, "Women as Political Animals? A Test of Some Explanations for Male–Female Political Participation Differences," *American Journal of Political Science* 21 (1977): 711–730.

19. Laurent Belsie, "Men Lag Women at the Voting Booth," *Christian Science Monitor,* February 28, 2002, p. 4.

20. Center for American Women and Politics, "The Gender Gap and the 2004 Women's Vote: Setting the Record Straight," October 28, 2004.

21. Belsie, "Men Lag Women at the Voting Booth," p. 4.

22. U.S. Census Bureau, "U.S. Voter Turnout up in 2004, Census Bureau Reports," May 26, 2005, http://www.census.gov/Press–Release/www/releases/archives/voting/004986.html (August 1, 2005).

23. *World Almanac and Book of Facts 2001* (New York: World Almanac Books, 2000), 40.

24. World Almanac, "Election 2004 Results," http://www.worldalmanac.com/index–m.htm (September 29, 2005).

25. M. Margaret Conway, Gertrude Steuernagel, and David W. Ahern, *Women and Political Participation* (Washington, DC: Congressional Quarterly Press, 1997), 81–82.

26. Ibid., 83.

27. Ibid., 91.

28. As cited in Ronald Inglehart and Pippa Norris, *Rising Tide: Gender Equality and Cultural Change Around the World* (New York: Cambridge University Press, 2003), 105.

29. International Institute for Democracy and Electoral Assistance, "Gender and Political Participation: Voter Turnout by Gender," www.idea.int/gender/turnout (April 23, 2003).

30. Yael Yishai, *Between the Flag and the Banner: Women in Israeli Politics* (Albany: SUNY Press Albany, 1997).

31. Hir Joseph, "WRAPA Prepares Women for Voting," April 11, 2003, http://allAfrica. com/stories/printable/200304120067.html (April 21, 2003).

32. Gehan Abu-Zayd, "In Search of Political Power—Women in Parliament in Egypt, Jordan, and Lebanon," 2002 update of case study originally published in *Women in Parliament: Beyond Numbers* (Stockholm: International IDEA, 1998), http://www. idea.int.

33. As quoted in Inglehart and Norris, *Rising Tide*, 77.

34. Ibid., 99–100.

35. Sidney Verba, Norman Nie, and Jae-on Kim, *Participation and Social Equality* (Cambridge, MA: Harvard University Press, 1978).

36. See Carol Christy, *Sex Differences in Political Participation: Processes of Change in Fourteen Nations* (New York: Praeger, 1987); Conway, Steuernagel, and Ahern, *Women and Political Participation*; David DeVaus and Ian McAllister, "The Changing Politics of Women: Gender and Political Alignments in Eleven Nations," *European Journal of Political Research* 17 (1989): 241–262; and Sidney Verba, Kay Schlozman, and Henry E. Brady, *Voice and Equality* (Cambridge, MA: Harvard University Press, 1995).

37. Inglehart and Norris, *Rising Tide*, 123–126.

38. Pippa Norris, "Women's Power at the Ballot Box," paper written for International Institute for Democracy and Electoral Assistance, *Voter Turnout from 1945–2000: A Global Report on Political Participation*.

39. Ibid.

40. Saleh al-Shaibani, "No Women Elected in Omani Vote," Reuters, October 28, 2007, http://uk.reuters.com/articlePrint?articleId=UKL2808041220071028 (October 14, 2008).

41. Louise Dunne and Kim Renfrew, "Women and Politics Worldwide: The Slow but Steady Struggle Goes On," Radio Netherlands, March 5, 2005, http://www2.rnw.nl/rnw/en/currentaffairs/region/internationalorganisations/wom050304?view5Standard.

42. Andrew Reynolds, "Women in the Legislatures and Executives of the World: Knocking at the Highest Glass Ceiling," *World Politics* 51, no. 4 (1999): 547–572.

43. Ibid., 547–572.

44. Ali Mari Tripp, *Women and Politics in Uganda* (Madison: The University of Wisconsin Press, 2000), 230.

45. For example, see Inglehart and Norris, *Rising Tide*, 130–131; Wilma Rule, "Electoral Systems, Contextual Factors and Women's Opportunities for Parliament in 23 Democracies," *Western Political Quarterly* 40 (1987): 477–498; Wilma Rule, "Why Women Don't Run: The Critical Contextual Factors in Women's Legislative Recruitment," *Western Political Quarterly* 34 (1988): 60–77.

46. Inglehart and Norris, *Rising Tide*, 130–131.

47. Pippa Norris, *Electoral Engineering: Voting Rules and Political Behavior* (New York: Cambridge University Press, 2004), 187.

48. Inter-Parliamentary Union, *Women in Parliament in 2007: The Year in Perspective* (Switzerland: IPU, 2007), 5.

49. Miki Caul, "Women's Representation in Parliament: The Role of Political Parties" (Irvine: Center for the Study of Democracy, UC Irvine, 1997): 6.

50. Norris, *Electoral Engineering,* 201–202.

51. Ibid., 202.

52. International IDEA and Stockholm University, "Global Database of Quotas for Women," http://www.quotaproject.org/system.cfm.

53. Ibid.

54. Inglehart and Norris, *Rising Tide,* 145.

55. Norris, *Electoral Engineering,* 193.

56. Ibid., 191–192.

57. International IDEA and Stockholm University, "Global Database of Quotas for Women," http://www.quotaproject.org/system.cfm.

58. Eileen McDonagh, "Assimilated Leaders: Democratization, Political Inclusion and Female Leadership," *Harvard International Review* 21 (Fall 1999): 3.

59. Pamela Paxton and Sheri Kunovich, "Women's Political Representation: The Importance of Ideology," *Social Forces* 82 (September 2003): 90.

60. Ibid., 87–114.

61. Inglehart and Norris, *Rising Tide,* 144.

62. Tripp, *Women and Politics in Uganda,* 230.

63. Saleh al-Shaibani, "No Women Elected in Omani Vote."

64. Inglehart and Norris, *Rising Tide,* 144.

65. International IDEA, "Gender and Political Participation: Gender Facts," http://www.idea.int.gender/facts.htm (April 23, 2003).

66. Adventure Divas, "Helen Clark," http://www.adventuredivas.com/divas/article.view?page5245 (May 1, 2003).

67. See Barbara Burrell, *A Woman's Place Is in the House: Campaigning for Congress in the Feminist Era* (Ann Arbor: University of Michigan Press, 1994); Janet Clark, "Women at the National Level: An Update on Roll Call Voting Behavior," in *Women and Elective Office: Past, Present, and Future,* ed. Sue Thomas and Clyde Wilcox (New York: Oxford University Press, 1998); Freida Gehlen, "Women Members of Congress: A Distinctive Role," in *A Portrait of Marginality: The Political Behavior of the American Woman,* ed. Marianne Githens and Jewell Prestage (New York: McKay Co., 1977); Susan Welch, "Are Women More Liberal Than Men in the U.S. Congress?" *Legislative Studies Quarterly* 10 (1985): 125–134.

68. Karin L. Tamerius, "Sex, Gender, and Leadership in the Representation of Women," in *Gender, Power, Leadership, and Governance,* ed. Georgia Duerst–Lahti and Rita Mae Kelly (Ann Arbor: University of Michigan Press, 1993).

69. See Clara Bingham, *Challenging the Culture of Congress* (New York: Times Books, 1997); Barbara Boxer, *Strangers in the Senate* (Bethesda, MD: National Press Books, 1994); Karen Foerstal and Herbert Foerstal, *Climbing the Hill: Gender Conflict in Congress* (Westport, CT: Praeger, 1996); Irwin Gertzog, *Congressional Women: Their Recruitment, Integration and Behavior,* 2nd ed. (Westport, CT: Praeger, 1995); Marjorie Margolies-Mezvinsky, *A Woman's Place: The Freshman Who Changed the Face of Congress* (New York: Crown, 1994).

70. See Edith Barrett, "The Policy Priorities of African-American Women in State Legislatures," *Legislative Studies Quarterly* 20 (1995): 223–247; Tamerius, "Sex, Gender, and Leadership in the Representation of Women."

71. Michelle Swers, "Are Congresswomen More Likely to Vote for Women's Issues Bills Than Their Male Colleagues?" *Legislative Studies Quarterly* 23 (1998): 445; and Michelle Swers, *The Difference Women Make: The Policy Impact of Women in Congress* (Chicago: University of Chicago Press, 2002).

72. Ibid., 445.

73. Debra L. Dodson and Susan Carroll, *Reshaping the Agenda: Women in State Legislatures* (New Brunswick: Center for American Women and Politics, Rutgers, The State University of New Jersey, 1991).

74. See Deborah Dodson, "Representing Women's Interests in the U.S. House of Representatives," in *Women and Elective Office: Past, Present, and Future*, ed. Sue Thomas and Clyde Wilcox (New York: Oxford University Press, 1998); Dodson and Carroll, *Reshaping the Agenda;* and Sue Thomas, *How Women Legislate* (New York: Oxford University Press, 1994).

75. Sue Thomas and Susan Welch, "The Impact of Gender on Activities and Priorities of State Legislators," *Western Political Quarterly* 44 (1991): 454–455.

76. See Barrett, "The Policy Priorities of African-American Women in State Legislatures"; Dodson, "Representing Women's Interests in the U.S. House of Representatives"; Dodson and Carroll, *Reshaping the Agenda;* and Thomas, *How Women Legislate.*

77. Michael B. Berkman and Robert E. O'Connor, "Do Women Legislators Matter? Female Legislators and State Abortion Policy," *American Politics Quarterly* 21 (January 1993): 102–124.

78. See Malcolm Jewell and Marcia Lynn Wicker, *Legislative Leadership in the American States* (Ann Arbor: University of Michigan Press, 1994); Cindy Simon Rosenthal, *When Women Lead: Integrative Leadership in State Legislatures* (New York and Oxford: Oxford University Press, 1998).

79. Carol Gilligan, *In a Different Voice: Psychological Theory and Women's Development* (Cambridge, MA; Harvard University Press, 1982).

80. Rosenthal, *When Women Lead.*

81. Burrell, *A Woman's Place Is in the House,* 153.

82. Jewell and Whicker, *Legislative Leadership in American States,* 177.

83. Rosenthal, *When Women Lead,* 76.

84. Dodson and Carroll, *Reshaping the Agenda.*

85. For an excellent discussion and overview of the gendered nature of legislatures, see Rosenthal, *When Women Lead.*

86. Alana Jeydel and Andy Taylor, "Are Women Legislators Less Effective? Evidence from the U.S. House in the 103d–105th Congress," *Political Research Quarterly* 56 (March 2003): 19–28.

87. Jill M. Bystydzienski, *Women in Electoral Politics: Lessons from Norway* (Westport, CT, and London: Praeger, 1995), 21.

88. Kathleen Bratton and Leonard Ray, "Descriptive Representation, Policy Outcomes, and Municipal Day-Care Coverage in Norway," *American Journal of Political Science* 46 (2002): 428–437.

89. Bystydzienski, *Women in Electoral Politics.*

90. Ibid.

91. Ibid., 54–56.

92. Ibid., 110.

93. Ibid., 109–110.

94. Sarah Childs, "In Their Own Words: New Labour MPs and the Substantive Representation of Women," *British Journal of Politics and International Relations* (June 2001): 173–190.

95. Sarah Childs, "Hitting the Target: Are Labour Women MPs 'Acting for' Women?" Paper for the 51st Political Studies Association Conference, April 10–12, 2001, Manchester, United Kingdom, 3–4.

96. Pippa Norris and Joni Lovenduski, "Blair's Babes: Critical Mass Theory, Gender, and Legislative Life," John F. Kennedy School of Government, Harvard University, Faculty Research Working Paper Series (September 2001).

97. Sandra Grey, "Does Size Matter? Critical Mass and New Zealand Women MPs," *Parliamentary Affairs* 55 (2002): 19–29.

98. A critical mass is generally considered to be 14 percent or more.

99. Nikki Craske, *Women and Politics in Latin America* (New Brunswick, NJ: Rutgers University Press, 1999), 56.

100. Ilja A. Lluciak, *After the Revolution: Gender and Democracy in El Salvador, Nicaragua, and Guatemala* (Baltimore, MD: Johns Hopkins University Press, 2001), 198.

101. Lluciak, *After the Revolution,* 201.

102. Karen Olsen de Figueres, "The Road to Equality—Women in Parliament in Costa Rica," 2002 update of case study originally published in *Women in Parliament: Beyond Numbers* (Stockholm, International IDEA, 1998): 3, http://www.idea.int.

103. Ibid., 3.

104. Maryam Poya, *Women, Work and Islamism: Ideology and Resistance in Iran* (London and New York: Zed Books, 1999), 144.

105. Ibid., 146.

106. Interparliamentarian Union, "Women in Parliaments: World Classification," http://www.ipu.org/wmn–e/classif.htm (June 1, 2005).

107. Poya, *Women, Work and Islamism,* 145.

108. Ibid., 145.

109. Azadeh Kian-Thiebaut, "Women and the Making of Civil Society in Post–Islamist Iran," in *Twenty Years of Islamic Revolution: Political and Social Transition in Iran Since 1979,* ed. Eric Hooglund (Syracuse, NY: Syracuse University Pres, 2002), 58.

110. British Broadcasting Corporation, "Guide to Iran's Presidential Poll," June 16, 2005, http://news.bbc.co.uk/1/hi/world/middle_east/4086944.stm (August 17, 2005).

111. Yishai, *Between the Flag and the Banner.*

112. Ibid., 100.

113. Peroshni Govender, "56 Female Candidates up for Election in Israel," January 28, 2003, Women's eNews, http://womensenews.org (January 28, 2003).

114. Shirin Rai, "Class, Caste and Gender—Women in Parliament in India," 2002 update of case study originally published in *Women in Parliament: Beyond Numbers* (Stockholm, International IDEA, 1998), http://www.idea.int.

115. The Inter-Parliamentary Union, *Women in National Parliaments,* September 30, 2008, http://ipu.org/wmn-e/classif.htm (October 22, 2008).

116. The British Broadcasting Corporation, "Indian Parliament Refuses Women Quotas," July 14, 1998.

117. Anuradha Sengupta, "Kashmiris Look to a Woman for Resolution of Strife," www.womensenews.org, January 24, 2003, p. 1.

118. Ibid.

119. The Inter-Parliamentary Union, *Women in National Parliaments*.

120. Ibid.

121. Ibid.

122. Mavivi Myakayaka–Manzini, "Women Empowered—Women in Parliament in South Africa," 2002 update of case study originally published in *Women in Parliament: Beyond Numbers* (Stockholm, International IDEA, 1998), http://www.idea.int.

123. Ibid., 1.

124. Ibid.

125. International Institute for Democracy and Electoral Assistance, "Global Database of Quotas for Women," http://www.quotaproject.org/displayCountry.cfm?CountryCode5ZA (August 18, 2005).

126. International Labor Organization, http://www.ilo.org/public/english/employment/gems/eeo/law/south/jmciqlsw.htm.

127. Myakayaka–Manzini, "Women Empowered."

128. Shirin Rai, "Class, Caste and Gender," 1.

129. Joni Saeger, *The State of the Women in the World Atlas* (Penguin Books, 1997). These countries are Sweden (50 percent), Norway (42 percent), Finland (41 percent), Seychelles (41 percent), Barbados (39 percent), Denmark (35 percent), Sri Lanka (29 percent), Gambia (25 percent), Netherlands (24 percent), Austria (22 percent), Luxemburg (21 percent), Bahamas, Bhutan, Fidischi, and the United States (all 20 percent).

130. United Nations Development Programme, *Human Development Report 2004* (New York: Oxford University Press, 2004), 234–237.

131. Carlos Lozada, "Colombia Gets Tough with a Woman's Touch," *Christian Science Monitor,* October 28, 2002.

132. International Women's Democracy Center, "Resources: Fact Sheet: Women's Political Participation," June 2008 http://www.iwdc.org/resources/fact_sheet.htm (October 22, 2008).

133. See Craske, *Women and Politics in Latin America;* de Figueres, "The Road to Equality"; Yishai, *Between the Flag and the Banner.*

134. Craske, *Women and Politics in Latin America,* 75.

135. Ibid., 67–68.

136. Tripp, *Women and Politics in Uganda,* 224.

137. Myakayaka–Manzini, "Women Empowered."

138. Craske, *Women and Politics in Latin America,* 68.

139. Tripp, *Women and Politics in Uganda,* 219.

140. Ibid., 219.

141. David S. Meyer, "Restating the Woman Question: Women's Movements and State Restructuring," in *Women's Movements Facing the Reconfigured State,* ed. Lee Ann Banaszak, Karen Beckwith, and Dieter Rucht (New York: Cambridge University Press, 2003), 279.

142. International Institute for Democracy and Electoral Assistance and Stockholm University, "Global Database of Quotas for Women," http://www.quotaproject.org (August 19, 2005).

143. Craske, *Women and Politics in Latin America,* 73.

144. Caroline Lambert, "French Women in Politics: The Long Road to Parity," The Brookings Institution, May 2001, http://www.brookings.edu/fp/cusf/analysis/women.htm (April 23, 2003).

145. Ibid.

146. Ibid.

147. Wilma Rule and Matthew Shugart, "The Preference Vote and Election of Women," Center for Voting and Democracy, 1995, http://www.fairvote.org/reports/1995/chp7/rule.html (April 21, 2003).

148. Inglehart and Norris, *Rising Tide,* 144–146.

149. Sophi Arie, "Elisa Carrio in Lead to Be Argentina's President," Women's eNews, July 18, 2002, http://www.womensenews.org (July 18, 2002).

CHAPTER 2

1. British Broadcasting Company News, "Talks to End Nigerian Oil Siege," July 11, 2002, http://news.bbc.co.uk/1/hi/world/africa/2119872.stm (February 5, 2003).

2. British Broadcasting Company News, "'Deal Reached' in Nigerian Oil Protest," July 16, 2002, http://news.bbc.co.uk/1/hi/africa/2129281.stm (February 5, 2003).

3. See Karen Beckwith for a longer discussion of definitions of women's movement. Karen Beckwith, "Beyond Compare? Women's Movements in Comparative Perspective," *European Journal of Political Research* 37 (2000): 431–468.

4. Jeffrey M. Berry, *Interest Group Society,* 3rd ed. (New York: Longman, 1997), 4–5.

5. Karen Beckwith, "Lancashire Women Against Pit Closures: Women's Standing in a Men's Movement," *Signs* 21, no. 4 (2000): 1034–1068.

6. Beckwith, "Beyond Compare?," 431–468.

7. Amrita Basu, "Introduction," in *The Challenge of Local Feminisms: Women's Movements in Global Perspective,* ed. Amrita Basu (Boulder, CO: Westview Press, 1995), 11.

8. See William Kornhauser, *The Politics of Mass Society* (Glencoe, IL: The Free Press, 1959); Neil Smelser, *Theory of Collective Behavior* (New York: The Free Press, 1962); Ralph H. Turner and Lewis Killian, *Collective Behavior* (Englewood Cliffs: Prentice Hall, 1957).

9. See Jo Freeman, *The Politics of Women's Liberation* (New York: McKay, 1975); J. Craig Jenkins, *The Politics of Insurgency* (New York: Columbia University Press, 1985); John D. McCarthy and Meyer Zald, eds., *Social Movements in an Organizational Society* (New Brunswick, NJ, and Oxford: Transaction Books, 1987).

10. See Anne Costain, *Inviting Women's Rebellion* (Baltimore, MD: Johns Hopkins University Press, 1992); Peter K. Eisenger, "The Conditions of Protest Behavior in American Cities," *American Political Science Review* 67 (1973): 11–28; J. Craig Jenkins and Charles Perrow, "Insurgency of the Powerless: Farm Workers Movements," *American Sociological Review* 42 (1977): 249–267; Mary Fainsod Katzenstein and Carol M. Mueller, *The Women's Movements of the United States and Western Europe* (Philadelphia: Temple University Press, 1987); Herbert P. Kitschelt, "Political Opportunity Structures and Political Protest: Anti-Nuclear Movements in Four Democracies," *British Journal of Political Science* 16, no. 1 (1986): 57–85; Doug McAdam, *Political Process and the Development of Black Insurgency 1930–1970* (Chicago and London: University of Chicago Press, 1985); David Meyer,

"Institutionalizing Dissent: The United States Structure of Political Opportunity and the End of the Nuclear Freeze Movement," *Sociological Forum* 8, no. 2 (1993): 157–179; Francis Fox Piven and Richard Cloward, *Poor People's Movements* (New York: Vintage Books, 1979); Sidney Tarrow, *Power in Movement* (Cambridge: Cambridge University Press, 1994).

11. Nancy McGlen and Karen O'Connor, *Women's Rights* (New York: Praeger, 1983).

12. Betty Friedan, *The Feminine Mystique* (New York: W.W. Norton & Co., 2001).

13. McGlen and O'Connor, *Women's Rights*.

14. British Broadcasting Company News, "Oil Deal 'Off,' Nigerian Women Say," July 16, 2002, http://news.bbc.co.uk/1/hi/world/africa/2132494.stm (February 5, 2003).

15. British Broadcasting Company News, "Nigerian Women Leave Oil Plant," July 18, 2002, http://news.bbc.co.uk/1/hi/world/africa/2136509.stm (February 5, 2003).

16. British Broadcasting Company News, "'Deal Reached' in Nigerian Oil Protest."

17. Jennifer Schirmer, "The Seeking of Truth and the Gendering of Consciousness," in *Viva: Women and Political Protest in Latin America*, ed. Sarah A. Radcliffe and Sallie Westwood (New York and London: Routledge, 1993), 32.

18. Tripp, Aili Mari, *Women and Politics in Uganda* (Madison: The University of Wisconsin Press, 2000), 108.

19. Schirmer, "The Seeking of Truth," 48–49.

20. Sheila Rowbotham and Stephanie Linkogle, eds., *Women Resist Globalization: Mobilizing for Livelihood and Rights* (London and New York: Zed Books, 2001), 2.

21. Tripp, *Women and Politics in Uganda*, 107–108.

22. Maxine Molyneux, "Mobilization Without Emancipation? Women's Interests, the State and Revolution in Nicaragua," *Feminist Studies* 11(1985): 227–254.

23. Temma Kaplan, "Uncommon Women and the Common Good," in *Women Resist Globalization*, 29.

24. Nikki Craske, *Women and Politics in Latin America* (New Brunswick, NJ: Rutgers University Press, 1999); Tripp, *Women and Politics in Uganda*.

25. UNESCO, "Baseline Definitions of Key Concepts and Terms," http://portal.unesco.org/en/file_download.php/9b8ae81bd5b2acba02fcec07cf7305c9Definitions.doc.

26. Craske, *Women and Politics in Latin America*, 119.

27. Jacqueline Adams, "Art in Social Movements: Shantytown Women's Protest in Pinochet's Chile," *Sociological Forum* 17 (2002): 30.

28. Tripp, *Women and Politics in Uganda*, 110.

29. Craske, *Women and Politics in Latin America*, 2–3.

30. Ibid., 112–113.

31. Helen I. Safa and Cornelia Butler Flora, "Production, Reproduction, and the Polity: Women's Strategic and Practical Gender Issues," in *Americas: New Interpretive Essays*, ed. Alfred Stepan (New York and Oxford: Oxford University Press, 1992), 127.

32. Schirmer, "The Seeking of Truth," 32–33.

33. Ibid., 39–41.

34. Anne Costain and Doug Costain, "Strategy and Tactics of the Women's Movement in the U.S.: The Role of Political Parties," in *The Women's Movements of the United States and Western Europe: Consciousness, Political Opportunity and Public Policy*, ed. Mary F. Katzenstein and Carol M. Mueller (Philadelphia: Temple University Press, 1987), 197.

35. Ibid.

36. Lee Ann Banaszak, Karen Beckwith, and Dieter Rucht, "When Power Relocates: Interactive Changes in Women's Movements and States," in *Women's Movements Facing the Reconfigured State*, ed. Lee Ann Banaszak, Karen Beckwith, and Dieter Rucht (New York: Cambridge University Press, 2003), 1–6.

37. Louise Krasniewicz, *Nuclear Summer: The Clash of Communities at the Seneca Women's Peace Encampment* (Ithaca, NY: Cornell University Press, 1992).

38. Maren Klawiter, "Racing for the Cure, Walking Women and Toxic Touring: Mapping Cultures of Action Within the Bay Area Terrain of Breast Cancer," *Social Problems* 46 (1999): 105.

39. Kaplan, "Uncommon Women," 37.

40. Myra Marx Ferree, "Equality and Autonomy: Feminist Politics in the United States and West Germany," in *The Women's Movements of the United States and Western Europe*, ed. Mary Fainsod Katzenstein and Carol McClurg Mueller (Philadelphia: Temple University Press, 1987), 172–177.

41. Paul Burstein, "Legal Mobilization as a Social Movement Tactic: The Struggle for Equal Employment Opportunity," *American Journal of Sociology* 96 (1991): 1201–1225.

42. Amy G. Mazur, *Theorizing Feminist Policy* (New York: Oxford University Press, 2002), 48.

43. Beckwith, "Beyond Compare?," 439–440.

44. As quoted in Dorothy McBride Stetson and Amy G. Mazur, "Introduction," in *Comparative State Feminism*, ed. Dorothy McBride Stetson and Amy G. Mazur (Thousand Oaks, CA: Sage Publications, 1995), 10.

45. Stetson and Mazur, "Introduction," in *Comparative State Feminism*, 1.

46. United Nations, "Fact Sheet No. 8: Institutional Mechanisms for the Advancement of Women," http://www.un.org/womenwatch/daw/followup/session/presskit/fs8.htm (September 14, 2005).

47. Cynthia Enloe, "Closing Remarks," *International Peacekeeping* 8 (Summer 2001): 111.

48. Costain, *Inventing Women's Rebellion*, xv.

49. Sarah L. Henderson, "Women in a Changing Context," in *Contemporary Russian Politics*, ed. Michael Bressler (Boulder, CO: Lynne Rienner Press, forthcoming).

50. Amy G. Mazur, *Gender Bias and the State: Symbolic Reform at Work in Fifth Republic France* (Pittsburgh: University of Pittsburgh Press, 1995), 1–4.

51. Tripp, *Women and Politics in Uganda*, 12.

52. Haya al-Mughni, "Women's Organizations in Kuwait," in *Women and Politics in the Middle East*, ed. Saud Joseph and Susan Slyomovics (Philadelphia: University of Pennsylvania Press, 2001), 176–182.

53. Banaszak, Beckwith, and Rucht, "When Power Relocates," 2.

54. Craske, *Women and Politics in Latin America*, 131.

55. Ibid., 131; Tripp, *Women and Politics in Uganda*, 110.

56. Nikki Craske, "Women's Political Participation in Colonias Populares in Guadelajara, Mexico," in *Viva: Women and Popular Protest in Latin America*, ed. Sarah Radcliffe and Sallie Westwood (London and New York: Routledge, 1993), 134.

57. David Meyer and Nancy Whittier, "Social Movement Spillover," *Social Problems* 41 (1994): 277.

58. Ronald Inglehart and Pippa Norris, *Rising Tide: Gender Equality and Cultural Change Around the World* (New York: Cambridge University Press, 2003), 29–48.

59. "Women's Studies Programs Worldwide," http://research.umbc.edu/~korenman/ wmst/programs.html (September 15, 2005).

60. As quoted in Nonna Mayer and Mariette Sineau, "France: The Front National," in *Rechtsextreme Parteien*, ed. Helga Amsberger and Brigitte Halbmayr (Opladen: Leske & Budrich, 2002), 80–81.

61. Ibid., 65.

62. Ibid., 68.

63. Ibid., 73.

64. Valentine M. Moghadam and Margot Badran, *Causes and Gender Implications of Islamist Movements in the Middle East* (Helsinki: World Institute of Development Economic Research, United Nations University, 1991).

65. al-Mughni, "Women's Organizations in Kuwait," 179.

66. Burcak Keskin, "Confronting Double Patriarchy: Islamist Women in Turkey," in *Right-Wing Women: From Conservatives to Extremists Around the World*, ed. Paola Bacchetta and Margaret Power (New York: Routledge, 2002), 245–247.

67. Nilufer Narli, "The Rise of the Islamist Movement in Turkey," *Middle Eastern Review of International Affairs* 3, no. 3 (1999).

68. Mayer and Sineau, "France," 70.

69. Ibid., 72.

70. Keskin, "Confronting Double Patriarchy," 251.

71. Henri Astier, "Le Pen's Voters," BBC News Online, April 23, 2002, http://news.bbc. co.uk/1/hi/world/europe/1946764.stm (September 30, 2005).

72. Mayer and Sineau, "France," 57.

73. Merve Kavakci, "Headscarf Heresy: For One Muslim Woman, the Headscarf Is a Matter of Choice and Dignity," *Foreign Policy* (May/June 2004): 66–67.

74. Marge Berer and T. K. Sundari Ravindran, "Fundamentalism, Women's Empowerment and Reproductive Rights," *Reproductive Health Matters* 4, no. 8 (1996): 10–15.

75. Rowbothom and Linkogle, *Women Resist Globalization*, 3.

76. David S. Meyer, "Restating the Woman Question: Women's Movements and State Restructuring," in *Women's Movements Facing the Reconfigured State*, 275–294.

CHAPTER 3

1. Susan Glasser, "Chechens Blamed in Moscow Attacks," *The Toronto Star*, July 6, 2003, p. A1.

2. Daniel Mclaughlin, "Bombing Shocks Russians: Muscovites Aghast at 'Black Widow' Attacks," *The Vancouver Sun*, July 7, 2003, p. A5.

3. John Solomon, "FBI Wary al-Qaeda May Begin Using Women in Attacks," The Associated Press, April 1, 2003.

4. Kevin Toolis, "The Revenger's Tragedy: Why Women Turn to Suicide Bombing," *The Observer*, October 12, 2003, http://www.guardian.co.uk/print/0,3858,4772634–103552,00.html (October 13, 2003).

5. Samuel P. Huntington, *Political Order in Changing Societies* (New Haven, CT: Yale University Press, 1968).

6. T. R. Gurr, *Why Men Rebel* (Princeton, NJ: Princeton University Press, 1970).

7. Theda Skocpol, *States and Social Revolutions* (Cambridge: Cambridge University Press, 1979).

8. Jack A. Goldstone, *Revolution and Rebellion in the Early Modern World* (Berkeley: University of California Press, 1991).

9. The dates listed refer to the year of regime change; the actual revolutionary movement started earlier and often continued to implement changes for several years afterward.

10. British Broadcasting News Corporation, "Country Profile: Algeria," http://news.bbc.co.uk/1/hi/world/middle_east/country_profiles/790556.stm (August 4, 2005).

11. Jack A. Goldstone, "Toward a Fourth Generation of Revolutionary Theory," *Annual Review of Political Science* 4 (2001): 142.

12. It is difficult to come up with an exact figure. Jane Jacquette estimated that about 30 percent of Salvadoran guerrillas were women. In her study of Nicaraguan guerrillas, Chinchilla estimated that women comprised about 20 percent of armed combatants. Chinchilla, Norma Stoltz. "Feminism, Revolution, and Democratic Transitions in Nicaragua" in *The Women's Movement in Latin America: Participation and Democracy* (2nd ed). Ed. Jane S. Jaquette. Boulder: Westview Press, 1994. 177–196. Karen Kampwirth estimated that perhaps a third of the combatants in the FSLN (Nicaragua), FMLN (El Salvador), and the FZLN (Zapatistas) were women, in contrast to the Cuban case, in which women made up 5 percent of armed combatants. Karen Kampwirth, *Feminism and the Legacy of Revolution: Nicaragua, El Salvador, Chiapas* (Athens: Center for International Studies at Ohio University Press, 2004), x.

13. As quoted in Christine Sylvester, "Simultaneous Revolutions and Exits: A Semi-Skeptical Comment," in *Women and Revolution in Africa, Asia, and the New World,* ed. Mary Ann Tetrault (Columbia: University of South Carolina Press, 1994), 38–39.

14. Nelson Mandela, *Long Walk to Freedom: The Autobiography of Nelson Mandela* (Boston: Back Bay Books, 1995).

15. Linda M. Lobao, "Women in Revolutionary Movements: Changing Patterns of Latin American Guerilla Study," in *Women and Revolution: Global Expressions,* ed. M. J. Diamond (Boston: Kluwer Academic Publishers, 1998), 260–265.

16. Beryl Williams, "Kollantai and After: Women in the Russian Revolution," in *Women, State and Revolution: Essays in Power and Gender in Europe Since 1789,* ed. Sian Reynolds (Amherst: University of Massachusetts Press, 1987), 68.

17. Michael Lynch, *Mao* (New York, Routledge Press, 2004), 209.

18. Kampwirth, *Feminism and the Legacy of Revolution,* 113.

19. Vladimir Ilyich Lenin, "Speech at the First All-Russia Congress of Working Women," November 19, 1918, http://www.marxists.org/archive/lenin/works/1918/nov/19.htm (April 21, 2006).

20. Lynch, *Mao,* 208.

21. Lois M. Smith and Alfred Padula, *Sex and Revolution: Women in Socialist Cuba* (New York: Oxford University Press, 1996), 4.

22. Margaret Randall, *Gathering Rage: The Failure of Twentieth Century Revolutions to Develop a Feminist Agenda* (New York: Monthly Review Press, 1992), 49.

23. As quoted in Kampwirth, *Feminism and the Legacy of Revolution,* 112.

24. As quoted in Karen Kampwirth, *Women and Guerilla Movements: Nicaragua, El Salvador, Chiapas, Cuba* (University Park: Penn State University Press, 2002), 114.

25. M. J. Diamond, "Olympe de Gouges and the French Revolution: The Construction of Gender as Critique," in *Women and Revolution: Global Expressions,* ed. M. J. Diamond (Boston: Kluwer Academic Publishers, 1998).

26. Valentine M. Moghadam, "Gender and Revolutions," in *Theorizing Revolutions,* ed. John Foran (New York: Routledge Press, 1997), 144.

27. Shana Penn, *Solidarity's Secret: The Women Who Defeated Communism in Poland* (Ann Arbor: University of Michigan Press, 2005), xiii.

28. Ibid., 23.

29. Sarah L. Henderson, "Women in a Changing Context," in *Understanding Contemporary Russia,* ed. Michael L. Bressler (Boulder, CO: Lynne Rienner Press, 2008).

30. As quoted in Penn, *Solidarity's Secret,* 332–333.

31. See Chapter 1 in Valentine M. Moghadam, *Modernizing Women: Gender and Social Change in the Middle East* (Boulder, CO: Lynne Rienner Publishers, 2003), 1–32.

32. Azadeh Kian-Thiebaut, "Women and the Making of Civil Society in Post-Islamist Iran," in *Twenty Years of Islamic Revolution: Political and Social Transition in Iran Since 1979,* ed. Eric Hooglund (Syracuse, NY: Syracuse University Press, 2002), 60.

33. British Broadcasting Corporation News, "Iran: Country Profile," August 3, 2005, http://news.bbc.co.uk/1/hi/world/middle_east/country_profiles/790877.stm (August 24, 2005).

34. As quoted in Kian-Thiebaut, "Women and the Making of Civil Society in Post-Islamist Iran," 60.

35. Roksana Bahramitash, "Revolution, Islamization, and Women's Employment in Iran," *The Brown Journal of World Affairs* 9 (Winter/Spring 2003): 233.

36. Moghadam, "Gender and Revolutions," 137–167.

37. Moghadam, *Modernizing Women,* 98.

38. As quoted in Ibid., 101.

39. Julia Shayne, *The Revolution Question: Feminisms in El Salvador, Chile, and Cuba* (New Brunswick, NJ: Rutgers University Press, 2004), 5.

40. Kampwirth, *Women and Guerilla Movements,* 6.

41. Kampwirth, *Feminism and the Legacy of Revolution,* 8.

42. British Broadcasting Corporation News, "Transcripts: The Guerilla's Story," January 1, 2001, http://news.bbc.co.uk/1/hi/in_depth/uk/2000/uk_confidential/1090986.stm (April 21, 2006).

43. Ilya Llukiak, *After the Revolution: Gender and Democracy in El Salvador, Nicaragua, and Guatemala* (Baltimore: Johns Hopkins University Press, 2001), 70.

44. Kampwirth estimated that up to a third of combatants of FSLN, FMLN, and FZLN were female. Kampwirth, *Feminism and the Legacy of Revolution,* x.

45. Juan Lazaro, "Women and Political Violence in Contemporary Peru," in *Women and Revolution: Global Expressions,* ed. M. J. Diamond (Boston: Kluwer Academic Publishers, 1998), 305.

46. Timothy Wickham-Crowley, *Guerillas and Revolution in Latin America: A Comparative Study of Insurgents and Regimes Since 1956* (Princeton, NJ: Princeton University Press, 1992), 216.

47. Lukiak, *After the Revolution.*

48. Kampwirth, *Feminism and the Legacy of Revolution,* xi.

49. Diamond, "Olympe de Gouges and the French Revolution."

50. Vera Figner, *Memoirs of a Revolutionist,* introduction by Richard Stites (DeKalb: Northern Illinois Press, 1991).

51. As quoted in Smith and Padula, *Sex and Revolution,* 46.

52. Sandra C. Taylor, *Vietnamese Women at War: Fighting for Ho Chi Minh and the Revolution* (Lawrence: University of Kansas Press, 1999).

53. Ibid., 127.
54. Smith and Padula, *Sex and Revolution*, 27.
55. As quoted in Ibid., 24.
56. Nikki Craske, *Women and Politics in Latin America* (New Brunswick, NJ: Rutgers University Press, 1999), 142.
57. Penn, *Solidarity's Secret*, 9.
58. Kampwirth, *Feminism and the Legacy of Revolution*, 175.
59. Roksana Bahramitash, "Revolution, Islamization, and Women's Employment in Iran," *The Brown Journal of World Affairs* 9 (Winter/Spring 2003), 232–233.
60. Mary Ann Tetrault, "Women and Revolution in Vietnam," in *Global Feminisms Since 1945*, ed. Bonnie G. Smith (New York: Routledge, 2000), 56.
61. Taylor, *Vietnamese Women at War*, 125.
62. As quoted in Smith and Padula, *Sex and Revolution*, 28.
63. Ibid., 30.
64. As quoted in Francesca Miller, *Latin American Women and the Search for Social Justice* (Hanover, NH: University of New England Press, 1991), 146–147.
65. Shayne, *The Revolution Question*, 164.
66. Craske, *Women and Politics in Latin America*, 142.
67. Randall, *Gathering Rage*, 44.
68. Ibid., 30.
69. As quoted in Molyneux, "Mobilization Without Emancipation? Women's Interests, the State and Revolution in Nicaragua," *Feminist Studies* 11 (1985): 227–254, footnote 19.
70. Kampwirth, *Feminism and the Legacy of Revolution*, 12.
71. Ibid., 14.
72. Sue Ellen M. Charlton, Jana Everett, and Kathleen Staudt, "Women, the State, and Development," in *Women, the State, and Development*, ed. Sue Ellen M. Charlton, Jana Everett, and Kathleen Staudt (Albany: SUNY Press, 1989), 10.
73. Barbara Wolfe Jancar, *Women Under Communism* (Baltimore: Johns Hopkins University Press, 1978), 113–114.
74. Craske, *Women and Politics in Latin America*, 139–140.
75. Beryl Williams, "Kollantai and After: Women in the Russian Revolution," in *Women, State and Revolution: Essays on Power and Gender in Europe Since 1789*, ed. Sian Reynolds (Amherst: The University of Massachusetts Press, 1987), 60.
76. Smith and Padula, *Sex and Revolution*, 32.
77. Craske, *Women and Politics in Latin America*, 145.
78. Karen Beckwith, "Beyond Compare? Women's Movements in Comparative Perspective," *European Journal of Policy Research* 37 (2000): 444.
79. Craske, *Women and Politics in Latin America*, 147.
80. Kampwirth, *Feminism and the Legacy of Revolution*, 176.
81. Penn, *Solidarity's Secret*, 199.
82. Marilyn Rueschemeyer, ed., *Women in the Politics of Postcommunist Eastern Europe* (Armonk, NY: M. E. Sharpe, 1994).
83. Sarah L. Henderson, "Women in a Changing Context," in *Understanding Contemporary Russia*, ed. Michael L. Bressler (Boulder, CO: Lynne Rienner Press, 2008).
84. Azadeh Kain, "Women and Politics in Post-Islamist Iran: The Gender Conscious Drive to Change," *British Journal of Middle Eastern Studies* 24, no. 1 (1997): 75–97.

85. As quoted in Ibid., 75–97.

86. Kian-Thiebaut, "Women and the Making of Civil Society," 65–67.

87. Charlton, Everett, and Staudt, "Women, the State and Development," 11.

88. Craske, *Women and Politics in Latin America,* 146.

89. Valentine Moghadam, ed., *Democratic Reform and the Position of Women in Transitional Economies* (Oxford: Clarendon Press, 1993).

90. Human Development Unit, Eastern Europe and Central Asia Region, World Bank, "Gender in Transition" (Washington, DC: World Bank, May 21, 2002).

91. Homa Hoodfar, "Bargaining with Fundamentalism: Women and the Politics of Population Control in Iran," *Reproductive Health Matters* 4, no. 8 (1996): 30–40.

92. Ibid.

93. United Nations Development Programme, *Human Development Report 2005* (New York: Oxford University Press, 2005), 312.

94. Ziva Galili, "Women and the Russian Revolution," in *Women and Revolution: Global Expressions,* ed. M. J. Diamond (Boston: Kluwer Academic Publishers, 1998), 63–77.

95. Marilyn B. Young, "Reflections in Women in the Chinese Revolution," in *Women and Revolution: Global Expressions,* ed. M. J. Diamond (Boston: Kluwer Academic Publishers, 1998), 357–361.

96. Taylor, *Vietnamese Women at War,* 31.

97. Kampwirth, *Feminism and the Legacy of Revolution,* 5–14.

98. As quoted in Shayne, *The Revolution Question,* 1.

99. Craske, *Women and Politics in Latin America,* 140.

100. Diamond, "Olympe de Gouges and the French Revolution."

101. Penn, *Solidarity's Secret,* 28.

102. Kian-Thiebaut, "Women and the Making of Civil Society," 60.

103. Hoodfar, "Bargaining with Fundamentalism."

104. Kian-Thiebaut, "Women and the Making of Civil Society," 63.

PART II INTRODUCTION

1. Amy G. Mazur and Susanne Zwingel, "Comparing Feminist Policy in Politics and at Work in France and Germany: Shared European Union Setting, Divergent National Contexts," *Review of Policy Research* 20, no. 3 (2003): 365–383.

2. For example, see Dorothy McBride Stetson and Amy G. Mazur, eds., *Comparative State Feminism* (Thousand Oaks, CA: Sage Publications, 1995); Amy G. Mazur, *Theorizing Feminist Policy* (New York: Oxford University Press, 2002).

CHAPTER 4

1. Kim Campbell, "Women Seek Solutions to Pension-System Bias," *Christian Science Monitor,* May 9, 1996, vol. 88, p. 9.

2. Diane Nicol, "Employers Face Rise in Equal Pay Claims," *The Scotsman,* April 19, 2003, p. 23.

3. Fiona Davidson, "Male Workers Say It's Unfair That Dress Rules Don't Apply to Women; Men Shirty About Ties," *The Express,* July 16, 2003, p. 7.

4. British Broadcasting Corporation News, "Wal-Mart Battles Huge Sexism Claim," September 25, 2003, http://news.bbc.co.uk/1/hi/business/3138188.stm (August 8, 2005).

5. OECD Economics Department, "Female Labour Force Participation: Past Trends and Main Determinants in OECD Countries," May 2004, http://www.oecd.org/dataoecd/25/5/31743836.pdf. (April 22, 2006).

6. United Nations Development Programme, *Human Development Report 2004* (New York: Oxford University Press, 2004), 221–224.

7. Ronnie Steinberg-Ratner, "The Policy and Problem: Overview of Seven Countries," in *Equal Employment Policy for Women,* ed. Ronnie Steinberg-Ratner (Philadelphia: Temple University Press, 1980), 41–42.

8. Amy G. Mazur and Susanne Zwingel, "Comparing Feminist Policy in Politics and at Work in France and Germany: Shared European Union Setting, Divergent National Contexts," *Review of Policy Research* 20, no. 3 (2003): 370.

9. Organization for Economic Co-operation and Development, *OECD in Figures: Statistics for the Member Countries* (Paris: OECD, 2007).

10. European Commission, "Gender Mainstreaming," http://europa.eu.int/comm/employment_social/gender_equality/gender_mainstreaming/employment/employment_labour_market_en.html (October 5, 2003).

11. Amy G. Mazur, *Theorizing Feminist Policy* (New York: Cambridge University Press, 2002), 80–87.

12. Bnet.com, "Labour Market Trends: Advancing Women in the Workplace," http://findarticles.com/p/articles/mi_qa3999/is_200408/ai_n9448236 (December 9, 2008).

13. Lynne E. Ford, *Women and Politics: The Pursuit of Equality* (New York: Houghton Mifflin Company, 2002), 199.

14. Commission of the European Communities, "Gender Pay Gaps in European Labour Markets—Measurement, Analysis and Policy Implications," Brussels, September 4, 2003.

15. Organization for Economic Co-operation and Development, *OECD in Figures: Statistics for the Member Countries* (Paris: OECD, 2007): 32.

16. Ibid., 33.

17. GlobeWomen, "Female Board Directors and Executive Officers, Fortune 500 Companies, 2008," http://www.globewomen.org/cwdi/2008%20CWDI/CWDI-ICD%20Event/united_states.htm (December 9, 2008).

18. "Helping Women Get to the Top," *Economist,* July 23, 2005.

19. Ibid.

20. World Bank, *Engendering Development: Through Gender Equality in Rights, Resources, and Voice* (New York: Oxford University Press, 2001), 1.

21. Carol Gilligan, *In a Different Voice* (Cambridge, MA: Harvard University Press, 1982).

22. Joyce Gelb, "The Equal Employment Opportunity Law: A Decade of Change for Japanese Women?" *Law & Policy* 22 (October 2000): 386.

23. M. Grazia Rossilli, "The European Union's Policy on the Equality of Women," *Feminist Studies* 25 (Spring 1999): 178–180.

24. National Organization for Women, "Facts About Pay Equity," http://www.now.org/issues/economic/factsheet.html (October 6, 2003).

25. Louise Nousratpour, "Hit out over Pay Injustice: Unions Urge Government to Confront Poverty," *Morning Star,* September 18, 2003, p. 1.

26. Hiromi Tanaka, "Equal Employment in Contemporary Japan: A Structural Approach," *Political Science* (January 2004): 66.

27. M. Margaret Conway, David W. Ahern, and Gertrude A. Steuernagel, *Women and Public Policy: A Revolution in Progress* (Washington, DC: Congressional Quarterly Press, 1999), 74.

28. See Eileen Applebaum et al., "Shared Work, Valued Care: New Norms for Organizing Market Work and Unpaid Care Work," Economic Policy Institute, June 2002.

29. Kia Franklin, "A Vote in Favor of Fairness; the Candidates' Opinions on Pay Discrimination Case Offers a Glimpse into Judicial Philosophy," *Newsday,* October 21, 2008, p. A35.

30. "Treaty Establishing the European Community," http://www.hri.org/docs/Rome57/ Part3Title08.html#Art119 (April 22, 2006).

31. "European Parliament Fact Sheet 4.8.7. Equality for Men and Women," http://www. europarl.eu.int/factsheets/4_8_7_en.htm (September 30, 2003).

32. M. Grazia Rossilli, "The European Union's Policy on the Equality of Women," *Feminist Studies* 25, no.1 (1999): 173.

33. European Union, "Equal Pay," http://europa.eu.int/scadplus/leg/en/cha/c10905.htm (April 22, 2006).

34. Ilona Ostern, "From Equal Pay to Equal Employment: Four Decades of European Gender Politics," in *Gender Policies in the European Union,* ed. Mariagrazia Rossilli (New York: Peter Lang, 2000), 28.

35. Catherine Hoskyns, "Four Action Programmes on Equal Opportunities," in *Gender Policies in the European Union,* 43–47.

36. Scottish Labour, "Women and the Changing European Union," November 4, 2002, http://www.scottishlabour.org.uk/helenliddell (September 30, 2003).

37. Reuters, "Women Paid 16% Less Than Men, Report Says; Gap Widest in Asia, Americas," *The Gazette (Montreal),* March 7, 2008.

38. U.S. General Accounting Office, "A New Look Through the Glass Ceiling: Where Are the Women?" January 2002.

39. National Women's Law Center, "The Paycheck Fairness Act: Helping to Close the Women's Wage Gap," May 2003, p. 1, http://www.nwlc.org (October 6, 2003).

40. Reuters, "Women Paid 16% Less Than Men, Report Says; Gap Widest in Asia, Americas," *The Gazette (Montreal),* March 7, 2008.

41. Commission of the European Communities, "Gender Pay Gaps in European Labour Markets—Measurement, Analysis, and Policy Implications," Brussels, 4.9.2003 SEC(2003)937: 10.

42. Hiroyuki Takahashi, "Working Women in Japan: A Look at Historical Trends and Legal Reform," Japan Economic Institute, no. 42, November 6, 1998, http://www.jei. org/Archive/JEIR98/9842f.html (November 13, 2003).

43. Rob Varnon, "Census Report on Earning: Struggling to Bridge the Wage Gap," *Connecticut Post,* August 17, 2003, Your Money section.

44. "Statement by Congresswoman Carolyn B. Maloney: Women's Equality Amendment— 11/14/2002," *Women's International Network News* (Winter 2003) 29–1, p. 73.

45. CEC, "Gender Pay Gaps in European Labour Markets," 11–17.

46. "Harman Pledges to Reduce the Widening Gender Wage Gap," *Birmingham Post,* September 6, 2007, p. 4.

47. CEC, "Gender Pay Gaps in European Labour Markets," 15.

48. "Japan's Salary Gap," *The Japan Times*, March 24, 2008.

49. James Graff et al., "Help Wanted for Europe," *Time*, June 19, 2000, vol. 155, issue 25, p. 18.

50. Ilse Lenz, "Globalization, Gender, and Work: Perspectives on Global Regulation," *Review of Policy Research* 20 (Spring 2003): 35–38.

51. Dongxiao Liu and Elizabeth Heger Boyle, "Making the Case: The Women's Convention and Equal Employment Opportunity in Japan," *International Journal of Comparative Sociology* 42 (2001): 389–390.

52. Tadashi Hanami, "Equal Employment Revisited," *Japan Labour Bulletin*, The Japan Institute of Labour 39 (January 1, 2000).

53. Joyce Gelb, "Japan's Equal Employment Opportunity Law: A Decade of Change for Japanese Women?" *Law and Policy* 22 (October 2000): 387.

54. M. Margaret Conway, David W. Ahern, and Gertrude A. Steuernagel, *Women and Public Policy: A Revolution in Progress* (Washington, DC: CQ Press, 2004), 95.

55. As quoted in Lynne E. Ford, *Women and Politics: The Pursuit of Equality* (New York: Houghton Mifflin, 2002), 211.

56. As quoted in Ibid., 213.

57. Executive Order 11246, 3 C.F.R. 169, 1974.

58. "The ERA: A Brief Introduction," http://www.equalrightsamendment.org/overview. htm (April 22, 2006).

59. Ostner, "From Equal Pay to Equal Employability," 28.

60. British Broadcasting Corporation, "Amsterdam Treaty," April 30, 2001, http://news. bbc.co.uk/1/hi/in_depth/europe/euro-glossary/1216210.stm.

61. Grazia Rossilli, "The European Union's Policy on the Equality of Women," *Feminist Studies* 25, no. 1 (1999): 171–172.

62. European Commission, Directorate-General for Education and Culture, *European Employment and Social Policy: A Policy for People* (Luxembourg: European Communities, 2000): 26.

63. Martin Fackler, "Career Women in Japan Find a Blocked Path, Despite Equal Opportunity Law," *New York Times*, August 6, 2007, A1.

64. Rossilli, "The European Union's Policy on the Equality of Women," 175.

65. Gelb, "Japan's Equal Employment Opportunity Law," 390–391.

66. Tanaka, "Equal Employment in Contemporary Japan," 66.

67. Fackler, "Career Women in Japan," A1.

68. Gelb, "Japan's Equal Employment Opportunity Law," 394.

69. Ibid., 396–397.

70. Akemi Nakamura, "Four Women Await Outcome of 10-Year Quest for Equal Pay," *The Japan Times*, March 27, 2005; "Four Women Win 63 Million Yen Ruling: Sumitomo Metal Guilty of Gender Bias," *The Japan Times*, March 29, 2005.

71. Ibid.

72. Fackler, "Career Women in Japan," A1.

73. "Only 8.9% of Managerial Positions Taken by Women in Japan," *Deutsche Press-Agentur*, September 13, 2003, Miscellaneous section.

74. Takahashi, "Working Women in Japan," p. 11 of 12.

75. Ibid., p. 11 of 12.

76. WomenOf.com, "Non-Profits Improve Numbers of Women CEOs," http://www. womenof.com/News/cn092500.asp (October 6, 2003).

77. GlobeWomen, "Female Board Directors and Executive Officers, Fortune 500 Companies, 2008," http://www.globewomen.org/cwdi/2008%20CWDI/CWDI-ICD%20Event/united_states.htm (December 9, 2008).

78. National Organization for Women, "Pay Equity Still a Dream Worth Pursuing: New Report Shows Glass Ceiling Intact," Summer 2002, http://www.now.org/nnt/summer-2002/payequity.html (October 6, 2003).

79. "The European Parliament Takes Stock," *Women's International Network News* 26, issue 4 (Autumn 2000) p. 59.

80. "EU Highlights Gender Equality," *Chinadaily.com.cn,* March 9, 2007.

81. "Women and Work: European Situation," http://www.etuc.org.EQUALPAY/UK/women_and_work/European-Union/default.cfm (November 11, 2003).

82. European Commission, "European Employment and Social Policy," 24.

83. *Christian Science Monitor,* August 8, 1997, vol. 89, issue 178, p. 10.

84. As cited in Heidi Gottfried and Laura Reese, "Gender, Policy, Politics, and Work: Feminist Comparative and Transnational Research," *The Review of Policy Research* 20, no. 1 (2003): 10.

85. Conway, Ahern, and Steuernagel, *Women and Public Policy,* 82.

86. U.S. Department of State, Bureau of Democracy, Human Rights, and Labor, "Japan: Country Reports on Human Rights Practices—2000," February 23, 2001, http://www.state.gov/g/drl/rls/hrrpt/2000/eap/709pf.htm (November 19, 2003).

87. As quoted in Ford, *Women and Politics,* 218.

88. Jeanne Gregory, "Sexual Harassment: The Impact of EU Law in the Member States," in *Gender Policies in the European Union,* 175–189.

89. Commission of the European Communities, "Report from the Commission to the Council, the European Parliament, the European Economic and Social Committee and the Committee of Regions: Annual Report on Equal Opportunities for Women and Men in the European Union 2002," Brussels, March 5, 2003, COM (2003) 98.

90. U.S. Department of State, Bureau of Democracy, Human Rights, and Labor, "Japan."

91. Ibid.

92. Ibid.

93. "Sexual Harassment," Encyclopedia Article from Encarta, http://www.encarta.msn.com/encyclopedia_761579949 (November 19, 2003).

94. "EU Tightens Sex Harassment Law," CNN.com, April 18, 2002, http://cnn.worldnews.printthis.clickability.com (November 20, 2003).

95. Ibid.

96. Commission of the European Communities, "Report from the Commission to the Council, the European Parliament, the European Economic and Social Committee and the Committee of Regions."

97. Social Security Administration, "Women and Social Security," October 3, 2005, http://www.ssa.gov/pressoffice/factsheets/women.htm (April 22, 2006).

98. "Women in Europe Towards Healthy Ageing," European Institute of Women's Health (1997), http://www.eurohealth.ie/report/index.htm, Introduction, p. 4 of 5 (September 29, 2003).

99. Ross Clare, "Women and Superannuation," The University of New South Wales, School of Economics and Actuarial Studies, paper presented at the Ninth Annual Colloquium of Superannuation Researchers, July 2001, p. 2.

100. Ayako Doi, "In Other Words," *Foreign Policy: The Magazine of Global Politics, Economics and Ideas* (November/December 2003), http://www.foreignpolicy.com/story/story.php?storyID=13976 (November 20, 2003).

101. "Women in Europe Towards Healthy Ageing," Introduction, p. 4 of 5.

102. Social Security Network, a Century Foundation Project, "Issue Brief #6: Social Security: A Women's Issue," http://www.socsec.org/facts/Issue_Briefs/ women.htm (October 3, 2003).

103. As quoted in Charles Pope, "Social Security Must Protect Women, Bush Told," *Seattle Post-Intelligencer,* June 13, 2001, http://seattlepi.nwsource.com/national/27227_socsec13.shtml (September 29, 2003).

104. Kim Campbell, "Women Seek Solutions to Pension-System Bias," *Christian Science Monitor,* May 9, 1996, vol. 88, p. 9.

105. "1 in 5 Women Relying on Partner's Pension," *The Financial Times,* August 16, 2003, Money section, p. 23.

106. "Women Given Unfair Choice of Babies or a Good Pension," *The Western Mail,* July 7, 2003, p. 1.

107. "Women in Europe Towards Healthy Ageing," European Institute of Women's Health, Introduction, p. 4 of 5.

108. Campbell, "Women Seek Solutions to Pension-System Bias," p. 9.

CHAPTER 5

1. Russell Shorto, "No Babies?" *New York Times Magazine,* June 29, 2008, p. 34.

2. For example, see Nancy Fraser, "After the Family Wage: Gender Equity and the Welfare State," *Political Theory* 22, no. 4 (1994): 591–618.

3. Diane Sainsbury, "Introduction," in *Gender and Welfare State Regimes,* ed. Diane Sainsbury (Oxford: Oxford University Press, 1999), 7.

4. The original delineation of welfare states into liberal, social capitalist, and social democratic welfare states was put forth by G. Esping Andersen, *The Three Worlds of Welfare Capitalism* (Cambridge: Cambridge University Press, 1990).

5. This framework is taken from Sainsbury, ed., *Gender and Welfare State Regimes.*

6. Organisation for Economic Co-operation and Development, *OECD in Figures: Statistics for the Member Countries* (Paris: OECD, 2002).

7. In addition, many women are also choosing to have fewer children later in life; one of the results of increased work activity among women has been a declining fertility rate in many of the OECD countries as well as an increase in the mean age of women at first childbirth (except for the United States). For example, fertility rates have dropped to an average of 1.68 in the OECD countries in the late 1990s and to 1.47 in the fifteen-country EU in 2001. Sheila B. Kamerman et al., *Social Policies, Family Types and Child Outcomes in Selected OECD Countries* (Paris: OECD; 2003), 8.

8. Part-time is defined as less than thirty usual hours worked per week in the main job. OECD, *OECD in Figures: Statistics of the Member Countries* (Paris: OECD, 2002), 18–19.

9. Ibid., 18–19.

10. J. O'Connor, "Gender, Class and Citizenship in the Comparative Analysis of Welfare State Regimes: Theoretical and Methodological Issues," *British Journal of Sociology* 44, no. 3 (1993): 501–518.

11. Wisensale, *Family Leave Policy,* 110.

12. Sheila Kamerman and Shirley Gatenio, "Mother's Day: More Than Candy and Flowers, Working Parents Need Paid Time-Off," Columbia University, the Clearinghouse on International Developments in Child, Youth, and Family Policies, Issue brief, Spring 2002.

13. Ibid.

14. Ibid.

15. Ibid.

16. International Labour Organization, *Condition of Work Digest 1994: Maternity and Work* 13 (1994): 20.

17. Ibid., 10.

18. International Labour Organization, *Time for Equality at Work: Global Report Under the Follow-up to the ILO Declaration on Fundamental Principles and Rights at Work* (Geneva: ILO, 2003), 76.

19. Sheila Kamerman and Shirley Gatenio, "Tax Day: How Do America's Child Benefits Compare?" Columbia University, the Clearinghouse on International Developments in Child, Youth, and Family Policies, Issue brief, Spring 2002.

20. The Clearinghouse on International Developments in Child, Youth, and Family Policies, "Section 18: Child and Family Allowances," Table 1: Child and Family Cash and Tax Benefits in Select Industrialized Countries, http://www.childpolicyintl.org (April 22, 2006).

21. The Clearinghouse on International Developments in Child, Youth, and Family Policies, "Section 18: Child and Family Allowances," http://www.childpolicyintl.org (April 22, 2006).

22. ILO, "Time for Equality at Work," 21.

23. Kamerman and Gatenio, "Tax Day."

24. Amy Mazur, *Theorizing Feminist Policy* (New York: Oxford University Press, 2002), 112.

25. Wisensale, *Family Leave Policy,* 109.

26. Kamerman and Gatenio, "Tax Day."

27. Erin Kelly and Frank Dobbin, "Civil Rights Law at Work: Sex Discrimination and the Rise of Maternity Leave Policies," *American Journal of Sociology* 105, no. 2 (1999): 455–492.

28. Amy Mazur, *Theorizing Feminist Policy* (New York: Oxford University Press, 2002), 112.

29. Wisensale, *Family Leave Policy,* 141

30. Kelly and Dobbin, "Civil Rights at Work."

31. George Bush, "The President's Veto Message," *Congressional Digest,* January 1993, p. 12.

32. Kelly and Dobbin, "Civil Rights Law at Work."

33. Wisensale, *Family Leave Policy,* 109.

34. OECD, *OECD in Figures.*

35. The Clearinghouse on International Developments in Child, Youth, and Family Policies at Columbia University, "Germany," http://www.childpolicyintl.org (August 9, 2005).

36. Karin Gottschall and Katherine Bird, "Family Leave Policies and Labor Market Segregation in Germany: Reinvention or Reform of the Male Breadwinner Model?" *Review of Policy Research* 20, no. 1 (2003): 115–135.

37. Maureen Baker, *Canadian Family Policies: Cross National Comparisons* (Toronto: University of Toronto Press, 1995).

38. United Nations, *Human Development Report 2004*, http://hdr.undp.org/reports/global/2004 (April 22, 2006).

39. The Clearinghouse on International Developments in Child, Youth, and Family Policies at Columbia University, "France," http://www.childpolicyintl.org (September 8, 2005).

40. Ibid.

41. The Clearinghouse on International Developments in Child, Youth, and Family Policies at Columbia University, "Sweden," http://www.childpolicyintl.org (September 8, 2005).

42. Wisensale, *Family Leave Policy*, 227.

43. Ibid., 218.

44. Kamerman and Gatenio

45. OECD, "Child Care in OECD Countries," in *Employment Outlook 1990* (Paris: OECD, 1990).

46. Sheila B. Kamerman, "Early Childhood Education and Care (ECEC): An Overview of Developments in the OECD Countries," unpublished paper, 3–6.

47. Sheila B. Kamerman, "Early Childhood Education and Care (ECEC)," 23–31.

48. Rachel Henneck, "Family Policy in the US, Japan, Germany, Italy, and France: Parental Leave, Child Benefits/Family Allowances, Child Care, Marriage/Cohabitation, and Divorce," unpublished paper, May 2003.

49. Abby J. Cohen, "A Brief History of Federal Financing for Child Care in the United States," *Financing Child Care* 6 (Summer/Fall 1996): 29.

50. Emilie Stoltzfus, *Citizen, Mother, Worker: Debating Public Responsibility for Child Care After the Second World War* (Chapel Hill: University of North Carolina Press, 2003), 8–10.

51. Gwendolyn Mink, *Welfare's End* (Ithaca, NY: Cornell University Press, 1998).

52. As quoted in Cohen, "A Brief History of Federal Financing for Child Care in the United States," 32.

53. Stoltzfus, *Citizen, Mother, Worker*, 14.

54. Martha Coven, "An Introduction to TANF," Center on Budget and Policy Priorities, October 24, 2003.

55. Henneck, "Family Policy in the US, Japan, Germany, Italy, and France."

56. Ibid.

57. Gottschall and Bird, "Family Leave Policies and Labor Market Segregation in Germany," 115–135.

58. German Federal Ministry of Health and Social Security, "Child Benefit, Child Raising Allowance, Parental Leave, Maintenance Advance and Supplementary Child Allowance," January 2005, http://www.bmgs.bund.de/downloads/Child_benefit-Kindergeld.pdf (April 22, 2006).

59. The Clearinghouse on International Developments in Child, Youth, and Family Policies at Columbia University, "Germany," http://www.childpolicyintl.org (September 8, 2005).

60. Ingela K. Naumann, "Child Care and Feminism in West Germany and Sweden in the 1960s and 1970s," *Journal of European Social Policy* 15, no. 1 (2005): 51–54.

61. Ibid., 51–54.

62. Ibid., 56–57.

63. "Germany to Bolster Child Care," *Deutsche Welle,* October 28, 2004.

64. Gottschall and Bird, "Family Leave Policies and Labor Market Segregation in Germany," 115–135.

65. Ibid., 115–135.

66. Marcia K. Meyers, Janet C. Gornick, and Katherin E. Ross, "Public Childcare, Parental Leave, and Employment," in *Gender and Welfare State Regimes,* ed. Sainsbury, 126.

67. Kamerman, "Early Childhood Education and Care (ECEC)," 15.

68. The Clearinghouse on International Developments in Child, Youth, and Family Policy at Columbia University, "France."

69. The Swedish Institute, "Childcare in Sweden," September 2004, http://www.sweden.se/templates/cs/BasicFactsheet (April 22, 2006).

70. Ibid.

71. Ibid.

72. Naumann, "Child Care and Feminism in West Germany and Sweden in the 1960s and 1970s," 54–58.

73. The Swedish Institute, "Childcare in Sweden."

74. The Clearinghouse on International Developments in Child, Youth, and Family Policy at Columbia University, Table 1.32, "Family and Child Allowance Programs: Coverage, Qualifying Conditions, Benefit Levels and other Related Allowances," http://www.childpolicyintl.org (April 22, 2006).

75. Naumann, "Child Care and Feminism in West Germany and Sweden in the 1960s and 1970s," 58–60.

76. Kamerman et al., "Social Policies, Family Types and Child Outcomes in Selected OECD Countries," 25.

77. Kamerman, "Early Childhood Education and Care (ECEC)," 8.

78. Janet C. Gornick, Marcia K. Meyers, and Katherin E. Ross, "Public Policies and the Employment of Mothers: A Cross-National Study," *Social Science Quarterly* 79, no. 1 (1998): 35–54.

79. Wisensale, *Family Leave Policy,* 219.

80. Diane Sainsbury, "Gender, Policy Regimes, and Politics," in *Gender and Welfare State Regimes,* ed. Sainsbury, 266–267.

81. Ibid., 267–268.

82. Ibid., 268–269.

83. Wisensale, *Family Leave Policy,* 185–212.

84. Shorto, "No Babies?," 39.

85. The Clearinghouse on International Developments in Child, Youth, and Family Policies at Columbia University, "Germany," http://www.childpolicyintl.org (March 16, 2009).

86. http://europa.eu.int/scadplus/printversion/en/cha/c10916.htm (April 22, 2006).

87. Arnlaug Leira, *Working Parents and the Welfare State: Family Change and Policy Reform in Scandinavia* (Cambridge: Cambridge University Press, 2002), 146.

88. Jet Bussemaker and Kees van Kinsbergen, "Contemporary Social Capitalist Welfare State and Gender Inequality," in *Gender and Welfare State Regimes,* ed. Sainsbury, 15–47.

CHAPTER 6

1. Andrew Stern, "US Pharmacist Sues, Refusing to Sell Contraceptive," Reuters News Service, June 10, 2005.

2. Judith Graham, "Illinois Supreme Court Revives Pharmacy Owners' Case Against Morning-After Pill," *Chicago Tribune,* December 19, 2008, http://archives. chicagotribune.com/2008/dec/19/health/chi-emergency-contraception-19dec19.3.

3. Dorothy McBride Stetson, "US Abortion Debates: 1959–1998: The Women's Movement Holds On," in *Abortion Politics, Women's Movements, and the Democratic State: A Comparative Study of State Feminism,* ed. Dorothy McBride Stetson (Oxford: Oxford University Press, 2001), 247.

4. Kristin Luker, *Abortion and the Politics of Motherhood* (Berkeley: University of California Press, 1984), 1–10.

5. Susheela Singh, Stanley K. Henshaw, and Kathleen Berentsen, "Abortion: A Worldwide Overview," in *The Sociocultural and Political Aspects of Abortion: Global Perspectives,* ed. Alaka Malwade Basu (Westport, CT: Praeger, 2003), 15–16.

6. Marina Calloni, "Debates and Controversies on Abortion in Italy," in *Abortion Politics, Women's Movements, and the Democratic State,* 181–203.

7. John C. Caldwell and Pat Caldwell, "Introduction: Induced Abortion in a Changing World," in *The Sociocultural and Political Aspects of Abortion,* 4.

8. The United Nations, *Abortion Policies: A Global Review* (New York: United Nations Press, 2002), http://www.un.org/esa/population/publications/abortion (August 10, 2005).

9. Luker, *Abortion and the Politics of Motherhood,* 16.

10. World Health Organization, Guttmacher Institute, "Facts on Induced Abortion Worldwide," October 2008, www.guttmacher.org (March 17, 2009).

11. Center for Reproductive Rights, "World Abortion Laws 2008 Fact Sheet," www. reproductiverights.org/sites/crr.civicactions.net/files/pub_fac_abortionlaws2008. pdf (March 17, 2009).

12. As cited in Caldwell and Caldwell, "Introduction," 1.

13. Ibid., 3.

14. Ibid., 2.

15. Evelyn Mahon, "Abortion Debates in Ireland: An Ongoing Issue," in *Abortion Politics, Women's Movements, and the Democratic State,* 157.

16. Ibid., 159.

17. United Nations Population Division, Department of Economic and Social Affairs, "Ireland," in *Abortion Policies: A Global Review* (New York: United Nations Press, 2002).

18. For information about abortion in Great Britain, see Dorothy McBride Stetson, "Women's Movements' Defense of Legal Abortion in Great Britain," in *Abortion Politics, Women's Movements, and the Democratic State,* 135–156.

19. United Nations Population Division, Department of Economic and Social Affairs, "Ireland."

20. Mahon, "Abortion Debates in Ireland," 161.

21. Shawn Pogatchnik, "Irish Bishops Reject Pregnancy Pamphlet," Associated Press, June 16, 2005.

22. Mahon, "Abortion Debates in Ireland," 162–163.

23. United Nations Population Division, Department of Economic and Social Affairs, "Ireland."

24. Mahon, "Abortion Debates in Ireland," 167.

25. Ibid., 165.

26. United Nations Population Division, Department of Economic and Social Affairs, "Ireland."

27. "Abortion Will Pop up Again on Political Radar Screen," *Irish Independent,* March 8, 2005.

28. "Rights Group Says Law Must Be Changed to Allow for Abortions," *Irish Independent,* March 8, 2005.

29. Mahon, "Abortion Debates in Ireland," 169.

30. "Voters in Ireland Reject Change in Abortion Law," *USA Today,* March 8, 2002, p. 7a.

31. Pogatchnik, "Irish Bishops Reject Pregnancy Pamphlet."

32. "Rights Group Says Law Must Be Changed to Allow for Abortions."

33. "Voters in Ireland Reject Change in Abortion Law."

34. CNN World News, "Abortion Ship Arrives in Ireland," June 15, 2001, http://cnn.worldnews.printthis.clickability.com (April 22, 2006).

35. "Abortion Will Pop up Again on Political Radar Screen."

36. Carl O'Brien, "Human Rights Court to Hear Irish Abortion Ban Case." *The Irish Times,* July 15, 2009, 1.

37. Mahon, "Abortion Debates in Ireland," 170.

38. Richard Oakley, "Irish Faith on Wane but Tolerance Rises," *The Times,* April 10, 2005.

39. As quoted in Lee Ann Banaszak, "The Women's Movement Policy Successes and the Constraints of State Reconfiguration: Abortion and Equal Pay in Differing Eras," in *Women's Movements Facing the Reconfigured State,* ed. Lee Ann Banaszak, Karen Beckwith, and Dieter Rucht (New York: Cambridge University Press, 2003), 154.

40. Irish Medical Council, "A Guide to Ethical Conduct and Behavior," 6th ed. (Dublin, Ireland: Irish Medical Council, 2004), 44.

41. Oakley, "Irish Faith on Wane but Tolerance Rises."

42. Banaszak, "The Women's Movement Policy Successes and the Constraints of State Reconfiguration," 148–155.

43. Stetson, "US Abortion Debates 1959–1998," 247.

44. Luker, *Abortion and the Politics of Motherhood,* 11–39.

45. United Nations Population Division, Department of Economic and Social Affairs, "United States of America," in *Abortion Policies: A Global Review* (New York: United Nations Press, 2002).

46. As quoted in Center for Reproductive Rights, *Roe v. Wade and the Right to Privacy* (2003), http://www.reproductiverights.org/pdf/roeprivacy.pdf (April 22, 2006), 30.

47. United Nations Population Division, Department of Economic and Social Affairs, "United States of America."

48. As quoted in Center for Reproductive Rights, *Roe v. Wade and the Right to Privacy,* 44.

49. United Nations Population Division, Department of Economic and Social Affairs, "United States of America."

50. Guttmacher Institute, "State Policies in Brief as of March 1, 2009," www.guttmacher.org (March 19, 2009).

51. Physicians for Reproductive Choice and Health and The Alan Guttmacher Institute, "An Overview of Abortion in the United States," June 2005, http://www.guttmacher. org/presentations/abort_slides.pdf (April 22, 2006).

52. As quoted in Find Law for Professionals, http://caselaw.lp.findlaw.com/scripts/get-case.pl?court=tx&vol=/sc/010061&invol=1.

53. United Nations Population Division, Department of Economic and Social Affairs, "United States of America."

54. Ibid.

55. The White House, "President Bush Signs Partial Birth Abortion Ban Act 2003," Nov 5, 2003, http://www.whitehouse.gov/news/releases/2003/11/print/ 20031105-1.html (April 22, 2006).

56. The Alan Guttmacher Institute, "State Policies in Brief as of August 1, 2005," http://www.guttmacher.org/statecenter/spibs/spib_BPBA.pdf (August 10, 2005).

57. United Nations Population Division, Department of Economic and Social Affairs, "United States of America."

58. Physicians for Reproductive Choice and Health and The Alan Guttmacher Institute, "An Overview of Abortion in the United States."

59. Joe Stumpe and Monica Davey, "Abortion Doctor Shot to Death in Kansas Church," The New York Times, June 1, 2009. http://www.nytimes.com/2009/06/01/us/01tiller. html.

60. Physicians for Reproductive Choice and Health and The Alan Guttmacher Institute, "An Overview of Abortion in the United States."

61. Ibid.

62. Ibid.

63. Evert Kettering, "Netherlands," in Abortion in the New Europe: A Comparative Handbook, ed. Bill Roston and Anna Eggert (Westport, CT: Greenwood Press, 1994), 173–186.

64. United Nations Population Division, Department of Economic and Social Affairs, "Netherlands," in Abortion Policies: A Global Review (New York: United Nations: 2002), http://www.un.org/esa/population/publications/abortion (August 10, 2005).

65. Kettering, "Netherlands," 173–174.

66. Ibid., 174–175.

67. Joyce Outshoorn, "Policy-Making on Abortion: Arenas, Actors, and Arguments in the Netherlands," in Abortion Politics, Women's Movements and the Democratic State, ed. Dorothy McBride Stetson (New York: Oxford University Press, 2001), 207.

68. Kettering, "Netherlands," 175; Outshoorn, "Policy-Making on Abortion," 209–213.

69. Kettering, "Netherlands," 175–176.

70. United Nations Population Division, Department of Economic and Social Affairs, "Netherlands."

71. Agence France Presse, "Dutch Women Go Abroad for Late-Term Abortions," April 12, 2005.

72. Trees A. M. Te Braake, "Late Termination of Pregnancy Because of Severe Foetal Abnormalities: Legal Acceptability, Notification and Review in the Netherlands," European Journal of Health Law 7 (2000): 387–403.

73. Netherlands Ministry of Foreign Affairs, "Questions and Answers on Dutch Policy on Abortion—2003," http://www.minvws.nl/en/themes/abortion/default.asp (August 10, 2005).

74. Agence France Presse, "Dutch Women Go Abroad for Late-Term Abortions."

75. Ibid.

76. Netherlands Ministry of Foreign Affairs, "Questions and Answers on Dutch Policy on Abortion—2003."

77. World Values Survey, "1999–2002 World Values Survey Questionnaire," http://www.worldvaluessurvey.org/statistics/index.html.

78. Ronnee Schreiber, "Injecting a Woman's Voice: Conservative Women's Organizations, Gender Consciousness, and the Expression of Women's Policy Preferences," *Sex Roles* 47 (October 2002): 337–339.

PART III   INTRODUCTION

1. United Nations Development Programme (UNDP), *Human Development Report 2003* (New York: Oxford University Press, 2003), 5.

2. Amartya Sen, *Development as Freedom* (New York: Anchor Books, 2000).

3. United Nations Development Fund for Women (UNIFEM), *Progress of the World's Women 2002: Gender Equality and the Millennium Development Goals* (New York: UNIFEM, 2002), vii.

4. United Nations Children's Fund (UNICEF) and Innocenti Research Centre, "Domestic Violence Against Women and Girls," *Innocenti Digest* 6 (June 2000): 2. http://www.unicef-icdc.org/publications/pdf/digest6e.pdf (October 12, 2005).

CHAPTER 7

1. "The List: The Worst Places to Be a Woman," *Foreign Policy,* www.foreignpolicy.com/story/cms.php?story_id=4319&print=1, posted May 2008.

2. UNIFEM, "Who Answers to Women? Gender and Accountability," *Progress of the World's Women 2008/09,* (New York: UNIFEM, 2009)117–133.

3. United Nations Development Program, *Human Development Report 2007/2008,* (New York: UNDP, 2008), 337.

4. World Bank, *Engendering Development: Through Gender Equality in Rights, Resources, and Voice* (New York: Oxford University Press, 2001), 8–14.

5. Ibid, 1.

6. United Nations Development Program, *Human Development Report 2007/2008,* 327–329.

7. For example, see GenderStats, at http://web.worldbank.org/WBSITE/EXTERNAL/TOPICS/EXTGENDER/EXTANATOOLS/EXTSTATINDDATA/EXTGENDERSTATS/0,,menuPK:3237391~pagePK:64168427~piPK:64168435~theSitePK:3237336,00.html.

8. UNIFEM, *Gender Equality Now. Accelerating the Achievement of the Millennium Development Goals. Part II of Progress 2008/2009* (New York: UNIFEM, 2009).

9. Irene Tinker, "Empowerment Just Happened: The Unexpected Expansion of Women's Organizations," in Jane S. Jaquette and Gale Summerfield, eds., *Women and Gender Equity in Development Theory and Practice: Institutions, Resources, and Mobilization* (Durham, NC: Duke University Press, 2006), 268.

10. Ester Boserup, *Women's Role in Economic Development* (New York: St. Martin's Press, 1970).

11. Janet Henshall Momsen, *Gender and Development* (New York: Routledge, 2004), 11.

12. As quoted in Jane S. Jaquette and Kathleen Staudt, "Women, Gender, and Development," in Jaquette and Summerfield, eds., *Women and Gender Equity in Development Theory and Practice*, 21.

13. United Nations, "United Nations International Decades Designated by the General Assembly, September 27, 2001, http://www.nalis.gov.tt/National-UN-Days/UN_INTERNATIONALDECADES.html (October 13, 2005).

14. Tinker, "Empowerment Just Happened," 277.

15. Valentine M. Moghadam, *Globalizing Women: Transnational Feminist Networks* (Baltimore: The Johns Hopkins University Press, 2005), 1–9.

16. Maxine Molyneux, "Mobilization Without Emancipation: Women's Interests, State, and Revolution in Nicaragua," *Feminist Studies* 11, no. 2 (1985): 227–254; Janet Henshall Momsen, *Gender and Development* (London: Routledge, 2004), 14.

17. United Nations, *Gender Mainstreaming: An Overview* (New York: United Nations, January 2002), v.

18. United Nations Development Fund for Women (UNIFEM), "Gender-Responsive Budgets,"http://www.unifem.org/gender_issues/women_poverty_economics/gender_budgets.php (August 12, 2005).

19. Elisabeth Rehn and Ellen Johnson Sirleaf, "Women War Peace," *Progress of the World's Women 2002*, vol. 1, Executive Summary (New York: UNIFEM, 2002), 3.

20. Moghadam, *Globalizing Women*, 13–17.

21. United Nations, "UN Action for Women," http://www.un.org/ecosocdev/geninfo/women/dpi1796e.htm (October 13, 2005), 3.

22. United Nations, Division for the Advancement of Women, "Convention on the Elimination of All Forms of Discrimination Against Women," http://www.un.org/womenwatch/daw/cedaw (October 13, 2005).

23. Ibid.

24. United Nations, Division for the Advancement of Women. *Women Go Global* (New York: UN Press, 2003).

25. Center for Reproductive Rights, "CEDAW: The Importance of U.S. Ratification," http://www.crlp.org/pub_fac_cedaw.html (October 13, 2005).

26. Human Rights Watch, "CEDAW: The Women's Treaty," January 31, 2005, http://hrw.org/campaigns/cedaw (October 13, 2005).

27. For example, see *Human Development Report 2005*, Table 28: Status of Major International Human Rights in the United Nations Development Program (New York: Oxford University Press, 2005), 311–314.

28. Margaret E. Keck and Kathryn Sikkink, *Activists Beyond Borders: Advocacy Networks in International Politics* (Ithaca, NY: Cornell University Press, 1998), 12–13.

CHAPTER 8

1. Qurratul Ain Tahmina, "South Asia: Working Women Get Poor Health Services," Inter Press Service, June 3, 2003.

2. United States State Department, *Trafficking in Persons Report* (Washington, D.C.: United States States Department, June 2008), 24.

3. Amartya Sen, *Development as Freedom* (New York: Anchor Books, 2000).

4. http://www.worldmapper.org/display.php?selected=181.

5. Food and Agricultural Organization, *Gender and Food Security: Division of Labor* (Rome, Italy: Food and Agricultural Organization, 2003).

6. As cited in "The List: The Worst Places to Be a Woman," *Foreign Policy,* posted May 2008, http://www.foreignpolicy.com/story/cms.php?story_id=4319.

7. World Bank, Gender and Development Group, *Gender Equality and the Millennium Development Goals* (New York: World Bank, April 4, 2003), 19.

8. Ibid., 19.

9. Naila Kabeer, *Gender Mainstreaming in Poverty Eradication and the Millennium Development Goals: A Handbook for Policy-Makers and Other Stakeholders* (London: Commonwealth Secretariat, 2003), 35.

10. Ibid., 31.

11. United Nations Development Programme, *Human Development Report 2004* (New York: Oxford University Press, 2004), 233.

12. International Labor Organization, "Global Employment Trends for Women Brief," March 2007, http://www.ilo.org/public/english/employment/strat/download/getw07.pdf.

13. United Nations Development Programme, *Human Development Report 2002* (New York: Oxford University Press, 2002), 23.

14. International Labour Office, *Women and Men in the Informal Economy: A Statistical Picture* (Geneva: ILO, 2002), 8.

15. Diane Elson and Hende Keklik, UNIFEM, *Progress of the World's Women 2002,* vol. 2, 37.

16. Thomas L. Friedman, *The Lexus and the Olive Tree* (1999), 7–8.

17. Leslie T. Chang, *Factory Girls: From Village to City in a Changing China* (Spiegel & Grau, 2008).

18. Jean-Pierre Singa Boyenge, *ILO Database on Export Processing Zones* (revised), Working Paper 251, International Labour Office, Geneva, April 2007, http://www.ilo.org/public/english/dialogue/sector/themes/epz/epz-db.pdf.

19. Kabeer, *Gender Mainstreaming in Poverty Eradication,* 69.

20. Oxfam International, *Trading Away Our Rights: Women Working in Global Supply Chains* (Oxford: Oxfam International, 2004), 17.

21. Kabeer, *Gender Mainstreaming in Poverty Eradication,* 70.

22. Norma Iglesias Prieto, *Beautiful Flowers of the Maquiladora: Life Histories of Women Workers in Tijuana* (Austin: University of Texas Press, 1997).

23. As quoted in Oxfam International, *Trading Away Our Rights,* 16.

24. Ibid.

25. Ibid.

26. Nicholas D. Kristof, "Where Sweatshops Are a Dream," *New York Times,* January 14, 2009.

27. United Nations Population Fund (UNFPA), *State of the World Population 2006. A Passage to Hope. Women and International Migration,* www.unfpa.org/swp/2006/english/chapter_2/print/chapter_2.html, Chapter 2, Page 2.

28. As cited in UNIFEM (2008), 58.

29. As quoted in United States State Department, *Trafficking in Persons Report,* 22.

30. UNFPA, *State of the World Population 2006,* 2.

31. Ibid., 11.

32. Ibid., 13–14.

33. Ibid., 8.

34. Arlie Russell Hochschild and Barbara Ehrenreich, eds., *Global Woman: Nannies, Maids, and Sex Workers in the New Economy* (New York: Metropolitan Books, 2004).

35. UNFPA, *State of the World Population 2006*, 8–9.

36. Ibid., 9–10.

37. Ibid., 5–6.

38. United States State Department, *Trafficking in Persons Report*, 6.

39. Vidyamali Samarasinghe, "Confronting Globalization in Anti-Trafficking Strategies in Asia," *Brown Journal of World Affairs* 10, no. 1 (2003): 91.

40. UNFPA, *State of the World Population 2006*, Chapter 3, 2.

41. United States State Department, *Trafficking in Persons Report*, 34.

42. UNFPA, *State of the World Population 2006*, Chapter 3, 2.

43. Ibid., Chapter 3, 3.

44. Ibid., Chapter 3, 1–2.

45. United States State Department, *Trafficking in Persons Report*, 11.

46. U.S. Department of Justice.

47. As quoted in U.S. Department of Justice, *Child Sex Tourism* (Washington, D.C.: U.S. Department of Justice, date not provided), www.usdoj.gov/criminal/ceos/sextour. html.

48. UN Department of Economic and Social Affairs, Division for Sustainable Development, http://www.un.org/esa/sustdev.

49. Shawn Meghan Burn, *Women Across Cultures: A Global Perspective*, 2nd ed. (New York: McGraw-Hill, 2005), 153–156.

50. United Nations, *Rural Women in a Changing World* (October 2008), 9.

51. Howard Handelman, *The Challenge of Third World Development*, 3rd ed. (Upper Saddle River, NJ: Prentice Hall, 2003), 121.

52. World Bank, "Women Dairy Farmers in Africa," http://www.worldbank.org/html/ cgiar/newsletter/june97/9dairy.html (April 22, 2006).

53. Women Watch, "International Day of Rural Women," October 15, 2008, www.un.org/ womenwatch/feature/idrw/index.html.

54. Oxfam International, *Trading Away Our Rights*, 17.

55. Ibid., 7.

56. As described in United Nations, *Rural Women in a Changing World*, 10–11.

57. United Nations, *Rural Women in a Changing World*, 7–9.

58. Kabeer, *Gender Mainstreaming in Poverty Eradication*, 31.

59. UNIFEM, *Who Answers to Women? Gender and Accountability*, (New York: UNIFEM, 2009), 60.

60. World Bank, Gender and Development Group, *Gender Equality and the Millennium Development Goals*, 4.

61. As cited in Denis Dreshsler, Johannes Jutting, and Carina Lindberg, "Gender, Institutions, and Development: Better Data, Better Politics," in *Poverty in Focus: Gender Equality*, no. 13, ed. International Poverty Centre (Brasilia, Brazil: ICP-UNDP, January 2008), no pagination.

62. World Bank, "Land Use Rights and Gender Equality in Vietnam," in *Promising Approaches to Engendering Development*, no. 1 (New York: World Bank, September 2002), 1–2.

63. Emily Kearney, "Reaching the Poorest with Microfinance: The Importance of Innovation in Program Design," unpublished thesis, Oregon State University, 2009.

CHAPTER 9

1. Women Deliver, "Real Stories About Women and Girls: Putting a Face on Women Deliver." Women Deliver Global Conference, October 18 – 20 2007, London. http://www.womendeliver.org/fact/Real_Faces_Real_Stories_%20factsheet_(A4).pdf

2. Women Deliver, "The Unfortunate Facts of Life in 2007," Women Deliver Global Conference, October 18 - 20 2007, London. http://www.womendeliver.org/resources/Unfortunate_Facts_Life.htm.

3. World Health Organization, UNICEF, and United Nations Population Fund, *Maternal Mortality in 2000: Estimates Developed by WHO, UNICEF, and UNFPA* (Geneva: World Health Organization, 2004), 2.

4. United Nations, *The Millennium Development Goals Report 2005* (New York: United Nations, 2005), 22.

5. World Health Organization (WHO), "Making Pregnancy Safer," February 2004, http://www.who.int/mediacentre/factsheets/fs276/en/print.html (October 13, 2004).

6. United Nations Population Fund (UNFPA), "Fast Facts on Maternal Mortality and Morbidity," http://www.unfpa.org/mothers/facts.htm (October 13, 2004).

7. Sneha Barot, "Back to Basics: The Rationale for Increased Funds for International Family Planning," *Guttmacher Policy Review* 11, no. 3 (2008), www.gutmacher.org/pubs/gpr/11/3/gpr110313.html.

8. United Nations Population Fund (UNFPA), "Population Issues Overview," http://www.unfpa.org/issues/index.htm (October 13, 2004).

9. UNFPA, "Reducing Risks by Offering Contraceptive Services," http://www.unfpa.org/mothers/contraceptive.htm (October 13, 2004).

10. World Health Organization (WHO), Department of Reproductive Health and Research, "Family Planning," http://www.who.int/reproductive-health/family_planning/index.html (October 13, 2005).

11. UNFPA, "Reducing Risks by Offering Contraceptive Services."

12. World Bank, *World Development Indicators 2002* (New York: World Bank, 2002).

13. Ibid., 16.

14. WHO, "Making Pregnancy Safer."

15. Women Deliver, "Saving Women's Lives: Leading Killers and Practical Solutions," www.womendeliver.org/resources/Saving_Women_Lives.htm.

16. http://www.snowcrest.net/freemanl/world/women/sons.htm.

17. United Nations Development Programme, "The State and Progress of Human Development," in *Human Development Report 2002* (New York: Oxford University Press, 2002), 23.

18. Naila Kabeer, *Gender Mainstreaming in Poverty Eradication and the Millennium Development Goals* (London: Commonwealth Secretariat, The International Development Research Center/CIDA 2003), 92.

19. Julia Duin, "Brides Bound by Traditions; Indian Women, Families Carry Costly Commitment of Dowry," *Washington Times,* February 27, 2007, A1.

20. Ibid.

21. Janet Bagnall, "When Women Become a Burden; Selective-Sex Abortions Threaten to Turn India into a Land Full of Angry, Lonely Young Men," *The Gazette (Montreal),* May 16, 2008, p. A15.

22. "Scans for Baby's Sex Illegal—but Rampant," *The Straights Times (Singapore),* July 14, 2007. http://www.asiaone.com/Just+Woman/Motherhood/Stories/Story/A1Story20070720–19064.html

23. Ibid.

24. "'Care for Girls' Gaining Momentum," *China Daily*, July 8, 2004, http://www.chinadaily.com.cn/english/doc/2004–07/08/content_346700.htm.

25. Valerie M. Hudson and Andrea M. Den Boer, *Bare Branches: The Security Implications of Asia's Surplus Male Population* (Cambridge, MA: The MIT Press, 2004).

26. World Bank, Gender and Development Group, *Gender Equality & the Millennium Development Goals* (New York: World Bank, 2003), 9.

27. WHO, "Women's Health in South-East Asia," February 2001, http://w3.whosea.org/women/regional_tablesf.htm.

28. UNAIDS, *Report on the Global Aids Epidemic Executive Summary* (Geneva, Switzerland: UNAIDS, July 2008), 5–8.

29. Ibid., 8.

30. Michael Kelly, "Hasten the Day When AIDS No Longer Has a Female Face," *The Irish Times*, March 13, 2007, p. 16.

31. Ibid., 16.

32. Noeleen Heyzer, "To Fight AIDS, Empower Women," *Chicago Sun-Times*, July 10, 2003, p. 35.

33. Aishwarya Rai, *Our Planet* (Nairobi, Kenya: United Nations Environmental Programme), volume 15, no. 2, p. 18.

34. Noeleen Heyzer, "Peace of Mind, Piece of Land," *Our Planet*, volume 15, no. 2, pp. 11–12.

35. Michael Fleshman, "Women: The Face of AIDS in Africa," *Africa Renewal* volume 18, no. 3 (October 2004): 6, http://allafrica.com/stories/printable/200410120768.html (October 13, 2004).

36. UNFPA, "Fast Fact—Maternal Mortality and Reproductive Health," www.unfpa.org/mothers/fact.htm (October 13, 2004).

37. United Nations Children's Fund (UNICEF), *Annual Report 2003* (New York: UNICEF, 2004).

38. UNAIDS, *Report on the Global Aids Epidemic: Executive Summary* (Geneva, Switzerland: UNAIDS, July 2008), 9.

39. UNFPA, "UNFPA: United Nations Population Fund," http://www.unfpa.org/about/index.htm (October 13, 2004).

40. UNFPA, "Who We Are," http://www.unfpa.org/publications/detail.cfm?ID=384&filterListType=.

41. International Planned Parenthood Federation, "About IPPF," http://www.ippf.org/about/what.htm (October 13, 2005).

42. WHO, "FamilyPlanning," http://www.who.int/reproductive-health/family_planning/index.html (January 30, 2004).

43. UNFPA, "International Conference on Population and Development," http://www.unfpa.org/icpd/icpd.htm (October 13, 2005).

44. Kirrin Gill, Rohini Pande, and Anju Malhotra, "Women Deliver for Development," October 2007, http://www.womendeliver.org.

45. Kate Benson, "Australia's Mother Theresa," *The Sydney Morning Herald*, March 29, 2008, http://www.smh.com.au/news/world/australias-mother-teresa/2008/03/28/1206207412966.html.

46. Nafis Sadik, "Practical Consensus," *Our Planet*, volume 15, no. 2, p. 6.

47. http://www.plannedparenthood.org/global/education/viewer.asp?ID=238.

48. Guttmacher Institute, "Bush Administration Withholds UNFPA Funding for Seventh Year," June 27, 2008, http://www.guttmacher.org/media/inthenews/2008/06/27/index. html.

49. Lois Abraham and Jane Roberts, "Citizen Engagement," *Our Planet,* volume 15, no. 2, p. 29. See also http://www.34millionfriends.org.

50. Raekha Prasad and Randeep Ramesh, "India's Missing Girls: Daughters Aren't Wanted in India," *The Guardian,* February 28, 2007, 4.

51. Randeep Ramesh, "India to Crack Down on Doctors Aborting Girls," *The Guardian,* April 25, 2008, 24.

52. Ibid.

53. "'Care for Girls' Gaining Momentum," *China Daily,* July 8, 2004, http://www. chinadaily.com.cn/english/doc/2004–07/08/content_346700.htm

54. UNAIDS, *A Joint Response to HIV/AIDS,* (Geneva: UNAIDS, 2004), 9.

55. UNAIDS, *Report on the Global Aids Epidemic: Executive Summary.*

56. The Alan Guttmacher Institute, "Beyond Slogans: Lessons from Uganda's ABC Experience," http://www.agi-usa.org/pubs/ib2004n02.html (October 14, 2005).

57. Holly Burkhalter, "The Politics of AIDS: Engaging Conservative Activists," *Foreign Affairs* (January/February 2004).

58. World Bank, *Engendering Development: Through Gender Equality in Rights, Resources, and Voice* (New York: Oxford University Press, 2001).

59. Lisa C. Smith and Lawrence Haddad, *Explaining Child Malnutrition in Developing Countries: A Cross-Country Analysis* (Washington, DC: International Food Policy Research Institute, 2000).

CHAPTER 10

1. Global Campaign for Education, "Must Try Harder: A School Report on 22 Rich Countries' Aid to Basic Education in Developing Countries," November 2003, http:// www.campaignforeducation.org (November 25, 2003).

2. Ibid.

3. World Bank, "Girls Education: How Are Girls Doing?" January 2009, http:// go.worldbank.org/1L4BH3TG20 (January 6, 2009).

4. National Institute for Literacy, "International Perspectives on Adult Literacy Education," 2006, http://www.nifl.gov/nifl/international/intro.html (January 6, 2009).

5. United Nations, *The Millennium Development Goals Report 2005* (New York: United Nations, 2005), 14.

6. Global Campaign for Education, "Must Try Harder."

7. World Education Forum, "Women and Girls: Education, Not Discrimination!," April 26–28, 2000, http://www2.unesco.org/wef/en-docs/press-kit/wome.pdf (April 23, 2006).

8. Karin Ronnow, "Journey of Hope: An In-Depth Report, Educate Girls, Change the World" (Central Asia Institute, 2008), 25.

9. World Education Forum, "Women and Girls."

10. United Nations, *The Millennium Development Goals Report 2005,* 14.

11. World Education Forum, "Women and Girls."

12. Ibid.

13. United Nations Educational, Scientific and Cultural Organization (UNESCO), "Girls Continue to Face Sharp Discrimination in Access to School," June 11, 2003 press release no. 2003–91, http://www.portal.unesco.org/en/ev.php (November 25, 2003).

14. UNESCO Institute for Statistics, "Gender Parity in Education: Not There Yet," March 2008, no. 1, http://www.uis.unesco.org/template/pdf/EducGeneral/UISFactsheet_2008_No%201_EN.pdf (January 6, 2009).

15. UN Integrated Regional Information Networks, "Togo; School Year Reopens with Free Primary Schools," *Africa News*, October 6, 2008.

16. The World Bank, "Girls' Education—Key Issues," 2009, http://go.worldbank.org/SP3Y3AHK10 (January 7, 2009).

17. Results, "2007 Basics: Global Education for All," 2007, http://www.results.org/website/article.asp?id=2566 (January 7, 2009).

18. UNESCO, "Girls Continue to Face Sharp Discrimination in Access to School."

19. UN Integrated Regional Information Networks, "Togo."

20. UNESCO, "Girls Continue to Face Sharp Discrimination in Access to School."

21. United States Agency for International Development (USAID), Office of Women and Development, "Girls' and Women's Education: A USAID Initiative," Fact Sheet (April 1998).

22. UNESCO, "Girls Continue to Face Sharp Discrimination in Access to School."

23. Human Rights Watch, "Guinea; Thousands of Girls Face Abuse as Domestic Workers," *Africa News,* June 15, 2007.

24. Global Campaign for Education, "Must Try Harder."

25. Aamir Latif, IslamOnline.net, "Taliban Divided on Girls Education," December 26, 2008, http://www.islamonline.net (January 8, 2009).

26. Karin Ronnow, "Journey of Hope: An In-Depth Report, Keeping Hope Alive" Central Asia Institute, 2008), 7.

27. USAID, Office of Women and Development, "Girls' and Women's Education."

28. Abdul Alim, Ben Abdallah, Solofo Ramaruson, Maman Sidikou, and Lieke Van de Wiel, "Accelerating Girl's Education in Yemen: Rethinking Policies in Teachers' Recruitment and School Distribution," February 2007, http://www.ungei.org/resources/files/Policy-Paper-Girls-education-Yemen.pdf (January 8, 2009).

29. World Education Forum, "Women and Girls."

30. UNESCO, "Girls Continue to Face Sharp Discrimination in Access to School."

31. Wellesley Centers for Research on Women and Development and Training Services, Inc., for USAID, September 2003, "Unsafe Schools: A Literature Review of School-Related Gender-Based Violence in Developing Countries," http://pdf.usaid.gov/pdf_docs/PNACU253.pdf (January 8, 2009).

32. UNESCO, "Girls Continue to Face Sharp Discrimination in Access to School."

33. "Kenya; Teenage Girls Targetted for Sexual Exploitation," *East African Standard,* Africa News, February 7, 2008.

34. UNICEF, *Gender Achievements and Prospects in Education: The GAP Report,* Part One, "South Asia Yawning Chasm," http://www.ungei.org/gap/reportSasia.php (January 8, 2009).

35. UNESCO, *EFA Global Monitoring Report 2003/4, Gender and Education for All, the Leap to Equality* (Paris: UNESCO Publishing, 2003), http://www.efareport.unesco.org (November 25, 2003).

36. Education for All—Fast Track Initiative, "About FTI," http://www.education-fast-track.org/ (January 13, 2009).

37. Education for All—Fast Track Initiative, "What's New," http://www.education-fast-track.org/ (January 13, 2009).

38. The United Nations, "The Millennium Development Goals Report 2008," September 2008, http://www.undp.org/publications/MDG_Report_2008_EN.pdf (January 13, 2009), 4.

39. Ibid.

40. Brendan O'Malley, "The Global Classroom," *South China Morning Post,* June 16, 2007, Education section, p. 6.

41. Ibid., 6.

42. UN News Service, "With UNICEF Help, Teens Show Girls in Uganda, Pakistan the Way to School," December 11, 2001, http://www.un.org/apps/news/printnews.asp?nid=9178 (December 15, 2003).

43. USAID, Office of Women and Development, "Girls' and Women's Education."

44. Department for International Development, "DFID and the G8 Presidency 2005: Progress on Debt Relief," http://www.dfid.gov.uk/g8/debtrelief.asp (January 15, 2009).

45. Associated Press, "The Debt Relief Tour," May 28, 2002, http://www.cbsnews.com/stories/2003/07/08/world/main562166.shtml (January 15, 2009).

46. "Uganda; Country's Debt Drops to $1 Billion," *The Monitor,* Africa News, February 28, 2007.

47. KatineChronicles, "Debate: The State of Education in Uganda," *The Guardian,* May 2008, http://www.guardian.co.uk/society/katineblog/2008/May/23/ugandawillachieveitsmillen (January 15, 2009).

48. Canadian International Development Agency, "Uganda," http://www.acdi-cida.gc.ca/uganda (January 12, 2009).

49. World Bank, "Uganda: Development Results," http://web.worldbank.org/WBSITE/EXTERNAL/COUNTRIES/AFRICAEXT/UGANDAEXTN/0,,menuPK:374871~pagePK:141159~piPK:141110~theSitePK:374864,00.html (October 15, 2005).

50. "Uganda; Country's Debt Drops to $1 Billion," *The Monitor,* Africa News, February 28, 2007.

51. Ibid.

52. James Button, "Rich Are Failing to Keep Their Word to Africa," *Sydney Morning Herald (Australia),* June 2, 2007, International News, p. 15.

53. World Bank, "World Bank's First-Ever Combination Grant-Credit Will Support Uganda Education, March 24, 1998, http://web.worldbank.org/WBSITE/EXTERNAL/NEWS/0,,contentMDK:20012678~menuPK:34466~pagePK:64003015~piPK:64003012~theSitePK:4607,00.html (October 15, 2005).

54. The World Bank, "Independent Evaluation Group," http://www.worldbank.org/ieg/education/findings.html (January 12, 2009).

55. "Uganda; Country's Debt Drops to $1 Billion."

56. KatineChronicles, "Debate: The State of Education in Uganda."

57. Ibid.

58. William Easterly, "Think Again: Debt Relief," *Foreign Policy,* November/December, 2001, p. 3.

59. Ibid.

60. Ibid., p.2 .
61. Global Campaign for Education, "Must Try Harder."
62. World Education Forum, "Women and Girls."
63. Ibid.
64. Ibid.
65. Ibid.
66. Ibid.
67. Global Campaign for Education, "Must Try Harder."
68. Ibid.
69. Ibid.
70. Ibid.
71. USAID, Office of Women and Development, "Girls' and Women's Education."

CHAPTER 11

1. Human Rights Watch, testimony from the press release "Serb Gang-Rapes in Kosovo Exposed," March 21, 2000, http://www.hrw.org/press/2000/03/kosrape.htm (November 7, 2003).
2. Ibid.
3. Peter W. Singer, 2006, *Children at War* (Berkley: University of California Press): 33–34.
4. Human Rights Watch, "Refugee and Internally Displaced Women; Gender-Based Asylum Claims," 2003, http://www.hrw.org/women/refugees.html (November 7, 2003).
5. Human Rights Watch, "Seeking Protection: Addressing Sexual and Domestic Violence in Tanzania's Refugee Camps," October 2000, http://www.hrw.org/reports/2000/tanzania (November 17, 2003).
6. Central Intelligence Agency, "Serbia and Montenegro," in *The World Factbook,* October 4, 2005, http://www.cia.gov/cia/publications/factbook/geos/yi.html (October 15, 2005).
7. Kitty McKinsey, "Yugoslavia: Crimes Against Women Become Focus of Tribunals," Radio Free Europe, May 13, 1998, http://www.rferl.org/nca/features/1998/05/F.RU.980513135425.html (December 3, 2003).
8. Ibid.
9. CNN.com, "Rape War Crime Verdict Welcomed," February 23, 2001, http://www.cnn.com/2001/WORLD/europe/02/23/hague.trial (December 2, 2003).
10. McKinsey, "Yugoslavia."
11. Human Rights Watch, testimony from the press release "Serb Gang-Rapes in Kosovo Exposed."
12. Central Intelligence Agency, "Congo, Democratic Republic of the," in *The World Factbook,* October 4, 2005, http://www.cia.gov/cia/publications/factbook/geos/cg.html (October 15, 2005).
13. Stephanie McCrummen, "Groups Sign Deal to End Long Fight in E. Congo; Accord Portrayed as Key Initial Step," *Washington Post,* January 24, 2008, p. A13.
14. Ibid., p. A13.
15. Omar El Akkad, "Civil War: Canada on Sidelines of Aims for Peace in Congo," *The Globe and Mail,* October 29, 2008, p. A13.

16. Institute for War and Peace Reporting, "Congo-Kinshasa; Rape a 'Weapon of War' in Eastern Congo," *Africa News,* December 23, 2007.

17. Human Rights Watch, "The War Within the War: Sexual Violence Against Women and Girls in Eastern Congo," June 2002, http://www.hrw.org/reports/2002/drc/index. htm (December 4, 2003).

18. Peter Goodspeed, "Rape Now War Strategy in Congo, Doctor Says; Sexual Terrorism," *National Post,* December 1, 2008, p A7.

19. Reseau des Femmes Pour un Developpement Associatif, "Women's Bodies as a Battleground: Sexual Violence Against Women and Girls During the War in the Democratic Republic of Congo, South Kivu (1996–2003)," *International Alert* 2005, p. 34.

20. Human Rights Watch, "The War Within the War."

21. Polly Markandya and Fionna Lloyd-Davis, "DRC: A Plaster on a Gaping Wound," Medecins Sans Frontieres, April 16, 2002, http://www.msf.org/countries/page.cfm (December 4, 2003).

22. Institute for War and Peace Reporting, "Congo-Kinshasa."

23. Human Rights Watch, "The War Within the War."

24. Institute for War and Peace Reporting, "Congo-Kinshasa."

25. Central Intelligence Agency, "Sierra Leone," in *The World Factbook,* October 4, 2005, http://www.cia.gov/cia/publications/factbook/geos/sl.html (October 15, 2005).

26. Physicians for Human Rights, "War-Related Sexual Violence in Sierra Leone: A Population-Based Assessment" January 23, 2002, *p.* 7, http://physiciansforhumanrights. org/library/2002–01-23.html.

27. Human Rights Watch, "Sierra Leone: Sexual Violence Widespread in War," January 16, 2003, http://www.hrw.org/press/2003/01/s10116.htm (November 17, 2003); Human Rights Watch, "Shocking War Crimes in Sierra Leone," June 24, 1999, http://www. hrw.org/press/1999/jun/s10624.htm (November 7, 2003).

28. Human Rights Watch, "Sierra Leone."

29. Central Intelligence Agency, "Burundi," in *The World Factbook,* October 4, 2005, http://www.cia.gov/cia/publications/factbook/geos/by.html (October 15, 2005).

30. Human Rights Watch, "Seeking Protection."

31. Sydia Nduna and Lorelei Goodyear, "Pain Too Deep for Tears: Assessing the Prevalence of Sexual and Gender Violence Among Burundi Refugees in Tanzania," International Rescue Committee, revised 1997, http://www.theirc.org/resources/ sgbv_1.pdf (January 23, 2009).

32. Human Rights Watch, "Seeking Protection."

33. Human Rights Watch, "The War Within the War."

34. Markandya and Lloyd-Davis, "DRC."

35. Ibid.

36. National Center for Post Traumatic Stress Disorder, "Rape of Women in a War Zone: a National Center for PTSD Fact Sheet," May 14, 2003, http://www.ncptsd.org/facts/ specific/fs_kosovo.html (December 2, 2003).

37. National Center for Post Traumatic Stress Disorder, "Rape of Women in a War Zone."

38. The Analyst, "Liberia; Fighters Exposed to Sexual Violence Have More Mental Health Disorders After War," *Africa News,* August 14, 2008.

39. Markandya and Lloyd-Davis, "DRC."

40. Institute for War and Peace Reporting, "Congo-Kinshasa."
41. Nirit Ben-Ari and Ernest Harsch, "Sexual Violence, an 'Invisible War Crime,'" *Africa Renewal* 18, no. 4 (January 2005): 1, http://www.un.org/ecosocdev/geninfo/afrec/v0118n04/184sierraleone.htm (January 23, 2009).
42. Louise Arbour, "War Crimes Against Women Go on with Impunity," *The Toronto Star* (March 11, 2007), p. A15.
43. UN High Commissioner for Refugees, "Basic Facts," http://www.unhcr.org (December 9, 2003).
44. Human Rights Watch, "Seeking Protection."
45. Susan McKay, "Girls as 'Weapons of Terror' in Northern Uganda and Sierra Leoneon Rebel Fighting Forces," *Studies in Conflict and Terrorism* (April 2005): 385–397.
46. Singer, *Children at War,* 32.
47. The News, "Liberia; Survey—Commanders Took Away Weapons from Ex-Female Fighters," *Africa News,* June 26, 2008.
48. Singer, *Children at War,* 33.
49. The News, "Liberia."
50. Ibid.
51. UN Integrated Regional Information Networks, "Liberia; Some Women Ready to Fight Again," *Africa News,* October 14, 2008.
52. Ben-Ari and Harsch, "Sexual Violence."
53. Dewi Cooke, "Women and the Hell of War: Justice," *The Age (Melbourne, Australia),* June 28, 2008, p. 8.
54. Ibid.
55. McKay, "Girls as 'Weapons of Terror.'"
56. Singer, *Children at War,* 15.
57. Singer, pp. 9–15.
58. Ibid., 15.
59. Ibid., 15.
60. Ibid., 16.
61. Ibid., 30.
62. Ibid., 31.
63. Ibid., 29.
64. Ibid., 62.
65. Nick Tattersall, "Savage Life of Boy Soldiers Made to Kill," *The Advertiser,* June 9, 2007, p. 76.
66. Singer, *Children at War,* 61.
67. Ibid., 194.
68. Michael Gerson, "Thorns in the Congo," *The Washington Post,* November 30, 2007: A23.
69. Ibid.
70. The Analyst, "Liberia."
71. Singer, *Children at War,* 195.
72. Vanessa Gezari, "Killing Our Fathers, Raising Our Sons," *St. Petersburg Times,* August 5, 2007, p. 1.
73. Ibid.
74. Tattersall, "Savage Life of Boy Soldiers Made to Kill."

CHAPTER 12

1. Testimony of Hannah Koroma, Sierra Leone, as quoted in Amnesty International, "Section One: What Is Female Genital Mutilation," http://www.amnesty.org/ailib/intcam/femgen/fgm1.htm (December 15, 2003).

2. Rena Singer, "Chastity Tests: Unusual Tool for Public Health," *The Christian Science Monitor*, June 2, 2000, http://www.csmonitor.com/durable/2000/06/ 02/fp1s4-csm.shtml (December 18, 2003).

3. Human Rights Watch, "Pakistan: Tribal Councils Source of Abuse," July 12, 2002, http://www.hrw.org/press/2002/pak0712.htm (November 7, 2003).

4. Amnesty International, "Section One: What Is Female Genital Mutilation."

5. Ibid.

6. World Health Organization, "Female Genital Mutilation," Fact Sheet no. 241, May 2008, http://www.who.int/mediacentre/factsheets/fs241/en/print.html (February 3, 2009).

7. Wairagala Wakabi, "Africa Battles to Make Female Genital Mutilation History," *The Lancet* 369 (March 31, 2007–April 6, 2007): 1069.

8. Sara Corbett, "A Cutting Tradition," *New York Times Magazine*, January 20, 2008, p. 44.

9. Amnesty International, "Section One: What Is Female Genital Mutilation."

10. Ibid.

11. Ibid.

12. Wakabi, "Africa Battles to Make Female Genital Mutilation History."

13. BBC News, "Senegal Village Rejects FGM," http://news.bbc.co.uk/go/pr/fr//1/hi/world/africa/3132350.stm (December 15, 2003).

14. Amnesty International, "Section One: What Is Female Genital Mutilation."

15. Omer Songwe, "Cameroon Princess Fights Mutilation," BBC News, December 9, 2002, http://news.bbc.co.uk/1/hi/world/africa/2547503.stm (December 15, 2003).

16. Amnesty International, "Section One: What Is Female Genital Mutilation."

17. Songwe, "Cameroon Princess Fights Mutilation."

18. BBC News, "South Africa Leader Urges Virginity Tests," http://news.bbc.co.uk/go/pr/fr/-/2/hi/africa/3683210.stm (February 3, 2009).

19. Karin Brulliard, "Zulus Eagerly Defy Ban on Virginity Test," Washingtonpost.com, September 26, 2008, http://www.washingtopost.com (February 2, 2009).

20. Ibid.

21. Ibid.

22. Ibid.

23. Stanley Karombo, "Rights-Zimbabwe: Virginity Testing Strips Girls of Their Dignity—Groups," Inter Press Service News Agency, February 2, 2009, http://ipsnews.net (February 2, 2009).

24. Ibid.

25. Stevenson Jacobs, "Jamaica: MPs Recommend Virginity Tests, Sterilization for Young Women," Associated Press, July 30, 2003, http://www.imdiversity.com/villages/global/article_detail.asp?Article_ID=18541 (December 18, 2003).

26. Associated Press, "Virginity Tests Protested in Turkey," July 17, 2001, http://www.jsonline.com/news/intl/ap/jul101/ap-turkey-virginit 071701.asp?fomrat=print (December 18, 2003).

27. Singer, "Chastity Tests."

28. Karombo, "Rights-Zimbabwe."

29. Ibid.

30. Associated Press, "Virginity Tests Protested in Turkey."

31. The Global Campaign to Stop Killing and Stoning, "Frequently Asked Questions About Stoning," http://www.stop-stoning.org/faq_stoning (February 6, 2009).

32. Jeff Koinange, "Woman Sentenced to Stoning Freed," CNN, September 26, 2003, http://www.cnn.com/2003/WORLD/africa/09/25/nigeria.stoning (December 18, 2003).

33. Human Rights Watch, "Nigeria: Teenage Mother Whipped," January 23, 2001, http://www.hrw.org/press/2001/01/nigeria0123.htm (November 17, 2003).

34. Thomas Erdbrink, "Iran Stones 2 Men to Death; 3d Flees; Sentences Carried Out Despite Judicial Moratorium in 2002," *Washington Post Foreign Service*, January 14, 2009, p. A14.

35. Ibid.

36. Amnesty International, "Campaigning to End Stoning in Iran," January 15, 2008, http://www.amnesty.org (February 2, 2009).

37. "Stoning Victim 'Begged for Mercy,'" *BBC News,* November 4, 2008, http://news/bbc.co.uk/go/pr/fr/-/2/hi/africa/7708169.stm (February 2, 2009).

38. Ibid.

39. Human Rights Watch, "Crime or Custom? Violence Against Women in Pakistan," August 1999, http://www.hrw.org/reports/1999/pakistan (November 7, 2003).

40. "Family Guilty in 'Honour Killing'; Turkish Clan Gets Life for Killing Rape Victim, 16," *The National Post,* January 13, 2009, p. A14.

41. Hillary Mayell, "Thousands of Women Killed for Family Honor," *National Geographic News* February 12, 2002, http://news.nationalgeographic.com/news/pf/15061734.html (February 2, 2009).

42. Ibid.

43. Ibid.

44. Ibid.

45. As quoted in Amnesty International, "Female Genital Mutilation—A Human Rights Information Pack," in Section Four, "A Human Rights Issue," http://www.amnesty.org/ailib/intcam/femgen/fgm4/htm (December 15, 2003).

46. Human Rights Watch, "Crime or Custom?"

Bibliography

"1 in 5 Women Relying on Partner's Pension." *The Financial Times.* August 16, 2003, Money section.

"Abortion Will Pop up Again on Political Radar Screen." *Irish Independent.* March 8, 2005.

Abraham, Lois, and Jane Roberts. "Citizen Engagement." Our Planet, United Nations Environmental Program, Nairobi Kenya vol. 15, no. 2, (2004), p. 29. http://www.34millionfriends.org.

Abu-Zayd, Gehan. "In Search of Political Power—Women in Parliament in Egypt, Jordan, and Lebanon." 2002 update of case study originally published in *Women in Parliament: Beyond Numbers.* Stockholm: International IDEA, 1998. http://www.idea.int.

Adams, Jacqueline. "Art in Social Movements: Shantytown Women' Protest in Pinochet's Chile." *Sociological Forum* 17 (2002): 21–56.

Adventure Divas. "Helen Clark." http://www.adventuredivas.com/divas/article.view?page=245 (May 1, 2003).

Agence France Presse. "Dutch Women Go Abroad for Late-Term Abortions." April 12, 2005.

The Alan Guttmacher Institute. "State Policies in Brief as of August 1, 2005." http://www.guttmacher.org/statecenter/spibs/spib_BPBA.pdf (August 10, 2005).

Aishwarya Rai. Our Planet, United Nations Environmental Programme, vol. 15, no. 2, (2004), p. 18.

Alim, Abdul, Ben Abdallah, Solofo Ramaruson, Maman Sidikou, and Lieke Van de Wiel. "Accelerating Girl's Education in Yemen: Rethinking Policies in Teachers' Recruitment and School Distribution," February 2007, http://www.ungei.org/resources/files/Policy-Paper-Girls-education-Yemen.pdf (January 8, 2009).

al-Mughni, Haya. "Women's Organizations in Kuwait." In *Women and Politics in the Middle East,* ed. Saud Joseph and Susan Slyomovics. Philadelphia: University of Pennsylvania Press, 2001.

al-Shaibani, Saleh. "No Women Elected in Omani Vote," Reuters, October 28, 2007, http://uk.reuters.com/articlePrint?articleId=UKL2808041220071028 (October 14, 2008).

Alvarez, Sonia E. *Engendering Democracy in Brazil: Women's Movements in Transition Politics.* Princeton, NJ: Princeton University Press, 1990.

Amnesty International. "Female Genital Mutilation—a Human Rights Information Pack," in Section Four, "A Human Rights Issue," http://www.amnesty.org/ailib/intcam/femgen/fgm4.htm (December 15, 2003).

———. "Campaigning to End Stoning in Iran." January 15, 2008. http://www.amnesty.org (February 2, 2009).

———. "Section One: What Is Female Genital Mutilation." http://www.amnesty.org/ailib/intcam/femgen/fgm1.htm (December 15, 2003).

Amsberger, Helga, and Brigitte Halbmayr, eds. *Rechtsextreme Parteien.* Opladen: Leske & Budrich, 2002.

Analyst. "Liberia; Fighters Exposed to Sexual Violence Have More Mental Health Disorders After War." *Africa News.* August 14, 2008.

Andersen, G. Esping. *The Three Worlds of Welfare Capitalism.* Cambridge: Cambridge University Press, 1990.

Applebaum, Eileen, Thomas Bailey, Peter Berg, and Arne L. Kalleberg. *Shared Work, Valued Care: New Norms for Organizing Market Work and Unpaid Care Work.* Washington, DC: Economic Policy Institute. June 2002.

Arbour, Louise. "War Crimes Against Women Go on with Impunity." *The Toronto Star.* March 11, 2007, p. A15.

Arie, Sophi. "Elisa Carrio in Lead to Be Argentina's President." *Women's eNews.* July 18, 2002. http://www.womensenews.org (July 18, 2002).

Associated Press, "The Debt Relief Tour," May 28, 2002, http://www.cbsnews.com/stories/2003/07/08/world/main562166.shtml (January 15, 2009).

———. "Virginity Tests Protested in Turkey," July 17, 2001. http://www.jsonline.com/news/intl/ap/ju101/ap-turkey-virginit071701.asp?fomrat=print (December 18, 2003).

Babb, Florence E. *After Revolution: Mapping Gender and Cultural Politics in Neoliberal Nicaragua.* Austin: University of Texas Press, 2001.

Bacchetta, Paola, and Margaret Power, eds. *Right-Wing Women: From Conservatives to Extremists Around the World.* New York: Routledge Press, 2002.

Bagnall, Janet. "When Women Become a Burden; Selective-Sex Abortions Threaten to Turn India into a Land Full of Angry, Lonely Young Men." *The Montreal Gazette.* May 16, 2008, p. A15.

Bahramitash, Roksana. "Revolution, Islamization, and Women's Employment in Iran." *The Brown Journal of World Affairs* 9 (Winter/Spring 2003).

Baker, Maureen. *Canadian Family Policies: Cross National Comparisons.* Toronto: University of Toronto Press, 1995.

Banaszak, Lee Ann. "The Women's Movement Policy Successes and the Constraints of State Reconfiguration: Abortion and Equal Pay in Differing Eras." In *Women's Movements Facing the Reconfigured State,* ed. Lee Ann Banaszak, Karen Beckwith, and Dieter Rucht. New York: Cambridge University Press, 2003.

Banaszak, Lee Ann, Karen Beckwith, and Dieter Rucht. "When Power Relocates: Interactive Changes in Women's Movements and States." In *Women's Movements Facing the Reconfigured State,* ed. Lee Ann Banaszak, Karen Beckwith, and Dieter Rucht. New York: Cambridge University Press, 2003.

———, eds. *Women's Movements Facing the Reconfigured State.* New York: Cambridge University Press, 2003.

Barrett, Edith. "The Policy Priorities of African-American Women in State Legislatures." *Legislative Studies Quarterly* 20 (1995): 223–247.

Barot, Sneha. "Back to Basics: The Rationale for Increased Funds for International Family Planning." *Guttmacher Policy Review* 11, no. 3 (2008). http://www.gutmacher.org/pubs/gpr/11/3/gpr110313.html.

Basu, Alaka Malwade, ed. *The Sociocultural and Political Aspects of Abortion: Global Perspectives.* Westport, CT: Praeger, 2003.

Basu, Amrita. "Introduction." In *The Challenge of Local Feminisms: Women's Movements in Global Perspective,* ed. Amrita Basu. Boulder, CO: Westview Press, 1995.

——, ed. *The Challenge of Local Feminisms: Women's Movements in Global Perspective.* Boulder, CO: Westview Press, 1995.

Beckwith, Karen. "Beyond Compare? Women's Movements in Comparative Perspective." *European Journal of Political Research* 37 (2000): 431–468.

——. "Lancashire Women Against Pit Closures: Women's Standing in a Men's Movement." *Signs* 21, no. 4 (2000): 1034–1068.

Belsie, Laurent. "Men Lag Women at the Voting Booth." *Christian Science Monitor.* February 28, 2002.

Ben-Ari, Nirit, and Ernest Harsch. "Sexual Violence, an 'Invisible War Crime.'" *Africa Renewal* 18, no.4 (January 2005): 1. http://www.un.org/ecosocdev/geninfo/afrec/v0118n04/184sierraleone.htm (January 23, 2009).

Berkman, Michael B., and Robert E. O'Connor. "Do Women Legislators Matter? Female Legislators and State Abortion Policy." *American Politics Quarterly* 21 (January 1993): 102–124.

Berry, Jeffrey. *Interest Group Society.* 3rd ed. New York: Longman, 1997.

Bingham, Clara. *Challenging the Culture of Congress.* New York: Times Books, 1997.

"Blair Puts Focus on Family-Friendly Reforms." *Guardian,* February 28, 2005.

Bnet.com. "Labour Market Trends: Advancing Women in the Workplace." http://findarticles.com/p/articles/mi_qa3999/is_200408/ai_n9448236 (December 9, 2008).

Boserup, Ester. *Women's Role in Economic Development.* New York: St. Martin's Press, 1970.

Boyenge, Jean-Pierre Singa. ILO Database on Export Processing Zones (revised). Working Paper 251, International Labour Office, Geneva, April 2007. Accessed at http://www.ilo.org/public/english/dialogue/sector/themes/epz/epz-db.pdf.

Bratton, Kathleen, and Leonard Ray. "Descriptive Representation, Policy Outcomes, and Municipal Day-Care Coverage in Norway." *American Journal of Political Science* 46 (2003): 428–437.

British Broadcasting Corporation News. "Amsterdam Treaty." April 30, 2001. http://news.bbc.co.uk/1/hi/in_depth/europe/euro-glossary/1216210.stm (April 30, 2006).

——. "Talks to End Nigerian Oil Siege." July 11, 2002. http://news.bbc.co.uk/1/hi/world/africa/2119872.stm (February 5, 2003).

——. "'Deal Reached' in Nigerian Oil Protest." July 16, 2002. http://news.bbc.co.uk/1/hi/africa/2129281.stm (February 5, 2003).

——. "Oil Deal 'Off,' Nigerian Women Say." July 16, 2002. http://news.bbc.co.uk/1/hi/world/africa/2132494.stm (February 5, 2003).

——. "Nigerian Women Leave Oil Plant." July 18, 2002. http://news.bbc.co.uk/1/hi/world/africa/2136509.stm (February 5, 2003).

——. "Wal-Mart Battles Huge Sexism Claim." September 25, 2003. http://news.bbc.co.uk/1/hi/business/3138188.stm (August 8, 2005).

British Broadcasting Corporation News. "Stoning Victim 'Begged for Mercy.'" November 4, 2008. http://news/bbc.co.uk/go/pr/fr//2/hi/africa/7708169.stm (February 2, 2009).

——. "South Africa Leader Urges Virginity Tests." http://news.bbc.co.uk/go/pr/fr//2/hi/africa/3683210.stm (February 3, 2009).

Brulliard, Karin. "Zulus Eagerly Defy Ban on Virginity Test." September 26, 2008. http://www.washingtopost.com (February 2, 2009).

Boxer, Barbara. *Strangers in the Senate.* Bethesda, MD: National Press Books, 1994.

Burkhalter, Holly. "The Politics of AIDS: Engaging Conservative Activists." *Foreign Affairs* (January/February 2004), pp. 8–14.

Burn, Shawn Meghan. *Women Across Cultures: A Global Perspective.* 2d ed. New York: McGraw-Hill, 2005, pp. 153–156.

Burrell, Barbara. *A Woman's Place Is in the House: Campaigning for Congress in the Feminist Era.* Ann Arbor: University of Michigan Press, 1994.

Burstein, Paul. "Legal Mobilization as a Social Movement Tactic: The Struggle for Equal Employment Opportunity." *American Journal of Sociology* 96 (1991): 1201–1225.

Bush, George. "The President's Veto Message." *Congressional Digest,* January 1993.

Bussemaker, Jet, and Kees van Kinsbergen. "Contemporary Social Capitalist Welfare State and Gender Inequality." In *Gender and Welfare State Regimes,* ed. Diane Sainsbury. Oxford: Oxford University Press, 1999.

Button, James. "Rich Are Failing to Keep Their Word to Africa." *Sydney Morning Herald (Australia).* June 2, 2007, International News, p. 15.

Buvinic, Mayra. "Promising Gender Equality." *International Social Science Journal* 162 (1999): 567–574.

Bystydzienski, Jill M. *Women in Electoral Politics: Lessons from Norway.* Westport, CT, and London: Praeger, 1995.

Caldwell, John C., and Pat Caldwell. "Introduction: Induced Abortion in a Changing World." In *The Sociocultural and Political Aspects of Abortion: Global Perspectives,* ed. Alaka Malwade Basu. Westport, CT: Praeger, 2003.

Calloni, Marina. "Debates and Controversies on Abortion in Italy." In *Abortion Politics, Women's Movements, and the Democratic State: A Comparative Study of State Feminism,* ed. Dorothy McBride Stetson. Oxford: Oxford University Press, 2001.

Campbell, Kim. "Women Seek Solutions to Pension-System Bias." *Christian Science Monitor,* May 9, 1996, p. 9.

Canadian International Development Agency. "Uganda." http://www.acdi-cida.gc.ca/uganda (January 12, 2009).

"'Care for Girls' Gaining Momentum." *China Daily.* July 8, 2004. http://www.chinadaily.com.cn/english/doc/2004–07/08/content_346700.htm.

Caul, Miki. *Women's Representation in Parliament: The Role of Political Parties.* Irvine: Center for the Study of Democracy, UC Irvine, 1997.

Center for American Women and Politics. "The Gender Gap and the 2004 Women's Vote: Setting the Record Straight." Advisory of October 28, 2004.

Center for Reproductive Rights. "CEDAW: The Importance of U.S. Ratification." http://www.crlp.org/pub_fac_cedaw.html (October 13, 2005).

——. "The World's Abortion Laws." www.crlp.org/pub_fac_abortion_laws.html (April 26, 2006).

Central Intelligence Agency. "Serbia and Montenegro," in *The World Factbook,* October 4, 2005. http://www.cia.gov/cia/publications/factbook/geos/yi.html (October 15, 2005).

Chang, Leslie T. *Factory Girls: From Village to City in a Changing China*. New York: Spiegel & Grau, 2008.

Charlton, Sue Ellen M., Jana Everett, and Kathleen Staudt. "Women, the State, and Development." In *Women, the State, and Development*, ed. Charlton, Everett, and Staudt. Albany: SUNY Press, 1989.

Childs, Sarah. "Hitting the Target: Are Labour Women MPs 'Acting for' Women?" Paper for the 51st Political Studies Association Conference. April 10–12, 2001. Manchester, United Kingdom, pp. 3–4.

———. "In Their Own Words: New Labour MPs and the Substantive Representation of Women." *British Journal of Politics and International Relations* (June 2001): 173–190.

Chowdury, Najma, and Barbara J. Nelson with Kathryn A. Carver, Nancy Johnson, and Paula L. O'Loughlin. "Redefining Politics: Patterns of Women's Engagement from a Global Perspective." In *Women and Politics Worldwide*, ed. Barbara J. Nelson and Najma Chowdury. New Haven, CT: Yale University Press, 1994.

Christy, Carol. *Sex Differences in Political Participation: Processes of Change in Fourteen Nations*. New York: Praeger, 1987.

Clare, Ross. "Women and Superannuation." The University of New South Wales, School of Economics and Actuarial Studies, paper presented at the Ninth Annual Colloquium of Superannuation Researchers, July 2001, p. 2.

Clark, Janet. "Women at the National Level: An Update on Roll Call Voting Behavior." In *Women and Elective Office: Past, Present, and Future*, ed. Sue Thomas and Clyde Wilcox. New York: Oxford University Press, 1998.

The Clearing House on International Developments in Child, Youth and Family Policies at Columbia University. "France." http://www.childpolicyintl.org (September 8, 2005).

———. "Germany." http://www.childpolicyintl.org (August 9, 2005).

———. "Sweden." http://www.childpolicyintl.org (September 8, 2005).

CNN.com. "EU Tightens Sex Harassment Law." April 18, 2002. http://cnn.worldnews. printthis.clickability.com (November 20, 2003).

CNN World News. "Abortion Ship Arrives in Ireland." June 15, 2001. http://cnn. worldnews.printthis.clickability.com (April 22, 2006).

Cohen, Abby J. "A Brief History of Federal Financing for Child Care in the United States." *Financing Child Care* vol. 6, no. 2 (Summer/Fall 1996)., pp. 26–40.

Commission of the European Communities. "Report from the Commission to the Council, the European Parliament, the European Economic and Social Committee and the Committee of Regions: Annual Report on Equal Opportunities for Women and Men in the European Union 2002." Brussels, March 5, 2003.

———. "Gender Pay Gaps in European Labour Markets—Measurement, Analysis and Policy Implications." Brussels, September 4, 2003.

Conway, Margaret, Gertrude Steuernagel, and David Ahern. *Women and Political Participation*. Washington, DC: CQ Press, 1997.

Cooke, Dewi. "Women and the Hell of War: Justice." *The Age (Melbourne, Australia)*. June 28, 2008, p. 8.

Corbett, Sarah. "A Cutting Tradition." *New York Times Magazine*. January 20, 2008, p. 44.

Costain, Anne. *Inviting Women's Rebellion*. Baltimore, MD: Johns Hopkins University Press, 1992.

Costain, Anne, and Doug Costain. "Strategy and Tactics of the Women's Movement in the U.S.: The Role of Political Parties." In *The Women's Movements of the United*

States and Western Europe: Consciousness, Political Opportunity and Public Policy, ed. Mary F. Katzenstein and Carol M. Mueller. Philadelphia: Temple University Press, 1987.

Cott, Nancy F. *The Grounding of Modern Feminism.* New Haven, CT: Yale University Press, 1987.

Coven, Martha. "An Introduction to TANF." Center on Budget and Policy Priorities, October 24, 2003.

Craske, Nikki. "Women's Political Participation in Colonias Populares in Guadelajara, Mexico." In *Viva: Women and Popular Protest in Latin America,* ed. Sarah Radcliffe and Sallie Westwood. London and New York: Routledge, 1993.

———. *Women and Politics in Latin America.* New Brunswick, NJ: Rutgers University Press, 1999.

Craske, Nikki, and Maxine Molyneux, eds. *Gender and the Politics of Rights and Democracy in Latin America.* New York: Palgrave, 2002.

Cronin, Stephanie, ed. *Reformers and Revolutionaries in Modern Iran: New Perspectives on the Iranian Left.* New York: Routledge Curzon, 2004.

Davidson, Fiona. "Male Workers Say It's Unfair That Dress Rules Don't Apply to Women: Men Shirty About Ties." *The Express.* July 16, 2003, p. 7.

de Figueres, Karen Olsen. "The Road to Equality—Women in Parliament in Costa Rica." 2002 update of case study originally published in *Women in Parliament: Beyond Numbers,* vol. 3. Stockholm: International IDEA, 1998. http://www.idea.int.

Department for International Development. "DFID and the G8 Presidency 2005: Progress on Debt Relief." http://www.dfid.gov.uk/g8/debtrelief.asp (January 15, 2009).

DeVaus, David, and Ian McAllister. "The Changing Politics of Women: Gender and Political Alignments in Eleven Nations." *European Journal of Political Research* 17 (1989): 241–262.

Diamond, M. J. "Olympe de Gouges and the French Revolution: The Construction of Gender as Critique." In *Women and Revolution: Global Expressions,* ed. M. J. Diamond. Boston: Kluwer Academic Publishers, 1998.

———, ed. *Women and Revolution: Global Expressions.* Boston: Kluwer Academic Publishers, 1998.

Dodson, Deborah. "Representing Women's Interests in the U.S. House of Representatives." In *Women and Elective Office: Past, Present, and Future,* ed. Sue Thomas and Clyde Wilcox (New York: Oxford University Press, 1998).

Dodson, Debra L., and Susan Carroll. *Reshaping the Agenda: Women in State Legislatures.* New Brunswick: Center for American Women and Politics, Rutgers, The State University of New Jersey, 1991.

Doi, Ayako. "In Other Words." *Foreign Policy: The Magazine of Global Politics, Economics and Ideas.* November/December 2003. http://www.foreignpolicy.com/story/story. php?storyID=13976 (November 20, 2003).

Dore, Elizabeth, and Maxine Molyneux, eds. *Hidden Histories of Gender and the State in Latin America.* Durham, NC: Duke University Press, 2000.

Dreshsler, Denis, Johannes Jutting, and Carina Lindberg. "Gender, Institutions, and Development: Better Data, Better Politics." International Poverty Centre. *Poverty in Focus: Gender Equality,* no. 13. January 2008 (no pagination).

Duin, Julia. "Brides Bound by Traditions; Indian Women, Families Carry Costly Commitment of Dowry." *The Washington Times.* February 27, 2007, p. A1.

Education for All—Fast Track Initiative. "About FTI." http://www.education-fast-track. org (January 13, 2009).

Easterly, William. "Think Again: Debt Relief." *Foreign Policy* 3 (Nov./Dec. 2001): 20–26.

Einhorn, Barbara. *Cinderella Goes to Market: Citizenship, Gender, and Women's Movements in Eastern Central Europe.* New York: Verso Press, 1993.

Eisenger, Peter K. "The Conditions of Protest Behavior in American Cities." *American Political Science Review* 67 (1973): 11–28.

El Akkad, Omar. "Civil War: Canada on Sidelines of Aims for Peace in Congo." *The Globe and Mail.* October 29, 2008, p. A13.

Elias, Diana. "Kuwait Appoints Its First Woman Cabinet Member." The Associated Press, June 12, 2005.

Enloe, Cynthia. "Closing Remarks." *International Peacekeeping* 8 (2001): 111–114.

Erdbrink, Thomas. "Iran Stones 2 Men to Death; 3d Flees; Sentences Carried Out Despite Judicial Moratorium in 2002." *The Washington Post,* January 14, 2009, p. A14.

European Commission. "Gender Mainstreaming." http://europa.eu.int/comm/employment_social/gender_equality/gender_mainstreaming/employment/employment_labour_market_en.html (April 30, 2006).

"European Parliament Fact Sheet 4.8.7. Equality for Men and Women." http://www.europarl.eu.int/factsheets/4_8_7_en.htm (September 30, 2003).

"The European Parliament Takes Stock." *Women's International Network News* 26, no. 4 (Autumn 2000): 59.

European Union. "Equal Pay." http://europa.eu.int/scadplus/leg/en/cha/c10905.htm (April 30, 2006).

Eurostat News Release. "The Life of Women and Men in Europe: A Statistical Portrait of Men and Women in All Stages of Life." October 8, 2002.

Fackler, Martin. "Career Women in Japan Find a Blocked Path, Despite Equal Opportunity Law," *New York Times.* August 6, 2007, p. A1.

"Family Guilty in 'Honour Killing'; Turkish Clan Gets Life for Killing Rape Victim, 16." *National Post.* January 13, 2009, p. A14.

Ferree, Myra Marx. "Equality and Autonomy: Feminist Politics in the United States and West Germany." In *The Women's Movements of the United States and Western Europe,* ed. Mary Fainsod Katzenstein and Carol McClurg Mueller. Philadelphia: Temple University Press, 1987.

Figner, Vera. *Memoirs of a Revolutionist,* introduction by Richard Stites. Dekalb: Northern Illinois Press, 1991.

Fleshman, Michael. "Women: The Face of AIDS in Africa." *Africa Renewal* 18, no. 3 (October 2004): 6. http://allafrica.com/stories/printable/200410120768.html (October 13, 2004).

Foerstal, Karen, and Herbert Foerstal. *Climbing the Hill: Gender Conflict in Congress.* Westport, CT: Praeger, 1996.

Food and Agricultural Organization. *Gender and Food Security: Division of Labor.* Rome: Food and Agricultural Organization, 2003.

Foran, John, ed. *Theorizing Revolutions.* New York: Routledge Press, 1997.

Ford, Lynne E. *Women and Politics: The Pursuit of Equality.* Boston: Houghton Mifflin Company, 2002.

"Four Women Win 63 Million Yen Ruling: Sumitomo Metal Guilty of Gender Bias." *The Japan Times.* Tokyo and Osaka,. March 29, 2005.

Franklin, Kia. "A Vote in Favor of Fairness; the Candidates' Opinions on Pay Discrimination Case Offers a Glimpse into Judicial Philosophy." *Newsday, Melville.* October 21, 2008, p. A35.

Fraser, Nancy. "After the Family Wage: Gender Equity and the Welfare State." *Political Theory* 22, no. 4 (1994): 591–618.

Freeman, Jo. *The Politics of Women's Liberation.* New York: McKay, 1975.

Friedan, Betty. *The Feminine Mystique.* New York: W. W. Norton & Co., 2001.

Friedman, Thomas L. *The Lexus and the Olive Tree.* New York: Farrar, Straus & Giroux, 1999, pp. 7–8.

Galili, Ziva. "Women and the Russian Revolution." In *Women and Revolution: Global Expressions,* ed. M. J. Diamond. Boston: Kluwer Academic Publishers, 1998.

Gehlen, Freida. "Women Members of Congress: A Distinctive Role." In *A Portrait of Marginality: The Political Behavior of the American Woman,* ed. Marianne Githens and Jewell Prestage. New York: McKay Co., 1977.

Gelb, Joyce. "The Equal Employment Opportunity Law: A Decade of Change for Japanese Women?" *Law & Policy* 22 (October 2000): 385–408.

"Gender Gap in Government." http://www.gendergap.com/governme.htm (April 21, 2003).

GenderStats. http://web.worldbank.org.

German Federal Ministry of Health and Social Security. "Child Benefit, Child Raising Allowance, Parental Leave, Maintenance Advance and Supplementary Child Allowance." January 2005. http://www.bmgs.bund.de/downloads/Child_benefit-Kindergeld.pdf (April 30, 2006).

"Germany to Bolster Child Care." *Deutsche Welle.* October 28, 2004.

Gerson, Michael. "Thorns in the Congo." *The Washington Post.* November 30, 2007, p. A23.

Gertzog, Irwin. *Congressional Women: Their Recruitment, Integration and Behavior.* 2d ed. Westport, CT: Praeger, 1995.

Gezari, Vanessa. "Killing Our Fathers, Raising Our Sons." *St. Petersburg Times.* August 5, 2007:, p. 1.

Gill, Kirrin, Rohini Pande, and Anju Malhotra. "Women Deliver for Development." Family Care International and the International Center for Research on Women. 2008, 2007. http://www.womendeliver.org.

Gilligan, Carol. *In a Different Voice: Psychological Theory and Women's Development.* Cambridge, MA: Harvard University Press, 1982.

Global Campaign for Education. "Must Try Harder: A School Report on 22 Rich Countries' Aid to Basic Education in Developing Countries." November 2003. http://www.campaignforeducation.org (November 25, 2003).

The Global Campaign to Stop Killing and Stoning. "Frequently Asked Questions About Stoning." http://www.stop-stoning.org/faq_stoning (February 6, 2009).

Goldstone, Jack. *Revolution and Rebellion in the Early Modern World.* Berkeley: University of California Press, 1991.

———. "Toward a Fourth Generation of Revolutionary Theory." *Annual Review of Political Science* 4 (2001): 139–187.

———, ed. *Revolutions: Theoretical, Comparative and Historical Studies.* 3rd ed. Belmont, CA: Thompson Wadsworth, 2003.

Goodspeed, Peter. "Rape Now War Strategy in Congo, Doctor Says; Sexual Terrorism." *National Post.* December 1, 2008, p. A7.

Gornick, Janet C., Marcia K. Meyers, and Katherin E. Ross. "Public Policies and the Employment of Mothers: A Cross-National Study." *Social Science Quarterly* 79, no. 1 (1998): 35–54.

Gottfried, Heidi, and Laura Reese. "Gender, Policy, Politics, and Work: Feminist Comparative and Transnational Research." *The Review of Policy Research* 20, no. 1 (2003).

Gottschall, Karin, and Katherine Bird. "Family Leave Policies and Labor Market Segregation in Germany: Reinvention or Reform of the Male Breadwinner Model?" *Review of Policy Research* 20, no. 1 (2003): 115–135.

Govender, Peroshni. "56 Female Candidates up for Election in Israel." January 28, 2003. Women's eNews. http://womensenews.org (January 28, 2003).

Graff, James, et al. "Help Wanted for Europe." *Time,* vol. 155, issue 25 (June 19, 2000).

Graham-Brown, Sarah. "Women and Power in the Middle East." In *Women and Politics in the Middle East,* ed. Suad Joseph and Susan Slyomovics. Philadelphia: University of Pennsylvania Press, 2001.

Gregory, Jeanne. "Sexual Harassment: The Impact of EU Law in the Member States." In *Gender Policies in the European Union,* ed. Mariagrazia Rossilli. New York: Peter Lang, 2000.

Grey, Sandra. "Does Size Matter? Critical Mass and New Zealand Women MPs." *Parliamentary Affairs* 55 (2002): 19–29.

Gurr, T. R. *Why Men Rebel.* Princeton, NJ: Princeton University Press, 1968.

Guttmacher Institute. "Bush Administration Withholds UNFPA Funding for Seventh Year." June 27, 2008. http://www.guttmacher.org/media/inthenews/2008/06/27/index. html.

Hanami, Tadashi. "Equal Employment Revisited." *Japan Labour Bulletin,* The Japan Institute of Labour 39 (January 1, 2000).

Handelman, Howard. *The Challenge of Third World Development.* Upper Saddle River, NJ: Prentice Hall, 2003.

"Harman Pledges to Reduce the Widening Gender Wage Gap." *Birmingham Post.* September 6, 2007, p. 4.

Hassim, Shireen. "'A Conspiracy of Women': The Women's Movement in South Africa's Transition to Democracy." *Social Research* 69 (Fall 2002): 693–732.

Henderson, Sarah L. "Women in a Changing Context." In Understanding *Contemporary Russia,* ed. Michael Bressler. Boulder, CO: Lynne Rienner Press, 2008.

Henneck, Rachel. "Family Policy in the US, Japan, Germany, Italy, and France: Parental Leave, Child Benefits/Family Allowances, Child Care, Marriage/Cohabitation, and Divorce." Unpublished paper, May 2003.

Heyzer, Noeleen. "Peace of Mind, Piece of Land." *Our Planet,* United Nations Environmental Program, Nairobi Kenya *vol.* 15, no. 2, 2004? pp. 11–12.

Hochschild, Arlie Russell, and Barbara Ehrenreich, eds. *Global Woman: Nannies, Maids, and Sex Workers in the New Economy.* New York: Metropolitan Books, 2004.

Hoodfar, Homa. "Bargaining with Fundamentalism: Women and the Politics of Population Control in Iran." *Reproductive Health Matters* 4, no. 8 (1996), pp. 30–40.

Hooglund, Eric, ed. *Twenty Years of Islamic Revolution: Political and Social Transition in Iran Since 1979.* Syracuse, NY: Syracuse University Press, 2002.

Hoskyns, Catherine. "A Study of Four Action Programmes on Equal Opportunities." In *Gender Policies in the European Union,* ed. Mariagrazia Rossilli (New York: Peter Lang, 2000).

Hudson, Valerie M., and Andrea M. Den Boer. *Bare Branches: The Security Implications of Asia's Surplus Male Population*. Cambridge, MA: The MIT Press, 2004.

Human Rights Watch. "Guinea; Thousands of Girls Face Abuse as Domestic Workers." *Africa News*. June 15, 2007.

———. "Crime or Custom? Violence Against Women in Pakistan." August 1999. http://www.hrw.org/reports/1999/pakistan (November 7, 2003).

———. Testimony from the press release "Serb Gang-Rapes in Kosovo Exposed." March 21, 2000. http://www.hrw.org/press/2000/03/kosrape.htm (November 7, 2003).

———. "Seeking Protection: Addressing Sexual and Domestic Violence in Tanzania's Refugee Camps." October 2000. http://www.hrw.org/reports/2000/tanzania (November 17, 2003).

———. "Nigeria: Teenage Mother Whipped." January 23, 2001. http://www.hrw.org/press/2001/01/nigeria0123.htm (November 17, 2003).

———. "The War Within the War: Sexual Violence Against Women and Girls in Eastern Congo." June 2002. http://www.hrw.org/reports/2002/drc/index.htm (December 4, 2003).

———. "Pakistan: Tribal Councils Source of Abuse." July 12, 2002. http://www.hrw.org/press/2002/pak0712.htm (November 7, 2003).

———. "Refugee and Internally Displaced Women; Gender-Based Asylum Claims." 2003. http://www.hrw.org/women/refugees.html (November 7, 2003).

Huntington, Samuel P. *Political Order in Changing Societies*. New Haven, CT: Yale University Press, 1970.

Inglehart, Ronald. *The Silent Revolution: Changing Values and Political Styles Among Western Publics*. Princeton, NJ: Princeton University Press, 1977.

———. *Culture Shift in Advanced Industrial Society*. Princeton, NJ: Princeton University Press, 1990.

———. *Modernization and Postmodernization: Cultural, Economic and Political Change in 43 Societies*. Princeton, NJ: Princeton University Press, 1997.

Inglehart, Ronald, and Pippa Norris. *Rising Tide: Gender Equality and Cultural Change Around the World*. New York: Cambridge University Press, 2003.

Institute for War and Peace Reporting. "Congo-Kinshasa; Rape a 'Weapon of War' in Eastern Congo." *Africa News*. December 23, 2007.

International Institute for Democracy and Electoral Assistance. "Gender and Political Participation: Gender Facts." http://www.idea.int.gender/facts.htm (April 23, 2003).

———. "Gender and Political Participation: Voter Turnout by Gender." www.idea.int/gender/turnout (April 23, 2003).

International Labor Organization. "Global Employment Trends for Women Brief." March 2007. http://www.ilo.org/public/english/employment/strat/download/getw07.pdf.

———. *Condition of Work Digest 1994: Volume 13 Maternity and Work*. Geneva: ILO, 1994.

———. *Women and Men in the Informal Economy: A Statistical Picture*. Geneva: ILO, 2002.

———. *Time for Equality at Work: Global Report Under the Follow-up to the ILO Declaration on Fundamental Principles and Rights at Work*. Geneva: ILO, 2003.

International Women's Democracy Center. "Resources: Fact Sheet: Women's Political Participation." http://www.iwdc.org/factsheet.htm (May 1, 2003).

Inter-Parliamentary Union. "Women in National Parliaments." March 28, 2003. http://www.ipu.org/wmn-e/classif.htm (April 21, 2006).

———. *Women in Parliament in 2007: The Year in Perspective* (Switzerland: IPU, 2007), p. 5.

Irish Medical Council. *A Guide to Ethical Conduct and Behavior.* 6th ed. Dublin: Irish Medical Council, 2004.

Jacobs, Stevenson. "Jamaica: MPs Recommend Virginity Tests, Sterilization for Young Women." The Associated Press, July 30, 2003. http://www.imdiversity.com/villages/global/article_detail.asp?Article_ID=18541 (December 18, 2003).

Jackson, Maggie. "Study: Part Time Work Is Widespread but Undervalued." The Associated Press, November 20, 1997.

Jaquette, Jane S., and Kathleen Staudt. "Women, Gender, and Development." In *Women and Gender Equity in Development Theory and Practice: Institutions, Resources, and Mobilization,* ed. Jane S. Jaquette and Gale Summerfield. Durham, NC: Duke University Press, 2006, p. 21.

Jancar, Barbara Wolfe. *Women Under Communism.* Baltimore, MD: Johns Hopkins University Press, 1978.

Jancar-Webster, Barbara. *Women and Revolution in Yugoslavia.* Denver, CO: Arden Press, 1990.

"Japan's Salary Gap." *The Japan Times.* March 24, 2008.

Jaquette, Jane. "Women in Power: From Tokenism to Critical Mass." *Foreign Policy* 108 (Fall 1997): 23–38.

Jehl, Douglas, and Michael R. Gordon. "American Forces Reach Cease-Fire with Terror Group." *New York Times,* April 29, 2003.

Jenkins, J. Craig. *The Politics of Insurgency.* New York: Columbia University Press, 1985.

Jenkins, J. Craig, and Charles Perrow. "Insurgency of the Powerless: Farm Workers Movements." *American Sociological Review* 42 (1977): 249–267.

Jewell, Malcolm, and Marcia Lynn Whicker. *Legislative Leadership in American States.* Ann Arbor: University of Michigan Press, 1994.

Jeydel, Alana, and Andrew Taylor. "Are Women Legislators Less Effective? Evidence from the U.S. House in the 103d–105th Congress." *Political Research Quarterly* 56 (March 2003): 19–28.

Joint United Nations Programme on HIV/AIDS (UNAIDS). *A Joint Response to HIV/AIDS.* Geneva: UNAIDS, 2004.

Jones, Del. "Few Women Hold Top Executive Jobs, Even When CEOs Are Female." *USA Today.* January 27, 2003. http://www.usatoday.com/money/jobcenter/2003-01-26-womenceos_x.htm (October 6, 2003).

Joseph, Hir. "WRAPA Prepares Women for Voting." April 11, 2003. http://allAfrica.com/stories/printable/200304120067.html (April 21, 2003).

Joseph, Saud. "Women and Politics in the Middle East." In *Women and Politics in the Middle East,* ed. Saud Joseph and Susan Slyomovics. Philadelphia: University of Pennsylvania Press, 2001.

Kabeer, Naila. *Gender Mainstreaming in Poverty Eradication and the Millennium Development Goals: A Handbook for Policy-makers and Other Stakeholders.* London: Commonwealth Secretariat, 2003.

Kain, Azadeh. "Women and Politics in Post-Islamist Iran: The Gender Conscious Drive to Change." *British Journal of Middle Eastern Studies* 24, no. 1 (1997): 75–97.

Kamerman, Sheila B. "Early Childhood Education and Care (ECEC): An Overview of Developments in the OECD Countries." Unpublished paper.

Kamerman, Sheila, and Shirley Gatenio. "Mother's Day: More Than Candy and Flowers, Working Parents Need Paid Time-Off." Columbia University, the Clearing House on International Developments in Child, Youth, and Family Policies. Issue Brief, Spring 2002.

———. "Tax Day: How Do America's Child Benefits Compare?" Columbia University, the Clearing House on International Developments in Child, Youth, and Family Policies. Issue Brief, Spring 2002.

Kamerman, Sheila B., Michelle Neuman, Jane Waldfogel, and Jeanne Brooks-Gunn. *Social Policies, Family Types and Child Outcomes in Selected OECD Countries*. Paris: OECD, 2003.

Kampwirth, Karen. *Women and Guerilla Movements: Nicaragua, El Salvador, Chiapas, Cuba*. University Park: The Pennsylvania State University Press, 2002.

———. *Feminism and the Legacy of Revolution: Nicaragua, El Salvador, Chiapas*. Athens: Ohio University Press, 2004.

Kaplan, Temma. "Uncommon Women and the Common Good." In *Women Resist Globalization*, ed. Sheila Rowbotham and Stephanie Linkogle. London and New York: Zed Books, 2001.

Karombo, Stanley. "Rights-Zimbabwe: Virginity Testing Strips Girls of their Dignity—Groups." Inter Press Service News Agency. February 2, 2009. http://ipsnews.net (February 2, 2009).

KatineChronicles. "Debate: The State of Education in Uganda." *The Guardian*. May 2008. http://www.guardian.co.uk/society/katineblog/2008/May/23/ugandawillachieveits-millen (January 15, 2009).

Katzenstein, Mary Fainsod, and Carol M. Mueller, eds. *The Women's Movements of the United States and Western Europe*. Philadelphia: Temple University Press, 1987.

Kavakci, Merve. "Headscarf Heresy: For One Muslim Woman, the Headscarf Is a Matter of Choice and Dignity." *Foreign Policy* (May/June 2004): 66–67.

Kearney, Emily. "Reaching the Poorest with Microfinance: The Importance of Innovation in Program Design." Unpublished thesis, Oregon State University, 2009.

Keck, Margaret E., and Kathryn Sikkinkh. *Activists Beyond Borders: Advocacy Networks in International Politics*. Ithaca, NY: Cornell University Press, 1998.

Kelly, Erin, and Frank Dobbin. "Civil Rights Law at Work: Sex Discrimination and the Rise of Maternity Leave Policies." *American Journal of Sociology* 105, no. 2 (1999): 455–492.

Kelly, Michael. "Hasten the Day When AIDS No Longer Has a Female Face." *The Irish Times*. March 13, 2007, p. 16.

"Kenya; Teenage Girls Targeted for Sexual Exploitation." *East African Standard*, Africa News. February 7, 2008.

Keskin, Burcak. "Confronting Double Patriarchy: Islamist Women in Turkey." In *Right Wing Women: From Conservatives to Extremists around the World*, ed. Paola Bacchetta and Margaret Power. New York: Routledge, 2002.

Kettering, Evert. "Netherlands." In *Abortion in the New Europe: A Comparative Handbook*, ed. Bill Roston and Anna Eggert. Westport, CT: Greenwood Press, 1994.

Kian-Kian-Thiébaut, Azadeh. "Women and the Making of Civil Society in Post-Islamist Iran." In *Twenty Years of Islamic Revolution: Political and Social Transition in Iran Since 1979*, ed. Eric Hoogland. Syracuse, NY: Syracuse University Press, 2002.

Kitschelt, Herbert P. "Political Opportunity Structures and Political Protest: Anti-Nuclear Movements in Four Democracies." *British Journal of Political Science* 16, no. 1 (1986): 57–85.

Klawiter, Maren. "Racing for the Cure, Walking Women and Toxic Touring: Mapping Cultures of Action Within the Bay Area Terrain of Breast Cancer." *Social Problems* 46, no. 1 (1999): 104–126.

Koinange, Jeff. "Woman Sentenced to Stoning Freed." CNN, September 26, 2003. http://www.cnn.com/2003/WORLD/africa/09/25/nigeria.stoning (December 18, 2003).

Kornhauser, William. *The Politics of Mass Society.* Glencoe, IL: The Free Press, 1959.

Krasniewicz, Louise. *Nuclear Summer: The Clash of Communities at the Seneca Women's Peace Encampment.* Ithaca, NY: Cornell University Press, 1992.

Kristof, Nicholas D. "Where Sweatshops Are a Dream." *New York Times,* January 14, 2009.

La Franiere, Sharon. "Nightmare for African Women: Birthing Injury and Little Help." *New York Times,* September 28, 2005.

Lambert, Caroline. "French Women in Politics: The Long Road to Parity." The Brookings Institution. May 2001. http://www.brookings.edu/fp/cusf/analysis/women.htm (April 23, 2003).

Latif, Aamir. "Taliban Divided on Girls Education." December 26, 2008. http://www.islamonline.net (January 8, 2009).

Lazaro, Juan. "Women and Political Violence in Contemporary Peru." In *Women and Revolution: Global Expressions,* ed. M. J. Diamond. Boston: Kluwer Academic Publishers, 1998.

Leira, Arnlaug. *Working Parents and the Welfare State: Family Change and Policy Reform in Scandinavia.* Cambridge: Cambridge University Press, 2002.

Lenz, Ilse. "Globalization, Gender, and Work: Perspectives on Global Regulation." *Review of Policy Research* 20 (Spring 2003).

"Liberia; Survey—Commanders Took Away Weapons from Ex-Female Fighters." *Africa News.* June 26, 2008.

"The List: The Worst Places to Be a Woman." May 2008. http://www.foreignpolicy.com/story/cms.php?story_id=4319&print=1.

Liu, Dongxiao, and Elizabeth Heger Boyle. "Making the Case: The Women's Convention and Equal Employment Opportunity in Japan." *International Journal of Comparative Sociology* 42 (2001).

Lluciak, Ilja A. *After the Revolution: Gender and Democracy in El Salvador, Nicaragua, and Guatemala.* Baltimore, MD: Johns Hopkins University Press, 2001.

Lobao, Linda M. "Women in Revolutionary Movements: Changing Patterns of Latin American Guerilla Study." In *Women and Revolution: Global Expressions,* ed. M. J. Diamond. Boston: Kluwer Academic Publishers, 1998.

Lovenduski, Joni, and Pippa Norris, eds. *Women in Politics.* New York: Oxford University Press, 1996.

Luker, Kristin. *Abortion and the Politics of Motherhood.* Berkeley: University of California Press, 1984.

Lynch, Michael. *Mao.* New York: Routledge, 2004.

Mahon, Evelyn. "Abortion Debates in Ireland: An Ongoing Issue." In *Abortion Politics, Women's Movements, and the Democratic State,* ed. Dorothy McBride Stetson. Oxford: Oxford University Press, 2001.

Mandela, Nelson. *Long Walk to Freedom: The Autobiography of Nelson Mandela.* United Kingdom: Back Bay Books, 1995.

Margolies-Mezvinsky, Marjoire. *A Woman's Place: The Freshman Who Changed the Face of Congress.* New York: Crown, 1994.

Markandya, Polly, and Fionna Lloyd-Davis. "DRC: A Plaster on a Gaping Wound." April 16, 2002. http://www.msf.org/countries/page.cfm (December 4, 2003).

Mayell, Hillary. "Thousands of Women Killed for Family Honor." February 12, 2002. http://news.nationalgeographic.com/news/pf/15061734.html (February 2, 2009).

Mayer, Nonna, and Mariette Sineau. "France: The Front National." In *Rechtsextreme Parteien,* ed. Helga Amsberger and Brigitte Halbmayr. Opladen: Leske & Budrich, 2002.

Mazur, Amy G. *Gender Bias and the State: Symbolic Reform at Work in Fifth Republic France.* Pittsburgh: University of Pittsburgh Press, 1995.

——. *Theorizing Feminist Policy.* New York: Oxford University Press, 2002.

Mazur, Amy G., and Suzanne Zwingel. "Comparing Feminist Policy in Politics and at Work in France and Germany: Shared European Union Setting, Divergent National Contexts." *Review of Policy Research* 20, vol. 1 (2003): 365–383.

McAdam, Doug. *Political Process and the Development of Black Insurgency 1930–1970.* Chicago and London: University of Chicago Press, 1985.

McCarthy, John D., and Meyer Zald, eds. *Social Movements in an Organizational Society.* New Brunswick, NJ, and Oxford: Transaction Books, 1987.

McCrummen, Stephanie. "Groups Sign Deal to End Long Fight in E. Congo; Accord Portrayed as Key Initial Step." *The Washington Post.* January 24, 2008, p. A13.

McDonagh, Eileen. "Assimilated Leaders: Democratization, Political Inclusion and Female Leadership." *Harvard International Review* 21 (Fall 1999): 64–69.

McDonald, Dearbhail. "Abortion—It's Back to Court." *Sunday Times of London.* August 14, 2005.

McGlen, Nancy, and Karen O'Connor. *Women's Rights.* New York: Praeger, 1983.

McKay, Susan. "Girls as 'Weapons of Terror' in Northern Uganda and Sierra Leoneon Rebel Fighting Forces." *Studies in Conflict and Terrorism* (April 2005): 385–397.

McKinsey, Kitty. "Yugoslavia: Crimes Against Women Become Focus of Tribunals." May 13, 1998. http://www.rferl.org/nca/features/1998/05/F.RU.980513135425.html (December 3, 2003).

Medecins Sans Frontiers. "The Crushing Burden of Rape: Sexual Violence in Darfur." A Briefing Paper. Amsterdam. March 8, 2005.

Meyer, David. "Institutionalizing Dissent: The United States Structure of Political Opportunity and the End of the Nuclear Freeze Movement." *Sociological Forum* 8, no. 2 (1993): 157–179.

——. "Restating the Woman Question: Women's Movements and State Restructuring." In *Women's Movements Facing the Reconfigured State,* ed. Lee Ann Banaszak, Karen Beckwith, and Dieter Rucht. New York: Cambridge University Press, 2003.

Meyer, David, and Nancy Whittier. "Social Movement Spillover." *Social Problems* 41 (1994): 277–298.

Meyers, Marcia K., Janet C. Gornick, and Katherin E. Ross. "Public Childcare, Parental Leave, and Employment." In *Gender and Welfare State Regimes,* ed. Diane Sainsbury. Oxford: Oxford University Press, 1999.

Miles, Alice. "Maybe Baby's Best with Dad." *The Times (London).* March 2, 2005.

Mink, Gwendolyn. *Welfare's End.* Ithaca, NY: Cornell University Press, 1998.

Moghadam, Valentine, ed. *Democratic Reform and the Position of Women in Transitional Economies.* Oxford: Clarendon Press, 1993.

——. "Gender and Revolutions." In *Theorizing Revolutions,* ed. John Foran. New York: Routledge Press, 1997.

———. "Revolution, Religion, and Gender Politics: Iran and Afghanistan Compared." *Journal of Women's History* 10 (Winter 1999): 172–195.

———. *Modernizing Women: Gender and Social Change in the Middle East.* 2d ed. Boulder, CO: Lynne Rienner Press, 2003.

———. *Globalizing Women: Transnational Feminist Networks.* Baltimore, MD: The Johns Hopkins University Press, 2005.

Moghadam, Valentine M., and Margot Badran. *Causes and Gender Implications of Islamist Movements in the Middle East.* Helsinki: World Institute of Development Economic Research, United Nations University, 1991.

Molyneux, M. "Mobilization Without Emancipation? Women's Interests, the State and Revolution in Nicaragua." *Feminist Studies* 11 (1985): 227–254.

Momsen, Janet Henshall. *Gender and Development.* London: Routledge, 2004.

Myakayaka-Manzini, Mavivi. "Women Empowered—Women in Parliament in South Africa." 2002 update of case study originally published in *Women in Parliament: Beyond Numbers,* vol. 1. Stockholm: International IDEA, 1998. http://www.idea.int (April 30, 2006).

Nakamura, Akemi. "Four Women Await Outcome of 10-Year Quest for Equal Pay." *The Japan Times.* March 27, 2005.

Narli, Nilufer. "The Rise of the Islamist Movement in Turkey." *Middle Eastern Review of International Affairs* 3, no. 3 (1999).

National Center for Post Traumatic Stress Disorder. "Rape of Women in a War Zone: A National Center for PTSD Fact Sheet." May 14, 2003. http://www.ncptsd.org/facts/specific/fs_kosovo.html (December 2, 2003).

National Organization for Women. "Facts About Pay Equity." http://www.now.org/issues/economic/factsheet.html (October 6, 2003).

———. "Pay Equity Still a Dream Worth Pursuing: New Report Shows Glass Ceiling Intact." Summer 2002. http://www.now.org/nnt/summer-2002/payequity.html (October 6, 2003).

National Women's Law Center. "The Paycheck Fairness Act: Helping to Close the Women's Wage Gap." May 2003. http://www.nwlc.org (October 6, 2003), p. 1.

Naumann, Ingela K. "Child Care and Feminism in West Germany and Sweden in the 1960s and 1970s." *Journal of European Social Policy* 15, no. 1 (2005).

Nduna, Sydia, and Lorelei Goodyear. "Pain Too Deep for Tears: Assessing the Prevalence of Sexual and Gender Violence Among Burundi Refugees in Tanzania." Revised 1997. http://www.theirc.org/resources/sgbv_1.pdf (January 23, 2009).

Nelson, Barbara J., and Najma Chowdury, eds. *Women and Politics Worldwide.* New Haven, CT: Yale University Press, 1994.

Netherlands Ministry of Foreign Affairs. "Questions and Answers on Dutch Policy on Abortion—2003." http://www.minvws.nl/en/themes/abortion/default.asp (August 10, 2005).

Nicol, Diane. "Employers Face Rise in Equal Pay Claims." *The Scotsman.* April 19, 2003, p. 23.

Norris, Pippa. "Women's Power at the Ballot Box." Paper written for International Institute for Democracy and Electoral Assistance, Voter Turnout from 1945–2000: A Global Report on Political Participation.

———. *Electoral Engineering: Voting Rules and Political Behavior.* New York: Cambridge University Press, 2004.

Norris, Pippa, and Joni Lovenduski. "Blair's Babes: Critical Mass Theory, Gender, and Legislative Life." John F. Kennedy School of Government, Harvard University, Faculty Research Working Paper Series (September 2001).

Nousratpour, Louise. "Hit out Over Pay Injustice: Unions Urge Government to Confront Poverty." *Morning Star*. September 18, 2003, p. 1.

Nzwili, Frederick. "Women Candidates in Kenya Assaulted, Under-Funded." December 27, 2002. www.womensenews.org (December 27, 2002).

Oakley, Richard. "Irish Faith on Wane but Tolerance Rises." *The Times*. April 10, 2005.

O'Connor, J. "Gender, Class and Citizenship in the Comparative Analysis of Welfare State Regimes: Theoretical and Methodological Issues." *British Journal of Sociology* 44, no. 3 (1993): 501–518.

O'Malley, Brendan. "The Global Classroom." *South China Morning Post*. June 16, 2007, Education, p. 6.

"Only 8.9% of Managerial Positions Taken by Women in Japan." *Deutsche Press-Agentur*. September 13, 2003, Miscellaneous section.

Organization for Economic Co-operation and Development. "Child Care in OECD Countries," in *Employment Outlook 1990*. Paris: OECD, 1990.

———. *OECD in Figures: Statistics for the Member Countries*. Paris: OECD, 2002.

Organization for Economic Co-operation and Development Economics Department. "Female Labour Force Participation: Past Trends and Main Determinants in OECD Countries," May 2004. http://www.oecd.org/dataoecd/25/5/31743836.pdf (April 30, 2006).

Ostner, Ilona. "From Equal Pay to Equal Employability: Four Decades of European Gender Policies." In *Gender Policies in the European Union*, ed. Mariagrazia Rossilli (New York: Peter Lang, 2000).

Outshoorn, Joyce. "Policy-making on Abortion: Arenas, Actors, and Arguments in the Netherlands." In *Abortion Politics, Women's Movements and the Democratic State*, ed. Dorothy McBride Stetson. New York: Oxford University Press, 2001.

Oxfam International. *Trading Away Our Rights: Women Working in Global Supply Chains*. Oxford: Oxfam International, 2004.

Paxton, Pamela, and Sheri Kunovich. "Women's Political Representation: The Importance of Ideology." *Social Forces* 82 (2003): 87–114.

Penn, Shana. *Solidarity's Secret: The Women Who Defeated Communism in Poland*. Ann Arbor: University of Michigan Press, 2005.

Physicians for Human Rights. "War-Related Sexual Violence in Sierra Leone: A Population-Based Assessment." Cambridge: Physicians for Human Rights, 2000, p. 7.

Piven, Francis Fox, and Richard Cloward. *Poor People's Movements*. New York: Vintage Books, 1979.

Pogatchnik, Shawn. "Irish Bishops Reject Pregnancy Pamphlet." Associated Press, June 16, 2005.

Pope, Charles. "Social Security Must Protect Women, Bush Told." *Seattle Post-Intelligencer*. June 13, 2001. http://seattlepi.nwsource.com/national/27227_socsec13.shtml (September 29, 2003).

Poya, Maryam. *Women, Work and Islamism: Ideology and Resistance in Iran*. London and New York: Zed Books, 1999.

Prasad, Raekha. and Randeep Ramesh. "India's Missing Girls: Daughters Aren't Wanted in India." *The Guardian*. February 28, 2007, p. 4.

Prieto, Norma Iglesias. *Beautiful Flowers of the Maquiladora: Life Histories of Women Workers in Tijuana.* Austin: University of Texas Press, 1997.

Rai, Shirin. "Class, Caste and Gender—Women in Parliament in India." 2002 update of case study originally published in *Women in Parliament: Beyond Numbers,* vol. 1. Stockholm: International IDEA, 1998. http://www.idea.int (April 30, 2006).

Ramesh, Randeep. "India to Crack Down in Doctors Aborting Girls." *The Guardian.* April 25, 2008, p. 24.

Randall, Margaret. *Gathering Rage: The Failure of Twentieth Century Revolutions to Develop a Feminist Agenda.* New York: Monthly Review Press, 1992.

Rehn, Elisabeth, and Ellen Johnson Sirleaf. "Women War Peace." In *Progress of the World's Women 2002,* vol. 1. New York: UNIFEM, 2003.

Reseau des Femmes Pour un Developpement Associatif. "Women's Bodies as a Battleground: Sexual Violence Against Women and Girls During the War in the Democratic Republic of Congo, South Kivu (1996–2003)." *International Alert* (2005): 34.

Results, "2007 Basics: Global Education for All." 2007. http://www.results.org/website/article.asp?id=2566 (January 7, 2009).

Reuters. "Women Paid 16% Less Than Men, Report Says; Gap Widest in Asia, Americas." *The Gazette (Montreal).* March 7, 2008.

Reynolds, Andrew. "Women in Legislatures and Executives of the World: Knocking at the Highest Glass Ceiling." *World Politics* 51, no. 4 (1999): 547–572.

Reynolds, Sian, ed. *Women, State and Revolution: Essays on Power and Gender in Europe Since 1789.* Amherst: The University of Massachusetts Press, 1987.

"Rights Group Says Law Must Be Changed to Allow for Abortions." *Irish Independent.* March 8, 2005.

Ronnow, Karin. "Journey of Hope: An In-Depth Report, Keeping Hope Alive." *Bozeman Daily Chronicle,* 2008, p. 7 (Central Asia Institute).

Rosenthal, Cindy Simon. *When Women Lead: Integrative Leadership in State Legislatures.* New York: Oxford University Press, 1998.

Rossilli, M. Grazia. "The European Union's Policy on the Equality of Women." *Feminist Studies* 25 (Spring 1999): 171–182.

Rossilli, M. Grazia, ed. *Gender Policies in the European Union* (New York: Peter Lang, 2000).

Roston, Bill, and Anna Eggert. *Abortion in the New Europe: A Comparative Handbook.* Westport, CT: Greenwood Press, 1994.

Rowbotham, Sheila, and Stephanie Linkogle, eds. *Women Resist Globalization: Mobilizing for Livelihood and Rights.* London and New York: Zed Books, 2001.

Rule, Wilma. "Electoral Systems, Contextual Factors and Women's Opportunities for Parliament in 23 Democracies." *Western Political Quarterly* 40 (1987): 477–498.

——. "Why Women Don't Run: The Critical Contextual Factors in Women's Legislative Recruitment." *Western Political Quarterly* 34 (1988): 60–77.

Rule, Wilma, and Matthew Shugart. "The Preference Vote and Election of Women." Center for Voting and Democracy. 1995. http://www.fairvote.org/reports/1995/chp7/rule.html (May 6, 2003).

Rueschemeyer, Marilyn, ed. *Women in the Politics of Postcommunist Eastern Europe* (Armonk, NY: M.E. Sharpe, 1994).

Sadik, Nafis, "Practical Consensus." *Our Planet.* United Nations Environmental Program, Nairobi Kenya, vol. 15, no. 2 (2004) p. 6.

Saeger, Joni. *The State of the Women in the World Atlas.* New York: Penguin Books, 1997.

Safa, Helen I., and Cornelia Butler Flora. "Production, Reproduction, and the Polity: Women's Strategic and Practical Gender Issues." In *Americas: New Interpretive Essays,* ed. Alfred Stepan. New York and Oxford: Oxford University Press, 1992.

Sainsbury, Diane. "Introduction." In *Gender and Welfare State Regimes,* ed. Diane Sainsbury. Oxford: Oxford University Press, 1999.

———, ed. *Gender and Welfare State Regimes.* Oxford: Oxford University Press, 1999.

Samarasinghe, Vidyamali. "Confronting Globalization in Anti-trafficking Strategies in Asia." *Brown Journal of World Affairs* 10, no. 1 (2003): 91.

"Scans for Baby's Sex Illegal—but Rampant." *The Straights Times (Singapore).* July 14, 2007.

Schirmer, Jennifer. "The Seeking of Truth and the Gendering of Consciousness." In *Viva: Women and Political Protest in Latin America,* ed. Sarah A. Radcliffe and Sallie Westwood. New York and London: Routledge, 1993.

Schreiber, Ronnee. "Injecting a Woman's Voice: Conservative Women's Organizations, Gender Consciousness, and the Expression of Women Policy Preferences." *Sex Roles* 47 (October 2002).

Scottish Labour. "Women and the Changing European Union." November 4, 2002. http://www.scottishlabour.org.uk/helenliddell (September 30, 2003).

Sen, Amartya. *Development as Freedom.* New York: Anchor Books, 2000.

Sengupta, Anuradha. "Kashmiris Look to a Woman for Resolution of Strife," January 24, 2003. http://www.womensenews.org/article.cfm?aid=1195 (January 24, 2003).

Shayne, Julie D. *The Revolution Question: Feminisms in El Salvador, Chile, and Cuba.* New Brunswick, NJ: Rutgers University Press, 2004.

Singer, Peter W. *Children at War.* Berkeley: University of California Press, 2006.

Singer, Rena. "Chastity Tests: Unusual Tool for Public Health." *The Christian Science Monitor.* June 2, 2000. http://www.csmonitor.com/durable/2000/06/02/fp1s4-csm.shtml (December 18, 2003).

Singh, Susheela, Stanley K. Henshaw, and Kathleen Berentsen. "Abortion: A Worldwide Overview." In *The Sociocultural and Political Aspects of Abortion: Global Perspectives,* ed. Alaka Malwade Basu. Westport, CT: Praeger, 2003.

Skocpol, Theda. *States and Social Revolutions.* New York: Cambridge University Press, 1979.

Smelser, Neil. *Theory of Collective Behavior.* New York: The Free Press, 1962.

Smith, Bonnie G., ed. *Global Feminisms Since 1945.* New York: Routledge, 2000.

Smith, Lisa C., and Lawrence Haddad. *Explaining Child Malnutrition in Developing Countries: A Cross-Country Analysis.* Washington, DC: International Food Policy Research Institute, 2000.

Smith, Lois M., and Alfred Padula. *Sex and Revolution: Women in Socialist Cuba.* New York: Oxford University Press, 1996.

Social Security Administration. "Women and Social Security," October 3, 2005. http://www.ssa.gov/pressoffice/factsheets/women.htm (April 30, 2006).

Social Security Network. "Issue Brief #6: Social Security: A Women's Issue." http://www.socsec.org/facts/Issue_Briefs/women.htm (October 3, 2003).

Songwe, Omer. "Cameroon Princess Fights Mutilation." December 9, 2002. http://news.bbc.co.uk/1/hi/world/africa/2547503.stm (December 15, 2003).

"Statement by Congresswoman Carolyn B. Maloney: Women's Equality Amendment—11/14/2002." *Women's International Network News* (Winter 2003): 29–31.

Steinberg-Ratner, Ronnie. "The Policy and Problem: Overview of Seven Countries." In *Equal Employment Policy for Women*, ed. Ronnie Steinberg-Ratner. Philadelphia: Temple University Press, 1980.

Stephen, Lynn. 1997. *Women and Social Movements in Latin America: Power from Below.* Austin: University of Texas Press.

Stern, Andrew. "US Pharmacist Sues, Refusing to Sell Contraceptive." Reuters News Service. June 10, 2005.

Stetson, Dorothy McBride. "US Abortion Debates: 1959–1998: The Women's Movement Holds On." In *Abortion Politics, Women's Movements, and the Democratic State: A Comparative Study of State Feminism*, ed. Dorothy McBride Stetson. Oxford: Oxford University Press, 2001.

———, ed. *Abortion Politics, Women's Movements, and the Democratic State: A Comparative Study of State Feminism*. New York: Oxford University Press, 2001.

Stetson, Dorothy McBride, and Amy G. Mazur. "Introduction." In *Comparative State Feminism*, ed. Dorothy McBride Stetson and Amy G. Mazur. Thousand Oaks, CA: Sage Publications, 1995.

———, eds. *Comparative State Feminism*. Thousand Oaks, CA: Sage Publications, 1995.

Stoltzfus, Emilie. *Citizen, Mother, Worker: Debating Responsibility for Child Care after the Second World War*. Chapel Hill: University of North Carolina Press, 2003.

The Swedish Institute. "Childcare in Sweden." September 2004. http://www.sweden.se/templates/cs/BasicFactsheet (April 22, 2006).

Swers, Michelle. "Are Congresswomen More Likely to Vote for Women's Issues Bills Than Their Male Colleagues?" *Legislative Studies Quarterly* 23 (1998): 435–448.

———. *The Difference Women Make: The Policy Impact of Women in Congress*. Chicago: University of Chicago Press, 2002.

Sylvester, Christine. "Simultaneous Revolutions and Exists: A Semi-Skeptical Comment." In *Women and Revolution in Africa, Asia, and the New World*, ed. Mary Ann Tetrault. Columbia: University of South Carolina Press, 1994.

Tahmina, Qurratul Ain. "South Asia: Working Women Get Poor Health Services." Inter Press Service, June 3, 2003.

Takahashi, Hiroyuki. "Working Women in Japan: A Look at Historical Trends and Legal Reform." Japan Economic Institute, no. 42. November 6, 1998. http://www.jei.org/Archive/JEIR98/9842f.html (November 13, 2003).

Tamerius, Karin L. "Sex, Gender, and Leadership in the Representation of Women." In *Gender, Power, Leadership, and Governance*, ed. Georgia Duerst-Lahti and Rita Mae Kelly. Ann Arbor: University of Michigan Press, 1993.

Tanaka, Hiromi. "Equal Employment in Contemporary Japan: A Structural Approach." *Political Science and Politics*, (January 2004), pp. 66–66.

Tarrow, Sidney. *Power in Movement*. Cambridge: Cambridge University Press, 1994.

Tattersall, Nick. "Savage Life of Boy Soldiers Made to Kill." *The Advertiser*. June 9, 2007, p. 76.

Taylor, Sandra C. *Vietnamese Women at War: Fighting for Ho Chi Minh and the Revolution.* Lawrence: University Press of Kansas, 1999.

Te Braake, Trees A. M. "Late Termination of Pregnancy Because of Severe Foetal Abnormalities: Legal Acceptability, Notification and Review in the Netherlands." *European Journal of Health Law* 7 (2000): 387–403.

Tetrault, Mary Ann. "Women and Revolution: A Framework for Analysis." In *Women and Revolution in Africa, Asia, and the New World,* ed. Mary Ann Tetrault. Columbia: University of South Carolina Press, 1994.

———. "Women and Revolution: What Have We Learned?" In *Women and Revolution in Africa, Asia, and the New World,* ed. Mary Ann Tetrault. Columbia: University of South Carolina Press, 1994.

———. "Women and Revolution in Vietnam." In *Global Feminisms Since 1945,* ed. Bonnie G. Smith. New York: Routledge, 2000.

Thomas, Sue. *How Women Legislate.* New York: Oxford University Press, 1994.

Thomas, Sue, and Susan Welch. "The Impact of Gender on Activities and Priorities of State Legislators." *Western Political Quarterly* 44 (1991): pp. 454–455.

Tinker, Irene. "Empowerment Just Happened: The Unexpected Expansion of Women's Organizations." In *Women and Gender Equity in Development Theory and Practice: Institutions, Resources, and Mobilization,* ed. Jane S. Jaquette and Gale Summerfield. Durham, NC: Duke University Press, 2006, p. 268.

"Treaty Establishing the European Community," http://www.hri.org/docs/Rome57/Part3Title08.html#Art119 (April 30, 2006).

Tripp, Aili Mari. *Women and Politics in Uganda.* Madison: The University of Wisconsin Press, 2000.

Turner, Ralph H., and Lewis Killian. *Collective Behavior.* Englewood Cliffs, NJ: Prentice Hall, 1957.

"Uganda; Country's Debt Drops to $1 Billion." *Monitor,* Africa News. February 28, 2007.

U.S. Department of Justice. "Child Sex Tourism." http//www.usdoj.gov/criminal/ceos/sextour.html.

U.S. Department of State, Bureau of Democracy, Human Rights, and Labor. "Japan: Country Reports on Human Rights Practices—2000." February 23, 2001, http://www.state.gov/g/drl/rls/hrrpt/2000/eap/709pf.htm (November 19, 2003).

U.S. Department of State. *Trafficking in Persons Report.* Washington, DC: U.S. Department of State,, June 2008, p. 24.

U.S. General Accounting Office. "A New Look Through the Glass Ceiling: Where Are the Women?" Washington, DC: U.S. General Accounting Office, January 2002, pp. 1–13.

UNAIDS. *Report on the Global Aids Epidemic Executive Summary.* Geneva, Switzerland: UNAIDS, July 2008, p. 8.

"The Unfortunate Facts of Life in 2007." Women Deliver Global Conference 2007.

UNFPA. "Selling Hope and Stealing Dreams: Trafficking in Women and the Exploitation of Domestic Workers." *State of World Population 2006,* New York: UNFPA, 2006.

———. "Who We Are." http://www.unfpa.org/publications/detail.cfm?ID=384&filterListType=.

UNIFEM. "Gender Equality Now. Accelerating the Achievement of the Millennium Development Goals." Part II of Progress 2008/2009, New York: UNIFEM, 2008/2009.

———. "Who Answers to Women? Gender and Accountability." Progress of the World's Women 2008/09. New York, UNIFEM, 2008/2009, pp. 117—133.

United Nations. "Charter of the United Nations." http://www.un.org/aboutun/charter (October 12, 2005).

———. *The United Nations and the Advancement of Women, 1945–1996.* New York: United Nations, Department of Public Information, 1996.

———. *Human Development Report 2007/2008,* New York: United Nations Development Programme, p. 337.

———. "United Nations International Decades Designated by the General Assembly." September 27, 2001. http://www.nalis.gov.tt/National-UN-Days/UN_INTERNA-TIONALDECADES.html (October 13, 2005).

———. *Women Go Global: The United Nations and the International Women's Movement, 1945—2000.* New York: United Nations, 2003.

———. *The Millennium Development Goals Report.* New York: United Nations, 2005.

———. "The Millennium Development Goals Report 2008." September 2008. http://www.undp.org/publications/MDG_Report_2008_EN.pdf (January 13, 2009), p. 4.

———. *Rural Women in a Changing World: Opportunities and Challenges.* New York: United Nations, October 2008.

United Nations Children's Fund (UNICEF). "Domestic Violence Against Women and Girls." Florence, Italy: Innocenti Research Centre, June 2000.

———. "Gender Achievements and Prospects in Education: The GAP Report, Part One, South Asia Yawning Chasm." http://www.ungei.org/gap/reportSasia.php (January 8, 2009).

UN Department of Economic and Social Affairs, Division for Sustainable Development. http://www.un.org/esa/sustdev.

———. *Annual Report 2003.* New York: UNICEF, 2004.

United Nations Development Programme. *Human Development Report 2002.* New York: Oxford University Press, 2002.

———. *Human Development Report 2003.* New York: Oxford University Press, 2003.

———. *Human Development Report 2004.* New York: Oxford University Press, 2004.

———. *Human Development Report 2005.* New York: Oxford University Press, 2005.

———. *Human Development Report 2007/2008.* New York: Oxford University Press, 2007/2008.

United Nations Development Fund for Women. *Progress of the World's Women 2002: Gender Equality and the Millennium Development Goals.* New York: UNIFEM, 2002.

United Nations, Division for the Advancement of Women. "Convention on the Elimination of All Forms of Discrimination Against Women." http://www.un.org/womenwatch/daw/cedaw (October 13, 2005).

United Nations Educational, Scientific and Cultural Organization (UNESCO). "Girls Continue to Face Sharp Discrimination in Access to School." June 11, 2003. Press release No 2003-91. http://www.portal.unesco.org/en/ev.php (November 25, 2003).

United Nations High Commissioner for Refugees. "Basic Facts." http://www.unhcr.org (December 9, 2003).

United Nations Integrated Regional Information Networks. "Liberia; Some Women Ready to Fight Again." *Africa News.* October 14, 2008.

———. "Togo; School Year Reopens with Free Primary Schools." *Africa News,* October 6, 2008.

United Nations Population Division, Department of Economic and Social Affairs. *Abortion Policies: A Global Review.* New York: United Nations Press, 2002.

United Nations Population Division, "Ireland." In *Abortion Policies: A Global Review.* New York: United Nations Press, 2002.

———. "Netherlands." In *Abortion Policies: A Global Review.* New York: United Nations: 2002. http://www.un.org/esa/population/publications/abortion/ (August 10, 2005).

———. "United States of America." In *Abortion Policies: A Global Review.* New York: United Nations Press, 2002.

United Nations Population Fund (UNFPA). "UNFPA: United Nations Population Fund." http://www.unfpa.org/about/index.htm (October 13, 2004).

———. "State of the World Population 2006. A Passage to Hope. Women and International Migration." http://www.unfpa.org/swp/2006/english/chapter_2/print/chapter_2.html.

United States Agency for International Development (USAID), Office of Women and Development. "Girls' and Women's Education: A USAID Initiative." Fact Sheet (April 1998).

Varnon, Rob. "Census Report on Earning: Struggling to Bridge the Wage Gap." *Connecticut Post.* August 17, 2003, Your Money section.

Verba, Sidney, Norman Nie, and Jae-on Kim. *Participation and Social Equality.* Cambridge, MA: Harvard University Press, 1978.

Verba, Sidney, Kay Schlozman, and Henry E. Brady. *Voice and Equality.* Cambridge, MA: Harvard University Press, 1995.

"Voters in United Arab Emirates Set to Vote in Historic Elections," http://www.dubaicity.com/news/historic-elections12-16.htm (October 14, 2008).

"Voters in Ireland Reject Change in Abortion Law." *USA Today.* March 8, 2002, p. 7A.

Wakabi, Wairagala. "Africa Battles to Make Female Genital Mutilation History." *The Lancet* 369 (March 31, 2007–April 6, 2007): 1069.

Wasserstrom, Jeffrey N. "Gender and Revolution in Europe and Asia, Part 2: Recent Works and Frameworks for Comparative Analysis." *Journal of Women's History* 6 (Spring 1994): 109–120.

Welch, Susan. "Women as Political Animals? A Test of Some Explanations for Male-Female Political Participation Differences." *American Journal of Political Science* 21 (1977): 711–730.

———. "Are Women More Liberal Than Men in the U.S. Congress?" *Legislative Studies Quarterly* 10 (1985): 125–134.

Wellesley Centers for Research on Women and Development and Training Services, Inc., for USAID. "Unsafe Schools: A Literature Review of School-Related Gender-Based Violence in Developing Countries." September 2003. http://pdf.usaid.gov/pdf_docs/PNACU253.pdf (January 8, 2009).

The White House. "President Bush Signs Partial Birth Abortion Ban Act 2003." http://www.whitehouse.gov/news/releases/2003/11/print/20031105-1.html (April 22, 2006).

Wickham-Crowley, Timothy. *Guerillas and Revolution in Latin America: A Comparative Study of Insurgents and Regimes Since 1956.* Princeton, NJ: Princeton University Press, 1992.

Williams, Beryl. "Kollantai and After: Women in the Russian Revolution." In *Women, State and Revolution: Essays on Power and Gender in Europe Since 1789,* ed. Sian Reynolds. Amherst: The University of Massachusetts Press, 1987.

Wisensale, Steven K. *Family Leave Policy: The Political Economy of Work and Family in America.* Armonk, NY: M.E. Sharpe, 2001.

Woloch, Nancy. *Women and the American Experience.* New York: Alfred A. Knopf, 1984.

Women Deliver. "Saving Women's Lives: Leading Killers and Practical Solutions." www. womendeliver.org/resources/Saving_Women_Lives.htm.

"Women and Work: European Situation." http://www.etuc.org.EQUALPAY/UK/women_ and_work/European-Union/default.cfm (November 11, 2003).

"Women Given Unfair Choice of Babies or a Good Pension." *The Western Mail.* July 7, 2003, p. 1.

"Women in Europe Towards Healthy Ageing." European Institute of Women's Health. 1997) http://www.eurohealth.ie/report/index.htm (September 29, 2003), Introduction, p. 4 of 5.

WomenOf.com. "Non-Profits Improve Numbers of Women CEOs." http://www.womenof. com/News/cn092500.asp (October 6, 2003).

Women Watch. "International Day of Rural Women." October 15, 2008. www.un.org/ womenwatch/feature/idrw/index.html.

World Bank. *Engendering Development: Through Gender Equality in Rights, Resources, and Voice.* New York: Oxford University Press, 2001.

——. "Girls Education—Key Issues." 2009. http://go.worldbank.org/SP3Y3AHK10 (January 7, 2009).

——. "World Bank's First-Ever Combination Grant-Credit Will Support Uganda Education, March 24, 1998. http://web.worldbank.org/WBSITE/EXTERNAL/NEW S/0,,contentMDK:20012678~menuPK:34466~pagePK:64003015~piPK:64003012~ theSitePK:4607,00.html (October 15, 2005).

——. "Uganda: Development Results." http://web.worldbank.org/WBSITE/EXTERNAL/ COUNTRIES/AFRICAEXT/UGANDAEXTN/0,,menuPK:374871~pagePK:141159~ piPK:141110~theSitePK:374864,00.html (October 15, 2005).

——. *Engendering Development: Through Gender Equality in Rights, Resources, and Voice.* New York: Oxford University Press, 2001.

——. *World Development Indicators 2001.* New York: World Bank, 2001.

——. *World Development Indicators 2002.* New York: World Bank, 2002.

——. "Land Use Rights and Gender Equality in Vietnam." *Promising Approaches to Engendering Development* 1 (September 2002): 1–2.

World Bank, Gender and Development Group. *Gender Equality and the Millennium Development Goals.* New York: World Bank, April 4, 2003.

World Bank, Independent Evaluation Group. http://www.worldbank.org/ieg/education/ findings.html (January 12, 2009).

World Health Organization. *Abortion: A Tabulation of Available Data on the Frequency and Mortality of Unsafe Abortion.* 2d ed. Geneva: Maternal Health and Safe Motherhood Program, Division of Family Health, World Heath Organization, 1994.

——. "Female Genital Mutilation," Fact Sheet no. 241, May 2008, http://www.who.int/ mediacentre/factsheets/fs241/en/print.html (February 3, 2009).

——. *Unsafe Abortion: Global and Regional Estimates of Incidence of and Mortality Due to Unsafe Abortion.* 3d ed. Geneva: World Health Organization, 1998.

——. "Making Pregnancy Safer," February 2004. http://www.who.int/mediacentre/ factsheets/fs276/en/print.html (October 13, 2004).

World Health Organization, UNICEF and United Nations Population Fund. *Maternal Mortality in 2000: Estimates Developed by WHO, UNICEF, and UNFPA.* Geneva: World Health Organization, 2004.

Worldmapper. http://www.worldmapper.org/display.php?selected=181.

World Values Survey. "1999–2002 World Values Survey Questionnaire." http://www.worldvaluessurvey.org/statistics/index.html (April 22, 2006).

Yishai, Yael. *Between the Flag and the Banner: Women in Israeli Politics.* Albany: SUNY Press Albany, 1997.

Young, Marilyn B. "Reflections on Women in the Chinese Revolution." In *Women and Revolution: Global Expressions,* ed. M. J. Diamond. Boston: Kluwer Academic Publishers, 1998.

Index